Private Capital Markets

Private Capital Markets

Valuation, Capitalization, and Transfer of Private Business Interests

Second Edition

ROBERT T. SLEE

WILEY

John Wiley & Sons, Inc.

Published by John Wiley & Sons, Inc., Hoboken, New Jersey.
Published simultaneously in Canada.

For general information on our other products and services or for technical support, please contact our Customer Care Department within the United States at (800) 762-2974, outside the United States at (317) 572-3993 or fax (317) 572-4002.

Wiley also publishes its books in a variety of electronic formats. Some content that appears in print may not be available in electronic books. For more information about Wiley products, visit our web site at www.wiley.com.

Library of Congress Cataloging-in-Publication Data:

Slee, Robert T.
    Private capital markets : valuation, capitalization, and transfer of private business interests / Robert T. Slee.—2nd ed.
        p. cm.
    Includes index.
      ISBN 978-0-470-92832-5 (hardback); ISBN 978-1-118-07542-5(ebk);
ISBN 978-1-118-07545-6 (ebk); ISBN 978-1-118-07544-9 (ebk)
    1. Corporations. 2. Private companies–Finance. 3. Capital investments. I. Title.
    HD2731.S6 2011
    332′.041—dc22

                                                                    2011002026

Printed in the United States of America.

10 9 8 7 6 5 4 3 2 1

To my girls

Contents

Foreword

Until the inaugural edition of *Private Capital Markets: Valuation, Capitalization, and Transfer of Private Business Interests* was published in 2004, private market players had only corporate finance theories to explain the behavior of the private capital markets. They were left to assume that corporate finance theories explain and predict actions in the private markets. As a corporate finance professor, I too was content to believe that public and private capital markets were substitutes.

An early skeptic, I have come to realize that private markets must be explained using theories tailored to experiences in those markets. This conclusion took me several years and active investigation to realize. I recall sitting in a business appraisal class in 2005 when an instructor introduced a relatively new and innovative book: *Private Capital Markets*. The instructor made several provocative claims about the book: (1) It contained an integrated theory that described the body of knowledge that applies to valuation, capitalization, and transfer of private companies; (2) businesses have more than one value at any point in time; and (3) it would ultimately change the way that business valuation for privately held companies would be performed.

Although these were interesting comments, I was unmotivated to investigate further. After all, I had a Ph.D. in finance and had been teaching corporate finance for nearly ten years. I was very confident that what I learned and taught in class about corporate finance also applied to privately held companies. Of course the capital asset pricing model applies to privately held companies. And capital structures of privately held companies mimic those of their publicly traded counterparts. And last but not least, companies have but one value. And why not: MBA finance books clearly state that the goal of all privately held companies is to go public!

Fast forward to one day in 2007 when I was reading a comment posted in a business valuation chat room by Rob Slee. Rob indicated that a goal of surveying the various segments of the private capital markets was to obtain a better understanding of the behavior of those providers and cost of capital for over 99% of businesses in our economy. My initial thought was "How silly." After all, we all know we can derive private company cost of capital by using public data as a proxy. And thankfully we have very rich data from the public markets to use for those kinds of projects. I then started to think about the private company business valuation consulting engagements I had over the preceding several years and realized that behaviors are unique with regard to business owners and capital providers and are not necessarily consistent with behaviors in the public markets. Furthermore, upon reflection, I started to doubt that the goal of every privately held company was to go public. Now I was motivated to investigate further.

After more contemplation, I replied to Rob that it was something in which I was personally interested and believed that I would have the support of the Graziadio School of Business and Management at Pepperdine University to pursue such an initiative. After getting the nod from Dean Livingstone and Associate Dean Smith, the Pepperdine Private Capital Markets Project was born and a proposal to teach a new class, "Private Capital Markets," was under way.

Now that I have taught the class for three years and have run the project for over four, I see things much more clearly. The Pepperdine Private Capital Markets Project hosts a semiannual survey that explores the behaviors exhibited by the major capital provider types and costs of capital on a simultaneous and comprehensive basis. The survey has grown from just 5 segments when originally launched in 2009 to 12: angel investors, venture capital, private equity, mezzanine, limited partners, cash flow lenders, asset-backed lenders, factors, investment bankers, business brokers, business owners, and business appraisers. The surveys, which are available at http://bschool.pepperdine.edu/privatecapital, ask questions about prior returns, expected returns, credit box parameters, acceptance rates, general behaviors, and industry and economic outlooks. With four reports now published, I am convinced the behavior in the private capital markets is unique—not only by capital type, but also within each capital type.

I have had many "Aha!" moments with regard to the behavior in the private capital markets that is addressed in this book and corroborated with survey data. For instance, unlike the way that investment opportunities are evaluated in the public markets, I learned that investments in the private markets are not made primarily with net present value analysis. That is, privately held business owners invest based mainly on payback and supplement their investment analysis with gut feel. To my surprise, gut feel was acknowledged by over 90% of survey participants. Activities like "being able to look the management team in the eyes and get a feel for their motivation" and "a general feeling that a particular product or service will gain market traction" are among many items that emerged as support for using gut-feel analysis. This contrasts considerably with behavior in the public markets, where investment decisions are made using a more formal and structured process.

I also learned that estimates of cost of capital by private business owners and private capital markets participants are very different. Interestingly, business owners have a tendency to see things more optimistically than those writing investment checks. Alternatively stated, the typical business owner frequently neglects to objectively assess all the risks on the horizon and therefore is unable to arrive at an appropriate risk-adjusted cost of capital.

I also learned just how segmented the capital providers are in the private capital markets. Each has investment preferences based on geography, industry, and size of investee companies. The implication is that a company may be worthy of financing, but if it does not approach a funding source that specializes in its industry, location, or size, the business is quite unlikely to obtain potentially vital growth capital.

Perhaps the most interesting observation is with regard to the use of earnings before interest taxes depreciation and amortization (EBITDA). It is the language of the middle markets and is the primary foundation upon which capital structures are built and value is determined. Senior lenders will lend at some multiple of EBITDA; mezzanine investments also will be extended at some multiple of EBITDA; and of course the same goes for investments by private equity groups. And to determine the value—you guessed it—capital providers in the middle markets also look to multiples for guidance.

Fortunately I have been able to leverage the survey findings in my private capital markets class as well. The foundation of this class is built on the *Private Capital Markets* book. Students in this class who have not been exposed to the middle markets often are shocked at the way business is done in this space. It seems that after even one corporate finance course, students grow accustomed to the efficiency and precision of the public markets and paint the economy in broad strokes. They frequently are amazed at many of the nuances of the private markets; for instance, the use of EBITDA as the driver for capital formation and valuation, the fact that a business can have more than one value at a singular point in time or that capital solutions are unique and not generalizable or transferrable from provider to provider. Initially they are immobilized by the subjectivity involved in evaluating capital prospects, arranging capital, and dealing with value relativity. Many feel as though they are "offroading" after becoming accustomed to driving on the "corporate finance freeway."

Now that four years have passed, I realize just how much of a transformation I have made with regard to my understanding of the private capital markets and just how convinced I am that the behaviors described in this book are unique and cannot always be explained by corporate finance theory. *Private Capital Markets* is a foundation for many of my professional activities. It is the primary source of information in my private capital markets class; it is the foundation upon which the Pepperdine Private Capital Markets Project surveys are built; and, most important, it has changed the way I view the private capital markets and the middle market in particular.

> JOHN K. PAGLIA, PH.D., CPA, CFA
> *Denney Academic Chair and Associate Professor of Finance*
> *Senior Researcher, Pepperdine Private Capital Markets Project*
> *Pepperdine University*

Private capital markets rely on a holistic body of knowledge that describes the valuation, capital structure formation, and transfer of private business interests. Far from the noise of Wall Street, this book focuses on Main Street and its business dilemmas and opportunities.

Private companies, particularly those with annual sales of $5 million to $350 million, have unique capital market needs. The key to understanding private capital markets is to realize that valuation, capitalization, and business transfer *rely* on each other for definition and support. Only by understanding each of these areas, and their connections, or *triangulation*, is it possible to use this body of knowledge.

This book is written with three groups of readers in mind:

1. It is a useful road map for owners of middle-market businesses.
2. It can guide professional advisors of middle-market business owners.
3. It may be used by academics who currently have no other book dealing with these large and dynamic markets.

Other potential readers include lawyers, trade association members, CPAs, estate planners, appraisers, intermediaries, investment bankers, capital providers, and various management consultants.

Owner-managers of private companies are the primary audience for this book. These people have built substantial businesses based on their market knowledge, their ability to manage operations, and lots of hard work. After dealing with owner-managers for more than 25 years, I recognize that they are an unusual group of people. They are driven by a vision. The fact that this vision is not apparent to anyone else, or that it might take a lifetime to realize, is not an impediment. They are out to prove something to somebody. Owners often view monetary rewards as the final effect of their efforts rather than motivation. They understand the link between money and learning, in that nothing really is learned in life until a checkbook appears. Finally, owner-managers are prudent. They believe it is easier and less risky to make money by controlling costs rather than by investing and earning. Ultimately, most owner-managers remain prudent even when they can afford to be otherwise. I am a big fan of owner-managers.

However, most owners are ill-prepared to deal with valuation, capital structure, and transfer issues. The private capital markets are sophisticated enough to be beyond the reach of part-timers. Owners, and most of their professional advisors, do not spend a majority of their time dealing with this body of knowledge. Lawyers, accountants, bankers, estate planners, and other professionals may know one facet of the private capital markets but are deficient in another area.

The owners' professionals are the second group that this book is intended to help. Finally, this book is aimed at academics, who are just warming to the idea that middle market finance is a separate and important field of study.

HOW TO READ THIS BOOK

After Chapters 1 and 2 introduce its framework, the book is broken into three parts: Valuation, Capital Structure, and Business Transfer. Each part contains an introduction and conclusion chapter. Chapter 3 introduces business valuation, Chapter 16 introduces capital structure, and Chapter 26 introduces business transfer. Subject matter chapters immediately follow each part's introductory chapter. A conclusion chapter summarizes the main themes of the book and raises a number of questions that are yet to be answered.

To obtain the proper perspective of middle-market finance theory, the main theory developed in this book, and the private capital markets, readers should first read the foreword, Chapters 1, 2, 3 and 36, and Appendix A. Readers interested in a particular subject, such as bank lending, should first read the introductory chapter for that part. The part conclusion chapters—15, 25, and 35—are also vital. These chapters reinforce information presented in each part and also extend the discussions in interesting and provocative ways.

Triangulation, the concept introduced in the book that refers to the use of two sides of the middle-market finance theory triangle to help fully understand a point on the third side, is dealt with in two ways. First, most chapters contain one or more constructs that relate the chapter topic to the broader body of knowledge. These constructs are called longitude and latitude for the valuation chapters, capital coordinates for the capitalization chapters, and transfer matrix for the transfer chapters. Second, each chapter concludes with a discussion of triangulation, which allows the reader to consider the impact of the body of knowledge on the topic at hand.

Several formatting conventions are used throughout the book to enrich the presentation. First, the exhibits depict charts, diagrams, tables, and examples that are pertinent to the specific discussion. Finally, a fictitious company called PrivateCo illustrates most of the mechanics presented herein. In a sense, information is presented and analyzed through the eyes of Joe Mainstreet, PrivateCo's majority shareholder.

MAJOR GOAL OF THIS BOOK

Middle-market finance theory organizes a holistic body of knowledge and requires a general understanding of the major constructs before specific techniques can be properly considered. For example, it makes little sense to raise venture or other equity capital before reviewing the relevant credit boxes and the Pepperdine Private Capital Market Line to determine if a less expensive form of capital is available.

Likewise, selling the entire business may not meet the goals of the owner. Other transfer methods might be more appropriate.

Understanding the private capital body of knowledge enables owner-managers and their professionals to solve difficult financial problems. This book provides enough information on private capital markets for owners to consider their possibilities. For the first time, owners can review an independent source of information on private capital markets and ascertain the best approach toward meeting their goals. Private business owners need, and deserve, this support. If this book helps owners take one step in that direction, the effort has been worthwhile.

Acknowledgments

It is fortunate that prospective authors and parents do not start out with perfect information. If they did, there would be fewer books and possibly fewer kids on the planet. In both cases, the initial notion quickly turns to a journey and finally a saga. I am still not sure what follows saga, but I remain hopeful that my grandfather was wrong when he described life to me 20 years ago: "Life, it's bad for a while, then it gets worse." He died at 89 years of age, insistent to the end that his situation had not materially improved throughout his life: only his ability to cope had improved.

A number of people definitely improved my ability to cope with this saga. The next "Chapter Champions" helped update subject matter content plus breathed life into otherwise inert technical matter.

Champion	Chapter	Title
Gary Fodor	8	Fair Market Value
Jim Lurie	9	Fair Value
Chris Cope	11	Insurable Value
Dat T Do	12	FASB Value Worlds
Chris Mellen	13	Intangible Asset Value
Phil Hamilton	14	Other Value Worlds
John Graham	17	Bank Lending
Bob Humber	19	Equipment Leasing
Dan Shaw	20	Asset-Based Lending
Brandt Brereton	27	Employee Stock Ownership Plans
Walter Putnam	29	Charitable Trusts
Dan Prisciotta	30	Family Transfers
Tim Rhine	34	Going Public, Going Private

Many people helped with the book beyond the subject matter champions. John Paglia not only wrote the foreword but helped with many conceptual issues throughout the book. Phil Hamilton provided great edits and much-needed spiritual support when it was desperately needed. Chris Cope and Dan Prisciotta both went beyond the call of duty. Ultimate thanks go to Sheck Cho and the editors at Wiley who patiently transformed something readable into something worth reading.

In alphabetical order, the next people provided insightful comments: Wayne Ackerman, Chris Blees, Ed Calt, KC Conrad, Ed Giardina, Chuck Knox, Frank Mainville, Kenneth Marks, Mike Nall, Randy Schostag, Sherry Smith, Dr. Stephen Spinelli, Tommy Thompson, Vincent Wolanin, and, last but not least, the Slee twins.

CHAPTER 1

Capital Markets

This book explores private capital markets, the last major uncharted financial markets. Private markets contain millions of companies, which generate more than half of the gross domestic product (GDP) of the United States and the world. Yet these markets are largely ignored, partly because of the difficulty obtaining information and partly because of the lack of a unified structure to approach them. This work offers such an approach. It provides a theoretical and practical framework that enables readers to make sound investment and financing decisions in the private capital markets.

A capital market is one in which businesses can raise debt and equity funds. Since the 1970s, public capital markets have received almost all of the attention from academics in the literature.[1] In 2004, the first edition of this book challenged the assumption that public and private capital markets are substitutes, showing instead that the two markets were different in most meaningful ways. Specifically, 12 factors differentiate public and private markets:[2]

1. Risk and return are unique to each market.
2. Liquidity within each market is different.
3. Motives of private owners are different from those of professional managers.
4. Underlying capital market theories that explain the behavior of players in each market are different.
5. Private companies are priced at a point in time, while public companies are continuously priced.
6. Public markets allow ready access to capital, while private capital is difficult to arrange.
7. Public shareholders can diversify their holdings, whereas private shareholders cannot diversify.
8. Private markets are inefficient, whereas public markets are fairly efficient.
9. Market mechanisms have differing effects on each market.
10. Capital market lines (costs of capital) are substantially different for each market.
11. The expected holding period for investors is different.
12. The transaction cost of either buying or selling the interest is different.

Several of the major differences between public and private markets require further discussion. Specifically, public and private markets differ in structure and

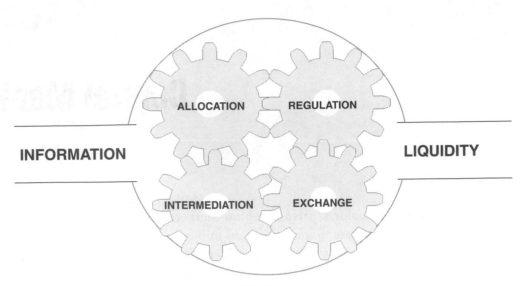

EXHIBIT 1.1 Mechanisms that Structure a Market

behavior, which necessitates unique capital market theories to better organize and predict behavior.

MARKET STRUCTURE

All markets are comprised of commercial activity where parties undertake an exchange because each expects to gain. In a free market, participants are able to meet and exchange for a mutually agreed price. Markets mechanisms are organized sets of activities enabling people to exchange or invest. Exhibit 1.1 depicts several market mechanisms as gears in a market that is greased by information and liquidity.

INFORMATION

The role of information is central in both public and private capital markets. Availability, accuracy, and access to information lubricate all market mechanisms. Information availability in public markets renders them more efficient. Theoretically, they are less likely to produce deals where one party takes advantage of another because of asymmetrical information. It takes government regulation and enforcement to ensure that public information is accurate and available to all.

Availability, accuracy, and access to information are significantly different in the private markets. Financial statements are the basic building blocks of information. Most private companies lack audited financial statements and are less likely to prepare their financial statements in compliance with generally accepted accounting principles. Even this lesser-quality information is not made publicly available. The absence of real-time, readily available information is a major difference between the markets.

Liquidity

Liquidity is the central value proposition of any market. Consider it as capital in motion, a necessary lubricant for movement between asset classes. The term refers to the amount of capital in a market and the flow of that capital internally as well as into and out of the market.

Markets are described as more or less liquid. For example, real estate and privately held businesses are typically illiquid investments, while investments in publicly held businesses are considered liquid. Public companies largely transfer fractional interests. Conversely, since there is no market to sell private minority interests, most private transfers involve enterprise sales. While an enterprise transfer of a private company can easily take a year or more, public enterprise sales normally require only six months. Investors in private companies factor a liquidity premium in their return expectations because they recognize that these investments are not easily exited.

Market Mechanisms

Market structure is comprised of several mechanisms; among them are:

- Allocation mechanism
- Regulatory mechanisms
- Intermediation mechanisms
- Exchange mechanisms

Market mechanisms provide a structured way to understand complex markets. These mechanisms are the activities or gears that enable a market to operate. Synchronization is possible because each mechanism contains elements of other mechanisms, all operate in a similar information environment, and all mechanisms tend toward equilibrium.

In equilibrium, the supply of companies for sale equals the demand for those companies. More sellers in a market lead to greater competition enabling buyers to get better value in the exchange. Fewer sellers mean less value for buyers. In short, a market is in equilibrium when supply equals demand.

Market mechanisms operate in an environment lubricated with information and liquidity, and one that tends toward equilibrium. This occurs, for example, in allocating scarce resources.

Allocation

Allocation is the market mechanism of rationing resources. Because resources are finite, markets allocate money, resources, effort, authority, and cooperation as well as tangible and intangible assets. Allocation decisions may be arrived at using a variety of criteria. For example, a first-come, first-served process benefits the fleet of foot. A political process, however, allocates benefits based on the ability to manipulate that process.

Resource allocation in the public markets is relatively efficient as demonstrated by both pricing and access to capital by public companies and investors. This is a distinct contrast with the relative inefficiency found in the private capital markets, as demonstrated by the inefficiency surrounding the Pepperdine Private Capital Market Line introduced in Chapter 2.

Regulation

"Regulation" refers to attempts to bring the market under the control of an authority. Regulation is provided by a number of sources, including government and competition.

Government regulation is pervasive, typically expressed as restrictions on behavior. It provides adjudication of disputes as well as rules for eligibility and participation. Governments may attempt to control all elements of the market. Yet in a free market system, governmental control itself operates under restrictions, which introduces competing authorities. Public companies are exposed to more extensive governmental regulation than are private companies.

Markets are also regulated through a severe discipline imposed by competition. Firms are not free to raise prices or salaries without facing economic consequences. Nor can a company pay its employees whatever it wants. Competition forces efficiency and ultimately causes supply and demand to balance. Competition regulates the market.

Intermediation

Specialization creates a need for intermediaries to serve as agents of exchange. This leads to increased efficiency based on developing expertise in disparate areas; however, it also breeds inefficiency through isolation. Specialization creates the need for information and trading expertise. Intermediaries act as *infomediaries* where information opacity exists.

Intermediaries add efficiency to a market in three ways:

1. They provide a communication system between parties.
2. They work to establish prices that often serve as the starting point in exchange discussions.
3. They might act as market makers by actually participating in the market as sellers or buyers in order to create a liquid market.

The public transfer market functions with agents *and* market makers. Public investment bankers are agents who advise on public enterprise transfers. Market makers are firms that stand ready to buy and sell a particular stock on a regular and continuous basis at a publicly quoted price. Public agents and market makers provide liquidity and efficiency to the public market. The private transfer market has agents, such as business brokers, merger and acquisitions (M&A) intermediaries, and private investment bankers. Yet none of these groups performs all the functions of public market makers.

Exchange

Market participants in a supply and demand economy are free to exchange something for an agreed price. Supply and demand in a market is affected by a host of factors. Shifts in supply or demand cause price increases and decreases. Changes in customer preferences or the cost of money may alter demand. Equilibrium is reached at the point where the greatest number of consumers and producers is satisfied.

An exchange is an institutionalizing mechanism. Institutionalized exchanges take many forms, including business-to-business, business-to-consumer, intermediated, and direct exchanges. The nature of the exchange mechanism is the most obvious difference between public and private markets. There is no single place or entity where an owner or investor might exchange an interest in a private company.

Comparison of the Markets

Market mechanisms explain the structure of the private capital markets. Exhibit 1.2 compares and contrasts transfer issues in the public and private capital markets. The private capital markets are a complex interacting network of discrete exchanges rather than a unified structure. They differ greatly from the unified structure of the public markets. For example, institutionalization in the public markets is developed more than in the private markets. In the public market, the players are licensed, highly regulated, and larger in size, and they tend to offer a wide range of financial services. In the private market, there is a host of smaller transfer players who provide discrete services. While these services are largely unregulated, the Securities and Exchange Commission and various state authorities provide some regulation.

Private markets are less mature than the public markets. They are considered emerging markets. While there are certain truths in the private–public comparison, there is more to private markets than the comparison implies. Private markets are driven by a wide variety of unique motives, and the markets have developed mechanisms enabling those unique objectives to be accomplished.

EXHIBIT 1.2 Comparison of the Capital Markets

Market Mechanism	The Public Market Enjoys	The Private Market Exhibits
Information	Symmetrical information Transparent information on the subject	Asymmetrical information Opaque information on the subject
Liquidity	Transfers of mainly minority interests Instant trading	Transfers of mainly enterprise interests Long-term planned exits
Allocation	Efficient allocation	Fairly inefficient allocation
Regulation	A regulated market	A mainly nonregulated market
Intermediation	An industry of agents and market makers	A segmented industry of agents
Exchange	Continuous pricing	Point-in-time pricing

Private capital markets are understandable in terms that apply to all markets. They are a collection of mechanisms, located in a free market system. No authority controls the overall structure and function of the market. Rather there are multiple authorities, with various levels of influence and control, operating in certain areas of the market.

So far this discussion describes markets from a high-level, monolithic viewpoint. Capital markets are not monolithic; rather, they are segmented based on a number of factors.

Segmented Markets

Private markets actually contain numerous marketplaces. For example, there are submarkets for raising debt or equity and for transferring business interests. This book consistently uses the collective term "markets" to describe activity within the private capital markets rather than attempting to describe particular submarkets with a confusing array of terminology. While there are no definitive size boundaries, Exhibit 1.3 depicts the market segmentation by size of business.[3]

Small businesses—those with annual sales of less than $5 million—are at the bottom of the ladder. There are more than 5 million small businesses that report having at least one employee in the United States. This group generates approximately 15% of the U.S. GDP. Lending to these businesses is generally handled by the business banking group of community or smaller regional banks. Small businesses are almost always owner managed. These businesses have limited access to the private capital markets beyond assistance from the Small Business Administration and business brokers. Capital access improves as the business moves into the upper segments.

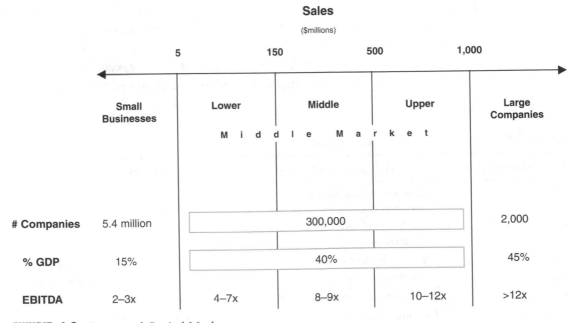

EXHIBIT 1.3 Segmented Capital Markets

EXHIBIT 1.4 Characteristics of the Lower Middle Market

- Owner management.
- Owner has unlimited liability and personally guarantees debt.
- Company has evolved from bookkeeper to controller or chief financial officer.
- Owner typically has more than 80% of personal wealth tied to business.
- About 80% of the businesses will not transfer to the next generation.
- Company has uncertain access to capital.
- Market value of the company can vary widely from year to year.

The entire U.S. middle market contains approximately 300,000 companies that generate roughly 40% of the U.S. GDP. The lower middle market includes companies with annual sales of $5 million to $150 million; and so on. The lower middle market is the main focus of this book. As Exhibit 1.4 portrays, companies in this segment have a number of unique characteristics.

The "middle" middle market includes companies with annual sales of $150 million to $500 million. They are serviced by regional investment banks and draw the attention of the banks' top lenders, their corporate bankers. Capital market access and efficiency improve at this level. Companies with sales over $150 million begin to have access to nearly all capital market alternatives.

The upper middle market is comprised of companies with sales of between $500 million to $1 billion. These companies have access to most of the capital market alternatives available to the largest public companies. This group of companies, which tends to be publicly held, attracts the secondary attention of the largest Wall Street investment banking firms. The largest regional bankers also take notice. In this tier, capital is accessible and priced to reflect the riskiness of the borrower.

Finally, the large-company market, which is comprised of about 2,000 mostly public companies, generates about 45% of the U.S. GDP. Large companies have the complete arsenal of capital alternatives at their disposal. They use discounted cash-flow techniques to make capital decisions because they can fund projects at their marginal cost of capital. Almost all are public. The few that are private have most of the financial capabilities of public companies. Wall Street bankers focus primarily on these companies, which flourish under the rules of corporate finance theory.

Each market segment yields information and liquidity, which form the basis for peculiar investor return expectations manifested by acquisition multiples paid for companies within it. Acquisition multiples based on earnings before interest, taxes, depreciation, and amortization (EBITDA) represent capital structure decisions. The reciprocal of EBITDA multiples yields a shorthand for expected return on total capital. For instance, equity investors *ordinarily* require 30% to 40% compounded returns from investments in the middle market and 10% to 20% from investments in large companies.[4]

Markets segment by investor return expectations because players within a segment view valuation parochially. The relationship between investor return expectations and valuation is straightforward: Greater perceived risk requires greater returns to compensate for the risk. Using a capital market–determined discount

EXHIBIT 1.5   Defining Characteristics by Segment

Characteristic	Small Market	Lower Middle Market	Middle Middle Market and Up
Revenue size	<$5 million	$5 million–$150 million	$150 million–$500 million
EBITDA size	<$500,000	$500,000–$15 million	$15 million–$50 million
Ownership profile	Owner managed	Owner managed–professionally managed	Professionally managed
Owner or manager capital motives	To manage cash in the business, not the balance sheet	To manage the business, not the balance sheet	To manage net assets on the balance sheet
Ownership goal	Lifestyle	Lifestyle–entity value creation	Entity value creation
Role of key manager	Wears all hats	Wears few hats—functional management	Functional management
Market orientation	Service	Service–market maker	Market maker–service
Capital access			
Debt	Business banking	Commercial banking	Corporate banking
Equity	Personal/family	Personal/private equity	Private equity
Intermediation	Business brokers	Local investment bankers	Regional/national investment bankers

rate is another way of looking at this risk/return relationship. The discount rate then is the expected rate of return required to attract capital to an investment, taking into account the rate of return available from other investments of comparable risk.

Since a number of factors form boundaries in the capital markets, observers must correctly identify the segment within which the subject will be viewed. Characteristics need to be weighed in their totality. For instance, some companies have annual sales of $3 million but meet other criteria that may allow them to be viewed as lower-middle-market entities. Companies with sales over $5 million may be viewed by the markets as small businesses, if they do not have the proper characteristics. An incorrect assessment will lead to improper valuation assessment. Exhibit 1.5 provides criteria appraisers can use to define the segment within which their subject should be viewed.[5]

Owners mainly decide the segment in which their company will be viewed. For instance, if an owner decides to personally manage every aspect of the business and desires to achieve only a good lifestyle from it, the market will probably view it as a small business. Conversely, owners who strive to create company value and build a functional organization may induce the markets to view the company as a lower-middle-market entity.

WHY ARE MARKETS SEGMENTED?

Markets, like individual firms, have a cost of capital that reflects the return expectations of capital providers in that market. But how do capital providers determine risk and return within a market? Capital markets are segmented for two primary reasons.

1. Capital providers are the authorities that set rules and parameters.
2. Owners and managers view and define risk and return differently in each market.

Capital Providers

Capital providers use credit boxes to define the criteria necessary to access capital. Credit boxes help capital providers filter asset quality and set return expectations. Loans or investments that meet the terms of the credit box should promise risk-adjusted returns that meets a provider's goal. Institutional capital providers use portfolio theory to diversify risk while optimizing return. Portfolio theory is built on the premise that the risk inherent in any single asset, when held in a group of assets, is different from the inherent risk of that asset in isolation. It is unlikely that even investments in a class, such as senior midmarket debt, will experience returns that covary.

Providers also use other devices to manage portfolio risk and return. Techniques like advance rates and loan terms enable providers to hedge risks. These techniques manage risk with interest rate matching and hedges and diversify investments across geography and industries. Loan covenants are a major risk/return management tool; by setting behavioral boundaries around the borrower, capital providers are better able to manage portfolios. Providers constantly monitor their portfolios, feeding back information through their credit boxes to adjust the characteristics of assets in their portfolios.

Debt providers' use of loan covenants further creates capital market segmentation. For example, as Exhibit 1.6 shows, the range of senior debt multiples and the ratio of senior debt to earnings before EBITDA are different for each segment. It is instructive to note a positive correlation between senior debt lending multiples and middle-market private acquisition multiples between 2003 and 2010.[6] During that period, lending multiples ranged from 2.1 to 3.3. During periods of restricted lending, M&A activity was depressed. In those deals, multiples

EXHIBIT 1.6 Correlation of Senior Lending and Acquisition Multiples

	2003–2005	2006	2007	2008	2009	2010
Senior Debt/EBITDA						
$10 million–$25 million	2.1	2.3	2.4	2.1	1.3	1.9
$25 million–$50 million	2.5	2.7	2.9	2.2	1.7	2.1
$50 million–$100 million	2.6	3.3	3.1	2.8	2.0	2.4
Total Enterprise Value/EBITDA						
$10 million–$25 million	5.5	5.7	5.4	5.3	5.1	4.8
$25 million–$50 million	6.0	6.0	6.2	5.9	6.1	6.3
$50 million–$100 million	6.1	6.5	6.6	6.4	6.1	6.2

Source: Copyright GF Data Resources LLC, used with permission.

tended to be lower. By comparison, in the late 2000s, both lending and acquisition multiples moved up together. There is a significant correlation between senior debt lending multiples and business transfer values, especially in larger transactions.

Markets are further segmented by the ability to accommodate perceived risk differences. In the middle market, there is a distinct difference between the portfolio risk experienced by equity providers and that of debt providers. Equity risk is generally greater, due to its legal structure; and it is likely to be a larger portion of a smaller portfolio, further increasing risk. Debt tends to be less risky, due to its substantial bundle of legal rights; and it is usually a smaller portion of a larger investment portfolio, diminishing the impact of risk. Middle-market equity investors generally spread their risk among relatively few investments contained in a given fund or portfolio. In contrast, debt investors spread the risk among a larger pool of investments in the portfolio. Mezzanine investors can assemble blended portfolios with an entirely different risk profile since they tend to make relatively smaller investments in a greater number of companies. Moreover, the debt portion of their investments diminishes mezzanine investors' risk, while the equity portion improves their return. Rounding out this discussion of the impact of portfolio risk, pity the poor business owner who has a portfolio of one company to absorb all risk.

Lenders' and investors' portfolios define the limit of their expected returns, and managing this limit creates market fluctuations. Similarly, owners manage a balance sheet with a blend of equity and debt. In other words, owners manage a portfolio of equity and debt in order to maximize utilization of capital and manage exposure to risk. It is the day-to-day operation of these portfolios of investments working through market mechanisms that defines the market at any point in time.

Owners' and Managers' View of Risk/Return

Business appraisal attempts to estimate the balance between risk and return, specifically the risk or likelihood of achieving a certain benefit stream. The preceding text illustrates that risk and return balance by market segment. Behavior of parties in the markets reinforces this premise. For instance, when a large public company, whose stock may be trading at 30 times earnings, acquires a lower-middle-market company, why does the larger company pay 4 to 7 times earnings and not 20? Paying any multiple less than 30 would be accretive, thus adding value to the shareholders. The reason is that the larger company views investments in the lower-middle market as riskier and therefore needs to pay less to balance risk and return.

Here is the key insight: Risk and return are viewed and defined differently by owners and managers in each market segment. At a minimum, both risk and return are comprised of financial, behavioral, and psychic elements. Financial risk/return indicates that the monetary results of an action must compensate for the risk of taking the action. Behavioral risk/return describes the fact that actions occur within a set of social expectations. For instance, loss of face in a community may be viewed as a behavioral risk. Psychic risk/return is personal to the decision maker and accounts for an individual's or an institution's emotional investment in a course of action.

Unlike shareholders in firms in larger markets, owners of small companies view risk/return more from a personal perspective. Many small and lower-midmarket company owners view the business as a means to a desirable lifestyle rather than an entity that creates purely financial value. Most small-firm owners do not measure investments in the business with the tools of corporate finance. They are more likely to use a "gut feel" approach to make an investment decision.

Mid-middle-market owner-managers tend to balance the financial and psychic elements of risk/return. They understand that cost of capital is relatively high, so financial returns must compensate for investment risk. However, personal pride and community standing still have great importance. Mid-middle- and larger-company managers are driven to realize risk-adjusted returns. This drives economic value-added approaches to managing, which have taken root only in larger companies. Behavioral and psychic decision making is less important to large-company managers, or at least it takes different forms.

The combination of capital providers that balance risk/return through portfolio management and owners-managers who view risk/return differently leads to market segmentation. The behavior and perceptions of players are unique in each market. Therefore, making proper financing, appraisal, and investment decisions requires using theories and methods appropriate to the subject's market. The next section discusses the ramifications of borrowing theories, tools, and data from a market other than the subject's.

Behavior of Players and Capital Market Theories

Studying the behavior of players in a system often begins with understanding their motives or goals. Motives of owners and managers are different in each market segment. Exhibit 1.7 illustrates behavioral differences, relating to capital and transfer motives, to help observers decide which market segment a company is likely to be viewed in.[7]

EXHIBIT 1.7   Owner and Management Motives

Motive	Small Market Owners Want:	Lower Middle Market Owners Want:	Middle-Middle Market and Up Managers Want:
Capital	No partners	As few shareholders as possible	To build equity in the business
	To remove equity from the business	To minimize equity in the business	To optimize the firm's capital structure
	To manage cash in business, not balance sheet	To stretch required equity	To borrow at the firm's marginal cost of capital
		To borrow without personal guarantees	To manage "net assets" on the balance sheet
		To manage the business, not the balance sheet	
Transfer	Simple transfer motives	To meet personal motives	To meet entity motives
	To create lifestyle business	To diversify the estate	To diversify the business
	To use the business to create a job	To create a family legacy	To create a business legacy
		To use transfer to create wealth	

Motives of small- and middle-market company owners are different from those of large-company managers. While most business owners want to maximize earnings, they differ in how they define and derive those earnings. Small-business owners want no partners; middle-company owners want few partners; large-company managers are motivated to increase the number of shareholders to build equity and reduce risk. Private owners want control and don't want to share equity. This limits growth because debt providers are reluctant to account for a company's total capitalization.

From the midrange of the middle market and up, managers are motivated to maximize earnings, thereby building the equity base. Smaller-business owners are motivated to reduce reported earnings to reduce taxes, which dilutes equity. Moreover, most private companies employ pass-through entities, such as limited liability companies and S corporations, to distribute money out of the company and further reduce equity.

Beginning in the mid-middle market, company managers seek to borrow at the firm's marginal cost of capital, thus optimizing the company's capital structure by always employing the least expensive capital. Private lower-middle-market and small-company owners want to avoid providing personal guarantees and are less concerned by the incremental cost of capital. Many gladly pay hundreds of extra basis points in interest to be relieved from the responsibility of personally guaranteeing a loan.

From the mid-middle market on up, managers are strongly motivated to manage the net assets of the business because companies have bonus systems tied to return on net assets. The more effectively a manager controls net assets, the bigger the bonus. On the contrary, small- and lower-middle-market private owners are compensated out of cash flow, not on a balance sheet metric. Therefore, they are motivated to manage the income statement, not the balance sheet.

There are distinct differences between transfer motives of players in various markets. Large-company managers have a corporate perspective; small-company owners have a personal perspective. Most small-firm owners have limited ability to build value in their business; therefore, they have limited transfer expectations. Most middle-market owners sell out because they are burned out. Large public companies do not get tired. Lower-middle-market owners cannot easily replace themselves because they tend to wear so many hats that no single person can replace them. Mid-middle-market and larger companies are organized functionally, so any one executive can be replaced without forcing a sale. Large companies can last a long time; small companies frequently do not outlast the current owner.

Large-company motives are different from personal owner motives relative to diversification, legacy building, and likely retirement vehicles. Most large-company managers seek to diversify their businesses because diversification reduces ownership risk and increases job security. As a result, a large-firm manager is more likely to diversify the business into unfamiliar territory. In contrast, lower-middle-market owners usually wish to diversify their estates, the majority of which are vested in the business. Therefore, a lower-middle-market owner is more likely to employ sophisticated estate planning techniques to transfer the business to children as a family legacy. Finally, lower-middle-market owners typically forgo some compensation to reinvest in the business, anticipating a major capital event. Professional managers look to maximize ordinary income and use 401(k) type plans or stock options to build retirement nest eggs.

Capital Market Theories

Until the first edition of this book was published in 2004, private market players had only corporate finance theories to explain the behavior of private capital markets.[8] They were left to assume that corporate finance theories explain and predict actions in the private markets. *Private Capital Markets* showed that corporate finance theories explain and organize the public capital markets but were never intended to explain nonpublic capital markets. Private markets must be explained using theories tailored to experience in those markets. Employing powerful theories in the wrong context leads to frustration and a loss of utility. For example, assessing risk using a theoretical structure applicable to one market while expecting a return in another market causes a serious disconnect.

At least three capital markets theories are needed to explain the broader capital markets. Exhibit 1.8 shows the linkage between each market and theory.

Small-company market theory does not yet exist in the literature. Elements of this emerging theory are extant, such as valuation standards for appraising small-business interests, capital-raising constructs such as the use of the Small Business Administration's programs, and various articles and writings on transferring small businesses. The behavior of many of the players at this end of the market relies more on psychology than on economics. At some point in the near future,

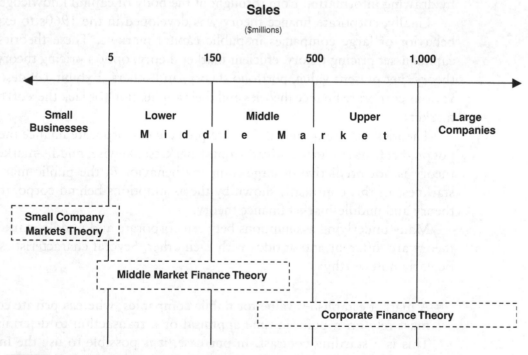

EXHIBIT 1.8 Capital Markets and Theories

EXHIBIT 1.9 Assumptions behind Corporate Finance Theory and Middle-Market Finance Theory

Corporate Finance Theory	Middle-Market Finance Theory
Use of a C corporation	Can be any type entity (S, limited liability corporation, etc.)
Value is established by a market	Value is established at a point in time
Ready access to public capital markets	No access to public capital markets
Owners have limited liability	Owners have unlimited liability
Owners are well diversified	Owners have one primary asset
Professional management	Owner management
Company has infinite life	Typical company life of one generation
Liquid securities efficiently traded	Illiquid securities inefficiently traded
Profit maximization as goal	Personal wealth creation as goal

institutions within the small-business market will mature sufficiently to enable a holistic theory to develop.

Middle-market finance theory is the integrated capital market theory unique to middle-market private companies, especially those with annual sales of $5 million to $350 million. This theory describes the valuation, capitalization, and transfer of private business interests. These three interrelated areas rely on each other in a triangular fashion. This interrelation not only provides strength to market architecture, but it also requires users of the body of knowledge to understand all three legs of the triangle. Just understanding valuation or capital structure or transfer will not get the job done in the marketplace. Employing triad logic generates what the private companies need most: holistic solutions. Typically a private business owner is faced with a financial problem that can be solved only by drawing information from throughout the body of capital knowledge.

Finally, corporate finance theory was developed in the 1960s to explain the behavior of large companies in public capital markets. These theories include capital asset pricing theory, efficient market theory, option pricing theory, agency theory, net present value, portfolio theory, and others. Exhibit 1.9 describes the various corporate finance theories and their application (or lack thereof) to private markets.

Theories are useful only if they are predictive. Corporate finance theory does not predict behavior in the private capital markets; likewise, middle-market finance theory is not predictive of large-company behavior in the public markets. The starkness of this contrast is shown by the assumptions behind corporate finance theory and middle-market finance theory.

Many underlying assumptions between corporate and middle-market finance theory are different and at odds with each other. Several characteristics are particularly noteworthy:

■ A market establishes value for public companies, whereas private companies must rely on a point-in-time appraisal or a transaction to determine value. This is a startling contrast. In one case, it is possible to use the Internet to obtain *real-time* pricing of a security. In the other case, much work is required to ascertain the value of a security at a particular point in time, probably in the past. If there were no other differences between public and private markets, this one issue would suffice to separate them.

■ Public companies have ready access to capital, but private companies must create capital solutions one deal at a time, with little certainty of success. Think of it as if public companies have access to a supermarket of securities. Within aisles of the supermarket can be found all of the available capital alternatives. The riskiness of the particular financing determines which aisle the public company can access. Private companies, however, have no access to the supermarket. Instead, they must visit a flea market of capital each time they need to access capital.

■ Shareholders in public companies are able to diversify, because of the high liquidity available in the public capital markets. They do not have all their eggs in one basket. Private owners have nearly all of their wealth tied up in one asset: the stock of their business. Increased risk is the main ramification of this lack of diversification. Both public and private capital markets treat risk similarly: The greater the risk of owning an asset, the greater the return required to compensate for the added risk.

The different assumptions that underlie corporate finance ultimately limit the utility of these theories to private markets, especially to the middle market.

Middle-Market Finance

Middle-market finance is the study of how managers of middle-market companies make investment and financing decisions. Chapter 2 describes this capital market theory.

NOTES

1. Unless otherwise stated, public companies are defined herein as those entities that trade on a public exchange and have a float of more than $500 million.
2. Robert T. Slee, "Public and Private Capital Markets Are Not Substitutes," *Business Appraisal Practice* (Spring 2005), p. 29.
3. Richard M. Trottier, *Middle Market Strategies: How Private Companies Use the Markets to Create Value* (Hoboken, NJ: John Wiley & Sons, 2009), Chapter 1.
4. John K. Paglia, Pepperdine Private Capital Markets Project Survey Report, April 2010, bschool.pepperdine.edu/privatecapital.
5. Robert T. Slee and Richard M. Trottier, "Capital Market Segmentation Matters," *Business Appraisal Practice* (Summer 2006), p. 46.
6. Correlations between senior lending multiples and acquisition multiples are: $10 million–$25 million category: .60; $25 million–$50 million category: −.05; $50 million–$100 million: .87.
7. Slee and Trottier, "Capital Market Segmentation Matters," p. 49.
8. Robert T. Slee, *Private Capital Markets: Valuation, Capitalization, and Transfer of Private Business Interests*, 1st ed. (Hoboken, NJ: John Wiley & Sons, 2004).

CHAPTER 2

Middle-Market Finance

A premise of this book is that private capital markets are unique. As such, unique capital market theories are required to explain and predict behavior of players in those markets. The main theory described in this book is middle-market finance theory, which is an integrated body of knowledge that applies to valuation, capitalization, and transfer of middle-market private companies. Several macro-events over the past 20 years have set the stage for the study of middle-market finance theory. These are:

- Private business valuation has become a career path. Dr. Shannon Pratt started this movement by publishing his landmark book, *Valuing a Business: The Analysis and Appraisal of Closely Held Companies* (McGraw-Hill) in 1981. Dr. Pratt was the first to bring structured thought to private business valuation. Partially due to his continued work, private business valuation has become quite sophisticated. There are now more than 5,000 practicing appraisers in the United States.
- Since the early 1990s, the private capital markets have developed many new capital alternatives. Prior to 1990, commercial lenders were the primary source of capital to private companies. In fact, if the local banker could not supply all of the capital needs of the owner-manager, the company probably went without necessary funding. Since that time, asset-based lenders, mezzanine players, private equity groups, and others have appeared. The variety of capital purveyors has enabled owner-managers to think in terms of capital structure and the various components of debt and equity that comprise it.
- Techniques to transfer private business interests have proliferated and become institutionalized. Transfer methods such as employee stock ownership plans, family limited partnerships, private auctions, and various other strategies are now available to owner-managers. Whether this transfer happens within the business to employees or a family member, or to an outsider, the owner-manager needs to become more knowledgeable. Owners often view transferring a business interest like grabbing the brass ring on a merry-go-round, but they need help improving their chances.

Most owner-managers and their professional advisors do not focus on the breadth of valuation, capital structure, and transfer issues, because they do not spend time dealing with this full body of knowledge. This book provides a resource

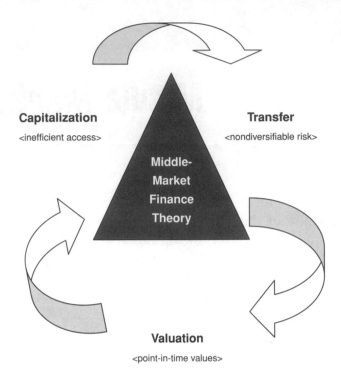

EXHIBIT 2.1   Structure of Middle-Market Finance Theory

for these individuals so they can structure and solve difficult financial problems in the private capital markets.

MIDDLE-MARKET FINANCE THEORY

Middle-market finance theory is the integrated capital market theory unique to middle-market companies, especially those with annual sales of $5 million to $350 million. This theory describes the valuation, capitalization, and transfer of middle-market private business interests. These three interrelated areas rely on each other in a triangular fashion, as shown in Exhibit 2.1.

Valuation forms the base of the triangle and is the foundation of middle-market finance theory. Valuation involves a rigorously defined process that ultimately derives what the company or business interest is worth. Valuation relies on input from the transfer leg of the triangle. The obvious transfer connections are selling multiples and other transactions that help derive values for similar situations. Without this feedback, much of valuation would be done in total isolation from the market and would quickly lead to nonsense. Since private securities do not have access to an active trading market, they rely on point-in-time appraisal or transactional pricing to determine value.

Capitalization, or capital structure formation, relies on valuation, the base of the triangle. The private capital markets allocate capital according to levels of risk and return. Private companies rely on proper valuations of assets, earnings, and cash flow to raise money. Unlike the public markets, private capital

EXHIBIT 2.2 Public and Middle Market Names

Public	Private Middle Market
Public capital markets (Wall Street)	Private capital markets (Main Street)
Corporate finance	Middle-market finance
Corporate finance theory	Middle-market finance theory

markets are characterized by inefficient access to capital. Private companies often cannot determine with any confidence whether they can access the funding they need.

Finally, transfer relies on capitalization. The business ownership transfer spectrum includes a broad range of alternatives. It spans the transfer of business interests to parties within the company to external parties. Transfer can occur only if capital is available to support the transaction. Transfer happens at a particular value that is determined using one of the defined valuation processes. Private investors cannot easily diversify their holdings due to the lack of liquidity in the private transfer market. This liquidity limitation increases the riskiness of the private transfer market, making things more difficult for private companies.

As Exhibit 2.2 shows, public and private markets use different names to describe key like-kind terms.

TRIADIC LOGIC

A compelling logic holds the three conceptual sides of the triangle together. Unlike most financial logic based on positives and negatives, a triadic logic operating here provides powerful cohesion between the moving parts. A system of logic with three bases is dynamic rather than static and serves to bring the three sides of the triangle into a coherent whole. This is the logic of a three-legged stool. The reason for introducing this triadic logical structure is to demonstrate that it is not possible to remove one of the tenets in a dynamic system without destroying the system. Legs can be added, but the logical system is necessary and sufficient on its own to provide coherence to middle-market finance theory.

For example, consider removing the capitalization side of the triangle and attempting to transfer the business. It is practically impossible. Or try transferring a business without a process of valuation. Again, it makes very little logical sense. Finally, an attempt to value a business without considering a possible transfer or how that transfer is capitalized is untenable.

MIDDLE-MARKET FINANCE THEORY IN PRACTICE

Middle-market finance theory is the integrated body of capital market theory that describes the valuation, capitalization, and transfer of middle market private business interests. Each of the three sides of the conceptual triangle exhibits a unique framework.

Value World Theory

Private securities do not enjoy access to an active trading market. Either a private valuation must be undertaken, or a transaction must occur to determine the value of a private security *for some purpose at some point in time.* "Purpose" is defined as the intention of the involved party or the reason for the valuation. Purpose leads to the function of an appraisal. "Function" is described as the intended specific use of an appraisal. Specific functions of a valuation require the use of specific methods or processes, each of which can derive dramatically different value conclusions. The purposes (sometimes called "reasons") for undertaking an appraisal are referred to herein as giving rise to *value worlds.* Therefore, here is the premise of value world theory:

> *A private business value is relative to the value world in which it is viewed.*

Every private company, therefore, has a number of different values at the same time, depending on the purpose *and* function of the valuation. The purpose of the appraisal governs the selection of a value world. Each value world follows a defined process to determine value under specific rules, based on the function of the appraisal. Each value world may have multiple functions. Each world also has an authority, which is the agent or agents that govern the world. The authority decides whether the intentions of the involved party are acceptable for use in that world as well as prescribes the methods used in that world.

Exhibit 2.3 lists a number of value worlds, with associated purposes, functions, and authorities.

Examples of authority are found in each appraisal world. For instance, the Financial Accounting Standards Board (FASB) is the authority in the world of impaired goodwill. FASB is responsible for developing criteria and administering methodology used to derive value and for sanctioning noncompliance.

By understanding the logic, definitions of process, and treatment of facts within each world, it becomes clear that private valuation is possible only within a set of parameters: a value world.

The intention or motive of the involved party leads to a purpose of an appraisal. This is the starting point in the valuation discussion. Purposes for undertaking an appraisal give rise to value worlds. The logical construct of a value world is independent of the experience of individual appraisers and individual assignments. Value then is expressed only in terms consistent with that world. Once the project is located in a value world, the function of the appraisal governs the choice of appraisal methods. The responsible authority in each value world prescribes these methods. The choice of appropriate appraisal methods ultimately may lead to a point in time singular value. Thus, a private business value is relative to the *purpose* and *function* of its appraisal.

EXHIBIT 2.3 Value Worlds Concept Chart

Appraisal Purpose	Value World	Appraisal Functions	Responsible Authority
To find the highest value in the open market	Market value	Sale of a minority or control interest, to support a merger	Financial intermediaries
To find a value for tax matters and for some legal reasons	Fair market value	Federal estate and gift taxes, employee stock ownership plans (ESOPs), charitable contributions	Federal law, administrative rulings
Shareholder actions	Fair value	To support a minority dissent, oppression claim	Statutory law
Shareholder value measurement	Incremental business value	To create/measure management bonus plans, company performance measurement, capital allocation systems	Management consulting industry
To determine insurance coverage	Insurable value	To fund buy/sell agreements, business interruption claims	Insurance industry, involved parties
To follow Financial Accounting Standards Board (FASB) ASC 350-20	Impaired goodwill	To determine impaired goodwill	FASB
To value intangible assets	Intangible asset	To value intellectual property, such as patents and copyrights, or to value intellectual capital	Intangible asset laws (patents, etc.)
To value the business from one investor's perspective	Investment value	Value specific to one investor, probably for purchase/investment	Investor
To value the business from an owner's perspective	Owner value	Value specific to owner, probably for sale	Owner
To determine the borrowing capacity of the business	Collateral value	To obtain a secured loan	Secured lending industry
To determine the value of a start-up	Early equity value	To derive the value of a start-up to determine equity splits	Venture capitalists
To determine the value of a business in bankruptcy	Bankruptcy value	To determine how much money creditors will receive	Bankruptcy judge and statutes
To determine the value of a public company	Public value	To set the price of an initial public offering	Public investment bankers

Private Capital

Capitalization, or capital structure formation, is the second leg of the private capital market triangle. "Capital structure" refers to the composition of the invested capital of the business, typically a mixture of debt and equity financing. For private companies, these securities range from placing industrial revenue bonds, to receiving mezzanine capital, to issuing common equity to venture capital firms. Private capital markets are much less efficient than their public counterparts. In fact, due to the lack of an organized market, private capital market solutions are created one at a time. In other words, private capital is assembled on a deal-by-deal basis.

Yet there is a structure of capital alternatives in the private markets. Unlike the organized structure that defines the public capital markets, private markets are more ad hoc, which leads to the next statement:

Private markets can be thought of as outdoor bazaars rather than public supermarkets of securities.

Nearly all capital alternatives are available in the private bazaar, but they are found in separate shops or discrete increments. Financing is more difficult in the private markets because capital providers in the bazaar constantly move around and may or may not rely on prior transactions to make current decisions. Fortunately for those in need of private capital, some organization in this *bizarre* bazaar can be discerned.

For assistance in empirically describing the private capital markets, the author partnered with Pepperdine University to conduct a series of surveys. These Pepperdine Private Capital Markets Surveys began in April 2009 and have continued every six months to the time of this writing.[1] These surveys help overcome a major shortfall in the first edition of this book, which was based mainly on anecdotal evidence.

The Pepperdine survey project is the first comprehensive and simultaneous investigation of the behavior of the major private *capital types*. The surveys specifically examine the behavior of senior lenders, asset-based lenders, mezzanine funds, private equity groups, venture capital, angel investing, and factoring firms. The Pepperdine surveys investigate, for each private capital type, the important benchmarks that must be met in order to qualify for capital (called "credit boxes"), how much capital typically is accessible, and what the required returns are for extending capital in the current economic environment. This book incorporates empirical data from the surveys into the discussion wherever possible.

Capital types are segmented into various capital access points (CAPs). The CAPs represent specific alternatives that correspond to *institutional* capital offerings in the marketplace. For example, asset-based lending is a capital type, and Tier 1 and Tier 3 are examples of capital access points within that type. Exhibit 2.4 shows the capital types with corresponding capital access points that were surveyed, along with one capital type—equipment leasing—and a number of capital asset points mentioned in this book that have not been surveyed. Examples of nonsurveyed CAPs are government lending programs, such as Small Business Association 7(a) or 504 loan programs. These nonsurveyed CAPs are derived mainly from programs that are readily observed in the marketplace.

Accessing private capital entails several steps. First, the *credit box* of the particular CAP is described. Credit boxes depict the criteria necessary to access the specific capital. Next, each CAP defines *sample terms*. These are example terms, such as loan/investment amount, loan maturity, interest rate, and other expenses required to close the loan or investment. Finally, by using the sample terms, an expected rate of return can be calculated. This rate is the expected or "all-in" rate

EXHIBIT 2.4 Structure of Capitalization

Capital Types	Capital Access Points
Bank lending	Industrial revenue bonds
	SBA 504 loans
	Business and industry loans
	SBA 7(a) loan guaranty
	SBA CAPLine credit lines
	Credit lines
	Export working capital loans
Equipment leasing	Bank leasing
	Captive/vendor leasing
	Specialty leasing
	Venture leasing
Asset-based lending	Tier 1 asset-based loans (ABLs)
	Tier 2 ABLs
	Tier 3 ABLs
Factoring	Low volume
	Medium volume
	High volume
Mezzanine	Mezzanine
Private equity	Angel financing
	Venture capital
	Private equity groups

of return required by an investor. It is not sufficient to consider the stated interest rate on a loan. Other factors, such as origination costs, compensating balances, and monitoring fees, add to the cost of the loan.

Once all of the capital types are described and their expected returns determined, it is possible to graph the Pepperdine Private Capital Market Line (PPCML), shown in Exhibit 2.5. The PPCML is empirically defined, since the capital asset pricing model or other predictive models are not suitable for use in

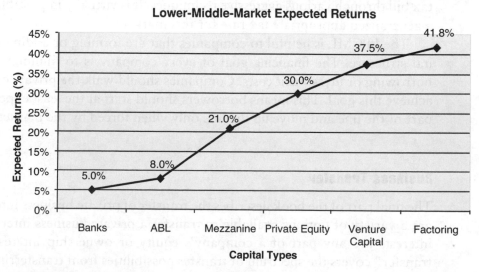

Lower-Middle-Market Expected Returns

EXHIBIT 2.5 Pepperdine Private Capital Market Line

EXHIBIT 2.6 Pepperdine Survey Capital Types by Quartiles

Capital Type	Description	1st Quartile	Median	3rd Quartile
Banks	$5 million equipment loan	4.1%	5.0%	6.3%
Asset-based loan	$5 million working capital loan	4.3%	8.0%	12.0%
Mezzanine	$5 million model pretax internal rate of return (IRR)	20.0%	21.0%	23.0%
Private equity	$5 million model pretax IRR	25.0%	30.0%	35.0%
Venture capital	Expansion model pretax IRR	30.5%	37.5%	40.0%
Factoring*	Medium monthly volume	–	41.8%	–

*Effective cost of medium-volume factoring; see Chapter 21 for the calculation.

creating the expected rates of return in the private markets. Somewhere on or near this line is the expected return of the major institutional capital alternatives that exist in the private capital markets.

Exhibit 2.5 encompasses various capital types in terms of the provider's all-in expected returns. The PPCML is described as median, pretax expected returns of institutional capital providers. For consistency, the capital types chosen to comprise the PPCML reflect likely capital options for mainly lower-middle market companies. For example, the PPCML uses the "$5 million loan/investment" survey category for banks, asset-based lending, mezzanine, and private equity. It should be noted that the PPCML could be created using different data sets.[2] The returns are further described as first and third quartiles, as shown in Exhibit 2.6.

The PPCML is stated on a pretax basis, both from a provider and from a user perspective. In other words, capital providers offer deals to the marketplace on a pretax basis. For example, if a private equity investor requires a 25% return, this is stated as a pretax return. Also, the PPCML does not assume a tax rate to the investee, even though many of the capital types use interest rates that generate deductible interest expense for the borrower. Capital types are not tax-effected because many owners of private companies *manage* their company's tax bill through various aggressive techniques. It is virtually impossible to estimate a generalized appropriate tax rate for this market.

The PPCML is helpful to companies that are forming or adding to their capital structure. The financing goal of every company is to minimize its effective borrowing or investment costs. Companies should walk the private capital line to achieve this goal. This means borrowers should start at the least expensive lowest part of the line and move up the line only when forced by the market.

Business Transfer

The final part of the book describes the transfer of private business interests. There are a variety of options available to transfer a private business interest. Business interests are any part of a company's equity or ownership interest. "Business transfer" covers the spectrum of transfer possibilities from transferring assets of a company, to transferring partial or enterprise stock interests.

Transfer channels represent the highest level of choice for private owners. Owner motives are the basis for selecting transfer channels. Transfer methods— the actual techniques used to transfer a business interest—are grouped under transfer channels.

An owner has seven transfer channels from which to choose. The channels are:

1. Employees
2. Charitable trusts
3. Family
4. Co-owners
5. Outside—retire
6. Outside—continue
7. Public

The choice of channel is manifested by the owner's motives and goals. For instance, owners wishing to transfer the business to children choose the family transfer channel. Owners who desire to transfer the business to an outsider then retire choose the outside—retire channel; and so on. Exhibit 2.7 is a schematic

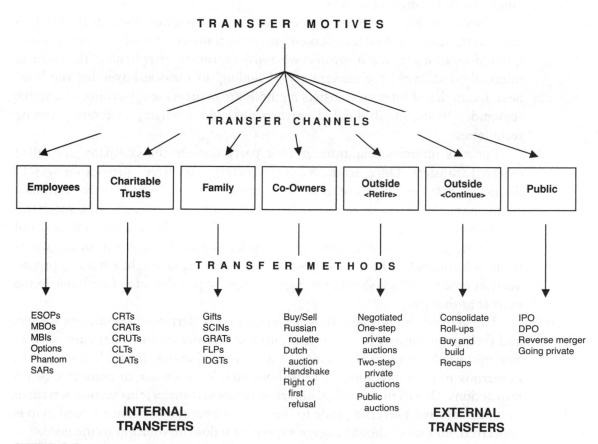

EXHIBIT 2.7 Business Ownership Transfer Spectrum

representation of transfer channels and transfer methods in the business ownership transfer spectrum.

Each transfer channel contains numerous transfer methods. A transfer method is the actual technique used to transfer a business interest. For example, grantor-retained annuity trusts, family limited partnerships, and recapitalizations are methods by which an interest is transferred. Certain methods are exclusively aligned with certain channels, such as an employee stock ownership plan (ESOP) within the employee transfer channel. Other methods can be applied across channels, such as the use of private annuities with either the family or outside channels.

Transfer methods correspond to specific value worlds. For instance, transferring stock into a charitable trust occurs in the world of fair market value. Selling stock via an auction happens in the world of market value; and so on. The connection between transfer methods and value worlds produces a major tenet of private business transfer:

The choice of transfer method yields a business interest's likely value.

An owner's motive for a transfer leads to the choice of a transfer method, which is linked to a value world. Each value world employs a unique appraisal process that yields a particular value. In other words, an owner can *plan* the timing and value of business in a transfer.

When a business interest transfers within the company itself, it is called an internal transfer. Internal transfers comprise the transfer methods that are custom-tailored solutions for use by owners who wish to transfer part or all of the business internally and avoid the uncertainty of finding an outside buyer for the business. Examples of internal transfers methods are management buyouts, charitable remainder trusts, family limited partnerships, and a variety of estate planning techniques.

Business interests that transfer to a party outside the company are called external transfers. Once again, the term "external transfer" provides a way to discuss transfer methods useful to an investor or buyer outside of the business. As the name implies, external transfers employ a process to achieve a successful conclusion. Examples of external transfers include negotiated sales, roll-ups, and reverse mergers. As an illustration, if an owner of a medium-size company wants to sell a business for the highest possible market price, he might employ a private auction process, which should produce the highest possible offers available in the market at that time.

The goal of the business transfer section is to alert private business owners and their professionals to the large number of transfer options that exist. Owner motives usually lead to the choice of a transfer channel. Each channel houses numerous transfer methods. The methods enable an owner to convert motives into actions. Due to the technical nature of business transfer, this section is written to give interested players a guide to the various alternatives. Once a road map is conceived, an owner should engage experts to tailor the solution to the need.

OWNER MOTIVES

A motive is a goal that initiates an action. The governing authority must sanction an owner's motive for a goal to be met.

Motives of private business owners initiate an action. Motives are not like dreams in that dreams do not lead to action. For example, many private business owners dream of going public, yet 99.9% never become public entities because authorities in the market must support the motive and provide it with additional momentum. No positive outcome is possible without this additional support. Authorities control both access and the rules of the game within their spheres of influence. In the case of going public, a private owner must convince a public investment banking firm, the authority, to take the company public.

Unintended consequences occur when private business owners act without considering the governing role of authorities. The owner who attempts to give stock to children, without acknowledging Revenue Ruling 59-60, may receive an unwelcome visit from the Internal Revenue Service (IRS). Or the owner attempting to raise venture capital money without regard to the venture capitalist's credit box may simply waste time and effort.

Private owners need to understand the mutually exclusive features and functions of the private capital markets. Once the motive initiates action, specific possibilities are opened and closed. This occurs because the owner's motives initiate action from each side of the triangular body of knowledge that forms connections between features and functions. By launching the initial motive without proper information, the owner unknowingly chooses a course of action that narrows future options. For instance, although owner's motives select the appropriate value world, once located in a value world, only a limited number of capital access points may be available. Within the value world and preselected capital access points, only a few transfer methods may be available. The available transfer methods, capital access points, and ultimate price an owner receives triangulate with the value world originally determined by the owner's motives.

For instance, an owner may be motivated to transfer the business to the employees via an ESOP. Since ESOPs are valued in the world of fair market value, the owner's motives cause the company to be valued in this hypothetical world without synergies. Most ESOPs are financed by bank lending. Further suppose the owner wants to transfer the company to the key managers. Managers live in the world of investment value and are constrained by their ability to finance the purchase price. The managers may access secured lending to finance the deal but may not be able to access private equity without losing control of the company. The owner may be able to increase the purchase price into the world of owner value if she is willing to finance the deal through seller notes. Finally, an owner who wishes to sell to a synergistic buyer in a consolidation makes the conscious decision to enter the synergy subworld of market value. An owner's motives drive the price she receives in a transfer.

EXHIBIT 2.8   Sources of Legitimacy for Authority

Government Action	Compelling Logic	Utility
Many authorities derive their legitimacy through government action. Government action often regulates the valuation process, capital allocation, and the methods by which to transfer business interests. State and federal authorities typically have strong sanctioning power due to the threat of legal action. Government-based authorities ultimately are limited by the consent of the governed.	Authority grounds the language and logic in the community it serves. Membership entails using this language and, when it is deemed useful, following the logic. The membership provides market feedback to the authority when it believes the compelling logic is not useful or could be improved. An example of an authority that fights to win the logic battle are the ERISA laws and the various ESOP service providers.	Authority derives legitimacy from the utility of its logic and actions. Utility is measured by how well it helps members accomplish their objective. Examples of utility in valuation is the management consultant's espousal of incremental business value. Unless constituents accept the utility of the authority's argument, incremental business value will not be adopted.

AUTHORITY

Once an owner sets a goal, the relevant authorities must be heeded. Authorities set the rules and processes regarding business valuation, capital structure formation and business interest transfer. Authorities in the private capital markets provide these rules and act as traffic cops to ensure compliance. The concept of authority helps explain how and why things happen the way they do.

"Authority" refers to agents or agencies with primary responsibility to develop, adopt, promulgate, and administer standards of practice within the private capital markets. Authority derives its influence or legitimacy mainly from government action, compelling logic, and/or the utility of its standards. Exhibit 2.8 describes the sources of legitimacy for authority. Authority sanctions its decisions by veto power or denying access to the market.

Each of the three areas of the private capital markets has dozens of authorities. For example, in valuation, the IRS and tax courts are the primary authorities in the world of fair market value. In capital, various capital providers such as banks and venture capitalists are authorities. Finally, in business transfer, authorities may be laws, such as the Employee Retirement Income Security Act laws for ESOPs, or investment bankers for reverse mergers.

Every authority has a boundary that forms the limit of its influence. The most obvious boundary is the utility of the logic or action that the authority promotes. In other words, if an authority promulgates rules that do not make sense to its constituency, the rules may be ignored or challenged. Even the mighty IRS is countered by the tax courts when members believe the former's rules are misdirected. This has been the case over the past 20 years regarding lack of marketability discounts. Tax courts have consistently ruled against the historic IRS position that private business interests suffer only slightly as compared to public interests.

Authorities have varying degrees of sanctioning power. The most direct sanction is veto power. Capital providers do not have to supply the requested money. Or the IRS can challenge an appraisal in court. Many authorities sanction noncompliance by denying access to information or a market. For instance, financial intermediaries who believe shareholders are overvaluing their company might choose not to represent it in a sale.

Each chapter discusses authority, especially as it relates to mandated processes and the legitimacy of the authority's position.

TRIANGULATION

The concept of triangulation demonstrates middle-market finance theory as a holistic body of knowledge. It requires an understanding of the entire framework before a specific technique or method can be properly considered and fully understood. That is why this work is consolidated into one book, covering valuation, capitalization, and business transfer as interrelated topics.

Points located on the various sides of the middle-market finance theory triangle do not exist in isolation. It is useful to borrow a loosely constructed concept of triangulation from navigation or civil engineering, where a point is located only with reference to other points. Once a point is identified and described, it can be used as a survey monument or control point to mark its location and relationship with other points. "Triangulation," graphically depicted in Exhibit 2.9, refers to the use of two sides of the middle-market finance theory triangle to help fully understand a point on the third side. Control networks can then be created using triangulation with various orders of accuracy. In economics, as in surveying,

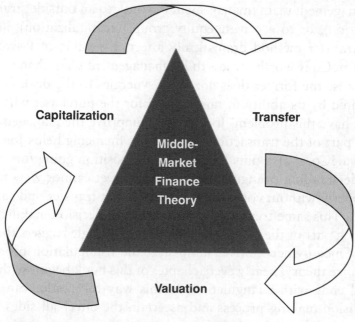

EXHIBIT 2.9 Triangulation

triangulation can help map out unknown territory by establishing relationships with what is known.

While there is no claim for mathematical accuracy or certainty in applying the concept of triangulation to the private capital markets, its application may bring useful insights. What is known about two control points on legs of the triangle can be used to locate and understand a third point. The process helps to think about relationships, understand interconnections, and eliminate errors.

On a macro level, triangulation can be summarized in three interrelated sentences:

1. Business value is directly affected by the company's access to capital and the transfer methods selected by or available to the owner.
2. Capitalization is dependent on the value world in which the company is viewed and the availability of transfer methods.
3. The ability to transfer a business interest is conditioned by its access to capital and the value world in which the transfer takes place.

Triangulation is a further embodiment of triadic logic, which describes middle-market finance theory using a three-legged conceptual stool. In other words, private valuation can be understood only relative to capital/transfer, capitalization must be viewed relative to the impact of valuation/transfer, and transfer is influenced by capitalization/valuation.

Perhaps an example of triangulation will help. Assume Joe Mainstreet, controlling shareholder of PrivateCo, the fictitious company described in this book, wants to diversify his estate and sell the business. Doing so typically calls for an appraisal in the world of market value. Joe has numerous transfer methods from which to choose that will meet his goal. For instance, he may sell to his management team (management buyout), to an outside strategic acquirer (private auction), or to a private equity group (recapitalization), and so on. The choice of transfer method dramatically affects the value of PrivateCo. It is likely that PrivateCo is worth far less to his management team than to a synergistic acquirer because the former does not bring synergies to the deal. Further, management is limited by its ability to raise capital for the purchase; whereas the acquirer may not have this problem. Joe may help improve the management's value by financing part of the transaction. While seller financing helps Joe get a higher value for PrivateCo, it also puts him in a riskier position going forward. This is the key to understanding triangulation. Joe Mainstreet cannot view the value of PrivateCo properly without considering the effect that transfer and capital has on the situation. This same triangulated framework of decision making is required no matter which part of the private capital market triangle triggers the action.

Since owner motives jump-start the triangulation process in middle-market finance theory, nearly every chapter of this book begins with motives of the owner and ends with triangulation. In this way the reader can establish the owner's decision-making process and ascertain the effect all sides of the middle-market finance theory triangle have on the decision.

NOTES

1. John K. Paglia, Pepperdine Private Capital Markets Project Survey Report, April, 2010, bschool.pepperdine.edu/privatecapital.
2. The Pepperdine surveys are delineated by quartiles and investment size, which allows for numerous capital market lines. The Pepperdine Private Capital Market Line (PPCML) shown is this book is representative of the capital alternatives available to lower-middle-market companies. Unless otherwise stated, the PPCML will use data from the "$5 million loan/investment" category of the April 2010 Pepperdine survey.

Business Valuation

CHAPTER 3

Private Business Valuation: Introduction

Private business valuation has only recently been viewed as a unique body of knowledge. In 1981, Dr. Shannon Pratt published *Valuing a Business: The Analysis and Appraisal of Closely Held Companies* (McGraw-Hill), the first major effort to legitimize private business appraisal as a stand-alone discipline. Before this work, private appraisal was driven by unsubstantiated opinion, and often the appraiser with the loudest opinion carried the day. During the 1990s, private valuation became sophisticated to the point where it is now a career path for thousands of business appraisers.

Professional business appraisers spend most of their time deriving fair market values of private business interests. This is understandable since fair market value is the most developed standard of value in the literature, the tax code, and the courts. Fair market value is often the default standard and is routinely employed for deriving value in a variety of scenarios, such as the value of a company to be sold or the value of a business interest in an insurable setting. It surprises many business owners and others outside of the appraisal community that a notional, hypothetical standard such as fair market value is so widely used to value actual interests. Rather than proposing a further stretch of fair market value into a one-size-fits-all standard, this book shows that the universe of private business appraisal is diverse and can be structured in a useful manner.

This chapter describes the fundamental concepts underlying private business valuation. In keeping with this book's premise, most of the tenets of private business valuation are drawn from middle-market finance theory, not corporate finance theory. The three major private valuation concepts covered are:

1. Private investor expectations drive private valuation.
2. Private business valuation can be viewed through value worlds.
3. Private valuation is a *range* concept.

These concepts form the basis for the ensuing chapters on private business valuation.

PRIVATE INVESTOR EXPECTATIONS DRIVE PRIVATE VALUATION

An underlying principle of all valuation is that risk is related to market rates on capital. The greater the perceived risk of owning an investment, the greater the return expected by investors to compensate for the risk. The desire to achieve a return that is at least commensurate with the corresponding risk is the primary motive for investors to bear the uncertainty of investing.

Investors *expect* to earn a certain return from an investment. Return expectations are the starting point in the valuation process. Expected returns convert a benefit stream to a present value. This conversion makes all investments comparable; that is, alternative investments with comparable risk can be valued on a common basis. Risk is the degree of uncertainty, in terms of the amount and timing, of realizing expected returns.[1]

Another way of looking at the risk/return relationship is through a discount rate, which is determined by the market.[2] The discount rate is the expected rate of return required to attract capital to an investment. It takes into account the rate of return available from other investments of comparable risk. The definition of "market" is especially important here, since it should encompass the universe of investors who are reasonable candidates to provide funds for a particular investment.[3] A fundamental premise of this book is that the market for *private* return expectations is determined by *private* investors. This is contrary to current appraisal methodology, which often looks to the public capital markets to determine private expectations. This difference is discussed at length later in this chapter. First, however, is a further delineation of private return expectations.

By answering the question "Return to whom?" private return expectations can be viewed from at least three different perspectives: market, firm, and investor. Each of these perspectives tells us something useful in the valuation process. Exhibit 3.1 shows the definition, terminology, and primary discovery process for each return perspective.

The private capital markets contain all of the return expectations of private investors. The market rate is an opportunity cost, that is, the cost of forgoing the next best alternative investment. Private *market* return expectations are found in the private capital markets by viewing the Pepperdine Private Capital Market Line. Terms such as discount rate, expected rate of return, and cost of capital describe the market return.

An individual firm attempts to meet its shareholders' return expectations. Firms typically use their weighted average cost of capital (WACC) as a minimum return required on investments. Management must take care to evaluate the risk of potential investments. The real return expectation should match the risk profile of the investment. This may mean a firm's WACC is 15%, yet the riskiness of a certain investment opportunity causes a return expectation of 25%. This is a typical situation for companies in multiple lines of business. Suppose PrivateCo owns three divisions, each operating with a different risk profile. PrivateCo has a single balance sheet that yields an 18% WACC. Should PrivateCo use 18% as the *hurdle rate*, the firm's minimum acceptable rate of return on an investment given

EXHIBIT 3.1 Private Return Expectations: Three Perspectives

Market

Definition:	The expected rate of return that the private capital markets require in order to attract funds to a particular investment.
Terms:	Discount rate, expected rate of return, required rate of return, cost of capital.
Process:	Found by viewing the Pepperdine Private Capital Market Line.

Firm

Definition:	The expected rate of return that a firm's shareholders require in order to fund a particular investment.
Terms:	Weighted average cost of capital (WAAC), hurdle rate.
Process:	Depends on the use to which the capital is put. The firm matches its expected return with the risk profile of the investment. At a minimum, however, the firm should receive its WACC.

Investor

Definition:	The expected rate of return that an investor requires in order to fund a particular investment.
Terms:	Cost of equity, return on equity, return on investment.
Process:	The investor's perception of the riskiness of the investment sets the expectation. Specifically, investor return is found by considering the total return received from the investment divided by the investment amount.

the risk of the particular investment, for all investment opportunities within the company? The answer is no. This subtle distinction between a firm's WACC and hurdle rate is important. Managers should match the return expectation with the project risk, which often means using a rate higher than the company's WACC.

Individual investors have return expectations that must be met before they will fund an investment. Cost of equity is peculiar to each investor. Most individuals determine required return on investment as the expected benefit stream divided by the amount of the investment.

The three return perspectives are central to understanding investment behavior in the private capital markets. The universe of individual investor and firm expectations comprise the market. Business valuation is essentially an exercise in measuring and matching risk and return. Investors view risk and return differently, which may also lead them to choose different valuation methods. This value measurement is then used to drive capital-raising and transfer methods. Deals do not happen without some agreement on risk/return.

A question remains: Why, then, do so many *private* appraisals performed in the United States look to the *public* capital markets to determine *private* return expectations? The capital asset pricing model and buildup methods are valuation tools that rely on public securities information to derive private discount rates. Using these models presumes that the return expectations in the public and private capital markets are the same. The next discussion indicates that they are not surrogates.

Is the Subject Company Similar?

The answer to the question of using public security information to derive private business values lies in Revenue Ruling 59-60, issued by the U.S. Treasury Department in 1959. It gives guidance on the valuation of closely held stock. Revenue rulings present the position of the Internal Revenue Service (IRS) on various matters, and Revenue Ruling 59-60 has become the benchmark decree regarding the government's view of private business valuation. Revenue Ruling 59-60 justifies considering the "market prices of . . . either on an exchange or over the counter" as one of eight factors to consider when valuing private businesses. Public companies comparable to the private subject are called *public guideline* companies. This begs a significant question: Does a private company have the attributes necessary to make a comparison to public companies relevant?[4]

Several key underlying theories of public corporate finance do not apply directly to private companies, as discussed in Appendix A. To the extent that corporate finance theories do apply, public and private companies often appear at opposite ends of the theoretical spectrum. Other theories, such as net present value, apply and are simply not used.

The next issue is whether public stock information is a relevant source for valuing private stocks. Most private companies have different foundations, both financially and organizationally, from those of most public companies. Perhaps a comparison can be found between two different industrial buildings. Assume both contain 100,000 square feet on five acres of land. Both are zoned the same, with approximately the same internal layout and capabilities. The only difference is that one sits on a shaky foundation and the other sits on bedrock. As long as their foundations are disregarded, they are equally desirable substitutes. But few would ignore such foundational consideration.

Principle of Substitution

The principle of substitution is a foundational concept underlying all economic appraisals. According to the principle of substitution, value is determined by the cost of acquiring an equally desirable substitute. In other words, no one would knowingly pay more for something than it would cost to obtain an equally desirable substitute. Guideline transactions are used to define the market for businesses that are equally desirable substitutes for the subject business. It is important to recognize that the principle of substitution does not call for "identical" businesses as substitutes for the subject company. Instead, it calls for investments whose desirability is equal to that of the subject business. From an investment viewpoint, guideline transaction prices are relevant to the value of private businesses when they are similar with respect to the degree of risk, the liquidity of the investment, and the involvement of management.[5]

A full discussion of the principle of substitution is found in Appendix B. It shows that public guideline transaction prices are not relevant to the valuation of private business interests. All three areas—risk, liquidity, and management involvement—point to major differences between public and private company stocks. Under this analysis, public stocks are *generally* not good substitutes or comparisons for private stocks. However, there are instances where it might be appropriate to compare a private company against its public counterparts.

To have a relevant private-to-public comparison, the private company should have the attributes necessary to go public. Following the analogy, it should have a foundation similar to that of a public company. These attributes alone do not overcome all of the problems, but the ability to go public does lessen the effect of most of the aforementioned differences. For example, company risk and management approach should be similar between could-be-public and public companies. Liquidity for could-be-public companies is probably enhanced over other private companies.[6] Could-be-public companies have more ability to attract minority interest capital than would otherwise be possible. This could indicate that holding period expectations may be shorter for these companies than other private companies.

The next characteristics make a private company more suitable for comparison to public companies. These attributes can be used to determine whether a private company could go public within a reasonable amount of time, say, 12 months.[7]

- Does the company have the look and feel of public companies in its market segment? Does it have a story for using the newly raised funds that would yield returns greater than expected in its market segment?
- Is there credentialed management depth? An active board of directors? Are both groups up to facing the public scrutiny that the process entails?
- Has strategic planning been developed to implement both short- and long-term goals?
- Can all public reporting requirements, especially in the financial area, be met with timeliness?
- Does the subject company perform financially above the average in its market segment?
- Can the stock be sold even if all of the preceding requirements are present? For example, there may be limited public capital access for a $3 million box converter. Is the subject company in a market segment that has historically been granted access to public monies?

If the owner or managers can answer these questions affirmatively, there is reason to believe it could access public money. This accessibility should be the basis for more relevant comparability. Companies that could go public but choose to remain private are the most relevant candidates for a public guideline valuation method. At least they have a similar foundation from which to compare.

PRIVATE BUSINESS VALUATION CAN BE VIEWED THROUGH VALUE WORLDS

Private securities do not have access to an active trading market and, therefore, must rely on point-in-time appraisal or transactional pricing to determine value. Either a private valuation must be undertaken or a transaction must occur to determine the value of a private security *for some purpose at some point in time.* "Purpose" is defined as the intention of the involved party regarding why a valuation is needed.

Intentions cover the range of owner motivations for needing to know the value of their business. For instance, an owner may need to know the value of her business because of the need to raise private equity. Or the owner may need to know the value of the business because she wants to employ an estate planning technique, such as a family limited partnership, to transfer shares of the company to her children. The motivation to know the value of the business is not just a curiosity. The initial motive launches the owner on a path that both opens and closes possibilities. For instance, an estate planning motive leads to a fair market valuation, which yields a financial, nonsynergistic value. Choosing this path limits the value of the business but may reduce taxation as well as meet other personal planning goals.

Motives further drive appraisal purpose because private owners should not undertake a capitalization or transfer without knowing the value of their businesses. To do so would be the business equivalent of flying blind. For example, without a current valuation owners cannot effectively raise capital, because they do not know what their assets or business is worth in a lending or investment context. Attempting to transfer the business without knowing what it is worth is usually an exasperating experience.

Purpose leads to the function of an appraisal. Function is the specific use of an appraisal. The function of a valuation requires the use of specific methods or processes, each of which can derive dramatically different value conclusions. As mentioned in Chapter 2, undertaking an appraisal gives rise to *value worlds*.

A private business value is relative to the value world in which it is viewed.

Every private company, therefore, has a large number of different values at the same time, depending on the purpose *and* function of the valuation. The purpose of the appraisal governs the selection of a value world. Each value world follows a defined process to determine value under specific rules, based on the function of the appraisal. Each value world may have multiple functions. Each world also has an authority, which is the agent or agents that govern the world. The authority decides whether the intentions of the involved party are acceptable for use in that world as well as prescribes the methods used in that world.

More specifically, "authority" refers to agents or agencies with primary responsibility to develop, adopt, promulgate, and administer standards of practice within that world. Authority decides which purposes are acceptable in its world, sanctions its decisions, develops methodology, and provides a coherent set of rules for participants to follow. Authority derives its influence or legitimacy mainly from government action, compelling logic, or the utility of its standards.

Sanctioning is the gatekeeping power of the authority to regulate access to the world. If the intention of the involved party, which leads to a purpose, does not meet the access criteria of an authority, the purpose will not be accepted. For example, an owner who pursues value in the owner value world may not access, or transact, in the world of early equity value. The latter world operates under a different set of valuation rules and will not recognize the owner's treatment of value.

Examples of authority are found in each appraisal world. For instance, secured lenders are the authority for the world of collateral value. They develop criteria for accessing their world and administering methodology used to derive value. Lenders sanction noncompliance by withholding funds.

Another example involves the world of investment value. The investor is the authority in this world since he governs both the rules within the world and methodology used to derive value. However, for these to have meaning outside the investor's view, they must be expressed in communally shared methods and standards. The investor can sanction noncompliant behavior by not investing. The reverse might be true as well. Investors who require too much return for the risk may not have opportunities to invest. Thus, for an authority to be effective, it must be widely recognized and accepted.

As explained in Chapter 2, private valuation is possible only within a set of parameters: a value world.

The conceptual hierarchy, graphically depicted in Exhibit 3.2, demonstrates the logical flow of decision making for an appraiser as the thought process moves from the general to the specific.

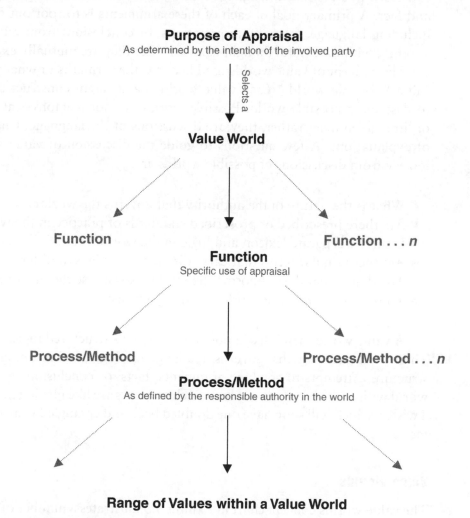

EXHIBIT 3.2 Private Valuation Conceptual Linkage

Value Worlds as Possible Worlds

To understand the concept of value worlds, it may be instructive to consider the discussion of "possible worlds" that philosophers have been engaged in for decades. The discussion can be traced back to Alfred North Whitehead and Bertrand Russell in their *Principia Mathematica*, where they argued that all of mathematics could be reduced to the logic of set theory.[8] Set theory is a way of organizing the primary concepts of a discipline. A similar concept was developed by Thomas Kuhn in his landmark book *The Structure of Scientific Revolutions*.[9] He coined the now-overused phrase "paradigm shift." Broadly speaking, it is the notion that the world can be seen through a structured prism of preconceived ideas, language, and logic. A paradigm is a set of embodied experiences. A possible world then is a logically consistent way of viewing and explaining the world.

More recently, the philosophical discussion centers around "structured propositions" that encapsulate a set of complex entities bound together in identifiable ways. Structured propositions perform a number of functions in addition to being the primary bearers of truth, falsity, and meaning. They are coherent arguments, expressed in a consistent language that excludes nonconforming language, logic, and fact. A primary goal of each of these arguments is to root out the fallacy of including language, factual interpretations, or conclusions from one world with another, without careful thought as to whether they are mutually exclusive.

The concept of value worlds used here has the earmarks of what philosophers call a "possible world." Each value world is a coherent construct that purports to describe a possible world. Possible worlds are not metaphysical speculations of little green men; rather, they are discussions of the language, truth, and logic of explanations. A few questions to guide the discussion of value worlds taken loosely from discussions of possible worlds are:

- What is the nature of the authority that governs the world?
- Are there prescribed or proscribed standards of practice in the world?
- Is there a separate lexicon and logic in the world?
- Are there similar terms that carry different meanings in different worlds?
- To what extent does choosing the world also choose the outcome?
- To what extent are the worlds mutually exclusive?

A value world then is like a possible world or a structured logical proposition. There is an authority that governs it, a language, logic, and meaning that provide structure. Attempts to combine arguments, facts, or conclusions from one value world with another are risky at best. Such attempts are like playing the parlor game Twister, which will soon have one doubled back and entangled in an embarrassing manner.

Value Worlds

The value worlds concept chart in Exhibit 3.3 illustrates a number of value worlds in terms of purposes, functions, and authorities within them. While this list is not

EXHIBIT 3.3   Value Worlds Concept Chart

Appraisal Purpose	Value World	Appraisal Functions	Responsible Authority
To find the highest value in the open market	Market value	Sale of a minority or control interest to support a merger	Financial intermediaries
To find a value for tax matters and for some legal reasons	Fair market value	Federal estate and gift taxes, ESOPs, charitable contributions	Federal law, administrative rulings
Shareholder actions	Fair value	To support a minority dissent, oppression claim	Statutory law
Shareholder wealth measurement	Incremental business value	To create/measure management bonus plans, company performance measurement, capital allocation systems	Management consulting industry
To determine insurance coverage	Insurable value	To fund buy/sell agreements, business interruption claims	Insurance industry, involved parties
To follow FASB ASC 350-20	Impaired goodwill	To determine impaired goodwill	FASB
To value intangible assets	Intangible asset	To value intellectual property, such as patents and copyrights, or to value intellectual capital	Intangible asset laws (patents, etc.)
To value the business from one investor's perspective	Investment value	Value specific to one investor, probably for purchase or investment	Investor
To value the business from an owner's perspective	Owner value	Value specific to owner, probably for sale	Owner
To determine the borrowing capacity of the business	Collateral value	To obtain a secured loan	Secured lending industry
To determine the value of a start-up	Early equity value	To derive the value of a start-up to determine equity splits	Venture capitalists
To determine the value of a business in bankruptcy	Bankruptcy value	To determine how much money creditors will receive	Bankruptcy judge and statutes
To determine the value of a public company	Public value	To set the price of an initial public offering	Public investment bankers

exhaustive, it indicates a universe of appraisal possibilities currently beyond the scope of most appraisers.

If the purpose of an appraisal involves finding the highest value of a business interest in the open market, the *world of market value* dictates the processes used to derive value. Every private company has at least three market values at the same time. Each market value alternative, called a subworld, represents the most likely selling price based on the most likely *buyer type*. In the world of market value, the subworlds are asset, financial, and synergy.

The asset subworld reflects what the company would be worth if the most likely selling price is based on net asset value, because the most likely buyer is not basing the purchase on the company's earnings stream but rather on the company's assets. In the asset subworld, the buyer is not giving credit to the seller for goodwill beyond the possible write-up of the assets; that is, no value for the operations of the subject. For our purposes here, goodwill is the intangible asset that arises as a result of name, reputation, customer patronage, and similar factors that result in some economic benefit a buyer is willing to pay for beyond the company's asset value.

The financial subworld reflects what an individual or nonstrategic buyer would pay for the going-concern enterprise, inclusive of goodwill. A financial buyer in the financial subworld must structure a deal using only the subject's income statement and balance sheet. Since the buyer brings no synergies to the deal, the deal itself must supply the earnings and the collateral that enable the transaction to be financed. This effectively creates a boundary around the valuation, in that there is a definable limit as to how much a financial buyer can pay for a business based on a capitalizing or discounting a benefit stream by an appropriate return expectation. The company itself provides much of the information used to create this boundary.

The synergy subworld is the market value of the subject when synergies from a possible acquisition are considered. Synergy is the increase in performance of the combined firm over what the two firms are already expected to accomplish as independent companies. The synergy subworld is mainly concerned with strategic or synergistic combinations, such as horizontal and vertical integrations, or any other combination where the acquirer can leverage the subject's capabilities.

APPRAISAL DEFINITIONS

Value world: A valuation construct that enables a private business value to be derived in a relevant setting that is relative to the purpose and function of the subject's appraisal.

Purpose: The intention of the involved party as to why a valuation is needed. The authority in the value world decides if the intention is acceptable in that world.

Function: The specific use of an appraisal, which leads directly to the choice of appropriate methods to employ.

Authority: "Authority" refers to agents or agencies with primary responsibility to develop, adopt, promulgate, and administer standards of practice within that world. Authority decides which purposes are acceptable in its world, sanctions its decisions, develops methodology, and provides a coherent set of rules for participants to follow.

Synergies can result from a variety of acquisition scenarios. Perhaps the most quantifiable group of synergies emanate from horizontal integrations, which can realize substantial synergies by cutting duplicate overhead and other expenses. Some of these savings *may* be shared with the seller. Vertical integrations also can create substantial synergies. These tend to be strategic, where the target helps the acquirer achieve some business goal. Synergies also can result from the different financial structures of the parties. For instance, the target may realize interest expense savings due to adopting the cheaper borrowing costs of the acquirer.

Value is determined in this subworld by capitalizing or discounting a synergized benefit stream at an appropriate rate of return expectation. For example, the synergy subworld stream may include recast earnings before interest, taxes, depreciation, and amortization (EBITDA) plus the amount of enjoyed synergies by the subject. The amount of enjoyed synergies is the estimated synergies that are credited to, or kept by, a party in a deal. The total expected synergies in a deal must first be forecast. Then the enjoyed synergies must be negotiated between the parties. The party most responsible for creating the synergies is usually the buyer. Buyers will not readily give these synergies away since the realization of the synergies happens while they own the business. A high level of mature judgment and experience is necessary when quantifying the enjoyed synergies.

If the purpose of the appraisal involves tax and many legal matters, the *world of fair market value* is in control. The process used in this world is systematic and follows the dictates of Revenue Ruling 59-60, which lists a number of items to consider when valuing a business interest in this world.

If the purpose for the appraisal involves legal matters, one of the other worlds *may* come into play. The lawyers or courts normally will provide the choice of the appropriate world, although it is surprising how much uncertainty remains in this area.

Some legal appraisal purposes may occupy several value worlds. For example, divorce appraisal is driven by the legal jurisdiction of the filing. Unfortunately, states do not always provide sufficient guidelines for valuation. In North Carolina, for instance, the statutes do not define and require a particular standard of value for divorce valuations. Nor is there a court of appeals case in North Carolina where the different standards have been specifically put before the court for its consideration.[10] This condition also exists in other states.

The *world of fair value* can be entered in one of two ways. Minority shareholders who believe the majority shareholders have taken corporate actions that negatively affect them are called *dissenters*. Examples of corporate actions include merging or selling assets of the corporation, or changing key tenets of the corporate bylaws. Every state has dissenter's rights statutes that serve to protect the minority, typically through the purchase of the dissenter's stock at fair value, called the *appraisal remedy*.

"Oppression" is a legal term that basically means the minority shareholder's reasonable expectations have not been met. Oppressed shareholders' statutes or dissolution statutes are meant to protect minority shareholders from oppressive action, fraud, and mismanagement by the majority. Oppression covers actions taken against a minority shareholder in his capacity as an employee, officer, director, or shareholder. If a minority holder proves to a court that he has been oppressed, the holder will receive *fair value* for his shares, which normally means

EXHIBIT 3.4   World of Incremental Business Value Process

Definition	Incremental business value (IBV) measures the result of generating a return on investment in excess of the company's corresponding cost of capital.
Purpose of appraisal	To measure the creation or incremental change to economic value in an entity, such as a company, product line, or financial management system.
Function of appraisal	For use in creating management bonus plans, project performance and subsidiary value measurement, as well as capital allocation systems and business planning.
Authority	Management consulting industry.
Valuation process summary	IBV = Returns − (Investment × Cost of Capital)
where:	IBV = incremental business value.
	Returns = recast EBITDA equals earnings before interest, taxes, depreciation, and amortization, recast for owner discretionary expenses and one-time company expenses.
	Investment = the greater of the total amount of investment made in a project or business or the financial market value of the company.
	Cost of Capital = the expected rate of return that capital providers in the private capital markets require in order to fund to a particular investment. Found by using the private cost of capital model.
	A positive IBV figure means that the number of dollars calculated creates shareholder value.

he will receive the pro rata share of the enterprise value, without any minority interest discount or lack of marketability discount.

The world of incremental business value measures the result of generating a return on investment in excess of the company's corresponding cost of capital. Investment equals the greater of all expenditures in a project or business that have a long-term impact, or the financial market value of the business. When a company generates positive incremental business value, it is generating revenues beyond the corresponding economic costs. This is important because positive incremental business value creates shareholder value; negative incremental business value destroys value (on a dollar-for-dollar basis). Further information on this world is provided in Exhibit 3.4.

The *world of insurable value* considers the value of a business or business interest to be covered by insurance. There are a variety of circumstances where business insurance is required, and as in the previous valuation worlds, within the insurable world, a business or business interest should be valued using a process that is specific to this world. By understanding how insurable value is determined and influenced, owners should be better prepared to purchase appropriate amounts of insurance to protect their business. Although there are numerous instances that require valuation for insurance purposes, three of the more important areas are to:

1. Derive the value needed to fund buy/sell agreements.
2. Determine the proper amount of key person insurance.
3. Value a claim in business interruption cases.

The *world of impaired goodwill* refers to the Financial Accounting Standards Board (FASB) ASC 350-20, which describes the accounting treatment of goodwill and other intangible assets. As opposed to amortizing goodwill over 40 years, the new rule does not allow for goodwill amortization. Rather, for just about every company that has engaged in business combinations in the United States, FASB requires an annual test for goodwill impairment, which basically means that if goodwill carried on the balance sheet is more than its current "fair value," the difference must be written off. Public *and* nonpublic companies are required to complete the impairment test each year, which suggests that this value world will be active in the foreseeable future.

The *world of intangible assets* describes the value of all elements of a business enterprise that exist beyond its monetary and tangible assets. The world of intangible asset value can be conveniently divided into two subworlds. The first is the more traditional valuation of intellectual property. The second, more recent and more intangible than the first, is known as intellectual capital. The two areas differ from each other in significant ways. Due to the increasing use of intangible assets, this world is expected to become more prevalent in the future.

The *world of investment value* describes the value of a business interest to a particular investor, given a set of specific investment criteria. This world may appear similar to market value, in that it is possible for the two worlds to derive the same value for an interest. Upon further consideration, however, the worlds are quite different. Market value measures the highest value available in the market, based on likely investor profiles; whereas investment value derives the value to a particular investor, based on this investor's benefit stream and specific return expectation.

The *world of owner value* is the value of a business or business interest to the current owner. Owners tend to highly value their businesses, mainly because they consider all compensation *and* all items that personally benefit them as part of the income stream. Examples of personal items include close business contracts, covered expenses such as insurances and business trips, and possibly even relatives on the payroll. Owners tend to capitalize this liberal benefit stream by a low return expectation, since they may view the equity risk as less risky than the market might perceive.

The *world of collateral value* measures the amount a creditor would be willing to lend given the subject's assets serving as security for the loan. A company enters the collateral value world when it seeks a secured loan, such as a commercial or asset-based loan, or if it uses its assets in some financial engineered way, such as a sales-leaseback arrangement.

The *world of early equity* depicts the valuation process for early round investors. This world mainly involves venture capital but also applies to any other investors in a start-up. Because early investors may not use historical earnings or assets by which to measure the initial value, they must look forward and *back into* a beginning value. Early investors do this by forecasting a likely terminal value (also known as exit value) and then determining the amount of equity they need to own to meet their return expectations. Investing in this world requires tremendous skill and market knowledge because the investment exit may not occur for five to seven years.

When a business is unable to service its debt or pay its creditors, the business or its creditors can file with a federal bankruptcy court for protection under either Chapter 7 or Chapter 11. The business then enters the *world of bankruptcy value*. In Chapter 7, the business ceases operations, and a trustee sells all of the business assets and distributes the proceeds to its creditors. Any residual amount is returned to the owners of the company. In Chapter 11, in most instances the debtor remains in control of its business operations as a debtor in possession and is subject to court oversight and jurisdiction. The bankruptcy court judge is the main authority in this world.

Finally, public companies, especially those with floats of more than $250 million, comprise the *public value world*. Public investment bankers are the valuation authorities in this world, as they use market knowledge to determine the price for initial offerings, secondary offerings, and, to some degree, pricing for mergers and acquisitions.

Occasionally book value is used as a benchmark in a shareholder matter, as in a buy/sell agreement. Book value does not constitute a value world, since it is an accounting term, determined by generally accepted accounting principles (GAAP). As an accounting concept, book value is a cost-based concept, and is not meant to represent the "value" of the assets less liabilities of the subject.

Each appraisal world has a definition of value, an exclusive purpose of the appraisal within the world, and functions that lead to unique processes to derive value. By way of example, the summarized process for determining incremental business value is shown in Exhibit 3.4.

This process is different in each value world and must be followed for a correct value determination.

The value worlds construct is important for several reasons. First, the range of possible values for a business interest at a *point in time* varies widely. An interest may be worth nearly nothing in one world while its value could be tremendous in another. Starting off in the correct world is paramount to understanding the value proposition. Keeping the worlds separate involves keeping the arguments, logic, and facts consistent in that world and separate from the other value worlds. For example, the fair market value world rotates with a fairly strict set of assumptions.

Second, with no ready market pricing for their private shares, owners must rely on point-in-time appraisals for most of their valuation decisions. Once the correct value world is chosen, a replicable valuation process is available. These processes provide relatively accurate answers to difficult questions.

Finally, the value worlds may collide. For example, owners often are faced with several decisions at the same time that require knowledge of the value worlds. This "war of the worlds" is important, mainly because it happens often to unsuspecting business owners. The subsequent chapters on valuation calculate values by world for PrivateCo, this book's fictitious example company. All values are derived on an equity enterprise basis using the same income statement and balance sheet. Exhibit 3.5 shows these values by value world in ascending order of value.

Subsequent chapters demonstrate that PrivateCo has a wide range of value possibilities on the same date, from a low of $2.4 million to a high of more than $18 million. Once again, the same original income statement and balance sheet

EXHIBIT 3.5 PrivateCo Valuation by World

World	Value
Asset market value	$2.4 million
Collateral value	$2.5 million
Insurable value (buy/sell)	$6.5 million
Fair market value	$6.8 million
Investment value	$7.5 million
Impaired goodwill	$13.0 million
Financial market value	$13.7 million
Owner value	$15.8 million
Synergy market value	$16.6 million
Public value	$18.2 million

is used as a starting point for the calculations. Of course, the presentation of the numbers and the processes to derive value are different, which fits with the value world premise.

If PrivateCo's owner Joe Mainstreet is advised that his company is worth a specific dollar value and that all of his decisions should revolve around that value, Joe and PrivateCo could suffer as a result of that advice.

The intention of the involved party leads to a purpose of an appraisal. Purposes for undertaking an appraisal are referred to as giving rise to value worlds. The logical construct of a value world is independent of the experience of individual appraisers and individual assignments. Value, then, is expressed only in terms consistent with that world. Once the project is located in a value world, the function of the appraisal governs the choice of appraisal methods. The responsible authority in each value world prescribes these methods. The choice of appropriate appraisal method ultimately may lead to a point-in-time singular value. Thus, a private business value is relative to the *purpose* and *function* of its appraisal.

Value World Quadrants

To consider the relations between value worlds, think of them in the value world quadrants in Exhibit 3.6. Each value world fits within one of the quadrants, depending on the world's relationship to the world categories. World categories represent the nature and effect of the authority within the worlds. The four main world categories are notional, empirical, regulated, and unregulated. Under this system, the fair market world lays in the *notional regulated* quadrant whereas market value lays in the *empirical unregulated* quadrant.

The authority decides which purposes are acceptable, sanctions its decisions, develops methodology, and provides a coherent set of rules for participants to follow. Authority derives its influence or legitimacy from three sources: government action, compelling logic, and/or the utility of its standards. The source of authority varies in each value world. Some authorities, such as the IRS and courts, are empowered by the government and have serious sanctioning power. Financial intermediaries and management consultants, in contrast, can only recommend and goad players in their spheres of influence. In the case of competing authorities,

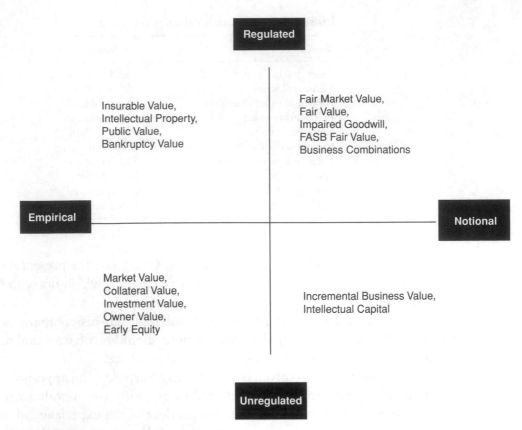

EXHIBIT 3.6 Value World Quadrants

such as asset appraisers and financial intermediaries, the authority with the most direct, relevant evidence is heeded. For example, in the asset subworld, the asset appraiser who specializes in an industry segment is likely to be the authority for that segment.

Is the authority located within the private capital market triangle? The purpose of authority is to accomplish an objective, usually within the triangle. All notional authorities live outside the triangle. These authorities, such as the FASB, state and federal courts and various laws, are not connected to the private capital markets. They often act in blatant disregard to the holistic interests of the capital markets. For example, FASB mandates the rules for determining fair value, yet it is not integrally involved in or constrained by the valuation, capitalization, or transfer side of the private capital markets. Notional authorities exist beyond the checks-and-balances of an integrated market.

Empirical authorities, by contrast, inhabit the private capital markets. These authorities, such as senior lenders, owners, investors, and financial intermediaries, have knowledge that emanates from the capital or transfer side of the triangle. Their behavior is routinely checked in the market. For instance, a senior lender in the world of collateral value who is too restrictive with its advance rates will not be competitive. Or an investor in the world of investment value who constantly underbids soon gets exasperated. The market feeds information back to these authorities, who then modify their behavior.

Each world category bears further discussion.

Notional World Category   Authorities in the notional world category do not inhabit the private capital markets. The validity of this world category is derived from the strength of its coherence to the logical structure established by an authority. For example, the IRS is an authority in the world of fair market value, which is a notional world. Over the past 30 years, it has taken the illogical position that private minority interests suffer only slightly from a lack of marketability. This untenable position has been altered and ultimately influenced by the other main authority in fair market value, the tax courts. The courts have consistently ruled against the IRS in this matter. But since the courts do not live in the private capital markets, they have not brought the full market reality into their decisions. Since they are notionally oriented, they do not have to abide by market expectations.

Empirical World Category   Value worlds and authorities in the empirical world category exist in the private capital markets. The most obvious example of an empirical value world is market value. The validity of this world category is derived from the strength of its correspondence to market experience. Information feedback mechanisms help establish the legitimacy of the authorities.

Regulated World Category   In this world category, authority has a high degree of influence tending toward control. Participants in the world must play by the authority's rules or be sanctioned. The world of fair value is highly regulated. It also demonstrates what happens when a participant does not play by the authority's rules. The appraisal remedy provides fair relief to the oppressed or dissenting shareholder.

Unregulated World Category   In the unregulated world category, authority has less influence because participants may or may not have to follow the rules. The world of early equity is an example of an unregulated value world. As the authority, venture capitalists value early-stage companies in this world. But venture capitalists can only suggest valuations through term sheet offers. Their only sanctioning power is to not invest.

Each valuation chapter contains a discussion of the corresponding value quadrant.

VALUATION AS A RANGE CONCEPT

Because each value world is likely to yield a different value indication for a business interest, private business valuation is a range concept. Thus, a private business interest has *at least* as many correct values at any given point in time as the number of value worlds. Within each world there are multiple functions of an appraisal calling for unique valuation methods. The spread of values can be quite large between worlds.

Beyond the different values determined by world, there are a nearly infinite number of values possible *within* each world. This observation is based on four factors. First, there is latitude regarding the application of a prescribed valuation process. For instance, in the world of fair market value, appraisers decide which methods are suitable among the asset, income, and market approaches. This decision-making process causes variability from one appraiser to the next. Most value worlds require judgment regarding the application of methods.

Second, once the appropriate value world is chosen, the next important valuation issue is the calculation of a suitable benefit stream. Each value world may employ a different benefit stream to value a business interest. A benefit stream may be designed by an authority to predict market behavior, as in the case of an intermediary's use of a synergized stream. Or a stream may be designed to meet an authority's goals, such as an owner's all-encompassing definition, which serves to increase the value of the firm. Benefit streams can differ substantially from world to world. Streams also vary greatly from the seller's and buyer's perspective. The difference in benefit stream definitions in each world is a key reason *value variability* exists between the value worlds.

Third, like benefit streams, private return expectations are determined within each value world. Private return expectations convert a benefit stream to a present value, so they are key to the value equation. While the private capital markets contain all of the return expectations of private investors, return requirements vary by world, as for an investor in the world of investment value, or an owner in the owner value world, or a venture capitalist in the world of early equity. Value variability between worlds is increased because each world employs a unique return expectation.

Finally, the probability of different value drivers occurring must be considered. For instance, if a company's EBITDA is $3 million, and this number is used in the valuation, it is assumed with 100% probability that the company will indeed achieve a $3 million EBITDA. What if, upon further due diligence and consideration of revenues and cost variables, it seems reasonable to presume the company has only a 50% chance of achieving a $3 million EBITDA? An independent analysis might further indicate that the company has a 25% chance of generating a $2 million EBITDA and a 25% chance of earning $3.5 million. Would each of these scenarios not lead to three different values, even in the same world?

Appraisers have some latitude in interpreting the correct valuation process, calculating the proper benefit stream and private return expectation, plus deciding on the probability of each variable occurring. These choices cause a wide range of possible expected values.

The existence of multiple variables in valuation leads to the idea of using probability-based scenario planning. In his article "How to Figure Odds in Forecasting Acquisition Results," Christopher Razaire makes the case for employing probabilities when valuing companies using discounted cash flow (DCF) analysis in the acquisition process.[11] Razaire believes two major flaws exist with current scenario planning methodology.

1. Current valuation methods lead to the choice of one value per assumption per period under consideration. As a result, the same weight of certainty is given to all assumptions, which of course can lead to misleading conclusions.

2. Multiple scenarios, such as "best case" and "worst case," can lead to flawed conclusions since, no matter how many scenarios are modeled, each scenario has such a small chance of occurrence. Even the "base case" scenario may have less than a 20% chance of coming true.

   Razaire correctly asserts that the objective of DCF is to find the value, or range of values, to which a higher number of possible scenarios lead.

3. Assign probabilities to numerous variables. Razaire uses an iterative computer program to generate a graph with percentages on the horizontal axis and values on the vertical axis.

   For example, the graph might show a 50% chance that the subject is worth $20 million but a 10% chance it is worth $40 million, and so on. This treatment enables an investor to quantify and visualize the risk profile of the valuation. If the valuation involves an acquisition offer, the use of probabilities allows the buyer to more fully understand the nuances of subtle changes to the offer. This can be especially beneficial if the offer changes in a bidding situation.

Razaire makes a strong case that calculating probabilities of a target's performance can help buyers determine appropriate valuations. In so doing, he supports the premise that private business valuation *within* a world is a range concept. However, this does not mean that some valuation engagements do not need to be stated as a singular figure.

Although not mentioned by Razaire, the next step in using probability analysis in business valuation could involve Monte Carlo simulation. Scientists who had worked on the Manhattan Project first developed Monte Carlo simulation in 1949. Originally used to determine the feasibility of nuclear fission, the technique has been advanced to more everyday usages with the advent of the personal computer.

Monte Carlo is a technique to calculate uncertainty in a forecast of future events. It assumes a mathematical model is used to determine a result. Instead of using a single value for each variable in a model, such as pretax earnings, it uses many values. A Monte Carlo *engine* runs the model over and over, each time using a different value for each of the variables in the model. Each run is called a trial. The outcomes are tabulated, and after a large number of trials (perhaps thousands), the forecast is shown not as a single value but as a *range* of values. In other words, the uncertainty is explicit.

An example using Monte Carlo to value a company may be helpful. Suppose the value of 100% of PrivateCo's stock is dependent on several underlying variables, pretax earnings, working capital investment, and capital expenditures. Monte Carlo simulation might be used to value the company by:

- Randomly generating 20,000 scenarios for the value of the underliers. In mathematical jargon, this simulation would be accomplished in a manner consistent with an assumed risk-neutral probability distribution of the three variables.
- Determining the value of the stock under each of the 20,000 scenarios.

■ Forming a histogram depicting the range of results. This diagram represents a discrete approximation of the probability distribution of the stock's value. The discounted mean of the histogram is the estimated value of the stock.

The solution in step 3 yields an approximate value. By using more scenarios, say, 50,000 instead of 20,000, the precision of the result could be improved. Typically, the precision of a Monte Carlo simulation is proportional to the square root of the number of scenarios used.

Although most private business appraisals generate a point-in-time singular value, the foregoing demonstrates private business valuation as a range concept. On a macro level, the range is defined by a host of different values that correspond to the various value worlds. Within each world, every company has a nearly infinite number of values based on the probability of the underlying valuation variables occurring. For appraisal to be useful, the derivation of a single value is typically necessary. The challenge, then, is to generate point-in-time appraisals within the range concept; that is, to derive singular values within the range of possible values. For the purposes of this book, doing this requires an understanding of the utility of the value worlds and awareness that the best single value may be only slightly more probable than a host of other values.

TRIANGULATION

Private business value is directly affected by the company's access to capital and the transfer methods available to the owner. Triangulation for valuation is depicted in Exhibit 3.7. Considering the value of a private business interest without reference

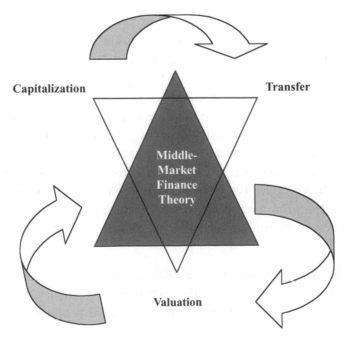

EXHIBIT 3.7 Triangulation

to capitalization or transfer quickly leads to an untenable position. For instance, the owner who ignores the return expectations of capital providers and his own willingness to act as an equity source, or the owner who fails to consider the spectrum of transfer alternatives, is truly "lost" in the conceptual value woods.

The choice of capital structure determines a firm's cost of capital that directly affects private business value. For example, companies with owners who forgo debt in the capital structure have very high costs of capital. Such owners create incremental business value only when they make investments that exceed this hurdle rate. This is a difficult concept for most private owners who believe value is created whenever their company makes a buck. These owners do not see the *value* in considering capital structure in the capital investment decision.

The choice of transfer methods is no less important to the value of a private firm. Regulated transfer methods, such as estate planning techniques, rely on the world of fair market value to derive value. This method typically has a dampening effect on value. However, nonregulated transfer methods in the world of market value, such as auctions, provide the highest level of market value. Many owners fail to recognize that in choosing a transfer method, they also choose the likely value world in which the company is valued, which directly affects business value.

NOTES

1. Shannon P. Pratt, Robert F. Reilly, and Robert R. Schweihs, *Valuing a Business: The Analysis and Appraisal of Closely Held Companies*, 5th ed. (New York: McGraw-Hill), p. 44.
2. Ibid., p. 159.
3. Shannon P. Pratt and Roger J. Grabowski, *Cost of Capital: Estimations and Applications*, 3rd ed. (Hoboken: John Wiley & Sons, 2008), p. 3.
4. Robert T. Slee, "Is the Subject Company Similar?" *Valuation Strategies* (May/June 1998).
5. Ray Miles, "Where to Find Transaction Data," Institute of Business Appraisers, 1996, www.go-iba.org.
6. Pratt, Reilly, and Schweihs, *Valuing a Business*, p. 408.
7. James B. Arkebauer and Ron Shultz, *Cashing Out: The Entrepreneur's Guide to Going Public* (New York: HarperBusiness, 1994), pp. 25–27.
8. Alfred North Whitehead and Bertrand Russell, *Principia Mathematica* (Cambridge: Cambridge University Press, 1910).
9. Thomas Kuhn, *The Structure of Scientific Revolutions* (Chicago: University of Chicago Press, 1970).
10. Thomas H. Elam, "Paradigms in Divorce Valuation Reports," *Business Appraisal Practice* (Fall, 2003).
11. Christopher Razaire, "How to Figure Odds in Forecasting Acquisition Results," *Mergers & Acquisitions* (November/December 1995): 6–12.

CHAPTER 4

Market Value

The world of market value describes the value of a business interest in the marketplace. Value is normally expressed as an equity enterprise value. The owner who says his business is worth $X is generally referring to the world of market value. By seeking a market value for his business, an owner is motivated to find the *open market* value, probably envisioning a transfer.

"Market value" is defined as:

> *The highest purchase price available in the marketplace for selected assets or stock of the company.*

This definition assumes the assets or stock of the company are valued on a debt-free basis, which means all interest-bearing debt must be deducted from the derived market equity values. Most market valuations are also done on a cash-free basis, meaning the seller keeps the excess operating cash and marketable securities in the company at the closing.

An owner whose motive is to derive the highest value obtainable in the marketplace focuses the appraisal process on the world of market value. Adapting a concept from commercial real estate appraisal, the market value focuses on determining the highest and best value for a business. No other value world has this goal or requires the combination of methods unique to this value world.

Rather than Internal Revenue Service (IRS) regulations, court precedents, or insurance company rules, financial intermediaries govern the market value. As with most private business valuation, market value requires a point-in-time expression of value. Determining value in this world requires a fair amount of market knowledge. In other words, the valuer needs to know what is really going on when two parties come together to make a deal.

Unlike the fair market value world, which employs the "willing buyer and seller" rule, the world of market value relies on the "unwilling buyer and seller" rule. Typically, these deals are struck in the real world when both parties are equally miserable with the resulting purchase price. Neither party is particularly willing to receive or pay what the other side is offering. Yet neither party is sufficiently unhappy to walk away from the deal. This tension allows deal makers to determine when the best possible deal is struck. This is the point of highest and best value because the buyer's company has the most identifiable synergies with the target company. The attraction is the strongest of all possible suitors, but if the terms were pushed any higher, the buyer would walk away from the deal.

Because financial intermediaries are the authority in market value, the language and concepts used in this world are those of the marketplace rather than legal or tax nomenclature. The parties take concepts such as synergy, cost reduction, market share, and leverage into consideration, but they are all in industry-specific language. No other theory of value fully attempts to account for these market considerations. Yet this is the world most interesting to owners. Many concepts in this world are simply not applicable in other value worlds. Moreover, many of these concepts are specifically restricted in other value worlds by the authorities and conventions of those value worlds. It is impossible to capture the world of market value using the lexicon and processes of other worlds.

While some of the processes of other value worlds are adapted here, there are distinct differences when they are used in the market value. Some processes have a general applicability across value worlds, with appropriate modifications. Yet they may have specific variations or interpretations within a given value world, and they may be combined with other conceptual approaches to yield quite different results.

For example, in fair market value, the subject of Chapter 8, there is a concept of market approach, which is one of the three main approaches used to determine fair market value. The market approach was originally linked to real estate appraisal, where information is used from transaction data of comparable properties to derive a value conclusion. Similarly in business appraisal, experts use transactional data from comparable or *guideline* business sales. These guideline transactions provide direction in determining applicable valuation parameters, or ratios. Then these are applied to the subject's performance and financial statements. For instance, typical ratios may include applying the guideline price/earnings or price/sales ratio to the subject company. Guidelines from public company data, which is voluminous and readily available, are frequently used despite difficulties in using public securities data to derive private value conclusions. Ultimately public data is not a relevant guide to valuing middle-market private stocks, especially in the world of market value.

Transactional data from private business sales is also used in the market approach. This is understandable since this type of data should be more relevant, and therefore more comparable, than the public data. With the advent of a number of private transactional databases, this data is also more available than ever before. There is definitely a place for private transactional data in determining the market value of private middle-market companies because these companies share a number of similarities. The use of transactional data is discussed in Chapter 2.

The goal of market approach in fair market value is to derive a hypothetical, defensible value in the middle of the road in terms of an indicated purchase price. In other words, the market approach generates a value the universe of potential buyers would be willing to pay for the subject company. In contrast, the world of market value generates the highest value the suitor with the greatest attraction would be willing to pay. Exhibit 4.1 compares the two worlds.

Potential deal synergies or special motivations by the parties are not considered in the fair market value world. This stands in direct contrast to the goal of market value, which is to derive the highest possible value obtainable in the

EXHIBIT 4.1 Comparison of Two Value Worlds

The World of Fair Market Value (market approach)	The World of Market Value
Notional (hypothetical) world	Actual world
Regulated by IRS/courts	Regulated by the market
"Willing buyer and seller . . . rule"	"Unwilling buyer and seller . . . rule"
World without special motivations	World characterized by special motivations
World without synergy	World with synergy

market. Potential synergies are valued in the world of market value. A deal in the private sector requires special motivations. More than likely, only one or two prospective buyers are willing to pay the market value of the subject. Theoretical assertions about the parameters of market synergies often shape highest and best value conclusions.

Exhibit 4.2 shows the process to determine market value.

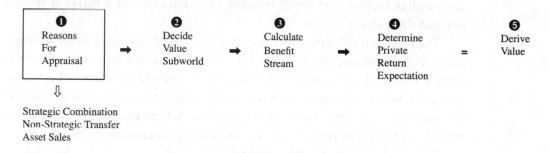

EXHIBIT 4.2 Market Value Process: Select Appraisal Reason

❶ Reasons for Appraisal

In step 1, market value encompasses the transfer of assets or stock in a market setting. Market valuations may be required for strategic combinations or non-strategic transfers. Unless otherwise stated, the valuation techniques described in this chapter do not apply to real estate or companies dominated by real estate. Real estate appraisal is a separate universe form business valuation. If the reason

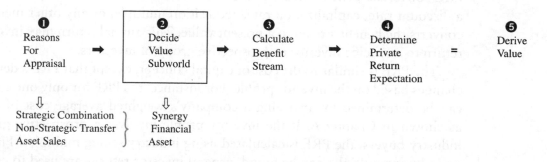

EXHIBIT 4.3 Market Value Process: Decide Subworld

calls for a valuation in market value, the next step, shown in Exhibit 4.3, is to decide what value *subworld* is appropriate to use.

❷ Decide Value Subworld

Every company has at least three market values at the same time. This is yet another example of why market value, like all business valuation, is a *range* concept. Each market value step, called a subworld, represents the most likely selling price based on the most likely buyer type. The subworlds are asset, financial, and synergy. In the asset subworld, the most likely buyer is not basing the purchase on the company's earnings stream but rather on its assets. Therefore, the most likely selling price is based on net asset value. In this subworld, the buyer gives no credit to the seller for goodwill beyond the possible write-up of the assets. No value is given for goodwill or the ongoing operations of the company. Goodwill is the intangible asset arising as a result of name, reputation, customer patronage, and similar factors that result in some economic benefit a buyer is willing to pay beyond the subject's asset value.

The financial subworld reflects what an individual or nonstrategic buyer would pay for the business. With either buyer, the valuation is based only on the company's financial statements. The synergy subworld is the market value of the company when synergies from a possible acquisition are considered. Synergy is the increase in performance of the combined firm over what the two firms are already expected or required to accomplish as independent companies.[1]

Exhibit 4.4 describes the subworlds.

The next two steps in the process for deriving market value, "Calculate the benefit stream" and "Determine the private return expectation," require some explanation. The benefit stream (stream) is the benefit stream that is pertinent to the value world in question. The Stream is economic in that it is either derived by recasting financial statements or determined on a pro forma basis. Streams may be comprised of earnings, cash flow, and/or distributions. To derive values in the financial or synergy subworlds, the benefit stream is either capitalized or discounted by the private return expectation.

Private return expectation (PRE) is the expected rate of return that investors in the private capital markets require in order to fund a particular investment. The PRE converts a benefit stream to a present value. Thus the PRE can be stated as a discount rate, capitalization rate, acquisition multiple, or any other metric that converts the benefit stream to a present value. This annual return may involve the return to a specific investor or prospective group of investors.

The PRE is similar to the cost of capital concept, except that PRE's derivation changes based on the investor profile. For instance, the PRE for only one company can be determined by analyzing a company's weighted average cost of capital, as shown in Chapter 6. If the investor profile involves a prospective group of industry buyers, the PRE is calculated using industry selling multiples. Finally, if no industry multiples can be found, general investor returns are used to calculate the PRE.

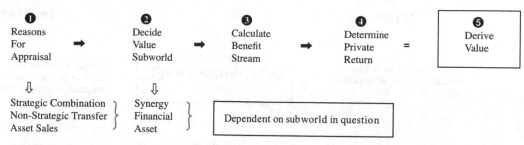

EXHIBIT 4.5 Market Value Process: Derive Value

Exhibit 4.5 illustrates the process to derive market value. By definition, the asset subworld does not use a benefit stream as part of the process to derive value. Benefit streams and PREs are discussed at length in Chapter 6.

LEVELS OF PRIVATE OWNERSHIP

Chapter 2 introduced the concept that private business values are relative to the reason for their appraisal and that appraisal reasons can be grouped into value worlds. Within each value world, there are levels of valuation that correspond to ownership groupings. Exhibit 4.6 shows the levels of private ownership that

EXHIBIT 4.4 Description of the Subworlds

Subworld	Buyer Profile	Comments
Synergy	Strategic/synergistic	Synergies can result from a variety of acquisition scenarios. Perhaps the most quantifiable group of synergies comes from horizontal integrations. A horizontal integrator can realize substantial synergies by cutting duplicate overhead and other expenses. Some of these savings *may* be shared with the seller. Vertical integrations also can create substantial synergies. These tend to be strategic; the target helps the acquirer achieve some business goal. Synergies also can result from the different financial structures of the parties. For instance, the target may realize interest expense savings due to adopting the cheaper borrowing costs of the acquirer.
Financial	Individual/nonstrategic	Most individual buyers are financial buyers. Any institutional buyer who is not participating in the subject's industry or cannot leverage the subject's business is also a financial buyer. Financial buyers do not bring synergies to a deal; therefore, goodwill is limited.
Asset	Value investor	When the subject has no current or future earnings prospects, or it is in an industry that does not give credit for *operating* goodwill, its asset value may be the highest value it can achieve or expect. Companies in the same industry may buy and deploy the asset base without pricing in goodwill.

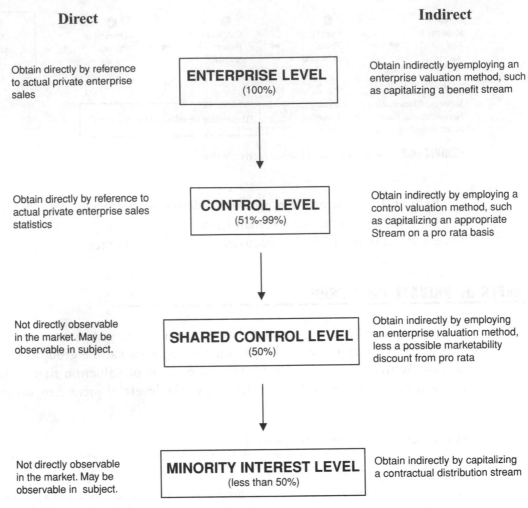

Direct

Obtain directly by reference to actual private enterprise sales

Obtain directly by reference to actual private enterprise sales statistics

Not directly observable in the market. May be observable in subject.

Not directly observable in the market. May be observable in subject.

ENTERPRISE LEVEL
(100%)

CONTROL LEVEL
(51%-99%)

SHARED CONTROL LEVEL
(50%)

MINORITY INTEREST LEVEL
(less than 50%)

Indirect

Obtain indirectly byemploying an enterprise valuation method, such as capitalizing a benefit stream

Obtain indirectly by employing a control valuation method, such as capitalizing an appropriate Stream on a pro rata basis

Obtain indirectly by employing an enterprise valuation method, less a possible marketability discount from pro rata

Obtain indirectly by capitalizing a contractual distribution stream

EXHIBIT 4.6   Levels of Private Ownership

correspond to the market value world. These ownership levels apply to most value worlds, except for fair market value, which employs a separate "Levels of Value" framework, discussed in Chapter 8.

The enterprise level corresponds to 100% ownership. The next level is the control level, which is 51% or greater ownership. The third level is 50%, or shared control ownership. Finally, an ownership interest less than 50% is a minority interest.

Ownership levels are valued directly or indirectly. Direct observation means the level is determined by direct reference to actual comparable data. An example of direct observation at the enterprise level is the use of actual private enterprise transactions, probably generated from a private transactional database. An indirect observation relies on a method that indirectly estimates the value. For instance, capitalizing the company's earnings, which is an indirect reference to what the market should be willing to pay for the subject's earnings stream, may derive an enterprise value.

Once a value world is chosen, a benefit stream is identified or estimated. Then the process of defining value begins. Value levels represent the level within a value world by which to value specific business interests. Each level determines how value is derived. For instance, a minority interest level valuation within market value is appraised differently than an enterprise valuation, and so on.

Enterprise Level (100%)

The enterprise level of market valuation denotes 100% of a company's value. Since enterprise information about private company transactions in the private markets exists, enterprise values are the easiest private values to derive. Enterprise values are determined both directly and indirectly.

Enterprise Level: Direct Enterprise values are obtained directly by reference to actual private enterprise sales. A number of databases contain information on enterprise sales. Chapter 6 focuses on the techniques used to derive values from private transactional information. Salient statistics from the main databases are presented next.

- *Institute of Business Appraisers Market Database.* The Institute of Business Appraisers maintains a database of information on actual sales of private businesses. The database has more than 30,000 records of enterprise transactions in over 650 Standard Industrial Classification (SIC) codes and is used mainly for smaller valuations (i.e., those less than $2 million). There are 13 points of information per transaction.
- *Bizcomps.* This database is published in two geographical editions: Eastern and Western. Each edition has about 5,000 transactions, with approximately 20 points of information per transaction. Bizcomps is used mainly for smaller valuations (those less than $5 million).
- *Done Deals.* Done Deals was started in 1996 and collects data from Securities and Exchange Commission filings. The database includes both public and private companies acquired by public companies. Approximately half of the deals are under $15 million and half over $15 million, and over 75% of the selling companies are privately owned. This database has over 9,000 transactions.
- *Pratt's Stats®*. Information is collected from a variety of deal-making sources. Most of the transactions reported in Pratt's Stats occur mainly in the $1 million to $30 million range. This database has the most detail per transaction, with approximately 88 data points.
- *GF Data.* GF Data's searchable database contains detailed information on business transactions ranging in size from $10 million to $250 million. This data is derived exclusively from more than 150 private equity groups, which ensures more reporting consistency than the other databases.

Other databases are used to supplement these sources, namely the Pepperdine Private Capital Markets reports.

Enterprise Level: Indirect   Enterprise values also are derived indirectly using methods that mirror what the market should be willing to pay for the business. There are a number of indirect valuation methods. Capitalizing the benefit stream of the enterprise is a frequently used method. Another example is net asset value method, which attempts to estimate market values of the company's assets and liabilities.

Indirect valuation is used when no direct valuation evidence is available or to complement direct findings.

Control Level (51%–99%)

In this book, a 51% to 99% ownership interest is considered a control value. Most states in the United States grant the rights of control in a private company at a minimum 51% interest level. Exhibit 4.7 lists powers that an owner with control can exercise.[2]

A controlling owner enjoys substantial benefits as compared to minority owners. Control transactions do not occur as often as enterprise deals. For this reason, it is more difficult to derive direct control valuations.

Control Level: Direct   Minority interest transactions typically are not reported to the private transactional databases mentioned earlier. Control transactions mainly occur as enterprise sales. Direct control valuation is a separate level because the 51%/49% partnership occurs quite often in the marketplace. Often the 49% owner does not realize the power and valuation difference between control and minority position when the entity is formed. Further, the articles of incorporation of the company usually do not grant the 49% holder any special rights. To protect their position, minority holders should structure an ownership agreement at the time of entity formation. Example tenets in ownership agreements include distribution rights, protections from orphan sales (the 51% holder cannot sell just the 51% interest without including the 49% holder), the ability to block major board

---

EXHIBIT 4.7   Control Powers and Rights

 1. Appoint or change operational management.
 2. Appoint or change members of the board of directors.
 3. Determine management compensation and perquisites.
 4. Set operational and strategic policy of the business.
 5. Acquire, lease, or liquidate business assets.
 6. Select suppliers and vendors with whom to do business.
 7. Negotiate and consummate mergers and acquisitions.
 8. Liquidate, dissolve, sell out, or recapitalize the company.
 9. Register the company's equity or debt securities for an initial public offering.
10. Declare and pay cash and/or stock dividends.
11. Change the articles of incorporation or bylaws.
12. Set one's own compensation, perquisites, and the compensation of related-party employees.
13. Decide what products and/or services to offer and how to price them.
14. Decide all matters relative to markets served.
15. Block any or all of the above actions.

---

of director decisions, and so on. Ownership agreements are described later in this chapter in the section titled "Ownership Agreement Tenets."

For those situations where the minority has no special ownership agreement, the control value tends toward the enterprise value. Under this scenario, the control holder solely benefits from the power of controlling the finances of the firm. If the minority enjoys empowered rights, some part of the enterprise value is allocated to the minority, as discussed in the sectioned titled "Minority Interest Level."

Control Level: Indirect Since private databases do not contain control value transactions, most control values are determined indirectly. A number of methods involve indirect valuation. One example is to capitalize a benefit stream applicable to the control value.

As with the enterprise level, indirect valuation is used when no direct valuation evidence is available or to complement direct findings.

Shared Control Level (50%)

Shared control occurs when no single holder owns more than 50% of the enterprise. This occurs at many private companies, when two partners each own 50% of the stock. Unless the parties execute well-thought-out ownership and operating agreements before going into business, shared control is a difficult way to operate. Often the partners are in such a hurry to get into business for the least money possible that no working relationship documents are created.

Consider the next examples of what can go wrong with a 50/50 ownership structure.

- A company with 50/50 owners was in a rapidly changing market. This necessitated growing to another level to remain competitive. One 50% shareholder was prepared for this, the other was not. As a result, the company did not meet market need, eventually lost its top two customers and ultimately liquidated.
- One 50% shareholder at retirement age wanted to fund his retirement plan through the sale of his stock. His much younger partner was not in a position to purchase the stock. There were no buyers for 50% of the company. The older partner continued working many years past his wishes.
- A small company with equal shareholders grew into a highly successful medium-size firm. One partner believed he was primarily responsible for the firm's success and should be compensated more than his partner. The other partner did not agree, leading to total fallout between the two. There was no process to resolve the situation, and the company suffered as a result.

Consider the commonalties in these scenarios. First, the partners did no up-front planning, which might have prevented problems. Second, disagreements between partners are exacerbated as a company becomes successful. Often the early lean years glue the partners together, but the many options success brings unglues them.

What can be done to prevent gridlock between equal owners? At the time of entity organization, the parties should create ownership agreements. These legal agreements, such as a buy/sell agreement, shareholder and operating agreements, contain the key provisions on how the parties operate the business and treat each other. These agreements are necessary for any entity with multiple owners but are especially important for 50/50 or minority interest position holders.

Ownership Agreement Tenets

Ownership agreements are usually outlined by the partners and drafted with help from advisors. Every agreement is different and must be tailored to the circumstances. Chapter 28 details the major tenets of these agreements, but a few ideas are highlighted here.

- Duties and compensation are described.
- The process for adding more partners is detailed.
- What happens when a partner dies or gets disabled? How are the shares valued?
- What happens if a partner is terminated? How are these shares valued?
- Within the buy/sell agreement, is there a buyout provision to help break a deadlock?
- Who is on the board? Is there a tiebreak director?

There are dozens of issues for partners to consider. Seasoned corporate lawyers can help formulate well-rounded ownership agreements. The foregoing tenets are not exhaustive; actual agreements may be 20 pages long with annual amendments adding to their length. Of course, an ownership agreement can be put into place at any point in a company's existence. Every company with 50/50 owners should implement an ownership agreement *before* issues arise. When the agreement is needed, it is too late to draft it objectively.

Shared Control Level: Direct   No market exists for trading 50% private stock interests. The only direct evidence for valuing shared control situations rests in the ownership agreement, if one exists. Even if an ownership agreement with a valuation provision exists, there may be a marketability discount from the determined value. This discount from a fair offer is often described in a buy/sell provision and calls for a marketability discount, reflecting the fact that the 50% interest is marketable to only one party.

Shared Control Level: Indirect   Valuing a shared control interest indirectly usually means deriving an enterprise value, either directly or indirectly, then figuring a pro rata interest. In other words, enterprise value is divided by two. There may or may not be a need to discount the interest further due to the limited selling market, depending on the ownership agreement in place.

EXHIBIT 4.8   Minority Interest Holder Protections

Protect Against:

- Excess owner salary
- Overpayment of family members
- Overpayment for control owner's assets
- Expense reimbursement
- Above-market lease payments to control holder
- Effective dilution of minority claims

Lessen Vulnerability By:

- Improving access to relevant information
- Avoiding risk of incurring costs to enforce minority rights
- Preventing diversion of profits
- Improving information reliability
- Providing for mediation resolutions
- Having board of director representation

Minority Interest Level (Less than 50%)

A minority interest represents less than 50% of the stock of the company. This is the lowest value level, and these interests cannot be readily sold, so they generally suffer from a serious lack of marketability. Exhibit 4.8 lists some issues minority holders should protect against when drafting ownership agreements with the majority holders.

Even with the protections just identified, the minority holder still suffers from a lack of control, especially as it relates to financial policy.

Minority Interest Level: Direct   No marketplace exists for exchanging private minority business interests. Direct comparison to other private minority interests is limited to similar transactions in the company. Generally a prior transaction must have occurred in the past two to three years to make it usable as a guideline. Even recent prior transactions may not be a good value guide if the original buyer has no interest in acquiring additional shares. If an agreement describes a process for the majority to purchase the minority shares, this would be the best valuation method.

Minority Interest Level: Indirect   Without an ownership agreement within the subject company giving the minority holder special empowering rights, most minority interests in private companies are nearly worthless. One exception to this premise is a minority holder in an enterprise where the control shareholders have a targeted exit date, such as a firm owned by a private equity group. For the most part, however, unless the minority interest has a legal claim on dividends, liquidations, or other contractual distributions, the minority position has value only to the extent it participates in an enterprise sale. Few buyers outside the company assign weight to this future event.

If the minority interest holder has a contractual distribution stream, it is possible to value the position. The expected stream is capitalized at an appropriate risk factor. Even with a contractual distribution stream, few outside buyers have an interest in acquiring a minority interest in a private company.

TRIANGULATION

"Triangulation" refers to using two sides of the middle-market finance theory triangle to help fully understand a point on the third side. Equity value is affected by the company's access to capital and the transfer methods available to the owner. Capital availability influences market value. For example, industries that cannot attract capital tend to suffer from depressed market values and vice versa.

Private return expectations drive the market value of a firm, evidenced by selling multiples of comparable private transactions. Market values represent the most direct value linkage from the transfer side of the triangle. The synergy sub-world of market value is the highest market value because of the transfer influence. The "market" determines the unique market valuation process. Financial inter-mediaries and asset appraisers are the authorities in this world. They enforce the process and provide feedback to the market. For instance, intermediaries use trans-fer experience to determine that, unless an empowering agreement exists, private minority interests are nearly worthless in the open market.

NOTES

1. Mark Sirower, *The Synergy Trap* (New York: Free Press, 1997), p. 20.
2. Jay E. Fishman, Shannon P. Pratt, J. Clifford Griffith, and D. Keith Wilson, *Guide to Business Valuations*, 9th ed. (Fort Worth, TX: Practitioners Publishing, 1999), chap. 7.

CHAPTER 5

Asset Subworld of Market Value

Market value is the highest purchase price available in the marketplace for selected assets or stock of the company. Every company has at least three market values at any given moment corresponding to the most likely selling price based on the most likely investor type. These *subworlds* are asset, financial, and synergy. This is another example of why market value, like all business valuation, is a range concept.

The asset subworld reflects what the company is worth if the selling price is based on net asset value. In this world, the most likely buyer does not base the purchase of assets on the company's earnings stream. The buyer in this subworld does not give credit to the seller for goodwill, the intangible asset that arises as a result of name, reputation, customer patronage, and similar factors, beyond the possible write-up of the assets.

An owner's motive to derive the highest value obtainable leads to appraisals in the world of market value. Commercial real estate appraisers often evaluate the "highest and best use of a property." Adapting this concept, the world of market value determines the highest and best value for a business. However, the asset subworld shows that the highest value for a business may be found by determining the market value of assets less liabilities.

Financial intermediaries and asset appraisers are the authorities governing the asset subworld, rather than Internal Revenue Service regulations, court precedents, or insurance company rules. Determining value in the asset subworld of market value requires substantial market knowledge, especially in terms of specific asset values.

A snapshot of the key tenets of the asset subworld is provided in Exhibit 5.1. The longitude and latitude construct enables the reader to get a fix on the subject matter, especially as it relates the chapter topic to the broader body of valuation knowledge.

To derive market value, the first step is to decide which subworld is most appropriate. The guidelines shown in Exhibit 5.2 help determine whether a company's highest value is found in the asset subworld.[1]

If the answer to most of the statements in Exhibit 5.2 is yes, then the asset subworld is appropriate to value the company. Typically, however, a company

EXHIBIT 5.1   Longitude and Latitude: Asset Subworld of Market Value

Definition	The highest purchase price available in the marketplace for the selected assets or stock of the company. The asset subworld values the net asset value of a company because the most likely buyer is not basing the purchase on the company's earnings stream but rather on its assets. In the asset subworld, the buyer gives no credit to the seller for goodwill beyond the possible write-up of the assets.
Purpose of appraisal	To value a company in a realistic market value setting, reflecting what knowledgeable buyers would actually pay for the company.
Function of appraisal	To value a company prior to a sale in the open market.
Quadrant	Empirical unregulated.
Authority	Financial intermediaries, asset appraisers, both located in the transfer side of the private capital markets.
Valuation process summary	The main method to derive value in this subworld is net asset value (NAV). With this process the company's assets and liabilities are adjusted to fair market values, which then derives an adjusted equity. It is appropriate to use fair market values for the company's assets and liabilities if it can be sold as an ongoing business. Depending on the circumstances, liquidation values may be used for the assets instead of fair market values. This would be the case if near-term liquidation of the company were the most likely event. PrivateCo's net asset value is determined on an ongoing basis as shown:

PrivateCo Example

FMV of assets	$4.0 million
– Market value of liabilities	$1.6 million
Net asset value =	$2.4 million

EXHIBIT 5.2   Asset Subworld Is Appropriate if . . .

1. The company has no earnings history and future earnings expectations cannot be reliably estimated. In this context, "earnings" are defined as recast earnings before interest, taxes, depreciation, and amortization (EBITDA). EBITDA is recast for one-time expenses and discretionary expenses of the owner. This lack of an earnings base prohibits the buyer from using the company's earnings as the basis for the valuation.
2. The company depends heavily on competitive contract bids, and there is no consistent, predictable customer base.
3. The company has little or no added value from labor or intangible assets.
4. A significant portion of the company's assets are composed of liquid assets or other investments (e.g., holding companies).
5. It is relatively easy to enter the industry.
6. There is a significant chance of losing key personnel, which could have a substantial negative effect on the company.
7. The company participates in an industry that does not typically price a goodwill component into the deal structure. This can be the case in certain businesses, such as sawmills, or smaller distributors, such as building material suppliers.

EXHIBIT 5.3 Companies Typically Valued in the Asset Subworld

Small contractors	Sawmills	Sales representatives
Used auto dealers	Small retail	Local hardware stores
Small consulting firm	Commodity distributors	Small machine shops

may exhibit some of these characteristics but not all. In these cases, the appraising party should:

- Use judgment as to which characteristics are most important in the context. For instance, the company's lack of recast EBITDA and industry segment are more important considerations than barriers to entry.
- Talk with knowledgeable people in the company's industry about potential buyers. Most industries are serviced by specialist investment bankers and other intermediaries who understand how companies are valued for selling purposes.

Some industries tend toward asset subworld valuations. Buyers tend not to pay goodwill for companies in these industries, especially for transactions less than $5 million. These companies generally are heavily dependent on a key person, usually an owner, are engaged in contract type work, or do not have a reliable recast EBITDA stream. In such cases, a buyer is unlikely to consider paying more than net asset value. Exhibit 5.3 lists types of companies that are typically valued in the asset subworld.

Once the subworld is selected, the next step is to employ a process to derive value. The asset subworld is different from the other subworlds since it does not rely on an earnings stream to derive value. The process for deriving value in the asset subworld is shown in Exhibit 5.4.

Regarding step 5 of Exhibit 5.4, "Derive Value," there is no need to calculate an earnings stream or return expectation in this subworld because the company is valued on a net asset value basis. With this method, the company's assets and liabilities are adjusted to fair market values, which then derive a net asset value, sometimes known as an adjusted equity. It is appropriate to use fair market values for the company's assets and liabilities if they can be sold as an ongoing business. At times, liquidation values are used to value the assets. This is the case if near-term liquidation of the company is the most likely event.

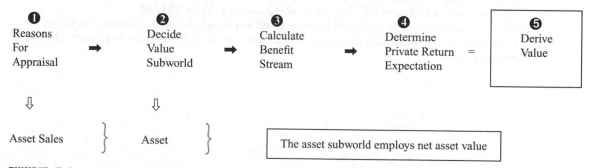

EXHIBIT 5.4 Asset Subworld Value Process: Derive Value

EXHIBIT 5.5   PrivateCo's Net Asset Value

	20X3	Adjustments	Net Asset Value
Current assets			
Cash in bank	$97,218	0	$97,218
Accounts receivables (a)	722,190	(36,110)	686,080
Inventories	450,057	0	450,057
Prepaid expenses (b)	39,729	(39,729)	0
Total current assets	1,309,194	(75,839)	1,233,355
Land (c)	23,700	676,300	700,000
Buildings (d)	417,673	1,082,327	1,500,000
Autos and trucks (e)	74,784	(24,784)	50,000
Machinery and equipment (f)	866,026	(416,026)	450,000
Office equipment (g)	95,526	(50,526)	45,000
Land improvements (h)	135,714	(135,714)	0
Accelerated depreciation (i)	(356,589)	356,589	0
Total	1,256,834	1,488,166	2,745,000
Other assets	2,322	0	2,322
Total assets	$2,568,350	1,412,327	$3,980,677
Current liabilities			
Customer deposits	$479,476	0	$479,476
Accounts payable	531,578	0	531,578
Accrued expenses	31,822	0	31,822
Total current liabilities	1,042,876	0	1,042,876
Long term debt	501,250	0	501,250
Total liabilities	1,544,126	0	1,544,126
Equity	1,024,224	1,412,327	2,436,551 ◄
Total liabilities and equity	$2,568,350	1,412,327	$3,980,677

Net Asset Value

Adjustments
(a) Accounts receivables are adjusted downward by 5% to reflect management's opinion of exposed bad debt expense.
(b) Prepaid expenses are reduced to zero since they have no ongoing value in this scenario.
(c) Fair market value of Land appraised by Jack Smith of Smith Realty Inc. on June 29, 2003 for $700,000.
(d) Mr. Smith appraised the building for $1,500,000 in the appraisal noted above.
(e) Management estimates the automobile and two trucks in the company could be sold for $50,000.
(f) Fair market value of machinery and equipment is appraised by ABC Appraisal Co. for $450,000.
(g) Management estimates the office equipment could be sold for $45,000.
(h) Land improvement account is reduced to $0 since it is included in the building's net asset value.
(i) Accumulated depreciation is reduced to zero since the underlying assets have been adjusted to market values.

STEPS TO DERIVE NET ASSET VALUE

Five steps are used to derive net asset value.[2]

Step 1. Obtain the company's balance sheet as near as possible to the valuation date.

Step 2. Adjust the balance sheet for known missing assets or liabilities.

Step 3. Adjust each tangible asset and identifiable intangible asset to its appraised value, which is generally fair market value. Examples of intangible assets are: patents and copyrights, franchise agreements, goodwill, covenants not to compete, and management or consulting agreements. Patents and franchise agreements usually are carried on the balance sheet at historical cost, which can be substantially different from appraised value.

Step 4. Adjust liabilities to their appraised or market values.

Step 5. After these steps, the amount of total equity is the value of the total stockholders' equity. If the company has preferred stock or other senior equity securities, then the equity value must be reduced by the value of those securities to determine the value of common equity.

Exhibit 5.5 demonstrates PrivateCo's net asset value determination.

Various assets are restated to fair market values, based on management estimates, real estate, and machinery appraisals. No adjustments are made to the liabilities of the company, which means they must be repaid at face value. In this example, PrivateCo has a rounded net asset value of $2.4 million and a book value of $1 million. The net asset value calculation presumes the assets of PrivateCo could be sold as an ongoing business rather than through a liquidation process. Liquidation values, on either a forced or an orderly basis, can be considerably less than ongoing values.

Income tax adjustments may be required when using the net asset value method. Although the details are beyond the scope of this book, the gains from the asset write-ups may need to be tax-effected. If tax adjustments are considered necessary, they are computed based on the difference between the market value and the tax basis of the company's assets and liabilities. Due to the vagaries and complexities of the tax laws, a pretax stance is taken throughout the book. Readers should confer with their tax professionals on these tax issues.

TRIANGULATION

Market value represents the most direct value linkage from the transfer side of the triangle. Market value authorities, financial intermediaries, and asset appraisers make their livings by transferring assets. They bring this experiential knowledge to the valuation process. For instance, ask any intermediary if they can sell a small sawmill for more than asset value. The answer will be no. In other words, companies viewed in the asset subworld are valued on a net asset value basis because this mirrors the open market.

PrivateCo's value in the asset subworld is $2.4 million.

World	PrivateCo Value
Asset market value	**$ 2.4 million**
Collateral value	$ 2.5 million
Insurable value (buy/sell)	$ 6.5 million
Fair market value	$ 6.8 million
Investment value	$ 7.5 million
Impaired goodwill	$13.0 million
Financial market value	$13.7 million
Owner value	$15.8 million
Synergy market value	$16.6 million
Public value	$18.2 million

Market value is located in the *empirical unregulated* value quadrant, where transactions occur in an unregulated marketplace. Profit-motivated players, free to choose from a host of investment alternatives, form the open market. The authorities then inform the involved parties of the market values based on actual transactions. In the case of competing authorities, such as asset appraisers and financial intermediaries, the authority with the most direct, relevant evidence is heeded. For example, in the asset subworld, the asset appraiser who specializes in an industry segment is likely to be the authority for that segment.

Capital availability directly influences market value. Industries that cannot attract capital tend to suffer from depressed market values and vice versa. This restricted access to capital affects the value at which a company can be transferred. For example, machine shops without proprietary product lines encounter capital restrictions. They may have access to equipment leasing or other asset-based financing but are unlikely to attract mezzanine or private equity. The earnings of the company and personal wealth of the owner are the only sources of growth capital. This condition almost always diminishes a company's ability to increase its market value beyond the value of its assets.

NOTES

1. Jay E. Fishman, Shannon P. Pratt, J. Clifford Griffith, and D. Keith Wilson, *Guide to Business Valuations*, 9th ed. (Fort Worth, TX: Practitioners Publishing, 1999), Chap. 7.
2. Ibid., pp. 6–7.

CHAPTER 6

Financial Subworld of Market Value

The world of market value is the value of a business interest in the marketplace. The owner who says her business is worth a certain price is generally referring to this world. These valuations determine possible open market selling prices for a business interest.

Every company has at least three market values at the same time. This is why market value, much like all of business valuation, is a *range* concept. Each market value level, called a subworld, represents the most likely selling price based on the most likely investor type. The subworlds are asset, financial, and synergy. The asset subworld reflects what the company is worth if the most likely selling price is based on net asset value. That is because the most likely buyer bases the purchase on the company's assets, not on its earnings stream. The financial subworld reflects what an individual or nonstrategic buyer would pay for the business. With either buyer type, the appraisal relies on the company's financial statements as the main source of information. The synergy subworld is the market value of the company when benefits from a possible acquisition are considered.

Market valuation focuses on an owner's wish to derive the highest value obtainable in the marketplace. The financial subworld reflects the market reality that the highest value for many businesses is found by selling to an individual or nonstrategic buyer. Financial intermediaries are the authorities governing the financial subworld, rather than Internal Revenue Service regulations, court precedents, or insurance company rules. Substantial market knowledge is required to determine value in the financial subworld.

Exhibit 6.1 provides the longitude and latitude for this subworld, which enables the reader to view all of the key tenets of the financial subworld.

As with other value worlds, the world of market value employs a unique process for determining value, shown in the Exhibit 6.2.

❶ Reasons for Appraisal

The reason (also called purpose) for the appraisal selects the appropriate subworld. If the subject is underperforming financially, the asset subworld is in control. If the likely buyer is an individual or nonstrategic company (financial buyer), the financial subworld is in control. Finally, if the buyer is likely to be synergistic with the subject, then the synergy subworld is used.

EXHIBIT 6.1   Longitude and Latitude: Financial Subworld of Market Value

Definition	The highest purchase price available in the marketplace for selected assets or stock of the company. The financial subworld value reflects what an individual or nonstrategic buyer would pay for the business. Valuation is based on the company's financial statements with either type of buyer.
Purpose of appraisal	To value a company in a market value setting, reflecting what a nonstrategic buyer actually would pay for the company.
Function of appraisal	To help an owner decide a likely selling price for a business in predication of a sale.
Quadrant	Empirical unregulated.
Authority	Financial intermediaries, located in the transfer side of the private capital markets.
Benefit stream	The stream that accrues to the financial buyer posttransaction. For the purposes of this book, that stream is recast earnings before interest, taxes, depreciation, and amortization (EBITDA).
Private return expectation	The expected rate of return that the private capital markets require in order to attract funds to a particular investment. In this subworld, there are three ways to determine this rate: specific investor return, specific industry return, and general return.
Valuation process summary	The financial buyer must structure a deal using only the company's income statement and balance sheet. This is a major determinant in selecting the financial subworld. Since the buyer brings no synergies to the deal, the deal itself must supply the earnings and collateral that will enable the transaction to be financed.
	The company's financial statements are recast for owner discretionary and one-time expenses. This process yields a recast EBITDA for the company, also called a benefit stream. This stream is either capitalized or discounted at the investor's required rate of return.

PrivateCo Example

	Financial Subworld	
Stream × Multiple	=	*Market Value*
$2,500,000 × 5.7	=	$14,250,000
less LTD*	=	$500,000
Market Value	=	$13,750,000

*Assumes a '5.7' multiple and a debt-free analysis.

The next step is to decide if the financial subworld is appropriate. Exhibit 6.3 shows this step within the market valuation process.

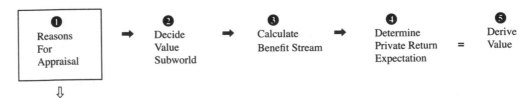

EXHIBIT 6.2   Market Value Process: Select Appraisal Reason

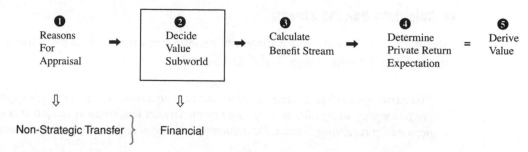

EXHIBIT 6.3 Market Value Process: Decide Subworld

➋ Decide Value Subworld

Exhibit 6.4 lists information that helps determine which subworld should be used for the valuation.

The facts and circumstances of the situation help determine in which subworld to view the subject.

EXHIBIT 6.4 The Financial Market Subworld Is Appropriate if . . .

1. Earnings are used as the basis for the valuation by the acquirer. No synergies are valued in the financial subworld.
2. The company is unlikely to attract a synergistic buyer, because the likely acquirer is either an individual, who brings no synergies to a deal, or a nonstrategic institution.
3. The company's owner-manager will not entertain a synergistic sale since it might result in staff reductions and other expense consolidations. Many owners are paternalistic regarding the people within their organizations and will not sell to a consolidator, even if doing so means receiving a higher selling price.

Within the financial subworld, the buyer brings no synergies to the deal. Because of this, the target itself must supply the earnings and the collateral for the transaction finances. This effectively creates a boundary around the valuation in the form of a definable limit as to how much a financial buyer can pay for a business, with the target providing most of this answer.

Once it is determined that the financial subworld is appropriate to use, the next step is to calculate the company's benefit stream. This is shown in Exhibit 6.5.

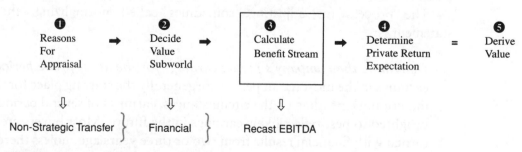

EXHIBIT 6.5 Calculate the Benefit Stream

❸ Calculate Benefit Stream

Each value world employs a different benefit stream (stream) to value a business interest. The benefit stream is defined as:

> *The earnings, cash flow, and distributions that an authority prescribes is appropriate to employ in a value world. The benefit stream is economic in that it is either derived by recasting financial statements or determined on a pro forma basis.*

The authority in each world determines the benefit stream to be used in that world. Streams often vary by industry based on deal-making convention. For instance, throughout the years sellers and buyers of public accounting practices have agreed to use net revenues as the stream whereas many segments of the software industry use subscription revenues as the stream. Some industries use gross margin dollars as the stream. The key here is that the appraiser needs to understand how stream is defined by authorities in the subject industry before a proper market valuation can be completed.

For the purposes of this book, the stream for financial market value is defined as:

> *Recast earnings before interest, taxes, depreciation and amortization (EBITDA)*

Recast EBITDA has been chosen here mainly for descriptive reasons. Once again, no single stream metric is usable across all industries.

EBITDA differs from the operating cash flow in a cash flow statement primarily by excluding payments for taxes or interest as well as changes in working capital. EBITDA also differs from free cash flow because it excludes cash requirements for replacing capital assets (capital expenditures).

Recast EBITDA includes adjustments for one-time expenses and various discretionary expenses of the seller. These earnings are measured before interest since valuation assumes a debt-free basis. Recast EBITDA is also stated on a pretax basis since the market value world typically does not consider the tax status of either party.

Private companies are non-tax-paying flow-through entities, such as S corporations or limited liability companies. Since there are significant differences in individual tax rates, valuators cannot determine tax rates for various parties with certainty. A pretax orientation enables the parties to view the business on a similar basis. Exhibit 6.6 lists some of the numerous recast adjustments.

The process for adjusting, sometimes called normalizing, the income statement is:

- *Determine the company's pretax earnings for the appropriate period.* Pretax earnings in the most recent period are generally the starting place for this determination. Depending on the circumstances, earnings of several periods may be weighted to best reflect likely earnings in the future. Most buyers are less concerned with financial results from two or three years ago, unless there is a negative trend. Some level of projections is used for the current year. For instance,

EXHIBIT 6.6   Recast Earnings Adjustments

Owner related:
- Excess compensation, compensation beyond what the owner is willing to receive postsale or the amount required to hire competent professional management
- Personal travel and entertainment
- Vehicle expense beyond what is considered normal
- Unearned family compensation, including wages, vehicles, trips, insurance
- Director's fees
- Insurances beyond what is considered normal
- Management fees
- Excessive rent

Employee related:
- Excessive bonuses or compensation beyond industry norms, if they can be eliminated
- Business practices that will be discontinued after a sale (extravagant automobiles, trips, etc.)

One-time expenses:
- Bad debt expense that is unusual compared to past averages
- Uninsured accident or casualty loss
- Trial advertising
- Legal (one time lawsuit, audits, etc.)
- Loss incurred in opening a new branch or launching a new product line
- Some research and development expenses

Discretionary business practices:
- Donations
- Accounting audits, if compilations or review will occur going forward
- All above-market close transactions
- Customer incentives that will be discontinued going forward

Accounting/finance:
- Depreciation added, normalized capital expenditures subtracted
- Discretionary overpaid expenses to reduce taxes

six months of projections generally can be used to supplement six months of actual results. Weighting is discretionary and sometimes controversial.

- *Adjust for owner-related discretionary items.* There are a variety of owner-related discretionary items, most of which are adopted to limit taxation. Not all owners' compensation is recast. Only excess compensation is added back to pretax earnings. This is compensation beyond what the owner is willing to receive postsale or the amount of difference required to hire competent professional management. For example, if an owner who did not plan to continue working after the sale of his business had been receiving $300,000 per year in compensation, and it would cost $200,000 per year to hire two managers to replace him, only $100,000 is added back to pretax earnings.
- *Adjust for employee-related items.* Certain employee-related items may be changed postsale, and they are added back to pretax earnings. It is important, however, to recast only those items that would not alter the company's morale or prospects postsale.
- *Adjust for one-time expenses.* As with the other adjustments, one-time expenses must be made judiciously. The items listed in Exhibit 6.6 are not encompassing, since these kinds of adjustments are peculiar to the circumstances of the company.

- *Adjust for discretionary business practices.* These adjustments are difficult to quantify, because judgment is required as to the business practices of the prospective buyer. The deciding factor should be: Is it reasonable for the business practice to continue beyond the sale?
- *Add interest expense and any noncash charges, such as depreciation and amortization.* The valuation assumes the company is debt-free at the valuation date, so interest expense is added to pretax earnings. Only interest expense associated with debt that will not survive the transaction should be considered. For instance, if the buyer as part of the transaction will assume a credit line, the interest on this line should not be recast. Noncash charges, such as depreciation and amortization, typically are added back since they reduce earnings but do not affect the cash position of the company.

Exhibit 6.7 provides an example of how these adjustments are used to recast the income statement of PrivateCo (our example company).

EXHIBIT 6.7   PrivateCo Recast EBITDA ($000)

Item	Y/E 20X3	Y/E 20X2	Y/E 20X1
Pretax profits	$1,800	$1,368	$1,950
Adjustments			
Depreciation	356	360	358
Normalized CapEx[a]	(300)	(300)	(300)
Excess owner comp[b]	250	250	250
Management fees[c]	200	189	304
Interest[d]	95	99	97
Officer insurances[e]	5.0	4.5	4.6
Excess accounting[f]	6.5	10.5	8.5
Excess legal[g]	8.7	0	0
Excess rent[h]	9.9	9.6	12
Excess health insurance	8.2	14	14
Casualty loss (fire)[i]	35	0	0
One time consulting[j]	0	55	0
Donations[k]	74	69	72
Employee incentives[l]	125	115	117
Total adjustments	873	876	937
Recast EBITDA	**$2,673**	**$2,244**	**$2,887**

[a]Normalized capital expenditures have been deducted from depreciation to offset noncash charges.
[b]Since the majority owner is passive, all his compensation will be added back.
[c]Management fees are charged each year by another company that the majority owner also controls.
[d]Interest expense is added back to accurately depict cash flow.
[e]Officer insurances are added back since the majority shareholder will not be on the payroll after the sale.
[f]Some accounting services are performed mainly for another company the majority owner controls but are billed to PrivateCo.
[g]One time expense. Former employee illegally took blueprints and PrivateCo successfully sued against this person.
[h]Assumes current rent will not continue under new ownership.
[i]The uninsured part of a fire (one time expense).
[j]A consultant was hired to perform design studies for a new product, which was not produced.
[k]The company gives donations each year to a charity the majority owner supports.
[l]Employee incentives includes bonuses that only a passive shareholder would instiute.

EXHIBIT 6.8 PrivateCo Weighted Recast EBITDA

Period	Recast EBIT	Weighted Factor	Weighted Value
Y/E 20X3 (current year)	$2,673,000	3	$8,019,000
Y/E 20X2	2,244,000	2	4,488,000
Y/E 20X1	2,887,000	1	2,887,000
		6	$15,394,000
	Weighted recast EBITDA:		$2,500,000 (as rounded)

The recast EBITDA is substantially higher than the reported pretax profits. This is not unusual. The key here is to add back only those expenses specific to the current ownership and not be incurred by a new owner.

Exhibit 6.8 shows the weighted recast EBITDA calculation for PrivateCo. The goal is to choose a recast EBITDA that is reasonable and reflects the company's likely earnings capacity in the future. The appraising party chooses how to weight the numbers, if at all. There will probably be a difference of opinion between the seller and buyer here. The seller wants the numbers weighted to show the highest possible value. The buyer, meanwhile, typically uses a scheme that shows the lowest number, even if it means going back into the history of the company. Many market valuations use the trailing 12 months' recast EBITDA as the basis for the appraisal. This approach often gives more weight to recent years, since they may be more indicative of the future prospects of the company. For presentation purposes, PrivateCo's recast EBITDA is weighted on a 3-2-1 basis, which means the current year's EBITDA has a weight of 3, the previous year has a weight of 2, and the earliest year has a weight of 1.

PrivateCo's weighted-average recast EBITDA using a 3-2-1 weighting is $2,500,000. This is achieved by taking the total weighted value of $15.4 million and dividing by the sum of the weighted factors, 6. Thus, for demonstration purposes, the financial subworld stream is $2.5 million.

The next step, shown in Exhibit 6.9, determines the return a prospective investor, or group of buyers, requires when undertaking an acquisition.

❹ Determine Private Return Expectation

Private return expectation (PRE or expectation) converts a benefit stream into a market value. The PRE introduces the concept of market risk and return into

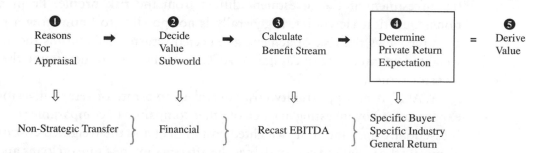

EXHIBIT 6.9 Determine Private Return Expectation

the valuation process. As explained in Chapter 4, PREs drive private valuation. The PRE is the quantification of these return expectations in the *private capital markets.*

The private return expectation is defined as:

The expected rate of return private capital markets require in order to attract funds to a particular investment

Thus, the PRE can be stated as a discount rate, capitalization rate, acquisition multiple, or any other metric that converts the benefit stream to a present value.

There are three different ways to calculate the private return expectation in the financial and synergy subworlds:

1. Specific investor return
2. Specific industry return
3. General return

It should be noted that the private return expectation (i.e., acquisition multiple) is typically the same in the financial and synergy subworlds. This is because the acquisition multiple is an assessment by the buyer of how likely it is that the benefit stream will be realized. Another way of saying this is that a multiple of 5 means that the buyer thinks the current benefit stream will continue for five years. This assessment is usually the same for both subworlds.

SPECIFIC INVESTOR RETURN

The returns required by individual investors differ from corporate investors. At least one study shows that, regardless of interest-rate levels or the general economic environment, individual financial buyers require about 30% returns on their investment. That corresponds to roughly a 3.3 selling multiple.[1] Since the corporate investor has already raised capital for its business, return expectations are driven by its capital structure.

If only one corporate prospective buyer is contemplated, the minimum PRE is determined by calculating the weighted average cost of capital for that investor. The actual return expectation depends on the capital's use. A company should not use a company return expectation to evaluate a potential investment if the investment differs from the risk profile. From a valuation/acquisition viewpoint, it generally is not possible to know how a potential acquirer views the risk of achieving expected returns. This means the acquirer's weighted average cost of capital (WACC) must be used to determine the specific investor return.

WACC is an opportunity cost equivalent to a rate of return investors could expect to earn by investing in stock of other companies of comparable risk. WACC is essentially the sum of the weighted cost of debt and the weighted cost of equity. Typically the weighted cost of debt is the after-tax interest rate on loans and bonds.

EXHIBIT 6.10   PrivateCo Private Cost of Capital Calculation

Capital Type	Market Value	% of Total	Return Expectation	Tax Effect	Rate Factor
Term loan	500,000	4%	5.7%	0%	.2
Equity	13,700,000	96%	25.0%	0%	24.0
			Weighted average cost of capital		24.2%

The cost of equity is more difficult to calculate. For public companies, it involves analyzing shareholders' expected return implicit in the price they have paid to buy or hold their shares. Investors have the choice of buying risk-free Treasury bonds or investing in other, riskier securities. They obviously expect a higher return for higher risk.

Private companies do not have access to the public securities market by which to calculate cost of equity. Chapter 2 introduced the Pepperdine Private Capital Market Line to show the effective cost of private debt and equity capital. Exhibit 2.5 shows private equity returns range from 25% to about 40%. If equity is the only component in the capital structure, equity holders must receive returns of 25% to 40% to compensate them adequately for the risk of ownership.

Purely for presentation purposes, the WACC for PrivateCo is determined in Exhibit 6.10.

To calculate a company's WACC, the market value of each capital type is calculated, then weighed based on its proportion of the whole. Market value of debt is typically its face value; PrivateCo's market value of equity of $13.7 million is calculated later in this chapter. If the benefit stream for market value was stated on an after-tax basis, the debt portion of the capital would be tax-effected at the marginal tax rates. Since the stream in this case is stated on a pretax basis (recast EBITDA), the debt is not tax-effected. For presentation purposes, an expected equity return of 25% is used. In this example, PrivateCo has a WACC of 24% (as rounded). This means Joe Mainstreet of PrivateCo creates shareholder value by investing in projects that return more than 24%.

Another way of considering expected investor returns is to calculate the reciprocal of the capitalization rate, which then becomes a selling multiple. For example, a 24% WACC corresponds to an acquisition multiple of approximately 4.2 (1/.24). In general terms, a prospective buyer could pay four times the stream for an acquisition candidate and still meet his or her return expectation. In this case, the buyer bets the benefit stream will continue for a minimum of four years. Increases in the benefit stream beyond four years add to the buyer's overall return.

Due to lack of information, it is difficult to calculate a potential buyer's WACC directly. Typically, WACC can be calculated only for public companies. In situations where more than one buyer is present, or if the single buyer's WACC cannot be determined, the next step is to calculate an industry-specific selling multiple.

SPECIFIC INDUSTRY RETURN

A private guideline acquisition search can be used to determine a private return expectation profile for the likely investor group. This method locates comparable acquisitions and then uses the resulting information to draw a value conclusion. Four steps are used for this method.[2]

Step 1. *Set criteria for collection of acquisition multiples, including time frames.* There is latitude here to decide how many years back to consider. Criteria to consider include:
  - Line of business. Transactions from companies may be usable if they are similar to the company from an investment perspective. Normally this is determined on an Standard Industrial Code (SIC) code basis.
  - Relative asset size and revenues comparable to the company.
  - Financial information relative to the company must be available.
  - Guideline transactions probably should have occurred in the past five years.

Step 2. *Identify the sources from which the data is gathered.* A number of databases contain acquisition multiples. The most useful include recast EBITDA multiples. All of the databases named below contain selling multiples helpful in the financial subworld. The key is to develop search criteria that match the valuation requirements. In other words, a company with a $1 million recast EBITDA should be compared against a company of similar size. The most appropriate databases are:
  - *Institute of Business Appraisers Market Database.* The Institute of Business Appraisers (IBA) maintains a database of information on actual sales of private businesses. The database, which contains over 30,000 records of enterprise transactions in over 650 SIC codes, is mainly usable for valuations of less than $2 million. There are 13 points of information per transaction. This database is especially useful for obtaining selling multiples for individual buyers in the financial subworld. Exhibit 6.11 shows data from a typical IBA market comparison.

    For discussion purposes, consider SIC code 3469, Metal Stampers. The example shows the results of a search for companies reporting profit. The transaction data does not factor into the decision on whether to use the data, since small financial subworld transactions tend not to be time sensitive (i.e., the earnings multiples paid tend not to vary as much as larger transactions).[3]

    The median price/earnings multiples for these qualifying transactions is 2.4 times. Buyers in these deals are willing to pay, on the average, 2.4 times the annual earnings to close the deal. "Annual earnings" are stated before owner's compensation, interest, and taxes. Unfortunately, it is impossible to determine if annual earnings are equivalent to recast EBITDA as defined earlier in the chapter.

EXHIBIT 6.11   Institute of Business Appraisers: Market Comparison Data

SIC CODE: 3469

The information below is supplied in response to your request for data to be used in applying the "Market Data Approach" to business appraisal. Because of the nature of sources from which the information is obtained, we are not able to guarantee its accuracy. Neither do we make any representation as to the applicability of the information to any specific appraisal situation.

The following explains entries in the data table:

Business type	Principal line of business
SIC CODE	Principal Standard Industrial Classification number applicable to the business sold
Annual gross	Reported annual sales volume of business sold
Annual earnings	Reported annual earnings before owner's compensation, interest, and taxes
Owner's compensation	Reported owner's compensation
Sale price	Total reported consideration, i.e., cash, liabilities assumed, etc., excluding real estate
Price/gross	Ratio of total consideration to reported annual gross
Price/earnings	Ratio of total consideration to reported annual earnings
Yr/Mo of sale	Year and month during which transaction was consummated

Business Type	Annual Gross $000's	Annual Earnings $000's	Owner's Comp. $000's	Sale Price $000's	Price/ Gross	Price/ Earnings	Geographic	Yr/Mo of Sale
Lawn/garden supply mfg	6000	480	80	1000	0.17	2.08	Midwest	97/9
Tool & die shop mfg	963	201		1200	1.25	5.97		97/3
Wash machine equip. mfg	496	109		149	0.30	1.37	Texas	87/2
Metal recycling	402	60		144	0.36	2.40	TX	93/1
Tool & die shop mfg	304	104		250	0.82	2.40		98/7
Tool & die mold shop	219	43		104	0.47	2.42		86/12

- *Pratt's Stats®*. This database lists approximately 88 different data fields. Most of the transactions reported in Pratt's Stats occur in the $1 million to $30 million range. Exhibit 6.12 represents a search result from Pratt's Stats, once again in SIC Code 3469. Also, companies reporting earnings of more than $500,000 are qualified for consideration.

    The Pratt's Stats information is summarized purely for descriptive purposes. In this case, the transactions summary shows a deal price/EBITDA mean multiple of 6.3 times and a deal price/EBITDA median multiple of 5.7 times.

Step 3. *Select the companies that meet the criteria.* As with the IBA Market Comparison Data and Pratt's Stats results, companies must meet the valuation criteria. Appraisers do not feel 100% comfortable that the transaction results are totally applicable. Also, any fewer than four to five transactions

EXHIBIT 6.12   Pratt's Stats Advanced Search Results: Summarized

No.	SIC Code	Business Description	Deal Price	Net Sales	Deal Price to EBITDA
1	3469	Manufacturing precision metal components	$7.085 MM	$14.2 MM	5.5 times
2	3469	Manufacturing mechanical enclosures	$8.75 MM	$16.8 MM	5.9 times
3	3469	Manufacturing metal stampings	$2.2 MM	$5.5 MM	5.0 times
4	3469	Milling machine parts	$3.8 MM	$7.5 MM	8.7 times

Transaction Summary
Deal Price/EBITDA Mean   6.3
Deal Price/EBITDA Median 5.7

may not reflect market expectation. It is better to have more than ten transactions, which would reliably reflect the market.

Step 4. *Apply the median multiple against the company's benefit stream.* The median multiple is better than the mean when applying a selling multiple to the benefit stream. A wide range of multiples within the reported transactions and medians tend to better reflect results.

Let us review the different preliminary values the IBA and Pratt databases yield for PrivateCo. Once again, due to the smaller size of its deals, the IBA database normally is best suited for individual financial subworld valuations, while the Pratt database typically is more appropriate for the nonstrategic financial subworld appraisals. The choice of database is determined by the earnings size of the company. That is because the appraisal should use database results with similar earnings levels. Exhibit 6.13 is an example that shows the ramifications of using different database results to derive a market value.

The IBA database is a good source of transactional data for smaller companies with reported earnings of less than $500,000. The Pratt Stats database, however, contains transactions larger than $2 million and can be used to determine values for larger companies. Users of transaction data need to ensure that they apply data consistently from the database to their subject company. For example, the Pratt's Stats benefit stream of recast EBITDA is consistent with how PrivateCo's stream

	Database	Stream	Multiple	Enterprise Market Value
Individual ⟶	IBA	$2,500,000	2.4	$ 6,000,000
⟶	Pratt's Stats	$2,500,000	5.7	$ 14,250,000

EXHIBIT 6.13   Comparison of IBA and Pratt Databases

was calculated in Exhibit 6.8; additional adjustments would have to be made to PrivateCo's stream to make the IBA database numbers meaningful.

GENERAL INVESTOR RETURNS

If no industry-specific selling multiples are available or the sample size is not large enough, the next step is to calculate a general investor return. This is accomplished either through the use of databases with general acquisition selling multiples or a general investor return matrix.

General Acquisition Selling Multiples   To determine a general acquisition selling multiple, start with general databases of private acquisition transactions. These databases provide summarized results rather than specific deal transactions. That information is useful when the private guideline industry return method does not yield comparable transactions. Alternatively, it can serve as a supplement to those results.

Exhibit 6.14 displays acquisition multiples over a period of years by transaction size.

There are several noteworthy items regarding Exhibit 6.14. First, larger transactions typically realize larger acquisition multiples. This means the market perceives lower risk of achieving the benefit streams of larger transactions and thus places a higher multiple. Second, the range for lower middle market transactions tends to be four to seven times EBITDA. This confirms the segmentation chart shown earlier in the book. Finally, acquisition multiples vary with the amount of senior lending available. For instance, 2009 was a lean year for senior lenders, and the multiples were relatively low as a result.

Exhibit 6.15 shows the final step in the market valuation process.

❺ Derive Value

After the appropriate benefit stream and private return expectations are determined, a final value is derived. The stream is either capitalized or discounted by

EXHIBIT 6.14   GF Data Resources General Acquisition Multiples: Summarized

Total Enterprise Value (TEV) / EBITDA
All Industries

	2006	2007	2008	2009	2010
TEV (MM)					
$10–25	5.7	5.4	5.3	5.1	4.8
$25–50	6.0	6.2	5.9	6.1	6.3
$50–100	6.5	6.6	6.4	6.1	6.2
$100–250	6.8	7.5	6.6	6.5	6.9

Source: Copyright, GF Data Resources LLC, used with permission.

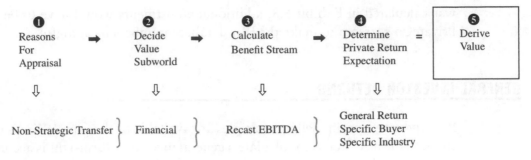

EXHIBIT 6.15 Derive Value

the private return expectation to create a present value. A review of capitalization versus discounting benefits follows.

Capitalizing versus Discounting

The end result of capitalizing and discounting a stream is the same: Both convert the stream to a present value. "Present value" is a financial term that describes what something received tomorrow is worth today. To calculate present value, a stream of earnings or cash is discounted, or "reverse compounded." Doing this requires a discount rate. Thus, $100 received a year from now is worth something less today. This is the present value. Assume money is invested at 5% a year right now with 5% chosen as the discount rate. The *present value*, then, of $100 promised a year from now using 5% as the discount rate is 95.24% or

$$((\$100 \div 105\%) \times 100\%)$$

Looking at it another way, $95.24 invested today at 5% interest yields $100 next year.

Consider this contrast between capitalization and discounting.

Capitalization = A method used to convert a single year's stream to a value, such as:

$$\text{Capitalized value} = \frac{\text{Benefit stream}}{\text{Capitalization rate}}$$

Using the example given in text:

$$\frac{\$5 \text{ (interest received per year} - \text{the stream)}}{5\% \text{ (capitalization rate)}} = \$100$$

In the market value world, another term for "capitalization rate" is the expected investment return of the buyer, expressed as a percentage.

Discounting = A method used to convert the expected future benefit streams to a present value, such as:

$$\text{Discounted Value} = \frac{\text{Cash}_1}{(1+i)^1} + \frac{\text{Cash}_2}{(1+i)_2} + \frac{\text{Cash}_3}{(1+i)^3} + \cdots$$

or

$$= \frac{\$5_1}{(1+5\%)^1} + \frac{\$5_2}{(1+5\%)^2} + \frac{\$5_3}{(1+5\%)^3} + \cdots$$

$$= \$100$$

When given the same stream, capitalization/discount rate and growth rate and capitalizing and discounting yield the same answer. The two rates are equal when the expected benefits into the future are the same as for the first period. The two rates are different when the benefits vary in the future. For an investment with infinite life, the difference between the discount rate and the capitalization rate is the annually compounded percentage rate of growth or decline in perpetuity in the stream being discounted or capitalized. In other words, in the open market where benefits change in unstable ways in the future, the capitalization rate equals the discount rate minus the annual compounded rate of growth of the stream.

Capitalizing a benefit stream is used for these reasons:

- *It is simple to use.* With only one calculation, it is easy to perform.
- *It is accurate.* If the stream is stable or growing at a fairly even rate, the capitalization of stream method determines a value as accurate as the discounted stream method.
- *It is accepted.* The use of selling multiples (the reciprocal of the capitalization rate) has been employed for many years and has wide acceptance among sellers and buyers.
- *It relies on what is known.* This method is not based on pie-in-the-sky–type futuristic estimates; rather, it uses historical or current numbers.

Earlier it was determined that PrivateCo's recast EBITDA was $2.5 million and the likely acquisition multiple was 5.7 (from Exhibit 6.12—Pratt's Stats median multiple). Now we can determine the financial market value for PrivateCo:

$$\text{Financial market value} = (\text{Recast EBITDA} \times \text{acquisition multiple}) - \text{long-term debt}$$
$$= (\$2,500,000 \times 5.7) - \$500,000$$
$$= \$13.7 \text{ million}$$

The financial market value of PrivateCo is $13.7 million. Since the long-term debt was deducted from the enterprise value, it is important to note that this figure is a 100% equity value for the company.

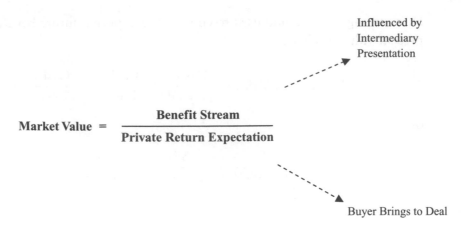

EXHIBIT 6.16   Control of Benefit Stream versus Expectation

Benefit Stream versus Private Return Expectation

Many appraisers and owners focus more on the selling multiple than on adjustments to the earnings. In other words, the parties often focus more on the private return expectation than on the benefit stream. However, investors bring the multiple in the form of their return expectation. Sellers cannot change this fact. What sellers can control is the presentation of the stream.

Professional financial intermediaries attempt to use a selling process to maximize a client's benefit stream. This is vital since the intermediary can influence *only* the numerator of the value equation. Exhibit 6.16 illustrates this difference.

The denominator of the valuation equation is the required rate of return needed by buyers to compensate for the risk of making a particular investment. Once buyers understand the risk of an investment, they bring this expectation to the deal.

TRIANGULATION

Financial intermediaries are the authority in the financial subworld. They "live" in the transfer side of the private capital markets triangle and bring their experience to the valuation process. They enforce the process and provide feedback to the markets. For instance, intermediaries gather and report transactional data that informs participants about acquisition multiples. They also help direct companies into the appropriate value world, including this subworld. This information is then used by the various market players to draw value conclusions. For example, intermediaries have learned that no market exists for the sale of private minority interests because they have tried, in vain, to sell such interests.

World	PrivateCo Value
Asset market value	$2.4 million
Collateral value	$2.5 million
Insurable value (buy/sell)	$6.5 million
Fair market value	$6.8 million
Investment value	$7.5 million
Impaired goodwill	$13.0 million
Financial market value	**$13.7 million**
Owner value	$15.8 million
Synergy market value	$16.6 million
Public value	$18.2 million

PrivateCo's value in the financial subworld is $13.7 million, which is almost six times greater than its value in the asset subworld.

Market value is located in the *empirical unregulated* value quadrant. This means that market transactions are observed within an unregulated marketplace. This is important because profit-motivated players who are free to choose from a host of investment alternatives form the open market. The authority then informs the involved parties as to likely market values based on actual transactions.

Capital availability directly influences market value. Since the likely buyer in the financial subworld is either an individual or a nonstrategic entity, access to capital constrains the valuation. Typically nonstrategic buyers can afford to pay only what they can finance while still receiving a risk-adjusted return. The balance sheet and income stream of the target provide most of the answers regarding financeability. In this subworld without synergies, deals are unlikely to attract growth capital, such as private equity, thereby limiting value.

NOTES

1. Robert Slee, "Different Buyers Pay Different Multiples," *Data Link* (May 1997).
2. Shannon P. Pratt, Robert F. Reilly, and Robert R. Schweihs, *Valuing a Business: The Analysis and Appraisal of Closely Held Companies*, 5th ed. (New York: McGraw-Hill), p. 268.
3. Ray Miles, "In Defense of 'Stale' Comparables," Publication P-299.1 (Plantation, FL: Institute of Business Appraisers, 1992).

CHAPTER 7

Synergy Subworld of Market Value

A business owner who wants to achieve the highest marketplace value focuses the valuation process on the world of market value. This world focuses on determining the highest and best value for a business. This principle is similar to the "highest and best use of a property" axiom in real estate appraisal.

The synergy subworld reflects the market reality that the highest value for many businesses is found by selling to a strategic buyer. Every company has at least three market values at the same time. This is another example of why market value, much like all business valuation, is a *range* concept. Each market value step, called a subworld, represents the most likely selling price based on the most likely buyer type. The subworlds are asset, financial, and synergy.

The asset subworld, the subject of Chapter 5, reflects what the company is worth if the most likely selling price is based on net asset value. The asset subworld assumes that the most likely buyer bases the purchase on the company's assets rather than on its earnings stream.

The financial subworld, the subject of Chapter 6, reflects what an individual or nonstrategic buyer might pay for the business.

The synergy subworld reflects the market value of the company when synergies from a possible acquisition are considered. "Synergy" is defined as the increase in performance of the combined firm over what the two firms are already expected to accomplish as independent companies.

Financial intermediaries are the authorities governing the synergy subworld. Determining value in the synergy subworld of market value, more than any other value world, requires substantial market knowledge, especially in terms of the dynamics that shape mergers and acquisitions.

A snapshot of the key tenets of the synergy subworld is provided in Exhibit 7.1.

The market value process for the synergy subworld is characterized by the flow chart in Exhibit 7.2.

❶ Reasons for Appraisal

The synergy subworld is concerned primarily with strategic or synergistic combinations, such as horizontal and vertical integrations, or any combination where

EXHIBIT 7.1   Longitude and Latitude: Synergy Subworld of Market Value

Definition	The highest purchase price available for selected assets or stock of the company. The synergy subworld applies when synergies from a possible acquisition are considered. Synergy is the increase in performance of the combined firm over what the two firms are already expected to accomplish as independent companies.
Purpose of Appraisal	To derive an open market value, probably to determine the likely selling price of a business to a synergistic buyer.
Function of Appraisal	To help an owner decide a likely selling price for a business in predication of a sale.
Quadrant	Empirical unregulated
Authority	Financial intermediaries, located in the transfer side of the private capital markets.
Benefit Stream	The stream that accrues to the financial buyer posttransaction. For the purposes of this book, that synergy subworld stream is recast earnings before interest, taxes, depreciation and amortization (EBITDA) plus enjoyed synergies.
Private Return Expectation	The expected rate of return that the private capital markets require in order to attract funds to a particular investment. In this subworld, there are three ways to determine this rate: specific investor return, specific industry return, and general return.
Valuation Process Summary	Value is determined in this subworld by capitalizing or discounting a synergized benefit stream at an appropriate rate of return expectation. The synergy subworld stream includes recast EBITDA plus the amount of enjoyed synergies by the target. The amount of enjoyed synergies means the estimated synergies are credited to, or kept by, a party in a deal.

PrivateCo Example

Stream	×	Synergy Subworld Multiple	=	Market Value
$3,000,000	×	5.7	=	$17,100,000
Minus LTD*			=	$500,000
Final Value			=	$16,600,000

*Assumes value on a debt-free basis

the acquirer can leverage the target's capabilities. Synergies result from a variety of acquisition scenarios. Perhaps the most quantifiable group of synergies emanates from horizontal integrations. A horizontal integrator realizes substantial synergies by cutting duplicate overhead and other expenses. Some of these savings *may* be shared with the seller. Vertical integrations also create substantial synergies. These tend to be strategic, in that the target helps the acquirer achieve some business

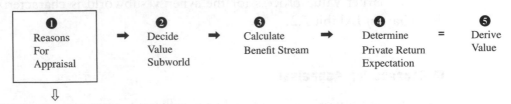

EXHIBIT 7.2   Market Value Process: Select Appraisal Reason

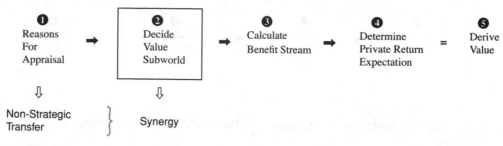

EXHIBIT 7.3   Market Value Process: Decide Subworld

goal. Synergies also result from different financial structures of the parties. For instance, the target may realize interest expense savings because of the cheaper borrowing costs of the acquirer.

The next step in the market valuation process, depicted in Exhibit 7.3, considers whether the synergy subworld is appropriate to use in the valuation.

❷ Decide Value Subworld

The synergy subworld is the market value of the company when synergies from a possible acquisition are considered. As such, this subworld is accessed only when a strategic or synergistic buyer or group of buyers is identified.

The guidelines listed in Exhibit 7.4 help determine whether a company's highest value is the synergy subworld.

If the answer to a number of the statements in Exhibit 7.4 is yes, then the company should be valued in the synergy subworld. Research on the company's industry should indicate if vertical or horizontal integrations or other strategic/synergistic acquisitions are taking place. The company's management team generally knows if the company is an attractive target to strategic buyers.

Once it is determined the synergy subworld is appropriate to use, the next step is to calculate a benefit stream. Exhibit 7.5 shows this step.

EXHIBIT 7.4   The Synergy Subworld Is Appropriate if . . .

1. The company participates in an industry that is being vertically or horizontally integrated, or it can be determined that a buyer can synergistically leverage the company's capabilities.
2. Synergies can be quantified with some level of certainty *prior* to a transaction.
3. Some of the following strategic motivations exist between the company and prospective acquirers:
   a. The company possesses technology or patents difficult or impossible to duplicate.
   b. The company employs a management team that is considered exceptional.
   c. The company has a strong market position that enjoys monopolistic attributes.
   d. The company uses business practices or processes dramatically more efficient than its counterparts.
   e. The company has developed a unique business model that is transferable to an acquirer.
   f. The company has access to worldwide markets that enables it to purchase and sell more effectively than the competition.

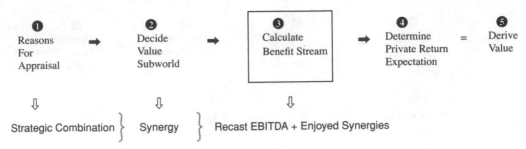

EXHIBIT 7.5   Calculate Benefit Stream

❸ Calculate the Benefit Stream

If the synergy subworld is the appropriate value level, the next step is to calculate a suitable benefit stream (stream). Each value world employs a different Stream to value a business interest. For these purposes, stream is defined as:

> *The earnings, cash flow, and distributions that an authority prescribes is appropriate to employ in a value world. The benefit stream is economic in that it is either derived by recasting financial statements or determined on a pro forma basis.*

The authority in each world determines the benefit stream to be used in that world. Streams often vary by industry based on deal-making convention. For instance, throughout the years sellers and buyers of public accounting practices have agreed to use net revenues as the stream whereas many segments of the software industry use subscription revenues as the stream. Some industries use gross margin dollars as the stream. The key here is that the appraiser needs to understand how the stream is defined by authorities in the subject industry before a proper market valuation can be completed.

Since the market value world signifies the value available in the marketplace, the stream should reflect the varied possibilities of that market. For demonstration purposes, the benefit stream for synergy subworld stream is:

Recast EBITDA + Amount of enjoyed synergies

Recast earnings before interest, taxes, depreciation, and amortization (EBITDA) is adjusted for one-time expenses and various discretionary expenses of the seller. These earnings are measured before interest since the valuation assumes a debt-free basis. Recast EBITDA is also stated on a pretax basis since the market value world typically does not consider the tax status of either party. This lack of tax consideration is driven by the fact that many private companies are non-tax-paying flow-through entities, such as S corporations and limited liability companies. There are significant differences within the individual tax rates, such that tax rates for other parties cannot be determined with certainty. A pretax basis enables the parties to view the business on a similar basis. The amount of enjoyed synergies represents the synergies that a party can reasonably expect to realize,

EXHIBIT 7.6   Recast Earnings Adjustments

Owner related:
- Excess compensation (compensation beyond what the owner is willing to receive postsale or the amount required to hire competent professional management)
- Personal travel and entertainment
- Vehicle expense beyond what is considered normal
- Unearned family compensation, including wages, vehicles, trips, insurance
- Director's fees
- Insurances beyond what is considered normal
- Management fees
- Excessive rent

Employee related:
- Excessive bonuses or compensation beyond industry norms, if they can be eliminated
- Business practices that will be discontinued after a sale (extravagant automobiles, trips, etc.)

One-time expenses:
- Bad debt expense that is unusual compared to past averages
- Uninsured accident or casualty loss
- Trial advertising
- Legal (one-time lawsuit, audits, etc.)
- Loss incurred in opening a new branch or launching a new product line
- Some research and development expenses

Discretionary business practices:
- Donations
- Accounting audits (if compilations or review will occur going forward)
- All above market close transactions
- Customer incentives that will be discontinued going forward

Accounting/finance:
- Depreciation added, normalized capital expenditures subtracted
- Discretionary overpaid expenses to reduce taxes

---

or receive credit for, in the acquisition. The adjustments to recast EBITDA are numerous. Exhibit 7.6 lists typical adjustments.

SYNERGIES

The synergy subworld stream includes adjusted EBITDA plus the amount of enjoyed synergies by the company. The amounts of enjoyed synergies are the estimated synergies credited to, or kept by, a party in a deal. First the total expected synergies in a deal are forecast. Then an estimate of the enjoyed synergies credited to each party is made. Usually the buyer is responsible for creating synergies. Buyers do not readily give the value of synergies away, since the realization of the synergies happens only while they own the business. A high level of realism and significant experience are necessary when quantifying enjoyed synergies.

The next synergy types, which are synergies with quantifiable certainty, may be available to the parties in a deal.

- Cost savings
- Revenue enhancements

- Gross margin enhancements
- Strategic combinations

Cost Savings

Cost savings are generally the easiest synergies to estimate with certainty. They are sometimes referred to as "hard synergies" since they emanate from hard numbers.[1] Examples of cost savings are elimination of jobs, facilities, and related expenses no longer needed due to consolidation. There are three primary types of cost savings grouped by the type of expected acquisition: horizontal integration, vertical integration, and financial structure.

Exhibit 7.7 lists synergies available in the cost savings category.

Exhibit 7.8 shows how cost savings synergies are developed in a valuation. This example assumes that several horizontal integrators are active in PrivateCo's industry segment and should have an interest in acquiring the company. The "Total Synergies" in the exhibit likely exist between PrivateCo and any of the consolidators; whereas, "Total Shared Synergies" shows the appraiser's estimate as to the percentage of the total synergies that is fair or reasonable for PrivateCo to enjoy.

A number of possible synergies may be realized if PrivateCo is acquired by a horizontal integrator. Unfortunately, synergy is often a euphemism for layoffs.

EXHIBIT 7.7 Cost Savings Synergies

Horizontal integration:	A variety of synergies are created with a horizontal integration. This type of acquisition is generally used to increase market share by purchasing a competitor. It is typically the least risky type of merger due to the buyer's familiarity with the industry and the likelihood of reducing operating expenses after the transaction. Examples of synergies are ■ Consolidating facility costs ■ Collapsing general administrative costs ■ Reducing marketing and selling expenses ■ Increasing buying power
Vertical integration:	Some synergies are realized from a vertical integration. Vertical integration is used to control production processes or to protect the technical core of the company, such as the material flow, distribution or marketing processes. Examples of synergies are ■ Reducing general and administrative costs (payroll, payables, receivable collections) ■ Increasing buying power ■ Increasing revenues through channel integration ■ Improving production or distribution capabilities
Financial structure:	The financial structure of the deal may allow for some synergies. ■ Tax benefits, such as sharing loss carryforwards ■ Interest expense savings from a lower cost of debt ■ Flotation cost savings in a reverse merger

EXHIBIT 7.8   Anticipated Cost Savings Synergies: PrivateCo/Horizontal Integrator

Synergy	Total $ Amount	% Enjoyed by PrivateCo	$ Synergy for PrivateCo
1. Eliminate payables clerk	$ 35,000	30%	$ 10,500
2. Eliminate receivables clerk	35,000	30%	10,500
3. Payroll savings	30,000	30%	9,000
4. Eliminate controller	75,000	30%	22,500
5. Reduced health insurance costs	290,000	30%	87,000
6. Other insurance savings	235,000	30%	70,500
7. Facility consolidations	900,000	30%	270,000
8. Selling expense savings	150,000	30%	45,000
9. Interest savings	30,000	30%	9,000
Total Synergies	$1,780,000	Total Shared Synergies	$534,000

Typically, a number of job positions are redundant in an acquisition. There should also be duplicate expenses that result in cost savings when eliminated. The ninth synergy listed, interest savings, results from the lower interest rate that the consolidator is expected to enjoy relative to PrivateCo's rate. This synergy is itemized under the strategic type of acquisition, but it may be employed in the horizontal or vertical integrated acquisition types as appropriate. Once again, a fair amount of work and market knowledge is required to estimate defensible synergies. But knowledgeable people working diligently in a market are able to achieve the highest and best value. These are the high-end outlying values that form the edge of the market. Rather than explaining them away or merely dismissing this value, the synergy subworld is a systematic method to document and achieve value.

This analysis shows the total synergies generated by PrivateCo and a horizontal integrator is $1,780,000. Under these estimates, PrivateCo would enjoy $534,000 of these synergies. Estimating shared synergies is a difficult task, since very little serious study is focused in this area. Exhibit 7.9 contains a rough guide for estimating shared synergies. From a seller's perspective, rarely does a buyer share more than 50% of total synergies. This is because buyers believe they are responsible for causing at least half of the realized synergies. Of course, this entire discussion is very seller-oriented. Buyers do not offer to share any synergies unless put under pressure to do so. If the company is a routine financial performer

EXHIBIT 7.9   Slee's Shared Synergy Guide

% Shared	Profile
0–10	Company is in the lowest quartile of its peers, and the certainty of potential synergy realization is low.
10–20	Company is in the middle of industry norms, and the certainty of potential synergy realization is less than compelling.
20–40	Company is in the top 10% of its peers, and the certainty of potential synergy is compelling.
50	Company is the top performer of its peer group, and the certainty of potential synergy realization is high.

relative to its industry peers, and the synergies are somewhat uncertain, it may only enjoy 10% to 20% or less of the total synergies. Top performers in an industry group, with a high degree of certainty regarding synergy realization, *may* be able to negotiate sharing 50% of the synergies generated by a deal. Companies can discover how they relate to their peers by reviewing the RMA Statement Studies or by checking with industry trade associations. The argument for synergy sharing must be made on a case-by-case basis.

There is some evidence to support a 50% synergy sharing in a strategic combination, at least in the form of a court case involving minority shareholders of a corporation that was controlled by the acquiring corporation. In the *Mills v. Electric AutoLite* case, the court decided that the acquisition had created synergistic benefits that must be shared equally between the parties.[2] In its opinion, the court discussed various types of synergy and expressed concern that synergistic benefits should be shared among the shareholders.

The benefit stream for PrivateCo on a cost-savings synergy subworld basis is:

Recast EBITDA	$2,500,000 (from Chapter 6)
Cost savings enjoyed synergies	534,000
PrivateCo synergy stream	$3,034,000

The synergy subworld stream for PrivateCo is rounded to $3 million. The recast EBITDA of $2.5 million was established in Chapter 6. The addition of $534,000 in enjoyed synergies may not seem considerable, but it makes a substantial difference when this enjoyed synergy number is capitalized or discounted.

Revenue Enhancements

Occasionally an acquirer and its target can achieve a higher level of sales growth together than either company could on its own. Revenue enhancements are difficult to quantify, but they can dramatically add synergy. The most quantifiable revenue enhancement occurs when the distribution channel of the company or acquirer can be used to increase sales of the other party. For example, if a large government supplier acquires a manufacturer of products that are not currently sold to the government, the acquirer might be able to enhance its revenues. An estimate of revenues generated by this combination is shown next.

Acquirer: $1 billion government supplier of clothing for the army.

Company: $50 million manufacturer of boots and accessories, with no government sales.

Estimate: The acquirer's revenues may increase $25 million by selling the company's products through the government channel (in addition to the $50 million revenue the company currently realizes).

The ultimate calculation for a revenue enhancement synergy involves calculating the profitability of the incremental revenues.

Gross Margin Enhancements

Occasionally business leaders can enhance gross margins by combining companies. This occurs when the buying power of the acquirer is far superior to the company. For instance, if PrivateCo considers an acquisition by a company that purchases a shared raw material 10% cheaper than PrivateCo, some part of this enhancement should be credited to PrivateCo as an enjoyed synergy.

> Synergy is the $2 + 2 = 5$ effect . . . such that the combined return on the firm's resources is greater than the sum of its parts

Gross margin enhancements through market pricing power are more difficult to rationalize. These enhancements happen when the acquirer increases market share to the point where sustainable price increases may be possible. Although gross margins are increased, the company cannot enjoy these synergies since the realization of the price increase comes only after the transaction. It may not be sustainable, and it may be realized in stages to test the market.

Strategic Combination Synergy

Sometimes deals are negotiated and valued under the belief that *strategic* reasons exist for a combination. A preemptive purchase is an example of a strategic acquisition that occurs when the transaction must be accomplished before competitors have an opportunity to move. Strategic synergies are almost always difficult to quantify and therefore are at the bottom of the certainty list. Exhibit 7.10 contains a number of specific strategic benefits.

Strategic synergy may be present when a company owns patents or other proprietary rights to technology, the acquisition of which would be prohibitively expensive for a competitor. This situation could give an acquirer a plausible reason for the acquisition as it attempts to fill the technology void in its operations

EXHIBIT 7.10 Specific Strategic Benefits

Synergistic acquisitions may generate some of the following benefits:

- The acquisition may improve the acquirer's geographic, marketing, or distribution advantage.
- The time required to take a product to market may be improved.
- The acquirer may gain buying power due to increased critical mass.
- Trade secrets or other proprietary information may be passed to the acquirer.
- A competitor may be taken out of the market.
- The culture of the acquirer may improve as a result of the transaction.
- The target may have better processes of systems that can be absorbed by the purchaser.
- Key managers from the acquired company may strengthen the management team.

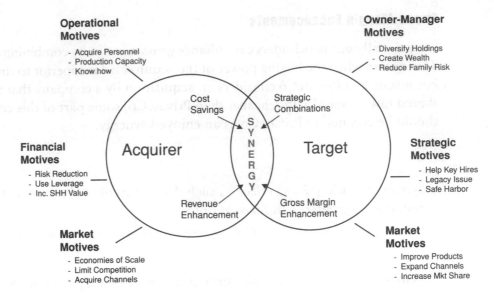

EXHIBIT 7.11   Synergy and Its Sources

or products. This synergy can be determined by measuring the difference between what the company is worth to a nonstrategic acquirer and what a strategic acquirer must pay to possess the missing technology without the acquisition. Say an acquirer needs to spend $20 million to develop a certain technology, and also it identifies a company for sale with the needed technology. In addition to its nontechnology value, the acquired company might receive credit for some part of the $20 million technology cost.

If this $20 million represents a capital expenditure, it can be quantified with some certainty. However, the treatment for this shared synergy is likely to be different. If the technology is primarily capital equipment, a shared value may be determined and built into the purchase price, perhaps by crediting $4 million to $6 million. If the technology is more process oriented and an income stream can be ascribed to it, however, the benefit may be capitalized and shared as discussed earlier.

Exhibit 7.11 depicts synergy and its various sources.

The next step in market valuation, shown in Exhibit 7.12, is to determine the return a prospective investor or group of buyers requires when undertaking an acquisition.

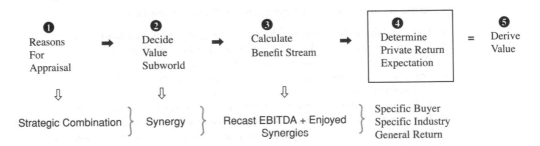

EXHIBIT 7.12   Determine Private Return Expectation

❹ Determine Private Return Expectation

Next, determine private return expectation (PRE or expectation). The expectation converts a benefit stream into a market value. PRE is defined as:

> *The expected rate of return that the private capital markets require in order to attract funds to a particular investment*

The PRE converts a benefit stream to a present value. The PRE can be stated as a discount rate, capitalization rate, acquisition multiple, or any other metric that converts the benefit stream to a present value. There are three different ways to calculate the PRE in the financial and synergy subworlds. These methods were explained in detail in Chapter 6 and can be summarized in this way:

1. *Specific investor return.* Returns required by individual investors differ from those of corporate investors. According to at least one study, individual financial buyers tend to require about 30% returns on their investment, which corresponds to roughly a 3.3 selling multiple.[3] Since the corporate investor has already raised capital for its business, return expectations are driven by its capital structure. It follows then that the expectation for a specific company is determined by analyzing the buyer's weighted average cost of capital (WACC).
2. *Specific industry return.* If merger and acquisition activity information is available in the company's industry, it may be possible to find acquisition multiples through a private guideline search. In this method, one locates comparable acquisition information, then uses the information to draw a value conclusion. A number of transactional databases support this method. Several examples are discussed in Chapter 6.
3. *General return.* If no industry-specific selling multiples are available, or if the sample size is not large enough, the next step is to calculate a general investor return. This is accomplished either through using databases containing general acquisition selling multiples or by using a general investor return matrix. In Chapter 6, GF Data Resources was shown as a source for general acquisition multiples.

The final step in the market valuation process is shown in Exhibit 7.13.

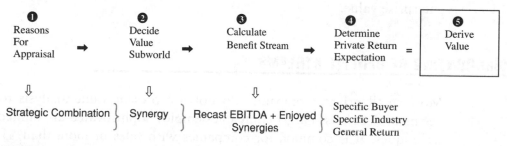

EXHIBIT 7.13 Derive Value

⑤Derive Value

After an appropriate benefit stream and private return expectations are determined, a final value can be derived. In an earlier example, PrivateCo's synergy stream is $3 million. Assuming the industry buyer group employs an acquisition multiple of 5.7, PrivateCo's synergy market value is:

$$(\text{Recast EBITDA} \times \text{acquisition multiple}) - \text{long-term debt}$$
$$= (\$3,000,000 \times 5.7) - \$500,000$$
$$= \$16.6 \text{ million}$$

The synergy market value of PrivateCo is $16.6 million. Since the long-term debt was deducted from the enterprise value, it is important to note that this figure is a 100% equity value for the company.

The stream is either capitalized or discounted by the private return expectation to derive a market value. It is useful to review the differences between capitalizing and discounting benefit streams.

CAPITALIZATION OF BENEFIT STREAMS

Capitalizing the benefit stream is a fairly simple calculation:

$$\text{Market value} = \frac{\text{Benefit stream}}{\% \text{ Return expectation}}$$

Assuming the industry buyer group employs a private return expectation of 17.5% (1 divided by 5.7 selling multiple), PrivateCo's market value is:

$$\text{PrivateCo market value} = \frac{\$3,000,000}{17.5\%}$$
$$= \$17.1 \text{ million}$$

Capitalizing a $3 million stream with a 17.5% capitalization rate yields a market value on an enterprise basis of $17.1 million. For purposes of the following presentation, PrivateCo's $500,000 in long-term debt is not deducted from the enterprise value.

DISCOUNTING OF BENEFIT STREAMS

Most small private companies do not use present value analysis to make investment decisions. Larger companies employ sophisticated discounted cash flow techniques. It is common for companies with sales of more than $150 million to use present value methodology when performing acquisition analysis. Since

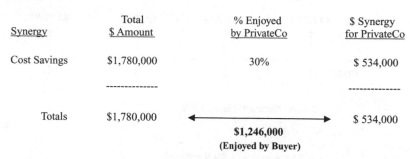

Synergy	Total $ Amount	% Enjoyed by PrivateCo	$ Synergy for PrivateCo
Cost Savings	$1,780,000	30%	$ 534,000
	--------------		--------------
Totals	$1,780,000		$ 534,000

$1,246,000
(Enjoyed by Buyer)

EXHIBIT 7.14 PrivateCo/Horizontal Integrator Synergies

larger companies tend to buy small companies, middle-market managers must understand the discounting process.

An interesting phenomenon, known as value perspective, occurs frequently in the world of market value regarding discounting benefit stream. Value perspective occurs when a seller values her company by capitalizing strategic or synergistic benefit streams and the buyer discounts the stream. Even if both parties use the same capitalization and discount rate, each party may experience distinct streams, causing substantially different market values. Exhibit 7.14 quantifies value perspective for the prospective seller and buyer of PrivateCo.

PrivateCo adds $534,000 to its benefit stream by sharing synergies with the hypothetical buyer group. What unshared synergies does the buyer enjoy? According to Exhibit 7.14, the buyer keeps $1,246,000 in synergies not shared with the seller. This has a dramatic valuation impact on the buyer's valuation. Assuming both sides start with recast EBITDA of $2.5 million and both use a 17.5% capitalization/discount rate, the following section shows the math.

SELLER/BUYER MARKET VALUATION

Sellers and buyers naturally view market valuation from opposite sides. These value perspectives can be explained quantitatively, which is extremely helpful during transfer negotiations. The next section discusses the sellers' value perspective.

Seller Value Perspective

A seller will almost always gravitate to the highest market valuation available, which in the next example is synergy market valuation.

$$\text{Market value} = \frac{\text{Benefit stream}}{\text{Return expectation \%}}$$

$$= \frac{\$3,000,000(\$2.5 \text{ million} + \$534,000 \text{ rounded})}{17.5\%}$$

$$= \$17.1 \text{ million}$$

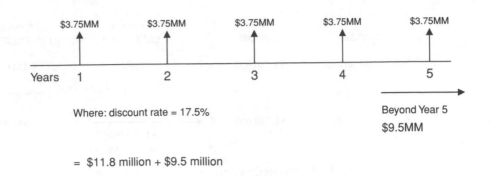

$$= \$11.8 \text{ million} + \$9.5 \text{ million}$$

$$= \$21.3 \text{ million}$$

EXHIBIT 7.15 Buyer Value Perspective

From the seller's perspective, the stream is $3 million, comprised of the recast EBITDA of $2.5 million plus the enjoyed synergies of $534,000. By capitalizing this stream at a 17.5% capitalization rate, the resulting market value is $17.1 million.

Buyer Value Perspective

The expected buyer group experiences the stream from a different perspective than the seller. The buyer believes its stream is about $3.75 million (recast EBITDA of $2.5 million plus shared synergies of $1.25 million). Assuming the expected buyer discounts the stream, instead of capitalizing it, Exhibit 7.15 shows a dramatic difference in valuation.

From the potential buyer's perspective, the $3.75 million stream is discounted for five years before a terminal value is calculated. This terminal value represents the present value as if the streams continue into perpetuity.[4] Discounting the stream of $3.75 for five years at a 17.5% discount rate yields a present value of $11.8 million. The terminal value has a present value of $9.5 million. Thus, the present value of this stream to the prospective buyer is $21.3 million. The present value of the stream to the buyer is rounded to $4 million more than the capitalized value to the seller. By paying $17 million to the seller, yet receiving $21 million in cash flow from the transaction, the buyer creates $4 million in shareholder value for the buyer's investors.

Another way of calculating this $4 million value difference between the seller's and buyer's perspective is to capitalize the difference in the enjoyed synergies between the parties. The seller and buyer in this scenario enjoy these synergies:

Buyer-enjoyed synergies	$1,246,000
Seller-enjoyed synergies	534,000
Difference	$ 712,000
Capitalized	17.5%
Present value	$4,000,000

EXHIBIT 7.16   Market Values by Subworld

| | PrivateCo | | |
Subworld	Stream	Multiple	Market Value
Asset subworld (net asset value)	–	–	$ 2,400,000
Financial subworld (weighted average)	$ 2,500,000	5.7	13,750,000
Synergy subworld (cost savings example)	3,000,000	5.7	16,600,000

The difference in enjoyed synergies is capitalized at 17.5%. This yields a present value of approximately $4 million. Value perspective is another indication that capitalizing and discounting a stream can yield equivalent answers. In this example, both methods return a $4 million difference in value based on the perspective of the party.

Subworld Comparisons   It is instructive to compare values across market value subworlds. Example market values for PrivateCo are calculated for the asset subworld in Chapter 5 and for the financial subworld in Chapter 6. It is interesting to compare the market values for each subworld, as shown in Exhibit 7.16.

Since the asset subworld is valued using the net asset value method, it does not rely on a benefit stream. For presentation purposes, a selling multiple of 5.7 is applied against the streams of the financial and synergy subworlds. The seller pays off the long-term debt at the closing, which reduces the values of the financial and synergy subworlds. In the example, there is more than a sevenfold difference between the lowest and highest market values. There is more than a $2.5 million difference between the synergy and financial subworlds. From a valuation perspective, this is substantial. It is important to realize that PrivateCo's financials are the same across the various value subworlds. By changing the presentation of the financial numbers, value has been identified, quantified, and recognized. If synergies are conservatively determined, these numbers remain valid during the valuation.

Unique Valuations   Some situations do not fit neatly into the market valuation process. For instance, companies with a heavy real estate component may not generate substantial annual benefit streams. Nevertheless, they have substantial value. A handful of other valuation situations do not fit the market value model. These are:

- *Some professional sports teams have negative streams but huge terminal values.* It is difficult for appraisers to place almost all of the value on an event that may not occur for ten years, such as the sale of the franchise. Some technology transfers, such as patents, are similarly difficult to appraise using this model. In these situations, appraisers rely on specific comparable transactions to derive value.
- *Monopolistic businesses do not necessarily follow these market valuation rules.* For instance, if a company produces a one-of-a-kind product with a global market, the private return expectation may not be predictable using standard

database searches. If PrivateCo owns a patent for a drug that cures the common cold, the expected selling multiple might be 20 or more to reflect the defensible position of the holder.

- *Companies that rely on an earn-out to realize value also require special treatment.* An earn-out is a contingent payment structure that pays a seller over time, based on certain events occurring. For example, if a seller has developed a new product that will not be available for sale until next year, a prospective buyer will not simply discount the stream at a large discount rate to derive a present value. Rather, more likely the buyer will structure an earn-out to pay the seller over time.

Brokers and intermediaries often use unique valuations to determine what market process is appropriate for a particular appraisal.

NONENTERPRISE MARKET VALUATIONS

This chapter describes market value in terms of enterprise values, or 100% valuations. Often market value must be derived for less than the enterprise. In most states, more than 50% stock ownership constitutes control. In these cases, the pro rata value of the position is computed using the market value process just defined. For example, if PrivateCo has a market value of $5 million and a 60% position is valued as part of an enterprise sale, the pro rata share is $3 million. If 60% of the stock is market valued as a separate block from the enterprise, it may have a value approaching 100%, or enterprise value. This beyond – pro rata valuation applies only when the 60% block has no constraints on its ability to control the company through an ownership agreement.

The more difficult market valuation occurs when less than 50% of the stock is valued. As indicated in Chapter 4, minority interests in a private company *may* have little or no value because there is no marketplace for private minority interests. Unless a contractual agreement is in place between the control and minority shareholders, the minority holders cannot be assured that their shares have value. If the minority interest holder has a contractual distribution stream via an ownership agreement, it is possible to value the position. Basically the expected stream is capitalized with an appropriate risk factor. It must be emphasized that even with a contractual distribution stream, few outside buyers are willing to acquire a minority interest in a private company.

TRIANGULATION

Financial intermediaries are the authority in the synergy subworld. They "live" in the transfer side of the private capital market triangle and bring their experience to the valuation process. They enforce the process and provide feedback to the market. For instance, intermediaries gather and report transactional data that informs participants about acquisition multiples. Intermediaries play a vital role in defining the synergistic benefit stream and guiding companies into this subworld. Then the various market players draw value conclusions. For example, intermediaries have learned that the synergy subworld is the highest level of market value because of the possibility of synergy sharing between seller and buyer in a transfer.

PrivateCo's value in the synergy subworld is $16.6 million. That is six times greater than its value in the asset subworld and more than 20% greater than in the financial subworld. Synergy sharing can dramatically add to a company's value.

World	PrivateCo Value
Asset market value	$2.4 million
Collateral value	$2.5 million
Insurable value (buy/sell)	$6.7 million
Fair market value	$6.8 million
Investment value	$7.5 million
Impaired goodwill	$13.0 million
Financial market value	$13.7 million
Owner value	$15.8 million
Synergy market value	**$16.6 million**
Public value	$18.2 million

The synergy subworld is created by financial intermediaries. Buyers do not offer to share synergies with sellers. Nor is it usually obvious which synergies are sharable. An experienced intermediary crafts a deal that treats each party fairly. This means neither side gains totally at the expense of the other.

Instead of fighting over acquisition multiples, the synergy subworld focuses on enhancements to the benefit stream. Owners who want more for their business are encouraged to consider what the buyer brings to the deal. Every dollar of enjoyed synergies increases the market value of a company by a factor of the acquisition multiple.

Market value is located in the *empirical unregulated* value quadrant. Market transactions are observed within an unregulated marketplace. Profit-motivated players, free to choose from a host of investment alternatives, create this open market.

Capital availability influences market value. By definition, the synergy subworld involves a high level of goodwill in the proposed value. The prospective buyer needs access to equity to close a synergistic transaction. By realizing substantial synergies and having sufficient access to growth capital, buyers can pay the high "synergistic" price yet still substantially add to shareholder value.

NOTES

1. Robert G. Eccles, Kersten L. Lanes, and Thomas C. Wilson, "Are You Paying Too Much for That Acquisition?" *Harvard Business Review* (July-August 1999): 141. Cost saving and revenue enhancement synergy ideas were taken from this paper.
2. Citation: 434 U.S. 1002; 98 S. Ct. 648; 54 L. Ed. 2d 499; 1977 U.S.
3. Robert Slee, "Different Buyers Pay Different Multiples," *Data Link* (May 1997).
4. The terminal value calculation is: Terminal value = present value (5 years, 18% discount)($3.75 million/18%).

CHAPTER **8**

Fair Market Value

The fair market value (FMV) world hypothetically embodies the value of a business interest. In terms of standards and process, FMV is the most structured value world. Examples include estate and gift appraisal, tax court cases, and the valuation of employee stock ownership plans (ESOPs). In some states, FMV is also the standard of value for equitable distribution cases. Finally, since FMV is so well established, it is often the default value world. Yet it is not the correct world in every valuation situation.

Fair market value is defined as:

The price at which the property would change hands between a willing buyer and a willing seller when the buyer is not under any compulsion to buy and the seller is not under any compulsion to sell, and both parties have reasonable knowledge of relevant facts. The hypothetical buyer and seller are assumed to be able and willing to trade and to be well informed about the property and concerning the market for such property.[1]

The "price" in the definition implies the value is stated in cash or cash equivalents. The "property" is assumed to have been exposed in the open market for a period long enough to allow the market forces to establish the value. The "willing buyer and seller" assumes an equal motivation between the hypothetical, but rational, parties. Finally, the derivation of FMV should follow a process that yields a *likely* point-in-time value, not a range of values. This value is concerned with the financial capacity of the subject *without* regard to possible acquisition synergies.

A snapshot of the key tenets of the fair market value world is provided in Exhibit 8.1.

Like the other value worlds, FMV relies on a rigorous process to determine value. In fact, the world of FMV is the most cohesive and fully developed of the value worlds. There are highly specific purposes for these appraisals, and each entails a specific process and set of standards. FMV appraisals are used to establish value in estate and gift valuation, tax court cases, and the creation and updates for ESOPs.

The authorities in this world include the powerful Internal Revenue Service (IRS) and the tax courts, among others. The weight of these authorities, their legitimacy, and the strength of their influence create an orderly world with strict boundaries.

Since FMV is used in a legal environment, standardization of the process is fairly rigid and especially important. The path toward industry standardization

EXHIBIT 8.1 Longitude and Latitude: Fair Market Value

Definition	The price at which the property would change hands between a willing buyer and a willing seller when the buyer is not under any compulsion to buy and the seller is not under any compulsion to sell, both parties having reasonable knowledge of relevant facts. The hypothetical buyer and seller are assumed to be able and willing to trade and to be well informed about the property and concerning the market for such property.
Purpose of appraisal	To derive a value that complies with Revenue Ruling 59-60 or other tax and legal reasons.
Function of appraisal	To value business interests for employee stock option plans, stock gifting, and many estate planning techniques.
Quadrant	Notional regulated.
Authority	Internal Revenue Service and tax courts. Neither is located in the private capital markets.
Benefit stream	For control valuations, this is normally the adjusted pretax earnings. For minority appraisals, this may be either reported pretax or after-tax earnings, depending on the appraisal.
Private return expectation	Typically a discount rate is derived by the capital asset pricing model or buildup method, both of which use public securities data.
Valuation process summary	The FMV valuation process is:

1. Define value premise (value to be determined as going concern or liquidation).
2. Determine size of the subject interest to be valued (using the levels of FMV).
3. Consider all elements of Revenue Ruling 59-60.
4. Use the three broad approaches.
5. Employ appropriate methods, given the facts and circumstances of the valuation.
6. Determine if any discounts or premiums need to be applied to the unadjusted indicated value.
7. Derive a value conclusion.

PrivateCo Example

Stream[a]	÷	PRE[b]	=	Fair Market Value
$1,900,000	÷	26%	=	$7,300,000
		less LTD[c]	=	$ 500,000
		Final value[d]	=	$6,800,000

[a]3-2-1 weighted average of pretax earnings (as rounded) adjusted for the control shareholder's discretionary expenses for years 20×1-20×3, taken from Exhibit 6.7. Calculation is shown as Footnote 2.
[b]Calculated later in this chapter
[c]Assumes a debt-free analysis
[d]For presentation purposes only. Typically the three approaches would be used to derive a final value.

really began in 1981, with the publication of *Valuing a Business*.[3] In this seminal book, Shannon Pratt defined the FMV process with a level of detail and precision unknown before.

Due to the work of Pratt and others, valuation has become a career path. Thousands of business appraisers now make their living performing valuations in the world of FMV. The sophistication of business appraisal requires that only that well-qualified, certified appraisers should be generating fair market valuations.

APPRAISAL ORGANIZATIONS

Several professional appraisal organizations grant certification to appraisers and provide education. Exhibit 8.2 describes these societies and lists the main certifications that each provides.

The various organizations use differing criteria to certify members. The organizations require candidates to pass written examinations, but only the IBA and ASA require a candidate to submit valuation reports for peer review before certification. References in this book to "certified" business appraisers apply to the main certifications listed in Exhibit 8.2.

Only accredited or certified business appraisers should be engaged for FMV appraisals. The appraisal body of knowledge is too sophisticated for noncertified appraisers to keep up. Further, many appraisers now specialize in certain areas of FMV. For instance, some appraisers only perform ESOP appraisals. Others specialize in family limited partnership appraisals. Appraisal organizations can help sort through the universe of specialized, certified appraisers.

The issue of appraisal "shelf life" comes into play, especially with regard to estate planning issues. Many shareholders gift shares of stock to children and grandchildren each year in an effort to reduce their estates. These gifts should be supported by an FMV appraisal. To be prudent, the subject should be appraised annually. Many shareholders have the stock appraised every few years or even use book value as the basis for the appraisal. This practice is not recommended because of possible IRS reviews and challenges. Most appraisers reduce their rates for annual updates after the first year.

Finally, a client may request to review the appraisal in draft form prior to final issuance. This review may clear up any factual errors or misstatements. Many appraisers do not grant this request until fully paid because they fear clients will not pay once they see the value conclusion. It is not appropriate, however, for clients to insist on interpretive changes to the draft that might improve their positions. Certified appraisers cannot advocate a client's position; rather, they can advocate only their own work.

EXHIBIT 8.2 Appraisal Organizations

Society	Main Certifications
Institute of Business Appraisers (IBA)	Accredited by IBA (AIBA) Certified Business Appraiser (CBA) Business Valuator Accredited For Litigation (BVAL)
American Society of Appraisers (ASA)	Accredited Member (AM) Accredited Senior Appraiser (ASA)
National Association of Certified Valuation Analysts (NACVA)	Accredited Valuation Analyst (AVA) Certified Valuation Analyst (CVA)
American Institute of Certified Public Accountants (AICPA)	Accredited in Business Valuation (ABV)

BUSINESS APPRAISAL STANDARDS

To support business appraisers, each organization has developed and published appraisal standards. These standards provide much of the structure for the practice of valuation. The IBA standards are contained in their entirety in Appendix C. Some of the more important tenets of these standards are summarized here.

- *Standard One: Professional Conduct and Ethics.* Appraisers must judge whether they are competent to perform assignments. Aside from acting professionally, appraisers cannot use rules of thumb or software programs as surrogates for individual competence. Appraisers must maintain strict confidentiality and have no contemplated interest in the property being appraised. Nonadvocacy is considered to be a mandatory standard of appraisal. The end product of the appraisal must be supportable and replicable. The amount of or method for calculating the appraisal fee must be stated. Finally, certification is extended to individuals, not firms.
- *Standard Two: Oral Appraisal Reports.* Oral reports are permitted only when ordered by the client. The appraisal should be followed by a written report that presents the salient features of the oral report.
- *Standard Three: Expert Testimony.* Appraisers should not take any position incompatible with the appraiser's obligation of nonadvocacy. Mandatory content, such as the standard of value, must be stated, and the appraiser must disclose any extraordinary assumptions or limiting conditions.
- *Standard Four: Letter Form Written Appraisal Reports.* Letter opinions are acceptable as long as they conform to all applicable business standards. Once again, there is mandatory content required. These include proper client identification, stated standard of value, appraisal use, the effective date of the appraisal, the preparation date, the report's assumptions, and limiting conditions and special factors that affect the opinion of value. The letter report must contain a value conclusion, which can be a specific opinion of value or a range of values.
- *Standard Five: Formal Written Appraisal Reports.* A comprehensive report should detail: distribution, purpose (stated standard of value), function, effective date, date of report preparation, assumptions and limiting conditions, and other factors that combine to make an acceptable report.
- *Standard Six: Preliminary Reports.* Under certain circumstances, a preliminary report may be issued; however, limitations on the use of the report must be stated by the appraiser.

As this overview indicates, the guidelines for professional business appraisal are direct and available. Aside from the individual organization standards, such as the IBA or ASA, there exists the Uniform Standards of Professional Appraisal Practice (USPAP). The USPAP standards are maintained by the Appraisal Foundation and pertain to real estate, personal property, and business valuation. Most business appraisers follow the USPAP standards in transactions involving federal regulations. Any appraisal performed for tax purposes, such as stock gifting or the appraisal of a family limited partnership, should follow the USPAP standards. Readers are encouraged to review the complete standards prior to engaging a business appraiser or reviewing a work product.

FAIR MARKET VALUE PROCESS

Like the other value worlds, the FMV world has a distinct process by which to derive value. This world is quite structured with standards and approaches, since the process must be replicable across a broad array of appraisal needs. The seven-step FMV process is:

1. Define value premise (value to be determined as going concern or liquidation).
2. Determine size of the subject interest to be valued (see Exhibit 8.3).
3. Consider all elements of Revenue Ruling 59-60.
4. Usc only three broad approaches—income, market, and asset—for generally accepted business appraisals.
5. Employ a number of different methods, based on the facts and circumstances of the valuation.
6. Determine if any discounts or premiums need to be applied to the unadjusted indicated value.
7. Derive a value conclusion.

Professional business appraisers must consider several other elements to meet the requirements of the standards. Some of these elements are proper identification of the client, stated value world (standard of value), effective date of the report, and contingent and limiting conditions of the report. For the purposes of this chapter, only these seven steps are discussed in detail.

Step 1: Define Value Premise

A going-concern value is the value of a business enterprise that is expected to continue to operate into the future. The intangible elements of going-concern value result from factors such as a trained work force, a customer list, an operational plant, and the necessary licenses, systems, and procedures in place. Liquidation value, however, is the net amount realized if the business is terminated and the assets are sold piecemeal. Liquidation can be either orderly or forced.

The selection of the correct premise of value is critical in determining an appropriate fair market value. Generally the appraiser considers the highest and best use of the subject's assets to determine a value premise, particularly for an enterprise appraisal. Ultimately the use of the appraisal helps determine the premise. For instance, an appraisal to support a reorganization or bankruptcy proceeding most likely presumes a liquidation premise. Likewise, if the subject is highly profitable and this is expected to continue, the likely value premise is as a going concern.

The reader can assume all discussions in this book center around going-concern values, unless otherwise stated.

Step 2: Determine Size of the Subject Interest to Be Valued

This second step in any fair market valuation is to determine *what* is being valued. The difference in value between a control interest and a minority interest in private companies is discussed in previous chapters. The levels of ownership concept is introduced in Chapter 4 to describe four levels that apply to the private business interest: enterprise, control, shared, and minority. These four levels apply to most value worlds. The world of fair market value, however, has its own levels, which are similar but different from those in Chapter 4. A primary difference is the reliance on public data in the FMV process to derive private values.

Exhibit 8.3 shows the levels of FMV, with references to the direct and indirect information, used to derive values.[4] Direct observation means the value level is determined by direct reference to actual comparable data. Direct observation for

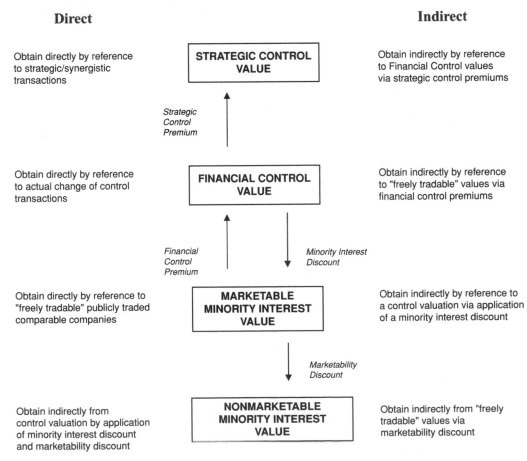

EXHIBIT 8.3   Levels of Fair Market Value

the financial control level uses a private transactional database of actual private enterprise transactions. Indirect observation refers to valuation methods using indirect estimates of the value. For instance, by capitalizing the subject's earnings, which is an indirect reference to what the market should be willing to pay for the subject's earnings stream, one may derive a financial control value.

Strategic control value is the value of 100% of the company based on strategic or synergistic considerations. As such, this level of value should reflect both the power of controlling the firm plus the added value arising from operational synergies. This value can be observed directly by reference to strategic/synergistic transactions or indirectly by grossing up a financial control value by a strategic control premium. Strategic control premiums represent the amount beyond pro rata value an investor will pay for control plus the amount of synergies credited to the subject's shareholders.

Financial control value represents the value of 100% of the enterprise based on financial returns. As such, this value should reflect the value the control holder exercises, especially in terms of financial policy control. Control value can be obtained directly by reference to other change of control transactions. A variety of databases contain transactions. Control value can be found indirectly by grossing up a minority interest publicly traded stock price by a financial control premium. Financial control premiums represent the amount beyond pro rata value an investor will pay for control. Although acceptable in the valuation standards, it is generally not proper to derive a control value by applying a control premium to a publicly traded stock price. There are now enough control transactions, both for public and private transactions, to derive control value directly.

The next level is marketable minority interest value. This level does not typically exist in the private value worlds. It represents the value of a minority interest assumed to be tradable in the marketplace. This level is attributable to publicly traded securities. This freely marketable level can be obtained either by reference to a comparable publicly traded security or by a capitalization or discount rate from a buildup method. The appropriate rate is built up through use of the capital asset pricing model (CAPM) or other technique, by using public securities data. This level can be determined indirectly by applying a minority interest discount to a control value. As is explained later, minority interest discounts are determined relative to control premiums by using this formula: $1-[1/(1+ \text{Control Premium})]$. Minority discounts reflect a lessening of the position due to the lack of rights typically associated with a minority position, as discussed in Chapter 4.

The lowest level is the nonmarketable minority interest value. This level reflects the value of minority interests in private businesses for which there is no active market. Holders at this level also lack control over the company's financial and operating policy. Since there is no active market for private minority interests, this level cannot be obtained by direct reference. It can be obtained indirectly by applying a lack of marketability discount (LOMD) to the marketable minority interest value. A LOMD represents the amount deducted from an equity interest to reflect lack of marketability. The determination of these discounts, relative to the restricted stock and pre–initial public offering (IPO) studies, is discussed in

Appendix A. It is also possible to obtain value at this level by applying successive minority interest discounts and LOMDs to a control value.

The levels of FMV chart is important because it reflects *what* is being valued in this world from a top-down perspective. All appraisals in the FMV world fit somewhere in this chart, and value is derived by applying direct and indirect methods described earlier. Once the *what-is-being-appraised* question has been answered, the next step in determining FMV begins.

Step 3: Consider All Elements of Revenue Ruling 59-60

More than 40 years ago, the U.S. Treasury Department outlined procedures for determining fair market value. Revenue Ruling 59-60 remains the main guide to determine the fair market value of private business interests. Exhibit 8.4 summarizes the revenue ruling's key points. The IRS lists eight "factors to consider" but proclaims that these should not be considered all-inclusive, without giving further guidance as to what else should be considered.

There is considerable room for judgment within these factors. For example:

- The earning capacity of a business is the future profit picture of a business *ignoring* extraordinary factors as well as cyclical and seasonal earnings changes.
- Prior transactions in the ownership of the company's stock are considered relevant as a guide if they occurred within the last two years or so of the appraisal and met the FMV standard of value.
- Minority interests (stock positions of less than 50% of the total outstanding shares) can be discounted substantially due mainly to the inability to control finances of the company. In some cases, small interests have been discounted by 70% to 90% in comparison to the control position.
- When comparing private companies to public companies, a LOMD is appropriate because private companies have no ready market for selling their stock. This discount is determined on a case-by-case basis but has averaged in the 35% to 40% range in many important court cases.
- The dividend-paying capacity of a business is generally considered a less important factor in determining value now than when the revenue ruling was drafted. For the most part, private companies do not routinely distribute

EXHIBIT 8.4   Revenue Ruling 59-60: Summarized Factors

1. The nature of the business and the history of the enterprise from its inception
2. The economic outlook in general and the condition and outlook of the specific industry
3. The book value of the stock and the financial condition of the business
4. The earning capacity of the company
5. The dividend-paying capacity of the business
6. Whether the enterprise had goodwill or other intangible value
7. Sales of the stock and the size of the block to be valued
8. The market price of stocks of corporations engaged in the same or a similar line business having their stocks traded in a free and open market, either on an exchange or over the counter

dividends due to the tax code. A typical private owner attempts to minimize corporate income tax payments while trying to maximize personal wealth. Dividends do not help the shareholder achieve this goal. Most appraisers tend to rely on the earning capacity of the business in lieu of dividends distributed as a determinant of value.

- There has been a considerable effort by valuation writers and appraisers to look to the public securities markets for valuation guidance for private business interests. This is understandable since there is ample data from more than 30,000 public companies. As argued in Chapter 2, however, this public-to-private method is not always relevant. Private transactions are typically more relevant than public security information for valuing private interests.

The next step in the appraisal process considers which valuation approaches to apply.

Step 4: Use the Three Broad Approaches

Nearly all appraisals in the FMV world employ three broad valuation approaches: income, asset, and market. These approaches form the framework of the valuation determination. The three approaches are like three legs of the appraisal table. Since the approaches are interrelated, all three need to be considered in a FMV appraisal, or the three-legged table does not stand. Each approach is defined in this way:

- *Income approach.* Uses methods that convert anticipated benefits into a present value.
- *Asset approach.* Uses methods based on the value of the underlying assets of the business, net of liabilities.
- *Market approach.* Uses methods that compare the subject to similar businesses, business ownership interests, securities, or intangible assets that have been sold.

The approaches may seem independent, but they are interrelated. The income approach requires a rate of return used to discount or capitalize the income. The marketplace drives these rates. All comparative valuation approaches relate some market value observation to either some measure of a subject's ability to produce income or to a measure of the condition of its assets. The asset approach uses depreciation and obsolescence factors that are based on some measure of market values of assets.

Business valuation standards require appraisers to utilize all three approaches in the valuation, or they must explain why an approach is omitted. It is up to the appraiser's judgment whether to incorporate the individual approach in the final value conclusion. The appraiser in the FMV world selects appropriate methods that best fit the circumstances of the appraisal, then reconciles the results to derive a final value conclusion.

Step 5: Employ Appropriate Methods, Given the Facts and Circumstances of the Valuation

A number of valuation methods are available within each approach. For instance, the capitalization of earnings method may be chosen within the income approach, or the net asset value method within the asset approach. Appraisers choose methods appropriate to the circumstances of the appraisal. Some of the more common methods used in the FMV world are:

Approach	Method	Appropriate to Use When...
Income	Discounted future earnings	Income is largely realized in the future.
	Capitalized earnings	Income is stable or evenly growing.
Asset	Net asset value	Substantial value difference between book value and fair market value of assets.
		Often used for capital-intensive business.
Market	Guideline publicly traded company	When the subject is a large private company comparable to a publicly traded company.
	Private company transactions	When the subject is similar to companies sold in private transactions.

There are a number of methods available other than those just listed. The next decision an appraiser makes is whether to employ discounts or premiums to the unadjusted indicated value generated by a particular method.

Step 6: Determine If Any Discounts or Premiums Should Be Applied to the Unadjusted Indicated Value

Each method generates an indicated value before adjustments, called an unadjusted indicated value. The adjustments may increase or decrease the value determined in the step. These adjustments take two primary forms: premiums or discounts. As Exhibit 8.3 shows, premiums and discounts may be necessary to adjust the indicated value to the correct value level of the subject interest. Some of the possible premium and discount adjustments are:

- Control premiums
- Minority discounts
- Lack of marketability discount
- Key person discount
- Nonvoting discount

The various methods yield indicated values at different levels. Exhibit 8.5 shows a number of methods as well as the type of value generated.

If the net asset value method is used, the indicated value is on the control/nonmarketable level of value. Likewise, the guideline publicly traded method yields a minority/marketable indicated value. Depending on the level being valued, a premium or discount may be needed. A brief review of premiums and discounts helps focus this discussion.

EXHIBIT 8.5 Value Type Generated by Different Methods

Method	Control/Minority	Marketable/Nonmarketable
Discounted future earnings	Control or minority	Marketable or nonmarketable
Capitalized earnings	Control or minority	Marketable or nonmarketable
Net asset value	Control	Nonmarketable
Guideline publicly traded	Minority	Marketable
Private company transactions	Control	Nonmarketable

Control Premiums Control premiums represent the amount an investor is willing to pay for the rights of control, as opposed to the minority position. The rights of control, such as setting distributions/dividends, electing board members, making acquisitions or divestitures, and so on, are so important that a control premium is intuitive. There is a way to measure control premiums. Studies by *Mergerstat Review*, a publication that measures control premiums, show the average control premium paid in the past ten years has typically been in the 8% to 33% range, with an average of 18%.[5]

The control premiums measured by Mergerstat involve only public companies. Control premiums are generally used to increase an unadjusted indicated value, which was derived from a comparison to the public securities market in the guideline publicly traded method.

Minority Discounts A minority discount is a reduction from the control value reflecting a lack of control that a minority holder suffers. If a control premium is intuitive, then it follows that the minority position should be discounted. In fact, one way to determine a minority discount relies on knowing the appropriate control premium:

$$\text{Minority interest discount} = 1 - (1/(1 + \text{Control premium}))$$

By way of example, assume the appraiser believes a 30% control premium is appropriate in an appraisal. The corresponding minority discount is:

$$= 1 - (1/(1 + .3))$$
$$= 23\%$$

By reference to the 30% control premium, there is an implied 23% minority discount. Quite often appraisers use this formula with the Mergerstat data to derive minority interest discounts.

Lack of Marketability Discount The LOMD is the amount or percentage deducted from the value of a marketable ownership interest to reflect the relative absence of marketability for private company. Of course, most private stocks suffer greatly from lack of marketability. To estimate the degree of discount for limited marketability, analyze the relationship between the share prices of companies initially offered to the public in IPOs and the prices at which their shares traded within a short period of time immediately before their public offerings. John Emory conducted the first comprehensive study of this type and showed private companies that could go public suffer from a lack of liquidity. The range of marketability discounts in the Emory studies was from 3% to 94%, with the median being 48%.[6] Appraisers also cite a number of other studies, such as the restricted stock studies and numerous tax court cases, that indicate that LOMDs of more than 25% are justifiable to apply against indicated private values.

In *Bernard Mandelbaum v. Commissioner*, Tax Court judge David Laro created significant discussion within the valuation community by raising key issues regarding marketability discounts and setting forth ten factors to be considered in determining an appropriate discount for lack of marketability.[7] These are:

1. Private versus public sales of stock
2. Financial statement analysis
3. Company's dividend policy
4. Nature of the company, its history, position in the industry, and economic outlook
5. Strength of company management
6. Amount of control transferred
7. Restrictions on transferability of stock
8. Holding period required in the stock
9. Company's redemption policy
10. Costs associated with making a public offering

More recently, Paglia and Harjoto matched sales transactions from Pratt's Stats with publicly traded counterparts to determine discounts for lack of marketability (DLOMs).[8] The estimated DLOMs based on matching criteria of net sales and EBITDA indicate that DLOMs for private firms average 68% for earnings before interest, taxes, depreciation and amortization (EBITDA) matches and 72% for revenues pairings. They also found that Food, Professional Services, Support, Finance, Retail, Wholesale, and Information areas of the economy exhibit the highest discounts. Furthermore, they reported that firm size (assets and sales), profitability (net income and EBITDA) are negatively related to the size of the discount. Overall, their findings suggest there is justification for larger discounts when preparing a valuation engagement.

Key Person Discount   Often the key person discount is applied when a key person is no longer going to be part of the business. This is often the case when the valuation is of a decedent's estate. No key person discount table helps determine the size of this discount. Most appraisers forecast the financial results of the business without the key person, which should decrease the future income. Another way to handle this loss is to increase the riskiness of achieving the future income by increasing the discount rate.

Perhaps the most famous court case involving a key person discount is the *Paul Mitchell* decision, where the court assigned a 10% key person discount to indicate the loss of value to the company after Paul Mitchell died.[9] Subsequent discussion on this case, especially by Larson and Wright, indicates the *Paul Mitchell* case is unique, partly in the fact that the key person's name coincided with the name of the firm.[10] Larson and Wright note that over an eight-year period, declines in value due to a key person's death in public companies were in evidence less than half the time and were only in the 4% to 5% range when a decline was noted.[11] It is generally not advisable to employ a key person discount of more than 10% to an appraisal's unadjusted indicated value. Unless no LOMD is taken, a large key person discount is difficult to justify.

Nonvoting Discounts   The concept of voting rights, or the lack thereof, attached to a minority interest ownership in a business is one of the most difficult variables to quantify. Theoretically, it is logical and supported by valuation theory and case law that if an ownership lacks the ability to elect directors and set the policy course of a business, any value attributable to control will be diminished accordingly, all other things being equal. This is the fundamental premise of a minority interest being worth less than a proportionate share of the business on a control basis.

First, if an additional class of shares are issued by a corporation, a dilution in ownership occurs, whether the shares are voting or nonvoting. Thus, the per-share claim of the stockholder on the earnings and assets of the business is diminished. Therefore, this dilution should result in a proportionate reduction in fair market value.

Next, the matter of voting rights is inseparable from the concept of control and should increase to the extent that these rights become meaningful. For extremely small minority interests, the market typically grants only a small amount of value to voting rights. But where swing votes or significant minority ownerships are involved, the impact can indeed be significant.

For example, if one were to hold only ten shares of a publicly traded corporation with 500 million shares outstanding, the impact of whether the ten shares are voting or not is insignificant. However, in the situation of a closely held business where a relatively small number of shares are outstanding, even small minority interests could combine to have an impact on voting issues whereas nonvoting shares would be prohibited from doing so regardless of the proportion of ownership.

Thus, nonvoting shares in a closely held business are inherently worth less than corresponding voting shares and should be subject to additional discount.

The quantification of a nonvoting discount arises from various studies of public securities markets and case law. A study by Kevin C. O'Shea and Robert M. Siwicki reviewed 43 publicly traded stocks with both voting and nonvoting shares of common stock outstanding.[12] They found a wide range of premiums of voting stocks over nonvoting stocks, or from a discount of 8.6% to a premium of 32.8% with an average of 3.8%. The authors noted that the context in which the minority ownership is placed, or whether the voting minority interest is significant, rather than the absolute question of voting versus nonvoting, that appears to impact the question of value. Nevertheless, the implication is that nonvoting shares do have an inherent discount of at least about 4% from voting shares, on a minority interest basis, in this study.

Other discounts may be appropriately applied to various methods. Examples include but are not limited to discounts for:

- Key customer dependence
- Obsolescence of technology
- Blockage
- Built-in capital gains
- Key product dependence

These and other unnamed discounts are beyond the scope of this book; readers should seek further information if needed.[13]

Step 7: Derive a Final Value Conclusion

Appraisers take two steps to derive a final value conclusion. First, they apply premiums and discounts to each method as appropriate. Application is made as appropriate on a specific method basis, since each method may yield an initial result at a different value level. If all methods yield an unadjusted indicated value at the same value level, for example, marketable, minority interest, then premiums or discounts are applied once.

Second, after the application of adjustments (called the adjusted indicated value), appraisers decide how to synthesize the various values. The application of premiums and discounts is usually multiplicative, not additive. The next example shows this calculation, from unadjusted indicated value to adjusted indicated value.

Unadjusted indicated value:	
Value on a control, marketable basis	$1,000,000
Less minority discount (30%)	300,000
Value on a minority, marketable basis	$700,000
Less LOMD (35%)	245,000
Adjusted indicated value	$455,000

The cumulative discount in this example is 54.5% (1 − ($455,000/ $1,000,000)).

Weighting and Final Value Conclusion   Reconciliation is one of the more difficult issues in a valuation. Normally, the appraisal yields several adjusted indicated values. The appraiser is not bound to include all of these values in the value conclusion. However, the appraiser discusses in the report the reasons for inclusions/exclusions of methods within the valuation. In this way, the reader at least knows the appraiser's reasoning.

Once the appraiser decides which values to include and has applied the necessary premiums and discounts to arrive at adjusted indicated values, the decision on how to weight the various adjusted indicated values is made. There are two primary ways to weight these values: explicit and implicit.

Explicit Weighting In explicit weighting, the appraiser assigns percentage weights to each adjusted indicated value. An example of explicit weighting follows.

Method	Adjusted Indicated Value per Share	Assigned Weight	Value Indication
Capitalized earnings	$20.00	0.2	$4.00
Net asset value	15.00	0.1	1.50
Private guideline	30.00	0.7	21.00
		Value conclusion per share	$26.50

In this case, the appraiser decides to weight the private guideline method the heaviest, with much lighter weighting given to the capitalized earnings and net asset value methods. Although this example does not show it, the appraiser might choose to weigh 100% of the value opinion using one method. This could happen if a subject was highly profitable but no guideline companies are found. In this case, the appraiser might assign all weight to the capitalized earnings method. Although once again, the appraiser must explain in detail the rationale for why this weighting is chosen, the final weighting is based on subjective reasoning by him or her.

Implicit Weighting Some appraisers use an implicit weighting scheme in the final reconciliation process. Adjusted indicated values from the various methods are presented and then a value conclusion is determined. Once again, the appraiser gives the reasons why one method's results are favored over another. Implicit weighting does not employ a quantitative presentation; rather, the appraiser chooses a final value and presents the reasoning. Here is an example of implicit weighting:

Method	Adjusted Indicated Value per Share
Capitalized earnings	$20.00
Net asset value	15.00
Private guideline	30.00
Value conclusion per share	$25.00

Ultimately the value conclusion is stated as a point estimate or a range of value. A point estimate is the typical result of a fair market valuation, whereas a value range is more typical for a market valuation.

KEY STEPS TO DERIVE FAIR MARKET VALUE

Exhibit 8.6 summarizes the key steps involved in deriving FMV. The three broad approaches utilize methods appropriate to the facts and circumstances of the appraisal. The methods yield unadjusted indicated values that may reside at the appropriate value level of the subject interest. If the unadjusted indicated values

APPROACHES

Income/asset/market

METHODS

Appropriate to facts/circumstances

UNADJUSTED INDICATED VALUES

Premiums/discounts

ADJUSTED INDICATED VALUES

Weighting

VALUE CONCLUSION

EXHIBIT 8.6 Key Steps to Derive Fair Market Value

need adjusting, premiums or discounts are applied to create adjusted indicated values. Finally, the adjusted indicated values are weighted according to the judgment of the appraiser to determine the value conclusion.

Business appraisers need to take special care when deriving fair market values. In 2010 the IRS issued a new IRC Section 6695A penalty, "Letter 4485, Appraiser Penalty Assessment Notification Letter." These "new" regulations could impose a significant monetary penalty on an appraiser for "significantly" under- or overvaluing a subject company in regard to IRS regulations.

DOES THE FAIR MARKET VALUE PROCESS MAKE SENSE?

Many owners have difficulty understanding the fair market valuation process. This difficulty emanates from the incongruence between the goal of the process, which is to estimate a likely price of a business interest, and the value conclusion, which may bear no resemblance to what the market actually would pay. An obvious example of this incongruence is the appraisal of a private minority interest. Since there is no market for these interests, does it make sense to draw a value conclusion

EXHIBIT 8.7   Appraisal Twister?

	P/E
Public guidelines per share average (daily stock prices)	15
Less marketability discount (30%)	(4.5)
Less key person discount (10%)	(1.0)
Private company minority per share	9.5

by comparing the private interest to a group of public securities using the market approach with a discount for lack of marketability and other factors? More than likely, the market value of the private minority interest is quite low, perhaps even zero. Yet the FMV of the interest may be quite high. Exhibit 8.7 depicts the problem with the market approach.

If a group of public guideline companies have an average price/earnings ratio of 15 and routine discounts are applied, a price/earnings ratio of 9.5 would be applied to the subject's minority interest–level earnings to derive a minority interest value. Many valuation analysts believe comparing private to public stocks consistently overvalues private minority interests. This process is somewhat like appraisal Twister because nonsensical rules of the game dominate actions of the participants and the ultimate outcome.

Another example of the disconnect between FMV and actual market reality can be found in the way that discount rates are derived. The buildup method (BUM) is a widely recognized method of determining the after-tax net cash flow discount rate, which in turn yields the capitalization rate. BUM is used primarily in the FMV world. It is called a "buildup" method because it is the sum of risks associated with various classes of assets. It is based on the principle that investors would require a greater return on classes of assets that are more risky. The BUM model is:

$$Ke = RF + ERP + SRP + IRP + CSRP$$

where: Ke = Required rate of return on equity
        RF = Risk-free rate of return
      ERP = Equity risk premium
      SRP = Size risk premium
       IRP = Industry risk premium
   $CSRP$ = Company-specific risk premium

The first element of the BUM model is the risk-free rate, which is the rate of return for long-term government bonds. Investors who buy large-cap equity stocks, which are inherently more risky than long-term government bonds, require a greater return, so the next element of the BUM is the equity risk premium. In determining a company's value, the long-horizon equity risk premium is used because the company's life is assumed to be infinite. The sum of the risk-free rate and the equity risk premium yields the long-term average market rate of return on large public company stocks.

Similarly, investors who invest in small-cap stocks, which are riskier than blue-chip stocks, require a greater return, called the "size premium." Size premium data is generally available from two sources: Morningstar's (formerly Ibbotson & Associates') Stocks, Bonds, Bills & Inflation and Duff & Phelps' Risk Premium Report.

By adding the RF, ERP, and SRP, the rate of return that investors would require on their investments in small public company stocks can be determined. These three elements of the BUM discount rate are known collectively as the systematic risks.

In addition to systematic risks, the discount rate must include unsystematic risks, which fall into two categories. One of those categories is the industry risk premium. Morningstar's yearbooks contain empirical data to quantify the risks associated with various industries. The other category of unsystematic risk is referred to as company-specific risk. No published data is available to quantify specific company risks. Instead, they are determined by the valuation professional, based on the specific characteristics of the business and the professional's reasonable discretion applied to appropriate criteria.

By way of example, PrivateCo's Ke can be determined in this way:

Ke	=	**RF**	+	**ERP**	+	**SRP**	+	**IRP**	+	**CSRP**
	=	3%	+	7%	+	6%	+	3%	+	4%
	=	23%								

PrivateCo's required rate of return on equity is 23%. Due to the nature of the variables used to derive BUM, this return on equity rate is stated on an after-tax basis. For the purposes of this chapter and book, we seek to determine a pretax capitalization rate. This will then be used to determine an enterprise fair market value, which will be comparable to the values derived for all other value worlds.

The next step in determining PrivateCo's capitalization rate is to derive its weighted average cost of capital (WACC), which is on an after-tax basis. The WACC tax-effects PrivateCo's debt to make it after tax, as shown:

PrivateCo Weighted Average Cost of Capital Calculation

Capital Type	Market Value	% of Total	Expected Return	Tax Effect	Rate Factor
Term loan	500,000	4%	4.1%	35%	.1
Equity	13,700,000	96%	23.0%	0%	22.1
			PrivateCo after-tax WACC		22.2%

Thus, PrivateCo's WACC is 22% (as rounded). Now we need to convert to a pretax capitalization rate. There are two steps in converting WACC to a pretax capitalization rate:

1. Convert the after-tax discount rate to an after-tax capitalization rate by subtracting the estimated growth rate. Assume PrivateCo's long-term growth rate

is expected to be 5%. The after-tax discount rate of 22% converts to an after-tax capitalization rate of 17%.

2. Convert the after-tax capitalization rate to a pretax capitalization rate by dividing the after-tax capitalization rate by 1 minus the tax rate. Assume PrivateCo's tax rate is 35%. The after-tax capitalization rate, when rounded, converts to a 26% pretax capitalization rate (17% ÷ (1 − .35)).

For this example, PrivateCo's pretax capitalization rate is 26%.

TEARING DOWN THE BUILDUP MODELS

There are several issues regarding the BUM (or CAPM) model.[14] Appraisers rely on the fungibility of capital argument to support the belief that investors can choose to substitute investments in public or private markets with equal ease. Thus, an investor in middle-market private equity could always achieve the risk-free rate by buying government securities. They use a BUM adding return to the risk-free rate to compensate for the additional risk of private market investing. There are several weaknesses with this argument.

The fungibility approach ignores market segmentation, investor return expectations, differences in access and cost of capital, and differences in how each market works as well as distinctly different behavior of players in each market segment who are guided by different market theories. This approach to valuation is misguided and introduces procedural and substantive errors that threaten to render appraisals irrelevant.

Appraisers use financial models—such as CAPM or the BUM—which are based on this fungibility theory. But these models are not designed to directly yield cost of capital for private companies; rather, they generate rates by reference to returns in another market, the public market. This is like drawing conclusions about a neighborhood pond by studying an ocean, then making "necessary" adjustments to describe the pond. Why not study the pond directly—or in the case of appraisal, why not use return expectations from the subject's market segment to derive cost of capital?

Appraisers rely on the fungibility of capital argument to support the belief that investors can choose to substitute investments in public or private markets with equal ease. Thus, an investor in middle-market private equity could always achieve the risk-free rate by buying government securities. They use a BUM, adding return to the risk-free rate to compensate for the additional risk of private market investing. There are several weaknesses with this argument, however.

The fungibility argument does not stipulate the necessity of adopting the risk-free rate as a standard. Why that standard rather than a variety of others? That money is fungible does not necessarily lead to the adoption of the risk-free rate as an objective standard, or even an adequate standard. The presence of elaborate retrograde calculations to make it fit the market indicates that it is not sufficient.

Once again, the logic of substitution governs this situation. Specifically, the relevant market of investors determines the cost of capital by defining and quantifying opportunity costs within a market. For example, private equity firms are frequently restricted by their charters and cost of funds from investments outside specific markets. They can never achieve the risk-free rate without abandoning the private equity market and investing in another market with fundamentally different risk and return expectations, information and liquidity functions, and value-creating models. Because there is no clear and necessary substitution, cost of capital is properly based on market costs, not book value, or firm value, or a standard appropriated from another market.

Players within a market do not approach the problem of calculating real-world investment decisions this way. Imagine private equity or mezzanine investors trying to decide whether they should invest in the private market or in a risk-free government instrument. They cannot do this because their capital is raised at lower cost and their mission is to reinvest it in a market with greater return expectations. That market necessarily has different risk and return characteristics.

The use of valuation models built on the fungibility argument uses functions and attributes of divergent markets, yielding fundamental contradictions. It conflates incompatible value worlds (standards of value) that operate with dissimilar rules and standards and are governed by diverse authorities, often with irreconcilable boundaries. Therefore, using the risk-free standard as a base is logically inadequate in that it purports to be an independent standard but is in fact systemically bound to a different, mismatched theoretical market. Capital may be fungible, but it is not fully substitutable. A scale derived from direct observation of the market is more accurate, useful, and responsible than a theoretical construct attempting to mimic that market.

TRIANGULATION

The language and lexicon of private business valuation started in the world of fair market value. Revenue Ruling 59-60 gave credence to a fairly structured appraisal process. Through the efforts of Shannon Pratt and others, fair market value represents the first concerted effort to apply the language and logic of economic theory to private business valuation.

World	PrivateCo Value
Asset market value	$2.4 million
Collateral value	$2.5 million
Insurable value	$6.5 million
Fair market value	**$6.8 million**
Investment value	$7.5 million
Impaired goodwill	$13.0 million
Financial market value	$13.7 million
Owner value	$15.8 million
Synergy market value	$16.6 million
Public value	$18.2 million

Unlike some of the other value worlds, FMV is a highly regulated value world. The main authorities in this world, the IRS and tax courts, have a high degree of influence tending toward control. Participants in this world must play by the authority's rules or be sanctioned. Regulated value worlds may exist in blind disregard to what really occurs in the marketplace. For instance, in the world of FMV, private minority business interests are presumed to have value, even if it means looking to the public capital markets to establish it. In the private capital markets, no such intrinsic value exists, unless an empowering agreement is in place between the shareholders. Even then the actual *market* for the minority interest may be limited to one or two other shareholders.

The regulated FMV world is linked to regulated transfer methods. ESOPs and various estate planning techniques, such as charitable trusts and family limited partnerships, are created and regulated by the government. All of the regulated transfer methods are valued in the world of FMV. This is an important insight. Government rules are present on both sides of the transaction. Likewise, FMV does not have standing with unregulated transfer methods, such as auctions and IPOs. Unregulated transfer methods are viewed through unregulated value worlds, such as market value and collateral value, which reflect values in a more dynamic setting.

An equally important consideration regarding triangulation is the lack of importance regarding FMV and the private capital markets. This market is driven by the actual exchange of debt and equity. Regulated value worlds are rarely employed in a market environment. This explains why FMV is rarely mentioned in a capital context.

NOTES

1. See Revenue Ruling 59-60, 1959-1 CB 237-IRC Sec. 2031.
2. **PrivateCo Pretax Earnings on a Control Basis ($000)**

Item	Year-end 20×3	Year-end 20×2	Year-end 20×1
Pretax profits	$1,500	$1,068	$1,650
Adjustments			
Excess owner compensation[a]	250	250	250
Management fees[b]	200	189	304
Excess accounting[c]	6.5	10.5	8.5
Excess rent[d]	8.7	0	0
Total Adjustments	465	450	563
Recast EBITDA	$1,965	$1,518	$2,213

[a] Since the majority owner is passive, all his compensation will be added back.
[b] Management fees are charged each year by another company that the majority owner also controls.
[c] Some accounting services are performed mainly by another company the majority owner controls and are billed to PrivateCo.
[d] Assumes current rent is above-market rent and will not continue under new ownership.

3. Shannon P. Pratt, Robert F. Reilly, and Robert R. Schweihs, *Valuing a Business: The Analysis and Appraisal of Closely Held Companies*, 5th ed. (New York: McGraw-Hill).

4. Christopher C. Mercer, *Quantifying Marketability Discounts* (Brockton, MA: Peabody Publishing, 1997), p. 19.

5. *Mergerstat Review*, 2007 (Santa Monica: Factset Mergerstat LLC, 2007), p. 24.

6. John D. Emory, "Expanded Study of the Value of Marketability as Illustrated in Initial Public Offerings of Common Stock," *Business Valuation News* (December 2001), pp. 4–20.

7. T.C. Memo 1995-255, June 12, 1995.

8. John K. Paglia and Maretno Agus Harjoto, "Can Publicly Traded Company Multiples Shed Insights on Discounts for Lack of Marketability?" *Business Valuation Review* 29, no. 1 (July 2010): 18–22.

9. *Estate of Paul Mitchell v. Commissioner*, WL 21805-93, TC Memo. 1997-461, October 9, 1997.

10. James A. Larson, and Jeffrey P. Wright, "Key Person Discount in Small Firms: An Update," *Business Valuation Review* (September 1998).

11. Ibid., p. 93.

12. Kevin C. O'Shea and Robert M. Siwicki, "Stock Price Premiums for Voting Rights Attributable to Minority Interests," *Business Valuation Review* (December 1991).

13. Pratt, Reilly, and Schweihs, *Valuing a Business*, p. 430.

14. Rob Slee and John Paglia, "Private Cost of Capital Model," *Value Examiner* (March 2010).

CHAPTER 9

Fair Value

The world of fair value is among the most tightly constricted value worlds. It applies only to minority shareholders who are either oppressed by the majority or dissent from majority actions. The governing authorities in this world are the laws and court systems of the various states. This world is entirely statutory. Each state has adopted laws to grant rights to minority shareholders. Further, each state is an independent authority regarding these matters. The definition and application of fair value can be quite different from state to state.

The language in this world is legalistic because a legal action has been taken by the minority shareholder to determine the value of the shares. Although some of the general concepts are similar to those in other worlds, a unique language and set of concepts are found in the world of fair value.

This world is especially important to minority shareholders in private companies since they have no public market in which to sell shares. Shareholders in this world are motivated to receive fair value for their shares and must assert their claim through court action.

A snapshot of key tenets of the fair value world is provided in Exhibit 9.1.

DISSENTING AND OPPRESSED SHAREHOLDERS

The fair value world can be entered in one of two ways: dissension or oppression. Minority shareholders who believe the majority has taken corporate actions that negatively affect them are called *dissenters*. Examples of corporate actions include merging or selling the assets of the corporation, or changing key tenets of the corporate bylaws. Every state has dissenter's rights statutes that serve to protect the minority, typically through the purchase of their stock at fair value, called the *appraisal remedy*.

"Oppression" is a legal term that means the minority shareholder's reasonable expectations have not been met. Oppressed shareholders' statutes or dissolution statutes are meant to protect minority shareholders from oppressive action, fraud, and mismanagement by the majority. Oppression covers actions taken against a minority shareholder in her capacity as an employee, officer, director, or

EXHIBIT 9.1   Longitude and Latitude: Fair Value

Definition	The value of the shares immediately before a corporate action to which the dissenter objects, excluding any appreciation or depreciation in anticipation of the corporate action unless exclusion would be inequitable. (From Model Business Corporation Act)
Purpose of appraisal	To derive the fair value of a business interest.
Function of appraisal	To value the interests of dissenting or oppressed shareholders in a lawsuit.
Quadrant	Notional regulated.
Authority	State laws and State courts. Each state deals with fair value as they wish. The authorities do not inhabit the private capital markets.
Economic benefit stream	Determined on a case-by-case basis.
Private return expectation	Determined on a case-by-case basis.
Valuation process summary	The definition of fair value leaves to the parties, and ultimately to the courts, the details by which fair value is to be determined within the broad outlines of the definition. Although case law provides guidance as to how each state interprets the definition of fair value, no state specifically equates fair value with fair market value. Fair value is determined on a case-by-case basis, depending on the facts of the suit plus the particular legal jurisdiction.

shareholder. The courts have recognized the special nature of shareholders in private corporations, such as:[1]

- Shareholders usually expect to be active participants in management.
- When dissention arises, the majority shareholder is likely to have the power to undermine or disappoint the minority shareholder's expectations and prevent the minority shareholder from obtaining a fair return on his investment.
- The lack of a ready market for the minority shareholder's stock restricts the holder from liquefying his position.

In oppression cases, some state courts can dissolve the corporation and award the fair value of the shares to the oppressed. Although the dissension and oppression statutes differ in terms of triggering events and latitude of the courts to deliver a remedy, both rely on the payment of fair value for the minority shareholder's stock.

"Fair value" usually is considered to mean the economic value of the securities assuming a continuing ownership and without consideration of diminished value in exchange associates with lack of control or marketability.

TRIGGERING EVENTS

Some action must be taken by an aggrieved party to initiate a fair value claim. Two such triggering events, minority dissent and oppression, are predominant in this world.

Dissent

Majority shareholders may take actions the minority has no control over, and these may reduce the value of the minority shareholders' shares. A number of *triggering events* may cause a minority shareholder to dissent. States have adopted different triggering events. Any party who believes he or she has a fair value claim should seek legal advice on this and the other issues in this chapter.

Some of the more common actions triggering dissent are:

- Consummation of a plan of merger
- Consummation of a plan of share exchange
- Consummation of a sale or exchange of substantially all of the assets used in the business
- Significant changes to the corporate bylaws

An appraisal remedy is available to those minority shareholders who can prove to the courts that they have been damaged by the actions of the control group of shareholders.

Oppression

A number of actions by the majority may trigger an oppressive suit by the minority. Two of these actions are:[2]

1. The minority shareholder has been terminated in an official role with the company, such as an employee or director.
2. The minority has been frozen out by the majority in a freeze-out or cash-out merger. In this case, a minority shareholder's interest is involuntarily eliminated when controlling shareholders create a new corporation, transfer their stock to that corporation, and then agree to merge the old corporation with the new one. The new corporation then acquires the assets and liabilities of the original corporation, with the majority owning the stock of the surviving corporation. The minority shareholders no longer have an equity interest in the new business and have the right to receive only cash for their shares in the original company.

Oppression does not necessarily mean the controlling shareholders have committed fraud or mismanaged the company. It often involves unreasonable compensation or insider transactions to benefit the majority.

To protect minority shareholders, states have enacted laws providing an appraisal remedy for dissenting or oppressed shareholders. The process is determined by each state to enable fair valuation to occur. Fair value is not determined differently based on a triggering event.

Perfecting the Dissenters' Appraisal Rights

Most states require a dissenting shareholder to perfect their appraisal rights before the appraisal remedy is available. This process typically is quite specific and must be followed exactly if the dissenter expects to bring the action to the courts. The Model Business Corporation Act (MBCA), which many states have adopted, outlines the process:[3]

- A shareholder who wishes to exercise appraisal rights must first give written notice of her intent to dissent prior to the meeting at which the matter giving rise to appraisal rights (e.g., a sale of the company's assets) will be voted on.
- The shareholder must not vote in favor of the action.
- If the action is approved, the shareholder must then demand payment for her shares and deposit her share certificates with the corporation.
- The corporation must then pay the shareholder the fair value of the shares.
- If the shareholder does not agree with the corporation's determination of value, the shareholder then is required to notify the corporation of her estimate of fair value and demand payment from the corporation.
- If the corporation disagrees with the shareholder's estimate, it must initiate a judicial appraisal proceeding.

Shareholders who fail to follow this process lose the right to the appraisal remedy.

Role of Inequitable Conduct

Dissenting shareholders tend to prevail if the court case involves an inequitable act by the majority. Most appraisal cases decided since 1983 that were litigated to a final disposition have resulted in favorable verdicts for the dissenting shareholders.[4] In most cases, the offered price to the dissenters or oppressed parties was obviously unfair.[5]

When the offered price was fair, the controlling shareholder typically breached a fiduciary duty or otherwise engaged in unfair conduct. Examples of bad conduct where dissenters achieved favorable outcomes include:

- Controlling shareholders who wrongfully usurped opportunities belonging to the corporation whose shares were being appraised.
- Insiders who froze out the dissenting shareholders, failed to disclose information with respect to the cash-out merger, and failed to use due care in effecting the merger.
- Controlling shareholders who did not even challenge the minority's claims of self-dealing, inadequate disclosure, and unfair dealing.

The courts appear to penalize inequitable conduct of the controlling shareholder in favor of the minority. In a typical dissent case, the dissenting shareholder claims his stock has a fair value between two and ten times the fair value claimed by the corporation.[6] Obviously, there is a large range of fair values in these cases.

DETERMINATION OF FAIR VALUE

Ultimately it is up to the courts in the appropriate jurisdiction to determine fair value. There is no consensus on a definition of fair value. The MBCA defines fair value as:

> *The value of the shares immediately before the effectuation of the corporate action to which the dissenter objects, excluding any appreciation or depreciation in anticipation of the corporate action unless exclusion would be inequitable.*[7]

According to the MCBA, the definition of fair value leaves to the parties, and ultimately to the courts, the process by which fair value is derived. Although case law provides guidance as to how each state interprets the definition of fair value, no state specifically equates fair value with fair market value.[8] Thus, the courts delineate between the worlds of fair market value and fair value.

Generally, however, the market value world is of little or no importance when determining the fair value within the context of a private company because the shares of stock are not traded on any public market. Moreover, a sale of its stock usually does not qualify as an arm's length transaction because the sale usually involves corporate officers, employees, or family members. The court may give no weight to market value if the facts of the case so require.

Although no single valuation method is employed in fair value cases, the discounted cash flow (DCF) method is well known by most courts. For example, Delaware courts describe the DCF method as "the preeminent valuation methodology."[9] The facts of each case determine the appropriate methods. Such methods have included net asset value, the private guideline method, valuation based on earnings and book value, and a combination.[10]

The valuation methods used by a court are dependent on the valuation evidence presented by the parties. The parties create the valuation methodology, and the court reacts to the processes. If both parties present evidence of fair value utilizing the net asset method, the court probably will incorporate a net asset value analysis in its decision. Similarly, if the parties agree on a market approach, the court typically will adopt it.

Appraisal experts usually are engaged by the opposing parties to render value opinions. Even though the appraisal organizations may require nonadvocacy among their certified members, expert opinions often reflect the client's position. The "dueling experts" problem has been dealt with by two Delaware Court of Chancery decisions in a non-Solomon-like way. Rather than "adding the competing valuations then dividing by two" to resolve the issue, the courts determine the stronger valuation argument and incorporate the argument into their final decision. This is a clear effort by the courts to differentiate between value worlds. Further, it shows the game of appraisal Twister can lead to conclusions based on hopelessly entangled logic. Unfortunately, not all courts have adopted this position, and many courts still rely on compromised valuations.

Proportionate Interests

The Delaware courts have held dissenting shareholders are entitled to a "proportionate interest in a going concern."[11] That value is determined on a going-concern basis rather than a liquidation basis. A famous Delaware court case, *Bell v. Kirby Lumber Corp.*, shows how important this use of value premise can be. Kirby Lumber owned a large amount of forestland, which it used to supply a sawmill and plywood plant. Kirby was asset-heavy but profit-poor. Court records showed Kirby was worth approximately $682 per share on a net asset value basis but less than $200 per share on an earnings basis. The dissenting shareholders argued Kirby should be valued based on what the shareholders would receive in a merger negotiated at arm's length with a third party, which presumably would allow for a sale at liquidation value.[12] The court concluded an arm's length sale analysis was inappropriate because it "presupposes an acquisition value based on the very fact that the company will not continue in business on the same basis."[13] In the *Kirby Lumber* decision, the court ruled that the dissenting shareholders were entitled to a proportionate interest in a going concern and fair value should not be based on liquidation value. The *Kirby* case is a prime example of how the courts, acting as an authority in a value world, prescribe the process in that world.

Valuation Date

According to the MCBA, fair value is "the value of the shares immediately *before* the effectuation of the corporate action to which the dissenter objects." Most state statutes provide the valuation date for a dissenting shareholder's fair valuation to be the day prior to the meeting of shareholders at which the action dissented from was opposed.[14] The MCBA goes on to define fair value "excluding any appreciation or depreciation in anticipation of the corporate action unless exclusion would be inequitable." The dissenting shareholder neither receives credit nor is penalized from the action from which he dissented.

As with any appraisal, the valuation date is critical: Only those facts known or knowable on the valuation date should be considered. Courts have accepted this principle, saying that "valuation of securities is in essence a prophecy as to the future, but this prophecy must be based upon facts available at the critical valuation date."[15] As two of the foremost writers in the field, Robert Reilly and Robert Sweighs, assert, "an investor's required return and the amount of available benefits usually is estimated at a single point in time. Also, the estimate of value is based solely on the information that is discernable and predictable at the valuation date."[16]

Minority Discounts

The primary issue facing the courts is whether the minority interest should be valued in isolation, which might call for a minority discount, or whether the corporation should be valued on an enterprise basis, without a minority discount. The Delaware courts have strongly preferred to value the corporation as a whole, with a pro rata share of that value awarded to the dissenting shareholder. This fits with the court's preference of the DCF method, which is primarily an enterprise valuation method. The no-minority-interest-discount reasoning makes sense for two main reasons:

1. The primary purpose of the appraisal remedy is to protect minority shareholders from unequal conduct. Applying a minority interest to the pro rata share would violate this purpose. Essentially the minority shareholder would be penalized by a lack of control.
2. In a cash-out merger, if a minority discount was applied, the controlling group would receive more than a pro rata share of the value of the corporation. This would enable the majority to benefit from such mergers.

While most courts have not applied minority discounts, a few court cases have allowed the appraised value of the stock to reflect such a discount.[17]

Lack of Marketability Discounts

Private companies have no market for their shares. As such, the courts must attempt to recreate a market and give the dissenter what he or she is giving up. In this process, some courts have applied a lack of marketability discount (LOMD) to reflect the fact that no ready market for the shares is available.

The LOMD is routinely used in the world of fair market value to quantify the relative absence of marketability of a private company's shares. LOMDs are applied when a preliminary value of business interest has been derived through comparison to a public security. There are several ways to calculate LOMDs, including the use of restricted stock studies, pre–initial public offering studies, and numerous court cases.

The problem with applying LOMDs to dissenting and oppression cases, however, is that fair value is not the same as fair market value. Fair value, a statutory term, enables shareholders to be fairly compensated, which may or may not equate with the *market's* judgment about the stock's value. Within this value world, "market value is, at most, one factor in determining fair value."[18] Without a comparison to the public market, there is probably no place for LOMDs in determining fair value.

The application of discounts can be significant to the ultimate fair value calculation. Chapter 8 shows typical minority and LOMDs in a fair market value setting. Fair market value and fair value are entirely different worlds. Purely for purposes of distinguishing this concept further, Exhibit 9.2 contrasts the adjusted indicated value from the fair market value world with typical discounts, versus the fair value world without discounts.

The minority interest holder in the fair value world would benefit by more than 50% over the fair market value minority holder if the discounts were not applied.

The world of fair value is quite legalistic. Success requires participants to understand and use statutory laws. Since the laws vary by state, readers who

EXHIBIT 9.2 Comparison of Fair Market Value versus Fair Value

	Fair Market Value	Fair Value
Unadjusted indicated value:		
Value on a control, marketable basis:	$1,000,000	1,000,000
Less minority discount (30%)	300,000	0
Value on a minority, marketable basis	$ 700,000	1,000,000
Less LOMD (35%)	245,000	0
Adjusted indicated value	$ 455,000	1,000,000

need to enter this world are strongly encouraged to confer with an expert in the appropriate jurisdiction.

Fair value is a highly legalistic value world; therefore, it is critical to check with legal counsel before taking any actions. Both statute and case law change. Some jurisdictions are very different from others. Ohio, for example, has case law that prescribes application of both minority and marketability discounts.

TRIANGULATION

Like the world of fair market value, the world of fair value is a regulated value world. This means the authorities in this world, state governments and state courts, have a high degree of influence tending toward control. Participants in this world must play by the authority's rules or be sanctioned. Regulated value worlds may exist in blind disregard to the dynamic interconnections of the private capital markets triangle. Fair value is a unique value world because it compensates individuals for losses they may have suffered relative to a majority action. In this sense, courts use valuation for purposes other than connecting to the markets. The *Kirby* case shows the court's reluctance to accept a higher, presumably market, value for the company because the goal of this world is fairness as determined by the court, not the markets.

The regulated fair value world is not linked to specific transfer methods or capital access points. Transfer has already occurred prior to fair value claim: The minority holder's shares have already been tendered. Further, pursuant to a successful claim, the court is not concerned with the defendant's choice of capitalization technique. The control shareholder simply pays the plaintiff fair value as determined by the court.

Fair value's lack of connection to transfer and capital only occurs in a regulated value world. Once again, the authorities in these value worlds are not concerned with how value fits within a broader capital markets context.

NOTES

1. Robert F. Reilly and Robert P. Schweihs, *Handbook of Advanced Business Valuation* (New York: McGraw-Hill, 2000), p. 299.
2. Ibid., p. 306.

3. Ibid., p. 298.
4. Barry Wertheimer, "The Shareholders' Appraisal Remedy and How Courts Determine Fair Value," 47 *Duke Law Journal* 613, p. 24.
5. Ibid., p. 24.
6. Ibid., p. 26.
7. Shannon P. Pratt, Robert F. Reilly, and Robert R. Schweihs, V*aluing a Business: The Analysis and Appraisal of Closely Held Companies*, 5th ed. (New York: McGraw-Hill), p. 790.
8. Wertheimer, "The Shareholders' Appraisal Remedy," p. 6.
9. Ibid.
10. Ibid., p. 7.
11. Ibid., p. 1.
12. Ibid., p. 18.
13. Ibid., p. 1.
14. Reilly and Schweihs, *Handbook of Advanced Business Valuation*, p. 304.
15. Ibid., p. 305.
16. Ibid., p. 305.
17. Wertheimer, "The Shareholders' Appraisal Remedy," p. 11.
18. Bobbie J. Hollis, "The Unfairness of Applying Lack of Marketability Discounts to Determine Value in Dissenter's Rights Cases," *Journal of Corporation Law* (October 1999): 3.

CHAPTER 10

Incremental Business Value

The world of incremental business value (IBV) considers the creation, measurement, and management of a company's IBV, that is, a return in excess of the corresponding cost of capital.[1] This is a dynamic valuation process based on a company's performance. By understanding how value is determined and influenced, owners are better prepared to increase the value of their business. Like the other value worlds (which business appraisers call "standards of value"), the IBV world follows a certain process for deriving value. However, unlike the other value worlds that rely on static valuation, the IBV world enables owners to value their firms on a constant and continuing basis using a dynamic methodology. This chapter shows how private firms can determine IBV, and how owners can increase that value.

The world of IBV is separate and distinct from all other value worlds. The authority here is the academic community and management consulting industry, which developed most of the IBV conceptual framework. Much of this world is defined by what it is not. Although it uses numbers from financial statements, it jettisons many of the accounting definitions of value. For example, book value does not play a part in determining IBV.

Years ago IBV was known as residual income analysis or, later, return on net assets. In many respects, this world is incommensurable with other value worlds. The primary difference is the IBV world generates and uses an incremental value calculus, as opposed to absolute values derived in the other value worlds. For example, if a company generates a positive IBV of $1 million, this means the company has bettered the shareholder's position by $1 million, not that the company is worth $1 million on an enterprise basis.

Exhibit 10.1 contains the longitude and latitude, or position of key tenets, of this world.

Although IBV uses language familiar in other worlds, its purpose renders it mutually exclusive to the purposes of other worlds. The purpose of the IBV world is to measure the incremental change to IBV in an entity over time. This is why IBV is a popular tool for use in bonus plans and capital allocation systems. This incremental measurement contrasts sharply with the absolute value measurements afforded in the other value worlds. IBV attempts to grasp the relationship among performance, return on investment, and value. Improving IBV may also improve the value of a business in another world, such as the world of market value,

EXHIBIT 10.1 Longitude and Latitude: Incremental Business Value

Definition	Incremental business value is the result of generating a return in excess of the corresponding cost of capital.
Purpose of appraisal	To measure the creation or incremental change to incremental business value in a company, product line, or financial management system.
Function of appraisal	For use in creating management bonus plans, project performance, and subsidiary value measurement as well as capital allocation systems and business planning.
Quadrant	Notional unregulated.
Authority	Management consulting industry.
Benefit stream	Recast earnings before interest, taxes, depreciation and amortization (EBITDA).
Private return expectation	Discount rate derived by the private cost of capital model.
Valuation process summary	IBV = Recast EBITDA − (Investment × Cost of Capital)

where: IBV = incremental business value.

Recast EBITDA = earnings before interest, taxes, depreciation, and amortization, recast for owner discretionary expenses and one-time company expenses.

Investment = greater of: (1) the total amount of investment made in a project or business; or (2) the financial market value of the company.

Cost of capital = expected rate of return that capital providers in the private capital markets require in order to fund to a particular investment.

A positive IBV figure means that shareholder value is created. A negative IBV means shareholder value is destroyed.

PrivateCo Example

IBV = Recast EBITDA − (Cost of Capital × Capital Employed)
     = \$2.8 million − (29% × \$13.7 million)
     = \$(1.1) million (as rounded)

---

but there is no direct linkage. However, it seems reasonable that if a company improves its net return on assets and adds more IBV, it may also be worth more in the other worlds.

NATURE OF INCREMENTAL BUSINESS VALUE

The prior chapters provide valuation processes that are static in nature. Their final result is stationary and does not indicate whether the owners have created value in their decision making. For example, if the fair market value of PrivateCo is \$100 per share, the fair market value process makes no attempt to measure if the return is adequate given the capital employed and the extent to which the company exceeds that minimal value-creating threshold. The world of IBV, however, measures the IBV of a business or project using a dynamic process. Unlike other value worlds, the IBV valuation process enables owners to determine if their investment is likely to create value before actually making the investment. Further, repeated usage of an IBV metric enables owners to monitor value-changing trends over time. The other value worlds do not afford such answers.

IBV is defined as generating revenues beyond the corresponding economic costs. No less a source than Peter Drucker voiced this connection when he said, "Until a business returns a profit that is greater than its cost of capital, it operates at a loss. Never mind that it pays taxes as if it had a genuine profit. The enterprise still returns less to the economy than it devours in resources.... Until then it does not create wealth; it destroys it."[2] Capital has a cost, and this cost can be measured via the private capital access line. If managers do not consider this cost when making investment decisions, they risk destroying IBV. At the least, managers should not invest in projects that are expected to return less than the company's weighted average cost of capital (WACC). More specifically, managers should match the cost of capital with the risk of the potential investment. Therefore, projects that are riskier than the company's risk profile should be evaluated using a higher rate than the WACC.

Some tenets behind IBV can be found in the early 1900s with the concept of residual income. Residual income is defined as operating profit less a capital charge. The idea of residual income first appeared in accounting literature in 1917, and it continued to be discussed well into the 1960s. By the late 1950s and early 1960s, the discussion of IBV was promoted by two economics professors, Miller and Modigliani. These academics viewed value from an economic rather than accounting framework. They showed that IBV is driven by required rates of return in the market to compensate for risk and economic income, which lays the framework for a discounted cash flow methodology. For the first time, managers could use an economic approach to determine the IBV of companies and specific projects. A positive net present value (NPV) adds value, while a negative NPV subtracts value from the ownership. From the 1960s to the 1990s, NPV was the dominant method used to determine IBV. Over the past 10 to 20 years, however, NPV has given way to other frameworks. This transition occurred largely because NPV is derived from future cash flows and therefore is not readily usable for incentive systems based on past performance and current results.

The most recent IBV metrics have focused on easily implemented measures, which can be used for many purposes. Most metrics are created and promoted by management consulting firms. Perhaps the best known is incremental economic value added (EVA) created by Stern Stewart & Co.[3] EVA is used to measure wealth changes to the shareholders. Similar to residual income, EVA says that earning a return greater than the cost of capital increases value while earning less than the cost of capital decreases value. Thus, EVA does not rely on accounting measures of investment, such as capitalized expenses for financial reporting purposes, but an economic view that captures and considers period costs such as advertising, ongoing research and development, and so forth as part of the "economic" investment.

Traditional accounting methods, such as earnings per share (EPS) or return on investment (ROI), have been used for years for evaluating strategic decisions. Over the last ten years, a key consideration has been that economic—not accounting—concepts drive value. There are several reasons for this.

PROBLEMS WITH USING TRADITIONAL METHODS

Because accounting methods traditionally have been cost oriented, as opposed to value oriented, they do not always align themselves with value creation. They can tell you what is spent and even what you made. But they do not necessarily tell you if you made enough relative to the company's cost of capital. In addition:[4]

- *Accounting measures ignore the time value of capital invested.* Each type of capital has a cost, based on the return expectations of the market. The time value of debt is reflected in the rate of interest charged while equity capital also has an opportunity cost. Investors require compensation for investing in the company and not in alternate assets.
- *Accounting methods are somewhat subjective, whereas cash is a matter of fact.* Managers may be motivated to manipulate accounting figures, whether to increase a bonus or pay less corporate taxes.
- *Accounting methods exclude consideration of risk.* If a company pronounces earnings of $5 million, it is entirely unclear if this earnings result is commensurate with the risk of owning this earnings stream.
- *Traditional measures ignore the investment requirements of the company in calculating earnings.* For instance, a company may invest $10 million per year to build a pipeline of products. A service company may require little investment in growing its business each year. Thus, to analyze an investment properly, the cash directed into the business must be considered relative to the returns.

A company is committed to maximizing shareholder returns if it uses value-based approaches. For most private companies, the managers are the shareholders. As the business grows and becomes more sophisticated, it becomes increasingly important to separate the concepts of an owner's personal wealth creation from the task of creating wealth in the business. IBV is an excellent tool in that process.

VALUE-BASED APPROACHES

A number of approaches measure IBV. The NPV method is probably the most frequently used because it has been around longest. However, many competing approaches are introduced in the IBV metric wars, including cash flow return on investment (CFROI), shareholder value added (SVA), cash flow added (CVA), and IBV added (IBVA).[5] Each measure offers a somewhat different orientation in the search for IBV. A description of all these metrics is beyond the scope of this chapter. Instead, NPV is compared and contrasted to IBV.

NET PRESENT VALUE

Understanding present value is the starting point to using NPV. Present value is a financial term that describes what something received tomorrow is worth today.

To calculate present value, a stream of earnings or cash is discounted or "reverse compounded." This requires a discount rate. Thus, $100 received a year from now is worth something less today. This is its present value. Assume money is invested at 5% a year right now with 5% chosen as the discount rate. The *present value*, then, of $100 promised a year from now using 5% as the discount rate is 95.24% or

$$((100 \text{ dollars} \div 105 \text{ percent}) \times 100 \text{ percent})$$

Looking at it another way, $95.24 invested today at 5% interest yields $100 next year.

NPV is calculated by adding the initial investment, represented as a negative cash flow, to the present value.

The discount rate is the expected rate of return offered by securities having the same degree of risk as the project. NPV is a key indication of whether a project or investment increases investor value. If NPV is positive, the financial value of the investor's assets should be increased. Thus, the investment is financially attractive. If NPV is zero, the financial value of the investor's assets does not change, producing an indifferent investment. And if NPV is negative, the financial value of the investor's assets should decrease. The investment would not be financially attractive.

Here is another example of how NPV is calculated. Assume a business wants to expand. The plans require $1 million in up-front cash to fund the expansion. For the five years following the expansion, the business will realize a cash flow of $350,000 per year. Beyond the fifth year, the business will realize a cash flow of $200,000 per year for the foreseeable future. Finally, assume the shareholders of the business require a 20% compounded return on their investments. This scenario is represented as shown:

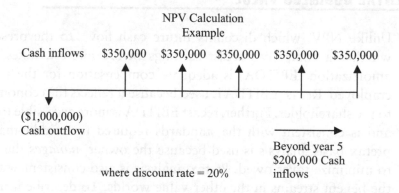

$$NPV = (\text{Cash outflow})_0 + \frac{\text{Cash inflow}_1}{(1 + \text{Return expectation})^1} + \frac{\text{Cash inflow}_2}{(1 + \text{Return expectation})^2}$$

$$NPV = (\$1,000,000)_0 + \frac{\$350,000_1}{(1 + 20\%)^1} + \frac{\$350,000_2}{(1 + 20\%)^2} + \frac{\$350,000_3}{(1 + 20\%)^3}$$

$$+ \frac{\$350,000_4}{(1 + 20\%)^4} + \frac{\$350,000_5}{(1 + 20\%)^5} + \frac{\$200,000_n}{(1 + 20\%)^n}$$

$$= \$450,000 \text{ (rounded)}$$

In this example, the shareholders are better off financially by $450,000 if they spend the $1 million and receive $350,000 in cash flow per year for five years and $200,000 per year thereafter. In other words, the shareholders have a NPV on their investment of $450,000.

NPV measures IBV in that it considers economic profits and the time value of money. Owners who invest in projects with a positive NPV create IBV because revenues exceed corresponding economic costs. But, as Appendix A shows, most private owners do not rely on NPV for their investment decisions. For them, IBV might be more beneficial.

There are several pitfalls involving the use of NPV. In short, they are:

- Forecasts of future cash flows tend to be overly optimistic, causing a hockey-stick pattern. This optimism often overvalues the project.
- The terminal value often represents more than 50% of the NPV, which captures value beyond the detailed planning horizon. Terminal value is the value beyond the detailed planning horizon. Terminal value in the prior example is the value from year 6 to the end of the project's useful life. Since the time frame is so far in the future, large terminal values can distort the value of a company or project. As most business owners realize, capturing value beyond five years is extremely difficult.
- NPV is a stock measure and not particularly useful for bonus or incentive programs.

So while NPV is theoretically correct, it may not be the best value-creating approach a private company can use.

INCREMENTAL BUSINESS VALUE

Unlike NPV, which discounts future cash flows to the present, IBV measures whether a company's recast earnings before interest, taxes, depreciation, and amortization (EBITDA) is adequate compensation for the total cost of capital employed. Recast EBITDA is used because it reflects the economic profits available to the shareholder. Further, recast EBITDA is more accessible to private companies and is consistent with the standards required for middle-market businesses. A pretax basis analysis is used because the owner *manages* the firm's tax position to minimize taxes owed. Pretax analysis is also consistent with the treatment of the benefit streams in the other value worlds. To describe it more clearly, IBV is defined as recast EBITDA less a capital charge, or

Recast EBITDA − Investment Cost employed

or

Recast EBITDA − (Investment × Cost of Capital employed)

Earnings before interest and taxes are adjusted for owner discretionary expenses and other one-time expenses, a recasting that follows the same market-value adjustment process defined in Chapter 6. Major exceptions to the IBV recasting include *not* adding back discretionary items that are expected to continue in the future. For example, special employee bonuses that are expected to continue for the foreseeable future would not be recast. Cost of capital for IBV purposes is the company's private cost of capital, as determined by the Private Cost of Capital (PCOC) model. The PCOC model determines the market value of both equity capital and interest-bearing debt, then weights each type of capital. For private companies, the cost of equity can be found on the Pepperdine Private Capital Market Line (PPCML). The cost of debt is explicit and does not include a tax shield due to the tax deductibility of interest because the earnings measure, EBITDA, is stated on a pretax basis.

Exhibit 10.2 contains an IBV calculation for PrivateCo. First, recast EBITDA is derived. Since this involves recasting the company's income statement, adjustments are made to show the discretionary expenses of the owner. Taken from a recast performed in Chapter 6, the example shows how these adjustments are used to recast an income statement. PrivateCo has recast EBITDA of $2.8 million (as rounded).

EXHIBIT 10.2 PrivateCo Recast EBITDA ($000)

Item	Y/E 20X3
Sales	$22,500
Gross profits	5,850
SG&A expenses	3,000
Depreciation	356
Interest expense	95
Other	599
Pretax profits	**$1,800**
Adjustments	
Depreciation	356
Interest	95
Excess owner comp[a]	250
Management fees[b]	200
Officer insurances[c]	5.0
Excess accounting[d]	6.5
Excess rent[e]	8.7
Excess health insurance	8.2
Casualty loss	35
Donations	74
Recast EBITDA	**$2,800**

[a]The majority owner is passive; therefore 100% of his compensation will be added back.

[b]Management fees are charged each year by another company that the majority owner also controls.

[c]Officer insurances are added back since the majority shareholder will not be on the payroll after the sale.

[d]Some accounting services are performed mainly for another company the majority owner controls but are billed to PrivateCo.

[e]Assumes current rent will not continue under new ownership.

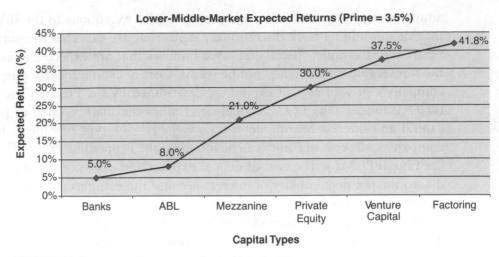

EXHIBIT 10.3 Pepperdine Private Capital Market Line

The next step in calculating IBV is to calculate cost of capital. PrivateCo's private cost of capital is shown in Exhibit 10.3. Every type of capital has a cost. These costs represent the expected returns of the particular capital providers. Several points must be made about the expected rate of return. First, this return is the expected rate of return *to the provider*. In other words, capital providers require a certain all-in return to compensate them for taking the risk of extending the credit or making the investment. This expected return is different from the effective cost to the borrower or investee. The major difference between the expected return to the provider and effective cost to the borrower are various transaction costs. For example, the borrower may incur legal, brokerage, environmental, and other costs in effecting the transaction.

Second, expected returns are used to feed IBV rather than realized returns, even though there are often substantial differences between the two rates. Expected returns are used because capital providers offer credit and structure deals based on what they expect to receive from the investment.

Third, it is now possible to graph expected returns for the major capital types, including banks, asset-based lenders, mezzanine providers, private equity, venture capital and factoring. This graph is called the PPCML, as shown in Exhibit 10.3. The return expectations of the investors who issue private securities are located on or near this line.

Exhibit 10.3 encompasses various capital types in terms of the provider's all-in expected returns. The PPCML is described as median, pretax expected returns of institutional capital providers. For consistency, the capital types chosen to comprise the PPCML reflect likely capital options for mainly lower-middle-market companies (i.e., companies that employ $5 million or more in outside capital).

The PPCML is stated on a pretax basis, both from a provider and from a user perspective. In other words, capital providers offer deals to the marketplace on a pretax basis. For example, if a private equity investor requires a 25% return, this is stated as a pretax return. Also, the PPCML does not assume a tax rate to the investee, even though many of the capital types use interest rates that generate deductible interest expense for the borrower. Capital types are not tax-effected because many owners of private companies *manage* their company's tax bill through various aggressive techniques. It is virtually impossible to estimate a generalized appropriate tax rate for this market.

PRIVATE COST OF CAPITAL MODEL

It is a premise of this book that public data typically should not be used to derive private discount rates. The argument is framed by answering these five questions:

1. Do privately held firms obtain capital from the public markets? (No)
2. Do the majority of privately held companies go public? (No)
3. Do we have robust sources for obtaining capital in the private capital markets? (Yes)
4. Do these capital sources price risk in their particular segments? (Yes)
5. Is it possible to learn what these return expectations are by segment? (Yes)

This book clearly shows private capital markets are unique yet dynamic; that less than .001% of private companies go public; that risk is priced by capital type or capital access point; and by surveying capital providers, we have learned decision-making behavior. Based on arguments in previous chapters and here, the author believes that public return data should not be used to derive private cost of capital.

A relevant private discount rate model should enable the user to determine the expected rate of return that the market of private capital providers requires in order to attract funds to a particular subject or investment. The PCOC model yields such a discount rate by positioning the user into the decision-making process of private capital providers. The author and John Paglia of Pepperdine University created this model to empower users of private capital market data, such as from the Pepperdine capital market surveys, to derive a discount rate that is generated from empirical data.[6]

The PCOC model is:

$$PCOC = \sum_{i=1}^{N} \left[(CAP_i + SCAP_i) \times \frac{MV_i}{\sum_{j=1}^{N} MV_j} \right]$$

where: N = number of sources of capital
CAP_i = median expected return for capital type i
$SCAP_i$ = specific CAP risk adjustment for capital type i
MV_i = market value of all outstanding securities i

PCOC depends on private cost of debt (PCOD), private cost of equity (PCOE), and private cost of preferred (PCOP) where applicable.

EXHIBIT 10.4   PrivateCo CAP$_e$ by Capital Type

Capital Type	Book Value	PPCML Cap Type	CAP$_e$
Term loan	$500,000	5.0%	6.0%
Equity	$1,000,000	30.0%	30.0%

There are four steps to determining PCOC. PrivateCo's discount rate will now be derived using this process:

1. To determine the appropriate capital types by which to compare, review the credit boxes described in the most current Pepperdine survey. Select the appropriate median CAP$_e$ from the survey results.

   PrivateCo has a relatively simple capital structure, as shown in Exhibit 10.4. CAP$_e$ is found for each capital type from the most recent Pepperdine survey. For existing debt, the analyst can calculate the expected (all-in) return directly from the loan agreement. (See Chapter 17 for guidance on this issue.) For presentation purposes, we will assume that PrivateCo's existing term loan is about to be renegotiated.

   By reviewing the PPCML in Exhibit 10.3and associated data, the CAP$_e$ for PrivateCo's term loan and equity is 5% and 30%, respectively. The term loan CAP$_e$ is 6%, as opposed to the 5% shown on the PPCML, because the PPCML shows the median return expectation for $5 million loans. PrivateCo's term loan is $500,000, which corresponds to a higher return expectation. The equity CAP$_e$ is 30%, the same number as shown for equity on the PPCML, because PrivateCo fits within the "$5MM equity" category of the Pepperdine survey.

2. Determine the market value of each capital type. The next step is to determine the market values of PrivateCo's capital types. Exhibit 10.5 shows these results. In PrivateCo's case, the face value of its debt is also its market value. The market value of PrivateCo's equity is calculated in Chapter 6 at $13.7 million.

3. Apply a specific capital type (SCAP) risk adjustment to the selected median capital type based on a comparison of subject results to the appropriate survey credit box. Use first- and third-quartile returns as a guide to this adjustment.

   In order to determine the SCAP risk adjustment, the appraiser must compare surveyed and subject credit boxes for each capital type. Exhibit 10.6 shows this comparison for the term loan.

   The surveyed results represent the qualifying minimum threshold for loan approval. For example, in order to make a loan, lenders require a current

EXHIBIT 10.5   PrivateCo Market Value by Capital Type

Capital Type	Book Value	Market Value
Term loan	$500,000	$500,000
Equity	$1,000,000	$13,700,000

EXHIBIT 10.6 Comparison of Surveyed and PrivateCo Term Loan Credit Boxes

	Term Loan					
	Pepperdine Survey					
	1st Quartile	Median	3rd Quartile	Very Important	Score (0–4)	PrivateCo
Current ratio	1.0	1.0	1.2	4.5%	1.9	2.5
Fixed charge coverage	1.1	1.2	1.4	50.0%	3.1	4.0
Senior debt service	1.2	1.4	1.7	45.5%	3.0	3.5
Total debt service ratio	1.2	1.3	1.4	65.0%	3.5	2.5
Senior debt to EBITDA	2.3	2.8	3.0	45.5%	2.9	.2
Total debt to EBITDA	2.4	3.5	4.2	40.9%	2.9	.6
Debt to net worth	1.9	2.5	3.3	18.2%	2.0	1.5
Debt to tangible net worth	2.0	2.5	3.0	27.3%	2.5	1.5

ratio of 1, fixed charge coverage of 1.2, and so on as a median. Not all credit box characteristics are considered equally important, as the "Very Important" and "Score" columns indicate. For instance, current ratio and debt to worth are less important variables to the lending decision than total debt service ratio and senior debt to EBITDA. The Pepperdine survey asked respondents to score their responses on a 4-point scale. Only fixed charge coverage, senior debt service, and total debt service scored a 3.0 or above. For purposes of deciding PCOD SCAP, greater weight should be put on these variables.

As the last column shows, PrivateCo compares favorably against median results for all metrics. Since PrivateCo generates a high level of EBITDA relative to investment in the business, its leverage ratios are outstanding, as witnessed by a low total debt to EBITDA of .6, which is substantially lower than median survey results. Further, PrivateCo's coverage ratios indicate low debt in the business yet high profitability. PCOD SCAP will reflect that PrivateCo's financial results compare favorably to first-quartile survey responses.

The next step in determining PCOC is to derive PCOE SCAP. This is accomplished by comparing surveyed private equity group expectations to PrivateCo's results. Exhibit 10.7 makes this comparison.

The surveyed results represent Private Equity's credit box (i.e., the criteria that prospects must display in order to qualify for investment). PrivateCo is expected to perform well in revenue and EBITDA growth when compared to median expectations. However, PrivateCo is not expected to surpass third-quartile expectations in these areas.

Private equity groups (PEGs) also scored various investment measures. PrivateCo compares in this way:

- PEGs are rightly concerned about customer concentrations. PrivateCo has no single customer that represents more than 20% of annual sales. The top 10ten customers represent 40% of annual sales. The top 50 customers represent 70% of sales. This diversity of customers and lack of customer concentration would be viewed as a positive by PEGs.

EXHIBIT 10.7   Comparison of Surveyed and PrivateCo Private Equity Credit Boxes

	Private Equity					
	Pepperdine Survey					
	1st Quartile	Median	3rd Quartile	Very Import.	Score (0–4)	PrivateCo
Revenue growth rate (minimum)	5%	5%	10%			7%
Revenue growth rate (expected)	9%	10%	15%			7%
EBITDA growth rate (minimum)	7%	10%	10%			12%
EBITDA growth rate (expected)	10%	15%	19%			12%
Customer concentrations				40.3%	3.2[a]	
Market leadership				18.6%	2.7[b]	
Historical operating performance				29.7%	3.1[c]	
Industry sector				29.9%	2.9[d]	
Future prospects of company				74.6%	3.7[e]	
Management team				67.5%	3.6[f]	

[a]Customer concentrations are relatively important to PEGs, but PrivateCo has a diversified customer base, with no single customer accounting for more than 15% of sales.
[b]PEGs are less concerned about market leadership than all of the other categories. PrivateCo is not viewed as a market leader in its space. Rather, it is considered a well-run, follow-the-leader company.
[c]Historical operating performance is moderately important to private equity investors. PrivateCo has a fairly stable operating performance over the past few years.
[d]PEGs view industry sector as moderately important. PrivateCo operates in a sector with relatively long periods of stability. This sector is not expected to change appreciably in the foreseeable future.
[e]PEGs are mostly concerned with the future prospects of a company. PrivateCo will perform well into the future but not at a breakneck pace. This is mainly due to conservative policies set by Joe Mainstreet.
[f]PrivateCo's management team is seasoned but mainly homegrown. The average tenure of direct reports to Joe Mainstreet is more than 20 years. While this offers stability, it may present a problem if a PEG invested in the company and wished to make major changes.

In summary, PrivateCo qualifies for private equity investment but would likely be viewed as an average performer, with average expectations. For this reason, PCOE SCAP is 0.

The next step is to determine PrivateCo's CAP by capital type, as shown in Exhibit 10.8.

By comparing survey results to PrivateCo actual or expected results, SCAP can be determined for PCOD and PCOE. PrivateCo compares favorably to first-quartile survey term debt results, as shown in Exhibit 10.6. Thus, PCOD SCAP is (.3)%, which is the number needed to convert CAP

EXHIBIT 10.8   Determination of PrivateCo's CAP by Capital Type

Capital Type	Market Value	CAPe	1st Quartile	3rd Quartile	SCAP	PCOD CAP	PCOE CAP
PCOD (loan)	$500,000	6.0%	5.7%	6.6%	(.3)%	5.7%	
PCOE	$13.7MM	30.0%	25%	35%	0%		30%

EXHIBIT 10.9 PrivateCo Private Cost of Capital Calculation

Capital Type	Market Value	% of Total	CAP	Tax Effect	Rate Factor
PCOD	500,000	4%	5.7%	0%	.2
PCOE	13,700,000	96%	30.0%	0%	29.0
			Private cost of capital		29.2%

to the first-quartile survey result of 5.7%. In other words, PrivateCo can expect to pay an all-in PCOD of 5.7%.

    Deriving PCOE SCAP requires comparing surveyed results from private equity groups to PrivateCo's actual and expected results. As Exhibit 10.7 shows, PrivateCo would likely be viewed by PEGs as an average candidate. Thus, PCOE SCAP is 0, and PCOE CAP is 30%.

4. Calculate the percentage of capital structure for each CAP. Add the individual percentages to derive PCOC.

    If the benefit stream for IBV was stated on an after-tax basis, the debt portion of the capital would be tax-effected at the marginal tax rates. Since the benefit stream in this case is stated on a pretax basis (EBITDA), the debt is not tax-effected. Exhibit 10.9 shows PrivateCo's PCOC calculation.

    In this example, PrivateCo has a private cost of capital of 29% (as rounded).

RAMIFICATIONS OF USING PCOC

The temptation to use readily available public information to value private companies is strong. Note that within the private capital markets, mainly academics and business appraisers use the guideline public company method. Other parties in the private capital markets—business owners, lenders, investors, estate planners, and so forth—rely on valuation methods that are specifically useful to making decisions in their markets.

    Why do parties in the private capital markets not employ public information in their decision-making process? Because these parties have real money in the markets; valuation is not notional to them. Making proper financing and investment decisions requires using theories and methods that are appropriate to the subject's market, such as choosing the correct value world and resulting process when making a valuation decision.

    Using a discount rate that is derived from empirically derived private data could alter professional, legalistic, and compliance business appraisal in four ways. First, adjustments such as lack of marketability discounts and control premiums may not be needed. These adjustments originally were created based on the faulty premise that public return expectations could be manipulated to derive private values. Once risk is defined using private return expectations, these public-to-private adjustments are unnecessary.

    Second, PCOC provides a risk definition that can be applied across value worlds (standards of value). Each world also has an authority, which is the agent or agents that govern the world. The authority decides whether the intentions of the involved party are acceptable for use in that world and prescribes the methods used in that world. More specifically, "authority" refers to agents or agencies with primary responsibility to develop, adopt, promulgate, and administer standards of practice within that world. Authority decides which purposes are acceptable in its world, sanctions its decisions, develops methodology, and provides a coherent set of rules for participants to follow. Authority derives its influence or legitimacy mainly from government action, compelling logic, and/or the utility of its standards. Authorities from the various value worlds will finally have an empirically derived method of defining risk. It is hoped that these authorities will prescribe use of PCOC in their respective worlds.

Third, business owners finally will have the ability to determine their companies' cost of capital. This knowledge will help them learn whether they are creating economic value, that is, generating returns on invested capital greater than this cost. This should promote economic value creation as a practical and useful tool. Plus it opens an avenue for business valuators to consult with business owners to help them make better investment and financing decisions.

Finally, the PCOC model will make business appraisal more relevant. Currently, an industry of business appraisers inhabits mainly the notional value worlds. Business owners need more help in competing in a global economy. Tools like the PCOC model will help the appraisal industry become more value added.

The last step to calculate IBV determines the amount of investment made in the business.

INVESTMENT

Investment is the greater of (a) all expenditures in a business (or project) that have a long-term impact or (b) the financial market value of the company. Young companies or those without positive benefit streams are likely to use the first definition; companies with substantial financial market values will use the second definition.

Relative to the first definition, the concept of investment is much more expansive than accounting terms such as book value. For example, investment incorporates spending on "nouns"—people, places, and things.

Examples of investments in people are:

- Forgone salaries of the owners during periods when the business does not generate sufficient cash flow to pay such.
- Training of productive employees.
- Long-term bonuses paid.

Examples of investments in places are:

- Leasehold improvements.
- Buildings owned by the business.
- Other structural improvements.

Examples of investments in things include:

- Subsidized losses from the business.
- Original acquisition cost of fixed assets (underappreciated).
- Expensed infrastructure for the business, such as computer systems.

Once a company generates a large benefit stream, investment equals the equity value of financial market value. This makes sense because IBV measures value created or lost, so financial market value is the correct benchmark. In other words, a company creates additional IBV when it adds to financial market value and loses IBV when it detracts from financial market value.

Joe Mainstreet works with his consultant, Nancy Value, to prepare Exhibit 10.10, which describes the investment in his company.

Investment in the business includes assets that would appear on the balance sheet as well as expensed items. Further, opportunity costs, such as forgone compensation by the shareholders, are included. These investments all have something in common: Regardless of accounting definitions, they were necessary to build the infrastructure and capabilities of the business.

Total investment in PrivateCo per Exhibit 10.10 is $4.6 million. PrivateCo's financial market value was determined in Chapter 6 as $13.7 million, which is the value that will be used in the next example. Now IBV for PrivateCo can be determined:

$$\text{Incremental Biz Value} = \text{Recast EBITDA} - (\text{Investment} \times \text{Cost of Capital})$$

$$= \$2.8 \text{ million} - (\$13.7 \text{ million} \times 29\%)$$

$$= \$2.8 \text{ million} - \$3.9 \text{ million}$$

$$= \$(1.1) \text{ million}$$

The company is generating $(1.1) million in IBV. Once again, this negative IBV number means that Joe is not generating returns that exceed his company's cost of capital. And generating negative IBV ultimately also should lead to a loss of market value.

EXHIBIT 10.10   Investment in PrivateCo

Item	Y/E 20X3
Original Acquisition Cost of Productive Assets	$3,000,000
+ Expensed Portion of Computer System	100,000
+ Training Programs for Existing Employees	350,000
+ Leasehold Improvements	400,000
+ Unpaid Compensation to Joe	250,000
+ Other Expensed Investment	500,000
Total Investment	$4,600,000

PROJECT DECISION MAKING

IBV could be used as a basis for management bonus plans, for project performance, and for subsidiary value measurement. For private companies, project investment decisions are an especially noteworthy application because the recast EBITDA of the project can be derived and applied against the cost of capital employed.

Assume Joe Mainstreet wants to hire a salesperson but first wants to understand if this new hire will add value to PrivateCo. Hiring the employee promises to add $75,000 per year in pretax profits. Project investment, or the cost of hiring the employee, is approximately $150,000. This investment includes the salary and fringe benefits of the employee, plus the cost of hiring the employee, plus the indirect labor to support the employee.

Joe uses this formula:

$$\text{Incremental Biz Value} = \text{Project Return} - (\text{Investment} \times \text{Cost of Capital})$$
$$= \$75,000 - (\$150,000 \times 29\%)$$
$$= \$75,000 - \$43,500$$
$$= \$31,500$$

This "employee" project promises to generate an IBV of $31,500. Let us stop here and review what IBV is telling us. It says that by undertaking this investment successfully, Joe will create $31,500 in positive IBV in his business; or, said in a different way, PrivateCo will generate returns on investment of $31,500 greater than its cost of capital.

PROBLEMS WITH INCREMENTAL BUSINESS VALUE

There are several problems associated with the IBV concept:

- IBV is an accounting-based concept. For multiperiod analyses, IBV may have some accounting distortions. For example, historical asset values that distort ROI also distort IBV values.
- There may be distortions caused by inflation. Historical asset values are distorted because inflation affects IBV values.
- The recast to EBITDA must be done correctly to obtain a proper result.

VALUE-CREATION STRATEGIES

In order to create value, owners must understand the variables that drive business value. Exhibit 10.11 contains value drivers tied to actions that owners can implement to increase IBV.[7]

EXHIBIT 10.11   Actions that Affect Economic Value

Goals	Value Drivers	Strategies
Increase recast EBITDA	Increase sales	Enter niche markets; patent new products to create barriers to entry; launch innovative products; consolidate competitors.
	Lower cost of goods sold	Develop scale economies; acquire captive access to raw materials; increase efficiencies in processes (production, distribution, services) and labor utilization; implement cutting-edge cost control systems.
	Control operating expenses	Budget and monitor expenses; identify fixed versus variable expenses; manage expenses at lowest level possible; keep track of recast items.
Reduce Risk	Reduce business risk	Perform at a higher operating level compared to competitors; establish long-term contracts whenever possible; institute financial transparency, including the retention of audited financial statements.
	Reduce cost of capital	Maximize use of debt to support equity, possibly use less costly equity subsitutes, such as mezzanine debt; reduce surprises (volatility of earnings); consistently test the market cost of debt.
	Reduce customer concentration	No single customer should account for more than 25% of sales.
	Form management structure	Create a functional organization so the owner is not central to the business; develop a strong backup manager.
Employ additional high-yielding capital	Improve investment decisions Decrease capital base	Invest only in positive NPV/EV projects. Implement product line profitability capabilities to determine winners and losers; withdraw or liquidate underperforming businesses.

INCREASE RECAST EBITDA

Increasing recast EBITDA is of primary importance since this is the metric that most directly affects IBV. Owners can increase sales through internal or external growth or through a combination of the two. In either case, capital is a constraint. Aggressive owners are constantly in search of acquisition opportunities that are accretive and self-financing. This means that consolidation math works in their favor, particularly with a deal structure requiring little or no out-of-pocket cash.

Owners who focus on maximizing their company's gross margins often unlock substantial value. By definition, this means minimizing cost of goods sold. The best investment most owners can make is upgrading the company's purchasing function. Professional materials management pays for itself many times over and helps create value. Companies can benefit greatly from installing cutting-edge inventory management and other throughput management systems.

Finally, most medium-size companies can create IBV by better controlling operating expenses. Unfortunately, many of these companies do not maintain a flexible budget or tie their budgets to longer-term planning. Professional managers, however, are obsessive about budgeting at the lowest possible level in the organization and then creating accountability for everyone involved. Ultimately, in most large companies, employee compensation is tied to success against the budget. This contrasts with many smaller private companies, which do not budget sales and expenses. Of course, always reacting to change is a management method that ensures that small companies remain small.

REDUCE RISK

IBV increases as a company reduces its operating and financial risk. An example of operating risk reduction is the ability to negotiate and implement long-term material purchase and sales contracts. Financial risk is reduced by meticulously decreasing a company's cost of capital.

Another risk-reducing attribute is the elimination of customer concentrations above 25% or so. Concentrations above 25% add risk to a company's financial prospects, which may serve to increase a company's cost of capital. Management concentration causes a similar increase in risk. Some owners are so central to the success of the business that it would take several additional people to replace them. This lack of management institutionalization not only has a negative recasting impact but also adds tremendous risk to an assessment. In either event, concentrations reduce IBV.

EMPLOY HIGH-YIELDING CAPITAL

Private managers should manage risk/return by implementing a disciplined capital allocation system. The payback method, an investment decision approach that considers the length of time it takes to recover the initial cost of a project, without regard to the time value of money, works well for projects that return the investment within a year or so; however, complicated projects require an NPV or IBV approach. Owning a company gets progressively easier and more profitable when assets are deployed correctly.

The single most glaring weakness for most medium-size companies is the lack of vision regarding product and service line profitability. Simply put, many companies do not know where they make money. Outsiders correctly view this lack of control as risky. Once again, companies that budget effectively typically do not have this problem. Proper financial controls enable companies to employ capital more effectively. A lack of these controls causes increased risk relative to the company's ability to achieve its financial goals. Increased risk translates to a lower valuation.

The key to creating value within the value worlds concept is to maximize the variables that determine value in a particular value world. These variables are determined by the authorities in a world. Thus, understanding the purpose for value creation is the proper starting point for the value discussion.

INCREMENTAL BUSINESS VALUE VERSUS MARKET VALUE

Exhibit 10.11 shows a variety of things owners can do to affect the IBV of their company. The question: Will the *market value* of a private company increase if it consistently invests in positive NPV and IBV projects? The answer: It should.

First, it is helpful to know if the market value of public companies expands with increases in IBV. In his classic book, *The Quest for Value*,[8] Stewart studies the IBV–market value relationship for 618 U.S. public companies. He states that positive EVA (the public company cousin of IBV) and market value correspond well with each other.[9]

In 1996, Lehn and Makhija studied 241 U.S. public companies and the correlation between EVA and market value. The researchers found a positive correlation higher than the correlation between traditional measures like return on assets (ROA), return on equity (ROE), and return on sales (ROS).[10]

Finally, in 1996 several researchers from Stern Stewart & Co. presented findings on the relationship between IBVA and market value for 100 bank-holding companies. They calculated regressions to five performance measures including earnings per share (EPS), net income, ROE, ROA, and EVA. The correlations between these performance measures and market value are: EVA, 40%; ROA, 13%; ROE, 10%; net income, 8%; and EPS, 6%. They used data from the ten-year period 1986 through 1995.[11]

But over the past 15 years academic research has not unilaterally established EVA's correlation to market value and stock returns. The evidence is mixed and has not resolved the debate over performance measures. The empirical results of one study, for instance, do not support the claims that EVA is a better financial tool than traditional accounting measurements in explaining market value. EVA did not significantly outperform traditional accounting measures in tests of relative information content.[12]

Should private companies expect to experience a positive financial impact with increases in their IBV? There are some direct ties from economic to market value. If a company increases its recast EBITDA substantially, market value should increase. Also, if a company reduces its long-term debt while still maintaining its benefit stream, the market value of shareholder equity is increased. Even if the owner never sells her business, an increase in IBV makes the company stronger and more profitable.

The correlation between IBV and market value for the private company is less than perfect, however. Both the company's industry segment and its desirability to competitors have a dramatic impact on its market value. For instance, if a company participates in an industry segment that does not pay operating goodwill for acquisitions, such as construction companies or machine shops, the company's management may create substantial IBV without a corresponding increase in market value. Yet IBV may understate market value. The synergy subworld of market value relies on increases in value relative to synergistic buyer types. This creation of synergies extends beyond the reach of IBV as measured by IBV. In such cases, IBV serves little purpose as it is designed to be an internal valuation metric. This does not mean that IBV has no market value use. Owner-managers find determining IBV useful because it is a *before-the-act* tool. This alone separates it from the other value worlds. While more work is needed to correlate a private company's market value with IBV, adopting an IBV framework for financial decision making is clearly beneficial to a private owner–managed company.

TRIANGULATION

IBV is an internal measure of value. Internal metrics are emerging techniques because they are dynamic, rather than static, value methods. In other words, managers can actively plan their activities based on a dynamic approach, as opposed to finding out what the value of the company was six months ago.

Incremental business value is a notional world. It is a value world whose validity is derived from the strength of its coherence to the logical structure established by an authority. As opposed to an empirical world, like market value, which is observed through market experience, or a regulated world, like fair market value, which gives the authority almost total control over value rules, notional worlds exist because an authority says so. The authority must prove its utility to potential participants. The academic community and management consulting industry are the authorities in the IBV world and constantly battle for the attention of their constituents.

Much like the other value worlds, access to capital affects incremental business value. A higher cost of capital increases a company's capital cost employed, which reduces IBV. Likewise, lowering cost of capital while maintaining the same benefit stream increases IBV. The most important connection between IBV and capital, however, is that productivity measures are applied to capital as rigorously as operating assets.

The effect of IBV on business transfer requires more study. Selling a premium business is often difficult because price expectations are so high by the shareholders. Also, an acquirer has to believe it can add value to a targeted business. Many buyers cannot justify paying a high price for a superior business because it is more likely that the target's financial performance will decrease rather than increase after the closing.

Companies that generate positive IBV should realize higher values in most of the value worlds. Like much of the IBV world, however, this area requires further study.

NOTES

1. Rob Slee, "Using the Incremental Business Value Model," *Valuation Strategies* (September 2010), pp. 20–25.

2. Peter Drucker, "Peter Drucker Takes the Long View," *Fortune* (September 1998).
3. IBVA is a registered trademark of Stern Stewart & Co.
4. David Neidell, "Shareholder Value as a Basis for Strategy," *Foresights Business Studies Journal*, Trinity College (2002).
5. The following metrics are registered trademarks: CFROI is a registered trademark of Boston Consulting Group and HOLT Value Associates. SVA is a registered trademark of LEK/Alcar Consulting Group. CVA is a registered trademark of Anelda AB.
6. Rob Slee and John Paglia, "Private Cost of Capital Model," *Value Examiner* (March 2010).
7. AICPA, Measuring and Managing Shareholder Value Creation, course offering.
8. G. Bennett Stewart, *The Quest for Value* (New York: HarperBusiness, 1991).
9. Esa Makelainen, "Economic Value Added as a Management Tool" (Helsinki School of Economics and Business Administration, 1998), p. 16.
10. Ibid.
11. Ibid.
12. Woo Gon Kim, "EVA and Traditional Accounting Measures: Which Metric Is a Better Predictor of Market Value of Hospitality Companies?" *Journal of Tourism and Hospitality Research* (2006): 30.

CHAPTER 11

Insurable Value

The world of insurable value considers the value of a business or business interest to be covered by insurance.[1] Business insurance is required in a variety of circumstances. In the insurable world, as in other valuation worlds, a business interest should be valued using a process specific to this world. By better understanding how value is determined in the world of insurance value, owners are better prepared to purchase insurance to protect their businesses. Although numerous instances require valuation for insurance purposes, this chapter focuses on three main reasons:

1. To fund buy/sell agreements
2. To determine the proper amount of key person insurance
3. To value a claim in business interruption cases

This world has dual authorities. Insurance companies determine value in many circumstances, such as business interruption claims. The involved parties also may authorize valuation actions, such as the formation of buy/sell agreements. This world employs its own lexicon of terms, including "provisions," "triggers," and "yardsticks." Some terminology used in this world is similar to that of other value worlds. For example, many buy/sell agreements use *market value* terms to describe the valuation process. However, insurable value then deviates and employs a unique process to derive ultimate value. This world is mutually exclusive from the other value worlds because it must carve out processes specific to its goals. The value conclusions from this world have meaning specific to this world and may have very little applicability beyond it.

A snapshot of the key tenets of this world is provided in Exhibit 11.1.

RISK AND INSURANCE

Most medium-size business owners are deluged with ever more sophisticated insurance alternatives. Often it is difficult to judge how much insurance is appropriate. With proper valuation methodology, owners can treat purchasing insurance like purchasing any other business asset, without the fear of over- or

EXHIBIT 11.1   Longitude and Latitude: Insurable Value

Definition	The appropriate value sought in an insurable setting.
Purpose of appraisal	To derive a value that meets an insurable need, such as funding a buy/sell agreement or business interruption claim.
Function of appraisal	To help an owner plan for the likely value of a business interest in an insured setting.
Quadrant	Empirical regulated for insurance companies. Empirical unregulated regarding the involved parties in a noninsurance setting.
Authority	Insurance companies and involved parties. Both authorities are located in the private capital markets.
Benefit stream	Defined by the authority specific to the circumstances.
Private return expectation	The expected rates of return that the private capital markets require in order to attract funds to a particular investment. In the insurable value world, this return is often specific to the shareholder.
Valuation process summary	The suitable valuation process usually is determined by the insurable event. For buy/sell agreements, value is derived by whatever process the involved parties deem appropriate. For business interruption claims, value is determined using a lost profits analysis, although no set methodology applies to all cases.

PrivateCo Example

Stream	×	Example Multiple	= Insurable Value
$1,400,000	×	5.0	= $7,000,000
	less LTD*		$500,000
	Final Value		= $6,500,000

*Assumes debt-free analysis

underinsuring. Owners of private companies have several goals in managing risk in their companies:

- Lessen their personal investment risk in the company by reducing the cost of capital
- Diminish operating risk
- Help control risk so that it is more likely for the return to exceed the riskiness of the investment
- Protect the company's ability to generate returns

Business insurance protects the company by reducing both owner's and investor's perception of risk. Investor's perception of achieving specific returns determines the cost of available capital. Controlling risk controls not only cost of capital but may impact capital availability as well.

Also, business insurance assists business owners in planning for liquidity to themselves and their families. Liquidity becomes increasingly important with age as often significant portions of business owners' net worth is represented by an illiquid business ownership interest. Insurance also assists the business entity with solvency concerns in the event of some type of loss. Business entities must attempt to protect and insulate as much as possible the day-to-day operations from extraordinary events.

BUY/SELL AGREEMENTS

Planning for the continuity of the enterprise is a critical task for every owner-manager. Buy/sell agreements are one tool used to achieve this goal. A buy/sell agreement is a binding contract between the various owners that controls when an owner can sell an interest, to whom, and for how much. The primary purposes of these agreements are to:

- Provide for transition while continuing to operate the business.
- Provide liquidity and create a market to sell a business interest.
- Determine the "triggering events" that will activate the buy/sell.
- Establish a price, or pricing formula, for the business interest.
- Protect against unwanted new partners.
- Provide dispute resolution procedures prior to such events occurring.
- Determine payment terms once the buy/sell is triggered.

A well-constructed buy/sell is similar to a premarital agreement because it is uncertain when one of the partners will want to leave the company. Every business with multiple owners should have a buy/sell agreement in force. A decision hierarchy can be used to construct a buy/sell agreement properly. Exhibit 11.2 shows this process.

As this hierarchy depicts, the type of buy/sell is chosen before decisions are made regarding the buy/sell provisions. Provisions are negotiated between the parties to reflect participant's intentions. As a practical matter, the provisions should be reviewed periodically to ensure that the original provisions currently reflect the intentions of the parties relative to the business. Valuation mechanics are then constructed to support the provisions. Finally, buy/sell triggering events are defined, which may influence the appropriate funding technique.

The type, provisions, and funding techniques descriptions of buy/sell agreements are discussed in detail in Chapter 31. Only the valuation and triggering events part of the hierarchy is discussed in this chapter.

EXHIBIT 11.2   Buy/Sell Decision Hierarchy

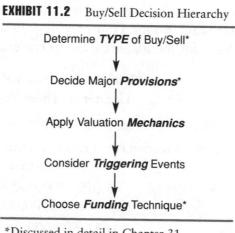

Determine **TYPE** of Buy/Sell*

↓

Decide Major **Provisions***

↓

Apply Valuation **Mechanics**

↓

Consider **Triggering** Events

↓

Choose **Funding** Technique*

*Discussed in detail in Chapter 31.

VALUATION MECHANICS

The valuation process is a key element in the buy/sell agreement. Because this is an unregulated world, parties have wide latitude to choose a valuation process. It may help the process to include a business appraiser in the discussions who is experienced in these matters. Most price-setting mechanics in these agreements employ one of three methods:

1. Negotiation between the parties
2. Formulas
3. Outside appraisal

Negotiation

Many buy/sell agreements contain provisions defining a process by which an ultimate price could be determined for the shares in question. In the absence of such a provision, negotiation between the parties is generally the best way to set a price. Current owners understand the risk of the investment and future prospects of their company better than anyone. Many companies set the buy/sell share price at the annual meeting and fix this price for the coming year. If no consensus is reached at the meeting, then another method is used to set the price, such as a formula or outside appraisal.

Formula

A formulaic approach may be used to value interests in a buy/sell agreement. A common method is to use the book value, or net asset value, of the company. This is unfortunate, since book value is generally not a surrogate for market value of most companies. Net asset value may be appropriate for distressed small companies or companies with exceptionally high asset value.

One approach gaining popularity is to employ a series of price-setting methods and use the highest derived value. One formula might be asset based, such as the net asset value at the time of the triggering event. Another formula might be income based, such as capitalizing the company's earnings before taxes. This method requires some up-front agreement by the parties on the definition of pretax earnings and the capitalization rate or selling multiple to be used. Finally, insurance might be in force for the triggering event. For example, assume for PrivateCo:

PrivateCo Buy/Sell Valuation
Greater of Three Values

Net asset value = $2,400,000 (from Chapter 5)

Capitalized earnings formula = (Pretax earnings avg last 3 years × 5)
  − Long-term debt at time of trigger

$$= (((\$1,500,000 + \$1,068,000 + \$1,650,000)/3) \times 5) - \$500,000$$

$$= \$6,500,000 \text{ (as rounded)}$$

Insurance in force = $2,000,000

In this example, the highest value of $5.5 million is derived using the capitalization of pretax earnings method. The pretax earnings average over the past three year-ends, using data for PrivateCo from Chapter 6, is $1.4 million, and is applied against a multiple, in this case 5. PrivateCo has long-term debt of $500,000 at the time of the triggering event. This is subtracted from the capitalized pretax earnings to reflect a debt-free value. It is preferable to select an earnings base that is an average of several years' results rather than a single period. The pretax earnings might also be adjusted for controlling owner compensation. The multiplier should be appropriate to the company in question. For example, some branded technology-based companies might be better suited with a 10 multiple, or higher. The deal databases introduced in Chapter 6 can assist in this selection.

The *insurance in force* assumes the triggering event, such as death of an owner, is covered by $2 million worth of insurance. If an insurable triggering event occurs valued beyond $2 million, the company must make up the difference between the required payout and the insurance coverage in effect. Normally the buy/sell establishes a note for a multiyear period so the company is not debilitated. This fact once again points to the need to maintain a proper level of insurance.

There are several advantages in employing a greater-of-several-methods approach to valuing a buy/sell agreement. First, the parties agree on the formulas at the buy/sell formation. This enables advance planning, which is always important when insurance is concerned. Second, since only the "greatest" valuation number is chosen, no party should feel as if it has been treated unfairly. Finally, the parties can engineer this approach to include methods they believe best fit the circumstances. For instance, if net asset value is considered too low to include in the mix, the parties may opt for a multiple of net asset value or some other measure that better suits the circumstances.

Outside Appraisal

An outside appraisal may be used to determine the price of the stock in question. Of course, the proper value world needs to be stated in the agreement. All instructions to the appraiser should be written. This is important since the buy/sell may stipulate how the stock is to be valued: as a minority interest; as a pro rata share of the enterprise value with no discounts, or at a percentage of the pro rata value. (See Exhibit 4.6 for a discussion on this topic.) The valuation is performed using an independent appraisal process. An outside appraisal agreement usually provides the appraisal is subject to agreement when it is updated. Appraisers are then brought in only if the owners have allowed the mutually agreed valuation to fall out of date. O'Neal and Thompson provide these guidelines regarding the selection of appraisers in a buy/sell:

> *If the price of shares is to be fixed by appraisal, the names of the appraisers or a method of choosing them must be specified; and a statement should be made that the decision of a majority of the appraisers will be binding. . . . A typical appraisal provision states that the optionee or purchaser, as the case may be, shall select one appraiser, the offeror or vendor a second, and that the two appraisers shall*

choose a third. . . . *Occasionally an independent third party, such as a corporate fiduciary, is given the power to appoint the third appraiser; or the third appraiser is designated by office.* . . . *Sometimes the appraisers are selected in advance and designated by name.* . . . *If that is done, provision must be made for a method of appointing substitutes should the designated appraisers die, become incapacitated, or refuse to serve.*[2]

Although O'Neal and Thompson do not say it, only certified business appraisers should qualify for the pool. All of the certifying bodies require their certified appraisers to take an oath of independence; therefore, no certified appraiser can advocate a client's position, only his or her own. Noncertified appraisers are free to take sides without fear of any governing oversight. This appraisal approach can be very expensive to implement, involving tens of thousands of dollars. To minimize costs, the parties to the agreement should be explicit in their instructions to the appraisers, identifying which standard of value and what premise of value will be used.

TRIGGERING EVENTS

The drafting of the buy/sell agreement is often on friendly terms. When certain triggering events occur, however, the interests of the parties involved often diverge and may become adversarial. A buy/sell agreement might sit idle for years until a triggering event occurs. There are a variety of triggering events that activate the buy/sell, some of which are listed in Exhibit 11.3.

Other than death, these events need some further explanation. Typically someone is deemed to be disabled on a long-term basis according to the definition used in the disability insurance contract in force at the time of the disabling event. A typical disability insurance policy pays as long as the insured cannot perform the material duties of any occupation for which he is suited by training, education, or experience for some continuous period of time, say six months. For example, if a night stockperson in a grocery store suffers injuries preventing him from performing that function, he will collect disability payments only if he takes a position at less than 60% (this varies) of his predisability income within 12 months of returning to work. This is called the "any occupation" definition, and many policies have provisions limiting payments in a variety of ways. In many cases, legal advice is necessary to create a disability definition appropriate to the user's circumstances.

EXHIBIT 11.3   Possible Buy/Sell Triggering Events

1. Death
2. Long-term disability
3. Voluntary termination
4. Involuntary termination
5. Third-party actions, such as personal bankruptcy or divorce

An insurance policy that covers individuals who become disabled and are unable to perform the majority of the occupational duties that they have been trained to perform are called "own-occupation." This type of insurance policy is contingent on the individual being employed at the time the disability occurs. Persons not working at the time of disablement will not be able to claim insurance under an own-occupation policy, but they will if they are covered under a modified own-occupational policy. Under a modified policy, the definition of "disabled" includes persons not working at the time of their disablement. These types of insurance policies apply to highly trained individuals, such as surgeons. Because the definition on own-occupation is very flexible, persons covered under an own-occupation policy may find another job and still receive full benefit payments.

Retirement with notice means that a retiring shareholder gives at least 12 months' notice. This much notice should be adequate time to find a replacement without doing damage to the company.

In a voluntary termination, the employee-owner decides to quit or retire based on individual free will. In any case, the company's board of directors may vote to purchase the shares of the exiting employee. The ownership agreement of the company controls the latitude of the board regarding this purchase option.

In the case of an involuntary termination, the owner, who is also an employee, is terminated against her will. This termination can be for "cause," meaning the owner violated her employment agreement, or "at will," meaning the employee was terminated without a specific reason. In either event, the ex-employee also becomes an ex-owner. This makes business sense because the employee probably became an owner due to efforts while an employee and once these contributions cease, all attachments to the company also cease.

Third-party actions, such as a personal bankruptcy or divorce, may also trigger a buy/sell action. Most company owners do not wish to have outsiders as owners; this trigger protects them and the company against those events. Once again, it is typical for the board to vote whether to call the shares, and the tenets of the ownership agreement help guide the decision.

Triggering actions are also important because they may help determine value for the shares. For instance, when an employee-owner decides to quit without notice, thereby triggering the buy/sell, should he receive full value for his shares? Many companies link the triggering event with total value received as well as payment terms. Here is one method for handling this issue. Assume a 10% owner triggers PrivateCo's buy/sell and the "greater of three methods" approach calls for an $6.5 million enterprise valuation. The valuation in each triggering event could be:

PrivateCo Buy/Sell Valuation

Event	Discount	Value
Death	No discount to pro rata value	$650,000 ($6.5MM × 10%)
Disability	Same valuation as death	$650,000
Retirement with notice	Same valuation as death	$650,000
Voluntary termination	35% discount to pro rata value	$422,500 ($650k × (1 − 35%))
Involuntary termination	50% discount to pro rata value	$325,000 ($650k × (1 − 50%))
Third-party action	Same as involuntary termination	$325,000

By linking discounts with some of the triggering actions, PrivateCo is attempting to penalize actions not in the company's best interest. Notice that there are no discounts associated with an owner's death or disability. A voluntary termination triggers a 35% discount, with the thought that someone should not be able to walk off the job and receive full value. In this example, involuntary termination receives a 50% discount because it is assumed that the owner has violated a major covenant of an agreement or this trigger would not occur. Finally, for this example, third-party actions are treated as involuntary terminations for valuation purposes.

PrivateCo's ownership agreement might contain a great deal of flexibility regarding the discounting issue. For instance, the agreement might let uninvolved owners decide the level of discount in the triggering events rather than enforce a hard-and-fast rule. Life insurance payable to the company also provides business continuity in case of the loss of a key person, which is covered next.

KEY PERSON INSURANCE

A key person insurance policy may be taken out on any employee whose contribution is considered uniquely valuable to the company. Most business failures occur because of management weakness or the loss of a key person. Although key person insurance will not replace a key manager, it gives the business financial flexibility as it deals with the loss. Valuing a key employee is difficult. Companies usually cover this need only for the owner-manager, and this typically is tied to life insurance without much thought to the quantification of the key person loss.

Key person insurance may serve five purposes.

1. Funds may be used to identify, attract, and train a replacement employee.
2. Funds may be used to redeem the stock that was owned by a deceased shareholder.
3. Insurance money may be used to fulfill contractual obligations to continue to provide a portion of a deceased employee's salary to family for a period of time.
4. Funds may maintain the stability of the stock price in the case no funds are available to purchase the deceased employee's shares.
5. Insurance funds may be used as a mitigation tool to comfort creditors and shareholders.

Three different methods are presented to help shareholders estimate the worth of an employee to the company:

1. Multiple compensation method
2. Contribution to profits method
3. Cost of replacement method

Multiple Compensation Method

The multiple compensation method is the simplest method of calculating the value of a key person. It assumes an employee's value is accurately reflected in his or her total compensation. Many companies multiply the total compensation by the number of years it takes to train someone to step into the role of the lost person. For example, if a key person was making $150,000, and it will take three years to hire and train a replacement, the proper amount of key person insurance is $450,000.

Contribution to Profits Method

This method estimates the impact an employee has on the company's profit. The company calculates the expected profit and considers excess profit as the result of key employees. The percentage of profit attributable to each key employee is estimated and then multiplied by the number of years it will take to hire and train a replacement.

This method works best when used to measure the value of key salespeople. For example, if a salesperson had a special relationship with a customer and was generating $1 million in business that generated a $200,000 profit, it might take two years to replace this individual. In this case, $400,000 of key person insurance is appropriate.

Cost of Replacement Method

The cost of replacement method calculates the direct costs required to interview, hire, and train a replacement. It also includes an estimate of opportunity costs due to the loss of the key employee. For example, assume a headhunting firm will be hired at a cost of $50,000 to help fill a key executive job. Training will take several months and cost $35,000. Finally, the company will be without this key executive for the three-month training period, at a cost of $50,000. In total, it will cost the company about $135,000 to replace the key person.

Many businesses use permanent life insurance to fund key person needs. These policies build cash value that appears as an asset on the company's books. Often the cash value is used to fund benefit plans for the owner or key individual in the event there is no death prior to retirement.[3]

Term insurance is an alternative life insurance product. While less expensive than permanent insurance, most companies use this only for short-term needs, such as an employee hired to perform duties for a specific, short time period.

As with all life insurance, death proceeds are received income tax free. This can be highly attractive to a business, as the earnings of the key person would have been taxable. This after-tax element is already built into the valuation methods outlined earlier.

There are two other important points to consider:

1. Premiums are a nondeductible business expense. If the business is a C corporation, there is a possibility the death proceeds could be subject to the alternative minimum tax.
2. If the owner is the insured, the receipt of the insurance could increase the stock value for estate purposes.

Once the value of the key person is derived, a key person plan can be created in a variety of ways. The most common is corporate ownership. With corporate ownership insurance coverage, the company is the owner and beneficiary of the policy. To the extent there is excess coverage, the death proceeds provide corporate-paid salary continuation benefits to the surviving family. Alternatively, if death does not occur before retirement, the cash value can be used to fund a nonqualified deferred compensation plan.

A properly established key person plan ensures the continuity of the business. Another threat to every company is business interruption from some external event.

BUSINESS INTERRUPTION

Unexpected disruptions to normal business operations may occur, often without warning. These interruptions may result from many sources, including contract violations or torts committed against the business. Incidents of casualty may also cause business interruptions. Protections against business interruptions may cover either the loss of business earnings or the loss of income sustained and costs incurred to resume normal operations. Business interruption insurance protects the prospective earnings of the insured business.[4] It is also designed to do for the insured, in the event of a loss, what the business would have done for itself if an interruption in the operation of the business had not occurred. If the interrupting cause is insurable, coverage is triggered by the total or partial suspension of business operations due to the loss of use of business assets.

Once a possible claim arises, the insured must follow the procedures laid out in the coverage. Many insurers have adopted procedures defined in the Insurance Services Office (1990), which describe the steps required to make a claim. Steps involve things like notifying the police, taking reasonable steps to protect the property from further damage, and cooperating with the investigation.[5]

The first issue in any business interruption claim is to determine whether the insured's loss arises out of an interruption of its business. Most policies use the phrase "necessary suspension of operations" to describe this precondition to coverage.[6] While this language is ambiguous, according to Chesler and Anglim, the insured must establish these elements in order to trigger coverage: a necessary suspension of operations due to physical damage to covered property and caused by a covered cause of loss. These elements must form a *causal chain* in order to establish coverage under the policy. The insured cannot recover merely by establishing the existence of a suspension of operations, covered property damage, and covered cause of loss; rather, the insured must also prove the requisite causal relationships.[7]

The causal chain requires two distinct steps:

1. A covered event must cause property damage.
2. The property damage must cause an interruption.

If a covered event directly causes both an interruption of the insured's business and property damage, it is not covered because the property damage, not the covered event, must cause the interruption. This area of the law is sufficiently complex that readers should seek professional guidance. The remainder of the chapter assumes the insured qualifies for interruption insurance.

Loss of Income

In addition to establishing a suspension of operations, an insured must also show it has suffered an actual loss of income. It is not enough to show just a loss of sales or capabilities; rather, the insured must establish it would have earned profits without the suspension of its operations. Without this proof, there can be no recovery. This can lead to the problem of a money-losing business or an emerging yet unprofitable business to successfully claim a recovery. This lack of record keeping and profitability was problematic after the BP oil spill in 2010. Fishermen in the Gulf of Mexico could not prove they had operated profitably prior to the spill, which prevented standard insurance policies from paying. Key court cases have held the promise of profitability is not enough.[8] It is the insured's responsibility, through proper accounting, to prove they deserve to be compensated for a business interruption.

Valuing the Claim

In quantifying the claim, reasonable certainty must exist as to the amount of the lost profits or the loss of business value. The valuation must be reasonable and likely to occur, given the facts and circumstances of the business's operations. There is no predetermined method for deriving the actual loss of profits and business expenses covered by business interruption insurance. The selected method should consider several aspects, including history of profitability, the nature of the business, and probabilities for the future. A key consideration is the intention of the parties. For instance, if the insured had just landed a large customer and was in the process of investing to meet the new sales demand, there is reason to believe that the profitability of the company was about to increase.

Under a business interruption policy, the insured's books and accounting system are tools to help determine the loss. The policy may be either *valued*, in which case the value of the loss is agreed on in advance and fixed by the policy, or *open*, in which case the amount of any loss sustained is to be determined by competent proof.[9] It is also possible for a policy to be partially valued and partially open.

It should be noted that businesses have a duty to keep damages as low as possible rather than allowing them to compound with time. Causation (or proximate cause) must be proven. The interruption must be shown to be caused by the wrongful party's actions.

Lost Profits Analysis

Because of the peculiarities of this type of appraisal, a specialized area has developed in business valuation called lost profits analysis. It deals with commercial damages due to business interruption. Essentially, lost profits equals what the business would have made minus what the business did make. The next overview of lost profit analysis is taken from the viewpoint of the court system, which ultimately settles these disputes. The courts seem to prefer the before-and-after method over the yardstick approach, each of which is discussed next.

Before-and-After Method

The before-and-after method compares revenues and profits before and after the business interruption.[10] This method is heavily influenced by past performance of the business. It assumes data is available to construct a reliable forecast and that economic and industry conditions are similar during the loss period and the period prior to the loss.

Gaughan, a leading author in this area, claims that the plaintiff must exercise discipline in applying this method or the courts will not rule favorably. He cites the example of a lack of rigor on the plaintiff's behalf in the case of *Katskee v. Nevada Bob's Golf*.[11] In this case, a lessee sued a lessor for lost profits on sales of merchandise resulting from the failure of the lessor to allow the lessee the right to renew a lease. The expert assumed the location in question and the replacement location were the same in all relevant aspects except for their square footage. The court ruled against the plaintiff because the expert used oversimplistic assumptions and did not undertake a serious analysis of the possible differences in the plaintiff's market position.

Yardstick Approach

The yardstick approach involves a comparison with similar businesses to determine if there is a difference in the level of the plaintiff's performance after a business interruption. This method is used if there is an insufficient track record to apply the before-and-after method.[12]

Difficulties of comparing one business to another are discussed earlier in this book in a private-to-public comparison. For this reason, the yardstick approach is used mainly for new businesses.

Because of the complexities surrounding these valuation issues, readers are encouraged to seek a text dedicated to business interruption.[13]

Period of Restoration

Business interruption policies generally use the term "period of restoration" to describe the period during which the coverage is triggered.[14] The period of restoration is the reasonable amount of time it theoretically should take the insured to repair the damage and resume operations. This period is somewhat hypothetical, since it might not be the same as the actual amount of time that it takes the insured to resume its operations at the damaged site. For example, if an insured wants to rebuild a destroyed facility larger that it was before the casualty, the additional time to rebuild falls outside the period of restoration and is not covered.

Readers who require a more detailed understanding of the issues are urged to seek a professional in this field.

TRIANGULATION

Insurable value is a hybrid world. This world is in the empirical regulated quadrant when viewed from one authority, the insurance industry. Insurance policies can be purchased in a heavily regulated marketplace; premium costs and benefits are known. This world is empirical unregulated when viewed from the perspective of the other primary authority, involved parties. Within a buy/sell, provisions are set by the involved parties. In other words, value in this context is whatever the parties say it is.

Funding in this world may include life insurance, a cash purchase, a seller's note, or a combination. When certain triggering events occur, the buyer may want a low price while the seller may want a high price. Further, the buyer may want lenient terms including payments over a long time horizon and low interest rates. The seller may want aggressive terms including cash up front, payments over a short time horizon, high interest rates or collateral, and security from the buyer.

This world is directly tied to the capital leg of the triangle. Various funding mechanisms exist, such as self-insurance and pledges of outside assets. This chapter focuses mainly on insurance companies to fund insurable events. For example, the death or disability of covered shareholders causes a business valuation, which ultimately is funded by insurance proceeds. The company and involved parties capitalize shareholder buyouts. For example, if the triggering event involves an employee-shareholder termination, the company usually takes on the liability of purchasing the stock. Typically the buy/sell agreement stipulates how the shares are purchased, which normally involves a financing period. In any event, the purpose of this world is to ameliorate capital as a constraint.

Likewise, insurable value is linked to business transfer. In some cases, the insurable event interrupts a business to the point that an insurance company pays to the shareholders the total value of the business. Also, triggering events in a buy/sell lead directly to a transfer. Once again, parties' interests may diverge in the future, so it is important that plans are kept current and funding mechanisms are instituted to effect the transfer.

PrivateCo's value in this world is $6.5 million.

World	PrivateCo Value
Asset market value	$2.4 million
Collateral value	$2.5 million
Insurable value (buy/sell)	**$6.5 million**
Fair market value	$6.8 million
Investment value	$7.5 million
Impaired goodwill	$13.0 million
Financial market value	$13.7 million
Owner value	$15.8 million
Synergy market value	$16.6 million
Public value	$18.2 million

NOTES

1. This chapter does not cover valuation of specific assets for property and casualty insurance purposes due to the broad scope of that topic.
2. F. Hodge O'Neal and Robert B. Thompson, *O'Neal's Close Corporations*, 3rd ed. (St. Paul, MN: West Group, 1996), pp. 134–135.
3. Anthony J. Capobianco, "Insurance Helps Compensate for Key Person Loss," *Business Review* (October 1997).
4. Rick Hammond, "Underlying Principles of Business Interruption Insurance," 1999, http://library.findlaw.com/1999/Jun/1/127909.html.
5. Ibid., p. 3.
6. Robert D. Chesler and Alexander J. Anglim, "Essentials of Business Interruption Insurance Law," *Mealey's Litigation Report* (December 2001): 18.
7. Ibid.
8. The most often cited case involves *Dictiomatic, Inc. v. United States Fidelity & Guaranty Co.*, 958 F. Supp., 594 (S.D. Fla. 1997).
9. Hammond, "Underlying Principles of Business Interruption Insurance," p. 4.
10. Patrick A. Gaughan, *Measuring Commercial Damages* (New York: John Wiley & Sons, 1999), p. 39.
11. Ibid., p. 40.
12. Ibid., p. 41.
13. The Gaughan text cited in note 10 is considered a good text on this subject.
14. Chesler and Anglim, "Essentials of Business Interruption Insurance Law," p. 20.

CHAPTER 12

FASB Value Worlds

The Financial Accounting Standards Board (FASB) is a private, not-for-profit organization whose primary purpose is to develop generally accepted accounting principles (GAAP) within the United States in the public's interest. The FASB, acting as an authority, has created a number of value worlds in the past few years, several of which are described in this chapter.

Specifically, this chapter discusses fair value, which gives guidance for post-transaction financial reporting compliance. The goal of the FASB's framework is to eliminate the inconsistencies between balance sheet (historical cost) numbers and income statement (fair value) numbers. Further, the fair value of the target company's identifiable assets and goodwill is reflected on the acquiring company's balance sheet. The fair value ultimately impacts the company's reported earnings in subsequent periods due to amortization of certain identifiable intangible assets.

FASB FAIR VALUE (ASC 820, FORMERLY FAS 157)

During the last decade, the use of fair value measurements in financial reporting has increased. In 2006, the FASB issued Financial Accounting Standard (FAS) 157 to provide a framework for how companies should measure fair value and sets out the required disclosures when GAAP requires the use of fair value. Note that the FASB is using the term "fair value" here, even though "fair value," the subject of Chapter 9, has been used to describe minority dissent and oppression cases for decades. Companies began using FASB's framework for nonfinancial assets and nonfinancial liabilities for the first time in 2009. Also in 2009, the FASB proposed, and in some cases finalized, additional guidance and disclosures relating to fair value measurements. This guidance was codified as Accounting Standards Codification (ASC) 820.

In accounting, fair value is used as an estimate of the market value of an asset (or liability) for which a market price cannot be determined (usually because there is no established market for the asset). Under GAAP (FAS 157), fair value is the amount at which the asset could be sold or the liability could be transferred in a hypothetical transaction between willing parties, or transferred to an equivalent party, other than in a liquidation sale. Note that the definition focuses on the exit price rather than the entry price. This is used for assets whose carrying value is based on mark-to-market valuations; for assets carried at historical cost, the fair value of the asset is not used. One example of where fair value is an issue is a restaurant with a cost of $2 million that was built five years ago. If the owners wanted to put a fair value measurement on the restaurant, it would be a subjective estimate because there is no active market for such items or items similar to this one. In another example, if ABC Corporation purchased a two-acre tract of land in 1980 for $1 million, then a historical-cost financial statement would still record the land at $1 million on ABC's balance sheet. If XYZ purchased a similar two-acre tract of land in 2005 for $2 million, then XYZ would report an asset of $2 million on its balance sheet. Even if the two pieces of land were virtually identical, ABC would report an asset with one-half the value of XYZ's land; historical cost is unable to identify that the two items are similar. This problem is compounded when numerous assets and liabilities are reported at historical cost, leading to a balance sheet that may be greatly undervalued. If, however, ABC and XYZ reported financial information using fair value accounting, then both would report an asset of $2 million. The fair value balance sheet provides information for investors who are interested in the current value of assets and liabilities, not the historical cost.

Exhibit 12.1 provides a snapshot of the key tenets of FASB fair value.

FAS 157 provides a framework for measuring fair value. This structure is described in five steps:

1. Determine unit of account.
2. Determine potential markets based on the highest and best use.
3. Determine markets for basis of valuation.
4. Apply the appropriate valuation technique(s).
5. Determine fair value.

EXHIBIT 12.1   Longitude and Latitude: FASB Fair Value

Definition	The price received to sell an asset or the price paid to transfer a liability in a transaction taking place in an active market.
Purpose of appraisal	To determine the fair value of a company's assets or liabilities, as described by FAS 157.
Function of appraisal	To determine the price that would be received to sell the asset or transfer the liability at the measurement date (an exit price).
Quadrant	Notional regulated.
Authority	FASB.
Benefit stream	Determined on a case-by-case basis.
Private return expectation	Determined on a case-by-case basis.
Valuation process summary	Valuation technique follows three broad levels of inputs (Level 1 being the highest priority).
	Level 1: Observable inputs that reflect quoted prices (unadjusted) for identical assets or liabilities in active markets (e.g., price × quantity).
	Level 2: Inputs other than quoted prices included in Level 1 that are observable for the asset or liability, whether directly or indirectly.
	Level 3: Unobservable inputs (i.e., a reporting entity's own data, financial projections, or when a financial model is relied on).

Step 1: Determine Unit of Account

The reporting entity must first determine the unit of account (i.e., what is being measured). Fair value is measured for a particular asset or liability and, thus, should incorporate its specific characteristics, such as condition, location, and restrictions, if any, on sale or use as of the measurement date.

Step 2: Determine Potential Markets Based on the Highest and Best Use

After determining the unit of account, the reporting entity must assess the highest and best use for the asset, based on the perspective of market participants. In accordance with FAS 157, paragraph 12, the fair value of an asset is based on the use of the asset by market participants that would maximize its value. The highest and best use for an asset must be determined based on the perspective of market participants, even if the reporting entity intends a different use.

Consideration of the highest and best use for an asset is an integral part of the identification of potential markets where the asset can be sold and establishes the valuation premise. The valuation premise may be either in use or in exchange.

Liabilities are valued based on the transfer of the liability to a market participant on the measurement date. However, reporting entities must still consider potential markets for the transfer of the liability.

Step 3: Determine Markets for Basis of Valuation

Once a reporting entity has considered potential markets, market participants, and the valuation premise, it must assess whether it has access to any potential markets. If access is available, a reporting entity must consider these points:

- *Is there a principal market for the asset or liability?* In accordance with FAS 157, paragraph 8, the principal market is the market in which the reporting entity would sell the asset or transfer the liability with the greatest volume and level of activity for the asset or liability. If there is a principal market, the fair value measurement represents the price in that market, even if the price in another market is potentially more advantageous.

  Furthermore, based on this guidance, if the reporting entity does have a principal market, it will be able to expedite steps 2 and 3. The reporting entity cannot incorporate potentially more advantageous markets in its fair value measurements when it has a principal market.
- *What is the most advantageous market?* If the reporting entity does not have a principal market, it should determine the most advantageous market for sale of the asset or transfer of the liability. As part of this determination, a reporting entity may need to consider more than one potential market. In each potential market, the entity should evaluate whether the appropriate valuation premise is in use or in exchange. In some cases, a reporting entity will need to determine the value in multiple markets and may need to consider both

valuation premises in one or more markets, in order to determine the highest fair value.

The market determination should incorporate the appropriate valuation technique(s), as further described in step 4. The reporting entity will determine the most advantageous market using valuation technique(s) consistent with market participant assumptions in each of the potential markets. The market that results in the highest value for the asset or the lowest amount that would be paid to transfer the liability (after transaction costs) will represent the most advantageous market.

In the application of the framework, it is important to note that the determination of highest and best use and development of the fair value measurement are based on market participant assumptions. However, the determination of the principal or most advantageous market is determined from the perspective of the reporting entity itself based on its business model and market access.

If there are no potential markets for the asset or liability, the reporting entity must develop a hypothetical market based on the assumptions of potential market participants.

Step 4: Apply the Appropriate Valuation Technique(s)

FAS 157 emphasizes the use of market inputs in estimating the fair value for an asset or liability. Quoted prices, credit data, yield curve, and so forth are examples of market inputs described by FAS 157. Quoted prices are the most accurate measurement of fair value; however, many times an active market does not exist so other methods have to be used to estimate the fair value on an asset or liability. FAS 157 emphasizes that assumptions used to estimate fair value should be from the perspective of an unrelated market participant. This necessitates identification of the market in which the asset or liability trades. If more than one market is available, FAS 157 requires the use of the "most advantageous market." Both the price and costs to transact must be considered in determining which market is the most advantageous market.

The framework uses a fair value hierarchy to reflect the level of judgment involved in estimating fair values. The hierarchy is broken down into three levels:

Level 1 Inputs. The preferred inputs to valuation efforts are quoted prices in active markets for identical assets or liabilities, with the caveat that the reporting entity must have access to that market. An example would be a stock trade on the New York Stock Exchange. Information at this level is based on direct observations of transactions involving the identical assets or liabilities being valued, not assumptions, and thus offers superior reliability. However, relatively few items, especially physical assets, actually trade in active markets. If available, a quoted market price in an active market for identical assets or liabilities should be used. To use this level, the entity must have access to an active market for the item being valued. In many circumstances, quoted market prices are unavailable. If a quoted market price is not available, preparers should make an estimate of fair value using the best information available in the circumstances. The resulting fair value estimate would then be classified in Level Two or Level Three.

Example inputs for Level 1 include: New York Stock Exchange prices for securities and New York Mercantile Exchange futures contract prices.

Level 2 Inputs. This is *valuation* based on *market observables*. The FASB acknowledged that active markets for identical assets and liabilities are relatively uncommon and that, even when they do exist, they may be too thin to provide reliable information. To deal with this shortage of direct data, the board provided a second level of inputs that can be applied in three situations. The first involves less active markets for identical assets and liabilities; this category is ranked lower because the market consensus about value may not be strong. The second arises when the owned assets and owed liabilities are similar to, but not the same as, those traded in a market. In this case, the reporting company has to make some assumptions about what the fair value of the reported items might be in a market. The third situation exists when no active or less active markets exist for similar assets and liabilities but some observable market data is sufficiently applicable to the reported items to allow the fair values to be estimated.

Example Level 2 inputs are posted or published clearing prices (if corroborated) and a dealer quote for a nonliquid security, provided the dealer is standing ready and able to transact.

Level 3 Inputs. The FASB describes Level 3 inputs as "unobservable." If inputs from Levels 1 and 2 are not available, the FASB acknowledges that fair value measures of many assets and liabilities are less precise. Within this level, fair value is also estimated using a valuation technique. However, significant assumptions or inputs used in the valuation technique are based on inputs that are *not* observable in the market and, therefore, necessitate the use of internal information. This category allows "for situations in which there is little, if any, market activity for the asset or liability at the measurement date." The FASB explains that "observable inputs" are gathered from sources other than the reporting company and that they are expected to reflect assumptions made by market participants.In contrast, "unobservable inputs" are not based on independent sources but on "the reporting entity's own assumptions about the assumptions market participants would use." The entity may rely on internal information only if the cost and effort to obtain external information is too high. In addition, financial instruments must have an input that is observable over the entire term of the instrument. While internal inputs are used, the objective remains the same: Estimate fair value using assumptions a third party would consider in estimating fair value. This method is also known as mark to management. Despite being "assumptions about assumptions," Level 3 inputs can provide useful information about fair values (and thus future cash flows) when they are generated legitimately and with best efforts, without any attempt to bias users' decisions.

Examples of Level 3 inputs are broker quotes that are indicative (i.e., not being transacted on) or not corroborated and models that incorporate management assumptions that cannot be corroborated with observable market data.

Step 5: Determine Fair Value

The outcome of the market determination and the application of valuation technique(s) will be a fair value measurement. To the extent that the valuation was applied to an asset that was valued in use, the total calculated value must be allocated to each unit of account in the asset grouping based on the specific facts and circumstances.

The FASB, after extensive discussions, has concluded that fair value is the most relevant measure for financial instruments. In its deliberations on Statement 133, the FASB revisited that issue and again renewed its commitment to eventually measuring all financial instruments at fair value.

BUSINESS COMBINATIONS (ASC 805, FORMERLY FAS 141R)

In December 2007, the FASB issued Statement of Financial Accounting Standards No. 141 (revised 2007), *Business Combinations*, (SFAS 141R), now codified in FASB ASC 805, which changes accounting and reporting requirement for business acquisitions. As part of the board's desire to align U.S. accounting practices with international financial reporting standards, FASB ASC 805 requires companies to measure certain contingent liabilities in a merger and acquisition transaction at fair value.

Goodwill is the excess of the purchase price of the acquired enterprise over the sum of the amounts assigned to identifiable assets acquired minus liabilities assumed. Intangible assets acquired in a business combination must be reported apart from goodwill in certain cases. This occurs if assets can be separated or divided from the entity and sold, transferred, licensed, rented, or exchanged. An intangible asset that cannot be sold, transferred, licensed, rented, or exchanged individually is considered separable if it can be sold, transferred, licensed, rented, or exchanged in combination with a related contract, asset, or liability (e.g., core deposit intangibles and the related deposit base) and arises from contractual or other legal rights. Intangible assets that meet the "separable" or "contractual-legal" criteria for recognition include:

- Marketing-related intangible assets, such as trademarks and trade names
- Customer-related intangible assets, such as customer lists and order backlogs
- Creative-type intangible assets, such as books, musical compositions, and photographs
- Contract-based intangible assets, such as licensing agreements, leases, and operating rights
- Technology-based intangible assets, such as patents, domain names, databases, and trade secrets

According to the FASB, the value of an assembled workforce of "at-will" employees acquired in a business combination should be included in the amount recorded as goodwill. "At-will employees" are those employees who are not subject to a contractual employment agreement.

Although goodwill intangibles with indefinite lives are not to be amortized, they must be tested for impairment annually at the reporting unit level. The new "reporting unit" concept refers to the level at which management reviews and assesses the performance of the operating segment. Goodwill-intangible assets are carried on the reporting unit's balance sheet. Nonpublic companies with only one legal entity need only one reporting unit.

FASB ASC 805 establishes these principles and requirements:

- With limited exceptions specified in the statement, an acquirer is required to recognize and measure in its financial statements the identifiable assets acquired, the liabilities assumed, and any noncontrolling interest in the acquiree, measured at their fair values as of the acquisition date. This replaces the original Statement 141's cost allocation method, which resulted not only in not recognizing some assets and liabilities but also in measuring some assets and liabilities at amounts other than their fair values at the acquisition date.

- An acquirer in a business combination achieved in a series of purchases (a step acquisition) is required to recognize the identifiable assets and liabilities as well as the noncontrolling interest in the acquiree at the full amounts of their fair values (or other amounts determined in accordance with this statement), which results in recognizing the goodwill attributable to the noncontrolling interest in addition to that attributable to the acquirer, improving the completeness of the resulting information and making it more comparable across entities.

- An acquirer is required to recognize assets acquired and liabilities assumed arising from contractual contingencies as of the acquisition date, measured at their acquisition-date fair values. An acquirer is required to recognize assets or liabilities arising from all noncontractual contingencies as of the acquisition date, measured at their acquisition-date fair values, only if it is more likely than not that they meet the definition of an asset or a liability in FASB Concepts Statement No. 6, *Elements of Financial Statements*. If that criterion is not met at the acquisition date, the acquirer instead accounts for a noncontractual contingency in accordance with other applicable generally accepted accounting principles, including Statement 5, as appropriate.

- An acquirer is required to recognize and measure the goodwill acquired in the business combination or a gain from a bargain purchase. FASB ASC 805 defines a bargain purchase as a business combination in which the total acquisition-date fair value of the identifiable net assets acquired exceeds the fair value of the consideration transferred plus any noncontrolling interest in the acquiree, and it requires the acquirer to recognize that excess in earnings as a gain attributable to the acquirer. The original Statement 141 required that "negative goodwill" amount to be allocated as a pro rata reduction of the amounts that otherwise would have been assigned to particular assets acquired, and there was no immediate impact to the acquirer's income statement.

- To allow users of the financial statements to evaluate the nature and financial effects of the business combination, the acquirer is required to make certain specific disclosures or, if disclosure of any of the information is impracticable, the acquirer is required to disclose that fact and explain why the disclosure is impracticable.

FASB ASC 805 applies to all transactions or other events in which an entity obtains control of one or more businesses, including those sometimes referred to as "true mergers" or "mergers of equals" and combinations achieved without the transfer of consideration (e.g., by contract alone or through the lapse of minority veto rights). It applies to all business entities, including credit unions and other mutual entities that previously used the pooling-of-interests method of accounting for some business combinations. It does not apply to (a) the formation of a joint venture, (b) the acquisition of an asset or a group of assets that does not constitute a business, (c) a combination between entities or businesses under common control, and (d) a combination between not-for-profit organizations or the acquisition of a for-profit business by a not-for-profit organization.

FASB ASC 805 applies prospectively to business combinations for which the acquisition date is on or after the beginning of the first annual reporting period beginning on or after December 15, 2008.

IMPAIRED GOODWILL (ASC 350-20)

Pursuant to accounting rules under Accounting Standards Codification Subtopic 350-20-35-1, goodwill and certain intangibles are not amortized; rather, these assets must be tested periodically for impairment under ASC 350, *Intangible–Goodwill and Other*.

Under ASC 350, companies must test their goodwill for impairment at three different points in time. The first is the transitional test, which was required at the beginning of the fiscal year in which the statement was adopted. In general, the valuation methods used for the transitional test must be consistent with all subsequent impairment testing. The second type of impairment testing is the interim test, which is required if certain "trigger events" occur, such as adverse changes in the business climate or market that might negatively impact the value of a reporting unit. Finally, companies must also perform annual tests for impairment. However, upon meeting certain criteria, some firms may not require a quantitative annual test.

The goodwill impairment tests consist of two steps. The step 1 impairment test compares the fair value of a reporting unit to its carrying value. If the fair value exceeds carrying value, there is no goodwill impairment and the test is complete. If not, impairment is indicated, requiring a step 2 impairment test. The step 2 test, which is similar to an allocation of purchase price performed pursuant to ASC 805, quantifies the amount of goodwill impairment.

Other hurdles within ASC 350 must be addressed to properly apply these standards. First, companies may have to reclassify their operations into so-called reporting units. Next, intangible assets need to be properly classified and allocated among a company's various reporting units. Additionally, impairment tests of other tangible and intangible assets may need to be conducted prior to performing tests under ASC 350.

Under ASC 805, goodwill should be recognized initially as an asset in the financial statements and measured initially as any excess of the fair value of the acquired business over the fair value of the net identifiable assets acquired. Any acquired intangible assets that do not meet the criteria for recognition as a separate asset should be included in goodwill. ASC 350-20 addresses the subsequent accounting for goodwill, including the requirement that goodwill should not be amortized but should be tested for impairment, at least annually, at a level within the company referred to as the reporting unit. Goodwill cannot be tested for impairment at any level within the company other than the reporting unit level. ASC 350-20 outlines the methodology used to determine if goodwill has been impaired and to measure any loss resulting from an impairment.

In accordance with ASC 350-20, goodwill is tested for impairment at the reporting unit level on an annual basis or upon a triggering event. Impairment is the condition that exists when the carrying amount of goodwill exceeds its implied fair value.

A snapshot of the key tenets of the impaired goodwill world is provided in Exhibit 12.2.

Impairment Test

Instead of amortizing goodwill, the new rules call for it to be tested *at least* annually for impairment at the reporting unit level. There are circumstances where the impairment test may be required more than once per year, including:

- A significant adverse change in legal factors or in the business climate
- An adverse reaction or assessment by a regulator
- Unanticipated competition
- A loss of key personnel
- A more-likely-than-not expectation that a reporting unit or a significant portion of a reporting unit will be sold or otherwise disposed of

If a reporting unit experiences none of these special cases, the impairment test should be performed at the same time each year. The requirement for an annual impairment test does not require that the fair value of each reporting unit would have to be recomputed every year. Companies may carry forward a detailed determination of the fair value of a reporting unit from year to year if all of the criteria listed in Exhibit 12.3 are met.

Once companies complete the initial detailed valuations of reporting units, it may be possible to update those valuations periodically without incurring the cost of the original valuations.

EXHIBIT 12.2   Longitude and Latitude: Impaired Goodwill

Definition	The amount at which an asset (or liability) could be bought (or incurred) or sold (or settled) in a current transaction between willing parties, that is, other than in a forced or liquidation sale.
Purpose of appraisal	To determine the fair value of a company's goodwill-intangible value, as described by SFAS No. 142.
Function of appraisal	An acquiring company must test goodwill and intangible assets with indefinite lives for impairment annually at the reporting unit level.
Quadrant	Notional regulated.
Authority	The FASB and SEC, both of which are located outside of the private capital markets.
Economic benefit stream	Operating cash flow (EBITDA minus capital expenditures).
Private return expectation	Risk-free rate.
Valuation process summary	Fair value constitutes the amount at which an asset or liability could be bought or sold in a current transaction between willing parties. Several methods can be used to determine this amount, such as a comparison to quoted market prices of similar assets. If market transactions are not available, the FASB suggests making a value estimate based on "the best information available under the circumstances." This generally involves using probability-weighted discounted cash flow techniques and other fundamental analyses. The cost approach is generally considered as a last resort.

PrivateCo Example

PrivateCo operating cash flow of $1.951 MM is grown by 10%, 15%, and 20% per year for five years. Management believes the chance of each scenario's growth rate occurring is 25%, 50%, and 25%, respectively. A discount rate of 5% is used.

Long-term debt at the time of the valuation is $500,000 and must be accounted for in the appraisal.

Probability-weighted present value minus LTD
$$= \$13,452,000 - \$500,000$$
$$= \$13 \text{ million (as rounded)}$$

The impairment test calls for the following steps:

Step 1: Determine the Fair Value of the Reporting Unit   The fair value of the reporting unit's equity, including goodwill, is compared to its book value. If the fair value of equity exceeds its book value of equity, then no impairment is indicated and no further testing is required.

EXHIBIT 12.3   Fair Value Carry-Forward Criteria

1. The assets and liabilities that comprise the reporting unit have not changed significantly since the most recent fair value determination. In other words, there has not been a recent acquisition or reorganization of an entity's reporting structure.
2. The most recent fair value determination resulted in an amount that exceeded the carrying amount of the reporting unit by a substantial margin.
3. Based on an analysis of events that have occurred and circumstances that have changed since the most recent fair value determination, it is unlikely that a current fair value determination would be less than the current carrying amount of the reporting unit. There have been no adverse changes in the key assumptions or variables used in the previous fair value computation.

Step 2: Calculate the Implied Fair Value of Goodwill   Calculate the implied fair value of goodwill by deducting the fair value of all tangible and intangible net assets of the reporting unit from the fair value of the reporting unit (as determined in step 1). In this step, companies must allocate the fair value of the reporting unit to all of the reporting unit's assets and liabilities, which is akin to a hypothetical purchase price allocation. The remaining fair value of the reporting unit after assigning fair values to all of the reporting unit's assets and liabilities represents the implied fair value of goodwill for the reporting unit.

If fair value is less than the book value, the implied fair value of goodwill is compared to its book value. Impairment loss is recognized equal to the excess of the book value of goodwill and the implied fair value of the goodwill. This becomes the new carrying value of goodwill for that reporting unit, which will be used in future impairment tests.

There are two noteworthy items here.

1. Public *and* nonpublic companies that follow GAAP are required to complete the impairment test each year.
2. Intangible assets with *indefinite* lives should not be amortized until their lives are determined to be finite. Intangible assets with finite lives should be amortized over their useful lives.

VALUATION

Fair value measurement constitutes the amount at which a reporting unit could be sold in a current transaction between willing parties. An independent valuation professional should perform this appraisal and probably will rely on:

- *Comparison to quoted market prices (public companies only).* The FASB states that the best evidence of fair value is quoted market prices in an active market and should be used if available.
- *Prices for similar assets.* When quoted market prices are not available, which is the typical situation, the estimate of fair value should be based on the best information available, including prices for similar assets and liabilities and the results of other valuation techniques.
- *Other valuation techniques, such as multiples of earnings.* A valuation technique based on multiples of earnings or revenue or a similar performance measure may be used if that technique is consistent with the objective of measuring fair value. Use of multiples of earnings or revenue in determining the fair value of a reporting unit may be appropriate, for example, when the fair value of an entity that has comparable operations and economic characteristics is observable and the relevant multiples of the comparable entity is known. Conversely, use of multiples would be inappropriate in situations in which an entity's operations are not of a comparable nature, scope, or size as the reporting unit.

■ *Present value techniques, with a reliance on probability-weighted analysis.* The FASB believes present value is often the best available technique with which to estimate the fair value of a group of net assets (such as a reporting unit). If a present value technique is used to measure fair value, estimates of future cash flows used in that technique shall be consistent with the objective of measuring fair value. Cash flow estimates shall incorporate assumptions marketplace participants would use in their estimates of fair value. If that information is not available without undue cost and effort, any entity may use its own assumptions. Those cash flow estimates shall be based on reasonable and supportable assumptions and shall consider all available evidence. The weight given to the evidence shall be commensurate with the extent to which the evidence can be verified objectively. If a range is estimated for the amounts or timing of possible cash flows, the likelihood of possible outcomes shall be considered.

The FASB believes these six elements should be incorporated into the discounted cash flow model:

1. An estimate of the future cash flow or, in more complex cases, a series of future cash flows at different times
2. Expectations about possible variation in the amount or timing of those cash flows
3. The time value of money, represented by the risk-free rate of interest
4. The price for bearing the uncertainty inherent in the asset or liability
5. Unidentifiable factors, such as illiquidity and market imperfections
6. The effect of an entity's credit standing on liabilities

According to the FASB, estimated cash flows and interest rates should reflect the range of possible outcomes rather than the single most likely, minimum, or maximum possible amount.

As an example, assume PrivateCo needs to be valued using probability-weighted present value analysis. Three scenarios are analyzed:

1. PrivateCo's EBITDA less capital expenditures (operating cash flow) is expected to grow by 10% per year. Management believes this has a 25% chance of occurrence.
2. PrivateCo operating cash flow grows by 15% per year, with a 50% chance of occurrence.
3. PrivateCo's operating cash flow grows by 20% per year with a 25% chance of occurrence.

By using a 5% risk rate, the weighted present value can be derived as shown in the next example.

EXAMPLE

PrivateCo Fair Value ($000)

Scenario 1: 10% operating cash flow growth, with 5% discount rate, 25% chance

Period	Cash Flow	PV	Extension
1	$2,146	$2,044	$2,044
2	$2,361	$2,141	$4,185
3	$2,597	$2,243	$6,428
4	$2,856	$2,350	$8,778
5	$3,142	$2,462	$11,240

Scenario 2: 15% operating cash flow growth, with 5% discount rate, 50% chance

Period	Cash Flow	PV	Extension
1	$2,244	$2,137	$2,137
2	$2,580	$2,340	$4,477
3	$2,967	$2,563	$7,040
4	$3,412	$2,807	$9,847
5	$3,924	$3,075	$12,921

Scenario 3: 20% operating cash flow growth, with 5% discount rate, 25% chance

Period	Cash Flow	PV	Extension
1	$2,341	$2,230	$2,230
2	$2,809	$2,548	$4,778
3	$3,371	$2,912	$7,690
4	$4,046	$3,329	$11,019
5	$4,855	$3,804	$16,725

Summary of present values:

	PV	Probability	Extension
Scenario 1:	$11,240	25%	$2,810
Scenario 2:	$12,921	50%	$6,461
Scenario 3:	$16,725	25%	$4,181
Probability-weighted present value			$13,452

The probability-weighted expected present value of $13.452 million is higher than the most likely estimate ($12.921 million has a 50% probability of occurrence).

The FASB provides little additional guidance to determine fair value. The regulators are silent on whether companies would be expected to obtain outside appraisals in certain situations.

Example of Measuring Impairment

Step 1 of the impairment test requires determining the fair value of the reporting unit. The results of the fair value determination are then used in the comparison of the fair value to the carrying value, including goodwill, of the reporting unit.

EXAMPLE

At the time of the annual test, BigPrivateCo is a reporting unit with a book value of $20 million, including goodwill of $6 million. The fair value of BigPrivateCo has also been determined to be $15 million. Also assume that none of the recognized assets of BigPrivateCo other than goodwill is impaired.

Book value of BigPrivateCo, including goodwill	$20 million
Fair value of BigPrivateCo	$15 million

Because BigPrivateCo's book value is greater than its fair value, step 1 of the test is failed, and BigPrivateCo will have to complete step 2 in order to measure the impairment loss. If the book value, including goodwill, of BigPrivateCo had been $13, no further action would have been required.

Step 2 of the impairment test requires a calculation of the implied fair value of goodwill. The implied fair value of goodwill is calculated in the same manner as goodwill in a business combination. The allocation is performed as if the reporting unit had just been acquired and the fair value of the reporting unit was the purchase price.

EXAMPLE

BigPrivateCo, after failing step 1, has determined these values:

Fair value of BigPrivateCo	$15 million
Net fair value of BigPrivateCo's assets and liabilities including unrecognized intangible assets	$10 million
Implied fair value of goodwill	$ 5 million
Carrying value of goodwill	$ 6 million
Impairment loss to be recognized	$ (1) million

BigPrivateCo reflects an impairment loss of $1 million in operating income and the new carrying value of goodwill for BigPrivateCo is $5 million.

If BigPrivateCo's implied fair value of goodwill increases in the subsequent years, say from $5 million to $7 million, there will be no write-up of goodwill. Goodwill can be written down but not written up.

TRIANGULATION

The FASB does not emanate from the capital or transfer sides of the private capital markets. It regulates a market it does not call home. Unintended consequences often occur in these circumstances. Since it oversees U.S.-based accounting standards, the FASB's main control and sanctioning power is over accounting auditors. Presumably auditors will not sign off on an audit unless the goodwill impairment test is completed properly. Because it is in management's interest to limit the amount of actual goodwill write-offs, this becomes one more negotiating item between management and its auditors. Since fair valuation is more art than science, this situation has the potential for conflicts of interest between auditors and owner-managers.

The FASB is a creator of value worlds. This chapter highlights several new worlds. These worlds are notional, as they cannot be observed in the market-place. These worlds are also highly regulated, as they are whatever the FASB says they are. An interesting sidebar concerning the FASB's motives in creating these new statements is its desire to converge with international accounting standards already put in place by the International Accounting Standards Board (IASB). The FASB and IASB are working toward the creation of global accounting standards. Of course, this makes sense, given the trend toward globalization of trade.

FAS 157 is having a major impact on private companies and how they determine and report asset and liability values. This is especially true for private equity groups and other larger private companies that are could-be-public entities. Transparency is important to these companies, as financial audits are routine, and going public may be a goal. It is not totally clear what effect FAS 157 will have on private companies that never receive an accounting audit.

ASC 805 addresses how companies should account for merger and acquisition transactions for financial reporting purposes. The acquirer must follow the dictates of this statement in order to record the fair value of the assets and liabilities it acquires. As with the other FASB value worlds, the goal of this world is to provide more consistency and comparability between reporting entities.

ASC 350-20 describes the process of determining if the fair values of any assets on the financials may have dropped below their carrying value after the transaction is closed. When such a condition exists, the entity is subject to an impairment test. According to the example in this chapter, PrivateCo's fair value in this world is $13 million. This world is unusual in its relationship to the transfer side of the triangle. Prior transfers cause this world to exist. Impaired goodwill can exist only if a prior acquisition caused goodwill to form on the acquirer's balance sheet. ASC 350-20 may affect future acquisitions, however. Because goodwill is not recognized in asset sales, buyers of smaller, private companies have one more reason to acquire the assets of the target rather than its stock. With asset sales of C corporations, sellers may realize less money on the sale of their business because taxes are generally higher on asset sales than stock transactions.

Purchase price allocation has become more important since the implementation of Statements 805 and 350. The purchase price is allocated between the tangible assets, and the remainder is allocated to intangibles. The private buyer will want to allocate as much as possible to intangibles with finite lives so amortization is maximized. This helps create a noncash expense in the future and reduces income taxes.

World	PrivateCo Value
Asset market value	$2.4 million
Collateral value	$2.5 million
Insurable value (buy/sell)	$6.5 million
Fair market value	$6.8 million
Investment value	$7.5 million
Impaired goodwill	**$13.0 million**
Financial market value	$13.7 million
Owner value	$15.8 million
Synergy market value	$16.6 million
Public value	$18.2 million

Under ASC 350, the pricing of deals with a high level of intangibles should decrease in the future because of the risk of impairment write-downs. Market volatility plays a part here because there is no reversal of an impairment loss should the fair value subsequently recover.

A company's capital structure is affected by impaired goodwill. A write-off due to impairment decreases shareholder equity. A reduction in equity, while not a cash loss, may affect a company's covenant position with its lenders. Certain ratios, such as debt to equity, are changed as a result of a write-off. Some banks use a covenant break to change the fee structure of the loan, which adds expense to the borrower. Of course, a lower equity figure makes it more difficult for a borrower to secure adequate financing.

CHAPTER 13

Intangible Asset Value

Most value worlds are based on tangible assets and their benefit streams. In contrast, the world of intangible asset value is based entirely on assets that do not have a physical reality. Intangible assets comprise all the elements of a business enterprise that exist in addition to monetary and tangible assets. This world is based on human capital, information, technical know-how, customer relationships, branding, intellectual property (IP)—in short, the collective experience that adds value to a company. This emerging world has grown in influence because of the increasing relative importance of the factors it encompasses.

The concept of IP is not new in the United States. At the urging of Thomas Jefferson, language was adopted by the Constitutional Convention in 1787 designed "to promote the progress of science and the useful arts, by securing for limited times to authors and inventors the exclusive right to their respective writings and discoveries." This statement became part of Article 1 Section 8 in the U.S. Constitution. The history of economic progress is the story of combining intellectual creativity with the physical world to produce the economic necessities of life.

Today, it is not unusual to find an increasing chasm between the tangible asset value of a company and its overall enterprise value. Increasingly, intellectual assets are not adequately reflected on companies' balance sheets. According to generally accepted accounting principles (GAAP), purchased intellectual assets, along with all other acquired intangible assets, are recorded properly on balance sheets, but if those same assets are developed internally, they are not adequately noted. Assets with an identifiable benefit stream, such as patents, copyrights, logos, or trademarks, may be reflected on a balance sheet. Other intellectual capital (IC) with less objectively defined benefit streams, such as the knowledge and experience of a company's assembled workforce, are not reflected on the balance sheet. Knowledge assets generally are not reflected in financial statements and other forms of information available to decision makers.

A snapshot of the key tenets of the intangible asset world is provided in Exhibit 13.1.

Unlike the situation in other business eras, intellectual value drives the benefit streams of most modern companies. Historically, companies could dominate industries by controlling access to natural resources and by managing manufacturing operations efficiently. Today, many heavy manufacturing concerns struggle to survive. In order to thrive, some manufacturing companies have turned to intellectual

EXHIBIT 13.1   Longitude and Latitude: Intangible Asset Value

Definition	Nonphysical assets that grant rights, privileges, and have economic benefits for the owner. The intangible asset world breaks into two subworlds: intellectual property and intellectual capital. Intellectual property (IP) includes patents, trademarks, copyrights, and trade secrets. Intellectual capital (IC) equals the sum of human capital and structural capital.
Purpose of appraisal	To determine the intangible asset value of a company's IP or IC.
Function of appraisal	To derive the value of specific IP like a patent, for legal reasons, such as setting a royalty rate; or for market reasons, such as the possible sale of an intangible asset. IC appraisals tend to be oriented towards efficiency measures (i.e., to generate an indication of how well management is utilizing company assets).
Quadrant	IP: empirical regulated; IC: notional unregulated.
Authority	IP: federal government agencies such as the Patent Office plus certain laws, such as trademark laws.
	IC: academics, consultants, and certain companies that have implemented IC methods.
Economic benefit stream	IP: the stream that emanates from the particular property.
	IC: not stream oriented.
Private return expectation	IP: the expected return based on the riskiness of achieving the economic benefit stream.
	IC: return expectations are unclear due to a weak identification of EBS.
Valuation process summary	IP: Depending on the type of IP (patent versus trade secret, etc.), the cost, income, and market approaches may be appropriate for use. The appraiser determines what approaches are suitable.
	IC: Two main methods are employed. The scorecard method identifies various components of intellectual capital, which are scored and graphed. No estimate is made of the dollar value of the intangible assets. The direct intellectual capital method estimates the dollar value of intangible assets by directly identifying and valuing the various components.

value or know-how. Many newer companies develop products and services not based on natural resources or a heavy balance sheet. These "service" companies have a heavier reliance on intellectual capital. Distribution businesses, software businesses, and consulting and training companies may develop significant value with relatively "light" balance sheets. Competitive advantage is increasingly based more on what is known than on what is owned. Companies today operate knowledge factories that convert raw knowledge into scalable and repeatable processes that create value for their customers.[1]

IC is of growing importance to companies today, but how can it be measured in a responsible and equitable fashion? What, for example, is the useful life of an intangible asset? Is there an intrinsic useful life? Certain intangibles, such as software, could be used indefinitely because they do not wear out. Yet often they become obsolete in 18 months or less. How can such intellectual assets be measured precisely?

In the world of impaired goodwill, the subject of Chapter 12, the Financial Accounting Standards Board (FASB) statements addressing some problems of adjusting and assessing goodwill were outlined. Accounting Standards Codification (ASC) Topic 350 (formerly known as Statement No. 142) describes the accounting treatment of goodwill and other intangible assets. As opposed to amortizing goodwill over 40 years, this accounting principle does not allow for goodwill amortization. Instead, FASB requires an annual test for *goodwill impairment*. If goodwill carried on the balance sheet is worth more than its current "fair value," the difference must be written off. The FASB intends to use this framework for future statements on intangible valuation issues. This framework relies on market comparisons to draw value conclusions.

There is international recognition of the growing importance of intellectual capital. The Organization for Economic Co-operation and Development (OECD) and the International Accounting Standards (IAS) Committee are working on the central issue. They want to develop standards for recognizing expenditures as legitimate long-term investments in intangible value, which in turn creates assets. In order for a proper judgment to be made, an intangible asset must be clearly identifiable and separable from other assets of the company, such as goodwill. If these expenditures cannot be segregated properly on the balance sheet, they must be expensed as incurred. For example, research and development and brand development may be capitalized and depreciated on the balance sheet, or they may be expensed as incurred. It depends on how they are recognized. OECD and IAS have been working for a number of years on developing international standards for treating this complex issue.

The world of intangible asset value can be divided into two distinct areas. The first is the more traditional subworld of IP. The second, more recent and less well defined, is the emerging subworld of IC. The two areas differ from each other in a number of significant ways.

SUBWORLDS

The authority governing the world of IP is comprised of various government or quasi-governmental agencies, such as the U.S. Patent Office, plus certain laws, such as trademark laws. The authority in the subworld of IC is the academic and consulting industry as well as a few large firms.

For an intangible taking shape in the subworld of IC to cross the bridge into the subworld of IP, it must meet the rigorous standards prescribed in GAAP. Essentially, the intangible asset must be describable in language acceptable to the accounting authorities, and it must conform to the logic embedded in the system of accounting standards.

Terminology in the two subworlds may be similar, but it carries different meanings. For example, the term "intangible" obviously is used in both subworlds. However, intangible property is more substantial and recognizable in accordance with a strict set of standards, while the intellectual assets found in the subworld of IC have not passed the recognition tests required by the authorities.

The subworld of IP excludes by definition the intangible assets that populate the subworld of IC.

IC authorities strive to recognize the sources of value and improve productivity. There is an international effort to identify and describe the intangibles in this world so that they can be recognized in a replicable fashion and admitted into the

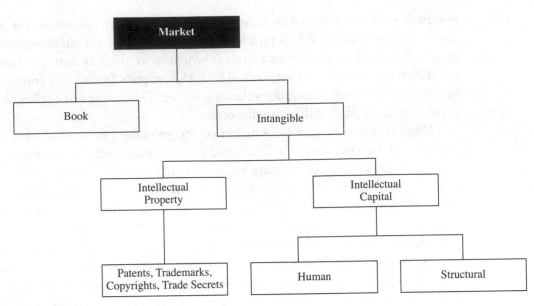

EXHIBIT 13.2   Value Scheme

subworld of IP. One of the weaknesses of the intangible property world is that no common language exists. As agreement on language develops, standards of practice become possible. Among the more interesting developments is Exhibit 13.2, adapted from a program started by the Skandia Company in the 1980s. It depicts the linkage between market value and the various types of capital.

In this schematic, market value equals the sum of a company's book value plus intangible assets. Intangible assets then become all other value of the company that is not identified on a company's financial statements. More precisely, intangible assets are comprised of IP and IC. IP includes patents, trademarks, copyrights, and trade secrets, with the latter item sometimes called *know-how* or *proprietary technology*. The components of IP are described in detail later in this chapter.

IC equals the sum of human capital and structural capital.[2] Bontis, a leading researcher in this field, defines human capital as "the combined knowledge, skill, innovativeness, and ability of the company's individual employees to meet the task at hand." It also includes the company's values, culture, and philosophy. The company cannot own human capital. Structural capital is the hardware, software, databases, organizational structure, and everything else of organizational capability that supports those employees' productivity.[3] In other words, structural capital is what gets left behind when the employees go home at night. Structural capital enables customer capital, which are the relationships developed with key customers. Unlike human capital, the company owns structural capital.

Valuing intangible assets is a difficult task. Yet measuring intangibles is an important exercise since they are becoming a larger part of many companies' value propositions. There are four categories for measuring intangibles on a general level.[4] The first two apply to the valuation of intangible assets in general; the final two apply to the measure of IC.

Intangible Assets Categories: General

The next methods derive the value of intangible assets in general.

- *Market capitalization methods (MCM).* The difference between a company's market capitalization and its stockholders' equity is calculated as the value of its IC or intangible assets.
- *Return on assets (ROA) methods.* The average pretax earnings of a company for a period of time are divided by the average tangible assets of the company. A company's ROA is then compared with its industry average. The difference is multiplied by the company's average tangible assets to calculate an average annual earnings from the intangibles. Dividing the above-average earnings by the company's average cost of capital or an interest rate, an estimate of the value of its intangible assets or IC is derived.

Intellectual Capital Categories

The next methods are used to value IC.

- *Scorecard (SC) methods.* The various components of intangible assets or IC are identified and indicators and indices are generated and reported in scorecards or as graphs. Scorecard methods are similar to direct IC methods, except that no estimate is made of the dollar value of the intangible assets. A composite index may or may not be produced.
- *Direct intellectual capital (DIC) methods.* The dollar value of intangible assets is estimated by identifying its various components. Once these components are identified, they can be directly evaluated, either individually or on a consolidated basis.

Within each category, a number of different methods exist. These methods enable the valuation of specific intangible assets. Exhibit 13.3 describes some of these methods with corresponding categories. There are advantages and disadvantages to methods offering dollar valuations, such as ROA and MCMs.[5]

Advantages of ROA and MCM Methods

- They are useful in merger and acquisition situations and for stock market valuations.
- They can also be used for comparisons between companies in the same industry.
- They are good for illustrating the financial value of intangible assets, a feature that tends to get the attention of chief executive officers.
- Because they build on long-established accounting rules, they are easily communicated in the accounting profession.

Disadvantages of ROA and MCM Methods

- By translating everything into monetary terms, they can be superficial.
- ROA methods are very sensitive to interest rate assumptions.

EXHIBIT 13.3   Sample Intangible Asset/Intellectual Capital Valuation Methods

Label	Major Proponent	Category/ Applies To	Description of Measure
Market-to-book value	Luthy (1998)	MCM (Intangibles)	The value of IC is considered to be the difference between the firm's stock market value and the company's book value.
Economic value added	Stewart (1997)	ROA (Intangibles)	Calculated by adjusting the firm's disclosed profit with charges related to intangibles. Changes in EVA provide an indication of whether the firm's IC is productive or not.
Skandia navigator	Edvinsson (1997)	SC (Intellectual capital)	IC is measured through the analysis of up to 164 metric measures (91 intellectually based and 73 traditional metrics) that cover five components: (1) financial; (2) customer; (3) process; (4) renewal and development; and (5) human.
Technology broker	Brooking (1996)	DIC (Intellectual capital)	Value of intellectual capital of a firm is assessed based on diagnostic analysis of a firm's response to twenty questions covering four major components of intellectual capital.

- Methods that measure only on the organization level are of limited use for management purposes below the board level.
- Several methods are of no use for nonprofit organizations, internal departments, and public sector organizations. This is particularly true of the MCMs.

Advantages and disadvantages of the direct IC and SC methods are listed next.

Advantages of Direct IC and SC Methods

- They can create a more comprehensive picture of an organization's health than financial metrics.
- They can be applied easily at any level of an organization.
- They measure closer to an event, so reporting can be faster and more accurate than pure financial measures.
- Since they do not need to measure in financial terms, they are useful for nonprofit organizations, internal departments, and public sector organizations as well as for environmental and social purposes.

Disadvantages of Direct IC and SC Methods

- The indicators are contextual and must be customized for each organization and each purpose, which makes comparisons very difficult.
- The methods are new and not readily accepted by accounting authorities and managers who are accustomed to seeing everything from a pure financial perspective.

INTELLECTUAL PROPERTY

The IP subworld is a more fully developed area of the world of intangible asset value. The term "intellectual property" refers to patents, trademarks, copyrights, and trade secrets[6] protected by law from unauthorized use by others. Each type of IP is defined as presented next.

- *Patents:* A patent is the grant of a property right by the U.S. government to the inventor by action of the Patent and Trademark Office.[7] The right conferred is a "negative right," in that it excludes others from making, using, or selling the invention.[8] There are numerous types of patents, with varying degrees of length of protection. Two of the major types are:

  1. *Utility patent.* This patent type is covered under Section 101 of the United States Code, which states: "Whoever invents or discovers any new and useful process, machine, manufacture or composition of matter, or any new and useful improvement thereof, may obtain a patent therefor." Utility patents have a term of 20 years from the date of filing the application.
  2. *Design patent.* "Whoever invents any new, original and ornamental design for an article of manufacture may obtain a patent therefor."[9] Design patents are issued for 14 years and protect only the appearance of an object, not its structural features.

- *Trademarks.* A trademark "includes any word, name, symbol or device or any combination thereof adopted and used by a manufacturer or merchant to identify his goods and distinguish them from those manufactured by others."[10] Registration under the Trademark Law Revision Act of 1988 continues for ten years and may be renewed for additional ten-year periods as long as the trademark is in use.

- *Copyright.* A copyright protects the expression of an idea, not the idea itself. Examples of copyrighted materials are literary works, musical works, motion pictures, sound recordings, and pictorial, graphic, and sculptural works. To be protected, the expression must be set to some tangible form. The copyright does not have to be registered with the Copyright Office to receive protection. Copyrights are protected for the life of the author plus 70 years.

- *Trade secrets.* There are a number of definitions for trade secrets, also called proprietary technology. One court decision defined trade secrets as "any information not generally known in the trade. It may be an unpatented invention, a formula, pattern, machine, process, customer list, or even news."[11] Trade secrets are governed by state laws, so the meaning and protection varies from jurisdiction to jurisdiction. Many trade secrets involve patentable inventions. The company may choose not to patent the secret in order to eliminate the need to educate the public regarding the secret. A trade secret does not have to be stated in tangible form to be protected.

Proprietary technology can take many forms. For proprietary technology to be classified as trade secrets, it must be used in the business, provide its owner with a competitive advantage, and be treated as a secret.[12] A few examples are listed next.

- Decision logic in computer software
- Formulas, recipes, methods of combination
- Technical experience captured in drawings, tooling, process designs
- Research and development information, such as laboratory logs and experimental designs
- Customer relationships
- Business knowledge—supplier lead times, names, alternate suppliers, cost and pricing data

Approaches to Valuation

There are three primary approaches for valuing IP: the cost approach, the market approach, and the income approach. Each approach has underlying methods that can be used to perform the valuation. Each of these approaches is especially well suited to certain types of IP. For instance, the cost approach is well suited for valuing copyrights as opposed to patents, which might be valued using a method within the income approach.

The *cost approach* calculates what it would cost another business to duplicate a given asset. More precisely, this approach seeks to measure the future benefits of ownership by quantifying the amount of money required to replace the future service capability of the subject property. Assets that can be valued using the cost approach include:

- Internal software
- Assembled workforce
- Customer relationships
- Corporate practices and procedures
- Distribution networks

For example, suppose PrivateCo owns a sophisticated, proprietary cost-estimating software system that took many years to create and is now central to the success of its business. No comparable off-the-shelf system is available for purchase. By using the cost approach, it is possible to measure what another company might need to spend to duplicate that cost-estimating package. In this way, PrivateCo would be able to establish a value for its own proprietary system.

The *income approach* measures, in today's dollars, the future benefits IP will bring to the holder. There are several methods underlying this approach: multiperiod excess earnings method, relief-from-royalty method, differential value method, profit split method, yield capitalization method, and direct capitalization method. The capitalization or discount rate used in this analysis should mirror the risk of achieving the income that is being capitalized or discounted. Assets that can be valued using this method are:

- Commercial software
- Brand names
- Copyrights
- Trademarks
- Patents
- Technology
- Favorable contracts
- Customer relationships
- Licenses and royalty agreements
- Employment agreements

Sometimes the income methods incorporate *savings to the holder* as part of, or in replacement for, the income stream. This savings feature occurs when a particular patent enables the holder *not* to pay a royalty. In such cases, the relief-from-royalty method is applied. For example, assume a company holds a patent that it is not currently using in its business. Another company might be able to use this patent in its core business, enabling it to discontinue the payment of a royalty to an outside holder. In this case, if the current royalty stream is $300,000 per year and the capitalization rate is 20%, the patent might be valued at $6 million.

The *market approach* is the most direct approach to value IP. This approach uses the measure of what others have paid for a comparable asset in an active public market. The sale of IP in the marketplace is completed most frequently as part of the sale of a company. While some of the purchase price may be allocated to intangible assets, it may not be directly applied to a particular IP asset. Occasionally IP is traded independently from the enterprise. Several examples are:

- Sale of Gloria Vanderbilt trademark by Murjani in 1988 for $15 million to Gitano
- Sale of the Hawaiian Punch brand from Procter & Gamble to Cadbury Schweppes PLC for a reported $203 million early in 1999
- Sale of the After Six trademark as part of bankruptcy liquidation for $7 million in 1993.
- Purchase of the Pet Smart logo for $10 million in 2002

As is the case with the guideline method, comparability is difficult to establish when comparing IP. Databases contain hundreds of IP sales. Using similar techniques to those found in the guideline method for determining enterprise value, it is possible to derive IP value using the market approach. The next assets can be valued using the market approach:

- Trademarks
- Impaired goodwill

- Patents
- Logos
- Brands

The next example illustrates a trade secret valuation.

EXAMPLE

PrivateCo has the opportunity to acquire a trade secret from CompetitorCo, which is converting one of its manufacturing lines to product lines not competitive with PrivateCo. The trade secret is the ability to run a production line at nearly twice the rate as PrivateCo, which runs a nearly identical line. Joe Mainstreet realizes the increased production capability will enhance PrivateCo's profits but is uncertain how to value such an opportunity. No tangible assets would be purchased since CompetitorCo keeps the equipment.

PrivateCo estimates it can save $3 million per year in manufacturing costs by implementing the trade secret. The market for PrivateCo's widgets is expected to decrease 20% per year for the next five years. Mainstreet believes PrivateCo's cost of capital for all new investments is 25%. How much can PrivateCo afford to pay for this secret?

If Joe Mainstreet is like every other red-blooded capitalist in America, he would try to figure out how to speed up his line without paying CompetitorCo. If this engineering attempt fails, he might consider making an offer for the trade secret.

PrivateCo receives the listed incremental savings from the acquisition:

Year	Savings	Present Value (25%)
1	$3,000,000	$2,400,000
2	$2,400,000	$1,500,000
3	$1,800,000	$900,000
4	$1,200,000	$500,000
5	$600,000	$200,000
	Total	$5,500,000 (as rounded)

PrivateCo could pay CompetitorCo $5.5 million for the trade secret and receive a 25% compounded return on its investment. In real life, Joe Mainstreet would offer $250,000 and be genuinely offended when CompetitorCo countered at $500,000.

INTELLECTUAL CAPITAL

The SC and direct IC categories of IC valuation are mentioned previously. The Skandia Navigator method is described in the SC methods category. Skandia is a pioneering company in the creation and use of IC measurement techniques. The

EXHIBIT 13.4   Sample of Skandia IC Measures

Financial focus	■ Revenues/employee ($) ■ Revenues from new customers/total revenue ($) ■ Profits resulting from new business operations ($)
Customer focus	■ Days spent visiting customers (#) ■ Ratio of sales contacts to sales closed (%) ■ Number of customers gained versus lost (%)
Process focus	■ PCs/employee (#) ■ IT capacity—CPU (#) ■ Processing time (#)
Renewal and development focus	■ Satisfied employee index (#) ■ Training expense/administrative expense (%) ■ Average age of patents (#)
Human focus	■ Managers with advanced degrees (%) ■ Annual turnover of staff (%)

Skandia report uses up to 91 new IC metrics plus 73 traditional metrics to measure the five areas of focus making up the Navigator model. Exhibit 13.4 summarizes some of these metrics.[13]

Scandia's Navigator uses 112 indices that offer direct counts, dollar amounts, percentages, and survey results. Navigator's five focus areas have 36 monetary measures that cross-reference each other. Skandia assigns no dollar value to its IC but uses proxy measures of IC to track trends in the assumed value.[14] The Navigator method is more of a management tool for assessing the effect of IC on the company, as opposed to a direct measurement technique. Because SC methods incorporate so many variables, they tend to be directionally accurate as measures of the overall value of IC.

The direct IC methods suffer from many of the problems associated with the SC methods. Most notably, the conversion from qualitative measures to quantitative values is difficult at best. One such method, Technology Broker created by Brooking, defines IC as the combined value of four components: market assets, human-centered assets, IP assets, and infrastructure assets. The value of these components is derived mainly from the organization answering a series of questions, such as:

- In my company, every employee knows his job and how it contributes to corporate goals.
- In my company, we evaluate return on investment on research and development.
- In my company, we know the value of our brands.
- In my company, there is a mechanism to capture employees' recommendations to improve any aspect of the business.
- In my company, we understand the innovation process and encourage all employees to participate within it.

This method then asks a series of specific audit questions to determine the amount of contribution relative to each of the four asset categories. In total, the Technology Broker IC Audit comprises 178 questions. Once again, many of these questions are qualitative in nature, such as: "To what extent are the patents owned by your company optimally exploited?" Once an organization completes its Technology Broker IC Audit, Brooking offers the cost, market, and income approaches to calculate a dollar value for the IC identified by the audit. Technology Broker's strength is to cause an organization to delve deeply into its intellectual underpinnings. Its weakness is that the conversion into quantitative values is not a direct line.

TRIANGULATION

The world of intangible asset value is an emerging world that will continue to increase in importance in the coming years. Global business models increasingly rely on intangible assets to meet goals and generate value. Managing and measuring these assets is a challenge for every business.

This world has two subworlds, intellectual property and intellectual capital. IP is the more familiar subworld, as it is comprised of well-known terms, such as patents, trademarks, and copyrights. The IP subworld lies in the empirical regulated quadrant. Since its elements are observable and traded in a market, it is empirical. For instance, numerous Web sites on the Internet routinely transfer patents. The authority's legitimacy in this subworld is grounded in government action. This subworld is highly regulated by various governmental agencies.

The IC subworld is more intangible than IP. This subworld lies in the notional unregulated quadrant. It is notional because it cannot be observed in a market; it exists only as a construct. Proponents of IC struggle to apply a coherent analysis that will be accepted and employed by the business community. IC is also highly unregulated. Companies cannot *borrow* against their IC. They may access equity investment due to the strength of their human capital.

This subworld is not directly tied to market value. It is uncertain whether increases in IC lead to increases in market value, especially for private companies. Similar to the creation of incremental business value, companies are probably better off by creating IC, but further study is required to understand how these benefits can be measured externally.

NOTES

1. Mary Adams and Michael Oleksak, *Intangible Capital* (Santa Barbara, CA: Praeger, 2010), p. xiii.
2. Nick Bontis, "Assessing Knowledge Assets: A Review of the Models to Measure Intellectual Capital," *International Journal of Management Reviews* 3, no. 1 (March 2001): 45.
3. Ibid.
4. Karl-Erik Sveiby, "Measuring Models for Intangible Assets and Intellectual Capital," Unpublished paper, October 2002, p. 1; available at: www.sveiby.com.
5. Ibid., p. 2.

6. Gordon V. Smith and Russell L. Parr, *Valuation of Intellectual Property and Intangible Assets*, 3rd ed. (New York: John Wiley & Sons, 2000), p. 27.
7. Ibid., p. 35.
8. Ibid.
9. Ibid., p. 36.
10. Ibid., p. 44.
11. Ibid., p. 28.
12. Ibid., p. 30.
13. Bontis, "Assessing Knowledge Assets," p. 46.
14. Ibid.

CHAPTER 14

Other Value Worlds

There are a number of value worlds beyond those described in other chapters. Worlds emanate from the multitude of reasons for which a private appraisal might be needed. These reasons may require using specific methods or processes for the valuation, which causes a host of different value worlds. Some of the other worlds are briefly summarized in this chapter. These other worlds are no less important than previously mentioned worlds; they simply require less space to explain. This chapter describes six worlds and discusses the processes used to derive value in each:

1. Investment value world
2. Owner value world
3. Collateral value world
4. Early equity value world
5. Bankruptcy value world
6. Public value world

INVESTMENT VALUE WORLD

The world of investment value describes the value of a business interest to a particular investor with a given defined set of individual investment criteria. The criteria usually are stated as a compounded return expectation. Although this world does not necessarily contemplate a sale, that is the dominant reason for valuing a business interest in this world. Although similar in concept, there is a difference between investment value and market value. Exhibit 14.1 shows the salient differences.

The two worlds are connected; it is possible for them to derive the same value for a company. For instance, if PrivateCo is valued using the synergy subworld of market value, it is possible a particular buyer could have nearly identical investment criteria as the group of synergistic buyers. It is more likely, however, that the specific investor values an interest somewhere within the market value world but not exactly in one of the market value subworlds. There are many reasons why investment value might differ from market value, including these differences between the specific investor and the market:

- Risk perception of the investment and the required rate of return
- Synergies with the subject company

EXHIBIT 14.1   Differences between Investment Value and Market Value

Investment Value World	Market Value World
Value attributable to one investor	Highest value available in the market
Derived based on a single investor	Derived based on likely investor "profiles"
Uses one investor return expectation	Uses return expectations of the investor profiles

- Estimates of earnings and cash flow
- Capital structures

Exhibit 14.2 summarizes the longitude and latitude for investment value. To determine investment value, an investor begins with a return expectation, usually stated on an annually compounded basis, and then personalizes the benefit stream. For example, assume PrivateInvestor has a 25% return expectation and views PrivateCo's benefit stream as $2 million per year to the investor for the foreseeable future. Capitalizing the $2 million by 25% yields an investment value for PrivateCo of $7.5 million ($8 million less $500,000 long-term debt). Both the return expectation and the return generated by the investment are specific to PrivateInvestor.

Quite often an investor becomes frustrated by an inability to complete transactions of private investment opportunities. Normally the investor does not bid high enough. The investor may be acting like an authority in a competing value world, such as market value. If the investor is relying on a business appraiser, that appraiser is likely thinking of and working in the fair market value world, not in the market value world. In these cases, the investor may not be successful until she modifies her valuation process to fit the value world where the investment is being transacted.

OWNER VALUE WORLD

The world of owner value measures the value of a business or business interest to the current owner. This world assumes the owner's current use of the interest and her ability to exploit the asset continue in the future unabated. Much like investment value, this world does not necessarily contemplate a sales transaction.

EXHIBIT 14.2   Longitude and Latitude: Investment Value

Definition	The value of a business interest to a particular investor.
Purpose	To determine the viability of an investment opportunity.
Function	To derive a value for the business interest based on a particular investor's estimate of the benefit stream and assessment of risk, probably for acquisition.
Quadrant	Empirical unregulated.
Authority	Investor.
Stream	Personalized to investor.
PRE	Personalized to investor.

EXHIBIT 14.3   Longitude and Latitude: Owner Value

Definition	The value of a business interest to the owner.
Purpose	To determine the viability of an exit opportunity or measure return on the business investment.
Function	To derive a value for the business based on the owner's personal needs and unique perspective on the benefit stream and the risk.
Quadrant	Empirical unregulated.
Authority	Owner.
Stream	Personalized to owner.
PRE	Personalized to owner.

The owner may need a value for reasons that cut across a number of value worlds. Owner value may incorporate the selfish motives of the owner and quite often involves a number of lifestyle issues.

Exhibit 14.3 describes the longitude and latitude for owner value. The first step in deriving owner value is to determine the benefit stream available to the owner. This stream is unique to every owner but has these common elements:

> Owner value benefit stream = Total compensation to owner
> + Pretax earnings of the business
> + Personal expenses passed through to the business
> + Effect of close business contracts
> + Covered expenses, such as insurances, business vacations, etc.
> + Any other items that personally benefit the owner

Although this definition of owner value benefit stream is liberal, it portrays the mentality of the typical owner-manager. By including all dollars in the stream that move in his direction, the owner generally values the business far beyond what it is worth to anyone else. Many owners also believe the risk of achieving and maintaining this stream is less than the market might measure. It is not unusual for an owner to use 10% to 20% as the capitalization rate in this situation, which often significantly understates the equity risk.

By way of example, assume Joe Mainstreet values PrivateCo's worth to him. He first calculates the company's benefit stream (some numbers are taken from Chapter 6):

PrivateCo Benefit Stream	
Total compensation to owner, including bonuses	450
+ Pretax earnings of the business	1,800
+ Personal expenses passed through to the business[a]	75
+ Effect of close business contracts[b]	9
+ Covered expenses such as insurances, business vacations, etc.	25
+ Any other items that personally benefit the owner[c]	90
Benefit stream to owner	2,449

[a]Personal expenses equal vacations and conferences charged to company.
[b]Excess rent charged to PrivateCo by a company controlled by Mainstreet.
[c]Total of donations ($74), legal ($9.9), and accounting ($6.5).

The benefit stream to Joe Mainstreet is $2.45 million (as rounded). This is the amount Joe expects to receive or control each year for the foreseeable future. He is likely to capitalize this benefit stream at a low rate, because he believes achieving this stream is fairly certain. Assume Joe uses a 15% capitalization rate. This creates an owner value on a total capital basis of $16.3 million ($2.45 million divided by 15%). After deducting PrivateCo's long-term debt of $500,000, the value of the equity in the owner value world is $15.8 million.

Since owners tend to perceive the economic benefits and risk of ownership different from the general market, they often feel insulted by offers for their businesses. Given the built-in differences in opinion, it is amazing that deals ever happen with this group.

COLLATERAL VALUE WORLD

The collateral value world measures the amount a creditor is willing to lend with the subject's assets serving as security for the loan. A company enters the collateral value world when it seeks a secured loan (e.g., a commercial- or asset-based loan) or if it uses its assets in some financially engineered way (e.g., a sale-leaseback arrangement). Exhibit 14.4 summarizes the longitude and latitude for collateral value.

"Collateral" is defined as property that secures a loan or other debt so the lender may seize the property if the borrower fails to make proper payments on the loan. When lenders demand collateral for a secured loan, they are seeking to minimize the risks of extending credit. To ensure that the particular collateral provides appropriate security, the lender wants to match the type of collateral with the loan. For example, the useful life of the collateral typically will have to exceed, or at least meet, the term of the loan; otherwise, the lender's secured interest would be jeopardized. Consequently, short-term assets such as receivables and inventory are not acceptable as security for a long-term loan. They are, however, appropriate for short-term financing, such as a line of credit.

To further limit their risks, lenders usually discount the value of the collateral so they do not lend 100% of the collateral's highest value. This relationship between the amount of money a lender extends to the value of the collateral is called the *loan-to-value* ratio. Another term for loan-to-value ratio is the *advance rate*. Advance rates reflect the percentage of each asset class a lender actually will loan against. For example, a lender may advance 80% against eligible receivables, 50% against eligible inventory, and so on. Eligibility varies from lender to lender and is explained in detail in Chapter 20.

EXHIBIT 14.4   Longitude and Latitude: Collateral Value

Definition	The value of a business interest for secured lending purposes.
Purpose	To determine how much a company can borrow using its collateral.
Function	To establish the borrowing base for a loan.
Quadrant	Empirical unregulated.
Authority	The lending industry.

There is no single definition of "value" of an asset to be appraised in the collateral value world. Many definitions of value exist, and the use of each depends on the circumstances. Lenders may choose to have an asset valued at replacement cost, fair market value in continued use, fair market value removal, orderly liquidation value, or forced liquidation value, just to name a few. An asset appraiser is given the appropriate standard of value, usually by the lender, prior to the start of the appraisal. Definitions of a few of the standards are presented next.[1]

> *Fair value* is "the cash price that might reasonably be anticipated in a current sale, under all conditions requisite to a fair sale. A *fair value* sale means that buyer and seller are each acting prudently, knowledgeably, and under no necessity to buy or sell, that is, other than in a forced or liquidation sale."
>
> *Orderly liquidation value* is "the estimated gross amount, expressed in terms of money, which could typically be realized from a sale, given a reasonable time to find purchasers, with the seller being compelled to sell on an as-is, where-is basis."
>
> This is the valuation standard most frequently used by asset-based lenders. Its primary attribute, "realized from a sale," provides maximum flexibility to the presumed liquidator in both the timing and the method of disposal.
>
> *Forced liquidation value* is "the estimated gross amount, expressed in terms of money, which could be typically realized from a properly advertised and conducted public auction sale, negotiated liquidation sale, or a combination of the two, with the seller being compelled to sell with a sense of immediacy, on an as-is, where-is basis, under present-day economic trends."

The facts and circumstances of the appraisal determine the actual advance rate a lender might offer. Typically, however, the closer the standard reflects a cash position, the higher the advance rate. For instance, a lender might advance 80% against a forced liquidation appraisal but only 60% against an orderly liquidation value.

Success in the collateral value world can be enhanced in two ways. First, the borrower should confer with a lender prior to hiring an asset appraiser to ensure the correct standard of value is used. In some cases, an appraiser might appraise an asset using multiple standards. This causes the appraiser to employ a different appraisal process for each standard. Second, the more information a borrower provides to a lender, such as professional asset appraisals, the more likely a positive result will occur, especially regarding advance rates.

The type of collateral used to secure the loan affects the lender's advance rates. For example, unimproved real estate yields a lower advance rate than improved occupied real estate. These rates vary among lenders, and lending criteria other than the value of the collateral may influence the rate. For example, a healthy

EXHIBIT 14.5   Typical Advance Rates

Asset	Advance Rate	Type of Value
Real estate		
Occupied	80%	Appropriately appraised value
Improve, not occupied	50%	Appropriately appraised value
Vacant and unimproved	30%	Appropriately appraised value
Inventory		
Raw materials	50%–60%	Eligible amount
Work-in-process	0%	
Finished foods	50%–60%	Eligible amount
Accounts receivable	70%–80%	Eligible amount
Equipment	65%–85%	Purchase price

cash flow may allow for more leeway in the rate. A representative listing of advance rates for different types of collateral at a typical secured lender is shown in Exhibit 14.5. This represents the method for determining the asset value that is then multiplied by the advance rate.

Margined collateral is the result of an advance rate applied against a qualifying asset. A borrower's total margined collateral value is calculated by applying the advance rates against qualifying asset groups. Exhibit 14.6 shows PrivateCo's calculations.

The "stated value" for each of the asset classes is taken from PrivateCo's balance sheet, as shown in Chapter 5. The "loanable value/fair market value" column shows the amounts eligible for secured lending. Accounts receivable are reduced from the stated value to reflect ineligible receivables, such as past dues or those due from related companies. Inventory is reduced to account for work-in-process inventory, which is not eligible for secured lending. Land, buildings, machinery, and equipment are adjusted to their fair market values. These changes are explained in Chapter 5.

Finally, margined collateral value is the sum of the various margined asset classes. For PrivateCo, margined collateral value equals about $2.5 million (as rounded). Financial ratios and earnings further determine the amount PrivateCo actually can borrow. Chapters 17 and 20 describe collateral issues in much more detail.

EXHIBIT 14.6   PrivateCo Collateral Value ($000)

Asset Class	States Value	Loanable Value/ Fair Market Value	Advance Rate	Margined Collateral Value
Accounts receivable	$722	686	80%	$549
Inventory	450	250	50%	125
Land/Building	442	2,200	70%	1,540
Machinery and Equipment	866	450	65%	293
Total				$2,500

EXHIBIT 14.7   Longitude and Latitude: Early Equity Value

Definition	The value of a business interest as a start-up.
Purpose	To determine how much a company is worth to an early investor.
Function	To determine equity splits for the early investors.
Quadrant	Empirical unregulated.
Authority	The venture capital industry.
Stream	Cash distributed plus cash terminal value.
PRE	37.5%.

EARLY EQUITY VALUE WORLD

The early equity value world describes the valuation process for early round investors. The early equity world is the domain of venture capitalists (VCs) and angel investors but also applies to any investor who gets in on the ground floor of a business opportunity. Exhibit 14.7 summarizes the longitude and latitude for early equity value. Traditional valuation metrics may not apply to start-ups. There are no earnings, so all historical income-based methods are out. Future forecasts for the company are typically so rosy that valuation decisions based on them become difficult. Normally there are not enough tangible assets to make a meaningful asset-based valuation. It may be possible to look to the market for like-kind start-ups, but this information normally is not available. Faced with this valuation dilemma, most early-stage investors back into the valuation based on an assumed terminal value.

Terminal value represents the expected value of the investment at the point of exit. Most early investors have five- to seven-year investment horizons, so terminal value is the value of their investments at that point. The return to the investor becomes the terminal value plus any distributions or dividends received along the way. Most early investors do not expect distributions before the exit event because it is generally assumed the company will need to reinvest the cash to grow. VCs win or lose the investment game based on accurately picking companies with terminal values that meet or exceed their required rates of return. Estimating the terminal value enables the VC to back into the value of the company and then decide equity splits. Equity splits are the percentages of the company each investor owns.

Exhibit 14.8 shows the assumptions and equity split determination for a typical VC investment. Suppose a VC invests $5 million today in the equity of a business.

EXHIBIT 14.8   Example Venture Capital Investment

Up-front investment	$ 5.0 million
Subject year 5 earnings	12.4 million
Projected selling multiple	5.0
Projected enterprise selling price in year 5	$62.0 million
Venture capitalist requirement in year 5 to obtain a 35% compounded rate of return	$22.4 million
Proposed VC equity split	36%

EXHIBIT 14.9   Longitude and Latitude: Bankruptcy Value

Definition	The value of a business in a bankruptcy proceeding.
Purpose	To derive a value that is in the best interests of the bankruptcy estate and its creditors.
Function	To determine how much value the creditors will receive in the proceeding.
Quadrant	Empirical regulated.
Authority	Bankruptcy judge.
Stream	Not meaningful.
PRE	Not meaningful.

The VC expects a 35% compounded rate of return over a five-year investment life. The VC needs to receive $22.4 million in year 5 to achieve its desired return. By employing conservative forecasts, managements believe the company will earn $20 million per year by its fifth anniversary. The VC firm does its own calculations and thinks the company will earn $12.4 million by the end of the fifth year. Further, the VCs believe the company will sell for five times earnings. This suggests an enterprise value of the company of $62 million in year 5 ($12.4 million × 5). The VC then backs into the required equity split of 36% (($22.4 million ÷ $62 million) × 100).

Early investors may request more or less equity depending on their calculations of the likelihood and amount of the exit value. Considering these numbers, it is easy to see why so many VC and other early investments fail to deliver expected returns.

BANKRUPTCY VALUE WORLD

When a business is unable to service its debt or pay its creditors, the business or its creditors can file with a federal bankruptcy court for protection under either Chapter 7 or Chapter 11. In Chapter 7, the business ceases operations. A trustee sells all of its assets and then distributes the proceeds to the business's creditors. Any residual amount is returned to the owners of the company. In Chapter 11, the debtor usually remains in control of its business operations as a debtor in possession and is subject to the oversight and jurisdiction of the court.

Exhibit 14.9 summarizes the longitude and latitude for bankruptcy value.

Recently 363 bankruptcy sales have become common. These sales, named after the section of the bankruptcy code dealing with the procedure, allow for a sale of assets more quickly than in a plan of reorganization. A 363 sale requires only the approval of the bankruptcy judge, while a plan of reorganization must be approved by a substantial number of creditors and meet certain other requirements to be confirmed. A plan of reorganization is much more comprehensive than a 363 sale in addressing the overall financial situation of the debtor and how the company's exit strategy from bankruptcy will affect creditors.

In a 363 sale, the assets will be conveyed to the purchaser free and clear of any liens or encumbrances. Those liens or encumbrances then will be attached to the net proceeds of the sale and paid as ordered by the bankruptcy court. Before approving a sale, the bankruptcy court must answer these questions:

- Do the terms of the sale constitute the highest and best offer for the assets to be sold?
- Were the negotiations concerning the terms and conditions of the proposed sale conducted at arm's length?
- Is the sale in the best interests of the bankruptcy estate and its creditors?
- Has the purchaser acted in good faith and is the sale itself being made in good faith?

All of these questions must be answered yes or the sale will not be approved. The bankruptcy judge is the authority in this world, as she presides over the case to determine if the requirements for approval of a 363 sale have been met.

Valuation in a 363 sale may begin with a stalking horse bid. A stalking horse is an interested buy who makes an initial bid for the bankrupt company's assets. Doing this can put prospective purchasers in a risky position, so they usually negotiate to receive a breakup or topping fee if they do not become the approved purchaser. This ensures that another party must bid significantly more than the initial prospective buyer did to buy the company's asset or assets. This overbid is sometimes called an upset bid.

Bidding procedures are proposed by the debtor concerning the process and form by which offers, if any, for the asset or assets to be sold should be made by parties other than the stalking horse. Often they are included as part of the 363 motion as a means of keeping the process orderly. Sometimes, however, other prospective purchasers see the bidding procedures as designed to cool competing offers by imposing onerous procedural requirements.

A credit bid occurs when a secured creditor can bid up to the amount of the debt owed to it by the debtor for the purchase price of the assets to be sold without having to pay any actual cash.

The bankruptcy value world is highly structured in that its authority—judges—have almost absolute power to administer and sanction behavior in their world.

PUBLIC VALUE WORLD

Public companies, especially those with floats of more than $500 million, comprise the public value world. Public investment bankers are the valuation authorities in this world. They use market knowledge to determine the price for initial offerings, secondary offerings, and, to some degree, pricing for mergers and acquisitions.

Exhibit 14.10 summarizes the longitude and latitude for bankruptcy value.

Valuing public equities primarily uses two approaches: discounted cash flow (DCF) and fundamental (market comparison) analysis. Free cash flow valuation and comparables (comps) are key tools in fundamental analysis, the process of

EXHIBIT 14.10   Longitude and Latitude: Public Value

Definition	The value of a business in the public markets.
Purpose	To derive a value of a public company.
Function	To determine the price of a stock in an initial public offering or secondary offering.
Quadrant	Empirical regulated.
Authority	Public investment bankers.
Stream	Net income.
PRE	Price/earnings ratio.

picking stocks that are undervalued by the stock market. An analyst attempts to discover and acquire stocks of companies that are undervalued in anticipation that other investors eventually realize the company's true value.

The process of valuing publicly traded equity using DCF involves three steps.

1. Pro forma statements are forecasted several years into the future.
2. The forecasted statements are used to calculate free cash flows for the entire company. These free cash flows are then discounted by the cost of capital for the company.
3. The equity value of the common stock is calculated as total company value minus the market value of its debt. Dividing that value by the number of outstanding shares produces the value of one common share. The resulting value of the shares can be compared with the current market price to make buy and sell decisions.

Fundamental stock analysts rely heavily on price/characteristics ratios using comparable companies to validate buy and sell decisions. Most of these ratios—for example, the price/earnings (P/E) ratio—include the quoted market price in the numerator and some measure of profitability or performance in the denominator. The analyst compares the ratio of the stock in question to the ratios for stocks of companies in the same industry and of similar size and financial leverage. The comparison tells the analyst if the stock is expensive or cheap relative to other stocks.

Assume Joe Mainstreet is considering taking PrivateCo public via an initial public offering. Joe engages Jerry Smith of PublBankers to value PrivateCo. Jerry uses fundamental analysis to determine how the public market of investors would value PrivateCo. He develops Exhibit 14.11, which shows financial metrics of comparable companies. The ideal set of comparable companies will be from the subject's industry and will have financial policies, including dividend yield and financial leverage, similar to the company being valued. The companies shown in the exhibit are hypothetical. For this discussion, assume they would be reasonable candidates for comparison with PrivateCo. The companies vary in size, dividend policy, and financial leverage.

The most popular characteristic ratio for comparison across stocks is the P/E ratio. But Jerry would also analyze growth rate comparisons, quality of earnings, as well as the other financial metrics. Assume Jerry completes his analysis and

EXHIBIT 14.11   Price/Characteristic Ratios for Comparable Companies

	Ticker			
	ABC	RST	XYZ	Industry
Market Cap ($billions)	2.16	1.42	0.90	NA
Dividend Yield	2.6%	3.3%	0.1%	1.9%
LT Debt/Capital Ratio	44%	26%	66%	40%
Beta	1.28	0.98	0.88	1.05
PE (trailing)	13.5	18.3	22.2	16.4
Price/Sales (trailing)	1.1	0.85	2.8	1.5
Price/Book	4.6	1.4	3.5	2.9
Price/Cash Flow (trailing)	9.9	10.5	22.3	10.3

determines the public markets would value PrivateCo's after-tax earnings at 11 times on a control basis. PrivateCo's pro forma earnings must be calculated by starting with pretax earnings and then adjusting for seller discretionary expenses, one-time expenses, and taxes. Exhibit 14.12 shows these calculations.

Jerry calculates PrivateCo's trailing pro forma net earnings as $1.7 million. Multiplying this amount by the 11 multiple just noted produces an enterprise value of $18.7 million. Once again, PrivateCo's $500,000 debt must be subtracted from this enterprise value to determine a 100% equity value. Thus, the equity value of PrivateCo in the public value world is $18.2 million.

Literally thousands of books have been written on valuing companies in the public value world. Readers who need more detail are encouraged to review that literature.

TRIANGULATION

Each of the value worlds discussed in this chapter deserves a separate triangulation discussion.

The investment value world lies in the empirical unregulated quadrant. The investor is the authority in this world. This world is empirical because investors observe acquisitions in the highly unregulated open market. This world's link to capital is dependent on the investor and the deal opportunity. An investor generally brings some level of equity to a transaction, along with managerial and other financial capabilities. The target usually supplies most of the collateral for debt capacity. By its nature, this world is transfer-oriented. Many transfer methods, such as auctions, recapitalizations, and management buy-ins, are available to the investor. The more capabilities an investor brings to a deal, the more sources of capital and transfer methods are accessible.

An owner in the owner value world is the ultimate authority. Owners make all the rules for other interested parties to follow. This is one reason why many owners are loath to use banks as a capital source. Banks restrict the owner's actions, something to be avoided by this control-oriented group. Transferring a business is difficult for this group. Owners tend to view their companies as

EXHIBIT 14.12   PrivateCo Pro Forma Earnings ($000)

Item	Y/E 20X3
Pretax Earnings	$1,800
Adjustments	
Excess Owner Comp[a]	250
Management Fees[b]	200
Interest[c]	95
Officer Insurances[d]	5.0
Excess Accounting[e]	6.5
Excess Legal[f]	9.9
Excess Rent[g]	8.7
Excess Health Insurance	8.2
Casualty Loss—Fire[h]	35
One-time Consulting[i]	0
Donations[j]	74
Employee Incentives[k]	125
Total Adjustments	817
Pro Forma Pretax Earnings	$2,617
Less corporate taxes[l]	(915)
Pro Forma Net Earnings	$1,702

[a]Since the majority owner is passive, all his compensation will be added back.

[b]Management fees are charged each year by another company that the majority owner also controls.

[c]Interest expense is added back to depict cash flow accurately.

[d]Officer insurance expenses are added back since the majority shareholder will not be on the payroll after the sale.

[e]Some accounting services are performed by another company the majority owner controls and are billed to PrivateCo.

[f]One-time expense. Former employee illegally took blueprints and PrivateCo successfully sued that person.

[g]Assumes current rent will not continue under new ownership.

[h]The uninsured part of a fire (one-time expense).

[i]A consultant was hired to perform design studies for a new product, which was not produced.

[j]The company gives donations each year to a charity the majority owner supports.

[k]Employee incentives includes bonuses that only a passive shareholder would pay.

[l]Assume corporate income taxes equal 35% of pretax earnings.

generating higher benefit streams than most outsiders do. Plus, since managing risk is an integral part of their everyday lives, owners see less risk in achieving the benefit streams than other observers do. These two facts often make it unlikely, from the owner's perspective, that the business will be valued for a fair price. Ultimately, many owner-managed businesses transfer only upon the earlier of two events: The owner is able to appreciate other value worlds, or she gets desperate to sell.

A strong authority also rules the collateral value world. Secured lenders invoke the *golden rule* (he with the gold makes the rules) in their dealings with borrowers. Lenders set the terms by which they will lend. While flexible around the edges, they tend to value assets in a way that favors them. Collateral value is the dominant world in private capital formation because it is the most pervasive level of capital. Banks, asset-based lenders, and even some mezzanine lenders live in this world.

Nearly all transfer methods are available to collateral value. In fact, most transfers start is this world.

Venture capitalists, for whom the golden rule is sacrosanct, are the primary authorities in the world of early equity. In this world, the authority values, capitalizes, and transfers private business interests. While it is an unregulated world, the veto power of VCs is very strong. They can choose not to invest. Because this is an extremely high-risk/high-return world, a high level of potential is necessary to attract early investment.

Bankruptcy judges are the authority in the bankruptcy value world. Valuation in this world is discovered based on a formal bidding process. Many sales occur in bankruptcy using the 363 section of the law. This section provides a quicker resolution to the process, thus possibly saving jobs. This is a highly regulated world.

Large public companies make up the public value world. Public investment bankers are the authorities in this world. Values in this world are determined mainly by analyzing what investors are paying for comparable companies.

World	PrivateCo Value
Asset market value	$2.4 million
Collateral value	**$2.5 million**
Insurable value (buy/sell)	$6.8 million
Fair market value	$6.8 million
Investment value	**$7.5 million**
Impaired goodwill	$13.0 million
Financial market value	$13.7 million
Owner value	**$15.8 million**
Synergy market value	$16.6 million
Public value	**$18.2 million**

NOTE

1. American Society of Appraisers, Definitions of Values Relating to Machinery, www. appraisers. org.

CHAPTER 15

Private Business Valuation: Conclusion

Chapters 3–14 cover the concepts underlying private business valuation. These concepts constitute more than a disparate group of approaches to value. Their cohesiveness is due to a number of fundamental theoretical constructs underlying private business appraisal. The concepts of private appraisal are derived, in large part, from risk and return. Consider these facts:

- Private investor return expectations drive private valuation.
- Private business appraisal can be viewed through value worlds.
- Private business valuation is a range concept.
- Valuation is triangulated to capitalization and business transfer.

PRIVATE INVESTOR RETURN EXPECTATIONS

Private return expectations, defined as the expected rate of return that the private capital markets require in order to attract investors, drive private business valuation. The private capital markets house all of the return expectations of private investors. Expected return in this context has many synonyms, including discount rate, expected rate of return, cost of capital, required rate of return, and selling multiples. All are used to describe expected return from a slightly different perspective.

Some observations are important relative to return expectations:

- *They emanate from the capital side of the private capital markets triangle.* In other words, private return expectations are found in the private capital markets by viewing the Pepperdine Private Capital Market Line (PPCML), as shown in Exhibit 15.1.

    Exhibit 15.1 encompasses various capital types in terms of the provider's all-in expected returns. The PPCML is described as median, pretax expected returns of institutional capital providers. For consistency, the capital types chosen to comprise the PPCML reflect likely capital options for mainly lower-middle-market companies. For example, the PPCML uses the $5 million loan/investment survey category for banks, asset-based lending, mezzanine

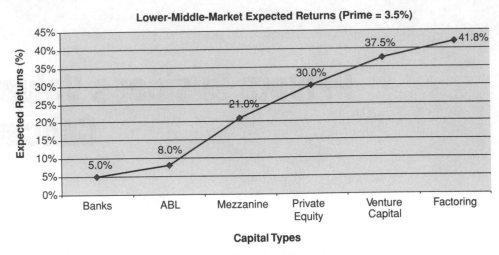

EXHIBIT 15.1 Pepperdine Private Capital Market Line

and private equity. It should be noted that the PPCML could be created using different data sets. The returns are further described as first and third quartiles, as shown in Exhibit 15.2.

The PPCML is stated on a pretax basis, both from a provider and a user perspective. In other words, capital providers offer deals to the marketplace on a pretax basis. For example, if a private equity investor requires a 25% return, this is stated as a pretax return. Also, the PPCML does not assume a tax rate to the investee, even though many of the capital types use interest rates that generate deductible interest expense for the borrower. Capital types are not tax-effected because many owners of private companies manage their company's tax bill through various aggressive techniques. It is virtually impossible to estimate a generalized appropriate tax rate for this market.

- *Private return expectations can be viewed from at least three different perspectives: market, firm, and investor.*
  - The market rate is an opportunity cost, which is the cost of forgoing the next best alternative investment.
  - An individual firm attempts to meet its shareholders' return expectations. Firms use their weighted average cost of capital as a minimum return required on investments.

EXHIBIT 15.2 PPCML Capital Types by Quartiles

Capital Type	Description	1st Quartile	Median	3rd Quartile
Banks	$5MM equipment loan	4.1%	5.0%	6.3%
Asset-based loan	$5MM working capital loan	4.3%	8.0%	12.0%
Mezzanine	$5MM model pretax IRR	20.0%	21.0%	23.0%
Private equity	$5MM model pretax IRR	25.0%	30.0%	35.0%
Venture capital	Expansion model pretax IRR	30.5%	37.5%	40.0%
Factoring*	Medium monthly volume	–	41.8%	–

*Effective cost of factoring (see Chapter 21).

- Individual investors have return expectations that must be met before they will fund an investment. Cost of equity is peculiar to each investor.

  Each of these perspectives tells us something useful in the valuation process.
- *Expected returns convert a benefit stream to a present value.* This is valuation distilled to its most basic definition. The ability to derive present values from the universe of investment options is crucial; it enables investors to compare the value of various assets on a common basis. This ability to evaluate investments on a common basis is a building block of valuation and the private capital markets.

Risk and return for private investments should be determined in the private capital markets. The greater the perceived risk of owning an investment, the greater the return expected by investors to compensate for that risk. Due to market inefficiency, risk and return are not perfectly aligned in the private markets. Some capital providers receive a return that is not commensurate with the investment risk. The desire to achieve a return at least commensurate with the corresponding risk is the primary motive for investors to bear the uncertainty of investing.

Many private appraisals performed in the United States look to the public capital markets to determine private return expectations. The capital asset pricing model and buildup methods use public securities information to derive private discount rates. These models presume that the return expectations in the public and private capital markets are the same. A premise of this book is that public and private return expectations are not the same and are not surrogates for one another.

Private return expectations govern all private business valuation. In a sense, they act as a boundary for the private capital markets. A graphic way to conceptualize this boundary is through the PPCML. Risk and return analysis provides the yardstick for the market. In its broadest intellectual sense, all of valuation in the private capital markets can be explained in terms of risk and return.

VALUE WORLDS

Either private valuations must be undertaken, or a transaction must occur to determine the value of a private security for some purpose at some point in time. "Purpose," also called "reason" in this book, is defined as the intention of the involved party as to why a valuation is needed. Purpose is the starting point in the valuation process.

Motives drive appraisal purpose because a private owner should not undertake a capitalization or transfer without knowing the value of her business. To do so would be the business equivalent of flying blind. For example, without a current valuation, owners cannot effectively raise capital, because they do not know what their assets or business is worth in a lending or investment context. To transfer the business without knowing its worth is usually an exasperating experience.

The purposes for undertaking an appraisal give rise to *value worlds*. Throughout this book, value worlds are offered as helpful constructs through which to view private business appraisal. Several key concepts describe value worlds. They are:

- One or more authorities govern each world.
- Each world employs a unique appraisal process.
- The choice of world determines the appraisal outcome.

Authority

"Authority" refers to agents or agencies with primary responsibility to develop, adopt, and administer standards of practice within a value world. Authority decides which purposes are acceptable, sanctions its decisions, develops methodology, and provides a coherent set of rules for participants to follow. Examples of authority are found in each appraisal world. For instance, secured lenders are the authority in the world of collateral value.

These lenders are responsible for developing the criteria and administering methodology used to derive value as well as for sanctioning noncompliance.

Another example involves the world of early equity value. Early investors, such as venture capitalists, are the authority in this world since they govern both the rules within the world and the methodology used to derive value. However, for these rules to have meaning outside the investor's view, they must be expressed in communally shared methods and standards. The venture capitalist can sanction noncompliant behavior by not investing in the business. However, for an authority to be effective, it must be widely recognized and accepted. The venture capitalist accomplishes this recognition and acceptance by developing professional management techniques, strategically positioning the company, and adopting generally accepted accounting principles through exercising authority granted in their investment documents.

Authority derives its influence or legitimacy from three primary sources: government action, compelling logic, and the utility of authorities' actions and standards. The boundary of an authority's influence often does not extend beyond a given value world. Each of these three sources of legitimacy can be found in valuation, as Exhibit 15.3 describes.

There are numerous authorities in every value world. However, some authorities exert more pull on their constituents than others. The nature of an authority's power and pull on its constituency helps position a world in a value quadrant. For instance, the Internal Revenue Service (IRS) and courts regulate fair market value through government action. Since these authorities do not inhabit the private capital markets, their actions may disregard the market's wishes. This lack of market checks and balances on the IRS position causes fair market value to be a notional world. The validity of IRS actions is derived from the extent to which this authority coheres to an intellectually consistent standard rather than the extent to which it corresponds to market activity and mechanisms.

EXHIBIT 15.3 Sources of Legitimacy for Authority

Value World	Quadrant	Primary Authorities	Government Action	Compelling Logic	Utility
Market value	Empirical unregulated	Intermediaries IRS	Secondary	Primary	Primary
Fair market value	Notional regulated	Tax courts	Primary	Secondary	Secondary
Fair value	Notional regulated	Statutory law	Primary	Secondary	Secondary
Incremental business value	Notional unregulated	Management consulting	Secondary	Primary	Primary
Insurable value	Empirical regulated	Insurance industry	Primary	Secondary	Secondary
	Empirical unregulated	Involved parties	Secondary	Primary	Secondary
Impaired goodwill	Notional regulated	FASB	Primary	Secondary	Secondary
Intellectual property	Notional regulated	Patent laws, etc.	Primary	Secondary	Secondary
Intellectual capital	Notional unregulated	Consultants	Secondary	Primary	Primary
Investment value	Empirical unregulated	Investor	Secondary	Secondary	Primary
Owner value	Empirical unregulated	Owner	Secondary	Secondary	Primary
Collateral value	Empirical unregulated	Secured lenders	Secondary	Secondary	Primary
Early equity value	Empirical unregulated	Venture capitalists	Secondary	Secondary	Primary
Bankruptcy value	Empirical regulated	Bankruptcy judge	Primary	Secondary	Primary
Public value	Empirical regulated	Investment bankers	Primary	Secondary	Primary

Typically an authority's influence is limited to the value world in which it is viewed. For instance, while state laws and courts make the rules in the world of fair value, they have little or no effect in the other worlds. Likewise, while secured lenders authorize the world of collateral value, they have no standing in early equity value. The limit of an authority's power is a boundary on their influence.

Yet outside parties can influence authorities' decisions. For example, the business appraisal community has educated and influenced the IRS and tax courts on a wide variety of issues over the years. Along these lines, the author hopes to use the Private Cost of Capital Model introduced in Chapter 10 to standardize the definition of private return expectation in a number of value worlds. This would simplify appraisal as well as make it more relevant.

Competing authorities may cause a world to split into different value quadrants. This is the case for the intangible asset and insurable value worlds. Each primary authority in these worlds derives its legitimacy from a different source. For example, the authority in the subworld of intellectual property—various intangible asset laws—provides a highly regulated influence on the world. In contrast, the subworld of intellectual capital, whose authority is the consulting industry, derives its authority from compelling logic and the utility of its ideas. This authority has an unregulated influence on intellectual capital. In the case of competing authorities, the authority with the stronger claim or more logical argument generally exerts the stronger gravitational pull on the parties. The authority with the stronger veto power is likely to prevail.

Sanctioning is the gatekeeping power of the authority to regulate access to the world. If the intention of the involved party, which leads to a purpose, does not meet the access criteria of an authority, the purpose will not be accepted. For example, an owner who pursues value in the owner value world may not access, or transact in, the world of collateral value. The latter world operates under a different set of valuation rules and will not recognize the owner's treatment of value.

Each World Employs a Unique Appraisal Process

Once the project is located in a value world, the function of the appraisal governs the method by which it is performed. The responsible authority in each value world prescribes these methods. Law, decree, custom, and various other means are used to develop methods. Perhaps the first comprehensive business valuation methodology was developed by the Treasury Department with its Revenue Ruling 59-60. This and subsequent rulings form the basis for valuation in the world of fair market value. Authorities in other worlds are constantly prescribing and proscribing valuation methodology. A new value world, impaired goodwill, was created in 2001 by the Financial Accounting Standards Board (FASB). As the authority, the FASB created the valuation process in this world. Authorities also proscribe certain methodology. For instance, financial intermediaries insist that asset-based methods are not suitable to value companies in the synergy subworld of market value.

Choice of Value World Determines the Appraisal Outcome

The choice of value worlds may be mutually exclusive. The reason for needing an appraisal selects the appropriate value world. For the most part, reasons point to only one world. Tensions arise because parties within one world might visit another world to accomplish a goal. For instance, an investor in investment value must visit an owner in the owner value world if he wants to acquire the business. The investor and owner are unlikely to agree on a business value, since each party employs a different valuation process. For a deal to occur, the investor and owner probably will need to abandon their own world and value the transaction in the world of market value. The appraisal rules used in market value are less reliant on a particular point of view; rather, the appraisal process attempts to mirror the behavior of the broader market of players.

In some cases, the involved party has a choice as to which value world to employ. For example, an owner operating in the world of owner value can value and transact in her world if she is willing to provide terms that enable the investor to increase his offer. In this case, the owner could offer favorable seller financing to the buyer. The right terms would provide the means for the buyer to pay more for the company without substantially increasing his risk in the deal.

The choice of value world determines the appraisal outcome. This is because each value world employs an appraisal process specific to that world. The range of values exemplifies the effect of using different methodologies in different worlds for PrivateCo. Exhibit 15.4 shows some of the values derived for PrivateCo throughout the chapters. The range of possible values is large, from $2.4 million to more than $18.2 million.

Parties that ignore a value world or are confused about the appropriate value world may suffer serious consequences. For instance, if Joe Mainstreet sold PrivateCo in the financial subworld instead of the synergy subworld, he would forgo more than $2 million. Joe might have good reasons to sell his business to a non-strategic acquirer. At the least, Joe should be aware that choosing a world has an opportunity cost.

The next practical example may help clarify the importance of the two concepts: Private investor return expectations drive valuation, and private business

EXHIBIT 15.4 PrivateCo Range of Values

World	PrivateCo Value
Asset market value	$2.4 million
Collateral value	$2.5 million
Insurable value (buy/sell)	$6.5 million
Fair market value	$6.8 million
Investment value	$7.5 million
Impaired goodwill	$13.0 million
Financial market value	$13.7 million
Owner value	$15.8 million
Synergy market value	$16.6 million
Public value	$18.2 million

appraisal can be viewed through value worlds. Buyers and sellers are confronted with this situation every day.

EXAMPLE

Joe Mainstreet finds himself in a pressurized situation sitting across the table from people who do not see the value of PrivateCo the way he does. Because Joe cannot understand their position, his only defense is to think the worst of them, and his anxiety builds. He concludes that they want to steal the business he spent a lifetime building.

Fortunately, Joe has Dan Dealmaker with him at the table to act as interpreter and to help overcome natural barriers between worlds. Dan explains that the different value worlds are completely understandable, defensible, and coherent, and all methodologies for deriving value are value-world specific. Dan goes on to say that negotiations improve when the parties are able to understand the motives, worldviews, and methodologies of those sitting across the table. He provides Joe with a toolbox of ideas allowing him to understand the legitimacy of the other positions.

Joe feels some of the tension going out of the situation and says, "I used to worry about the world and all of its people; now I have to worry about the people and all of their worlds."

Equipped with this new insight, Joe still thinks they want to steal the business . . . he is just a little less sure of it.

This text does not describe all the known value worlds. In fact, there are many others, limited only by the number of reasons a valuation is needed. For example, real estate is a value world. There is also the issue of value premise to consider. The preceding discussion assumes value on a going-concern basis. Nearly all of the value worlds can be viewed on a liquidation basis, which alters the valuation processes significantly. Although these issues are important, they will be discussed in a future edition.

PRIVATE BUSINESS VALUATION IS A RANGE CONCEPT

Because each value world is likely to yield a different value indication for a business interest, private business valuation is a range concept. Thus, a private business interest has *at least* as many correct values at a given point in time as the number of value worlds. Within each world there are a multitude of functions of an appraisal that call for unique valuation methods. As Exhibit 15.4 shows, the spread of values can be quite large between worlds.

Beyond the different values determined by world, there are nearly an infinite number of values possible *within* each world. This observation is based on four factors. First, even though appraisers are interpreters of authority's decisions, there is latitude regarding the application of a prescribed valuation process. For instance, in the world of fair market value, appraisers decide which methods are suitable within the asset, income, and market approaches. This decision-making process causes variability from one appraiser to the next. Most value worlds require judgment regarding the application of methods.

Second, once the appropriate value world is chosen, the next important valuation issue is the calculation of a suitable benefit stream. Each value world employs a different benefit stream to value a business interest. Streams can differ substantially from world to world. Streams also vary greatly from the seller's and buyer's perspective. The difference in the benefit stream definitions in each world is a key reason why value variability exists between the value worlds.

Third, much like benefit streams, private return expectations are determined within each value world. This can be seen by the particular return requirement of an investor in the world of investment value, or to an owner in the owner value world, or to a venture capitalist in the world of early equity. Private return expectations convert a benefit stream to a present value, so they compose one-half of the value equation. Value variability between worlds is increased because each world employs a unique return expectation.

Finally, the probability of different value drivers occurring must be considered. For instance, if PrivateCo's earnings before interest, taxes, depreciation and amortization (EBITDA) is $3 million, and this number is used in the valuation, it is assumed with 100% probability that PrivateCo will indeed achieve a $3 million EBITDA. What if, upon further due diligence and consideration of revenues and cost variables, it seems reasonable to presume PrivateCo has only a 50% chance of achieving a $3 million EBITDA? An independent analysis might further indicate PrivateCo has a 25% chance of generating a $2 million EBITDA and a 25% chance of earning $3.5 million. Wouldn't each of these scenarios lead to three different values, even in the same value world?

This concept of value variability is an integral part of the larger idea that business value is a range concept. This is another example where value world theory translates to practical considerations in business valuation and transfer. The concept of ranges provides a way for valuations in various value worlds to overlap in a way that creates the possibility for deals to get done. For example, if parties cannot agree on a specific benefit stream, a deal will not consummate unless an economic bridge is built. Economic bridges come in many forms, such as earn-outs, ratchets, options, look-backs, and other contingent payment plans. These bridges enable parties to come to agreement even though they may still have a foot in their home world. Bridge techniques are covered in detail in Part Three.

TRIANGULATION

A compelling logic holds the three conceptual sides of the private capital market triangle together. Triadic logic provides a powerful cohesion among the moving parts. An idea that originates on the valuation leg of the triangle finds its opposite in the transfer leg and capitalization leg. Triadic logic is a synchronizing function much like harmony in a musical composition. In music, tension is created by the interchange of dissonance and consonance. It is resolved by harmony. Harmony is a logical function imposing a network of transitions, progressions, and modulations to bring opposing forces into a workable system of understanding and communication. The ultimate legitimacy of authorities is the extent to which they contribute to market harmony or equilibrium.

Similarly, triadic logic captures equilibrium in economic theory as markets work to synchronize the thoughts and activities of disparate entities. In a practical sense, this balancing act links private valuation, capitalization, and transfer. Private business value is directly affected by the company's access to capital and the transfer methods available to the owner. Considering the value of a private business interest without reference to capitalization or transfer quickly leads to an unharmonized position.

FINAL THOUGHTS ON VALUATION

Many say that private business valuation involves more art than science. Yet there is a definite structure to this discipline that must be heeded. Active authorities who define suitable valuation processes shape this structure. While some authorities have more sanctioning capabilities than others, involved parties who ignore the structure of this system do so at their own risk.

A private business's value is not fixed; rather, it is relative to the purpose, function, and various other variables of the appraisal. Every private business interest has a range of likely values. The determination of the most likely value from this range constitutes the artful part of the exercise.

Finally, a private value is influenced by a company's access to capital and the transfer methods available to the owner. This interrelationship among value, capital, and transfer is captured in this book by the concept of triangulation. Attempts to value business interests in isolation of the triangulated body of knowledge are similar to sitting on a one-legged stool. It can be done, but most likely it will result in a great fall.

Capital Structure

CHAPTER 16

Capital Structure: Introduction

The term "capital structure" refers to the mix of debt and equity financing in a business. Private debt and equity are raised in the private capital markets. Because these markets are quite different from their public counterparts, comparison and analysis is fraught with uncertainty. Investment bankers for large public companies access the public capital markets somewhat predictably. This enables financial managers of public companies to plan their capital structure. Private companies, however, must *create* capital structure solutions one deal at a time. This difference is monumental. The public capital markets structure helps public companies plan and execute capital solutions with certainty. The private capital markets have much less structure and, even with expert guidance, may not yield any capital.

Yet there is a structure of capital alternatives in the private capital markets. Unlike the organized structure of public capital markets, private markets are more ad hoc. Private markets are more like an outdoor bazaar while public markets resemble a supermarket. Nearly all capital alternatives are available in the private bazaar, but they are found in separate shops or discrete increments. To make financing in private markets even more difficult, capital providers in the bazaar constantly move around and may or may not rely on prior transactions to make current decisions. Fortunately, for those in need of private capital, some organization in this bizarre bazaar is discernible. To understand private markets, we first review public capital markets, then compare and contrast the two markets.

PUBLIC CAPITAL MARKETS

Public capital markets are fairly efficient. Since security pricing and risk/return are more nearly in alignment, access to capital is predictable. By either of these measures, public markets are relatively efficient. Typically, pricing differences between public capital alternatives are measured in basis points (a basis point is .01%) rather than percentage points. The public capital market line, shown in Exhibit 16.1, depicts the expected investor rates of return relative to U.S. public securities.

The public capital market line is determined by the capital asset pricing model (CAPM).[1] As expected, the riskier the capital type, the higher the return

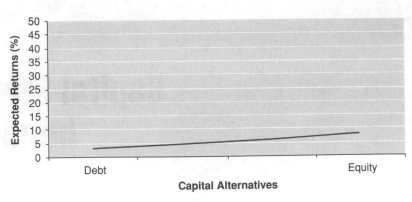

EXHIBIT 16.1 Public Capital Market Line

expectation. For example, as of this writing, public equity holders require returns of 8% or so, but debt holders require less than a 4% return. The line is viewed as the expected returns on portfolios of investments, as opposed to returns on single securities. A multitude of capital portfolios comprise the public capital market line.

The rates of return required by private investors also can be graphed through the Pepperdine Private Capital Market Line (PPCML). This line is created empirically since it must be observed in the marketplace. No widely accepted predictive private capital model, such as the CAPM, is used to determine the risk/return equilibrium of private portfolios of securities. The details of the PPCML are described later in this chapter. Exhibit 16.2 shows the summarized line as graphed against the public capital market line.

There are three noteworthy things about this chart.

1. The PPCML is quite steep compared to the public capital market line. Private investors perceive substantially more risk in private capital markets and require commensurate returns.

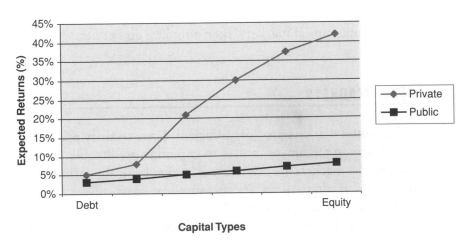

EXHIBIT 16.2 Public Capital Market Line versus Pepperdine Private Capital Market Line

2. If public and private markets enjoyed the same level of efficiency, the two lines would run parallel to each other separated only by liquidity differences.
3. Both lines represent portfolios of expected returns that group around a point on the line. Individual investors' experience in either market might not fit on a line. Rather, their experience may fit within a larger portfolio of expected returns averaged to a reference point.

Pricing Differences

There are built-in differences between public and private investor return expectations. The early chapters of this book identify and quantify many of these disparities. They largely break into two groups: the cost of being a public entity and the additional return requirement from private equity ownership due to lack of marketability.

The cost of obtaining access to an established trading market is substantial. The flotation cost, which is the cost of selling stock for a public offering, represents the initial cost of gaining access to cheaper public capital. These flotation costs can amount to 10% to 15% of the offering when all underwriting expenses are considered.

John Emory began comprehensive studies of the relationship between a company's initial public offering (IPOs) and the price its shares traded immediately prior to the IPO, for the purpose of analyzing marketability differences between public and private securities.[2] Emory examined 593 IPOs and all private transactions occurring within five months prior to those offerings between January 1, 1980, and December 30, 2000. None of the 593 companies were development-stage companies. In fact, all were financially sound before the offering. The private sales and transactions took place at a 47% average discount from the price at which the stock subsequently came to market. The range of marketability discounts was from 3% to 94%, with a median of 48%.

The combination of flotation costs and lack of marketability differences indicate a built-in pricing difference of more than 50% between public and private capital markets.

Efficiency Differences

Compared to public markets, private capital markets are inefficient. They are hampered by information opacity, manager orientation and risk?, and motives of managers and owners.

Information Opacity

Inefficiency in private capital markets is caused by information opacity. Private shareholders, as a group, do not provide outside parties with adequate information about their company's financial outlook, current operations, or future prospects. This lack of information prohibits capital providers from creating an efficient market. For example, most private businesses do not obtain audited financial statements. Further, owner-managers have a larger incentive to merge their personal life with the business in order to reduce taxes. They have very little incentive to provide financial transparency. Often it is not entirely clear who owns the collateral pool, the business or the owner. Outside capital providers strongly prefer to finance businesses with assets separate from the owner.

Manager Orientation and Risk

Owner management results in implied unsystematic risks. Unsystematic risks are company specific and attributable to management. These risks are in addition to systematic risks affecting the overall corporate environment. Unsystematic risk also exists in public companies but to a lesser extent. For example, a private company is more likely to rely on the skill of one or two individuals for profitability. Their skills probably are not easily transferable. Most small private companies do not employ a chief financial officer; rather they have either a controller or bookkeeper that closes the books. Yet this "money-saving" decision often costs the company because it leads to inadequate financial management. Private companies also frequently rely on outside vendors to provide critical services and skills. Since unsystematic risks typically are high for private companies, capital providers perceive greater risk.

Manager and Owner Motives

Public managers and private owners often have different motivations for capitalizing a business. Exhibit 16.3 compares a few of the capital motives. Understanding the individual motives further explains efficiency differences in the markets.

Public managers are motivated to increase the number of shareholders in the company and build equity. A small number of shareholders is risky to the public manager because a group may usurp control of the company. Private owners want to control the company. They do not want to share equity. In many cases, this limits the private company's growth because debt providers will not form the total capitalization of the company.

Further, public managers are encouraged by Wall Street to maximize earnings, thereby building the equity base. Private owners are motivated to reduce reported earnings in order to reduce taxes, which dilutes equity. Moreover, private companies employ pass-through entities, such as limited liability companies and S corporations, to distribute money out of the company, reducing equity further.

EXHIBIT 16.3   Comparison of Capital Motives

Public Managers Want	Private Owners Want
As many shareholders as possible	As few shareholders as possible
To build equity in the business	To minimize equity in the business
To optimize the firm's capital structure	To stretch their equity as far as possible
To borrow at the firm's marginal cost of capital	To borrow without personal guarantees
To manage "net assets" on the balance sheet	To manage the business, not the balance sheet

Public company managers seek to borrow at their firm's marginal cost of capital by receiving investment at the next least expensive capital point available. Ultimately public managers wish to optimize their company's capital structure by always employing the least expensive cost of capital. Private owners are motivated more by the desire to avoid providing personal guarantees and less by the incremental cost of capital. Many private owners would gladly pay hundreds of basis points in extra interest if it means they are relieved from the responsibility of personally guaranteeing a loan.

Public managers are strongly motivated to manage the net assets of the business because most public companies have bonus systems tied to return on net assets. The more effectively a public manager controls the net assets, the bigger his bonus. But private owners are compensated out of cash flow, not on a balance sheet metric. They are motivated to manage the business, not the balance sheet.

Authority

The concept of authority is central to this book's premise that rules and processes observed in the private capital markets are not randomly set. Authorities develop and promulgate standards of practice. Then the constituents follow within the authority's sphere of influence. Nowhere is this power more obvious than in capital structure formation. Capital providers are authorities that possess strong sanctioning ability: They do not have to fund the capital need.

Utility is the strongest source of an authority's legitimacy. This is because there is no reason for prospective borrowers or investees to be concerned with a capital authority unless they need capital. A capital authority's boundary is established by its marginal utility. In other words, personal guarantees notwithstanding, borrowers typically will seek the cheapest capital alternative while capital authorities or sources offer funding only on tightly defined terms. This concept of marginal utility explains why factoring is a funding option of last resort because it typically is the most expensive form of capital.

Capital authorities promulgate their credit requirements through the use of credit boxes. Credit boxes depict the criteria necessary to access the specific capital. Borrowers that do not qualify for credit at one capital access point must continue to move up the PPCML until they can access an authority's capital. From the authority's perspective, a credit box effectively creates a boundary around its return expectation.

A New Private Line Developing?

Reducing these inefficiencies ultimately should flatten the PPCML. In fact, Exhibit 16.4 shows several PPCMLs based on size of loan/investment.[3] Larger loan/investments typically require lower return expectations. Further institutionalization of the lower middle market should help flatten the private capital market line over time.

Since private equity groups and other institutional investors entered the market in the 1990s, financial transparency is more common in the lower-middle market.

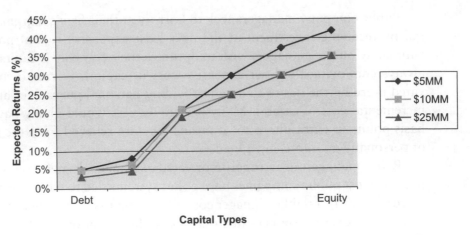

EXHIBIT 16.4 Pepperdine Private Capital Market Lines by Loan/Investment Size

They have implemented financial control systems and disciplined reporting. They also bring sophisticated management techniques to companies, which benefit from the attention in three ways.

1. Increased financial transparency enables the company to create layered capital structures that support aggressive growth plans.
2. Unsystematic risks are reduced, primarily through the implementation of functional management organizations. This approach lessens reliance on one or two key managers.
3. Outside investor's capital motives are more aligned with public managers.

Because of these reasons, company value creation and deployment of optimal capital structures is a goal.

Even with more professional management, however, public and private capital lines remain separate. Short of a secondary market for private securities, there are still liquidity differences between the public and private markets because of built-in pricing differences. Many sophisticated private investors benefit from this *arbitrage* play. They are astute enough to invest in inefficient private companies at relatively cheap prices and, by dramatically increasing the size and sophistication of the companies, can exit these investments at much higher pricing levels.

The next section discusses the structure of private capital markets. It is offered as a guided tour through the bazaar.

PRIVATE CAPITAL MARKETS

The six broad categories of capital available in the private capital markets are called capital types. The capital types are:

1. Bank lending
2. Equipment leasing

3. Asset-based lending
4. Factoring
5. Mezzanine
6. Private equity

These capital types are segmented into various capital access points (CAPs). The CAPs represent specific alternatives that correspond to *institutional* capital offerings in the marketplace. For example, equipment leasing is a capital type whereas, captive-vendor, specialty, and venture leasing are examples of capital access points within that type. Exhibit 16.5 shows the capital types with corresponding capital access points.

Accessing private capital entails three steps.

1. Determine the *credit box* of the particular CAP. Every capital provider uses a credit box to make lending and investment decisions.
2. Use CAP to define *sample terms*. These are example terms, such as loan or investment amount, loan maturity, interest rate, and other terms required by the provider.
3. Calculate an expected rate of return using the sample terms. This is the rate of return required by an investor for making the loan or investment. It is not enough to consider the stated interest rate on a loan. Other factors, such as origination costs, compensating balances, and monitoring fees, add to the cost of the loan.

EXHIBIT 16.5   Structure of Capitalization

Capital Types	Capital Access Points
Bank lending	Industrial revenue bonds
	SBA 504 loans
	Business and industry loans
	SBA 7(a) loan guaranty
	SBA CAPLine credit lines
	Credit lines
	Export working capital loans
Equipment leasing	Bank leasing
	Captive/vendor leasing
	Specialty leasing
	Venture leasing
Asset-based lending	Tier 1 asset-based loans
	Tier 2 asset-based loans
	Tier 3 asset-based loans
Factoring	Small volume
	Medium volume
	Large volume
Mezzanine	Mezzanine
Private equity	Angel financing
	Venture capital
	Private equity groups

EXHIBIT 16.6   Credit Box for Industrial Revenue Bonds

To qualify for an IRB, an applicant must:

- Have a capital need of at least $2 million.
- Use the proceeds for a manufacturing facility.
- Show capability to operate the business successfully.
- Get local support for the project (inducement).
- Pay a wage above the county average manufacturing wage or 10% above the state average manufacturing.
- Wage or obtain a wage waiver because the project is located in an area of "especially severe unemployment."
- Obtain the required environmental permits.
- Save or create enough jobs to have a measurable impact on the area.

Credit Boxes

This book employs credit boxes to describe access to most of the CAPs. Credit boxes embody the access variables a borrower must exhibit to qualify for the loan or investment. Unless a borrowing entity meets these criteria, it is not likely to be considered for a loan or investment.

Exhibit 16.6 illustrates the credit box for industrial revenue bonds (IRBs).

There is a significant variance in the nature of the credit criteria from CAP to CAP. The credit boxes of some capital access points are more qualitative, as shown in the IRB box in Exhibit 16.6. Many of the credit boxes are primarily quantitative, such as asset-based lending and factoring. Once again, each credit box indicates the criteria necessary to access that CAP.

Sample Terms

Once the credit box is shown, sample terms for most CAPs are illustrated. Sample terms are intended to reflect typical market terms for the CAP. With the proliferation of providers within each CAP, it is impossible to define sample terms for a CAP that represents the entire market. However, the various terms are discussed to help prospective users of credit generally understand each CAP. The sample terms for IRBs are shown in Exhibit 16.7.

The sample terms for each CAP show the example loan or investment amount with typical terms associated with the CAP. All of the terms are fully described in later chapters.

EXHIBIT 16.7   Sample Terms for Industrial Revenue Bonds

Example loan	$10 million. $2 MM Land/Buildings $8 MM M&E
Terms	20 years real estate 7 years M&E
Interest rate	2.5% (prime rate of 3.5% less 30%)
Letter of credit fees	1% per year
Placement fee	1% of loan amount

EXHIBIT 16.8   Expected Rate of Return for Industrial Revenue Bonds

1.	Total interest cost ($10 million loan × 2.5% interest rate)	$250,000
2.	Letter of credit fee ($10 million loan × 1%)	100,000
3.	Placement fee ($10 million loan × 1% ÷ 10 years)	10,000
	Annual returns of loan	$360,000
	Expected rate of return ($360,000/$10,000,000)	**3.6%**

Expected Rates of Return

Finally, the *expected rate of return* is calculated, normally from the sample terms. This calculation can be complex, so the details of the computation are shown within each CAP. Exhibit 16.8 contains the expected rate of return calculation for the IRB.

The stated interest rate of 2.5% is increased by the "terms cost" of 1.1%, which yields an expected rate of return of 3.6%. The interest rate and letter of credit fees are assumed to stay at the same percentages for the life of the loan. It is assumed that the placement fee is financed over ten years, with only the annual cost shown.

Two points must be made about the expected rate of return. First, this return is the expected rate of return *to the provider*. In other words, capital providers require a certain "all-in" return to compensate them for taking the risk of extending the credit or making the investment. This expected return is close to the effective cost to the borrower or investee. The major difference between the expected return to the provider and effective cost to the borrower are various transaction costs. For example, the borrower may incur legal, brokerage, environmental, and other costs in effecting the transaction. These costs are considered when calculating an effective or all-in cost to the borrower or investee.

Second, the expected rate of return to the provider may or may not represent a *compounded rate of return*. Except for mezzanine and private equity returns, the expected rates described in the book are determined on a noncompounded basis. In most cases, the difference between expected and compounded rates is small. This difference is apparent in the example in Exhibit 16.9 that compounds the industrial revenue bond cash flows.

Assuming the provider receives the placement fee at time zero, instead of over ten years, the compounded return would be 3.72%. This compares to the 3.6% expected rate of return calculated earlier. It makes sense that the return to the provider is larger if it receives money from its investment sooner.

Expected rates are shown in this book because it is easier for the reader to duplicate the math as opposed to the more complicated process of compounding. Determining the compounded rate of 3.72% necessitates performing an internal rate of return calculation and requires a financial calculator or computer. The expected return calculations throughout this book can be accomplished by hand. This enables readers to replicate the math to suit their own circumstances.

EXHIBIT 16.9   Compounded Rate of Return for IRBs ($000)

	Time Periods (Months)				
	0	1–12	13–24	25–36	...	121–132
Note principal	(10,000)				
Interest received	0	20.8	20.8	20.8		20.8
Principal received						10,000
Letter of credit fee received	100	8.3	8.3	8.3		8.3
Placement fee received	100				
Total	(9,800)	350	350	350	350	10,350
Compounded rate of return:		3.72%			

PEPPERDINE PRIVATE CAPITAL MARKET LINE

Once all of the capital types are described and their expected returns determined, it is possible to graph the PPCML, shown in Exhibit 16.10. The PPCML is empirically defined, since the CAPM or other predictive models are not suitable for use in creating the expected rates of return in the private markets. Somewhere on or near this line is the expected return of the major institutional capital alternatives that exist in the private capital markets.

Exhibit 16.10 encompasses various capital types in terms of the provider's all-in expected returns. The PPCML is described as median, pretax expected returns of institutional capital providers. For consistency, the capital types chosen to comprise the PPCML reflect likely capital options for a lower-middle-market company. As shown in Exhibit 16.4, the PPCML could be created using different data sets.[4]

Throughout the capital chapters, return expectations are generated directly from the Pepperdine Capital Market Surveys or from sample term sheets that use data from the Pepperdine surveys. The marketplace is quite varied as to these returns. The "sample terms/expected returns" combination enables readers to understand the calculations.

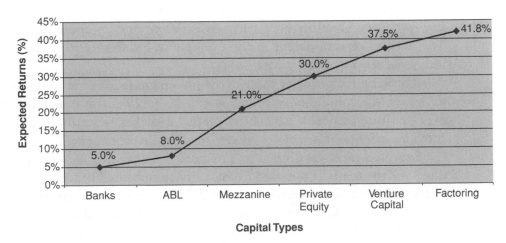

EXHIBIT 16.10   Pepperdine Private Capital Market Line

EXHIBIT 16.11   Expected Returns by Capital Access Point (Prime = 3.5%)

Capital Access Point	Description	Expected Return
IRBs	Industrial Revenue Bonds	3.6%
504	SBA 504 loan	4.0%
B&I	Business and Industry loan	4.8%
7(a)	SBA 7(a) loan	5.8%
ABL 1	Tier 1 asset-based loan	6.2%
CAPLine	SBA CAPline credit line	6.7%
Bank leasing	Bank equipment leasing	7.0%
Captive leasing	Captive/vendor equipment leasing	7.0%
ABL 2	Tier 2 asset-based loan	8.8%
Bank C/L	Bank credit line	9.0%
EWCP	SBA export working capital program	9.7%
Specialty leasing	Specialty equipment leasing	10.0%
Venture leasing	Venture capital leasing	16.5%
ABL 3	Tier 3 asset-based loan	17.3%
Mezzanine	Equity mezzanine capital	19.5%
PEG	Private equity group	30.0%
Factoring L	Large-volume factoring	34.6%
V/C	Venture capital	37.5%
Angel	Angel investing	40.0%
Factoring M	Medium-volume factoring	41.8%
Factoring S	Small-volume factoring	49.5%

Risk and return are matched more closely in private capital markets than previously possible. Most secured lenders receive a lower return than unsecured lenders. But private capital markets are still relatively inefficient in two major ways. In theory, private equity returns should form the highest part of the PPCML, since the investment risk is greatest. Exhibit 16.10 demonstrates that this is not the case. The most expensive capital type involves factoring, which *should* fall closer to asset-based lending in overall returns. The other inefficiency refers to the pricing between the capital types. In an efficiently priced market, the capital alternatives should be priced fairly close to each other, say 20 to 50 basis points (bps) apart. The PPCML can have 900-bps spreads or more from one capital type to the next. An example of this is the difference between the expected rates of return for mezzanine capital (21%) and private equity (30%). A 900-bps is unlikely in an efficiently priced market. The capital access points, with the corresponding expected rates of return (derived from sample term sheets), are listed in Exhibit 16.11.

Although all of these CAPs are described in detail in later chapters, next we present a brief summary of each CAP, in order of increasing expected return percentage.

■ *Industrial Revenue Bonds* (3.6%). Industrial revenue bonds (IRBs) are municipal bonds whose proceeds are loaned to private persons or to businesses to finance capital investment projects. Even though they are municipal bonds, IRBs are not general obligations of the municipality. The municipality is not responsible for debt service, nor is it liable in case of default. The borrower has sole responsibility for paying the principal and the interest on the bonds. Exempt from federal income tax, IRBs have lower interest rates than most comparable capital sources. The bond proceeds can be used to finance entire projects, including land, buildings, and machinery and equipment. Finally, the terms of the agreement among the municipality, the bond buyer, and the borrower can be negotiated to conform to the needs of the borrower. (See Chapter 18.)

■ *SBA 504 Loans* (4.0%). The Small Business Administration (SBA) works with certified development companies around the country who directly oversee the 504 program. A 504 project includes: (a) a loan from a private-sector lender covering up to 50% of the project cost; (b) a loan from the certified development company (CDC), backed by a 100% SBA-guaranteed debenture, covering up to 40% of the cost; and (c) a contribution of at least 10% equity from the small business. As of this writing, the maximum SBA debenture is $1 million for meeting the job creation criteria or a community development goal. (See Chapter 18.)

■ *Business and Industry Loans* (4.8%). The Business and Industry (B&I) Guaranteed Loan Program helps create jobs and stimulates rural economies. This program provides guarantees up to 90% of a loan made by a commercial lender. Loan proceeds may be used for working capital, machinery and equipment, buildings and real estate, and certain types of debt refinancing. The primary purpose is to create and maintain employment and improve the economic climate in rural communities. This is achieved by expanding the lending capability of private lenders in rural areas, helping them make loans that provide lasting community benefits. (See Chapter 18.)

■ *SBA 7(a) Loans* (5.8%). The 7(a) Loan Guaranty Program is one of the SBA's primary programs. It provides loans to small businesses unable to secure financing on reasonable terms through normal lending channels. The program operates through SBA-guaranteed, private-sector lenders. (See Chapter 18.)

■ *Tier 1 Asset-Based Loan* (6.2%). Tier 1 asset-based lenders (ABLs) typically comprise the larger commercial banks' ABL divisions. This tier usually requires a break-even earning capacity, although sometimes a negative earning capacity expected to turn positive is acceptable. Tier 1 ABLs also typically want initial fundings of at least $10 million and preferably more than $15 million. (See Chapter 20.)

■ *SBA CAPLines* (6.7%). CAPLines is the umbrella program under which the SBA helps small businesses meet their short-term and cyclical working capital needs. (See Chapter 18.)

■ *Bank Leasing* (7.0%). Banks are a major source of equipment leases. Because of their relatively cheap cost of funds, banks may offer the least expensive lease. Banks require a strong credit position and usually already have a lending or other relationship with the borrower. Banks are at a disadvantage when it comes to residual value of the equipment because they are not active players in the equipment market. Because of this, banks are not competitive when residual value is difficult to predict. (See Chapter 19.)

■ *Captive/Vendor Leasing* (7.0%). Many large manufacturing companies provide financing to their customers, sometimes in the form of an equipment lease. Captive-leasing companies typically are divisions or subsidiaries of these manufacturers leasing only the larger company's products. Since captive lessors are generally part of a large company, their cost of funds tends to be low, making them highly competitive. (See Chapter 19.)

- *Tier 2 Asset-Based Loan* (8.8%). Tier 2 ABLs tend to fund riskier borrowers, that is, those that may have negative earning capacities but are expected to break even in the next year. As compensation for this additional risk, tier 2 ABL lenders require a higher interest rate than the tier 1 lenders. In a typical market, this interest rate is generally 1 to 2 points above the prime rate. Tier 2 lenders tend to be ABL divisions of midsize banks or independent arms of larger finance companies. Tier 2 ABLs prefer initial fundings of $3 million to $15 million but may bid on smaller deals if the possibility of strong loan growth exists. (See Chapter 20.)
- *Bank Credit Line* (9.0%). This is a standard credit line offered by a bank. The borrower pays interest on the money it actually borrows, instead of the committed amount. (See Chapter 17.)
- *Export Working Capital Program* (9.7%). The Export Working Capital Program (EWCP) provides short-term working capital to exporters. The SBA's EWCP supports export financing to small businesses when they cannot find loans elsewhere. The program encourages lenders to offer export working capital loans by guaranteeing repayment of up to $1 million or 90% of a loan amount, whichever is less. A loan can support a single transaction or multiple sales on a revolving basis. (See Chapter 18.)
- *Specialty Equipment Leasing* (10.0%). Some equipment lessors specialize in an industry or with certain types of equipment. These lessors have an advantage in situations where the underlying equipment has an uncertain secondary market (i.e., where specialized knowledge about equipment obsolescence creates a lessor advantage). Specialized equipment lessors may be more expensive than other lessor types at the outset, because of their higher cost of funds and the lack of reliance on residual value. However, for specialized equipment, this lessor ultimately may be cheaper than the other lessors. This is because this lessor works with the lessee over time and absorbs some of the obsolescence risk of the equipment. (See Chapter 19.)
- *Venture Capital Leasing* (16.5%). Venture leasing provides general-purpose equipment, such as computers, telecommunication systems, and office equipment, to start-up and early-stage companies. In exchange for the lease financing, the venture lessor receives monthly equipment payments, the equipment's residual value, and possibly equity warrants in the company. Even without accounting for the warrant cost, this lessor type may offer the highest-cost lease to lessees. (See Chapter 19.)
- *Tier 3 Asset-Based Loan* (17.3%). Tier 3 ABLs are driven less by the earning capacity of the borrower and more by collateral liquidation values. It is not unusual for tier 3 lenders to fund companies that do not expect to make money in the foreseeable future. Tier 3 lenders have the highest interest rates of the three tiers as well as the most restrictive lending arrangements. Tier 3 ABLs may loan less than $1 million per transaction but normally do not loan more than $2 to $3 million. (See Chapter 20.)

- *Mezzanine Capital* (19.5%). Mezzanine capital is subordinated debt that provides borrowing capability beyond senior debt while minimizing the dilution associated with equity capital. Mezzanine investors provide financing with a lower-than- adequate running yield but a higher equity kicker offsetting the risk-capital aspects of the investment. The trigger for the mezzanine investor is often the case in pre-IPO-situations, acquisitions of small and medium companies, and high-growth situations. (See Chapter 22.)
- *Private Equity Groups* (30.0%). Private equity groups (PEGs) are direct investors in the equity of private companies, especially in later-stage firms. PEGs tend toward control investments through recapitalizations or direct buyouts; however, many take a minority position in the right deal. (See Chapter 24.)
- *Factoring, Large Volume* (34.6%). This type of financing involves factoring relationships over $500,000 per month in volume. (See Chapter 21.)
- *Venture Capital* (37.5%). Venture capital is money provided by professionals who invest alongside management in early- to expansion-stage companies that have the potential to develop into significant economic contributors. Venture capital is an important source of equity for start-up companies. (See Chapter 23.)
- *Angel Investing* (40.0%). Angel investors tend to be wealthy investors who wish to participate in high-risk deals to satisfy some entrepreneurial urge and make a risk-adjusted return at the same time. (See Chapter 23.)
- *Factoring, Medium Volume* (41.8%). This type of financing involves factoring relationships between $100,000 to $500,000 per month in volume. (See Chapter 21.)
- *Factoring, Small Volume* (49.5%). This type of financing involves factoring relationships between $20,000 to $100,000 per month in volume. (See Chapter 21.)

This list describes most of the institutional CAPs available to finance private businesses. However, due to space limitations, not all CAPs in the private capital markets are discussed. An example is floor plan loans. Floor plans are used by various dealers to finance higher-priced items, such as automobiles, appliances, and boats. Floor planning enables dealers to maintain large inventory levels without making large out-of-pocket investments.

Floor plans typically are supplied by the finance company of a manufacturer. This arrangement solves several problems for the manufacturer. It enables the manufacturer to smooth its production schedule because dealers are required to take a certain number of units each month. Since dealers have minimal investment in the inventory, they can manage the inflows, even if it takes many months to sell. Manufacturers also make money on the financing relationship. In many cases, for example, the financing arms of automotive companies make more money than the manufacturing divisions. Finally, by flooding the market with numerous models, colors, and options, manufacturers are better able to service customers.

Although programs vary, in a typical floor planning arrangement, the lender advances a large percentage, sometimes 80% to 95%, of the cost of inventory but retains title to the assets. The finance company pays the manufacturer upon delivery of the inventory. This action also creates an outstanding loan balance to the dealer. To encourage aggressive marketing, manufacturers often incentivize dealers by offering interest-free periods or rebates through the financing company.

Dealers repay specific loans as the assets are sold. Failure to pay within the specified time may cause the dealer to be considered out of trust. This situation usually causes all of the floor plan loans to accelerate and, if left unresolved, may cause a termination of the financing relationship. Finance companies implement sophisticated inventory-control and repayment systems at dealerships to overcome miscommunications between the parties.

Floor plan financing is also available from banks and other lending institutions. However, vendors have more of a strategic interest to finance their goods than do outside lenders. Similar to vendor leasing, expected returns of vendor-supplied floor planning may be quite attractive since manufacturers make money from financing and manufacturing, and may subsidize the former activity.

Floor plan financing is not available to every private company. The type of business or its relationship with its vendors determines applicability. Companies that do qualify for this financing live in the details of these programs. Because these plans are used for a number of purposes and motives, there are no standardized expected returns from the capital providers. For all of these reasons, floor plan financing is not treated as a CAP and is not shown on the PPCML.

There are a number of noteworthy issues regarding the PPCML.

KEY ISSUES REGARDING THE PEPPERDINE PRIVATE CAPITAL MARKET LINE

The PPCML assumes transaction sizes of roughly in the range between $1 million and $50 million. Beyond $50 million, a borrower begins to have more sophisticated capital alternatives, such as loans from insurance companies and securitizations.

For presentation purposes, the expected returns plotted on the PPCML reflect a prime interest rate of 3.5%. Interest rate changes tend to affect the bottom half of the line (venture leasing and below) more than the top half (debt mezzanine capital and above). For instance, banks and asset-based lenders index to either the prime rate or LIBOR (London Interbank Offered Rate). The mezzanine and equity part of the private markets tend to require returns somewhat independent of interest rate indices. This fact can be corroborated by the behavior of high-yield players throughout the past 20 years. Regardless of the interest rate level or the other macroeconomic conditions, mezzanine investors require compounded returns around 20% while equity players require returns in the 30% to 40% range.

The PPCML is helpful when companies form or add to their capital structure. The financing goal of every company is to minimize its effective borrowing or investment costs. To achieve this, companies should *walk* the PPCML. This means borrowers should start at the least expensive lowest part of the line and move up the line when forced to do so by the market.

Some owners *skip* along the PPCML, incurring opportunity costs. An "opportunity cost" refers to the added capital cost to the company for not acquiring the least expensive cost of capital available. There is little reason to pay 34% for factoring, for instance, if tier 3 ABL is accessible at 17%. In this example, the company suffers an opportunity cost of 17 percentage points.

Many owners unknowingly incur opportunity costs. The cost of trade credit is laden with hidden opportunity costs. A brief example demonstrates how the timing of an invoice payment can result in an opportunity cost. Assume PrivateCo has a $1,000 invoice with payment terms of 2/10, net 30. If the firm does not pay within 10 days, it pays a finance charge of $20 for the use of the goods for the next 20 days. The effective cost of this decision not to take the discount is seen when viewed in annual terms. The next equation shows how to quantify the annual interest expense of this lost opportunity.

$$\text{Trade credit interest}\% = \left(\frac{\text{Percentage discount}}{\text{100\% minus percentage discount}} \right) \times \left(\frac{360}{\text{Payment period minus discount period}} \right)$$

$$= \left(\frac{.02}{1 - .02} \right) \times \left(\frac{360}{30 - 10} \right)$$

$$= 36.7\%$$

On an annual basis 2/10, net 30 costs approximately 36.7%, which puts not taking this discount in the same cost neighborhood as private equity and venture capital. Yet many owners forgo taking a discount rather than use a credit line to pay the invoice. Meanwhile, the credit line may have an expected cost of less than 10%. The opportunity cost of not taking the discount in this example is quite large. The key point here is for owners to consider costs of capital in a comparative setting. The PPCML is a tool for focusing this thought process and, hopefully, reducing opportunity costs.

CAPITAL STRUCTURE TREATMENT

A number of assumptions and perspectives guide this book's treatment of capitalization. Various capital categories are described as capital types. The capital types are then broken into specific alternatives, or CAPs. The other major perspectives are presented next.

First, keep in mind that this is not a how-to-write-a-business-plan book. Many such books already exist, most of which can be located with an Internet search. The key premise for borrowers to attract capital is to demonstrate that the capital provider gets the required return with the least risk possible. As long as the presentation focuses on this risk/return correlation, the investee is well served.

Second, this is not a list-of-capital-providers book. Within each capital type, there are sometimes thousands of different capital providers, and they change daily. The Internet contains up-to-date lists.

Third, the PPCML describes the expected rates of return required by various capital providers. This line is stated on a pretax basis, from both a provider and a user perspective. In other words, capital providers offer deals to the marketplace on a pretax basis. For example, if a private equity investor requires a 35% return, this is stated as a pretax return. Also, the PPCML does not assume a tax rate to the investee, even though many of the CAPs use interest rates that generate deductible interest expense for the borrower. CAPs are not tax-effected because many owners of private companies manage their company's tax bill through various aggressive techniques. It is virtually impossible to estimate a generalized appropriate tax rate for this market.

Borrowers should consider the tax-deductible features of CAPs when making investment decisions, however. Fortunately, this is just a matter of using the information provided in the chapters and applying a specific tax rate.

Finally, the required or expected returns of private capital providers are different from returns actually realized. Investors hope all of their investments live up to expectations. Of course, the end result is often quite different. Exhibit 16.12, taken from data published by Thomson Reuters, shows actual returns for a variety of private equity sources.[5]

The Private Equity Performance Index is based on the latest quarterly statistics from Thomson Reuters' private Equity Performance Database analyzing the cash flows and returns for over 2,044 U.S. venture capital and private equity partnerships with a capitalization of $982.6 billion. Sources are financial documents and schedules from limited partner investors and from general partners. All returns are calculated by Thomson Reuters from the underlying financial cash flows. Returns are net to investors after management fees and carried interest.

Exhibit 16.12 shows riskier investments return more than less-risky investments. For example, early/seed venture capital returns more than later-stage venture capital, which itself returns more than mezzanine capital.

Yet a substantial difference exists from these realized returns and the expected returns discussed earlier. This chapter suggests that mezzanine capital providers seek expected returns of about 20%, buyout firms (PEGs) expect returns of about

EXHIBIT 16.12 Thomson Reuters U.S. Private Equity Performance Index (PEPI)*

Fund Type	5 Year	10 Year	20 Year
Early/seed venture capital	1.1	−3.6	23.2
Balanced venture capital	7.0	−.1	14.8
Later-stage venture capital	8.3	.3	15.5
All venture capital	5.2	−1.5	17.8
All buyouts	5.4	4.0	9.0
Mezzanine capital	2.7	2.3	6.7
All private equity	5.8	2.8	11.3

*As of March 31, 2010.

30%, and venture capitalists target approximately 40% returns. Over a 10-year period, the realized returns for these groups are 2%, 3%, and (1.5)%, respectively. What explains these rather large differences between expected and realized returns?

Perhaps most of the difference lies in the nature of *picking winners* in the private capital markets. Given the uncertainty surrounding the companies that qualify for private equity, providers may need to shoot for 30% to actually receive a positive return (although 3% is not an acceptable risk-adjusted return). There may be insufficient information about the investee's prospects at the time of the investment for the capital provider to make winning decisions. Whatever the reasons for the difference, companies in need of private capital are subjected to the provider's expected returns, not realized returns, when the deal is structured.

Private capital markets are fairly inefficient, in terms of both capital access and pricing consistency. There is a structure to this market, however. Institutional capital alternatives are identifiable and definable. A handful of capital types comprise dozens of CAPs. Access to CAPs is determined through credit boxes. Sample terms indicate likely deal terms. Expected rates are calculated from the sample terms and represent the return required by the capital providers. Finally, the expected rates are graphed to form the PPCML.

TRIANGULATION

Capitalization is dependent on the value world in which the company is viewed and the availability of transfer methods. Triangulation is graphically depicted in Exhibit 16.13. Specific CAPs are linked to value worlds. Once located within a value world, a company's value can be determined. Capital availability affects

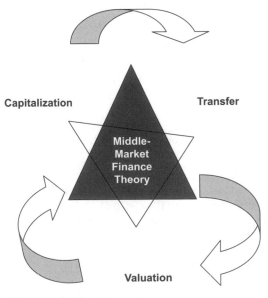

EXHIBIT 16.13 Triangulation

transfer options and pricing. The type of capital employed by a company directly impacts its transfer alternatives.

The lower half of the PPCML is tied to the world of collateral value. Secured lenders rely on collateral of a borrower to make credit decisions. Mezzanine lenders and private equity providers primarily look at the company through the world of market value to make investment decisions. It is important to understand through which value world a capital provider views the company since, in the eyes of the provider, the company has value only in that world. For instance, a bank will not view the subject in the world of market value because, if liquidation occurs, the bank must look to the company's assets for repayment.

Equity availability affects the firm's value. Limited access to equity necessarily impairs access to debt and thereby limits growth. The return expectation of institutional private equity is too high to allow a company to grow on equity alone. Achieving these return expectations requires leveraging equity and debt. If an owner cannot or will not increase equity, others are unlikely to invest equity or debt. The equity portion of a firm's capital structure affects its ability to attract debt, its ability to grow, and ultimately, its value.

The availability of capital to finance private transactions is a driving force behind private acquisition multiples. Debt typically constitutes 60% to 70% or more of a buyer's capital structure. Access to debt affects an acquirer's ability to price an acquisition.

Consider service industries, which do not rely on large asset bases to generate earnings. Contractors and professional service providers fit into this category. Due to the lack of a collateral base and reliable income streams, senior lending is quite limited in these industries. As a result, the pricing multiples for these businesses tend to be less than for companies in asset-heavy industries. For example, a contractor may sell for three times its benefit stream, as compared to four to seven times for a proprietary manufacturer.

NOTES

1. The public capital markets line shown in the text depicts expected returns for investors in the largest public companies. Further, this line is presented in a historical context. The actual line may vary significantly from the presentation based on market conditions.
2. John D. Emory, "Expanded Study of the Value of Marketability as Illustrated in Initial Public Offerings of Common Stock," *Business Valuation News* (December 2001), pp. 4–20.
3. John K. Paglia, Pepperdine Private Capital Markets Project Survey Report, April 2010, bschool.pepperdine.edu/privatecapital.
4. Ibid.
5. Thomson Reuters Corporation, thomsonreuters.com, August 10, 2010.

CHAPTER 17

Bank Lending

There are a variety of senior lenders in the marketplace. This group typically has a first, or senior, position in the collateral pool of a company. Commercial banks, the primary players in this group, are the focus of this chapter. Owner-managers are motivated to seek bank lending for several reasons. Banks historically have been the largest source of capital for small to medium-size businesses. Banks also typically have been the cheapest source of borrowed funds. Over the past 15 years, banks have broadened their offerings to include a spectrum of financial alternatives appealing to owners in need of more sophisticated services. Banks now serve as financial intermediaries. They lend, arrange, advise, and directly invest capital in private companies.

Bank credit is rationed based on the return needs of the institution. Banks seek to maximize the spread between deposits received and income-producing assets. Business lending is an example of the latter. Banks lend to small businesses only when it is likely that the loans will be repaid. Credit quality is enhanced by sophisticated underwriting techniques, such as credit scoring for individual loans and repayment projections for commercial loans. Even with these methods, lending to small businesses remains risky. This fact in part explains banks' hierarchical decision-making structures. Most banks require a handful of bank officer signatures on the loan request as an experiential hedge against this risk.

This chapter describes the types of loans banks extend, interest rate options and hedges, loan costs, loan covenants, risk ratings, and negotiating points to consider. Exhibit 17.1 provides a snapshot of bank lending.

TYPES OF FACILITIES

Most banks offer loans such as term loans, credit lines, and letters of credit, although the terminology may change from bank to bank. Banks frequently offer government-sponsored loans, the subject of the next chapter. The next sections discuss each type of bank loan with an emphasis on required collateral and payment terms.

EXHIBIT 17.1 Capital Coordinates: Bank Lending (Credit Line)

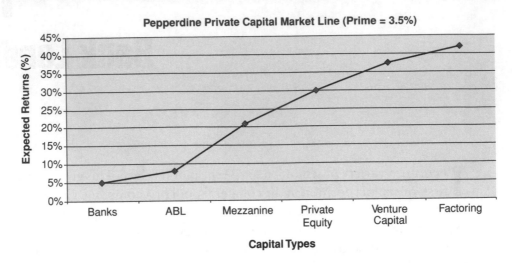

Capital Access Point	Credit Line
Definition	A credit line allows a company to borrow against an established credit limit to meet short-term working capital needs. There are various costs for a credit line in addition to the stated interest rate. Borrowers should consider closing points, compensating balances, unused line fees, and float days as additional costs of the loan. The credit box for a credit line requires a borrower to possess sufficient collateral and cash flow to service the loan.
Expected Rate of Return	9.0%
Likely Provider	Banks
Value World(s)	Collateral value
Transfer Method(s)	Credit lines may be involved with any or all transfer methods.
Appropriate to Use When . . .	A borrower's cash flow fluctuates within a month or season, causing short-term working capital needs. Credit lines should be used only when the capital need is also short term.
Key Points to Consider	Banks are less obtrusive to healthy borrowers than most other capital providers. Financial reporting is periodic and not as demanding. A credit line may or may not provide adequate growth capital. Credit lines are usually for fixed amounts and are not intended to mirror a company's growth curve. Many banks require an annual cleanup period where the credit line must be reduced to zero for at least one month.

Term Loan

Term loans are used most often to finance fixed-asset purchases, such as equipment, vehicles, furniture, and fixtures. They also can be used to finance permanent working capital or debt consolidation. Term loan features include:

- A choice of a fixed or variable interest rate, which is discussed later.
- Various terms to meet borrowers' needs. Usually terms are no more than five years with the exception of commercial real estate loans that offer longer terms.

- The advantage of spreading the cost of the fixed asset over its useful life, providing the borrower with a manageable monthly payment.

Term debt is collateralized by a first lien on the current and long-term assets of the company. Because term loans have specific time and terms, repayment must be made within the useful life of the financed asset.

Credit Line

A credit line allows a company to borrow against an established credit limit for short-term working capital. Borrowings are payable on demand, and interest rates usually are tied to an index, such as the prime rate. A credit line can be secured or unsecured. If the line is secured, the collateral base is comprised of "short-term" assets, such as receivables or inventory. Credit lines are subject to review at least annually.

These loans enable a company to borrow up to a specified amount of money whenever it is needed. The company pays interest on the money it actually borrows, instead of the committed amount. Some banks charge commitment fees and unused line fees, but these are negotiated up-front between the bank and the borrower. A typical line of credit is seasonal, in that it helps to supply a company's seasonal cash needs. Seasonal lines usually require a company to pledge specific assets, such as receivables and inventory, to collateralize the loan.

Letter of Credit

A letter of credit (L/C) is a written agreement issued by a bank and given to the seller (exporter) at the request of the buyer (importer) to pay up to a stated sum of money. The L/C is good for a stated period of time (the expiration date) and is payable upon presentation of stipulated documents. Payment may be made immediately or after a specified period of time. In effect, the issuing bank is substituting its credit for that of the buyer. Since an experienced bank has a broad correspondent base, the letter of credit can travel directly from the buyer's bank to the exporter's bank without passing through multiple banks.

If the buyer requests a letter of credit from its bank, it is granted only if the buyer has established an adequate line of credit with the bank. On behalf of the buyer, the bank then promises to pay the purchase price to a seller, or the seller's appointed bank, if the stipulated and highly detailed conditions are met. Example conditions include complete shipment, onboard, ocean bills of lading, a commercial invoice and original packing slip, and proof of adequate insurance.

An element of L/Cs that surprises novice users is the attention to detail required. There is no item too small to consider. Export managers learn to take great care to correct every misspelling in original documents. Some banks use whatever excuse possible to delay processing documents while holding their customers' money.

L/Cs are available in a variety of forms. Some of these are confirmed irrevocable L/Cs, confirmed L/Cs, and acceptance L/Cs. Irrevocable L/Cs are the most common form.

Collateral

Collateral is property that secures a loan, or other debt, so the lender may seize the property if the borrower fails to make proper payments on the loan.

When lenders demand collateral for a secured loan, they are seeking to minimize the risks of extending credit. To ensure the collateral provides appropriate security, the lender matches the type of collateral with the loan being made. For example, the useful life of the collateral typically needs to meet or exceed the term of the loan, or the lender's secured interest would be jeopardized. Consequently, short-term assets, such as receivables and inventory, are not acceptable as security for a long-term loan, but they may be appropriate for short-term financing, such as a line of credit.

In addition, many lenders require their claim to the collateral in the form of a first-secured interest. This means no prior or superior liens exist, or may be subsequently created, against the collateral. As a priority lien holder, the lender ensures its share of any foreclosure proceeds before any other claimant.

Lenders further limit their risks by discounting the value of the collateral and not lending 100% of the collateral's highest value. This relationship between the amounts of money a lender extends and the value of the collateral is called the *loan-to-value* ratio, also known as *advance rates*. Advance rates reflect the percentage of each asset class a lender actually will loan against. For example, a lender may advance 80% against eligible receivables, 50% against eligible inventory, and so on. Eligibility varies from lender to lender and is explained in detail in Chapter 20.

The type of collateral used to secure the loan affects the lender's advance rates. For example, unimproved real estate yields a lower advance rate than improved occupied real estate. These rates vary between lenders, and lending criteria other than the value of the collateral may also influence the rate. For example, a healthy cash flow may allow for more leeway in the rate. A representative listing of advance rates for different types of collateral at a typical secured lender is shown in Exhibit 17.2. *The type of value* represents the method for determining the asset value that is then multiplied by the advance rate.

Margined collateral is the result of an advance rate applied against a qualifying asset. A borrower's total margined collateral value is determined by applying advance rates against qualifying asset groups.

Loan Payments

Loan repayment schedules are highly negotiable based on the needs of the parties. However, borrowers sometimes forget that the longer it takes to pay back the principal. the higher the total interest payment will become. Some payment options are:

EXHIBIT 17.2 Typical Advance Rates

Asset	Advance Rate	Type of Value
Real Estate		
Occupied	80%	Appraised value
Improved, not occupied	50%	Appraised value
Vacant and unimproved	30%	Appraised value
Inventory		
Raw Materials	50%–60%	Eligible amount
Work-in-process	0%	
Finished goods	50%–60%	Eligible amount
Accounts receivable	70%–80%	Eligible amount
Equipment	75%–85%	Purchase price

- *Equal payments.* This type of loan requires the borrower to pay the same amount each period (monthly or quarterly) for a specified number of periods. Part of each payment is applied to interest, and the balance is applied to principal. The loan is fully repaid after the specified number of periods.
- *Equal payments with a final balloon payment.* This type of loan requires the borrower to make equal monthly payments of principal and interest for a relatively short period of time. After the last installment payment, the borrower must pay the balance in one payment, called a balloon payment.
- *Interest-only payments and a final balloon payment.* With this type of loan, the borrower's regular payments cover only interest. The principal is unchanged. At the end of the loan term, the borrower makes a balloon payment to cover the entire principal and any remaining interest. Borrowers often prefer this payment structure because of the lower periodic payments. However, borrowers ultimately pay more interest because they are borrowing the principal for a longer time.
- *Equal principal payments.* This type of loan requires the borrower to pay the same amount of principal each period for a specified number of periods. The total payment for each period is variable, and it should decline as the borrower pays interest only on the outstanding principal at the beginning of the period. With this payment structure, borrowers pay larger payments at the beginning of the loan.

INTEREST RATES

Most business borrowers still associate interest rates with the prime rate, the rate banks have historically charged their most creditworthy customers. Over the past decade or so, however, the prime rate has given way to different market indices, such as LIBOR (London Interbank Offered Rate) and swap rates. There are two options to set interest rates:

1. *Fixed rate.* With a fixed-rate loan, the interest rate applied to the outstanding principal remains constant throughout a predetermined period that may or

may not equal the length of the loan. The interest rate is set at the beginning of a loan by examining the risk involved and the current market rates. The advantage of a fixed-rate loan is that the interest rate is fixed. The payments are constant and will not rise if the market rate rises. But the borrower does not benefit from a decline of the market rate. Many lenders will incorporate prepayment penalties into their loan terms to protect yield. As an aside, some banks will quote fixed interest rates using a 360-day year, which helps to increase the bank's yield.

2. *Variable interest rate.* With a variable interest rate, the interest rate applied on the outstanding principal amount fluctuates in line with changes to the prime rate or LIBOR and, as a result, so will the amount of the borrower's payments. The interest rate for each period is the current market rate plus a predetermined premium, which remains constant during the life of the loan. With a variable interest rate loan, the borrower saves money when the market rate decreases. The disadvantage, however, is the interest the borrower pays will increase with the market rate.

Fixed Rates

Most banks will not offer loans with fixed interest rates for a term longer than five to seven years because its cost of funds may increase significantly above the fixed rate on the loan. However, banks can "match funds" by locking in a rate on a certificate of deposit or other liability for the same amount and term as the loan.

Variable Rates

Banks may offer many different types of "floating" interest rates. Some of the more common are:

- *Prime rate.* Most banks follow the lead of the major money center banks in setting their own prime rates. Unless the borrower's loan agreement specifies "New York prime," a bank's prime rate may be different from the prime announced by such money center banks. Furthermore, increases or decreases in a borrower's rate may lag the market leaders by a day, a weekend, or even longer. Most banks define their prime rate as the rate of interest established by the bank from time to time whether or not such rate shall be otherwise published. The borrower's loan agreement also specifies how quickly its rate changes after prime changes. Usually it is immediately, but sometimes it is not until the first of the next month.
- *LIBOR.* LIBOR is the rate on dollar-denominated deposits, also known as Eurodollars, traded between banks in London. The index is quoted for one month, three months, six months, or one-year periods. LIBOR is the base interest rate paid on deposits between banks in the Eurodollar market. A Eurodollar is a dollar deposited in a bank in a country where the currency is not the dollar. The Eurodollar market has been around for decades and is a

major component of the international financial market. London is the center of the Euromarket in terms of volume.

The LIBOR rate quoted in the *Wall Street Journal* is the LIBOR posted by the British Bankers' Association (BBA). Each day the *Wall Street Journal* publishes the prior day's BBA LIBOR rate as part of the Money Rates table in the Money and Investing section.

■ *Swap rates.* Swap rates are derived from interest rates set in derivative contracts, or swaps, which trade every day in the multitrillion-dollar international market. Although a swap can take many complex forms, the transaction is fundamentally an agreement between two parties to exchange short-term interest payments for long-term interest payments, or vice versa. Each party agrees to assume the interest rate payments of the other's loan, based on the particular party's desire to hedge its interest rate risk. The fixed rate, of 1 to 30 years, that the floating rate borrower has assumed is his "swap rate." The Federal Reserve publishes average swap rates for appropriate fixed-term periods. Because the parties involved in such swaps are high-grade corporate and municipal entities, swap rates represent an active and liquid schedule of rates between highly creditworthy institutions.

As an example, suppose a borrower has a seven-year commercial mortgage tied to one-month LIBOR. The company is concerned about rate volatility during the life of the loan. The borrower decides to swap its floating rate for a fixed rate to mitigate the risk. In the swap transaction, the company pays a fixed rate of 3% to its swap counterpart, SwapCo, in exchange for receiving LIBOR. The swap cash flows are based on a principal schedule matching the outstanding loan. In other words, the LIBOR payment the company receives from SwapCo offsets the LIBOR payment the company owes to its lenders.

Note that the borrower has engaged in two separate transactions: a loan and a swap. In the loan transaction, the company is making floating-rate interest payments (LIBOR plus borrowing spread) to its lenders. In the swap transaction, the company is making or receiving payments based on the difference between LIBOR and the swap rate. The borrower, in effect, has created a fixed rate on the loan and is immunized against movements in LIBOR.

LIBOR versus Prime

Historically, the LIBOR interest rate has been much lower than the prime rate. As Exhibit 17.3 shows, since 1995, the difference ranged from 220 to 320 basis points (bps; a basis point is .01%).[1]

LIBOR is usually priced in the marketplace at some premium, such as +200. This means the quoted rate is LIBOR plus 200 bps (or LIBOR plus 2%). This raises the question whether LIBOR with a premium is actually cheaper than borrowing at prime. At least one study has shown that it is cheaper. The study conducted by the Loan Pricing Corporation found that prime borrowing is more expensive by roughly 125 to 150 bps. This difference is known as the *prime premium*. The study also shows that the added volatility of LIBOR does not account for difference. In other words, even with the added risk of greater LIBOR rate swings, which are

EXHIBIT 17.3   Prime versus LIBOR Rates

Date	Prime	3-Month LIBOR	Difference (Basis Points)
6/95	9.0%	6.0%	300
6/96	8.3%	5.6%	270
6/97	8.5%	5.8%	270
6/98	8.5%	5.8%	270
6/99	7.8%	5.4%	240
6/00	9.5%	6.8%	270
6/01	7.0%	3.8%	320
6/02	4.8%	1.9%	290
6/03	4.2%	1.1%	310
6/04	4.2%	1.6%	260
6/05	6.2%	3.5%	270
6/06	8.2%	5.5%	270
6/07	7.7%	5.4%	230
6/08	5.0%	2.8%	220
6/09	3.2%	.6%	260
6/10	3.2%	.5%	270

more intense than prime in the near term, it is still substantially cheaper to borrow at LIBOR.[2]

Economists claim that markets eventually correct an imbalance. Why has the prime premium not been reduced or eliminated? The main reason involves competition. Historically, LIBOR borrowers were public companies with the ability to issue commercial paper or public bonds. These companies had established credit ratings, and the spread above LIBOR represented a premium for default risk only. Prime-based lending, however, adds additional spread to pay for the cost of investigating and monitoring privately owned borrowers. With increased competition, lenders have chosen to introduce LIBOR pricing to the private sector apparently without getting paid for the added cost of fully monitoring these borrowers.

Competitive pressure increasingly will lead to long-term stability in the spread between prime and LIBOR. The cost of capital for most major lenders is similar, leading to similar consumer interest rates. Since most lenders publish the interest rates they charge, there is little reason for one major lender to undercut the others on price, since it knows that the others will quickly match rates. Any advantage will be short-lived. Aside from branding, marketing, and other secondary factors, debt is a commodity. Since money is fungible, it matters less on who the lender is, and more on the general health of companies so they can afford to repay the loans.

But interest rates can be managed by employing sophisticated hedging techniques, as discussed next.

INTEREST RATE HEDGES

There are methods by which interest rates can be hedged, or controlled, by the borrower for a price. Due to the complexity of some of these strategies, some

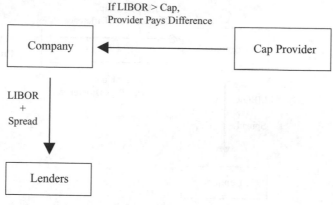

EXHIBIT 17.4 Interest Rate Cap

techniques may be limited to accredited investors. Three hedging techniques are shown here: cap, collar, and lock.

Interest Rate Cap

An interest rate cap is used by companies to set a maximum interest rate they will pay on their borrowings. Exhibit 17.4 illustrates an interest rate cap. If the floating rate rises above a cap level, the company is credited for the difference. If the floating rate remains unchanged or declines, the company benefits from lower borrowing rates. The cap is purchased with a one-time up-front fee, usually referred to as a premium. Typically a cap can be purchased for a minimum of 90 days and a maximum term of five years. Once the premium is paid, there are no other costs or risks associated with the hedge.

As an illustration, suppose PrivateCo has a $20 million, two-year revolving credit facility tied to LIBOR. Core outstandings are $12.5 million. PrivateCo uses one-month LIBOR, assumed at 3.5%, as its primary borrowing index. For planning purposes, the company has assumed that LIBOR will not rise above 4.5%.

Without any hedge, PrivateCo is vulnerable to rising rates. To protect its projections, PrivateCo decides to purchase a cap on one-month LIBOR at 4.5%. The contract will cover a core amount of $12.5 million. PrivateCo pays an initial premium for two years of protection. If LIBOR rises above 4.5% during the two-year contract period, PrivateCo will be reimbursed by the cap provider for the difference.

Interest Rate Collar

Borrowers use interest rate collars to set the minimum (floor) and maximum (cap) interest rates they will pay on their borrowings. Exhibit 17.5 illustrates an interest rate collar. If the floating rate rises above the cap level, the company is credited for the difference. If the floating rate falls below the floor level, the company is debited for the difference.

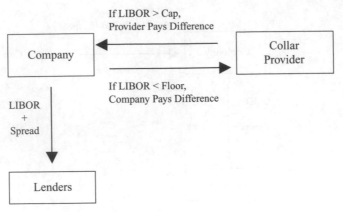

EXHIBIT 17.5   Interest Rate Collar

By way of example, suppose PrivateCo just completed a midsize acquisition financed with a syndicated bank credit facility. The facility is a $25 million, six-year combined reducing revolving credit and term loan with LIBOR pricing. The financing includes a 50% hedge requirement for a minimum term of three years.

PrivateCo and its lenders have agreed that the maximum LIBOR rate threshold to support cash flow projections is 3.5%. Management believes that three-month LIBOR, currently (in this example) at 2.5%, is headed higher over the foreseeable future but eventually may reverse course. PrivateCo enters a $12.5 million, three-year collar with a cap of 3.5% and a floor of 1.5%. If during the three-year collar agreement period LIBOR rises above 3.5%, PrivateCo will be reimbursed by the collar provider for the difference. If LIBOR declines below 1.5% to, say, 1.0%, PrivateCo will owe (1.5% − 1.0%) = .50% on the collar.

Forward Rate Locks

Forward rate locks enable a company to borrow at a certain interest rate at a specified date in the future. Exhibit 17.6 illustrates a forward rate lock. On the specified future date, if the actual interest rate is higher than the lock rate, the

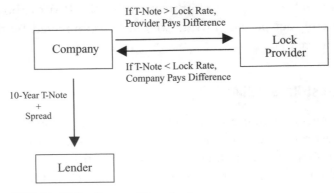

EXHIBIT 17.6   Forward Rate Lock

company is credited for the difference. If the actual interest rate is lower than the lock rate, the company is charged for the difference.

As an example, a forward rate lock is often used by a company to hedge a future borrowing need. For example, suppose management of PrivateCo believes it will need to borrow heavily in the next 90 days but that interest rates may spike upward during this period. Further, assume that PrivateCo borrows at the prime rate, and this rate currently is 3.5%.

To protect against an increase in rates, PrivateCo enters into a forward lock agreement with BankCo for three months forward at a fixed rate of 3.5%. In three months, PrivateCo would borrow the anticipated funds at a variable rate. If the prime interest rate at that time was higher than 3.5%, BankCo would compensate PrivateCo for the difference in rates, and vice versa.

LOAN COVENANTS

Loan covenants are used by lending institutions to influence borrowers to comply with the terms in the loan agreement. If the borrower does not act in accordance with the covenants, the loan may be considered in default and the lender may have the right to demand payment in full. Loan agreements between banks and customers generally contain several types of covenants: Affirmative covenants require the borrower do certain things; negative covenants restrict the borrower in some way; and financial covenants require the borrower to maintain certain financial characteristics during the term of the loan agreement.

Affirmative covenants generally require the borrower to comply with basic rules. Examples of affirmative covenants include:

- Maintain legal existence.
- Stay current with all taxes.
- Maintain appropriate insurances.
- Keep an accurate financial reporting system.
- Provide the bank with reports as required.
- Possibly maintain compensating balances with the bank.

Negative covenants usually restrict the actions of the corporation and ownership. Examples of negative covenants include:

- Limits to level of indebtedness.
- Limits to distributions, dividends, or management fees.
- Do not merge with or acquire another company.
- Do not allow other liens on company assets.
- No changes in ownership.
- Restrict corporate guarantees.

Financial covenants measure company ratios against projections the management provided before or during the loan process. Examples of financial covenants include:

- Maintain a current ratio (current assets divided by current liabilities) of not less than 1.5 to 1.
- Maintain tangible net worth in excess of $1 million.
- Maintain a ratio of total liabilities to tangible net worth of no greater than 3 to 1.

Covenant requirements can be extensive, depending on the amount and term of the loan and the credit standing of the borrower. Most banks monitor compliance with loan covenants on a quarterly basis with the receipt of quarterly and annual financial statements. Sometimes the bank requires a periodic certification by a corporate officer or independent accountant that no covenant violation has occurred, called a compliance certificate.

HOW BANKS DEAL WITH COVENANT VIOLATIONS

Banks take loan covenants quite seriously and generally are careful to watch for violations. Sometimes violations may go undetected, but once they are detected, the bank may:

- Waive the provisions of the violated covenant for a certain period of time. This waiver period generally lasts for up to one year, at which time the covenant would be in full force and effect again.
- Amend the covenant so that the borrower will not be in continuing violation.
- Demand a cure of the violation within a certain period of time. The cure period is specified in the loan agreement between the borrower and the bank and generally runs from 10 to 30 days. Sometimes no cure period is permitted with respect to certain covenants.
- If compliance, waiver, or amendment has not cured the violation, or if no cure period is permitted, the bank may declare an event of default has occurred and demand payment of the loan.

If drafted properly, bank loan covenants should not interfere with a company's normal operations. Both the bank and the borrower come up with mutually agreeable covenants that each can live with for the length of the loan agreement.

LOAN COSTS

A variety of costs are associated with a bank loan. A brief review of some of the more routine fees is presented next.

Points

Up-front bank charges for a loan can be assessed for reviewing and preparing documents, performing credit checks, or simply agreeing to grant a loan. Points are one-time charges computed as a percentage of the total loan amount.

Compensating Balances

Some banks require a short-term borrower to establish and maintain a specified balance in an account at the institution as a condition of the loan. For example, the bank may require the borrower to keep at least 10% of the outstanding loan balance in an account. This "compensating balance," often in a low-interest-bearing account, is a way the bank makes a loan more profitable. In effect, the bank is reducing the principal amount of the loan and increasing the effective rate of interest.

A compensating balance is negotiable, and some banks simply request an informal "depositor relationship" with the borrower. This relationship requires the borrower to use the bank for some other type of business, such as maintaining a credit card or opening some type of traditional savings account. Usually no set balances are required.

Unused Line Fees

An additional cost is the unused line fee, which is some percentage of the difference between a credit line's facility amount and the funded amount. Like other fees, this one is negotiated. Unused line fees typically range from .25% to 1% of the unused portion of the credit line.

Credit Boxes

This book uses the term "credit boxes" to describe access to most of the capital access points (CAPs) described in the following chapters. Credit boxes depict the access variables a borrower must exhibit to qualify for the loan. In other words, unless borrowers meet certain criteria, they will not be considered for the loan. In connection with the credit box, a summary of terms is offered representing the terms likely to be offered by the lender if the borrower's quantitative and qualitative characteristics fit within the credit box. Examples of these terms include interest rate, closing fees, monitoring fees, audit fees, and so on. By considering all of the terms of the deal, the expected rate of return is determined. As shown later in this chapter, these expected rates often are substantially greater than the stated interest rates.

Exhibit 17.7 depicts the credit box for a bank credit line as well as sample terms.[3] These terms were taken from a Pepperdine survey, but it should be noted that terms fluctuate because of market conditions and changing motivations of the players.

EXHIBIT 17.7   Bank Credit Line Credit Box and Sample Terms

Credit Box

Earning Capacity	Collateral
Positive at funding	Initial funding of at least $1 million
	Sufficient collateral base
Financial Boundaries	**Covenants**
No more than 2.3 times debt/EBITDA	Fixed charge of at least 1.4 to 1
Total liabilities to net worth of less than 3.5 to 1	Total debt to tangible net worth of 1.5

Sample Terms

Example loan	$5 million facility; $3 million funded
	3-year commitment
Interest rate	Prime rate + 4% (Prime = 3.5%)
Commitment fee	.5% of the facility amount
Closing fee	1% of facility amount
Unused line fee	.3% per annum on unused portion

The credit box is broken into four quadrants: earning capacity, collateral, financial boundaries, and covenants. A prospective borrower must meet each of the specified quadrant requirements to secure credit from the bank. An explanation of these terms is presented next.

Earning Capacity   The earning capacity of a company is the reported pretax profits of the borrower, adjusted for extraordinary items. Banks generally require a borrower to exhibit a positive earning capacity at the time of funding, with the expectation that earnings will continue during the life of the loan.

Collateral   Banks require a sufficient, stable collateral base. The preferred entry is at least $1 million in initial funding. Adequate assets secure most small loans. "Adequate," in this case, means conservative advance rates are applied to the various pledged assets to determine loan size. A detailed discussion on eligibility of assets occurs in Chapter 20. Banks typically monitor the collateral at least quarterly.

Financial Boundaries   Banks require borrowers to meet several "boundary" ratios. These boundaries help define the overall riskiness of the lender's portfolio, which ultimately provides feedback to its credit box. One such boundary might state no deal is undertaken with a "Total Debt to EBITDA" ratio of more than 2.3 times. In this case, "total debt" means the total interest-bearing debt of the company. "EBITDA" means the earnings before interest, taxes, depreciation, and amortization. This boundary is a technique for the bank to disqualify companies with excessive leverage. Another boundary is total liabilities to tangible net worth of not more than 3.5. "Tangible net worth" is defined as stockholders' equity less book value of intangible assets, such as goodwill. Once again, the lender is setting up a financial fence to filter out overly risky transactions.

Covenants   Nearly all loans have financial covenants, which restrict the borrower in some way. These covenants vary greatly from one institution to another and must be negotiated with care. As an example, two covenants are offered in the credit box. The first covenant, fixed charge of at least 1.4 to 1, requires some definition. The fixed charge coverage ratio is defined as the ratio of:

- EBITDA minus capital expenditures not financed by the lender minus taxes to
- Current maturities of long-term debt plus interest expense.

This covenant shows whether current earnings on a cash basis are adequate to cover current fixed obligations on a cash basis. This covenant is tailored to meet the needs of the situation.

This credit box depiction illustrates some of the quantitative criteria needed to gain credit access to banks. Each lender is somewhat unique in its approach to making credit decisions. In other words, its credit box is engineered to meet its return on investment requirements. Of course, various qualitative aspects factor into the lending decision. Prospective borrowers should interview representatives of the institution about the characteristics of their credit box. Doing this saves everyone a lot of time and effort.

The sample terms show a possible deal offering for a credit line from a bank if a borrower successfully traverses the credit box. In this case, assume a $5 million facility is sought, with $3 million funded at closing. Typically, the facility begins with excess capacity, mainly so the credit has room to grow. Normally banks grant a credit line loan term of one to three years, with annual renewability at the option of the lender. The interest rate normally is computed and payable monthly and pegged to some known source, such as published in the *Wall Street Journal*. In the example, the interest rate is prime + 4%, with prime assumed at 3.5%. Thus the example uses 7.5% as the interest rate.

Most banks charge a closing fee at the time of funding. This fee, sometimes called a closing or origination fee, generally is expressed as an absolute number or a percent of the facility amount, not the funded amount. The commitment fee, which some banks charge for providing the loan, is .5% of the facility amount in this example. The closing fee in the example is $50,000 ($5 million facility amount times 1%). This fee, which is negotiable, varies from lender to lender. An additional cost is the unused line fee, which is some percentage of the difference between the facility amount and the funded amount. In the example, this fee is .3% per annum applied against $2 million ($5 million facility amount minus $3 million funded amount), or $6,000 annually, payable monthly. The next table shows a computation of the expected return to the bank from the sample terms.

1. Total interest cost	$240,000
($3 million loan × 7.5% interest rate)	
2. Commitment fee	
($5 million facility amount × .5%) ÷ three years	8,333
3. Closing fee	16,666
($5 million facility amount × 1% ÷ three years)	
4. Unused line fee	6,000
(($5 million facility amount − $3 million funded amount) × .3%)	
Annual returns of loan	271,000
Expected rate of return	**9.0%**
($271,000/$3,000,000)	

The stated interest rate of 3.5% increases by the "terms cost" of 5.5%, which yields an expected rate of 9.0%. This assumes the closing fee is spread over the three-year life of the loan.

RISK RATINGS

Banks rate their borrowers through a risk rating system. Exhibit 17.8 shows a typical risk rating matrix. Although these systems vary by bank, many large banks use the 10-point scale shown in the exhibit.[4]

Bank officers use the grading points to generate a borrower's risk rating. Companies are unlikely to exhibit characteristics uniformly at a single level across the grid. For instance, a company might be in a class 4 industry, with a class 5 position. Ultimately it is a judgment call by the lending officer as to the final risk rating assigned to a borrower.[5] Risk ratings of 4 and lower tend to be large public companies. Many banks move a borrower into the special assets part of the bank once a risk rating hits 7. Most banks do not share current risk ratings with the customers. This practice makes it difficult for borrowers to know exactly where they stand with the bank.

It should be noted that most banks use risk ratings as well as other criteria to determine loan pricing. These criteria involve both qualitative issues, such as management strength and type of business (such as a niche versus commodity supplier of parts), as well as quantitative measures, such as return on capital requirements.

NEGOTIATING POINTS

There are a number of negotiable bank loan issues. Prospective borrowers should consider incorporating the next terms into the deal before closing a loan.

Interest Rate Pricing Matrix

Borrowers can negotiate an interest rate pricing matrix that lessens the interest rate over time as the borrower's financial condition improves. The matrix can tie to any of a variety of financial ratios. Typically only one ratio is chosen, and

EXHIBIT 17.8 Borrower Grade Criteria (10-Point Scale)

Borrower Grade	Industry Segment	Position within Industry	Earnings/Cash Flow Trends	Asset/Liability Values
1 Risk free	Governments of major countries, top banks, major multinationals	Leader with significant share in stable industry	Very strong earnings record	Highest quality assets
2 Minimum risk	Minimal industry cyclicality, highly favorable outlook	Reasonable market share, may dominate local market	Consistent earnings and cash flow with acceptable growth	High asset quality
3 Modest risk	Industry not overly cyclical, favorable outlook	Well-positioned, leader in local market	Consistent earnings and cash flow with modest growth	Assets above average quality, little reance on intangibles
4 Better than average	Moderate link to business cycle, neutral long term outlook	Tends to be price follower with average market share	Adequate earnings, cash flow	Assets of average quality
5 Average risk	May be susceptible to unfavorable changes in economy	Position within industry is deteriorating, increasing reliance of untested products	Earnings and cash flow are strained, outlook is uncertain	Assets below average quality, significant intangibles exist
6 Acceptable risk	Intensely competitive industry, outlook is uncertain	Market share and performance ratios well below industry average, smaller borrower	Earnings and cash flow are strained, subject to volatility	Low asset quality, liability type may be mismatched with assets
7 Special mention	Industry may be in start-up or long-term decline outlook is unfavorable	Industry has significant problems that adversely affect high percentage of participants. Borrower ranks in the bottom of its industry.	Earnings and cash flow may not cover fixed charges	Lowest quality assets, liability type may be greatly mismatched with assets
8 Substandard	Industry has significant problems that adversely affect high percentage of participants. Borrower ranks in the bottom of its industry.			
9 Doubtful	Industry has major longer-term problems that adversely affect majority of participants. Borrower ranks in the bottom of its industry.		Excessive degree of risk. Financial and management deficiencies well defined. Collection is highly improbable. Timing of loss uncertain.	
10 Loss	Severe permanent industry problems exist that adversely affect virtually all participants.		Unsecured debts considered uncollectible and should not be continued as active bank assets.	

it corresponds to a problem in the borrower's position at the loan closing. For instance, if the prospective borrower is leveraged at the closing, the lender might give the borrower incentives to pay down debt by offering the next matrix.

Pricing Matrix Based on Improving Leverage		
Leverage	Prime Margin	LIBOR Margin
3.0 or higher	1.00%	3.50%
2.50 to 2.99	0.50%	2.50%
2.5 or lower	0.00%	2.00%

For this example, leverage is defined as the ratio of total liabilities divided by tangible net worth. The lender might offer this pricing matrix if the borrower had a leverage ratio of more than three times at the closing, which would correspond to an interest rate of prime + 1% or LIBOR + 3.5%. The interest rate decreases as the leverage decreases, which normally is measured annually. Instituting a pricing matrix before the closing saves a borrower from renegotiating rates later. It may be possible to tie the pricing matrix into quarterly financial reporting.

Repayment Terms

Borrowers should negotiate repayment terms that match their ability to repay the loan. For instance, an interest-only period may be necessary before the principal is amortized. The key here is for the borrower to understand its cash flow well enough to tailor repayments to its ability to repay the loan.

Loan Covenants

Borrowers often overlook the opportunity for negotiating loan covenants. Most bankers are willing to tailor the covenants to a borrower's projections plus provide for breathing room. It is the borrower's responsibility to understand her financial ratios well enough into the future to negotiate these items.

Several covenants require special attention, such as:

- Limitations on shareholder compensation
- Limitations on acquisition of additional fixed assets
- Minimum or compensating cash balance
- Minimum equity level

Borrowers can have some covenants either limited or removed based on certain positive events occurring in the borrower's business. For instance, with proper negotiation, shareholder compensation can be increased once the borrower reaches a certain equity level.

Personal Guarantees

Typically, shareholders who own 20% or more of the borrower must personally guarantee the loan. In the heat of battle, most borrowers do not think to negotiate

EXHIBIT 17.9 Personal Guarantee Requirement

Annual Sales Size	Yes	No
$.5 million	16%	84%
$1 million	25%	75%
$5 million	30%	70%
$10 million	45%	55%
$25 million	52%	48%
$50 million	67%	33%
$100 million	65%	35%

releases from the guarantee before the closing. Releases can be achieved through benchmarking the loan. For example, the guarantee could be either partially or fully released when the company reaches a certain profitability level or when the leverage of the company is reduced by a certain amount. Releasing, or "burning," a personal guarantee, as it is sometimes called, is nearly impossible once a loan closes because there is no incentive for the lender to give on this issue.

Exhibit 17.9 shows the results of a recent Pepperdine Capital Market survey regarding bank personal guarantee requirements.[6] Respondents were asked whether they would lend without personal guarantees to companies of various sales sizes. As might be expected, bankers tend to view personal guarantees as less important as company size increases.

Financial Statements

Many lenders require annual audited financial statements as a condition of closing the loan, especially for loans greater than $5 million. This is a negotiated item and a fairly important consideration when it comes to expense. Borrowers can agree to provide "reviewed" financial statements in many cases and save themselves more than $10,000 per year. Regardless of the level of outside accounting diligence, borrowers can expect to supply internally generated monthly financial statements to the bank each month.

Loan Closing Fees

The borrower pays the lender's cost of closing the loan. This fee includes legal, recording, appraisal, and other closing costs. If left unchecked, these fees can be substantial. For example, the closing fees for a $5 million funding can easily exceed $20,000. Borrowers can negotiate caps on these fees, such that the lender must receive permission from the borrower to exceed a certain amount. Sometimes the borrower can negotiate a fixed fee for the legal fees part of the closing. The borrower also incurs its own legal fees for reviewing loan documents, which are in addition to the lender costs.

The key to negotiating a deal with a bank is to consider all of the terms and conditions of the deal before executing a term sheet. Many borrowers focus on the interest rate to the exclusion of the other terms. As the examples show, there are many costs associated with these deals, and together they comprise the expected return.

TRIANGULATION

Capitalization is dependent on the value world in which the company is viewed and the availability of transfer methods. Banks view borrowers in the world of collateral value. Banks use this world to determine the value of the firm from a collateralized lending perspective. To these capital providers, margined collateral of a borrower is what matters most.

Access to capital affects the value of a firm. Banks provide a broad array of capital products and services that help companies grow. However, banks regulate capital access by imposing loan covenants and credit boxes that restrict a borrower's ability to access various types of capital.

In a recent meeting with an owner of a sporting goods manufacturer, the owner expressed his frustration with bank financing by saying "I can grow my business as fast as the bank will let me." This owner would qualify for most capital access points on the Pepperdine Private Capital Market Line, but he chooses bank lending because of its low cost and infrequent intrusions. In addition, he does not want partners or to fund growth out of his own pocket. The owner figured he could grow his business by an additional 20% per year if the bank would fund it.

Bank lending is available to most transfer methods. Banks use covenants to protect their collateral position, which may prohibit a business transfer. Borrowers still prefer bank lending because often it represents the most effective capital source.

Many sellers do not disclose their business transfer plans to bankers because of the lower- and middle-market paranoia that only troubled businesses are for sale. Unfortunately, many owners believe bankers are more likely to withdraw or call their loans than they are to have empathy with the owner's desire to get out.

NOTES

1. Source: wsjprimerate.com.
2. This study is described by Robert T. Slee, "A Secret Your Banker May Not Be Telling You," *Business Journal* (November 1996).
3. John K. Paglia, Pepperdine Private Capital Markets Project Survey Report, April 2010, bschool.pepperdine.edu/privatecapital.
4. Robert Morris Associates, *A Credit Risk-Rating System* (1994). Due to space limitations, the 10-point scale contains three columns not shown in the chapter. These columns are Financial Flexibility/Debt Capacity, Management and Controls, and Financial Reporting.
5. Ibid., p. 25.
6. John K. Paglia, Pepperdine Private Capital Markets Project Survey Report.

CHAPTER 18

Government Lending Programs

Federal, state, and local governments administer numerous lending programs. Many of these programs are intended to enable private capital providers to participate in riskier lending, mainly to smaller companies. These programs typically involve government lending guarantees rather than direct loans. With assurances for most of the loan principal, banks and other lending sources are enticed to participate in the loan process.

Borrowers are motivated to seek government lending programs for three reasons.

1. Most important, they cannot access the required capital without using the particular lending program. This is almost always the case with the guarantee programs of the Small Business Administration (SBA).
2. A government loan program may represent the cheapest source of capital. Industrial revenue bonds, for example, are the least expensive type of institutional capital.
3. The program may better fit their needs than other programs. This is often the case with the Certified Development Company 504 program.

Only national government lending programs are described in this chapter. Readers can contact the appropriate state and local economic resource centers for help with these programs. These loan programs are reviewed here:

- Industrial Revenue Bonds
- Business and Industry Loans, from the U.S. Department of Agriculture
- Small Business Administration Programs, such as the 7(a) loan guaranty program, the Certified Development Company 504 program, the CAPLines program, and the Export Working Capital Program

Exhibit 18.1 depicts the capital coordinates for industrial revenue bonds and the Business and Industry program.

EXHIBIT 18.1   Capital Coordinates: Government Lending Programs

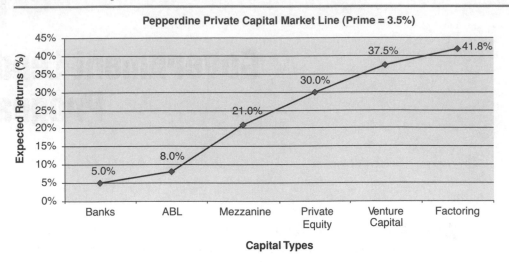

Capital Access Points

Capital Access Point	Industrial Revenue Bonds	Business and Industry Loans
Definition	Municipal bonds whose proceeds are loaned to private persons or to businesses to finance capital investment projects.	This program helps create jobs and stimulates rural economies by providing financial backing for rural businesses. This program provides federal guarantees for a loan made by a commercial lender.
Expected Rate of Return	3.6%	4.8%
Likely Provider	Municipalities	Banks
Value World(s)	Collateral value	Collateral value
Transfer Method(s)	Outside transfers	Outside transfers
Appropriate to Use When ...	The lowest interest rate is sought and the project involves the acquisition of fixed assets and real estate.	A rural company needs to borrow money to create or retain jobs.
Key Points to Consider	Only projects with higher-paying jobs than the local area average qualify.	A minimum 10% equity is required for existing businesses and 20% for new businesses.

INDUSTRIAL REVENUE BONDS

Industrial revenue bonds (IRBs) are municipal bonds whose proceeds are loaned to individuals or to businesses to finance capital investment projects. Even though they are municipal bonds, IRBs are not general obligations of the municipality. The municipality is not responsible for debt service, nor is it liable in case of default. The borrower has sole responsibility for paying the principal and interest on the bonds. Because IRBs are municipal bonds, they are exempt from federal income tax, so they have lower interest rates than most comparable capital sources. The bond proceeds are used to finance entire projects, including land, buildings and machinery, and equipment. Finally, the terms of the agreement among the municipality, the bond buyer, and the borrower are negotiated to conform to the needs of the borrower.

Although IRBs have a variety of names and purposes, such as industrial development bonds (IDBs) and qualified small issue bonds, there are essentially three basic types. The states' principal interest in these bonds is assisting new and expanding industry in an effort to provide residents with good jobs and wages. The regulations governing bond issuance combine federal regulations and particular statutes. The amount of IRBs each state may issue annually is based on population.

The three types of bond issuances are:

1. *Tax exempt* (small-issue IDBs). Because the income derived by the bondholder is not subject to federal income tax, the maximum bond amount is $10 million in any given jurisdiction. According to federal regulations, the $10 million total includes the bond amount and capital expenditures over a six-year period going both backward and forward three years. The maximum any company may have is $40 million nationwide outstanding at any given period.
2. *Taxable*. Taxable bonds are not exempt from federal tax. They are, however, exempt from most state taxes. The essential difference is that the taxable bond rate is more costly to the borrower, is not subject to the federal volume cap, and may exceed $10 million in bond amount.
3. *Exempt facility/solid waste disposal bond*. These bonds are subject to a volume cap although there is no restriction on amount, and the interest on these bonds is federally tax exempt.

All three bond types are processed and approved in the same manner. The state supervises, approves, and guides bond applications. The county bond authority issues the bonds where the facility will be located. The county authority may select bond counsel for the project. Three of the more significant regulations are:

1. Only a company engaged in some manner of manufacturing can use IRB funds. Some states also allow for pollution control facilities to qualify.
2. IRB proceeds may be used only for land, building, and equipment. Other costs that typically qualify include existing equipment, which is in place and installed as part of an integrated production line; architects' and engineers' fees; and issuance costs. While land can be included, it generally can comprise up to 25% of the total project cost. Specific rules govern the inclusion of the various asset classes. These rules vary from state to state, and readers should perform the necessary due diligence to ensure compliance.
3. The company must agree to pay its employees greater than or equal to the average weekly manufacturing wage of the county or the state average weekly manufacturing wage plus 10%.

In most states, IRBs can be used to finance an acquisition. For this to happen, the jobs involved must be in jeopardy because of an imminent plant closing. The acquisition must be structured as a purchase only of fixed assets and must meet the used building and equipment requirements. The bond proceeds cannot be used to refinance existing debt or as venture capital. With start-ups, the applicant must contribute an amount equal to 25% of the bond amount for beginning working capital.

For most states, it takes eight to ten weeks for an application to be approved. To handle the numerous requirements, a client should have an inducement agreement signed between his company and the county. There is neither financial nor legal liability involved with the agreement for either party. Bond counsel prepares this and other documents so the client should make an early contact. It is also appropriate to discuss the required letter of credit with a bank at the same time; it must be rated investment grade or better. The applicant negotiates the letter of credit with his bank. The bank sends the applicant a commitment letter with a copy to the local government commission. All bond issues must be supported by a letter of credit so it is important that the borrower secures a commitment early in the process.

It is the applicant's responsibility to find a buyer for the bonds. Often the bank that provides the letter of credit also places the bonds and may purchase them.

Interest rates range from a low of 40% of the prime rate to 75% of prime. The term of the loan ranges up to 30 years for real estate and up to 10 years for equipment, depending on the estimated useful life of the equipment.

Exhibit 18.2 depicts the credit box for an IRB as well as sample terms that might be offered. This credit box illustrates some of the criteria needed to gain credit access to an IRB. Each state and municipality is unique in its IRB approach. Each state is allocated a certain amount of tax-exempt bonds annually, so applicants need to make sure there is open capacity.

EXHIBIT 18.2 Industrial Revenue Bonds Credit Box and Sample Terms

Credit Box

To qualify for industrial revenue bonds, an applicant must:
- Have a capital need of at least $2 million.
- Use the proceeds for a manufacturing facility.
- Show that it has the capability to successfully operate the business.
- Get local support for the project (inducement).
- Pay a wage above the county average manufacturing wage or 10% above the state average manufacturing wage or obtain a wage waiver because the project is located in an area of "especially severe unemployment."
- Obtain the required environmental permits.
- Save or create enough jobs to have a measurable impact on the area.

Sample Terms

Example loan	$10 million loan. $2 MM land/buildings $8 MM machinery and equipment (M&E)
Terms	20 years real estate 7 years M&E
Interest rate	2.5% (prime rate of 3.5% less 30%)
Letter of credit fees	1% per year
Placement fee	1% of loan amount

Exhibit 18.2 also shows the possible sample terms for an IRB. In this case, it is assumed that a $10 million loan is sought, with $8 million needed for machinery and equipment and $2 million needed for real estate. In the example, the machinery is financed for 7 years, while the real estate is financed over 20 years. The interest rate is the prime rate less 30%, so with prime assumed at 3.5%, the sample rate is 2.5%. The sample terms indicate the likely deal terms for an IRB. The letter of credit fee is annual and typically costs about 1% of the outstanding loan. The placement fee is charged by the placement agent and typically costs 1% to 2% of the amount raised.

The next table shows the expected rate of return to the provider of the sample terms.

1. Total interest cost	$250,000
($10 million loan × 2.5% interest rate)	
2. Letter of credit fee	100,000
($10 million loan × 1%)	
3. Placement fee	10,000
($10 million loan × 1% ÷ 10 years)	

Annual returns of loan	$360,000
Expected rate of return	**3.6%**
($360,000/$10,000,000)	

The stated interest rate of 2.5% is increased by the "terms cost" of 1.1%, which yields an expected rate of return of 3.6%. The interest rate and letter of credit fees are assumed to remain the same percentages for the life of the loan. The example assumes the placement fee is financed over ten years, and only the annual return is shown.

Another government program is the Business and Industry loan program, administered by the Rural Development division of the U.S. Department of Agriculture (USDA).

BUSINESS AND INDUSTRY LOAN PROGRAM

The Business and Industry (B&I) Guaranteed Loan Program helps create jobs and stimulates rural economies by providing financial backing for rural businesses. This program provides federal guarantees for a loan made by a commercial lender.

Loan purposes must be consistent with the general purpose contained in the regulation. They include but are not limited to:

- Business and industrial acquisitions when the loan will keep the business from closing, prevent the loss of employment opportunities, or provide expanded job opportunities.
- Business conversion, enlargement, repair, modernization, or development.
- Purchase and development of land, easements, rights-of-way, buildings, or facilities.
- Purchase of equipment, leasehold improvements, machinery, supplies, or inventory.

The primary purpose is to create and maintain employment and improve the economic climate in rural communities by expanding the lending capability of private lenders in rural areas, helping them make and service quality loans.

B&I loan guarantees are extended to loans made by recognized commercial lenders or other authorized lenders in rural areas. Rural areas include all areas other than cities or unincorporated areas of more than 50,000 people and their immediately adjacent urban or urbanizing areas. Generally, recognized lenders include federal or state chartered banks, credit unions, insurance companies, savings and loan associations, farm credit banks, or other farm credit system institutions with direct lending authority.

Individual borrowers must be citizens of the United States or reside in the United States after being legally admitted for permanent residence. Corporations or other nonpublic body organization-type borrowers must be at least 51% owned by persons who are either citizens of the United States or reside in the United States after being legally admitted for permanent residence. B&I loans normally are available in rural areas, which include all areas other than cities or towns of more than 50,000 people and the contiguous and adjacent urbanized area of such cities or towns.

The total amount of agency loans to one borrower must not exceed $10 million. The administrator may, at the administrator's discretion, grant an exception to the $10 million limit for loans of $25 million under certain circumstances. For instance, the administrator may approve guaranteed loans in excess of $25 million, up to $40 million, for rural cooperative organizations that process value-added agricultural commodities. The percentage of guarantee, up to the maximum allowed, is a matter of negotiation between the lender and the agency. The maximum percentage of guarantee is 80% for loans of $5 million or less, 70% for loans between $5 and $10 million, and 60% for loans exceeding $10 million.

Maximum repayment terms are 7 years for working capital, 15 years (or useful life) for machinery and equipment, and 30 years for real estate. Collateral, which usually includes personal and/or corporate guarantees, must be sufficient to protect the interests of the lender and the government. A minimum of 10% tangible balance sheet equity is required for existing businesses and 20% for new businesses. Feasibility studies may be required. The interest rate is negotiated between the lender and borrower, and it may be fixed or variable. The lender addresses the business adequacy of equity, cash flow, collateral, history, management, and the current status of the industry in a written credit analysis. Lenders are expected to service, and if necessary, liquidate loans, with concurrence of USDA's Rural Development. There is a one-time guarantee fee equal to 2% of the guaranteed portion of the loan at the time the guarantee is issued.

Exhibit 18.3 illustrates the credit box and sample terms regarding a B&I loan.

In this case, it is assumed a $5 million loan is sought, with $3 million needed for machinery and equipment and $2 million needed for real estate. The machinery is financed for 7 years while the real estate is financed over 20 years. The interest rate is prime + 1%, with prime assumed at 3.5%. Thus, the example uses 4.5% as the interest rate.

EXHIBIT 18.3　　Business and Industry Loan Guaranty Program Credit Box and Sample Terms

Credit Box

To qualify for a B&I loan, an applicant must:
- Be an eligible business.
- Be located in a rural area.
- Have a loan need less than $10 million ($40 million in limited circumstances).
- Have a minimum 10% tangible book equity; start-ups should have a tangible book equity of 20% to 25%.
- Have sufficient collateral and cash flow to attract a lender.

Sample Terms

Example loan	$5 million loan. $2 MM land/buildings
	$3 MM M&E
Terms	20 years real estate
	7 years M&E
Interest rate	4.5% (prime rate of 3.5% + 1%)
Bank closing fee	1% of loan amount
Guaranty fee	2% of guaranty portion

The next table shows the expected return of a B&I loan.

1.	Total interest cost	$225,000
	($5 million loan × 4.5% interest rate)	
2.	Bank closing fee	5,000
	($5 million loan × 1% ÷ 10 years)	
3.	Guaranty fee	8,000
	($5 million loan × 80% guarantee × 2% ÷ 10 years)	
	Annual returns of loan	$238,000
	Expected rate of return	**4.8%**
	($238,000/$5,000,000)	

The stated interest rate of 4.5% is increased by the "terms cost" of .3%, which yields an expected rate of return of 4.8%. The bank closing fee and guaranty fee are treated as if they are financed over ten years. The guaranty fee is actually paid to the USDA for supplying the guarantee. This fee adds to the return expectation of the deal but not to the bank's return. It is assumed the bank would not make the loan at the stated interest rate, or perhaps not at all, without the government guarantee.

SMALL BUSINESS ADMINISTRATION PROGRAMS

The U.S. Small Business Administration, established in 1953, provides financial, technical, and management assistance to help Americans start, run, and grow their businesses. With a portfolio of business loans, loan guarantees, and disaster loans worth more than $80 billion, the SBA is the nation's largest single financial backer of small businesses.

The SBA enables its lending partners to provide financing to small businesses when funding is otherwise unavailable on reasonable terms. It guarantees major portions of loans made to small businesses. The SBA does not currently have funding for direct loans nor does it provide grants or low-interest-rate loans for business start-up or expansion.

The eligibility requirements and credit criteria of the program are very broad in order to accommodate a wide range of financing needs. When a small business applies to a lending partner for a loan, the lender reviews the application and decides if it merits a loan on its own or if it requires an SBA guaranty. The lender then requests SBA backing on the loan. By guaranteeing the loan, the SBA assures the lender that the government will reimburse it for a portion of its loss, in the event the borrower does not repay the loan.

By providing this guaranty, the SBA enables tens of thousands of small businesses to get financing every year that they would not otherwise obtain. To qualify for an SBA guaranty, a small business must meet SBA criteria, and the lender must certify that it could not provide funding on reasonable terms without an SBA guaranty.

Exhibit 18.4 shows the capital coordinates for the 7(a) and 504 SBA loan programs.

The SBA administers more than a dozen programs. This chapter focuses on four of them: the 7(a) Loan Guaranty Program, the Certified Development Company (504) loan program, the CAPLines loan program, and the Export Working Capital program.

7(a) LOAN GUARANTY PROGRAM

The 7(a) Loan Guaranty Program, SBA's primary lending program, provides loan guarantees to small businesses unable to secure financing on reasonable terms. It operates through private-sector lenders that provide loans, which are in turn, guaranteed by the SBA.

Information on SBA loan programs is available on the Internet at www.sba.gov as well as through the management counseling and training services offered by the agency available from local SBA offices.

As of this writing, this SBA program can guarantee as much as 85% on loans of up to $150,000 and 75% on loans of more than $150,000. 7(a) loans have a maximum loan amount of $2 million. SBA's maximum exposure is $1.5 million. Thus, if a business receives an SBA-guaranteed loan for $2 million, the maximum guaranty to the lender will be $1.5 million, or 75%. The ability of the business to repay the loan from cash flow is a primary consideration in the SBA loan decision process; however, good character, management capability, collateral, and owner's equity contribution are also important considerations. All owners with a 20% or greater interest are required to personally guarantee SBA loans.

Although most small businesses are eligible for SBA loans, some types of businesses are ineligible, and a case-by-case determination must be made by the agency. Eligibility is generally determined by three factors: business type, business size, and use of the loan.

EXHIBIT 18.4   Capital Coordinates: SBA 7(a) and SBA 504 Programs

Pepperdine Private Capital Market Line (Prime = 3.5%)

Capital Access Points

Capital Access Point	SBA 7(a)	SBA 504
Definition	Provides loan guarantees to small businesses unable to secure financing on reasonable terms through normal lending channels	Provides growing businesses with long-term, fixed-rate financing for major fixed assets, such as land and buildings
Expected rate of return	5.8%	4.0%
Likely provider	Banks	Banks, certified development companies
Value world(s)	Collateral value	Collateral value
Transfer method(s)	All but public	All but public
Appropriate to use when ...	A loan guaranty is the only way to obtain the required financing	A borrower wants to minimize the equity investment
Key points to consider	Personal guarantees required of borrower and spouse; the SBA sets maximum interest rates	Personal guarantees required; low blended interest rates

Business Type

Most businesses are eligible for SBA assistance. An applicant business must operate for profit; be engaged in, or propose to do business in, the United States or its possessions; have reasonable owner equity to invest; and use alternative financial resources first, which includes personal assets. Ineligible businesses include real estate investment and other speculative activities; lending activities; pyramid sales plans; illegal activities; gambling activities; and charitable, religious, or certain other nonprofit institutions.

Size of Eligible Businesses

The Small Business Act defines an eligible small business as one that is independently owned and not dominant in its field of operation. In determining what a small business is, the definition shall vary from industry to industry to reflect market differences. Most businesses are eligible under the act; however, potential borrowers should check the SBA Web site for exact size eligibility descriptions.

Use of Proceeds

The proceeds of SBA loans can be used for most business purposes. These may include the purchase of real estate to house the business operations; construction, renovation or leasehold improvements; acquisition of furniture, fixtures, machinery, and equipment; purchase of inventory; and working capital.

Proceeds of an SBA loan cannot be used to:

- Finance floor plan needs.
- Purchase real estate where the participant has issued a forward commitment to the builder/developer, or where the real estate will be held primarily for investment purposes.
- Make payments to owners or pay delinquent withholding taxes.
- Pay existing debt unless it can be shown that the refinancing will benefit the small business and that the need to refinance is not indicative of imprudent management. (Proceeds can never be used to reduce the exposure of the participant in the loans being refinanced.)

SBA loan programs generally are intended to encourage longer-term small business financing. Actual loan maturities are based on the ability to repay, the purpose of the loan proceeds, and the useful life of the assets financed. However, maximum loan maturities have been established: 25 years for real estate and equipment and, generally, 7 years for working capital.

Interest rates are negotiated between the borrower and the lender but are subject to SBA maximums, which are pegged to the prime rate, LIBOR (London Interbank Offered Rate), or an optional peg rate. Interest rates may be fixed or variable. These are the interest rates for fixed-rate loans:

- Fixed-rate loans of $50,000 or more must not exceed the base rate plus 2.25% if the maturity is less than seven years and the base rate plus 2.75% if the maturity is seven years or more.
- For loans between $25,000 and $50,000, maximum rates must not exceed the base rate plus 3.25% if the maturity is less than seven years and the base rate plus 3.75% if the maturity is seven years or more.
- For loans of $25,000 or less, the maximum interest rate must not exceed the base rate plus 4.25% if the maturity is less than seven years and the base rate plus 4.75% if the maturity is seven years or more.

Variable-rate loans may be pegged to the lowest prime rate, LIBOR, or the SBA optional peg rate. The optional peg rate is a weighted average of rates the federal government pays for loans with maturities similar to the average SBA loan.

It is calculated quarterly and published in the Federal Register. The lender and the borrower negotiate the amount of the spread, which will be added to the base rate. An adjustment period is selected that will identify the frequency at which the note rate will change. It must not be more often than monthly, and it must be consistent (e.g., monthly, quarterly, semiannually, annually, or any other defined period).

To offset the taxpayer costs of SBA's loan programs, the agency charges lenders a guaranty and a servicing fee for each loan approved. These fees can be passed on to the borrower once the lender has paid them. The amounts of the fees are determined by the amount of the loan guaranty. For loans more than $150,000 but up to and including $700,000, a 3% guaranty fee will be charged. For loans greater than $700,000, a 3.5% guaranty fee will be charged. In addition, all loans will be subject to a 50 basis point (0.5%) annualized servicing fee, which is applied to the outstanding balance of SBA's guaranteed portion of the loan.

Processing fees, origination fees, application fees, points, brokerage fees, bonus points, and other fees that could be charged to an SBA loan applicant are prohibited. A commitment fee may be charged only for a loan made under the Export Working Capital Loan Program.

Prepayment

There is a prepayment penalty for those loans that meet the next criteria:

- Have a maturity of 15 years or more where the borrower is prepaying voluntarily.
- The prepayment amount exceeds 25% of the outstanding balance of the loan.
- The prepayment is made within the first three years after the date of the first disbursement (not approval) of the loan proceeds.

The prepayment fee calculation is:

- During the first year after disbursement, 5% of the amount of the prepayment.
- During the second year after disbursement, 3% of the amount of the prepayment.
- During the third year after disbursement, 1% of the amount of the prepayment.

Exhibit 18.5 shows the credit box and sample terms for the 7(a) program. The sample terms assumes a $2 million loan is sought, with $1 million needed for machinery and equipment and $1 million needed for real estate. Machinery is financed for 7 years while the real estate is financed over 20 years. The interest rate is prime plus 1.5%, with prime assumed at 3.5%. Thus, the example uses 5% as the interest rate.

EXHIBIT 18.5   SBA 7(a) Loan Guaranty Program Credit Box and Sample Terms

Credit Box

To qualify for an SBA loan guaranty, an applicant must:
- Be an eligible business, as defined by the SBA.
- Have a loan need less than $2 million.
- Personally guarantee the loan if he/she owns more than 20% of the borrower.
- Have sufficient collateral and cash flow to attract a lender.
- Meet the type, size, and use of proceeds conditions as defined by the SBA.

Sample Terms

Example loan	$2 million loan. $1 MM land/buildings $1 MM M&E
Terms	20 years real estate 7 years M&E
Interest rate	5% (prime rate of 3.5% + 1.5%)
Bank closing fee	1% of loan amount
Guaranty fee	3.5% of guaranty portion
Servicing fee	.5% annual service fee

The next table computes the expected rate of return to the provider based on the sample terms.

1. Total interest cost ($2 million loan × 5% interest rate)	$100,000
2. Bank closing fee ($2 million loan × 1% ÷ 10 years)	2,000
3. Guaranty fee ($2 million loan × 75% guarantee × 3.5% ÷ 10 years)	5,250
4. Servicing fee (annual) ($2 million loan × .5%)	10,000
Annual returns of loan	$117,250
Expected rate of return ($117,250/$2,000,000)	**5.8%**

The stated interest rate of 5% is increased by the "terms cost" of .8%, which yields an expected rate of return of 5.8%. The bank closing fee and guaranty fee are amortized over 10 years.

CERTIFIED DEVELOPMENT COMPANY 504 LOAN PROGRAM

The 504 Certified Development Company (CDC) Program provides growing businesses with long-term, fixed-rate financing for major fixed assets, such as land and buildings. A CDC is a nonprofit corporation set up to contribute to the economic development of its community. CDCs work with the SBA and private-sector lenders to provide financing to small businesses. Each of the 250 or so CDCs nationwide covers a specific geographic area.

Typically, a 504 project includes a loan secured with a senior lien from a private-sector lender covering up to 50% of the project cost, a loan secured with a junior lien from the CDC (backed by a 100% SBA-guaranteed debenture) covering up to 40% of the cost, and a contribution of at least 10% equity from the small business being helped.

In order to qualify for the program, the borrower must meet the SBA's definition of "small business" and must plan to use over half (51%) of the property for its own operations within one year of ownership; if the building is to be newly constructed, the borrower must use 60% at once and plan to occupy 80%. The borrower may form a real estate holding company that lease 100% to the operating business, which then subleases surplus space (up to 49%). To qualify for this program, U.S. citizens or permanent residents must hold a majority of the ownership of the operating companies and the holding company. There are three criteria for eligibility:

1. The company's average net income cannot surpass $2.5 million after taxes for the preceding two years.
2. The anticipated project size must be greater than the personal, nonretirement, unencumbered liquid assets of the guarantors/principles.
3. The company does not have a tangible net worth in excess of $7.5 million.

Proceeds from 504 loans must be used for fixed-asset projects, such as purchasing land and improvements, including existing buildings, grading, street improvements, utilities, parking lots, and landscaping; construction of new facilities, or modernizing, renovating or converting existing facilities; or purchasing long-term machinery and equipment. The 504 program cannot be used for working capital or inventory, consolidating or repaying debt, or refinancing.

The maximum SBA debenture is $1.5 million when meeting the job creation criteria or a community development goal. Generally, a business must create or retain one job for every $65,000 provided by the SBA except for small manufacturers, which have a $100,000 job creation or retention goal.

The maximum SBA debenture is $2.0 million when meeting a public policy goal. These include:

- Business district revitalization
- Expansion of exports
- Expansion of minority business development
- Rural development
- Increasing productivity and competitiveness
- Restructuring because of federally mandated standards or policies
- Changes necessitated by federal budget cutbacks
- Expansion of small business concerns owned and controlled by veterans (especially service-disabled veterans)
- Expansion of small business concerns owned and controlled by women

The maximum debenture for small manufacturers is $4.0 million. A "small manufacturer" is defined as a company that has its primary business classified in sector 31, 32, or 33 of the North American Industrial Classification System (NAICS) and all of its production facilities located in the United States. To qualify for a $4.0 million 504 loan, the business must meet the definition of a small manufacturer and either (a) create or retain at least one job per $100,000 guaranteed by the SBA or (b) improve the economy of the locality or achieve one or more public policy goals.

Interest rates on 504 loans are pegged to an increment above the current market rate for 5- and 10-year U.S. Treasury issues. Maturities of 10 and 20 years are available. Fees total approximately 3% of the debenture and may be financed with the loan. Generally, the project assets being financed are used as collateral. Personal guarantees of the principal owners are also required.

To be eligible, the business must be operated for profit and fall within the size standards set by the SBA. Under the 504 program, the business qualifies as small if it does not have a tangible net worth in excess of $6 million and does not have an average net income in excess of $2 million after taxes for the preceding two years. Loans cannot be made to businesses engaged in speculation or investment in rental real estate.

Exhibit 18.6 shows the credit box and sample terms for the SBA 504 program.

This example assumes a $2 million project, with $1 million needed for machinery and equipment and $1 million for real estate. The machinery is financed for 7 years while the real estate is financed over 20 years. The interest rate is prime plus 1% for the bank part of the loan and prime minus .5% for the SBA debenture, with prime assumed at 3.5%. Thus, the example will use 4.5% as the interest rate for the bank portion and 3% for the debenture. On a weighted average basis, the blended rate is as shown in the next table.

EXHIBIT 18.6   SBA 504 Loan Program Credit Box and Sample Terms

---

Credit Box

To qualify for a 504 loan, an applicant must:
- Be an eligible business, as defined by the SBA.
- Have a loan need typically less than $5.5 million.
- Connect with a local CDC to help package the loan.
- Contribute at least 10% of the project in equity.
- Personally guarantee the loan if he/she owns more than 20% of the borrower.
- Have sufficient collateral and cash flow to attract a lender.
- Not have a tangible net worth in excess of $7.4 million and not have an average net income in excess of $2.5 million.

Sample Terms

Example loan	$2 million project. $1 MM land/buildings $1 MM M&E
Terms	20 years real estate 7 years M&E
Interest rate	3.8% (prime rate of 3.5%, blended)
Bank closing fee	1% of loan amount
Debenture fee	3% of debenture amount

	Loan Amount	Interest Rate	Loan Weight	Rate
Bank	$1,000,000	4.5%	56%	2.5%
Debenture	800,000	3.0%	44%	1.3%
Equity	200,000			
			100%	3.8%

For a 504 loan of $1.8 million, the bank loans $1 million, the SBA offers a debenture of $800,000, and the borrower contributes $200,000 in equity. The blended interest rate between the bank and debenture rates is 3.8%. A computation of the expected rate of return to the provider based on the sample terms is shown next.

1. Total interest cost $68,400
   ($1.8 million loan × 3.8% interest rate)
2. Bank closing fee   1,000
   ($1 million loan × 1% ÷ 10 years)
3. Debenture fee   2,400
   ($800,000 SBA loan × 3% debenture fee ÷ 10 years)

Annual returns of loan	$71,800
Expected rate of return	**4.0%**
($71,800/$1,800,000)	

The blended interest rate of 3.8% is increased by the "terms cost" of .2%, which yields an expected rate of return of 4.0%. The bank closing fee and debenture fee are amortized over ten years.

CAPLINES LOAN PROGRAM

CAPLines is the umbrella program under which the SBA helps small businesses meet short-term and cyclical working capital needs. A CAPLines loan can be for any dollar amount, except for the small asset-based line. There are five short-term working-capital loan programs for small businesses under the CAPLines umbrella:

1. *Seasonal line.* Advances against anticipated inventory and accounts receivable help during peak seasons when businesses experience seasonal sales fluctuations. Can be revolving or nonrevolving.
2. *Contract line.* Finances the direct labor and material cost associated with performing assignable contract(s). Can be revolving or nonrevolving.
3. *Builders' line.* Used by small general contractors to finance direct labor and material costs. The building project serves as the collateral, and loans can be revolving or nonrevolving.
4. *Standard asset-based line.* An asset-based revolving line of credit for businesses unable to meet credit standards associated with long-term credit. It provides financing for cyclical growth, recurring, and/or short-term needs. Repayment comes from converting short-term assets into cash, which is remitted to the

lender. Businesses continually draw from this line of credit, based on existing assets, and repay as their cash cycle dictates. This line generally is used by businesses that provide credit to other businesses. Because these loans require continual servicing and monitoring of collateral, additional fees may be charged by the lender.

5. *Small asset-based line.* An asset-based revolving line of credit of up to $200,000. It operates like a standard asset-based line except that some of the stricter servicing requirements are waived, providing the business can consistently show repayment ability from cash flow for the full amount.

Except the small asset-based line, CAPLine loans follow SBA's maximum loan amounts. Thus, SBA can guarantee as much as 85% on loans of up to $150,000 and 75% on loans of more than $150,000. 7(a) loans have a maximum loan amount of $2 million. SBA's maximum exposure is $1.5 million. Thus, if a business receives an SBA-guaranteed loan for $2 million, the maximum guaranty to the lender will be $1.5 million, or 75%. Eligibility for this program is the same as for the SBA 7(a) guaranty loan program, discussed earlier in this chapter.

Each of the five lines of credit has a maturity of up to five years. A shorter initial maturity may be established to suit individual business needs. CAPLines funds can be used as needed throughout the term of the loan to purchase assets, as long as sufficient time is allowed to convert the assets into cash at maturity.

Exhibit 18.7 displays the capital coordinates for the CAPLines and Export Working Capital programs.

Interest rates, guaranty amounts, and fees are the same for CAPLine loans as with the 7(a) loan program mentioned earlier. Exhibit 18.8 contains the credit box and sample terms for the CAPLines program.

In this example, it is assumed a $1 million loan is sought. The interest rate is prime plus 2%, with prime assumed at 3.5%. Thus, the example uses 5.5% as the interest rate. The next table computes the expected rate of return to the provider of the sample terms.

1.	Total interest cost	$55,000
	($1 million loan × 5.5% interest rate)	
2.	Bank closing fee	2,000
	($1 million loan × 1% ÷ 5 years)	
3.	Guaranty fee	5,250
	($750,000 SBA guaranty × 3.5% guaranty fee ÷ 5 years	
4.	Servicing fee (annual)	5,000
	($1 million loan × .5%)	
	Annual returns of loan	$67,250
	Expected rate of return	**6.7%**
	($67,250/$1,000,000)	

The stated interest rate of 5.5% is increased by the "terms cost" of 1.2%, which yields an expected rate of return of 6.7%. The bank closing fee and guaranty fee are amortized over five years.

EXHIBIT 18.7   Capital Coordinates: SBA CAPLines and SBA EWCP Programs

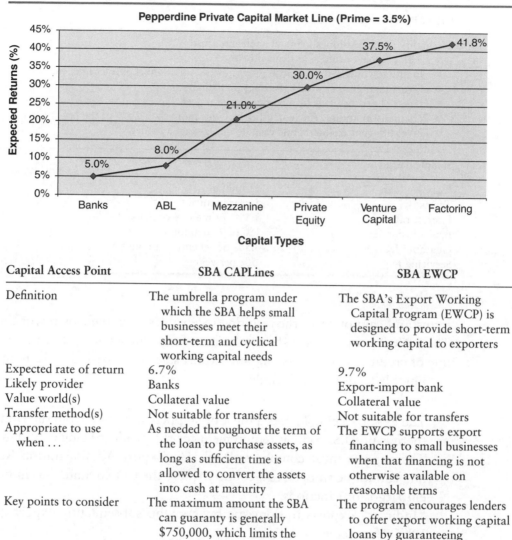

Capital Access Point	SBA CAPLines	SBA EWCP
Definition	The umbrella program under which the SBA helps small businesses meet their short-term and cyclical working capital needs	The SBA's Export Working Capital Program (EWCP) is designed to provide short-term working capital to exporters
Expected rate of return	6.7%	9.7%
Likely provider	Banks	Export-import bank
Value world(s)	Collateral value	Collateral value
Transfer method(s)	Not suitable for transfers	Not suitable for transfers
Appropriate to use when …	As needed throughout the term of the loan to purchase assets, as long as sufficient time is allowed to convert the assets into cash at maturity	The EWCP supports export financing to small businesses when that financing is not otherwise available on reasonable terms
Key points to consider	The maximum amount the SBA can guaranty is generally $750,000, which limits the CAPLine to $1 million	The program encourages lenders to offer export working capital loans by guaranteeing repayment of up to $1 million, or 90% of a loan amount, whichever is less

EXPORT WORKING CAPITAL PROGRAM

The SBA's Export Working Capital Program (EWCP) provides short-term working capital to exporters. The EWCP supports export financing to small businesses when that financing is not otherwise available on reasonable terms. The program encourages lenders to offer export working capital loans by guaranteeing repayment of 90% of a loan amount, or $750,000, whichever is less. A loan can support a single transaction or multiple sales on a revolving basis.

EWCP loans are used for transaction financing. For example, an EWCP loan will support 100% of supplier costs for an export transaction. EWCP loans can also be used to even out cash flow when exporters have negotiated longer sales

EXHIBIT 18.8   CAPLines Loan Program Credit Box and Sample Terms

Credit Box

To qualify for a CAPLines loan, an applicant must:
- Be an eligible business, as defined by the SBA.
- Qualify for one of the five loan programs (seasonal line, contract line, etc.).
- Have a loan need typically less than $2 million.
- Have a short-term, cyclical working capital need.
- Personally guarantee the loan if he/she owns more than 20% of the borrower.
- Have sufficient collateral and cash flow to attract a lender.

Sample Terms

Example loan	$1 million
Terms	5-year maturity
Interest rate	5.5% (prime rate of 3.5% + 2%)
Bank closing fee	1% of loan amount
Guaranty fee	3.5% of debenture amount
Servicing fee	.5% per year

terms and cannot carry the resulting receivables with their own working capital. The EWCP loan can be a short-term loan for a single contract or in the form of a line of credit that supports ongoing export sales for a period of 12 months.

Eligible transactions include:

- The exports being financed must be shipped and titled from the United States; there is no U.S. content requirement for the product being exported.
- The exports must comply with all U.S. Export Administration Regulations and cannot be shipped to a country where the United States has imposed trade embargos or sanctions.
- "Indirect" exports to domestic buyers who subsequently export qualify for EWCP financing.

Financing is available for manufacturers, wholesalers, export trading companies, and service exporters. EWCP loan borrowers must meet SBA 7(a) eligibility and size standards (less than 500 employees for manufacturers, less than 100 employees for wholesalers) and have been in business for at least one year. SBA can waive the one-year-in-business requirement if the applicant can demonstrate sufficient export expertise and business experience.

The maximum EWCP line of credit/loan amount is $2 million. Participating banks receive a 90% SBA guaranty provided that the total SBA-guaranteed portion to the borrower does not exceed $1.5 million. In those instances where the SBA-guaranteed portion reaches the $1.5 million cap, banks can still get a 90% guaranty thanks to a coguaranty program between SBA and the Export-Import (EXIM) Bank of the United States. Under this program, the bank still submits only one loan application to the SBA and receives a 90% U.S. government guaranty that is backed by both agencies. For the EXIM Bank guaranteed portion, a higher fee may apply.

EXHIBIT 18.9   EWCP Credit Box and Sample Terms

Credit Box

To qualify for an SBA Export Working Capital Loan Guaranty, an applicant must:
- Be an eligible business, as defined by the SBA.
- Be in business for at least one year prior to application.
- Be primarily an exporter.
- Have sufficient collateral and cash flow to attract a lender.
- Have a loan of no more than $2 million.
- Personally guarantee the loan if he/she owns more than 20% of the borrower.
- Have collateral located in the United States.

Sample Terms

Example loan	$1 million
Terms	1-year maturity
Interest rate	5.5% (prime rate of 3.5% + 2%)
Bank closing fee	1% of loan amount
Guaranty fee	3% of guarantee portion
Servicing fee	1% annual service fee

EWCP loans are typically issued for one year. The SBA does not establish or subsidize interest rates on loans. The interest rate can be fixed or variable and is negotiated between the borrower and the participant lender.

The SBA fee for an EWCP loan with a 12-month maturity or less is $\frac{1}{4}$ percent (0.25 percent) assessed on the guaranteed portion of the loan. For example, for a one-year $1 million line of credit with a 90% guaranty ($900,000 guaranteed portion), the guaranty fee is $2,250 ($900,000 × 0.25 percent). The SBA can reissue EWCP loans on an annual basis, and the guaranty fee remains $\frac{1}{4}$ percent.

The export-related inventory and the receivable generated by the export sales financed with EWCP funds will be considered adequate collateral. The SBA also requires the personal guarantee of owners with 20% or more ownership.

Exhibit 18.9 shows the credit box and sample terms for this program.

In this example, it is assumed a $1 million loan is sought and the interest rate is prime plus 2%, with prime assumed at 3.5%. Thus, the example uses 5.5% as the interest rate. The next table computes the expected rate of return to the provider of the sample terms.

1. Total interest cost ($1 million loan × 5.5% interest rate)	$55,000
2. Bank closing fee ($1 million loan × 1%)	10,000
3. Guaranty fee ($1 million loan × 75% SBA guaranty × 3%)	22,500
4. Servicing fee (annual) ($1 million loan × 1%)	10,000
Annual returns of loan	**$97,500**
Expected rate of return ($97,500/$1,000,000)	**9.7%**

EXHIBIT 18.10   Summary of Interest Rates by Government Lending
Program

	Stated Rate	Expected Return
IRBs	2.5%	3.6%
B&I loans	4.5%	4.8%
7(a) loans	5.0%	5.8%
504 loans	3.8%	4.0%
CAPLines	5.5%	6.7%
EWCP	5.5%	9.7%

The stated interest rate of 5.5% is increased by the "terms cost" of 4.2%, which yields an expected rate of return of 9.7%. Since this example assumes a one-year term for the loan, the bank closing fee and guaranty fee are paid at the closing.

NEGOTIATING POINTS

Most of the negotiating points regarding government lending programs occur at the underlying bank level. For instance, nearly all of the negotiating points mentioned in Chapter 17 can be applied to the bank portion of the government programs. Since the governmental part of the programs generally follows bureaucratic rules, it is unlikely to be negotiated.

Other Government Programs

There exist other government lending and investment programs than the ones mentioned earlier. Many of these are local or state sponsored. These can be found by reviewing local and state Internet sites.

Exhibit 18.10 summarizes the stated interest rates and expected returns for the programs presented in this chapter.

TRIANGULATION

Government lending programs position government as an active player in the private capital markets. The government's intentions are market oriented, and they are designed to improve capital access for companies that otherwise might not be able to fund their business plans. This contrasts with the role of government in valuation, where its interests are tax/revenue based. In other words, government intentions regarding valuation issues are directed outside of the market and may or may not reflect market reality.

Access to capital affects the value of a firm. Government lending programs dramatically improve capital access. In some cases, such as IRBs, the borrower substantially reduces its cost of capital by implementing a government loan program. In most cases, such as the SBA programs, the borrower reduces its cost of capital but, more important, increases its capital base to provide for future growth.

Government lending programs help fledgling companies grow into middle-market companies. This is no small feat. Desperately needed capital is the most difficult to arrange. Small companies have a difficult time attracting capital for this reason. Joe Mainstreet likely started out in business by securing a bank loan with an SBA guarantee. Once a company grows beyond $10 million to $20 million in revenues, its options increase relative to funding alternatives.

Most of the government programs mentioned in this chapter support business transfer needs. In some cases, the government program seals the deal. Recently, a buyer group became so enamored with the seller's low rate on an IRB that it upped its bid dramatically so the building and IRB would be included in the deal.

Two SBA programs, the 7(a) and 504, are especially useful in supporting business transfers. A large percentage of small business transfers would not be possible without these government programs. Although it is not the purpose of this book to extol the virtues of the SBA, this agency became much more user-friendly in the 1990s and now is highly responsive to its constituents' needs.

CHAPTER 19

Equipment Leasing

Most businesses in the United States lease equipment at some point. Many of these companies use leasing to finance the eventual purchase of the equipment. This chapter discusses the various types of leases, the advantages and disadvantages of leasing over purchasing, the lease process, the effective costs of leasing, and negotiating points.

An equipment lease is a legally binding and generally noncancellable document that details an agreement between two parties: The lessor is the party that owns the asset, and the lessee is the party that uses the asset. Lessees choose the asset they wish to use and the vendor(s) they want to supply it. They also negotiate the purchase price and performance requirements directly with the vendor of their choice. The lessor, on behalf of the lessee and at the lessee's instruction, purchases the specific asset from the specified vendor.

The lessee agrees to keep and use the asset for a specific time period defined as the lease term. During this period, the lessee must pay a predetermined periodic rental, usually monthly; pay any and all taxes or other equipment assessments; maintain the required insurance; and keep the asset in good working condition.

Companies are motivated to seek equipment leasing primarily because leases tend to be relatively easy to obtain. Just about every company can obtain an equipment lease. Lessors not only finance the equipment for the lessee, expecting to earn a fair return for providing this service, but also may commingle the financing and sale of the equipment, which often results in a good deal for the lessee.

Lessors are the authorities in equipment leasing: They make the rules. Lessors have the power to veto all transactions, which gives them authority over lessees. Five different equipment lessor types are discussed in this chapter. Exhibit 19.1 depicts the capital coordinates for bank and captive/vendor equipment leasing. The Pepperdine Private Capital Market Line is not shown because equipment leasing has not yet been surveyed.

TYPES OF LEASES

There are a number of different types of leases, and this chapter describes three general types. The first type is a *true lease*, defined as

> *A lease in which the lessor takes the risk of ownership, as determined by various Internal Revenue Service (IRS) pronouncements, and, as owner, is entitled to the*

EXHIBIT 19.1   Capital Coordinates: Bank and Captive/Vendor Equipment Leasing

Capital Access Point	Bank	Captive/Vendor
Definition	Banks are a major source of equipment leases. Because of the bank's cheap source of funds, they may offer the least expensive lease terms.	Many large manufacturers provide financing to their customers, often in the form of an equipment lease.
Expected rate of return	5%–7%	5%–7%
Authority	Banks	Vendors
Value world(s)	Collateral value	Collateral value
Transfer method(s)	Available to all transfer methods	Available to all transfer methods
Appropriate to use when . . .	The least expensive lease is sought and residual value of the equipment is fairly predictable.	A vendor subsidizes equipment sales with favorable lease terms.
Key points to consider	Finance leases become part of a borrower's capital structure, having the same balance sheet effect as a loan.	The lease versus purchase analysis should be performed to determine the cheapest method of financing.

benefits of ownership including tax benefits. This type of lease is sometimes called a tax lease.

Structuring a lease as a true lease is important because the lessor becomes the tax owner of the property, with all of the rights and privileges this confers. Improper structuring may cause the lease to be recognized as a conditional sale or secured loan. Instead of payments being recognized as rent, as is the case with a true lease, improper structuring would cause the lessee's payment be broken into imputed principal and interest, which does not offer tax advantages to the lessor.

To help taxpayers determine the type of lease, the IRS issued Revenue Ruling 55-540 in 1955, which defined what was not a true lease for tax purposes, commonly referred to as a lease intended as a security. This ruling holds that a transaction is not a true lease if any one or more of these conditions are present:

- Any portion of the periodic lease payment is applied to an equity position in the asset to be acquired by the lessee.
- The lessee automatically acquires title to the property upon payment of a specified amount of "rentals" he or she is required to make.
- The total amount, which a lessee is required to pay for a relatively short period of use, constitutes an inordinately large proportion of the total sum required to be paid to secure the transfer of the title.
- The agreed "rental" payments materially exceed the current fair rental value.
- The property may be acquired for a nominal purchase option in relation to the value of the property at the time the option may be exercised.
- Some portion of the periodic payment is specifically designated as interest or its equivalent.

Readers should consult their leasing professional and CPA to determine if a proposed lease is a true lease or not.

The second type of lease described here is a *finance lease*, probably the most common type of lease used worldwide, defined as:

> *A lease agreement that requires the lessee to remit payments of lease rentals, which total the cost of the asset plus the lessor's required profit. It is noncancellable and requires the lessee to pay all of the taxes and other assessments, provide insurance, and maintain the asset according to the manufacturer's guidelines. It provides that the lessee will acquire title to the asset at the conclusion of the lease term.*

Like nearly every lease, the finance lease probably contains a *hell-or-high-water* clause that states the lessee's commitment to pay rent is unconditional during the term. In other words, the lessee must pay regardless of what may occur during the term.

The third type of lease mentioned here is the *operating lease*, which extends for a relatively small part of the useful life of the equipment. Unlike the finance lease, lessors expect lessees to return the equipment at the end of the lease term. In some cases, an operating lease can last a day or two, such as a short-term truck rental, or several years, such as a long-term truck rental. An operating lease is almost always a true lease and may have a hell-or-high-water provision.

A difficulty with lease terminology is that the perspective of the participants determines which terminology to use. There are three main participants involved in the leasing discussion, and they are focused on different aspects of the lease. These participants are the:

1. *Leasing industry.* This group is most concerned with earning an economic return on the lease. They may use terms such as a "full payout lease," which means the total lease payments back to the lessor for the entire cost of the equipment including financing, overhead, and a reasonable rate of return, with little or no dependence on the residual value.
2. *Tax people.* This group, which consists of the people who are most concerned with the after-tax cost of the lease such as the IRS and tax CPAs, tries to ascertain whether the lease is a true lease or finance lease. The tax ramifications are extreme, depending on the type of lease that this group mainly focuses on.
3. *Accountants.* Accountants focus on the accounting treatment of the lease. Once again, different terminology is used to describe their perspective, such as a capital lease and an operating lease (different from the type described earlier, of course). A capital lease (accounting perspective) is the same as a finance lease (tax perspective). An operating lease (accounting) is the same as a true lease (tax).

Since the lease ultimately affects both the lessor's and the lessee's financial statements, the accounting treatment deserves extra mention here. Accountants typically refer to a finance lease as a capital lease. The accounting definition of a capital lease is:

A lease that meets at least one of the criteria outlined in paragraph seven of FASB [Financial Accounting Standards Board] 13, the standard for accounting and reporting of leases and, therefore, must be treated essentially as a loan for book accounting purposes. The four criteria are

1. *Title passes automatically by the end of the lease term.*
2. *Lease contains a bargain purchase option (i.e., less than the fair market value).*
3. *Lease term is greater than 75% of the estimated economic life of the equipment.*
4. *The present value of the lease payments is equal to or greater than 90% of the equipment's fair market value.*[1]

A capital lease is used by the lessee both to borrow funds and to acquire an asset to be depreciated. Thus, the equipment is recorded on the lessee's balance sheet as an asset and the lease as a corresponding liability. Periodic lessee expenses consist of interest on the debt and depreciation of the asset.

Accountants also view operating leases in specific terms. Operating leases, from a financial reporting perspective, have the characteristics of a true rental agreement and must meet certain criteria established by FASB. These criteria are:

- Title to the asset may not automatically transfer to the lessee at any time during the lease term or immediately after the lease term.
- There is no provision for a bargain purchase option.
- The lease is noncancellable for its term, and that term is less than 75% of the economic life of the asset.
- The present value of lease payments is less than 90% of the equipment's fair market value.

The lessee accounts for an operating lease without showing an asset or a liability on the balance sheet. The lessee accounts for periodic payments as operating expenses of the period on the profit and loss statement. Payments due in the periods following the preparation of the financial statement must be footnoted in the financial report.

A subtype of the operating lease is the sale-leaseback. The sale-leaseback occurs when an asset that is owned by the lessee is sold to the lessor and then leased back to the lessee. This can be an effective way for a lessee to raise cash for its business or to effect a change in asset utilization strategy. This type of lease is chosen as part of the sale-leaseback negotiations. For example, if PrivateCo sells $2 million of used equipment to LeaseCo, which then turns around and leases the equipment back to PrivateCo, it is necessary to negotiate what type of lease is involved. Most sale-leasebacks are structured as operating leases because the equipment is fairly old by the end of the lease.

LEASE RATE FACTORS

The lease factor is a shorthand mathematical expression that describes the lease payment as a decimal or fraction of the equipment acquisition cost. In other words, the lease factor is the fraction of the equipment cost each month that is paid to lease the equipment. For example, in a 36-month lease, a lease factor of .035 means that the lessee will pay 3.5% of the equipment cost per month. For equipment costing $100,000, the monthly payment would be $3,500. When added together and measured against the equipment's cost, it is possible to calculate the lease rate, or the effective interest rate implicit in the payments.

LEASE FACTORS

36-Month Lease

Monthly Factor	Noncompounded Equivalent Financing Rate	APR
.03	8%	5.1%
.035	26%	15.7%
.04	44%	25.5%

Lease rate factors simplify calculating the cost of leasing. Using the example of 3.5% of equipment cost per month for 36 months, we get 126% in all. This 126% consists of two components: 100% represents the cost of the equipment, and 26% is the lease finance charge for the three-year period. Lease factors are stated in noncompounded terms; that is, the 26% finance charge in the example is spread monthly over three years rather than considered as a present value.

Lease rates are negotiated between the parties and are affected by many considerations. Some of these factors are:

- The cost of the leased asset
- The financial strength of the lessee, including term debt requirements and available cash flow
- The credit profile of the lessee, including historical reduction of other term debt
- The forecasted value of the leased asset at lease end or if it is sold in a distressed situation
- The lease term
- The lessor's cost and availability of funds
- Charges and documentation fees

LEASING PROCESS

The generic lease process consists of eight steps.

1. The lessee selects the equipment and the vendor or supplier, and then the lessee negotiates the best price with that supplier.
2. The lessee submits an application to a leasing company and provides the credit and other information required by the leasing company.
3. The leasing company conducts a credit investigation and evaluation.
4. If the lessee's credit is approved, the leasing company conveys, in writing, all of the terms and conditions of the lease to the lessee.
5. Once the terms and conditions are agreed, the supplier of the equipment is contacted and asked for a pro forma invoice, which details the exact equipment configuration and the exact cost.
6. Once the leasing company receives the executed documents and a check from the lessee to cover any up-front costs, it will issue a purchase order to the supplier.
7. The lessee signs all documents except the acceptance notice. This is not signed until the equipment is installed to the lessee's satisfaction.
8. Once the installation is complete and insurance on the equipment is in force, the lessor pays for the equipment and the lease starts.

LESSOR TYPES

There are a number of lessor types in the market. Each has a unique business model that may or may not fit the needs of a particular lessee. The next sections summarize each lessor type, then compare them relative to the major leasing characteristics.

Banks

Banks are a major source of equipment leases. Because of their relatively cheap cost of funds, banks may offer the least expensive lease. Banks require a lessee with strong credit and usually already have a lending or other relationship with the borrower. Banks are at a disadvantage when it comes to residual value of the equipment, since they are less active players in the equipment market. For this reason, banks tend not to be competitive in situations where residual value is difficult to predict.

Captive and Vendors

Many large manufacturing companies provide financing to their customers, sometimes in the form of an equipment lease. *Captive* leasing companies tend to be divisions or subsidiaries of these manufacturers, and are dedicated to offering leasing primarily for the manufacturer's products. Since captive lessors generally are part of a large company, their cost of funds tends to be low, making them highly competitive.

With *vendor* leasing, the manufacturer does not use a subsidiary leasing company; rather, the manufacturer offers the lease to customers directly. Many vendors earn higher lease rates in this scenario, with the hope of bundling the leases and selling them to other lessors.

It should be noted that both captive and vendor lessors exist for the purpose of supporting the manufacturers and may, from time to time, offer very aggressive lease plans as part of a sales promotion driven by the manufacturer.

Specialty Equipment Lessors

Some lessors specialize in an industry or in certain types of equipment. These lessors have an advantage in situations where the underlying equipment has an uncertain secondary market (i.e., where specialized knowledge about equipment obsolescence can create a lessor advantage). *Specialized* equipment lessors may be more expensive than other lessor types at the outset, because of the higher cost of funds and the lack of reliance on residual value. However, for specialized equipment, this lessor may be cheaper over time than the other lessors. This is because this lessor works with the lessee over time and absorbs some of the obsolescence risk of the equipment. Exhibit 19.2 provides a snapshot of specialty and venture leasing.

Independent Lessors

These general leasing companies may be affiliated with a larger finance company. *Independent* lessors offer leases on most types of equipment and may find

EXHIBIT 19.2 Capital Coordinates: Specialty and Venture Equipment Leasing

Capital Access Point	Specialty	Venture
Definition	These lessors specialize in an industry or with certain types of equipment.	Venture leasing provides equipment to start-up and early-stage companies.
Expected rate of return	8%–10%	15%–20%
Authority	Specialized lessors	Venture lessors
Value world(s)	Collateral value	World of early equity value; collateral value
Transfer method(s)	Available to all transfer methods	Available to all transfer methods
Appropriate to use when . . .	Residual value is not predictable, thereby making this lessor cost competitive.	Traditional leasing methods are unavailable.
Key points to consider	This lessor generally absorbs some of the obsolescence risk of the equipment, which may benefit the lessee in certain circumstances.	Warrant costs add to the required rate of return listed above and must be negotiated separately from the standard lease terms.

equipment niches where banks cannot participate. These lessors are more likely to offer creative solutions than the competition. Independent lessors usually have a higher cost of funds than the competition.

QUESTIONS TO ASK BEFORE SIGNING A LEASE

Here is a list of ten questions that should be asked prior to signing a lease.

Before the Lease

1. How am I planning to use this equipment in my business, and how long will I need it?
2. Does the leasing representative understand my business and how this transaction helps me do business?

During the Lease Period

3. What is the total lease payment, and are there any other costs that I could incur before the lease ends?
4. What happens if I want to change this lease or end the lease early?
5. How am I responsible if the equipment is damaged or destroyed?
6. What are my obligations for the equipment (such as insurance, taxes, and maintenance) during the lease?
7. Can I upgrade the equipment or add equipment under the lease?

After the Lease Ends

8. What are my options at the end of the lease?
9. What procedures must I follow if I choose to return the equipment?
10. Are there any extra costs at the end of the lease?

Venture Lessors

Venture leasing provides general-purpose equipment, such as computers, telecommunication systems, and office equipment, to start-up and early-stage companies. In exchange for the lease financing, the venture lessor receives monthly equipment payments, the equipment's residual value, and, in some cases, equity in the company. Even without accounting for the warrant cost, this lessor type probably offers the highest-cost lease to lessees.

Exhibit 19.3 compares lessor types across a number of characteristics. The exhibit raises four issues.

1. Because leasing is so varied as to the providers and deal structures, it is difficult to draw definitive conclusions by lessor types. Thus, the exhibit needs to be viewed in *directionally accurate* terms.
2. It is important for prospective lessees to understand the underlying different approaches used by the various lessor types. For instance, some lessors have

EXHIBIT 19.3 Comparison of Lessor Types

	Bank	Captive/ Vendor	Specialty	Independent	Venture
Preferred lease type	True/capital	True/operating	True	All	Finance/capital
Tailored terms?	Rarely	Rarely	Sometimes	Rarely	No
Negotiated lease?	Rarely	Rarely	Sometimes	Sometimes	No
Residual guaranty	No	Yes	Sometimes	Sometimes	N/A
Importance of residual value?	Minimal	High	High	Varies	Minimal
Cost of funds	Lowest	Low	Moderate	Moderate/high	Risk based
Expected return	5%–7%	5%–7%	8%–10%	10%–13%	15%–20%

a preferred lease type, some negotiate lease terms, and some rely heavily on residual value for their return.

3. The lessors have different costs of funds. Banks generally have the lowest cost of funds, whereas venture lessors may have the highest.
4. Expected returns are quite varied in equipment leasing. Deals in this market are not as standardized as many of the other capital access points. For this reason, expected return is shown as ranges, with only venture leasing (described in the next section) shown as an exact return.

Expected Returns

Equipment leasing is too varied relative to pricing and terms to employ the credit box depiction that this book uses to describe most of the other capital access points. Each lease should be analyzed separately to determine the expected returns. Little research has been done to determine lease returns by lessor type. At least one study was done to show expected lease returns to the lessor.[2] This study involved venture leasing, which provides general-purpose equipment, such as computers, telecommunication systems, and office equipment, to start-up and early-stage companies. In exchange for the lease financing, the venture lessor receives monthly equipment payments, the equipment's residual value, and equity warrants in the company. Exhibit 19.4 shows pretax yields assuming a residual value of 15%.

EXHIBIT 19.4 Venture Leasing Study

Pretax Yields on 44 Lease Agreements

Assumes residual value of 15%

	Yield
Maximum	37.2%
Minimum	11.1%
Average	17.7%
Median	16.5%

A couple of items are noteworthy regarding this study. The median yield of 16.5% might be higher than nonventure leasing, since lessors might require an extra return for the risk of leasing to early-stage companies. Also, the median yield for this study when assuming a zero residual value is 9.4%. Finally, the warrants associated with the leases were not considered in the yield pricing.

COMPARISON OF LEASING AND PURCHASING

There are a number of advantages when comparing leasing with purchasing equipment. Exhibit 19.5 shows the major differences.

Cost of Lease versus Purchase

The costs of the lease versus purchase can be determined through discounted cash flow analysis. This analysis compares the cost of each alternative by considering the timing of the payments, tax benefits, the interest rate on a loan, the lease rate, and other financial arrangements. Of course, the ultimate cost is dependent on the validity of assumptions about future values and changes in the value of money.

To perform the analysis, certain assumptions about the economic life of the equipment, residual value, and depreciation need to be made. To evaluate a lease, the net cash outlay in each year of the lease term is determined. These amounts are derived by subtracting the tax savings from the lease payment. This calculation

EXHIBIT 19.5   Comparison of Leasing and Borrowing (Purchasing)

Item	Leasing	Borrowing
Effective Cost	May be lowest cost when all tax savings are considered.	Normally the lowest pretax effective cost.
Ongoing Fees	May have service fees.	No service fees unless loan origination or compensating balances are required.
Ownership of Asset	No ownership with operating lease; ownership eventually with capital lease. Also, leasing may better match the duration need of the lessee.	Ownership from the outset. This may or may not match the lessee's duration need.
Down Payment	Some leases provide 100% financing	Normally requires a 20%–25% down payment
Borrowing Capacity	Operating leases do not affect a company's capacity since they are off the balance sheet. Also, the lessee can avoid loan covenant restrictions that may exist with a loan.	Loans reduce borrowing capacity. Loan covenants must be negotiated and complied with.
Hedge Against Inflation	By delaying the outlay of funds until the lease payment, the lessee benefits from increases in equipment costs.	Ownership absorbs devaluation and inflation risk.
Residual Value	Accrues to the lessor with a true lease.	Accrues to the purchaser with a finance lease.
Tax Benefits	For true leases, rent expense is deducted as payments are made.	Depreciation and interest expense reduce taxable income.

yields the net cash outlay for each year of the lease. Each year's net cash outlay is discounted to take into account the time value of money. This discounting derives the present value of each of the amounts. The sum of the discounted cash flows is called the net present value of the cost of leasing. This figure is compared with the final sum of the discounted cash flows for the loan and purchase alternative.

Evaluation of the borrow/buy option is a little more complicated because of the tax benefits that go with ownership through loan interest deductions and a depreciation method called Modified Accelerated Cost Recovery System (MACRS). The interest portion of each loan payment is found by multiplying the loan interest rate by the outstanding loan balance for the preceding period.

As noted earlier, a claim on the residual value is one of the advantages of ownership. It is discounted at a higher rate than the cash outlays. In the next example, the firm's assumed average cost of capital is 15%. This rate is used because the residual value is not known with the same certainty as are the loan payment, depreciation, and interest payments.

The major difference in cost, of course, comes from the residual value. If that value is ignored, the alternatives are very close in their net present value of costs. Naturally, it is possible that residual costs for each asset could be very high or be next to nothing. Residual value assumptions need to be made carefully. Outside sources that offer residual valuations can assist in the determination.

The next sections analyze the differences between purchasing and signing an operating lease. Assuming that PrivateCo needs a machining center, Exhibit 19.6 contains estimates for this equipment.

Purchase Option

Several items listed in the chart in Exhibit 19.6 require further explanation. First, the interest rate represents the incremental borrowing rate of the firm. The net cash flows are discounted by this rate. The discount rate, however, represents the weighted average cost of capital of the firm. The residual value is discounted by the discount rate to reflect the additional risk of estimating this value five years before realization.

EXHIBIT 19.6 Purchase versus Lease Terms Estimates

Item	Cost	Purchase	Lease
Machining Center	$1,000,000	☐	
Down Payment	$200,000	☐	
Residual Value	$160,000	☐	
Interest Rate	8%	☐	
Discount Rate	15%	☐	☐
Term	5 years	☐	☐
Monthly Loan Payment	$16,221	☐	
Monthly Lease Payment	$21,000		☐
Income Tax Rate	30%	☐	☐
Depreciation	7-year property	☐	

Second, for most business property placed in service after 1986, the owner either claims the equipment expensing deduction for the full cost of the item (for small-ticket items) or uses MACRS. This method categorizes all business assets into classes and specifies the time period over which the assets can be written off. The equipment used in this example qualifies under "7-year property" and therefore can be written off over a seven-year period using these percentages: 14.29%, 24.49%, 17.49%, 12.49%, 8.93%, 8.92%, 8.93%, and 4.46% for the last year (called the "half-year convention").

Finally, this example does not incorporate maintenance costs into the calculations. Although the lessee is normally responsible for maintaining the equipment, this is a negotiated item between the parties.

To determine the net present value of the purchasing cash flows, the calculations in Exhibit 19.7 are necessary. The cost of purchasing in this example, on a present value basis, is $(683,802). This present value number represents the net cost, in today's dollars, of financing the purchase of the equipment.

The interest was calculated based on end-of-period principal and interest payments. Beginning balance: $800,000. Interest rate: 8%. Depreciation was calculated using the MACRS tables with 7-year property. The tax benefit is calculated by adding the interest and depreciation expenses and multiplying by the assumed 30% tax rate.

EXHIBIT 19.7   Cost of Purchasing

Period	Down PMT/ Loan PMT	Total Payments	Tax Benefits[a]	Net Cash Flow	Present Value[b]
Time Zero	$(200,000)	$(200,000)	—	$(200,000)	$(200,000)
1	(195,000)	(195,000)	59,098	(135,902)	(125,835)
2	(195,000)	(195,000)	86,198	(108,802)	(93,280)
3	(195,000)	(195,000)	61,408	(133,592)	(106,050)
4	(195,000)	(195,000)	42,302	(152,698)	(112,238)
5	(195,000)	(195,000)	27,177	(167,823)	(114,217)
Residual[c]		160,000	(3,132)	156,868	67,818
Total					$(683,802)

[a]The tax benefit equals the tax shield generated by depreciation and interest expense, taxed at 30%.
[b]The period 1–5 net cash flows are discounted at 8%, while the residual value cash flow is discounted at 15%.
[c]The residual value sale of $160,000 causes a gain of $10,441, which causes taxes paid of $3,132.

1. The Tax Benefits listed in the cost of purchasing table are calculated as follows:

Year	Interest	Depreciation	Tax Benefit
1	$54,093	$142,900	$59,098
2	42,426	244,900	86,198
3	29,792	174,900	61,408
4	16,108	124,900	42,302
5	1,289	89,300	27,177

EXHIBIT 19.8   Cost of an Operating Lease

Period	Lease PMT	Tax Benefits[a]	Net Cash Flow	Present Value[b]
Time Zero	0	—	0	0
1	(252,000)	75,600	(176,400)	(163,333)
2	(252,000)	75,600	(176,400)	(151,234)
3	(252,000)	75,600	(176,400)	(140,032)
4	(252,000)	75,600	(176,400)	(129,659)
5	(252,000)	75,600	(176,400)	(120,055)
Residual[c]				0
Total				$(704,313)

[a]The tax benefit equals the tax shield generated by the lease payment taxed at 30%.
[b]The period 1–5 net cash flows are discounted at 8%.
[c]The lessee does not benefit from residual value with an operating lease.

1. The tax benefits listed in the cost of an operating lease table are calculated as follows:

Year	Lease Payment	Tax Benefit
1	$252,000	$75,600
2	$252,000	$75,600
3	$252,000	$75,600
4	$252,000	$75,600
5	$252,000	$75,600

Lease

The calculation regarding the present value of an operating lease is much simpler than the cost of purchasing presentation. With an operating lease, the lessee does not have benefit of claiming depreciation or interest expense. However, the lease expense is tax-deductible. Exhibit 19.8 shows the present value calculations for this example.

The lease payments are provided in the example. The tax benefit is calculated by adding the lease payment and multiplying by the assumed 30% tax rate.

The present value of the operating lease cash flows is $(704,313), which is slightly more expensive than the cost of purchasing shown in the previous example. It should be noted, however, that residual value is extremely important to the cost of purchasing calculations. For example, if PrivateCo believes it can sell the machining center in year 6 for $250,000, instead of the $160,000 used in the example, the present value of purchasing becomes $(653,857), which is considerably less than the present value cost of purchasing example.[3]

Several of the variables are sensitive enough in this purchase versus lease analysis so that slight changes in an estimate yield a different result. Aside from residual value, changes in the required down payment, lease payments, tax rates, and discount rate all can change the ultimate decision. Although this sort of analysis is useful, a lease/buy decision should not be made solely on cost analysis figures. The advantages and disadvantages, while tough to quantify, may outweigh differences in cost, especially if costs are reasonably close.

Aside from the stated costs, there can be hidden costs in a lease, such as:

- *Document fees*. These fees are administrative costs due upon signing the lease and can amount to hundreds of dollars, depending on the complexity of the lease contract and size of the transaction.
- *Broker fees*. Some leasing companies are not full-service lessors; rather, they are leasing brokers that charge a fee by marking up the lease rate factor.
- *UCC-1 fees*. These are fees required by the secretary of the state where the equipment is being leased. A UCC-1 fee is a one-time fee due at signing.
- *Title fees*. Some lessors charge a fee to obtain clean title to the equipment in the event the option to purchase the equipment is exercised at the end of the lease.
- *Taxes*. In most states, there is a tax on goods purchased. Some states tax at 5% to 6% or more. The tax is factored into lease payments, so this cost should be considered, because it could increase the monthly lease payments, depending on the total cost of the equipment and the state of purchase. Also, if the lease is structured as an installment sale, tax may be due up front or as part of the amount to be financed.

NEGOTIATING POINTS

Leases contain many variables that are negotiated. Therefore, there are many negotiating points to consider. Some of the more important points are described in the next sections.

Start Period

Most equipment leases start with acceptance or commencement. Lessees should not begin paying for an equipment lease until the equipment is operating successfully. This is all the more important since most equipment leases include a nonnegotiable hell-or-high-water clause that takes effect regardless of whether equipment works.[4]

ABC Lease

Some lessors try to lock up lessees forever whereby the lessee can escape only by paying an inordinate fee. With an ABC lease, the lessee can exercise only one of three options: (1) buy the equipment at a mutually acceptable price, (2) extend the lease at a mutually acceptable price, or (3) return the equipment to the lessor only if a new deal is negotiated with the lessor at a mutually acceptable price.[5]

Changes

Lessees need to know whether they can move equipment to a new location without written consent for which they must pay. Computers and other technology products need upgrades more than every three to five years. Lessees should negotiate strong lease language if they want the lessor to pay for upgrades, which adds to the cost of the lease.

Termination

Early termination probably is the most common equipment leasing problem because the lessee's needs may change during the lease term, but the termination cost may be high. Often the termination price is the total of all payments remaining. Other approaches involve preserving the lessor's originally anticipated yield. Provisions for early termination, early buyout, subleasing, and assignment can protect lessees. They are not, however, part of the written lease unless the lessee puts them there.

Along a similar line, most lessors require some type of notification period near the end of the lease term. If the leasing company is going to remarket the equipment successfully, it probably needs to know 60 to 90 days in advance of its return. The lease may even mandate an automatic extension of the lease term if adequate notice is not given. For example, it may mandate an additional 90 days if the lessee waits until the very end of the lease to notify the lessor of its intent to return leased equipment. If a lease requires notification or extension clauses substantially longer than 90 days, the leasing company may be trying to take advantage of the lessee.

If a lessee chooses to return the equipment, it is fairly standard practice to require the lessee to crate and ship it back to the lessor at the lessee's expense. Making the return provisions too difficult is a way to increase the likelihood that the lessee will elect to purchase the equipment at lease end rather than return it. Such provisions as the way the equipment must be crated, the return of manuals and cables, how it must be shipped and to what location(s) can all impact that decision.[6]

Purchase Rights

Most leases give the lessee an end-of-lease purchase or release option at the then-current fair market value. Prudence requires that fair market value (FMV) is defined up front. Some of the largest leasing companies use FMV as the purchase standard of value, but *they* determine what that fair market value is! The lessee has a right to buy the equipment but only at the number the lessor stipulates. It is almost always better to have FMV determined through independent appraisals.

Maintenance Responsibility

Lessees should clarify which service and maintenance programs are included in the lease. If lessees are responsible for service and maintenance, they should make sure the expectation is reasonable.

Master Lease versus Schedules

Another point of consideration is to review both the master lease and specific equipment schedules.[7] When reviewing copies of documents, the master lease usually gets most of the scrutiny, as it governs virtually all of the standard terms of a lease. The schedules usually define specific equipment, payments, lease length, and so on. Since terms and conditions of the schedule often take precedence over the master lease, lessees need to review them both.

TRIANGULATION

Equipment leasing is the most readily available type of capital for businesses. Since access to capital affects the value of a business, equipment leasing probably does more to increase the value of private companies than any other capital type. As the private capital access line demonstrates, equipment lessors expect returns somewhat in the middle of the line. In other words, equipment leasing is not the cheapest or the most expensive form of capital.

Lessees consciously make a trade-off between time and money with regard to equipment leasing. Many lessees spend a fair amount of time and effort to finance the required equipment through their normal banking relationship, probably by purchasing the equipment up front. Other lessees choose to pay extra for a lease because it is easier to accomplish than dealing with the bank, and they find that that it is just not that much more expensive than a bank loan. As one owner of a wood kilning and planing operation explained, "For an extra point or two, I get the leased equipment delivered to me within days. It might take weeks or months to get the same response from my banker."

The leasing market is bifurcated by lessor return expectations. Companies that lease with banks or captive/vendors, typically the lessors with the lowest return expectations, usually have the choice as to whether to purchase or lease. Lessees that deal with specialty or venture lessors, however, may not have the luxury of moving down the access line. Within the leasing industry, companies shop for the least expensive credit available.

Equipment leases are also the most tailored form of capital. With the variety of lessors in the market, the needs of the borrower can almost always be met. Since lessors maintain a security interest in the equipment, they can regain possession of the equipment in case of payment or other default. Lessors view lessees in the world of collateral value because the residual value of equipment tends to have greater value when in place and operating.

Equipment leasing often eases transfer of a business because operating leases tend to slide through to the new owner. Even finance leases typically can be reworked to suit to the next owner. Some buyers employ an equipment sale-leaseback as a source for a cash down payment.

NOTES

1. FASB 13, paragraph 7(a)
2. Robert T. Kleiman, "The Characteristics of Venture Lease Financing," *Journal of Equipment Lease Financing* (Spring 2001).

3. The $653,857 present value based on a $250,000 residual value is calculated as:

> Residual value = $250,000
>
> Gain over book value = $79,559
>
> Tax on gain = $23,868 (taxed at 30%, which might be an overstatement)
>
> Net cash flow of residual value = $226,132 ($250,000 residual value − $23,868 gain)
>
> Present value of $226,132 = $(97,763), which is shown as a negative because it improves the cash flow
>
> Present value of net cash flows = $653,857 ($200,000 + 125,835 + 93,280 + 106,050 + 112,238 + 114,217 + (97,763)

4. Michael J. Fleming, *A Guide to Equipment Leasing*, February 17, 2000, www.bpubs.com.
5. The first several points were taken from Martin Paskind, "Act with Care When You Lease Equipment," SOHO America, 2000, www.soho.org.
6. Robb Aldridge, "Gotcha! Be Wary of Leasing Documentation," *AS400 Technology Showcase* (August 1998).
7. Ibid., p. 2.

CHAPTER 20

Asset-Based Lending

The asset-based lending industry makes loans secured by a variety of assets. These loans are used for a number of purposes ranging from growth to turnaround financing. Typically, asset-based lenders (ABLs) lend against the current assets of a business, such as the accounts receivable (A/R) and inventory. Other asset classes, such as property, plant, and equipment, may also serve as collateral. It should be noted that commercial banks make asset-based loans as well. But pure ABLs are much more interested in underlying asset values for securing their loans than a commercial bank would be. Conversely, ABLs are less interested in a company's earnings and financial loan covenants than a bank. Another major difference between asset-based lending and commercial banking is that state and federal governments regulate the latter. Since ABLs are not regulated, they have more autonomy to structure deals. Asset-based lending is sometimes called *commercial finance* or *secured lending*.

Owner-managers are motivated to seek asset-based lending for a variety of reasons. They may have no choice because their bank requests the migration. Or asset-based lending may be the least expensive source of funds available to their company. Thousands of companies that otherwise would not qualify for traditional bank lending receive asset-based loans each year. Even if the bank says yes, borrowing capacity is often greater with an asset-based loan than with a bank credit line. Also, ABLs can engineer terms that specifically meet a borrower's needs. Since ABLs fully collateralize their positions, they can be more lenient on certain soft items than other secured lenders. Items such as such as personal guarantees and covenants may be negotiable.

HOW ASSET-BASED LENDING WORKS

Normally the ABL loan is a revolving credit facility, known as a *revolver*. A revolver is a loan that can be drawn down and repaid. The borrower grants a security interest in its receivables, inventory, and/or other assets to the ABL as collateral to secure the loan. A security interest means the lender is granted possession of and ownership in the assets in the event of default. As receivables are paid, the cash is turned over to the lender to pay down the loan balance. When the borrower needs additional working capital, he requests another advance.

The lender manages a revolving credit facility and the related collateral to offer the borrower the largest possible loan amount at any given time. Because the borrower's customers generally are not notified of the assignment of the accounts to the lender, the borrower continues to service its receivables.

ASSET-BASED LENDING

Flow of Activities/Funds

1. The company sells a product or service.
2. The ABL advances funds to the company, based on predetermined advance rates. Applying the advance rates against the eligible assets creates a borrowing base.
3. The company's customers send payments to a lockbox or blocked account controlled by the lender.
4. The ABL credits the company's loan balance for payments received less cost of the loan.

ABLs loan varying amounts against different asset classes. These "advance rates" differ from lender to lender. For a typical borrower, it would not be unusual for an ABL to loan 75% to 85% against eligible receivables and 40% to 60% against eligible raw and finished goods inventory. Lending eligibility rules vary by ABL, but they are stated up front by each lender. Normally there is no advance against work-in-process (WIP) inventory, mainly because in the event of liquidation, the WIP inventory has little or no value to the lender. Advance rates applied against eligible assets compose the borrowing base, or the amount that can be borrowed at a given time. Exhibit 20.1 shows a typical borrowing base certificate. Companies complete this certificate at least monthly and possibly more often, depending on the lender's requirements.

Asset Eligibility

Asset eligibility, which is always described in loan agreements, differs between lenders. "Eligible receivables" usually refers to receivables that the ABL has a perfected first secured interest until collection, arise out of the normal course of the business, and do not exhibit any of these characteristics:

- Receivables 60 days or more past invoice date, typically with a limit of 90 to 120 days from invoice date
- Intracompany or personal receivables
- Foreign source receivables, unless backed by credit insurance or letter of credit
- Receivables subject to any claim or lien other than the primary lender
- Receivables from shipments against a U.S. government contract (unless the borrower can obtain an assignment of claims from the government, which is difficult to do)

EXHIBIT 20.1   Borrowing Base Certificate

ABLCo Borrowing Base Certificate

Customer Name:	**PrivateCo**	
Certificate Number:	50	
1.	Accounts receivable control (from prior month's report)	$6,000,000
2.	Additions to accounts receivable control since last certificate	
	(A) New sales $500,000	
	(B) Other additions $0	
	(C) Total additions	$ 500,000
3.	Reductions to accounts receivable control since last certificate	
	(A) Gross reductions $300,000	
	(B) Credit memos $0	
	(C) Total reductions	$ 300,000
4.	Accounts receivable control (Line 1 + 2C − 3C)	$6,200,000
5.	Total ineligible accounts	$1,000,000
6.	Eligible accounts receivable (Line 4 − line 5)	$5,200,000
7.	Accounts receivable availability (80% of Line 6)	$4,160,000
8.	Inventory availability (from Line 12 of Recapitulation Inventory)	$3,000,000
9.	Other availability	$ 0
10.	Total gross availability (The lesser of the totals of lines 7, 8, and 9, OR credit line of _____)	$7,160,000

Loan Position

11.	Beginning loan balance (from previous certificate)	$5,000,000
12.	Plus borrowing requested	$1,400,000
13.	Less cash remitted against loan since last certificate	$1,200,000
14.	Adjustments to loan balance	$ 0
15.	New loan balance (Line 11 + 12 less 13 ± 14)	$5,200,000
16.	Net availability (Line 10 − line 5)	$1,960,000

- Progress billings
- Contra or short-period accounts
- Customer concentrations, which may cause ineligibility beyond a set amount, say 25% to 30% of A/R to one customer
- Offset relationships, which exist when a company purchases from its customers (Lenders are concerned if these relationships involve large amounts of money because A/R may be offset with payables to the same customer.)
- A receivable more than 50% ineligible for any of the reasons just cited (called a "cross-aged" receivable)

Eligible receivables are generally reduced by all finance charges accrued against receivables.

A variety of factors can cause invoices not to be collected. Some of these factors are bad debt write-offs, warranty returns, fraud, prompt payment discounts, and incorrect invoices. Since ABLs are driven by the actual amount of cash collected, they attempt to quantify the difference between total invoices and cash actually collected. This difference is called *dilution,* also known as all noncash reductions to A/R. Simply stated, dilution is expressed as a percentage of the total invoices uncollected, as the next example illustrates.

PrivateCo has $5 million in invoices, of which $4.7 million is collected.

- $100,000 is subtracted for prompt payment discounts.
- $100,000 is subtracted for warranty claims.
- $100,000 is subtracted for returned goods.

The diluted amount is $300,000 (amount uncollected); dilution is 6% ($300,000 ÷ $5,000,000).

In this example, the dilution rate is 6%. Dilution is important to ABLs since it is the major factor in setting the advance rate on receivables. No ABL knowingly advances an amount equal to 1 minus the dilution rate. To help determine advance rates against receivables, many ABLs use this formula:

$$\text{A/R advance rate} = (1 - ((2 \times \text{dilution rate}) + 5\%))$$

With a dilution rate of 6%, PrivateCo could expect a maximum A/R advance rate of

$$\text{A/R advance rate} = (1 - ((2 \times .06) + .05))$$
$$= 83\%$$

As with most lending sources, ABLs tend to view this situation conservatively, and they may desire a cushion even after accounting for dilution. In this case, PrivateCo could expect an A/R advance rate of 75% to 80% of eligible receivables.

"Eligible inventory" typically means marketable raw or finished goods inventory in which the ABL has a perfected security interest, reduced by the obsolescence reserves of the borrower and excluding

- Inventory that is subject to any lien or assignment other than the ABL
- Inventory that is obsolete, damaged, unsalable, or otherwise unfit for use
- Inventory in transit or located outside the United States
- WIP inventory
- Supplies, packaging, and so on
- Inventory on consignment
- Inventory that is located at third-party premises or out of control of the borrower
- Specialized products that can be sold only to a limited number of purchasers

Many ABLs limit inventory to less than 50% of the total revolver. Most ABLs also limit eligible inventory in a general way, to whatever they say is eligible.

Advance rates for inventory rely less on a formula and more on a number of variables peculiar to the customer asking for the loan. These include the method of tracking inventory (cycle counting versus annual physical inventories or perpetual inventory), the number of inventory turns, the weighting of inventory held between raw and finished goods, and the experience of lenders actually liquidating inventory in that industry. A prospective customer with a reliable cycle counting program and a heavy mix toward high-turning finished goods should be awarded a higher advance rate than a company that does not have those characteristics. Advance rates within industries tend to aggregate around fairly tight numbers, mainly because of liquidation history. Finally, many ABLs will limit the total dollar amount of inventory that can be borrowed against. This "cap" prevents borrowers from adding unnecessary inventory just to increase the amount of the borrowing base.

Other criteria used by ABLs to determine an advance rate against inventory are:

- Age or turns of the inventory
- Price variance of the inventory
- Quality of the inventory
- Ability to return inventory to vendor

As with a receivables advance-rate setting, the ABL considers a variety of factors to determine an appropriate advance rate on inventory.

Asset-based lenders typically make term loans based on fixed assets only in conjunction with a revolving loan against current assets. The borrower needs to supply, at its cost, current fixed-asset appraisals. The ABL normally lends against the estimated liquidated value of the fixed assets less some discount for the effort of selling a distressed asset. Advance rates for fixed assets tend to fall in the 60% to 70% of orderly liquidation value range, or 75% to 80% of forced liquidation value. The fixed-asset loan part of the overall financing is generally less than 30% of the total. Finally, the term for the fixed-asset loan is usually amortized over five years and generally not more than seven years.

LANGUAGE OF ASSET-BASED LENDING

Advance rate. The percentage of funds extended to a client against eligible collateral as stated in a lending contract.

Airball. The portion of an asset-based loan that is not covered by collateral.

Availability. The amount of money a client has available to borrow, determined by the sum of collateral values less all ineligibles multiplied by the agreed advance rate.

Boot collateral. Collateral that is not used to support the transaction, such as intangible assets.

Borrowing base certificate. A form prepared by the borrower that reflects the current status of the collateral. Borrowing base certificates may be due on a daily, weekly, or monthly basis.

Contra. An account created when a company both buys from and sells to the same client and, therefore, has payables and receivables that offset.

Cross aging. When past due receivables exceed a given percentage of a debtor's total A/R, the current portion of receivables is also classified as ineligible.

Dilution. Returns, allowances, credit losses, discounts, and other offsets against A/R. Dilution drives the advance rate in a transaction.

Eligible accounts. Sometimes called "acceptable accounts" or "prime accounts." These are receivables that satisfy the criteria specified in the security agreement so that they are acceptable to the secured party and included in the borrowing base as eligible collateral and entitle the debtor to an advance.

Grid loan. A secured but not heavily monitored loan. As long as the borrower's company performs according to the loan agreement, collateral monitoring is minimal.

Holdback. The balance of an invoice in excess of the advance. The holdback becomes equity when the invoice is paid.

Jumbo account concentration. A debtor having a balance in excess of 5% of a company's total receivables.

Negative pledge. A promise not to secure certain assets of a company, such as inventory or receivables.

Over advance. A lender's unsecured position that occurs when funds are advanced in excess of contracted terms.

Participation. Occurs when portions of a loan, usually up to 50%, are shared by different lenders.

Progress billing. Billing made on a percentage-of-completion basis and generally found in service, construction, and other industries.

Repurchase period. The period of time, generally 90 to 120 days beyond invoice date, beyond which a sale becomes ineligible for assignment in accordance with contract terms.

Reserve (holdback). The balance of an invoice in excess of the advance. The reserve becomes equity when the invoice is paid.

Retention. The percentage held back by a debtor on a service contract to ensure adequate performance.

Security interest. An interest in, or lien upon, collateral that secures payment or performance of an obligation.

T/A (trade acceptance). A negotiable instrument for the amount of a specific purchase and bearing

ASSET-BASED LENDERS

There are numerous ABLs in the United States, with many specializing in certain industry segments or loan sizes. The hierarchy for deal pricing among ABLs is based on the size of the deal and the perceived riskiness of the borrower. A three-tiered system exists within the ABL industry. These tiers represent broad niches where the various ABL competitors have found some level of success.

ASSET-BASED LENDING TIERS

Tier 1: Funded deals of $15 million or more
Tier 2: Funded deals of $3 to $15 million
Tier 3: Funded deals of less than $3 million

Tier 1 ABLs are those ABLs desiring the least risky credit opportunities. This tier contains most of the larger commercial banks' ABL divisions. Typically, tier 1 ABLs require borrowers to exhibit a break-even earning capacity, although at times a negative earning capacity expected to turn positive may be acceptable. The earning capacity of a company is the reported pretax profits of the borrower, adjusted for extraordinary items. Tier 1 ABLs also typically want initial fundings of at least $10 million, preferably more than $15 million.

Tier 2 ABLs tend to fund smaller, possibly riskier, borrowers than tier 1 ABLs. As compensation for this additional risk, tier 2 ABL lenders require a higher interest rate than tier 1 lenders. Tier 2 lenders tend to be ABL divisions of midsize banks or independent arms of larger finance companies. Tier 2 ABLs prefer initial fundings of $3 million to $15 million but may bid on larger or smaller deals if the borrower meets its credit box.

Finally, tier 3 ABLs, sometimes called "hard asset lenders," are driven less by the earning capacity of the borrower and more by liquidation values. It is not unusual for tier 3 lenders to fund companies that have current negative earning capacity and expect to remain so for the foreseeable future. The key for this group is the *cash burn rate*, which signifies the monthly rate of cash loss in the business. A tier 3 ABL measures the burn rate and determines how long the company can sustain its asset base. Tier 3 lenders have the highest interest rates of the three tiers as well as the most restrictive lending arrangements. For instance, while most tier 1 and 2 lenders lend against 80% of qualifying A/Rs, tier 3 lenders may lend against only 70% to 75%. Tier 3 ABLs may loan as little as $500,000 but normally do not loan more than $2 million to $3 million.

The remainder of this chapter fully describes the three tiers relative to:

1. *The credit box for each tier.* Credit boxes depict the access variables that a borrower must exhibit to qualify for the loan. Unless borrowers meet certain criteria, they will not be considered for the loan at that tier.
2. *A summary of terms likely to be offered by the tier lenders if the borrower meets the lending criteria stated in the credit box.* Examples of these terms include advance rates, interest rate, closing fees, monitoring fees, and audit fees.

EXHIBIT 20.2   Capital Coordinates: Asset-Based Lending Tier 1

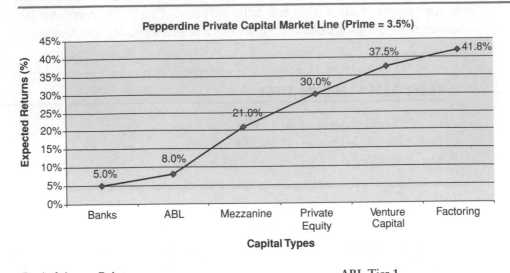

Capital Access Points	ABL Tier 1
Definition	Tier 1 ABLs are those ABLs desiring the least risky credit opportunities. Typically a break-even earning capacity is required, although at times a negative earning capacity expected to turn positive may be acceptable. Tier 1 ABLs typically want initial funding of at least $10 million and preferably more than $15 million.
Expected rate of return	6.2% (based on sample terms)
Likely provider	Tier 1 asset-based lenders include the larger commercial banks' ABL divisions.
Value world(s)	Collateral value
Transfer method(s)	Available to most transfer methods
Appropriate to use when . . .	A borrower with earnings and a stable current asset base has a moderate growth need. Banks have either said no to the loan or cannot provide enough capacity. This can be caused by internal or external growth.
Key points to consider	Tier 1 ABLs probably will require audited financial statements from the borrower. Reporting requirements will be heavier than with a bank loan but modest compared to the other tier lenders.

3. *The expected rate of return of the loan, as reflected by the sample terms.* The expected rate to the provider considers all of the terms of the deal, such as closing costs, monitoring fees, and various holdbacks. Expected rates are often substantially greater than the stated interest rate.

Exhibit 20.2 provides the capital coordinates for ABL tier 1 lenders.

TIER 1 ASSET-BASED LENDERS

Most large banks have divisions that specialize in making asset-based loans. These tier 1 lenders tend to reflect the conservatism of the parent bank, and they are likely

EXHIBIT 20.3   Tier 1 Asset-Based Lender Credit Box and Sample Terms

Credit Box

Earning Capacity	Collateral
Break-even at funding	Initial funding of at least $10 to $15 million
Positive within first year	Somewhat stable collateral base
Financial Boundaries (1st quartile)	**Covenants**
No more than 2.5 times debt/EBITDA	Fixed charge of at least 1.0 to 1
Total liabilities to net worth of less than 2.8 to 1	EBIT to interest expense of at least 1.5 to 1

Sample Terms

Example loan	$10 million facility—$7 million funded
	3-year commitment
Interest rate	Prime rate + 2% (Prime = 3.5%)
Advance rates	80%–85% of eligible A/R
	50%–60% of eligible inventory
	60%–75% of eligible fixed assets
Closing fee	1% of facility amount
Modification fee	.3% of modified amount
Unused line fee	.3% per annum on unused portion
Audit fees	$7,500
Prepayment penalty % (year 1, 2)	2.8%, 1.5%

to cater to *migrated* customers. Migrated customers have been in the commercial or corporate part of the bank, but they are moved into the more strictly monitored asset-based lending group. This generally occurs to borrowers with a good track record but that have exhibited declining, possibly negative, earnings and breaks in other financial ratios. Banks may also migrate borrowers who are exhibiting too much growth. The tier 1 ABL probably monitors the credit each month, as opposed to using quarterly reviews, by using a borrowing base report as well as a review of monthly financial statements.

Exhibit 20.3 depicts the credit box for tier 1 ABLs and sample terms that might be offered to a borrower. Although these terms fluctuate in all tiers due to market conditions and changing motivations of the players, the terms data is taken from a recent Pepperdine survey.[1]

The credit box is partitioned into four quadrants: earning capacity, collateral, financial boundaries, and covenants. A prospective borrower must meet each of the specified quadrant requirements to access credit from the tier 1 ABL. The next list presents an explanation of the exhibit.

- *Earning capacity.* The earning capacity of a company is the reported pretax profits of the borrower, adjusted for extraordinary items. Tier 1 ABLs generally require a borrower to exhibit break-even earnings level at the time of funding, with expectations that the earning capacity will turn positive during the first year after the closing.
- *Collateral.* Size matters with this lending group. The preferred entry is $15 million in initial funding, but a smaller amount may be considered for companies with a growing collateral base. More than the other tier lenders, tier 1

ABLs want a stable collateral base. For this reason, tier 1 ABLs monitor the collateral less closely than the other tiers, perhaps no more than once a month.

- *Financial boundaries.* Tier 1 ABLs require the borrower to meet several "boundary" ratios. These boundaries help define the overall riskiness of the lender's portfolio, which ultimately affects its credit box. Many of these boundaries are surveyed in the Pepperdine Private Capital Markets Survey and are presented here. One such boundary might be that no deal is undertaken that has a total debt to EBITDA ratio of more than 2.5 times. "Total debt" means the total interest-bearing debt of the company. "EBITDA" is the earnings before interest, taxes, depreciation, and amortization. ABL lenders use these boundaries to filter out companies that are too highly leveraged. Another boundary ratio is the total liabilities to tangible net worth of not more than 2.8 to 1. "Tangible net worth" is defined as stockholders' equity less the book value of intangible assets, such as goodwill. Once again, the lender is setting up a financial fence to filter out overly risky transactions.

- *Covenants.* Nearly all loans have financial covenants that in some way restrict the borrower. These covenants vary greatly from one institution to another and should be negotiated with care. As an example, two covenants are offered in the credit box. The first, fixed charge of at least 1.0 to 1, requires some explanation. The "fixed charge coverage ratio" is defined as the ratio of (1) EBITDA minus capital expenditures not financed by the lender minus taxes to (2) current maturities of long-term debt plus interest expense. This covenant shows whether current earnings on a cash basis are adequate to cover current fixed obligations on a cash basis. Once again, this covenant is tailored to meet the needs of the situation. The second covenant, EBIT (earnings before interest and taxes) to interest expense of at least 1.5 to 1, assures the lender of adequate earnings support for the loan. This covenant is also tailored to the particular borrower. For instance, a company operating at break-even may have a less restrictive covenant for the first year, followed by ever more restrictive covenants in succeeding years.

Exhibit 20.3 illustrates some of the quantitative criteria needed to gain credit access to tier 1 ABLs. Each lender is somewhat unique in its approach to making credit decisions. In other words, its credit box is engineered to meet its return on investment requirements. Of course, various qualitative aspects also factor into the lending decision. Prospective borrowers should interview representatives of the institution about the characteristics of their credit box. Further, borrowers should ask prospective lenders these questions:

- Who has the authority to approve the loan?
- Can we meet that person?
- Will we have access to that decision maker after the loan has closed?

In other words, borrowers should not blindly accept the salesperson's answers to their questions.

The sample terms show a possible deal offering from a tier 1 ABL for a borrower that successfully traverses the credit box. In this example, it is assumed a $10 million facility is sought, with $7 million funded at the closing. It is typical for the facility to begin with excess capacity, mainly so the credit has room to grow. Normally tier 1 ABLs grant a loan term of one to three years, with annual renewability at the option of the lender. The interest rate is normally computed and payable monthly and pegged to some known source, such as that published in the *Wall Street Journal*. Interest rates generally are described as either the prime rate or LIBOR (London Interbank Offered Rate). In the example, the interest rate is prime plus 2%, with prime assumed at 3.5%. Thus, the example uses 5.5% as the interest rate.

Most tier 1 ABLs charge a closing fee at the time of closing. This fee, sometimes called an origination fee, generally is expressed as an absolute number or a percentage of the facility amount, not the funded amount. The closing fee in the example is $100,000 ($10 million facility amount × 1%). This fee is entirely negotiated and varies from lender to lender. Most ABLs also charge a collateral monitoring fee, which normally is an absolute number paid monthly. An additional cost is the unused line fee, which is some percentage of the difference between the facility amount and the funded amount. In the example, this fee is .3% per annum applied against $3 million ($10 million facility amount – $7 million funded amount), or $9,000 annually, payable monthly. Almost all ABLs charge an audit fee at some stated daily rate. The audits generally are performed quarterly, with a daily rate of $500 to 1,000 per day per person. It should be noted that the borrower must support the audit personnel. It is not unusual for a controller or CFO to spend 30% to 50% of their time supporting these audits.

The expected rate of return to the tier 1 provider based on these sample terms is shown in the next table:

1.	Total interest cost ($7 million loan × 5.5% interest rate)	$385,000
2.	Closing fee ($10 million facility amount × 1% ÷ 3 years)	33,000
3.	Unused line fee (($10 million facility amount – $7 million funded amount) × .3%)	9,000
4.	Audit fees	7,500
	Annual returns of loan	$434,500
	Expected rate of return ($434,500/$7,000,000)	**6.2%**

The stated interest rate for the sample terms of 5.5% is increased by the "terms cost" of .7%, which yields an expected rate of return of 6.2%.

TIER 2 ASSET-BASED LENDERS

Tier 2 lenders tend to be ABL divisions of midsize banks or independent arms of larger finance companies. They typically fund deals in the $3 million to $15 million range. Tier 2 ABLs overlap in deal size with both tier 1 and tier 3 lenders. Tier 2 lenders fund riskier borrowers than tier 1 ABLs, in terms of both collateral and financial position of the borrower. As compensation for this additional risk, tier 2 ABL lenders require a higher interest rate. Tier 2 lenders also are more restrictive on eligible assets than tier 1 lenders but may provide higher advance rates on eligible collateral. Tier 2s may also monitor the collateral more strictly than the larger lenders. Exhibit 20.4 displays the capital coordinates for ABL tier 2 lenders

Exhibit 20.5 depicts the credit box and sample terms that might be offered by a tier 2 ABL. The order of importance regarding making a loan for most tier 2 ABLs is quality and amount of collateral, financial wherewithal of the borrower, and the experience and depth of the management team. As long as these characteristics are present, covenants are less important to the tier 2 ABL. For instance, if a borrower

EXHIBIT 20.4   Capital Coordinates: Asset-Based Lending Tier 2

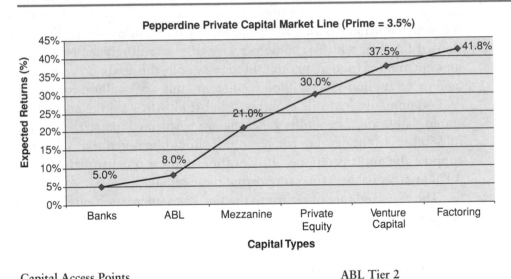

Capital Access Points	ABL Tier 2
Definition	Tier 2 ABLs tend to fund smaller, and possibly riskier, borrowers than tier 1 ABLs. Tier 2 ABLs prefer initial fundings of $3 to $15 million but may bid on larger or smaller deals if the borrower meets its lending criteria.
Expected rate of return	8.8% (based on sample terms)
Likely provider	Tier 2 lenders tend to be ABL divisions of midsize banks, or independent arms of larger financial companies.
Value world(s)	Collateral value
Transfer method(s)	Available to most transfer methods
Appropriate to use when . . .	A midsize borrower does not qualify for bank financing, probably because of an earnings problem; most of these borrowers live off the revolver, which means they run their business off the line and never totally pay it off.
Key points to consider	Prospective borrowers should show their deal to tier 1 lenders because they may provide smaller loans than they advertise. Some banks also own tier 2 lenders, under a different name from that of the bank. This is the hardest tier to identify a strong group of lenders because the players are constantly changing their lending criteria.

EXHIBIT 20.5   Tier 2 Asset-Based Lender Credit Box and Sample Terms

Credit Box

Earning Capacity	Collateral
Can be negative at funding	Initial funding of $3 to $15 million
Break-even within first year	Heavily monitored collateral base
Financial Boundaries (median)	**Covenants**
Likely not more than 3 times debt/EBITDA	Fixed charge of at least 1.1 to 1 by second year
Margined collateral is the key	EBIT to interest expense of at least 1.25 to 1

Sample Terms

Example loan	$7 million facility—$4 million funded
	3 year commitment
Interest rate	Prime rate + 4% (Prime = 3.5%)
Advance rates	75%–80% of eligible A/R
	40%–60% of eligible inventory
	50%–60% of eligible fixed assets
Closing fee	1.0% of facility amount
Unused line fee	.5% per annum on unused portion
Audit fees	$12,000 per year

is at break-even earnings and collateral is adequate for the loan size, the financial boundaries and covenants may be less restrictive than those shown in the credit box. Tier 2 terms fluctuate depending on market conditions and the changing motivations of the players.[2]

Once again, the credit box in Exhibit 20.5 is broken into four quadrants: earning capacity, collateral, financial boundaries, and covenants. A prospective borrower must meet each of the specified quadrant requirements to access credit from the tier 2 ABL.

The next list explains the terms.

- *Earning capacity.* Tier 2 ABLs may fund a company with a negative earning capacity if they expect the capacity will turn to break-even during the first year after the closing. Once again, this characteristic is less important than the collateral position of the borrower.
- *Collateral.* The preferred entry is $3 million to $5 million in initial funding, but a smaller amount may be considered for companies with growing collateral. Tier 2 ABLs expect to monitor the collateral base intensively. For this reason, Tier 2 ABLs monitor the collateral at least monthly, and perhaps weekly, until the lender is comfortable with the asset base. Sufficient collateral is the most important characteristic of the loan.
- *Financial boundaries.* Tier 2 ABLs require the borrower to meet several "boundary" ratios. These boundaries help define the overall riskiness of the lender's portfolio. One such boundary might be that deals will not be undertaken with a "total debt to EBITDA" ratio of more than three times. In this case, "total debt" means the total interest-bearing debt of the company. The primary boundary, however, is the margined collateral of the borrower. Margined collateral is calculated by multiplying the eligible assets against the

advance rates of the loan agreement. Therefore, a borrower cannot borrow more than its margined collateral.

- *Covenants.* Most ABL loans have financial covenants that in some way restrict the borrower. These covenants are tailored to the borrower and vary greatly from deal to deal. As an example, two covenants are offered in the credit box. The first covenant, fixed charge of at least 1.1 to 1 by the second year, requires some definition. The fixed charge coverage ratio is the ratio of (1) EBITDA minus capital expenditures not financed by the lender minus taxes to (2) current maturities of long-term debt plus interest expense. This covenant is meant to show that current earnings on a cash basis are adequate to cover current fixed obligations on a cash basis. Many ABLs use a covenant break to trigger demand or acceleration of the note. Once again, this covenant is tailored to meet the needs of the situation. The second, EBIT to interest expense of at least 1.25 to 1, is meant to assure the lender of adequate earnings support for the loan. This covenant is tailored to the particular borrower. For instance, a company operating at break-even may have a less restrictive covenant for the first year, followed by ever more restrictive covenants in succeeding years.

In the example, the interest rate is prime plus 4%, with prime assumed at 3.5%. The example uses a 7.5% interest rate. Some of the other sample terms are different from those presented with the tier 1 example. Typically, tier 2 loans have more restrictive advance rates because these loans generally are made to riskier borrowers than in the tier 1 portfolio. Tier 2 ABLs tighten the reins through more restrictive advance rates and get paid more for taking the risk through a higher interest rate and higher fees.

The next table illustrates the computation of the tier 2 ABL expected rate of return based on the sample terms.

1.	Total interest cost	$300,000
	($4 million loan × 7.5% interest rate)	
2.	Closing fee	23,333
	($7 million facility amount × 1% ÷ 3 years)	
3.	Unused line fee	15,000
	(($7 million facility amount − $4 million funded amount) × .5%)	
4.	Audit fees	12,000
	Annual returns of loan	$350,333
	Expected rate of return	**8.8%**
	($350,333/$4,000,000)	

For this example, the stated interest rate of 7.5% is increased by the "terms cost" of 1.3%, which yields an expected rate of return to the tier 2 ABL of 8.8%.

TIER 3 ASSET-BASED LENDERS

Tier 3 ABLs tend to be small, independent lenders. Exhibit 20.6 provides capital coordinates for this lender. Borrowers that fall into this net are going to pay dearly

EXHIBIT 20.6   Capital Coordinates: Asset-Based Lending Tier 3

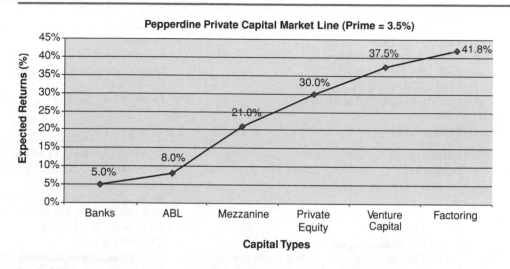

Capital Access Points	ABL Tier 3
Definition	Tier 3 ABLs are less driven by the earning capacity of the borrower and more concerned with liquidation values. It is not unusual for tier 3 lenders to fund companies that have a current negative earning capacity and expect to remain so for the foreseeable future. Tier 3 ABLs may loan as little as $500,000 but normally do not loan more than $2 to $3 million.
Expected rate of return	17.3% (based on sample terms)
Likely provider	Independent, commercial finance companies
Value world(s)	Collateral value
Transfer method(s)	Available to most transfer methods
Appropriate to use when . . .	No other debt alternative exists. Some tier 3 lenders offer deals far more expensive than the expected return shown.
Key points to consider	A tier 3 ABL measures the burn rate and determines how long the company can sustain its asset base. Tier 3 lenders usually have the most restrictive advance rates of the three tiers.

for not being able to attract cheaper capital. Tier 3 ABLs are driven mainly by the liquidated value of the borrower's collateral. It is not unusual for tier 3 lenders to fund companies that have current negative earning capacity and expect to remain so for the foreseeable future. Tier 3 lenders have the highest interest rates of the three tiers as well as the most restrictive lending arrangements. For instance, while most tier 1 and 2 lenders lend against 80% of eligible A/Rs, tier 3 lenders may lend against only 65% to 75%. Tier 3 ABLs may loan as little as $500,000 but normally do not loan more than $2 million to $3 million in total.

Tier 3 lenders analyze a borrower's cash burn rate to decide if a deal is feasible. If lenders believe the burn rate will not abate, they are unlikely to fund the deal. However, if a tier 3 ABL believes the burn rate will eventually subside, then the collateral is analyzed to determine a safe loan amount.

Exhibit 20.7 depicts the credit box for tier 3 ABLs and sample terms that might be offered. The credit box is partitioned into four quadrants: earning capacity,

EXHIBIT 20.7   Tier 3 Asset-Based Lender Credit Box and Sample Terms

Credit Box

Earning Capacity	Collateral
Can be negative at funding	Initial funding of $500,000 to $3 million
Cash burn rate is key	Highly monitored collateral base
Financial Boundaries	**Covenants**
Liquidated collateral is the key	Demand loan payment

Sample Terms

Example loan	$2 million facility—$1 million funded
Interest rate	Prime rate + 9% (Prime = 3.5%)
Advance rates	65%–75% of eligible A/R
	30%–50% of eligible inventory
	30%–40% of eligible fixed assets
Closing fee	1.1% of facility amount
Collateral monitoring fee	$30,000 per year
Unused line fee	.5% per annum on unused portion
Audit fees	$6,000 per year

collateral, financial boundaries, and covenants. A prospective borrower must meet each of the specified quadrant requirements to access credit from the tier 3 ABL. An explanation of these terms is presented next.

- *Earning capacity.* Tier 3 ABLs are much less concerned with earning capacity than the other tier lenders. The key concern is that negative cash flow caused by negative earnings does not consume the collateral base.
- *Collateral.* Tier 3 ABLs monitor the collateral closely, perhaps even daily, until the borrower is stable enough to be reviewed less often.
- *Financial boundaries.* These lenders are concerned mainly with liquidated collateral. The combination of liquidated collateral and burn rate drives the tier 3 decision-making process.
- *Covenants.* Tier 3 lenders have few financial covenants that restrict the borrower. Some lenders have a demand loan payment covenant, which basically entitles the lender to call the loan at its discretion with timely notice. This covenant is intended to protect the lender from further collateral deterioration.

The sample terms describe a possible deal offering from a tier 3 ABL. In this case, assume a $2 million facility is sought with $1 million funded at the closing. It is typical for the facility to begin with excess capacity, mainly so the credit has room to grow. Normally tier 3 ABLs grant a loan term of one to two years, with annual renewability at the option of the lender. In the example, the interest rate is prime plus 9%, with prime assumed at 3.5%. Thus, the example uses 12.5% as the interest rate. To protect their collateral position, tier 3 lenders offer restrictive advance rates. Since liquidation of the collateral is more likely than with the other tiers, these lenders exhibit the highest expenses per dollar loaned. These loans are heavily monitored, often on a daily or weekly basis.

The next table shows the computation of the expected rate of return to the provider based on the sample terms.

1. Total interest cost ($1 million loan × 12.5% interest rate)	$125,000
2. Closing fee ($2 million facility amount × 1.1% ÷ 3 years)	7,333
3. Collateral monitoring fee	30,000
4. Unused Line Fee (($2 million facility amount – $1 million funded amount) × .5%)	5,000
5. Audit fees	6,000
Annual returns of loan	$173,333
Expected rate of return ($173,333/$1,000,000)	**17.3%**

For this example, the stated interest rate of 12.5% is increased by the "terms cost" of 4.8%, which yields an expected rate of return to the tier 3 ABL of 17.3%.

NEGOTIATING POINTS

Beyond the terms just stated for each tier, there are other items that must be negotiated. Prospective asset-based borrowers should negotiate the next terms before closing a loan.

Personal Guarantees

Typically all shareholders who own 20% or more of the borrowing company must personally guarantee the ABL loan, although there may be a waiver of this guarantee for large tier 1 loans. In the heat of battle, most borrowers do not think to negotiate releases from the guarantee before the closing. Releases can be achieved through benchmarking the loan. For example, the guarantee can be either partially or fully released when the company reaches a certain profitability level or when the leverage of the company is reduced by a certain amount. Releasing, or *burning*, a personal guarantee is nearly impossible once a loan closes, because there is no incentive for the lender.

Interest Rate Pricing Matrix

Borrowers can negotiate an interest rate pricing matrix that lessens the interest rate over time as the borrower's financial condition improves. The matrix can tie to any of a variety of financial ratios. Typically only one ratio is chosen, and it corresponds to a problem in the borrower's position at the loan closing. For instance, if the prospective borrower is highly leveraged at the closing, the lender might incentivize the borrower to pay down debt during the loan term by offering the next matrix:

Pricing Matrix Based on Improving Leverage		
Leverage	Prime Margin	LIBOR Margin
5.0 or higher	0.50%	3.00%
4.50 to 4.99	0.25%	2.75%
4.50 or lower	0.00%	2.50%

For this example, "leverage" is defined as the ratio of total liabilities divided by tangible net worth. The lender might offer this pricing matrix if the borrower has a leverage ratio of more than five times at the closing, which corresponds to an interest rate of prime plus .5% or LIBOR plus 3%. The interest rate decreases as leverage decreases, normally measured annually. Instituting a pricing matrix before the closing saves a borrower from having to renegotiate rates later.

Prepayment Charges

For most ABL loans, the loan term ranges from one to three years. If a borrower wishes to terminate the loan agreement before the loan term expires, there may be a sizable prepayment penalty. A frequently quoted prepayment penalty is 3-2-1, meaning there is a 3% charge of the total loan if the borrower cancels the first year, a 2% penalty in the second, and so on. For some tier 2 and tier 3 lenders, this prepayment penalty may be closer to 5%. Borrowers should negotiate these prepayment charges to reasonable levels.

Financial Statements

Many lenders require annual audited financial statements as a condition to closing the loan, especially for loans greater than $5 million. This is a negotiated item and a fairly expensive consideration. Borrowers can agree to provide "reviewed" financial statements in many cases and save themselves more than $10,000 per year.

Loan Closing and Other Fees

The borrower pays the lender's cost of closing the loan. This includes legal, recording, appraisal, and other closing costs. If left unchecked, these fees can be substantial. Closing fees for a $5 million funding can easily exceed $20,000. Borrowers can negotiate caps on these fees such that the lender must receive permission from the borrower to exceed a certain amount. Sometimes the borrower can negotiate a fixed fee for the legal fees part of the closing. The borrower also incurs its own legal fees for reviewing loan documents, in addition to the lender costs.

Further, unused line fees can be negotiated with lenders. Since these fees are opportunity costs, they tend to be viewed by many lenders as something that can be waived.

Covenant Breaks

Most ABLs utilize an acceleration clause that calls the note upon a major covenant violation. Borrowers should review this clause carefully. One negotiating strategy is to limit the major covenants to those that the borrower believes it is unlikely to break. Another strategy is to negotiate a cure period before the acceleration is triggered. For example, upon the covenant violation, the borrower has 60 days to cure the default.

The key to negotiating a deal with an ABL is to consider the terms and conditions of the deal before executing a proposal letter. Many borrowers focus on the interest rate part of the deal to the exclusion of the other terms. As the various examples show, there are many costs associated with these loans, and together they compose the expected return.

Managing a company that uses asset-based lending must be done with foresight. All new initiatives or projects must be viewed relative to the borrowing base capacity and the other rules of asset-based lending. In effect, managers must negotiate and plan the growth of their companies with a view on asset borrowing availability. This may greatly influence the types of customers a company can sell or the types of inventory it buys. A premise of this book is that capital availability and cost of capital directly influence value creation. Judicious use of asset-based lending is yet another example of this connection.

TRIANGULATION

Capitalization is dependent on the value world in which the company is viewed and the availability of transfer methods. Asset-based lending is viewed in the world of collateral value. ABLs use this world to determine the value of the firm from a collateralized lending perspective. To these capital providers, margined collateral of a borrower is what matters most.

Growing businesses that rely on asset-based lending may limit their future growth opportunities. This limitation is algebraically based on the reciprocal of their advance rates. An example will help explain this concept. Suppose ABLCo grants PrivateCo advance rates of 80% of eligible A/Rs and 50% of eligible inventory. If PrivateCo grows quickly, say, more than 25%, the reciprocal of the advance rates, or 20% of A/R and 50% of inventory, may prohibit the company from financing its growth. In other words, unless profits are extremely high, PrivateCo can literally grow itself out of business. This is yet another indication that access to capital affects business value.

Asset-based lending is available to most transfer methods. Borrowers use asset-based lending to fund a transfer when conventional bank financing is not available or does not meet their needs. In these cases, asset-based lending often represents the most effective capital structure alternative. Of course, it matters if one accesses the least expensive lending tier. It costs more than twice as much to borrow from a tier 3 lender than it does to borrow from a tier 1 lender. To accomplish a successful transfer, prospective borrowers must accurately plan the amount of money that can be accessed and the return expectations of the most likely capital provider.

A recent management buyout illustrates the utility of asset-based lending in financing a transfer. The managers were attempting to acquire their division of a larger company; however, due to the lack of equity or equity sponsor, no bank would finance the deal. Fortunately, the division had substantial A/Rs and inventory on its books. The managers arranged an asset-based loan covering the required down payment while the parent issued a subordinated debt note for the remainder of the purchase price. This financing structure facilitates deals unlikely to attract other financing approaches.

NOTES

1. John K. Paglia, Pepperdine Private CapitalMarkets Project Survey Report, April 2010, bschool.pepperdine.edu/privatecapital. Tier 1 data uses first-quartile asset-based lending survey results.
2. Ibid. Tier 2 data uses median asset-based lending survey results.

CHAPTER 21

Factoring

Factoring is the process of selling accounts receivable at a discount. It is a credit service designed to turn assets into cash, but it is not a loan. The client business benefits from factoring its account receivables in three ways.

1. The sale improves the *business's* liquidity because the company receives cash almost immediately upon the creation of the invoice.
2. The client business does not need to incur the expense of a credit and collections department because these functions are performed by the factor.
3. Conventional financing may not be available to these companies, which leaves factoring receivables as their only source of growth financing.

HOW FACTORING WORKS

Most business sales result in the creation of an invoice, which states the terms and conditions for payment of the goods or service. Sometimes these invoices are paid immediately. More often, however, they are paid over some period of time, typically 30, 60, or 90 days. At the time of invoice creation, the selling company books an entry to its accounts receivable. Factors takes advantage of the value created by the invoice or receivable by paying cash for the right to receive future payments from the client's customers (called "debtors" in the factoring world).

Factoring solves the problem for growing businesses that tie up cash through added working capital requirements. For example, if PrivateCo grows its sales by $3 million from one year to the next, and its customers pay in 60 days after receipt of the invoice, PrivateCo will need additional cash to support this receivables growth of $500,000 ($3 million in new receivables divided by 12 months times 2 months to pay). This $500,000 cash need might be considerably greater if PrivateCo has increased inventory needs as well. Exhibit 21.1 provides the capital coordinates for factoring.

Through the use of factoring, companies may outsource some or all of the credit activities shown in Exhibit 21.2. This decision is the essence of whether to factor or not. Companies that manage the entire credit process in-house typically do not factor their receivables. However, companies that need substantial help in the credit process may choose to factor.[1]

EXHIBIT 21.1 Capital Coordinates: Factoring

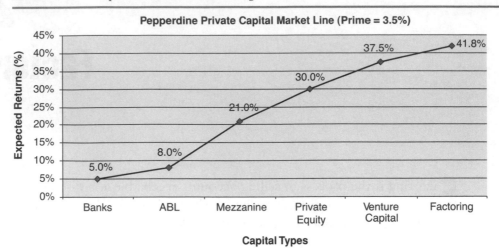

Pepperdine Private Capital Market Line (Prime = 3.5%)

Capital Access Point	Large Volume	Medium Volume	Small Volume
Definition	Factoring receivables of more than $500,000 per month	Factoring receivables of $100,000–$500,000 per month	Factoring receivables of less than $100,000 per month
Expected rate of return	34.6%	41.8%	49.5%
Authority	Independent factors, divisions of finance companies		
Value world(s)	Collateral value	Collateral value	Collateral value
Transfer method(s)	Supports most transfer methods	Supports most transfer methods	Supports most transfer methods
Appropriate to use when . . .	Less expensive financing is not available.		
Key points to consider	The higher the factoring volume, the more likely the client can negotiate lower commissions and reserves.	Clients should concentrate on the terms of the fee clock and the various miscellaneous fees associated with factoring.	Clients should seek just about any other source of capital. This is the most expensive capital access point on the private capital access line.

EXHIBIT 21.2 Credit Functions

Factors may peform these functions for clients:
1. Assessment of the credit risk
2. Making the credit-granting decision with regard to credit terms and credit limits
3. Collecting the receivables as they become due and taking actions against defaulters
4. Monitoring customer behavior and compiling management information
5. Bearing the risk of default or bad debt
6. Financing the investment in receivables

There is confusion about the role of factoring relative to a bank or asset-based lender. The most obvious difference is that factoring is not a loan; rather, it is the sale of an asset for cash. Beyond this, financing institutions tend to look at the viability of the business as a means of loan repayment. Factors consider the financial soundness of the client's customers as a source of payment. In an ironic twist, the client might be uncreditworthy, but because it sells to a creditworthy customer, a factoring transaction can occur. Of course, there is an accounting difference when a company factors its receivables rather than borrowing needed funds. Borrowing creates a balance sheet liability for the amount of the loan whereas factoring creates no obligation to repay. Factored receivables do not appear on the balance sheet whereas loans are reflected as a liability.

MECHANICS OF FACTORING

Assume that PrivateCo has a $1 million invoice it would like to factor. In this case, the customer has been given 30-day payment terms. Instead of waiting 30 to 60 days to receive payment from this customer, FactorCo may offer these terms:

- An advance of 85% of the invoice amount, meaning that PrivateCo receives $850,000 from FactorCo in one business day of tendering the invoice.
- A fee of 1.5%, or $15,000, as a commission for arranging the transaction.
- Interest at a rate of prime plus 2% is charged by FactorCo from the time of the advance to the client to the time the FactorCo receives payment from the debtor.
- Repayment of the remainder of the advance, less the fee, when the debtor pays the invoice. If the customer pays in 30 days, PrivateCo receives $135,000 from FactorCo in 1 to 3 business days after FactorCo receives payment.

By receiving $850,000 immediately and $135,000 when the customer finally pays the invoice to FactorCo, PrivateCo is able to meet its immediate cash obligations.

Other variables make this simple example more complex. The first variable involves the risk of noncollection. If a factor buys an invoice that later goes unpaid, who owns this risk? It all depends on the terms that the factor and client have agreed to upfront. There are two choices:

1. *Recourse factoring.* Under this arrangement, the factor establishes how long it will wait to be paid before the receivable reverts back to the client. This period is usually 60, 90, or 120 days. In case of default, the factor is owed the unpaid balance, expenses, and fees.
2. *Nonrecourse factoring.* With nonrecourse factoring, the factor does not have a claim against the client if the debtor defaults. It is usually the debtor's inability to pay that drives the reversion decision. For instance, if the debtor goes out of business through bankruptcy or liquidation, the factor generally keeps the receivable. If, however, there is a dispute over payment and the debtor refuses

to pay, the factor may have recourse. Thus, it is the responsibility of the client to satisfy the customer so it will pay. Factors purchase most receivables on a nonrecourse basis.

Invoice size and party negotiations dictate whether recourse or nonrecourse factoring is offered. Typically invoices of more than $100,000 may have a nonrecourse option, depending on the relationship with the factor and the quality of the debtor. Since nonrecourse factoring is tantamount to credit insurance, there is an extra cost for offering this service. Clients are less likely to have a nonrecourse option for invoices less than $100,000. Factors have a legitimate concern with offering recourse factoring to small businesses, because if there is a default, the client may not be able to cover the reverted receivable.

Since the factor acts as the credit department of the client, the factor has power over the credit process. Factors establish policies regarding the receivables they purchase. Factors can choose not to buy older accounts, accounts with a poor credit rating, or any account they believe is too risky. This means the client needs to check with the factor before selling to certain customers. Most factors have particular expertise in making initial credit-granting decisions and monitoring ongoing credit status. The more the client and factor work together, the more likely the client will benefit from the relationship.

Once the issue of risk ownership is decided, it is necessary to determine how the factor pays the client for the purchased invoice. There are two payment options:

1. *Nonmaturity factoring*. This type factoring, also called conventional or standard factoring, is the most prevalent method of payment. The factor's credit department checks the creditworthiness of all orders received from the client. When orders are filled, merchandise is shipped, and delivery is verified, the factor purchases the sales invoices and notifies the debtors that bills are payable directly to the factor. The client is charged interest from the date of shipment until the date payment is made on the account.
2. *Maturity factoring*. Maturity factoring occurs when a factor agrees to purchase an accounts receivable on the date payment is due on the account. For example, if a debtor's credit terms are "net 45 days," the factor must pay the client for the invoice within 45 days. With this arrangement, the factor is motivated to collect the account before paying the borrower. In this case, if the account is not collected within 45 days, the factor incurs the cost. No interest is charged here, because the client has taken no advances against receivables prior to the maturity date.

FEES AND TERMS

Factoring comes with numerous fees and terms. As with most business transactions, past relationships and expected volumes help determine negotiation positions. Since both fees and terms are considered to determine the cost of factoring, they are discussed here somewhat interchangeably.

EXHIBIT 21.3   Sample Factoring Commissions Based on Monthly Volumes

		$50,000	$250,000	$1,000,000
Commissions	0–30 days	3.0%	2.5%	1.8%
	31–45 days	4.5%	4.0%	3.1%
	46–60 days	6.0%	5.5%	4.2%

- *Discount fee.* The discount fee typically involves two costs: a commission charge expressed as a percentage of the receivables factored and an interest rate for the cash advances. The commission charge covers the credit process that a client wishes a factor to perform. Credit insurance, if purchased, is part of this service charge. The main consideration in determining the commission is the length of time it takes a debtor to pay. The longer an invoice is unpaid, the higher the fee. Other considerations are the annual volume, the number of invoices, and the number of customers.

  Commissions range from 1% to 10%, depending on these variables. Exhibit 21.3 shows an example pricing matrix based on factoring volumes.[2] The longer it takes a customer to pay, the higher the commission. Factoring prospects should get several quotes before entering into a business relationship.

  The interest rate part of the discount fee generally ranges from the prime rate to prime plus 5%. Once again, this is a negotiated item.
- *Reserve.* The reserve, sometimes called the *holdback*, is the invoice amount minus the advance, plus the fee, which a factor holds until the factor rebates the client. This holdback is meant to protect the factor from customer returns or disputed accounts. Reserves range from 5% to 50% of receivables, depending on the circumstances of the client and its debtors. Reserves generally are set based on the factor's history either with that client's accounts or with that client's industry. If it is likely that many accounts will be disputed, the reserve will be high.
- *Clearance days.* Clearance days, sometimes called *float* days or *collection* days, indicate the number of days that a client waits to receive monies after a factor has received payment from a debtor. Each day in float can be expensive to the client. This is exaggerated with factoring, because fees are accumulating until the factor pays the client.
- *Audit fees.* Most factors require an annual audit of the client's books and records; in some cases they require more frequent audits. The client pays this cost, which normally ranges from $1,000 to $5,000 per year.
- *Invoice fees.* Some factors charge for each invoice submitted for funding. There may be a minimum number of invoices required for submittal each month. Clients should multiply the per-invoice charge by the minimum number of invoices per month to ascertain the minimum monthly cost for invoice fees.
- *Filing fees.* Some factors pass along all charges they incur with respect to perfecting their security interest with the secretary of state's office in the state where the business is located.

EXHIBIT 21.4 Sample Factoring Terms Based on Monthly Volumes

Items	Small Volume	Medium Volume	Large Volume
Monthly volume	$50,000	$250,000	$1,000,000
Cash advance	80%	80%	85%
Commission			
0–30 days	3%	2.5%	1.8%
Interest rate (prime = 3.5%)	+3%	+2.5%	+2%
Clearance days	2	2	1
Cost of funds	59.4%	54.9%	34.0%

As can be seen from the terms just defined, time is a major component in determining fees in a factoring arrangement. The amount of time invoices are outstanding directly affects fees. In addition to helping determine the amount of the fee, time also helps determine when that fee starts and when it stops. Time is controlled in factoring through use of a *fee clock*. The fee clock begins once the invoice is received by the factor and the factor sends the client the advance on that invoice. Clients should make sure the contract indicates that they get credit for the invoice the day it is received by the factor.

Sample Terms

Exhibit 21.4 shows sample terms for three different volume points: $50,000, $250,000, and $1,000,000 per month in factored invoices.[3] The more a company factors, the less it costs per dollar factored. Several of the items require explanation. For example, it is assumed that all invoices are collected within 30 days. Commissions are higher than those stated if it takes longer to collect. Interest is charged against the advanced amount for the period from the time of the advance to the client to the time the factor receives payment from the debtor. Finally, the example assumes that the number of clearance days decrease as the factored amounts increase.

The cost of funds for factoring is high, ranging from 34% for large volume to more than 59% for small volume. An explanation of this calculation is required. Using the small-volume factored situation as an example, the next figures show the cost of funds calculation.

1. Commission ($50,000 × 3%)	$1,500
2. Interest ($40,000 × 6.5% ÷ 12)	217
3. Clearance period: 2 days[4]	170
Total monthly expense	$1,887

The factor also holds a reserve of $10,000 ($50,000 × 20%). If it is assumed that that the reserve is returned at the end of the month, the firm has paid $1,887 for the use of $38,113 ($40,000 − $1,887) for one month, which has an annual cost before compounding of:

$$\frac{\text{Monthly expense}}{\text{Use of Funds}} \quad \frac{\$1,887}{\$38,113} \times \frac{12}{1} = 59.4\%$$

Of course, a higher reserve or additional fees increase this rate, and vice versa. The following example shows a positive usage of factoring.

EXAMPLE

PrivateCo establishes a factoring relationship with two unusual business characteristics. In one component, which PrivateCo calls "deals," it purchases large quantities of an overstocked product from one company and resells to a number of others. In another component, which PrivateCo calls "flips," it purchases an entire inventory from one retailer and resells it to another. In both cases, the products are normally presold before PrivateCo purchases them. Although both practices are a routine part of the business, PrivateCo is opportunistic. Some months may present five to ten opportunities, which are handled out of cash flow. Other months may present an unusually high number of opportunities, or more costly opportunities, and may not be able to be handled out of current cash flow.

Dan Dealmaker, PrivateCo's investment banker, obtains a factoring arrangement that allows PrivateCo to do any number of both deals and flips. PrivateCo is financially well disciplined and therefore is able to draw the funds only as needed and repay them promptly from sale proceeds. For a number of reasons, this arrangement is not appropriate for a normal line of credit. It is possible, however, for PrivateCo to calculate the cost of funds into the deals and flips and select only profitable opportunities.

This creative arrangement allows PrivateCo to capitalize on opportunities that would not be available otherwise. In this case, factoring can be viewed as a profit-making opportunity rather than a cost.

The 59% cost calculated for small-volume factoring is overstated because the factor provides much of the credit function as part of these fees. To determine the effective cost of factoring, the cost of this credit function must be considered. Exhibit 21.5 estimates the client expense incurred, had the credit function been internalized, once again broken down by three volume sizes.

The next assumptions are used to estimate the credit function cost of several different firm sizes:

- A credit department is created and staffed by credit clerks and credit managers, the number of each decided by the size of the firm. According to the U.S. Bureau of Labor Statistics, a credit clerk earns on average $30,940 per year.[5] It is assumed that a firm with revenues of less than $2.5 million per year would require 50% of a clerk; firms with revenues $2.5 million to $15 million would require 1.5 clerks.
- According to the U.S. Bureau of Statistics, a credit manager earns $101,190 per year.[6] It is assumed that only the large-volume factoring client can afford a credit manager.

EXHIBIT 21.5 Credit Function Expenses by Monthly Volume Size

Items	Small Volume ($50,000)	Medium Volume ($250,000)	Large Volume ($1,000,000)
Credit clerk—$30,940	50%	150%	150%
	$15,470	$46,410	$46,410
Credit manager—$101,190	0%	0%	100%
	$0	$0	$101,190
Fringe benefits—20%	$0	$9,282	$29,520
Credit reports/other	$3,000	$20,000	$35,000
Total cost of credit function	$18,470	$75,692	$212,120
Total cost of commissions	18,000	75,000	216,000
Annual cost difference	$(470)	$(692)	$3,880
Monthly cost difference	(39)	(58)	323
Cost of funds (from above)	59.4%	54.9%	34.0%
Effective cost of funds[a]	49.5%	41.8%	34.6%

[a]The effective cost of factoring funds calculation for small-volume factoring is

1. Commission ($40,000 × 3%)	$1,200
2. Interest ($40,000 × 6.5% ÷ 12)	217
3. Clearance period: 2 days	170
4. Added cost of the credit function over commissions	(39)
Total Monthly Expense	$1,584

The factor also holds a reserve of $40,000 ($50,000 × 20%). If it is assumed that that the reserve is returned at the end of the month, the firm has paid $1,584 for the use of $38,416 ($40,000 − $1,584) for one month, which has an annual cost before compounding of:

$$\frac{\text{Monthly expense}}{\text{Use of funds}} \quad \frac{\$1,584}{\$38,416} \times \frac{12}{1} = 49.5\%$$

- Fringe benefit costs of 20% are applied to the clerk and manager salaries for medium and large firms. It is assumed that fringe benefits would not be paid on a part-time clerk for a small firm.
- Credit reports and other costs are stated in the table in Exhibit 21.5.
- The total cost of commissions equals the sample terms percentage times the expected annual volume. For example, the small-factoring annual volume is assumed to be $600,000 times 3%, which equals $18,000.
- The difference between the total cost of the estimated credit function and the total cost of annual commissions represents the incremental costs (as a negative) of a company providing its own credit function beyond the commissions a factor would charge for this service. A positive figure means that the client could conceivably do its own credit checks and collections more cheaply than the factor. In this example, only the large-volume factoring client could save by having its own credit function.

In this example, once the cost of an estimated credit function is considered, the effective cost of factoring ranges from 34% for large volumes to 49% for small volumes. This example does not fit all circumstances. Factoring clients should quantify the details of their arrangement and calculate their specific cost of funds.

Even though the cost of factoring is high, it is possible to still make money by controlling the variables, as the following example demonstrates.

EXAMPLE

PrivateCo exclusively represents a number of companies in an industry with several peculiarities, including 90-day billing, customers' right to return products, and consignment inventory. PrivateCo is unable to attract less costly conventional financing. It is possible to arrange a factoring relationship where invoices are submitted shortly before funds are needed for monthly settlement with represented companies. Further, not all invoices have to be submitted, and invoice payments can be substituted. They also negotiate a provision for no termination penalty.

Although the cost of factoring is still high, controlling the fee clock, the number of invoices submitted, and the right of substitution allows PrivateCo significant control over costs. Further, because it is anticipated that the need for factoring may be short term, the provision for no termination fee allows PrivateCo to return to conventional financing without paying large penalties.

In this case, factoring allows PrivateCo to work out of a short-term financial situation where no other form of financing is available. Although factoring is often viewed as the financing of last resort, it has a role and can solve real problems effectively.

NEGOTIATING POINTS

Beyond the terms discussed previously, a number of other issues can be negotiated. Prospective clients of factors should consider incorporating the next terms into the deal before the closing.

Length of Contract (Terms)

First-time clients should try to negotiate a short contract period, certainly no more than six months. Experienced clients should limit the contract to no more than one year. This shortened time allows clients to maintain flexibility in case more conventional financing becomes possible. As part of the contract negotiations, a key concern should be termination penalties. A penalty of 3% is typical in the industry. This means that if the client terminates the contract early, a penalty of 3% of the average monthly factored amounts is assessed.

Clients should negotiate the ability to collect some accounts themselves and not turn over all accounts to the factor. If clients do not need the advance for all of its accounts up front, it makes no sense to pay hefty factoring fees.

Clients should also negotiate flexibility to exchange an invoice, which is similar to holding back an invoice. Exchanging longer-paying customers with a shorter-paying one saves money. For example, if a client has a customer who has been paying in 30 days but suddenly changes its payment terms to 75 days, the client may want to exchange this longer-paying customer with a 30-day payer. The net result is that the client pays only a 30-day fee, rather than a 75-day fee, which should result in substantial savings.

Fee Clock

Clients can use time to reduce factoring fees. Many factors quote a fee schedule based on how long invoices are outstanding. The longer it takes the customers to pay, the higher the fee. Some clients save money by not sending an invoice to the factor until they really need the money. In this way, the fee clock does not begin until the money is needed. The fee clock stops the day the debtor's check *arrives* at the factor's office, not the day the check *clears* the bank. Because float days can be quite expensive to a client, this is a key consideration that should be incorporated into the factoring contract.

Arrange a Credit Line

Many factors provide a credit line to clients, based on the total amount factored each month. All invoices are sent in each month. The total amount of these invoices, minus the fee and reserve, becomes the credit line. Unlike an advance, which is taken in one lump sum, the credit line is drawn as needed. Using this line can save money if the client times its draws with actual needs.

For example, assume a client has customers who pay, on average, 45 days after invoice. Further assume the client does not need the money until 15 days after sending invoices to the factor, at which time it will need 50% of the factored amount. In this example, the client pays a 30-day fee on the 50% draw, provided the customers pay in 45 days. Fifteen days later, or 30 days after sending invoices to the factor, the client draws the remaining 50%. As a result, when the debtor pays at the end of the 45-day term, the client is charged a 15-day fee for this half of the draw, thereby being charged only a 15-day fee for this half of the draw.

Miscellaneous Fees

Some factors charge fees for a variety of activities, such as

- Application fees
- Due diligence fees
- Credit checking
- Invoice processing
- Wire transfer fees
- Filing fees

Considered individually, these fees generally are not substantial. As a group, however, they can be large. Prospective factoring clients should understand what fees are included in the contract. Perhaps the best way to negotiate these fees is to compare the terms of several factors before selecting a source.

Factoring is not for everyone. Yet worldwide factoring is almost a $1 trillion industry a year. Companies with an established credit function do not factor their receivables. Companies that have access to cheaper types of capital also do not typically use a factor. In fact, factoring often is considered the capital source of "last resort." Yet for companies that cannot access conventional forms of capital, factoring may enable them to grow their business and, it is hoped, get to a point where less expensive capital is available.

TRIANGULATION

Factoring affects the value of firms. This effect is positive for companies that can generate returns in excess of the cost of factoring, but it is negative for companies that are unable to generate such returns. Because the cost of factoring is so high, many firms have a cost of capital that prohibits them from achieving positive incremental business value. For these unfortunate companies, factoring ultimately replaces equity in the business.

It is very difficult to disengage from factoring for financial, rather than contractual, reasons. Most companies that factor do so because they are not creating enough incremental business value to finance operations out of cash flow. It usually takes an equity infusion before a company can migrate from factoring. Most companies that must factor are unable to attract equity capital.

Factoring affects the ability to transfer a business. Factoring may help a transfer in the case of a borrower with a lower cost of capital than the seller. Factoring may hurt a transfer if the buyer has an equal or greater cost of capital than the seller. This explains why factored companies generally cannot acquire other factored companies. Typically, the acquirer must be a larger company that is conventionally financed.

Factoring is typically the highest cost of capital in private capital markets. Some industries, such as textiles and furniture, used to use factoring as a standard financing tool. But the high cost of factoring ultimately restricted the competitiveness of these industries. With a dramatically increased cost of capital, many players in these industries were financially unable to modernize, which, when combined with a more competitive worldwide landscape, likely contributed to their worsening financial positions.

NOTES

1. Barbara Summers and Nicholas Wilson, "Why Do Firms Use Factoring?" *Credit Management*, February 1, 1998. (Exhibit 21.2 was taken from this article.)
2. John K. Paglia, Pepperdine Private Capital Markets Project Survey Report, April 2010, bschool.pepperdine.edu/privatecapital. "Volumes" correspond to median result for $50,000, $250,000, and $1 million volumes.
3. Ibid.

4. The two-day clearance period calculation is:

Average loan balance outstanding		$480,000
Average interest rate	×	6.5%
Annual cost of funds		$31,200
Number of days in year	÷	365
Average daily cost of funds		$85
Number of clearing days	×	2
Number of turns of accounts receivable	×	12
Cost of funds due to clearing days		$2,040
Cost per month (as rounded)		$170

5. Taken from *The Occupational Outlook Handbook, 2009–10*, available at www. bls.gov.
6. Ibid.
7. See note 4.

CHAPTER 22

Mezzanine Capital

Mezzanine capital is subordinated debt that provides borrowing capability beyond senior debt while minimizing the dilution associated with equity capital. It may be secured through a second lien on assets, or it may be secured by company stock. Since it forms an additional layer of debt, it carries more risk for the lender than normal or senior debt. It ranks behind senior debt for purposes of principal and interest repayment. Mezzanine capital is generally the lowest-ranking debt obligation in a borrower's capital structure. Compared to a bank loan, it contains a fairly loose covenant package. These factors make mezzanine debt more expensive than senior debt for the borrower. Nevertheless, it remains cheaper than institutional equity investment and may be available when the supply of equity is limited.

The mix of senior and mezzanine debt is influenced by a borrower's cash flow projections, because mezzanine capital typically is repaid either in installments or in one balloon payment at the end of the term. Mezzanine capital is an appropriate financing option in situations where access to conventional bank debt may be limited because of a lack of tangible assets or strong guarantor, an unduly conservative assessment of a company's prospects, or when the dilution implied by raising additional equity capital is unattractive. This chapter describes mezzanine capital for private companies in need of $1 million to $25 million.

Mezzanine financing is used during transitional periods in the life of a company when extra financing is required. It is not the answer for day-to-day operations needs. Mezzanine loans are used for long-term or permanent working capital, equipment purchases, management buyouts, strategic acquisitions, recapitalizations, new product development, and other worthwhile business purposes. In situations where a company's banker is unable to fully meet its credit needs, business owners have three options for raising additional capital: (a) sell equity in the business, (b) borrow from a mezzanine lender, or (c) invest further in the business, which typically is only considered after the first two options have been exhausted. Business leaders who need a substantial investment, yet do not want to concede large amounts of equity or control, find mezzanine financing attractive. Exhibit 22.1 provides capital coordinates for mezzanine capital.

LOAN STRUCTURE

The structure of mezzanine loans accommodates the financing needs of growing companies. The mezzanine investor predicates the investment decision on the

EXHIBIT 22.1 Capital Coordinates: Mezzanine Capital

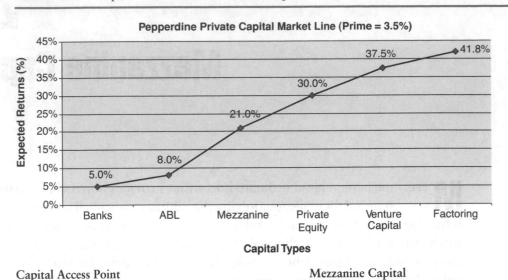

Capital Access Point	Mezzanine Capital
Definition	Subordinated debt that relies on cash interest, payment in kind, plus warrants for its return
Required rate of return	19.5% (based on equity mezzanine example)
Likely provider	SBICs, private funds
Value world(s)	Market value
Transfer method(s)	Private and public auctions
Appropriate to use when . . .	The investee is experiencing high growth and possible profitability but has little free liquidity. Mezzanine is often the next type of capital to add to the capital structure if senior lending becomes restricted because mezzanine is less expensive than equity.
Key points to consider	Beyond the 12% to 15% cash and payment-in-kind interest rate, a provider will structure a warrant position. The longer this warrant goes unexercised, the more costly it becomes to a growing investee.
	Performance ratchets may be used to incentivize management to reach performance targets.

firm's cash flow and projected growth rather than on collateral. Regardless of whether the mezzanine loan is secured, the mezzanine investor presumes there will be little or no recovery of principal from liquidation. The investment is priced accordingly. However, the investor may require a subordinate claim on corporate assets to the senior secured lender or a senior claim on the stock of the *investee*, which is the company that receives the investment. The terms of a mezzanine deal are usually flexible, generally involving 5- to 7-year maturities combined with amortizations ranging from 5 to 15 years. Repayment of principal usually is deferred until later in the loan term, and it is scheduled to fit the borrower's needs and cash flow projections.

Mezzanine providers earn a return by making investments with any of the next combinations:

- *Cash interest*. A periodic payment of cash (called a coupon) based on a percentage of the outstanding balance of the mezzanine financing. The interest rate can be either fixed throughout the term of the loan or can fluctuate (i.e., float) along with prime or LIBOR (London Interbank Offered Rate) or other base rates.

- *Payment-in-kind (PIK) interest.* Payment-in-kind interest is a periodic form of payment in which the interest payment is not paid in cash but rather by increasing the principal amount by the amount of the interest (e.g., a $10 million bond with an 3% PIK interest rate will have a balance of $10.3 million at the end of the period but will not pay any cash interest).
- *Warrant.* Along with the typical interest payment associated with debt, mezzanine capital often includes an equity stake in the form of attached warrants, similar to that of a convertible bond. Mezzanine providers use warrants as a way to increase their return, as opposed to converting into the investee's stock.

Cash Interest

According to the Pepperdine Private Capital Markets survey, cash interest varies slightly by size of funding, with a median for all deal sizes of 12% to 13%.[1] For some mezzanine deals, the loan will be interest-only for one to two years, then the principal will be amortized over some period, with a balloon payment due at maturity. Mezzanine providers are extremely flexible in structuring deals to meet the needs of the borrower, and in many cases the loan will be interest-only for the life of the loan.

Payment in Kind

PIK is used to describe interest or dividend income that is paid by a borrower through the issuance of a new security instead of through periodic cash payments. Instead, the mezzanine lender receives cash when the new security is liquidated or repaid at the end of the loan term.

Here is a basic example of how PIK works: Assume MezzCo lends PrivateCo $10 million. MezzCo charges the company 12% in current cash interest and 2% in PIK interest. For this example, assume the lender does not receive any warrants in PrivateCo, and, as a result, the stated interest rate is 14% (or 12% plus 2%). If the note is due in five years, MezzCo will earn interest income from the $10 million note as shown in Exhibit 22.2.

EXHIBIT 22.2   Mezzanine PIK Interest

	Beginning	Year 1	Year 2	Year 3	Year 4	Year 5	Total Interest
Note Balance	$10,000,000	$10,200,000	$10,404,000	$10,612,080	$10,824,322	$11,040,808	
Current Cash Interest	12%	1,200,000	1,224,000	1,248,480	1,273,450	1,298,919	$6,244,849
PIK Interest	2%	200,000	204,000	208,080	212,242	216,486	$1,040,808
							$7,285,657

The current interest, $1.2 million, is paid in cash as required by the note. The PIK interest, $200,000, is paid in a security and is added to the principal amount of the note, increasing that amount to $10.2 million after Year 1. MezzCo will receive the PIK interest in cash when the note is paid at maturity. The PIK effectively increases the lender's return beyond the stated 14% interest rate due to compounding interest.

Mezzanine lenders use a PIK interest component when they want to improve the certainty of their investment return. The PIK portion of the return is contractually certain. Since it also compounds the return, this method allows the lender to lock in an investment return. An added benefit to PIK is that it is paid in a debt security that is senior in the portfolio company's capital structure to the equity securities that otherwise would have been received upon exercise of a warrant. In other words, PIK notes have preference in liquidation to equity securities.

Warrant

In addition to the loan feature, most mezzanine deals also include warrants to help increase the yield to the investor. A warrant is a right to buy a security at a fixed price, also known as the exercise or strike price. Warrants can be traded as independent securities. Mezzanine investments may include *detachable* warrants, which means the warrants can be repurchased by the borrower, normally at a predefined strike price or under defined valuation procedures, or sold to other investors. As an enticement to the investor, typically the warrants are nominally priced, which causes them to be called *penny warrants*.

Mezzanine investors often work backward to determine the number of warrants they need in a deal. For example, if a mezzanine investor desires a 25% return from a particular investment, she may consider the return from the coupon and then analyze the most likely projections from the borrower to determine the required warrant valuation to achieve the return.

Exhibit 22.3 describes cash interest, PIK, and warrant terms for various loan sizes for nonsponsored deals.[2]

Nonsponsored deals are those that have no private equity group or other institutional funding participation. By way of reference, sponsored deals tend to achieve better terms for the borrower.

EXHIBIT 22.3   Mezzanine Terms by Loan Size for Nonsponsored Deals

	$1M	$5M*	$10M	$25M
Cash interest rate	12.5%	12.3%	12.0%	12.0%
PIK %	0.0%	2.0%	2.0%	2.0%
Total interest rate %	12.5%	14.3%	14.0%	14.0%
% of deals with warrants	100.0%	90.0%	75.0%	na
Warrant coverage (% of total diluted equity)	16.0%	10.0%	8.8%	7.0%
Expected return kicker from warrants %	10.0%	6.0%	5.0%	3.0%
Total model return (gross cash on cash pretax IRR on new investments)	24%	21%	21%	19%

*Median total model return for a $5M loan represents the mezzanine-expected return on the PPCML.

There are three noteworthy items regarding mezzanine terms:

1. The cash interest rate is surprisingly similar for such a wide spread of deal sizes.
2. All small deals employ warrants to help generate returns to the provider. But larger deals rely more on the total interest rate percentage than on the warrant for a return.
3. Median expected returns on a pretax basis decrease with deal size. Another way of stating this return is as a gross cash-on-cash pretax internal rate of return.

MEZZANINE INVESTORS

Several types of institutional providers offer lower-middle-market mezzanine capital. These companies make mezzanine investments usually in amounts of $500,000 to $50 million per deal. Investor types are funds, frequently organized as Small Business Investment Companies (SBICs); insurance companies; banks; and other providers, composed of economic development boards, including state and local commissions. According to Private Equity Information, a private equity information database, there are approximately 160 mezzanine providers in the market, not including SBICs.[3] As of this writing, there are about 300 SBICs in operation. Many SBICs provide mezzanine capital. They are the most uniformly structured of the mezzanine players, so they are described at some length here.

Small Business Investment Companies

More than 50 years ago, an entrepreneur looking for the capital to launch a small business had few capital alternatives. Very few institutional resources were available to back up promising but untried ideas. In 1958, the U.S. Congress created the Small Business Investment Company (SBIC) program to help solve this problem. Licensed by the Small Business Administration (SBA), SBICs are privately owned, profit-motivated investment firms. They are participants in a partnership between government and the private sector economy. Using their own capital and funds borrowed at favorable rates through the federal government, SBICs provide loans and venture capital to new and established small, independent businesses.

Loans and Debt Securities

SBICs make long-term loans to small businesses for their sound financing, growth, modernization, and expansion. An SBIC may provide loans independently or in cooperation with other public or private lenders. SBIC loans to small business concerns may be secured, but the SBA does not mandate this. Such loans may have a maturity of no more than 20 years, although under certain conditions the SBIC may renew or extend a loan's maturity for an additional 10 years.

An SBIC may elect to loan or invest money in a small business concern in one of three ways: loans, debt security, or equity. *Debt securities* are loans for which the small business concern issues a security, which may be convertible into equity or contain rights to purchase equity in the small business concern. These securities also may have special amortization and subordination terms. By law, the SBIC must work only with small, private business concerns and may do so by purchasing the small business concern's equity securities. The SBIC may not, however, become a general partner in any unincorporated small business concern or become otherwise liable for the general obligations of an unincorporated concern. The average loan size for an SBIC is approximately $1.2 million.[4]

Types of Businesses

SBICs may invest only in qualifying small business concerns as defined by SBA regulations. SBICs may not invest in:

- Other SBICs
- Finance and investment companies or finance-type leasing companies
- Unimproved real estate
- Companies with less than one-half of their assets and operations in the United States
- Passive or casual businesses
- Companies not engaged in a regular and continuous business operation
- Companies that will use the proceeds to acquire farmland

An SBIC is not permitted to control, either directly or indirectly, any small business on a permanent basis. Nor may it control a small business in participation with another SBIC or its associates. In certain instances, the SBA may allow an SBIC to assume temporary control to protect its investment. But in those cases the SBIC and the small concern must have an SBA-approved plan of divestiture in effect. Without written SBA approval, an SBIC may invest no more than 20% of its private capital in securities, commitments, and/or guarantees for any one small concern.

Loans made to and debt securities purchased from small concerns should have minimum terms of five years. The small concern has the right to prepay a loan or debt security with a reasonable penalty when appropriate. Loans and debt securities with terms less than five years are acceptable only when they are necessary to protect existing financings, are made in contemplation of long-term financing, or are made to finance a change of ownership.

Other Mezzanine Providers

Many private mezzanine funds are unaffiliated with the federal government. State or local economic development boards control some of these funds. Other funds are offered through private equity groups or finance companies looking to provide most or all of the capital structure needs of the borrower. Finally, some insurance companies invest in larger deals involving higher-quality companies. Insurance companies tend to view mezzanine lending from an institutional, debt-oriented point of view and therefore are more concerned with current interest payments and scheduled return of capital. The remainder of this chapter does not differentiate between various structures of mezzanine funds. Rather, it focuses on the investment orientation of mezzanine funds in general.

TARGETED INVESTMENTS

Mezzanine investors look for businesses that have high potential for growth and earnings but currently are unable to obtain sufficient bank funding to achieve their goals. This may be because of a lack of collateral or guarantor, higher balance sheet leverage, or a variety of other reasons. As risk lenders, mezzanine investors consider investment opportunities outside conventional commercial bank parameters. Ideally mezzanine investors prefer companies that, in a three- to five-year period, can exit mezzanine financing through debt from a senior lender, an initial public offering (IPO), or sale of the company. In addition to these financial criteria, SBIC investors view the quality of the people involved as critical.

Strong management is important, and mezzanine investors look closely at an entrepreneur's hands-on operating achievement and proven management ability. The track record of a company's management team is a valuable indicator of its ability to achieve future success. Mezzanine investors are not interested in situations such as seed capital funding, early-stage financing, research and development funding, and problem situations.

Investment Preferences

Mezzanine capital is the flexible bridge between secured senior debt and equity capital. Flexibility is very important since the mezzanine capital may be close to senior debt, herein called debt mezzanine capital (DMC), or closer to equity, called equity mezzanine capital (EMC). The marketplace does not refer to DMC or EMC; rather, mezzanine funds tend to focus on one or the other and structure deal terms based on how they view the subject. Since all-in returns for DMC and EMC can be quite different, each will be described separately. Exhibit 22.4 describes characteristics of each mezzanine type.

EXHIBIT 22.4   Investor Preferences

Debt Mezzanine Capital	Equity Mezzanine Capital
Subject has adequate free cash flow.	Subject has little free liquidity.
For stable, high-profit companies.	For high-growth companies.
Mezzanine fills the "stretch" piece.	Mezzanine fills the equity piece.
Capital preservation is goal.	Capital appreciation is goal.
Partners incentivized partly on upside.	Partners incentivized mainly on upside.
Bank-driven deals.	Equity-driven deals.

DMC is the debt-oriented type of mezzanine capital used where the invested company is profitable with continuing growth prospects. Typical applications for DMC are strong management buyout or management buy-in transactions as well as later-stage company expansions, where a strong operating leverage can be achieved.

EMC is the type of mezzanine financial instrument available for growth companies with an ambitious business plan resulting in less financial liquidity. Therefore, the mezzanine investor provides the financing with a lower-than-adequate running yield but a higher-equity kicker, offsetting the risk-capital aspects of the investment. Equity mezzanine investors seek to fund pre-IPO situations, acquisitions of small and medium-size companies, and high-growth situations.

PRICING

Mezzanine financing presents a fairly high degree of risk to the investor, so it is far more expensive than a bank loan. The price of mezzanine debt typically includes a base interest or "coupon" rate on the loan with an additional pricing vehicle to ensure that the investor participates in the success (or failure) of the business. This vehicle takes the form of a stock warrant or a royalty, often called a *success* or *revenue participation* fee, which is based on the growth of the business. The pricing is structured to fit the unique characteristics of the business and the deal.

The portion of the pricing that rewards the investor based on the firm's success should be carefully considered. A high warrant position may have disadvantages and costs similar to those of a straight equity investment. Mezzanine investors that do not use a high level of warrants usually have a lower cost, have fewer management control features, and employ an easier exit strategy. Instead of using an equity-based vehicle, these investors base a portion of the pricing on the firm's measurable financial success during the loan term, using a fee-based formula tied to the firm's income statement.

If the company wishes to exit the mezzanine investment prematurely, it may face sizable costs, including a prepayment penalty or a yield maintenance calculation to ensure that the investor is guaranteed a minimum return on the investment. These costs should be defined up front to ensure a smooth exit strategy.

Pricing terms are different between debt and equity mezzanine deals. This is reasonable since the riskiness of the investment positions can be quite different.

DEBT MEZZANINE CAPITAL

Debt-oriented mezzanine investors tend to focus their investments on capital preservation, investing in transactions with consistent historical cash flows, conservative capital structures, and a strong equity sponsor. Insurance companies often fill this role. In spite of having large amounts of capital to invest, they tend

EXHIBIT 22.5 Debt Mezzanine Credit Box and Sample Terms

Credit Box

To qualify for debt mezzanine capital, an applicant must:

- Have a mezzanine need of at least $10 million, and probably more than $20 million
- Have enough critical mass that the mezzanine capital is not at undue risk for bankruptcy
- Have consistent historical cash flows
- Have total debt to EBITDA no more than 3.5
- Have growth prospects and sufficient cash flow to enable the payment of a 14%+ return
- Employ a fairly conservative capital structure
- Have a relatively stable management and market
- Have a strong equity sponsor

Sample Terms

Example loan	$25 million loan
Cash interest rate	12% fixed (prime = 3.5%)
PIK rate	2% fixed
Term	5 years
Principal amortization	Equal quarterly payments
Detachable warrants	None
Commitment fee	.3% of loan
Closing fee	1% of loan

to operate with relatively small staffs and therefore have less time to devote to understanding a potential investment.

Exhibit 22.5 shows the credit box and sample terms for DMC.[5] Since there are numerous debt mezzanine players with constantly changing investment appetites, prospective investees should canvass the market to determine the current credit box and terms offered.

The credit box describes the qualities necessary to access DMC. While many of the characteristics are qualitative in nature, each has a quantitative corollary. For example, "employ a conservative capital structure" might also be stated as "mezzanine debt to net worth shall not exceed 3.5 to 1." Also, historical and future cash flows coverage ultimately breaks down to ratios and numbers. A strong equity sponsor may be the most important item in the credit box. This equity partner may represent a private equity group or current ownership with financial depth. Since debt mezzanine investors do not knowingly put themselves at equity risk, they must have a capable equity partner.

Exhibit 22.5 is an illustration of the terms a typical debt mezzanine deal might convey. In this case, the interest rate is fixed at 14%, with 12% representing the cash interest rate and 2% in PIK interest. At the end of five years, the borrower's option to defer interest shall cease, and all deferred interest shall be due and payable. With a $25 million loan, this means that the current coupon is paid at $250,000 per month ($25 million × 12% ÷ 12 months), with the PIK adding $500,000 per year to the note ($25 million × 2%). The borrower will pay the PIK interest at the maturity of the note. In this example, the mezzanine provider is not using warrants to enhance the return.

The next figures show the expected return to the debt mezzanine provider.

1. Total interest cost ($25 million loan × 14% interest rate)	$3,500,000
2. Commitment fee ($25 million loan amount × .3% ÷ 5 years)	15,000
3. Closing fee ($25 million loan amount × 1% ÷ 5 years)	50,000
Annual returns of loan	$3,565,000
Expected rate of return	**14.3%**
($3,565,000/$25,000,000)	

The cash interest rate of 12% plus the PIK rate of 2% and the "terms cost" of .3% yields an expected rate of return of 14.3%. For ease of presentation, the amortization of the PIK interest and fees are shown on a noncompounded basis.

EQUITY MEZZANINE CAPITAL

Equity-oriented mezzanine investors tend to be more interested in capital appreciation. They focus on companies with more volatile earnings, less experienced equity sponsors, and riskier future projections. Most mezzanine funds favor this approach because the general partners are incentivized by upside capital growth. Exhibit 22.6 shows a credit box and sample terms for EMC.[6]

The credit box describes the qualities necessary to access EMC. Perhaps the most important combination of factors is a strong management team that can scale the business model. "Scalability" means that as the company grows, profits grow at an increasing rate. This usually creates substantial stock appreciation in a fairly short period of time. An example of a scalable business model is the creation

EXHIBIT 22.6   Equity Mezzanine Credit Box and Sample Terms

Credit Box

To qualify for equity mezzanine capital, an applicant must:

- Have terrific growth prospects, at least 20% compounded per year
- Have a management team experienced in high-growth situations
- Have sufficient cash flow beginning in year 2 to enable payment of principal and interest
- Have total debt to EBITDA no more than 3.5
- Employ a capital structure that puts the mezzanine in no worse than a second lien position
- Possess a scalable business model
- Have some equity support

Sample Terms

Example loan	$7 million loan
Interest rate	12% fixed, payable monthly (prime = 3.5%)
PIK interest	2%
Term	Interest only for 12 months; monthly principal + interest on 10-yearamortization, with all principal due in 5 years
Detachable warrants	5% of the fully diluted common
Commitment fee	1% of loan
Closing fee	2% of loan

of an interrelated family of software programs. Once the platform program is written, other similar programs can be created for other sales channels. Since most of the cost is incurred for the initial launch, future sales have a much smaller cost component.

Sample terms illustrate terms that a typical equity mezzanine deal might convey. In this case, the interest rate is fixed at 14% (cash interest rate of 12% and PIK interest of 2%), interest only is charged for the first 12 months, and then principal is amortized using a 10-year amortization schedule. Principal repayment is due in full at the end of the fifth year.

In this example, detachable warrants of 5% of the common stock are included in the deal. These warrants are valued separately from the loan, and the terms for the equity valuation normally are predefined in the agreements. The enterprise equity value is determined as the *greater* of these valuation procedures:

- The company's book value
- Eight times the company's average net profits before taxes for the prior two years (restated for shareholder compensation greater than $150,000) less long-term debt
- Six times the company's earnings before interest, taxes, depreciation, and amortization (EBITDA) for the prior year (restated for shareholder compensation greater than $150,000) less long-term debt

Warrant value is 5% of the equity value for this example. To illustrate the determination of this equity value, the year 5 numbers for the three valuation criteria are given. By that point, book value is estimated at $9 million, annual average net profits are $4.2 million, and the restated EBITDA is $5.75 million. Once again, it is assumed that the company has no long-term debt. The expected equity value in year 5 is:

Book value = $9 million

Net profits calculation: 8 × $4.2 million = $33.6 million

EBITDA calculation: 6 × $5.75 million = $34.5 million

The highest valuation is the EBITDA formula, or $34.5 million. The warrants are therefore expected to be worth $1.73 million in year 5 ($34.5 million × 5%). The expected rate of return to the equity mezzanine can now be calculated:

1. Total interest cost ($7 million loan × 14% interest rate)	$980,000
2. Warrant cost ($1.73 million spread over 5 years)	346,000
3. Commitment fee ($7 million loan amount × 1% ÷ 5 years)	14,000
4. Closing fee ($7 million loan amount × 2% ÷ 5 years)	28,000
Annual returns of loan	$1,368,000
Expected rate of return	**19.5%**
($1,368,000/$7,000,000)	

The stated interest rate of 14% is increased by the "terms cost" of 5.5%, which yields an expected rate of return to the provider of 19.5%. Once again, for purposes of this presentation, the various costs and fees are amortized on a noncompounded basis.

OTHER DEAL TERMS

Numerous terms and conditions are involved in closing a mezzanine loan. These are described in the term sheet and legal documentation.

Tranches

Borrowers may have capital needs that need funding over several years, such as a project or division build-out. In these cases, the borrower still wants to arrange the entire capital structure but to draw the funds as needed. In mezzanine terms, a funding commitment describes the entire amount of capital needed by the borrower and committed by the mezzanine provider. The borrower then draws tranches as needed. Normally there are minimal tranche amounts available. For example, a mezzanine provider may make a $10 million commitment, with $2.5 million tranches available to the borrower. The borrower may not be required to draw all of the tranches, but the commitment by the mezzanine provider will be available for some period of time. The terms of each tranche are negotiated between the parties at the time of the total commitment.

Warrant Terms

To avoid the possibility that the borrower may not repurchase the warrants, investors create warrants with a variety of equity features, such as:

- *Tag-along rights.* A procedure used to protect a minority shareholder when a majority shareholder sells his stake. The minority shareholder has the right to join the transaction and sell his minority stake in the company.
- *Drag-along rights.* A right that enables a majority shareholder, in the sale of a company, to force a minority shareholder to join in the sale. The majority owner doing the dragging must give the minority shareholder the same price, terms, and conditions for the security being sold as any other seller.
- *Piggyback registration.* When an underwriter allows existing holdings of shares in a corporation to be sold in conjunction with an offering of new shares.
- *Antidilution rights.* An investor's shares in a company cannot be diluted if the company issues more stock, such as in issuing grants to employees. Chapter 23 describes these rights in detail.
- *Voting rights.* An investor requests certain rights in governing activities, such as a right to veto in decisions concerning whether a company sells itself or merges with another.

- *Registration rights.* These rights govern how a company goes public, who pays the costs associated with the process, and how many times a company can file an IPO. In general, these rights are determined much further along in the process, and in many cases the investment bank handling the offering sets the terms.

All of these warrant terms are explained further in Chapter 23.

Prepayment Premiums

Most mezzanine loans have prepayment penalties. These penalties usually are stated as a percentage of the unpaid loan balance. According to the Pepperdine survey, median prepayment penalties by year are: 5%, 3.5%, 3.0%, 2.0%, and .8% respectively. Nearly all loans require payment in full, including penalties, if the loan is prepaid.[7]

Covenants

Mezzanine investors rely on covenant protection because there probably is insufficient collateral coverage. Typical covenants include:

- Cross-default and cross-acceleration provisions
- Minimum fixed-charge and interest-coverage tests
- Total debt, capital expenditure, dividend, and management fee limitations
- Maximum total indebtedness to cash flow test
- Change in business management and control restrictions
- Limitations on dividends and distributions
- Caps on compensation and pay raises to senior management
- Sale of assets and merger and acquisition limitations

It is also typical for the lender to charge a default interest rate in the event of a major default. This rate may be 5% to 6% above the stated rate and is in force until the default is cured.

Subordination

The mezzanine lender must work out a subordination agreement with the senior lender before closing the loan with the borrower. The subordination agreement spells out the relative rights and responsibilities of each lender. These include cross default; cross acceleration; and a standstill period, which is a limited period of suspension of rights and remedies. Some collateral of the subordinated or junior lenders can be specifically excluded from the agreement, such as life insurance and stock pledges, provided the senior lender does not claim the same collateral.

Debt subordination is a contractually established relationship between lenders to a single borrower. Subordination terms set the relationships between the parties. Primarily, the junior creditor "subordinates" to the senior creditor its right to receive payments from the debtor. In extreme cases, subordinated debt will be placed so low in the capital structure that it is tantamount to equity. Basically, there are three types of subordination:[8]

1. *Total or complete subordination.* No payments on junior debt at all until senior debt is paid in full. Definitions of Junior and senior debt are worded broadly. This level of subordination is often accompanied by a complete block on remedies.
2. *Partial subordinations.* Certain specific payments are permitted to be made to the junior creditor (e.g., interest). In a closely held corporation, salary, dividends, and the like might also be permitted. Principal payments may be allowed, although in a limited fashion. Payments can be stopped, however, upon the occurrence of certain events, such as a senior loan default.
3. *Contingent subordination.* This level of subordination allows all scheduled payments to be received until the occurrence of certain events, such as insolvency.

In almost all cases, a well-written subordination agreement prohibits prepayments of subordinated debt.

Subordination, also called intercreditor agreements, must be negotiated with care. Some banks also offer mezzanine capital along with the senior loan, which makes the subordination issues easier.

Board Seats and Visitation

Investors usually get one or more seats on the board of directors, or they have visitation rights to attend board meetings and meet with management on a periodic basis. They also receive information such as monthly operating reports and quarterly unaudited and annual audited financial statements. Separate approval of the directors appointed by the investor may be required for items such as major capital expenditures, borrowing from banks, approving management compensation and stock option plans, and deviations from previously approved business plans.

NEGOTIATING POINTS

Raising mezzanine capital is a complicated process. This is not a good time to "learn on the job." It is recommended that those inexperienced in this area should hire an investment banker or other professional who has already completed many deals. The next negotiating points help cut a better deal.

Warrant Position and Valuation

The size of the warrant and its valuation are totally negotiated items. The mezzanine lender proposes a certain warrant position in an attempt to meet its return expectation. Typically, warrants have a nominal price to the investor (i.e., penny warrants). Usually the size of a lender's warrant position is inversely related to the interest rate; that is, the higher the interest rate, the fewer the warrants required. Since the interest from a mezzanine loan is tax deductible and a warrant payoff is not, it may make sense for a borrower to put more weight on the coupon and less on the warrant.

The valuation procedures for the warrant are tailored to each deal and therefore have a lot of room for negotiation. Borrowers should not blindly accept formulas for valuing the warrant. The proper deal should mirror the marketplace for similar equity interests.

Warrant Exercise Date

Typically, the cost of buying a detachable warrant increases the longer it is in force. For example, borrowers should seek to purchase the warrant sooner rather than later, but in any event, they must prepay the corresponding loan first. Although most mezzanine lenders do not offer to sell the warrant before three years, a borrower with a good deal might negotiate this down to two years.

Deferred-Interest Balloons

Some debt-oriented mezzanine lenders employ a deferred-interest balloon as part of the loan. A *deferred-interest balloon* is a structure that stalls a stated amount of interest into the future, at which point it is due in full. This balloon payment may be in the borrowers' best interest for two reasons.

1. If borrowers are tight on cash flow during the first few years of the loan, the deferral of a large part of the interest may enable them to achieve their business plan goals without a liquidity crunch.
2. The deferred interest balloon *may* be deductible on a current period basis for taxes, even though it actually will be paid in the future. This may be the case if the balloon is a legal contract that is an obligation of the borrower, and the company is on an accrual basis for tax reporting. For instance, if a $3 million deferred-interest balloon is due five years after the closing, the borrower may be able to write off $600,000 per year in interest deductions. Readers are encouraged to check with their tax professionals to confirm whether this deduction is possible for their situation.

PRICING QUESTIONS TO ASK A MEZZANINE INVESTOR

- What is the cash interest or "coupon" rate of the loan?
- What are the other pricing components?
- Is there an equity component to the price?
- What are the costs to exit the relationship and pay off the loan?

Default Interest Rates

Most lenders increase the interest rate during the period of covenant default. As stated, it is not unusual for the interest rate to increase by 5% to 6% until the default is cured. Borrowers should negotiate each covenant and determine whether the default interest rate should apply. For instance, certainly the default rate should apply for payment defaults. But should it apply if capital expenditures exceeded the plan by $20,000? It may be desirable to separate major and minor defaults, with the default rate applying only to the more serious infractions.

Performance Ratchets

Performance ratchets sometimes are structured into mezzanine financing, especially in an equity mezzanine deal. Such ratchets are a matter for discussion and agreement between the parties. In essence, performance ratchets encourage management to perform against defined targets. These targets usually are defined by reference to profits but additionally or alternatively can be related to the time of exit.

Performance ratchets are designed to give the management team an enhanced proportion of the shares if performance reaches agreed levels. A reverse ratchet reduces the management's proportion of the shares if performance falls below agreed levels. It is important to have a clear, shared understanding between the parties of what is being agreed and how it is to be measured. Because there are many variables and alternative methods of measuring and interpreting accounting concepts, contentious situations will arise unless very precise terms of agreement are laid down up front.

Other Items

A handful of other items are negotiated with mezzanine deals. A majority of investors prefer the investee to use a C corporation legal structure. Few mezzanine players prefer investing in pass-through entities, such as limited liability companies, because tax distributions disrupt the target's cash flow. Most mezzanine investors prefer to have cash reinvested in the company to enable growth, thereby making the company and the warrant more valuable. Also, stock pledged as collateral for a mezzanine loan by a company owner is open for discussion. Many mezzanine deals occur without any pledge. If an owner is forced to pledge stock, it should have limits, such as a limit on the amount pledged and the performance benchmarks that trigger a release of the pledge.

Comparison to Other Capital

Mezzanine capital fills the capital void between secured debt and equity capital. Compare various characteristics of mezzanine capital to other capital types. Exhibit 22.7 compares mezzanine capital to bank debt and equity.

EXHIBIT 22.7   Comparison of Mezzanine Capital to Bank Debt and Equity

Item	Bank Debt	Mezzanine	Equity
Dilution	No	Maybe no	Yes
Term	3–7 years	3–7 years	Indefinite
Personal Guarantees	Yes	Probably not	No
Management control	No	No	Maybe
Warrants	No	Probably	No
Return expectation	4%–10%	14%–25%	22%–40%
Exit	Predefined	Predefined	Can be predefined

Mezzanine capital is characterized by a fairly high coupon rate of interest, a defined term, and attributes that lead to a lack of management control. Quite often shareholders do not guarantee mezzanine debt, which is an advantage over bank debt. Equity mezzanine might be dilutive, but typically investors prefer to sell their warrant position back to the investee rather than exercising the warrant. Mezzanine return expectations fall between bank debt and equity. Companies probably should use bank debt when it is available but employ mezzanine capital rather than add equity.

TRIANGULATION

Capital availability directly affects the value of a firm. High-growth companies often suffer from lack of capital because banks prefer conservative growth scenarios. Further, owners often do not want to dilute their ownership positions, so private equity is viewed as less desirable. Mezzanine capital may be a good option for companies experiencing earnings' growth rates of more than 20% per year.

Companies in need of mezzanine capital are viewed in either the collateral value or market value world. DMC providers consider the collateral position of the company, with an eye on market value. EMC investors are more concerned with open market values than they are with collateral values. With both types of investors, warrants are structured based on the market value of the company.

The real power of mezzanine financing is realized through the added leverage it provides to the borrower. For a typical company, every dollar of mezzanine capital can be leveraged, with up to three dollars of additional bank debt capacity. This is because banks normally view mezzanine capital as a form of quasi-equity, which expands the borrower's effective equity base. Thus, banks can lend more to the company without exceeding the borrower's existing debt-to-equity ratio. A corrugated box manufacturer recently used this added leverage to its advantage. By raising $5 million in equity mezzanine financing, its bank committed to an additional $10 million in low-cost financing. The blended cost of the total financing enabled the company to meet its business plan, which created substantial wealth for the shareholders.

If a company obtains mezzanine capital, it is forced to seek cheaper sources of capital to pay off the mezzanine at the end of its term. Most mezzanine investments are satisfied either through a change-of-control sale or a recapitalization of the company. A sale of the company is especially likely when the warrant position is too high to refinance. A recapitalization is likely when the company meets or exceeds its expectations. It is clear that obtaining mezzanine capital, like obtaining private equity, ultimately puts a company in play.

NOTES

1. John K. Paglia, Pepperdine Private Capital Markets Project Survey Report, April 2010, bschool.pepperdine.edu/privatecapital.
2. Ibid.
3. See the SBA Web site, www.sba.gov.
4. Ibid.
5. John K. Paglia, Pepperdine Private Capital Markets Project Survey Report.
6. Ibid.
7. Ibid.
8. Taken from: www.Archadvisors.com.

CHAPTER 23

Owners, Angels, and Venture Capitalists

Private capital markets begin with early-stage equity investing. These investors come in many shapes and sizes, including operating owner-managers, angels, and venture capitalists (VCs). Each of these groups plays a different role in the funding process, and each expects something different from the investment. This chapter describes how early-stage investors approach the problem.

People have been funding their own business start-ups since commercial activity began. Funding in the United States began to institutionalize in the 1930s and 1940s when wealthy families, such as the Rockefellers and Bessemers, began investing in private companies. Thus began venture capital. These original investors were far from "angels," but they had money, connections, and know-how. Perhaps the first venture firm was J.H. Witney & Company, which was founded in 1946 and survives to the present day. General Georges Doriot, a teacher and innovator from Harvard, institutionalized venture capital. In the early 1950s, he had raised money for a dedicated fund and realized tremendous returns from investments in Digital Equipment Corporation and other early technology titans. Finally the U.S. government entered the early-stage investing picture, when in 1958 it launched Small Business Investment Companies via the Small Business Administration.

More modern angel investors tend to be wealthy investors who wish to participate in high-risk deals to satisfy some entrepreneurial urge and make a risk-adjusted return at the same time. The term "angel" was coined by Broadway insiders to describe the financial backers of Broadway shows. These angels invested as much to display their wealth as for the return on the investment.

Private equity comes in many forms. Exhibit 23.1 contains a schematic that describes various private equity investors.

Chapter 24 describes later-stage equity investment.

Five characteristics differentiate all private equity investing from other types of investing.

1. The private equity investor identifies, negotiates, and structures the transaction. Beyond the transaction, the private investor may be a manager, board member, or consultant.

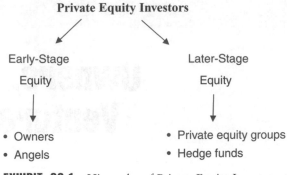

EXHIBIT 23.1   Hierarchy of Private Equity Investment

2. The private equity investor has a finite holding period, normally five to seven years. Generally, it takes several years to position the company and at least one to two years to realize a maximizing exit.

3. Private investors seek high returns on their capital. The private investor seeks 25% to 40% returns or more, as opposed to 10% to 20% return expectations from public equity securities.

4. Private equity professionals invest in a company only when they are convinced the company's management team can execute the business plan. The conversion from initial idea to profit recognition is the wealth-creating activity, and managers who can conclude this conversion successfully tend to get funded.

5. Most private investors require some control over their investment. This control may involve contractually given rights rather than merely a majority stock position. For example, most private investors negotiate certain rights, such as antidilution, registration, tag-along, and so on. Taken together, these moves grant them a certain amount of control.

STAGES OF PRIVATE EQUITY INVESTOR INVOLVEMENT

There are five generally recognized stages of private equity investor involvement; the first three stages are generally considered the realm of early investors. This stage concept is important because it enables the equity market to match the appropriate funding source with the capital need, creating efficiency in the capital allocation process. The stages are:

Stage 1: Seed stage. This is the initial stage. The company has a concept or product under development.

Stage 2: Start-up stage. The company is now operational but is still developing a product or service. There are no revenues. The company has usually been in existence less than 18 months.

Stage 3: Early stage. The company has a product or service in testing or pilot production. In some cases, the product may be commercially available. The company may or may not be generating revenues and usually has been in business less than three years.

Stage 4: Expansion stage. The company's product or service is in production and is commercially available. The company demonstrates significant revenue growth but may or may not be showing a profit. The company usually has been in business more than three years.

Stage 5: Later stage. The company's product or service is widely available. The company is generating ongoing revenue and probably positive cash flow. The company is more than likely profitable and may have been in business for more than 10 years.

Various equity providers align with each of the five stages of capital needs. Personal and family or friends are the primary funding sources for seed or start-ups. Angel investors invest in early-stage companies that are in business with a product or service in production. VCs tend to favor Stage 3 and 4 companies. Those firms expect to achieve substantial revenue growth, but they have not yet shown a profit. Private equity groups, hedge funds, and family offices typically provide capital for Stage 5 companies.

Owner-Managers

For most companies, private capital is assembled initially by an owner-manager. These entrepreneurs are the backbone of the economy and have the most to gain or lose in the success or failure of their businesses. This group has limited resources to start-up a business. Small businesses use several sources available for start-up *capital.*

- Self-financing by the owner through cash, equity loan on his or her home, and or other assets
- Loans from friends or relatives
- Grants from private foundations
- Personal savings
- Private stock issue
- Forming partnerships
- Angel investors
- Banks
- Venture capital
- Private placements

Many small businesses are further financed through credit card debt. Although this debt is quite expensive, it may be the only capital available to the owner. Many owners seek a bank loan in the name of their business; however, banks usually insist on a personal guarantee by the business owner. Chapter 18 describes a number of government loan guarantee programs, all of which require personal guarantees from major shareholders.

Since private placements constitute a major source of capital for emerging companies, they will be further examined next.

PRIVATE PLACEMENTS

A private placement is a nonpublic offering of securities exempt from full Securities and Exchange Commission registration requirements. Placements usually are made directly by the issuing company stock, but they may also be made by an underwriter. The offering may be of debt or equity. Specific state and federal laws govern private placements. While placements occur that involve tens or hundreds of millions of dollars, this chapter primarily focuses on placement alternatives that enable a company to raise $5 million or less. Various chapters describe the various high-yield debt and equity capital providers, such as mezzanine, angels, and VCs. Prior to formally offering private securities to the market, companies should understand and follow the appropriate securities laws. Appendix F gives an overview of the laws and various types of private placements and discusses marketing strategies for a successful offering. Assuming that the promoter is in compliance with the securities laws, the next section suggests ways to market a private placement offering.

FINANCIAL BARN RAISINGS

Much like the physical barn raisings of the past, some of the most success placements occur within the community where the issuer resides. These *financial barn raisings* leverage relationships that transcend financial requirements. This technique works especially well in small communities, where other businesspeople are in position to assess the risk of the offeror's character and background. A financial barn raising is accomplished in these ways:

- *Meet with the city fathers/mothers.* This often involves the mayor and other businesspeople who know who has discretionary income and a pro-community outlook. The role of city fathers/mothers in the process is to make introductions to wealthy individuals.
- *Orchestrate town meetings.* Once a large list of potential investors is compiled, the next step is to organize a series of town meetings. These meetings usually are held at local country clubs, Rotaries, and other clubs that are suitable. These meetings are social gatherings; imagine a "wine and cheese" meets "soft sell" process.
- *Close the deal.* Soon after the four or five social gatherings, the company principals should personally meet with the top prospects. Most private placements fail in this step; the money does not just find its way to the company. It must be guided.

Many of these investors qualify as financing angels, which is covered later in this chapter. Financial barn raisings take place within a series of fairly complicated securities laws, so readers should engage a securities attorney before undertaking one.

WITHIN EXISTING BUSINESS RELATIONSHIPS

Quite often customers, vendors, and other business relationships comprise a potential group of investors. An issuer may be able to combine a private placement within the terms of a business relationship. For instance, when a new supply contract is negotiated, the issuer may be able to get a customer to invest in the issuer's security, especially when the money is needed to fulfill the contract.

WHY PRIVATE PLACEMENTS FAIL

Most private placements fail because either the offeror does not present the market with a security that promises enough return for the risk or the investors cannot ascertain the risk of the investment. Most of these offerors are very small companies, with business models that are unproven. With this as a backdrop, it is reasonable for investors to expect at least 25% to 35% effective returns on their investments. Individual investors typically are not in a position to measure the risk of most private placements. Protecting individual investors from themselves explains why the blue-sky laws exist to begin with. Offerors can be successful with their placements if they:

- *Provide the necessary information.* Investors need basic information before they will consider investing.
  - Does the product or service solve a problem or need?
  - How many competitors are already in the marketplace?
  - Who are potential customers, and how will they be reached?
  - Is the management capable of delivering the business plan?
  - What does the investor get for her investment?
    It is the entrepreneur's responsibility to supply this information in a clear and concise fashion.
- *Are honest about the risk/return proposition.* It is the offeror's responsibility to offer potential investors a reasonable return for the risk. This may mean postponing an offering until the business is stable enough to merit outside investment.
- *Treat all investors at arm's length.* Even if the offering is targeted at family and friends, the offeror should treat the entire process as if all of the investors are outsiders. There should be no special deal to the offerees because they are family.
- *Beware of costly professionals.* Many brokers and lawyers are willing to take an offeror's money for doing the up-front work. Some of this expense is necessary, but prospective offerors should be wary and ask questions about experience and successful past offerings. As with any professional services purchase, potential offerors should talk with past clients before engaging the professional.

- *Market ... market ... market.* Offerors should access the market in every way possible. This means employing the marketing techniques just mentioned simultaneously. Throwing numerous financial barn raisings with an active board is a good way to access the market. Networking is the key to success.

It is extremely difficult to raise money through private placement. Prospective offerors who view this entire process as hand-to-hand financial combat will not be disappointed. At the end of the day, the hidden hand of capitalism helps determine winners from losers.

But for certain owners, finding an angel is the best way to go.

Angel Investors

Angels typically invest their own funds, unlike VCs, who manage the pooled money of others in a professionally-managed fund. The Center for Venture Research at the University of New Hampshire (www.wsbe.unh.edu/cvr), which does research on angel investments, has developed the next profile of angel investors.

- The "average" private investor is 47 years old with an annual income of $90,000, a net worth of $750,000, is college educated, has been self-employed, and invests $37,000 per venture.
- Most angels invest close to home and rarely put in more than a few hundred thousand dollars.
- Informal investment appears to be the largest source of external equity capital for small businesses. Nine out of ten investments are devoted to small, mostly start-up firms with fewer than 20 employees.
- Nine out of ten investors provide personal loans or loan guarantees to the firms they invest in. On average, this increases the available capital by 57%.
- Informal investors are older, have higher incomes, and are better educated than the average citizen, yet they are not often millionaires. They are a diverse group, displaying a wide range of personal characteristics and investment behavior.
- Seven out of ten investments are made within 50 miles of the investor's home or office.
- Investors expect an average 26% annual return at the time they invest, and they believe that about one-third of their investments are likely to result in a substantial capital loss.
- Investors accept an average of three deals for every ten considered. The most common reasons given for rejecting a deal are insufficient growth potential, overpriced equity, lack of sufficient talent of the management, or lack of information about the entrepreneur or key personnel.
- There appears to be no shortage of informal capital funds. Investors included in the study would have invested almost 35% more than they did if acceptable opportunities had been available.

For the business seeking funding, the right angel investor can be the perfect first step in formal funding. It usually takes less time to meet with an angel and to receive funds, due diligence is less involved, and angels usually expect a lower rate of return than a VC. The downside is finding the right balance of expert help without the angel totally taking charge of the business. Structuring the relationship carefully is an important step in the process.

There are at least five types of angel investors.[1]

1. Business owners
2. Key executives
3. Self-employed professionals
4. Sales and marketing professionals
5. All others

Business owners tend to make the best angels for the emerging business. They understand the problems better than others and often mentor the founder. Key executives offer a different set of solutions from the business-owner angel, but they are nearly as valuable and important. Executives bring the professional management techniques needed by many early-stage companies. Self-employed professionals, such as doctors, dentists, lawyers, and the like, may be more benign for the entrepreneur because they are not as likely to call the loan or demand their money back. But they may have less to contribute to the venture in the form of helpful advice, information, and contacts. They care about the founder and what he or she is trying to achieve; however, they may not focus as much on the return on their investment as VCs would. Sales and marketing professionals may fill a major gap in the entrepreneur's skill set. All business begins with a sale, and small businesses are even more dependent on this expertise.

Successful entrepreneurs also can be angels. They can be an entrepreneur's best bet because their business advice and contacts may make the difference between success and failure. However, they can become meddlesome, or their advice may not be worth much if the business they run is very different from the entrepreneur's business.

Exhibit 23.2 provides capital coordinates for angel investors.

Many major cities have bands of angels, or organized groups of early-stage investors. These groups generally invest from $100,000 to $2 million per deal. Angels tend to rely more on intuition than analytical investment techniques. They bet more on the entrepreneur and less on the product and market opportunity. Angels often host Internet sites but are also found through lawyers and accountants who specialize in new venture legal or accounting work. Angels are particularly helpful to entrepreneurs on a personal level, since many band members are professionals with similar backgrounds as the investee. Some angels are themselves VCs with their own firms, which invest as angels for early access to good deals.[2]

Exhibit 23.3 shows the credit box that describes the characteristics necessary to obtain angel financing.

Obtaining angel financing relies on leveraging personal contacts. More than the other types of institutional private equity, angel financing money is raised for

EXHIBIT 23.2   Capital Coordinates: Angel Investors

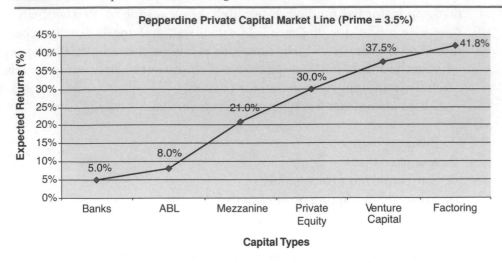

Capital Access Point	Angels
Definition	Angel investors tend to be wealthy investors who wish to participate in high-risk deals to satisfy some entrepreneurial urge and make a risk-adjusted return.
Expected rate of return	Seed: 60%; start-up: 45%; early: 35%
Authority	Angels come in five basic types: business owners, key executives, self-employed professionals, sales and marketing professionals, and all others.
Value world(s)	Early equity
Transfer method(s)	Negotiated, possibly via a private placement
Appropriate to use when . . .	Angels are start-up or early investors. They bet more on the entrepreneur and less on the product and market opportunity.
Key points to consider	Angel financing may take the form of a promissory note or preferred or common stock. Most angels are likely to remain passive, except for a board position. Founders should choose the type of angel that provides the greatest assistance to the company in meeting its goals.

more than purely economic reasons. Some angels may invest because of paternal instinct or just for the thrill of playing the game. But financial returns are important. Since this group enters a deal early, they require a high return. Exhibit 23.4 shows expected return and other data from a survey of angels.[3]

EXHIBIT 23.3   Angel Financing Credit Box

Credit Box

To qualify for angel financing, an applicant must:
- Have a private equity capital need of $100,000 to $2 million
- Be able to show that the initial funding need will enable the company to move to the next level
- Have terrific growth prospects, at least 20%–30% compounded sales growth per year
- Have a management team capable of creating and realizing the business plan
- Have salesmanship skills to entice angels into hearing the story

EXHIBIT 23.4   Angel Terms by Stage of Investment

	Seed	Start-up	Early	Expansion
Avg % of total equity purchased	20%	20%	20%	15%
Expected returns	60%	45%	35%	30%
Time to exit (months)	72	60	60	44
Avg % of investments likely to become worthless	60%	50%	40%	20%
Avg company value at time of investment	$500,000	$1.3M	$2.5M	$5.0M

Angels are minority investors with a five- to six-year investment horizon. Expected returns range from 60% for Seed investments to 30% for the expansion stage. A large percentage of early-stage investments are expected to become worthless.

Exhibit 23.5 shows an example term sheet. Angel terms usually are structured in one of three ways:[4]

1. They initially take a promissory note, with deferred monthly or quarterly interest payments for the first year or two. The note may be convertible into options that are exercisable at various performance benchmarks, such as when sales or profits reach a certain level. Ultimately, the options may be worth 15% to 30% of the equity, depending on the deal. Angels typically begin as passive creditors during the formative launch phase but want to see detailed financial statements at least quarterly beyond the first year. They also require at least one seat on the board of directors and will actively oversee the entrepreneur's implementation of the business plan.

2. Angels initially may take a cumulative convertible preferred stock position. They allow the firm to defer fixed-cash dividends for at least a year or two. Once again, they seek a role on the board and help implement the business plan.

3. They take a common voting equity position up front, have their place on the board, and may be actively involved in company management. They may want to add to the management team or, at the least, hire consultants to help work on key projects. Depending on the entrepreneur's perspective, this approach may be the best or worst of the three formats. It can be the best situation for entrepreneurs who need hands-on help and connection to the broader business community. It is less than ideal for entrepreneurs who want their own team of managers in place.

Overall, the deal hinges on the quality of the relationship between the angel and the entrepreneur. Angel financing is best suited for early-stage opportunities where the owner-manager needs capital plus guidance from experienced business-people. Owners of middle-market companies are not normally searching for angel investors. However, they may choose this financing route for a new product or business that is spun off from the existing company, thereby diversifying risk.

Exhibit 23.5 shows an example term sheet.[5]

EXHIBIT 23.5 Example Angel Term Sheet

This term sheet is being offered to the Company and will remain in effect until day of XX, 20XX.

Offer of Investment

The Fund will purchase, together with any syndicated investors, (collectively the "Investors"), common shares (the "Shares") at a price of $* per Share. The total round for all Investors will be $* of which the Fund will invest $* to acquire a total of * Shares. So long as the Investors hold their Shares and until a liquidity event, they shall have the right to exchange them for the same kind and class of securities issued by the Company (the "New Securities") in any follow on financings should such New Securities have rights superior to the Shares. The Investment will be made pursuant to an Investment Agreement made between the Investors, the Company and certain of its principals (the "Principals"). The capital structure on closing will be as described in the attached Share Register.

Board of Directors

The Fund believes that early-stage investments need strong mentoring and governance provided by a high-quality, engaged Board. On the completion of the investment, the Board will be comprised as follows:

- A total of five members, being the CEO, one nominee of the Fund and three nominees independent of management that the Company and the Fund agree on; and
- Each director must have made a meaningful investment in the Company.

Share and Option Vesting

The Fund believes that it is important that the Principals' interests align with the Investors. In this regard the parties agree that all stock options and all nominally priced previously issued shares will vest on the following basis:

- 50% of the shares will vest daily and linearly over a three year period; and
- the other 50% will not vest unless and until there is a sale of the Company.

All share and option vesting will accelerate on a sale of the Company. An Escrow Agreement will be entered into to provide for the vesting.

Liquidity Event

To ensure that a return can be provided to all of the Company's shareholders when an opportunity presents itself to sell the Company, the Fund will require a "drag-along" right be added to the Company's constating documents to allow the holders of 51% of the issued shares of the Company to cause the sale of all of the shares of the Company.

Reporting to Shareholders

The company will send a CEO Update monthly to all shareholders. Financial statements are also available upon request.

Investor Rights

Investors have the right of first refusal to participate in future financings. Any changes to the capital structure, new shares, options, or debt requires the approval of the majority of the investors in this round.

General

The Company will pay the legal costs of the Fund not to exceed $6,500, plus taxes and disbursements thereon. The Company will keep confidential this Term Sheet and all discussions with the Fund for a period of two years.

Binding Nature

This Term Sheet will terminate on *[date], unless terminated earlier by the Fund. The Company will not seek alternate financing unless and until this Term Sheet has terminated or been terminated by the Fund. The confidentiality provisions will survive termination of this Term Sheet. Acknowledged and agreed to by the Company and by the Fund this XX day of X, 20XX by: [Signatures]

Venture Capital

Venture capital is money provided by professionals who invest alongside management in early- to expansion-stage companies that have the potential to develop into value-creating enterprises. Venture capital is an important source of equity for early companies and less important for established middle-market companies.

Venture capital firms are pools of capital typically organized as limited partnerships. The VC may look at several hundred investment prospects before investing in only a few companies. VCs help grow companies using skill sets obtained from other similar ventures. The most successful VCs tend to be entrepreneurs first and financiers second.

VCs generally:

- Finance new and rapidly growing companies.
- Purchase equity securities.
- Assist in the development of new products or services.
- Add value to the company through active participation.
- Take higher risks with the expectation of higher rewards.
- Have a long-term orientation.

When considering an investment, VCs carefully screen the technical and business merits of the proposed company. Venture capitalists employ a strict filtering process, depicted in Exhibit 23.6.[6]

VCs mitigate the risk of venture investing by developing a portfolio of young companies in a single venture fund. They often coinvest with other professional venture capital firms, called syndicating a deal. In addition, many venture

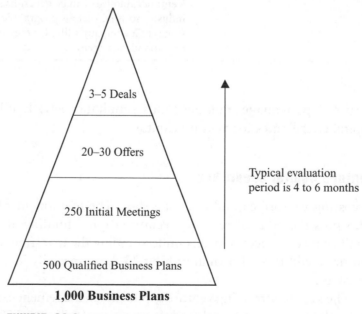

EXHIBIT 23.6 Venture Capital Investment Filter

EXHIBIT 23.7   Capital Coordinates: Venture Capital

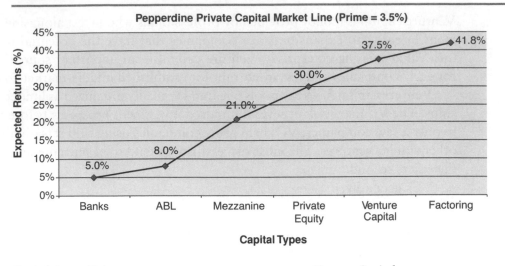

Capital Access Point	Venture Capital
Definition	Venture capital is money provided by professionals who invest alongside management in early- to expansion-stage companies with potential to develop into significant economic contributors.
Expected rate of return	Seed/Start-up: 40%; early: 36%; expansion: 30%; later: 25%
Authority	Institutional venture capitalists
Value world(s)	Early equity value
Transfer method(s)	Venture capitalists create their own transfer by valuing in the world of early equity, then capitalizing the valuation for shares of the investee.
Appropriate to use when . . .	An entrepreneur needs capital and strategic management support to meet a business plan's objectives.
Key points to consider	Venture capitalists help companies grow, but they eventually seek to exit the investment, usually in three to seven years. Venture capitalists can be generalists, investing in various industry sectors, various geographic locations, or various stages of a company's life. Or they may be specialists in one or two industry sectors.

partnerships manage multiple funds simultaneously. Exhibit 23.7 provides the capital coordinates for venture capital.

Venture Capital Credit Box

Accessing venture capital is a long shot. The investment filter shown in Exhibit 23.6 puts the odds of receiving venture capital funding at less than 1%. Such a small chance of success means understanding the investment characteristics of the venture credit box, shown in Exhibit 23.8, is especially important for prospective investees.[7]

The keys to attracting venture capital are management experience, the presence of a scalable business model, and the promise of at least a 35% compounded return on the investment. VCs are drawn to management teams that have previously

EXHIBIT 23.8   Venture Capital Credit Box

Credit Box

To qualify for venture capital, an applicant must:
- Have a private equity capital need of $1 million to $50 million.
- Be able to show that initial funding will enable the company to move to the next level.
- Demonstrate a successful business plan that will generate equity returns of at least 35% per year on a compounded basis.
- Have a management team capable of creating and realizing the business plan.
- Have a scalable business model.
- Have salesmanship skills to entice venture capitalists into hearing the story.

achieved like-kind results. Scalable business models are essential. Scalability means that the company can grow benefit streams at an increasing rate as revenues grow. The minimum 35% compounded rate of return expectation is extremely difficult to achieve. To put this in perspective, assume a VC invests $5 million in PrivateCo with a five-year exit strategy. If the VC is successful in meeting its return expectation, its position in PrivateCo will be worth more than $22 million at the time of exit. How many companies can increase their value by this much in a five-year period? It is little wonder that the venture filter is so stringent.

Exhibit 23.9 shows surveyed results by stage of investment.[8]

VCs are minority investors in private companies, but they acquire more of a company on the average than do angels. Similar to angels, VCs expect to be invested for five years or so. But VCs are much more confident than angels regarding the percentage of investments that will become worthless, possibly because VC investments are made to more valuable companies.

Structure of the Venture Deal

Investments by venture funds into companies are called *disbursements*. A company receives capital in one or more rounds of financing. The venture firm provides capital and management expertise and usually takes a seat on the board to ensure that the investment has the best chance of success. The VC calls an investee a portfolio company. Typically, portfolio companies receive several rounds of venture financing in their life. Later-round investments are linked to the investee's ability to meet negotiated benchmarks. This incremental investing process enables a venture firm to reserve some capital for later investment in some of its successful companies with additional capital needs.

EXHIBIT 23.9   Venture Capital Terms by Stage of Investment

	Seed/Start-up	Early	Expansion	Later
Avg % of total equity purchased	30%	25%	15%	12.5%
Total model returns*	55%	50%	37.5%	30%
Time to exit (months)	75	60	48	42
Avg % of investments likely to become worthless	35%	25%	17.5%	10%
Avg company value at time of investment	$2M	$5M	$10M	$18M

*Median total model returns for expansion stage represents venture capital on the PPCML.

The following example gives an inside look at various venture capital issues.

EXAMPLE

PrivateCo has developed a special technology it believes will revolutionize a segment of its industry. Joe Mainstreet creates a new company, NewCo, which contains the associated patents and specialized equipment. His goal is to raise $10 million to fund the business plan. A local venture capital company, VentureCo, agrees to invest $10 million in the form of convertible preferred stock. But VentureCo believes the opportunity is riskier than its normal investment profile and is asking for an added return. In addition to the typical preferred features, VentureCo wants participating preferred stock.

PrivateCo's investment banker, Dan Dealmaker, explains that participating preferred is a form of convertible preferred stock that provides the holder with extraordinary rights in the event NewCo is sold or liquidated. If VentureCo receives back its purchase price for the stock and possibly some guaranteed return on that purchase price, it then receives an additional pro rata share of the remaining sale or liquidation proceeds from NewCo.

Dealmaker uses the next example to illustrate how a "participating" feature in a convertible preferred stock affects the return on investment for both VentureCo and NewCo. The example assumes VentureCo purchases 2 million shares of convertible preferred stock for $10 million and NewCo owns 8 million shares of common stock. The illustration shows the return to VentureCo and NewCo if the company later sells for $20 million.

Preferred Stock Comparison		
	Nonparticipating	Participating
Preferred purchase price	$10 million	$10 million
Number of shares	2 million	2 million
Other shares—common	8 million	8 million
Sale price distribution on a $20 million sale		
Preferred	$4 million	$12 million
Common	$16 million	$8 million

The participating preference is meaningful. In the case of a $20 million sale, the preferred holder gets $12 million, as opposed to $8 million for the common stockholders. This is considerably richer than the $4 million that would be distributed to a nonparticipating preferred holder.

Dealmaker recommends that NewCo negotiate a sunset provision into the preference that makes it inoperative after a passage of time or in a sale or liquidation that would generate an agreed-on minimum return without the preference.

Venture capital investing involves both art and science, as the following lessons suggest.

LESSONS FROM A SUCCESSFUL VENTURE CAPITALIST

- *Manage the "three risks."* Technology risk, market risk, and financing risk all can threaten the success of a potentially lucrative scientific discovery.

- *Invest with a teaspoon.* When putting first money into a new discovery, start with small amounts.

- *Remember your tape.* A person's life and the life of an enterprise are the sum total of actions and decisions over a period of time—a tape that never stops rolling, according to Georges Doriot.

- *Control the technology.* Take an ownership interest, not a license, in new technology in order to ensure it is maximized in commercial application.

- *Avoid potholes.* Associate only with quality people. Avoid unproductive, intramural bickering. Let science lead the way.

Source: Robert Finkel and David Greising, *The Masters of Private Equity and Venture Capital* (New York: McGraw-Hill, 2009), p. 219.

PRE- AND POSTMONEY VALUATION

Private equity investors tend to talk about premoney and postmoney valuation. When a private investor invests money in a company, it establishes the company's postmoney valuation. A postmoney valuation equals the premoney valuation of the company plus the amount of the investment. This difference in terminology seems harmless, but it can cause serious misunderstandings. Consider these formulas:

$$\text{PreMoney Valuation} = \text{PostMoney Valuation} - \text{New Investment}$$

$$\text{PostMoney Valuation} = \text{New Investment} \times \frac{\text{Total Post Investment Shares Outstanding}}{\text{Shares Issued for New Investment}}$$

By way of example, suppose Joe and Jane Mainstreet own 1,000 shares of PrivateCo, which is 100% of the equity. If an investor makes a $2 million investment into PrivateCo in return for 200 newly issued shares, the implied *postmoney valuation* is:

$$\text{Post Money Valuation} = \text{New Investment} \times \frac{\text{Total Post Investment Shares Outstanding}}{\text{Shares Issued for New Investment}}$$

$$\text{PostMoney Valuation} = \$2 \text{ million} \times \frac{1,200}{200}$$

$$= \$12 \text{ million}$$

To calculate the premoney valuation, the amount of the investment is subtracted from the postmoney valuation. In this case, it is:

$$\text{PreMoney Valuation} = \text{PostMoney Valuation} - \text{New Investment}$$

$$= \$12 \text{ million} - \$2 \text{ million}$$

$$= \$10 \text{ million}$$

The initial shareholders dilute their ownership to $10/12 = 83.33\%$.

NEGOTIATING POINTS

Investees should not begin to negotiate a term sheet with private equity investors until they understand the offered terms. This is also a good time to get legal and other professional advice. The entire deal should be comprehended before specific clauses or provisions are discussed. Once the deal is understood, investees can expect to negotiate the next points.

Process of Developing the Valuation

Different investors value an interest quite differently, depending on their understanding of the risk of the investment. Investees should not negotiate a value or price offered for their shares until they understand the process used by the prospective investor. Even after the process is well understood, the valuation *process* should be negotiated rather than the final value.

For example, suppose an equity investor offers to invest $10 million in a series B convertible preferred round and values the company at $75 million. The investee believes the enterprise value is closer to $100 million. The investor has valued the company using net present value analysis. The investor has employed a higher discount rate and lower cash flows than the investee thinks reasonable. One possible solution is to make the investment less risky for the investor. This might be accomplished by creating a revenue benchmark or milestone, causing the investor to tranche the investment over a period of time. The ultimate dilution might split the difference between the investee and investor valuations.

Managing Multiple Offers

It is difficult to run auctions or other methods of generating multiple offers from equity investors. Part of the problem is that institutional investors talk to each other and often syndicate their deals. Another constraint is the time required by the investee to initiate and manage multiple offers. Managing multiple offers is more likely to be successful if the investee has engaged a representative. Even with professional assistance, it probably is wise to deal with investors who are widely separate geographically.

Board and Governance Issues

When investors have legal control, the board is mainly ceremonial. Minority equity investors often want the right to appoint a designated number of directors to a company's board. This enables investors to better monitor their investment and have a say in running the business. Companies often resist giving equity investors control of, or a blocking position on, a company's board. A frequent compromise is to allow outside directors, acceptable to the company and investors, to hold the balance of power. Occasionally, board visitation rights, in lieu of a board seat, are granted.

A variety of governance issues should be described in the term sheet. In this context, the term "governance" means how the major financial and legal issues of the company will be managed. In many cases, these issues are broken into majority and supermajority terms, as shown next.

- *Corporate Governance.* The PrivateCo board will have five members: three will be appointed by the series A common holders and two by the series B common holders. The series A holders will appoint the chairman and chief financial officer of the company. These decisions will require a supermajority approval of the board (at least four board votes):
  - Elections of directors
  - Issuance of new interests
  - Sale of entire business
  - Changes to share rights
  - Distributions or dividends, except for normal tax distributions
  - Incurring debts of more than $1 million
  - Acquisition of another business
  - Dissolution of the company
  - Key employee hires
  - Major changes in the employee benefits
  - Optional buyouts
  - Changes to the employment contracts, noncompete agreements, operating agreement, shareholder agreement, and buy/sell agreement
  - Job termination of a shareholder
  These decisions will require a majority (at least three board votes):
  - Expenditures on capital items in excess of $75,000 per item
  - Minor changes in the employee benefits package

Management should negotiate all of the major actions it can undertake without any board interaction.

Vesting of the Founders' Stock

Equity investors often insist that all or a portion of the stock owned or to be owned by the founders and key employees vest only in stages after continued employment with the company. This condition is often called an *earn-in* of stock. This is an especially contentious issue for early-stage companies because the value of the company is so uncertain. Vesting of founder stock is less of an issue in later-stage companies. If forced to earn-in over time, managers should negotiate benchmarks that are within their control to achieve without further actions by the equity investor.

Additional Management Members

Additional key managers sometimes are required as part of the equity investment. This is a highly negotiated item, because neither the current management team nor the equity investor wants to dilute their position. Perhaps the best compromise is to employ a deferred compensation plan, such as phantom stock, for the new players. After a period of several years, the added managers may participate in stock option plans that include all of the managers.

Employment Agreements with Key Founders

Management should negotiate employment agreements as part of the funding. Key issues often are compensation and benefits, duties of the employee and under what circumstances those duties can be changed, the circumstances under which the employee can be fired, severance payments on termination, the rights of the company to repurchase stock of the terminated employee and at what price, term of employment, and restrictions on postemployment activities and competition.

Special care should be taken to tie the employment agreement to the buy/sell agreement. For instance, if a manager is terminated without cause, that manager's stock should be repurchased at full value. However, if the manager is terminated with cause, the shares probably will be repurchased at a discount to full value. Managers also should negotiate to have the company pay for life and disability insurance that will fund the employment agreement and buy/sell.

Investor Transfer Rights

A number of investor transfer rights are negotiated. Some of these are:

- *Preemptive rights.* The right of the investor to acquire new securities issued by the company to the extent necessary to maintain its percentage interest on an as-converted basis.
- *Registration rights.* Investors typically receive certain registration rights for public offerings. Negotiations center around whether the investor receives piggyback and/or demand registration rights, and who pays the expenses of each such registration. Piggyback rights allow investors to have their securities

included in a company-initiated registration. Demand rights mean that holders can require the company to prepare, file, and maintain a registration statement. Normally, investors require the company to pay all of the holder's expenses regarding registrations.

- *Right of first refusal.* Right of the investor to be first offered securities to be sold by other shareholders and/or the company.
- *Right of cosale.* Right of the investor to sell its securities along with any securities sold by the company or the other shareholders.
- *Tag-along or drag-along right.* Right to obligate other shareholders to sell their securities along with securities sold by the investor.

These rights should be set forth in the term sheet and generally terminate upon an initial public offering of common stock by the company.

Antidilution Provisions

Investors require protection against dilution from future additional investment in the company. Antidilution provisions entitle an investor to obtain additional equity in a company without additional cost when a later investor purchases equity at a lower cost per share. These provisions come in two primary forms: ratchets and weighted average.

Ratchets give investors additional shares of stock for free if the company later sells shares at a lower price. For example, if an investor who has a ratchet purchases 100,000 shares of company stock for $200,000, or $2 a share, and the company later sells another investor 100,000 shares for $1 each, the first investor would receive another 100,000 shares for free. The result would be the same if the second investor bought only one share for $1.

The weighted average method uses a formula to determine the dilutive effect of a later sale of cheaper securities and grants the investor enough extra shares for free to offset that dilutive effect. Assume that an investor buys 600,000 shares of company stock for $4 per share when management owns 1,400,000 shares. A later investor buys 400,000 shares from the company for $2 per share. A ratchet would give the first investor 600,000 new shares for free to reduce the average price per share to $2.

The weighted average antidilution method is usually more favorable to management shareholders than the ratchet method. Under the ratchet method, the protected investor is entitled to get enough free shares to reduce his or her price per share to the same price paid by the later investor regardless of the number of shares sold to the later investor.

TRIANGULATION

Private equity investors provide various types of capital to growing companies. The various equity providers align with the five stages of capital needs. Owners, angels, and venture capitalists typically invest in start-up, early, and expansion-stage companies, respectively. Many companies evolve from one capital provider to the next as their capital needs change.

Companies in need of early-stage equity are viewed in the world of early equity or the world of market value, depending on the stage of investment. As the name suggests, early-stage companies are valued by angels and venture capitalists in the world of early equity, whereas private equity groups—the subjects of the next chapter—use market value to determine deal parameters. Value world collisions are the norm when private equity is sought. Founders and other shareholders tend to view value from the owner value world perspective, which often results in an overvaluation, at least from the perspective of the particular private equity provider. Many deals fail because this collision cannot be reconciled.

From the moment a company receives private equity, it is *in play* to be transferred. Private equity providers are driven to invest by the probability of successful exits. They negotiate deals that increase the odds of a profitable transfer. As a last resort, the provider will transfer its shares back to the company at some future date. The more profitable exit for the investor, however, usually involves a public offering or sale to a synergistic acquirer. This can be another source of friction between shareholders and investors: Shareholders may wish to grow and hold while investors want to grow and harvest. Both parties need to understand the other's motivations and plan accordingly.

NOTES

1. Mark Long, *Raising Capital* (San Diego: Promotions Publishing, 1998), pp. 129–130.
2. A good online tool for angel financing is: www.vfinance.com.
3. John K. Paglia, Pepperdine Private Capital Markets Project Survey Report, April 2010, bschool.pepperdine.edu/privatecapital.
4. David Newton, "An Explanation of Angel Investors," *Entrepreneur* (July 2000).
5. www.angelblog.net/The_One_Page_Term_Sheet.html
6. Dante Fichera, *The Insider's Guide to Venture Capital* (Roseville, CA Prima Venture, 2002), p. 292.
7. John K. Paglia, Pepperdine Private Capital Markets Project Survey Report.
8. Ibid.

Private Equity

The term "private equity investors" refers to the various individuals and organizations that provide equity capital to private companies. Chapter 23 focused on three early-stage equity investors: business owners, angels, and venture capitalists. The term "private equity," for our purposes here, refers to institutional entities that mainly provide capital to mainly later-stage companies. This chapter describes several private equity sources: private equity groups (PEGs), hedge funds, and family offices.

In the last 20 years, an organized assemblage of equity providers to companies with revenues in the range of $0 to $1 billion has emerged. Currently, thousands of equity capital providers offer hundreds of billions of capital to private companies. Given the effect of leverage, this investment potential has had an impact on the private equity market several orders of magnitude larger.

Private equity traces its roots to federal government regulations, tax laws, and security laws. For example, the U.S. Department of Labor modified the "prudent man" provision of the Employment Retirement Income Security Act in 1979–1980 to allow regulated pension funds to be invested in private businesses. Increased investment began flowing through the legal structure of limited partnerships, whose investment activities are regulated or governed by their own charters. Those charters typically both prescribe and proscribe the types of investment activities that the limited partners authorize their agents, the general partners, to engage in. Governmental authorities permitted this increased investment. However, the reduction in capital gains taxation from $49\frac{1}{2}\%$ to 28% in 1978, and subsequently to 20% in 1981, significantly increased the effective return of private equity investments, thereby encouraging increased funds to flow into this market. PEGs, hedge funds, and family offices bring to the private arena the intellectual equipment, language tools, and concepts found in public market companies.

Five characteristics differentiate private equity investing from other types of investing.

1. The private equity investor identifies, negotiates, and structures the transaction. Beyond the transaction, the private investor may be a board member or consultant.
2. The private equity investor has a finite holding period, normally five to seven years. Generally, it takes several years to position the company and at least one to two years to realize a maximizing exit.

3. Private investors seek high returns on their capital. The private investor seeks 25% to 40% returns, as opposed to 10% to 20% return expectations from public equity securities.

4. Private equity professionals invest in a company only when they are convinced that the company's management team can execute the business plan. The conversion from initial idea to profit recognition is the wealth-creating activity, and managers who can successfully conclude this conversion tend to get funded.

5. Most private investors require some control over their investment. This control may involve contractually given rights rather than merely a majority stock position. For example, most private investors negotiate certain rights, such as antidilution, registration, tag-along, and so on. Taken together, these moves grant them a certain amount of control.

STAGES OF PRIVATE EQUITY INVESTOR INVOLVEMENT

There are five generally recognized stages of private equity investor involvement. These stages are important because they enable the equity market to match the appropriate funding source with the capital need, creating efficiency in the capital allocation process. The stages are:

Stage 1: Seed stage. This is the initial stage. The company has a concept or product under development.

Stage 2: Start-up stage. The company is now operational but is still developing a product or service. There are no revenues. The company is usually in existence less than 18 months.

Stage 3: Early stage. The company has a product or service in testing or pilot production. In some cases, the product may be commercially available. The company may or may not be generating revenues and is usually in business less than three years.

Stage 4: Expansion stage. The company's product or service is in production and is commercially available. The company demonstrates significant revenue growth but may or may not be showing a profit. The company usually has been in business more than three years.

Stage 5: Later stage. The company's product or service is widely available. The company is generating ongoing revenue and probably positive cash flow. The company is more than likely profitable and may have been in business for more than 10 years.

Various equity providers align with each of the five stages of capital needs. Personal and family or friends are the primary funding sources for seed or start-ups. Angel investors invest in early-stage companies that are in business with a product or service in production. Venture capitalists tend to favor expansion-stage companies. Those firms expect to achieve substantial revenue growth, but they have not yet shown a profit. PEGs, hedge funds, and family offices, private companies that manage investments for wealthy families, provide capital for later-stage companies.

Private Equity Groups

A new type of equity investor began in the 1980s and came to prominence in the 1990s. PEGs are the largest direct investors in the equity of private companies, especially in later-stage firms. PEGs tend toward control investments; however, 61% of surveyed PEGs report that with appropriate shareholder protections, they would be receptive to taking minority positions.[1]

PEGs provide strategic capital for a number of activities, including recapitalizations, leveraged buildups, management buyouts, and management buy-ins. PEGs are opportunistic investors and look at many deals before making an investment. Frequently PEGs will create investment opportunities by sponsoring an executive team to target an industry in which the team has relevant experience and a strong track record. Most PEGs are comfortable investing in family businesses. Exhibit 24.1 displays the capital coordinates for PEGs.

PEG Investment Activities

A PEG's investment activities are divided into four phases:

1. *Selecting investments.* Includes obtaining access to a high-quality deal flow and evaluating potential investments. This stage involves acquiring a large quantity of information and sorting and evaluating it.
2. *Structuring investments.* Refers to the type and number of securities issued as equity by the portfolio company and to other substantive provisions of investment agreements. These provisions affect both managerial incentives at portfolio companies and the partnership's ability to influence the company's operations.
3. *Monitoring investments.* Involves active participation in the management of portfolio companies. General partners exercise control and furnish portfolio companies with financial, operating, and marketing expertise as needed through membership on boards of directors and less formal channels.
4. *Exiting investment.* Divesting can involve taking portfolio companies public or, more frequently, selling them privately. Because the investment funds of PEGs have finite lives, and investors expect repayment in cash or marketable securities, an exit strategy is an integral part of the investment process.

Like other investors, PEGs assess the general suitability of investment opportunities based on a credit box, shown in Exhibit 24.2.[2]

PEGs prefer to invest in companies with niche, proprietary products or services. These companies should enable the PEG to earn above-average returns during the investment as well as create an exit opportunity within five to seven years. About one-third of responding PEGs plan to sell to another private equity

EXHIBIT 24.1 Capital Coordinates: Private Equity Groups

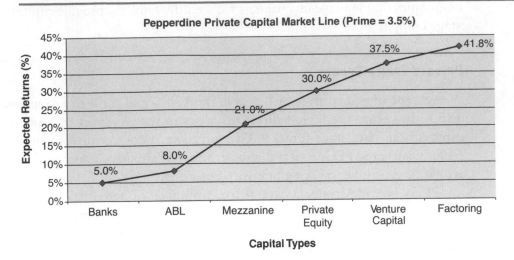

Capital Access Point	Private Equity Groups
Definition	PEGs are direct investors in the equity of private companies, especially later-stage companies.
Expected Rate of Return	25% to 35%, depending on size of deal
Value World(s)	Market value
Transfer Method(s)	Nearly all transfer methods are supported by PEGs.
Appropriate to Use When . . .	Private equity groups provide strategic capital for a number of activities, including recapitalizations, leveraged buildups, management buyouts, and management buyins. Recapitalizations are an ideal transfer method for PEGs because it enables a "win-win" for owner and investor.
Key Points to Consider	Few companies qualify for PEG investment. Private equity groups focus on investing in companies with niche, proprietary products or services. Private equity groups tend toward control investments but may make minority investments for deals that meet their expected returns.

EXHIBIT 24.2 Private Equity Groups Credit Box

Credit Box

To qualify for private equity group capital, an applicant must:
- Have a private equity capital need of $1million to $100 million, or more
- Prove that the initial funding will enable the company to move to the next level
- Demonstrate that a successful business plan will generate *at least* a 20% to 30% compounded return
- Have a management team capable of creating and realizing the business plan
- Have a differentiated product or service with a large market opportunity
- Have a path to a maximizing exit

EXHIBIT 24.3 PEGs Terms by Deal Size

	$1M	$5M	$10M	$25M	$50M	$100M
Avg % of total equity purchased	75.0%	80.0%	80.0%	70.0%	67.5%	62.5%
Multiple of EBITDA paid	4.0	5.0	5.5	6.3	7.1	na
Total model returns*	30%	30%	25%	25%	25%	20%
Time to exit (months)	60	60	60	48	48	36
Total debt as a % of purchase price	50.0%	50.0%	52.5%	50.0%	50.0%	50.0%

*Median total model returns of $5M deal size represents the PEG expected return on the PPCML.

group; 29% plan to sell to another private company; 28% plan to exit via a sale to a public company; and the remainder plan to take their companies public or exit in another way.[3]

Exhibit 24.3 shows various statistics by deal size.[4]

It may come as a surprise to some that PEGs typically do not acquire 100% of the companies in which they invest; rather, they use the equity recapitalization transfer method to make most of their investments. Deal size matters relative to pricing: the larger the deal, typically the larger the acquisition multiple that is paid. Finally, PEGs are using equity for about half of the capital structure, which indicates that at the time of the most recent Pepperdine survey, banks had taken a conservative approach to acquisition lending. If given the choice, most PEGs would prefer a total debt % of the purchase price of 75% or so.

Successful Investment Practices

Bain & Co, an international consulting firm, has identified a handful of disciplines that high-performing PEGs use to add value to their investments.[5] Consider the summary in Exhibit 24.4.

Top PEGs tend to define their investment focus by stressing a few critical success factors. Growth-oriented business plans are the order of the day for these investors. Cash flow, as opposed to earnings, is the key metric. Finally, the investment is divested based on achieving a desired return, even if the exit possibility occurs sooner or later than expected.

After the Investment

PEGs actively tend to their portfolios. For the most part, day-to-day operations are the responsibility of the portfolio company managers. PEGs typically serve as strategic business advisors, assisting management in these activities:

- Developing a strategic business plan
- Organizing and recruiting a well-balanced management team, board of directors, and professional service providers
- Determining appropriate capital structures, arranging equity and debt financings, and providing financial advice
- Developing strategic partnerships

EXHIBIT 24.4   Four Disciplines of Top Private Equity Groups

Define an Investment Thesis	Do Not Measure Too Much	Work the Balance Sheet	Make the Center the Shareholder
Have a 3- to 5-year plan.	Prune to essential metrics.	Redeploy or eliminate unproductive capital, both fixed assets and working capital.	Focus on optimizing each business.
Stress 2 or 3 key success levers.	Focus on cash and value, not earnings.	Treat equity capital as scarce.	Don't hesitate to sell when the price is right.
Focus on growth, not just cost reductions.	Use the right performance measures for each business.	Use debt to gain leverage and focus, but match risk with return.	Act as unsentimental owners. Get involved in the hiring and firing decisions in portfolio companies. Appoint a senior person to be the contact between the corporate center and a manager or employee.

- Planning and executing appropriate exit strategies
- Identifying and evaluating potential acquisition opportunities

Nearly all PEGs have substantial experience helping companies through initial public offerings as well as through merger and sale transactions. Later chapters on recapitalizations and roll-ups further describe the PEG investment model.

The following example describes the PEG investment process.

EXAMPLE

Joe Mainstreet believes he has an opportunity to grow PrivateCo substantially in a short time. A number of PrivateCo's competitors have approached him about a buyout. Joe believes he can double the size of PrivateCo by buying a handful of these companies and moving all of their business into PrivateCo's existing facility. Joe has been to BankCo, his bank of 20 years, and learned that too much growth is a bad thing, at least from the bank's perspective. On the way out the door, a BankCo vice president introduces Joe to PEGCo, a local PEG.

Joe provides PEGCo with this summary:

PrivateCo before and after the Acquisitions

	Before	After
Sales	$25.0 million	$45.0 million
EBITDA	3.5 million	8.5 million
Cost of acquisitions		$9.0 million

After convincing themselves that Joe's assumptions are correct, PEGCo determines its equity split based on making a $9 million investment in PrivateCo. While in the world of market value, PEGCo determines that PrivateCo is worth about 5.5 times earnings before interest, taxes, depreciation, and amortization (EBITDA), or $19.25 million, before the acquisition. Following this math, PrivateCo should be worth $46.75 million after the acquisitions. This is equal to about 47% of PrivateCo's equity on a before-acquisition basis ($9MM ÷ $19.25MM), or about 19% of the equity on an after-acquisitions basis ($9MM ÷ $46.75MM). PEGCo has been through these discussions with various private owners before and knows that Joe will fight for every last equity percentage point.

PEGCo expects PrivateCo to increase EBITDA by 10% per year. PEGCo requires a minimum $1 million per year in management fees. Finally, PEGCo believes the business could be sold for $68.2 million in year 5 following an investment ($12.4MM × 5.5).

PrivateCo Cash Flows after the Acquisitions (in $millions)

	Year 1	Year 2	Year 3	Year 4	Year 5
EBITDA	8.5	9.4	10.3	11.3	12.4
Management fees	1.0	1.0	1.0	1.0	
Terminal event					68.2

PEGCo has a 30% return expectation on its investments. Based on the expected fees and terminal value, PEGCo discovers that it must own about 35% of the PrivateCo stock to achieve its desired return. As part of the equity split negotiations, PEGCo also negotiates ownership agreements with Joe to enable it to have a claim on the distributions shown here.

Equity providers have high compounded-return expectations. For the most part, increased risk is correlated with increased return expectations. As might be expected, start-up investor return expectations are the highest, in the 50% to 60% range. Given a five-year investment horizon, a 60% compounded return correlates to about ten times the seed investor's capital. Angels invest mainly in companies that survived the start-up stage and therefore the riskiness has lessened to some degree. Given a five-year horizon, a 40% compounded return correlates to about five times the angel's investment. Venture capitalists and PEGs structure their participation to get 25% to 35% compounded returns on an expected case basis. Once again, using a five-year horizon, a 30% compounded return correlates to about three and a half times the investment. Each group wants to realize much higher returns from the *winners* in their portfolios.

Five-Year Investment Returns

	Compounded Returns		
Original Investment	25%	35%	50%
$3MM . . . becomes	$9.2MM	$13.4MM	$24.8MM

There is a major difference between the deals that draw venture capitalist (VC) and PEG investment. VCs place bets on business models, that is, on the likelihood that a company's business model will succeed. PEGs, however, place bets on proven management teams. The PEG bet is based on executing a certain strategy, such as a roll-up or other growth vehicle.

The next control-of-company spectrum shows that the owner-manager normally has operating and legal control in the early years of the company. This may change as the company's funding needs grow.

Stage	Seed/ Start-Up	Early	Expansion	Later
Control Of Company	Owner-Manager			Capital Provider

HEDGE FUNDS

Hedge funds are rather recent players in making investments in private companies. A hedge fund can take both long and short positions, use arbitrage, buy and sell undervalued securities, trade options or bonds, and invest in almost any opportunity in any market where it foresees impressive gains at reduced risk. Hedge fund strategies vary enormously—many hedge against downturns in the markets—which is especially important today with volatility and anticipation of corrections in overheated stock markets. The primary aim of most hedge funds is to reduce volatility and risk while attempting to preserve capital and deliver positive returns under all market conditions. While most hedge fund activities involve trading in public markets, hedge fund managers increasingly view larger private company securities as a potential source of returns.

The first hedge fund in the United States was set up by Alfred W. Jones in 1949. Jones was the first to use short sales and leverage techniques in combination. In 1952, he converted his general partnership fund into a limited partnership investing with several independent portfolio managers and created the first multimanager hedge fund. In the mid-1950s, other funds started using the short-selling of shares, although for the majority of these funds, the hedging of market risk was not central to their investment strategy.

Hedge funds traditionally have been limited to sophisticated, wealthy investors. Over time, the activities of hedge funds broadened into other financial instruments and activities. Today, the term "hedge fund" refers not so much to hedging techniques, which hedge funds may or may not employ, as it does to their status as private and unregistered investment pools. As of this writing, there are more than 8,000 registered hedge funds, with more than $1 trillion assets under management.[6]

The following further describes hedge funds:

Key Characteristics of Hedge Funds[7]

- Hedge funds utilize a variety of financial instruments to reduce risk, enhance returns, and minimize the correlation with equity and bond markets. Many hedge funds are flexible in their investment options (can use short selling, leverage, derivatives such as puts, calls, options, futures, etc.).
- Hedge funds vary enormously in terms of investment returns, volatility, and risk. Many, but not all, hedge fund strategies tend to hedge against downturns in the markets being traded.
- Many hedge funds have the ability to deliver non-market-correlated returns.
- Many hedge funds have as an objective consistency of returns and capital preservation rather than magnitude of returns.
- Most hedge funds are managed by experienced investment professionals who generally are disciplined and diligent.
- Pension funds, endowments, insurance companies, private banks, and high-net-worth individuals and families invest in hedge funds to minimize overall portfolio volatility and enhance returns.
- Most hedge fund managers are highly specialized and trade only within their area of expertise and competitive advantage.
- Hedge funds benefit by heavily weighting hedge fund managers' remuneration toward performance incentives, thus attracting the best brains in the investment business. In addition, hedge fund managers usually have their own money invested in their fund.

Converging with Private Equity Groups

Hedge funds are almost always opportunistic investors, meaning they typically do not have a static credit box like other equity investors. In fact, hedge funds value liquidity more than other equity players and normally will make an investment in a private company only if the exit strategy is apparent. Exhibit 24.5 compares hedge funds and PEGs on a number of investment factors.

Private equity firms generally invest in a company's equity, with a long-term view seeking large "equity-upside" returns. Hedge funds, however, may invest in secured debt, unsecured debt, or equity and may hedge those investments through intracompany hedges or industry hedges while seeking extraordinary returns. The hedge fund exit strategy may be a simple trade, as opposed to a complete corporate disposition. However, when loan-to-own hedge funds invest in debt securities of portfolio companies owned by private equity funds, the different risk tolerance, hold periods, and leverage and liquidity issues of the funds inevitably will result in a culture clash.

Approaching Hedge Funds

Even though there are thousands of hedge funds, it can be difficult to approach this group with an investment opportunity. Hedge fund managers tend to deal only

EXHIBIT 24.5   Hedge Funds versus Private Equity Groups

	Hedge Funds	Private Equity Groups
Due diligence	Quick based mainly on the metrics of the security and exit	Slow based on a large number of factors, including management and industry
Holding period	Usually less than 18 months	Usually 5–6 years
Participation	Yield players, may not be actively involved	Strategic investors, certain to be involved
Risk tolerance	High	Medium
Return definition	Return is based on the difference between invested value and sales proceeds.	Return on an investment may be adjusted based on several factors, including market share, profitability, revenues and valuation metrics.
View of financial metrics	Only metrics that directly convert an investment to a return are important.	A variety of financial metrics are important and monitored.
Management fees	Set based on the company's ability to pay; probably more aggressive than PEGs	Typically 2% management fees

with existing relationships. These managers are not in the position or inclined to perform long due diligences. Further, since hedge funds do not always employ consistent credit boxes, it is best to contact them through an intermediary that they already know.

FAMILY OFFICES

A family office is the organization that is created, often after the sale of family business or realization of significant liquidity, to support the financial needs (ranging from strategic asset allocation to record keeping and reporting) of a specific family group.

The modern concept and understanding of family offices was developed in the nineteenth century. In 1838, the family of J.P. Morgan founded the House of Morgan, which managed the family's assets. In 1882, the Rockefellers founded their family office, which exists today.

No formal data exists, but it is estimated that there are between 2,500 and 3,000 family offices in the United States; perhaps another 6,000 exist informally inside privately controlled businesses in the United States. For Europe and Asia, the concept of a family office is just evolving, with new family offices being formed monthly in these areas.

Family office services vary depending on the goals of the office. Some offices offer strictly strategic and investment services while others offer everything from strategic to convenience services like travel planning. Most offices provide these services:

- Investment advice, management, monitoring
- Financial and tax planning

- Wealth transfer planning
- Financial record keeping and compliance
- Family foundation management
- Client education and goal development

There are two types of family offices: single-family offices (SFOs) and multi-family offices (MFOs). SFOs serve one wealthy family, while MFOs operate more like traditional private wealth management practices with multiple clients. MFOs are much more common because they can spread heavy investments in technology and consultants among several high-net-worth clients instead of a single individual or family.

MFOs tend to have these characteristics:

- *Independence.* MFOs typically do not sell traditional products that a family typically might encounter from a brokerage firm and generally are not compensated for the products utilized by clients. MFOs usually follow a service delivery model, holding themselves out as an objective provider of advice that places the interests of their clients first.
- *Breadth and integration of services.* MFOs provide a wide array of services and typically oversee their clients' entire financial universe. MFOs will have full information about their clients' investments, tax situation, estate plan, and family dynamics. With this information, MFOs can assist in structuring and administering the clients' financial universe in an optimal fashion.
- *Professionals with diverse skills and deep specialties.* MFO professionals provide a wide array of advice and assistance to their clients. MFOs also have to be able to provide specialty knowledge on certain topics, such as income taxation, estate planning, and investments.
- *High-touch services.* MFOs have high average account sizes (usually in the tens of millions) and low client-to-employee ratios (in around the 3-to-1 range). Large account sizes combined with low client-to-employee ratios allows a great deal of focus and attention on each client family. Meetings with clients often occur many times a year.
- *Multigenerational planning.* MFOs typically work with an entire family: the patriarch/matriarch, their children and grandchildren. Planning encompasses the family's goals, which typically includes passing wealth down to younger generations in a tax-efficient manner. Children and grandchildren are clients and are counseled on investments, taxes, estate planning, and philanthropy from an early age. MFOs often coordinate and moderate family meetings for their client families.
- *Outsourcing.* MFOs do not typically provide all services in-house. It is common for some of the investment management to be outsourced to independent money managers. Custody and tax return preparation are also commonly outsourced.
- *Focus on taxable investor.* Most MFOs have a myopic focus on taxable investors, as the bulk of their client's assets are subject to short- and long-term capital gains. This is unique to very-high-net-worth families. Most investment

research (academic and financial service industry) is geared toward the institutional investor and foundations (with very different tax concerns from those of individuals and families). The bulk of the research done for the individual investor relates to 401ks and Individual Retirement Accounts.

Family offices have trillions of dollars in assets under management and will likely play a more meaningful role in private equity going forward.[8]

TERM SHEET

In the world of private equity, the *term sheet* outlines the tenets of the deal. The term sheet summarizes all the important financial and legal terms in the contemplated transaction, and it quantifies the value of the financing. Although generally a legally nonbinding agreement, the parties have an implied duty to negotiate the term sheet in good faith. Ultimately, an executed term sheet serves as the basis for the legal documents. Most of the terminology used in term sheets is the same whether the deal involves an angel, venture capitalist, or private equity group. Appendix E contains an example term sheet for a preferred stock financing.

The process of preparing and negotiating a term sheet helps to solidify the transaction and create a sense of momentum between the parties. A well-drawn and complete term sheet helps to minimize the time and efforts required to draft and negotiate the final agreements. In addition, an executed term sheet often assists the company in its negotiations with lenders, creditors, suppliers, customers, and others. A number of issues need to be negotiated between the parties, some of which are highlighted in the next sections.

Exhibit 24.6 compares various private equity sources based on a number of different criteria.

The exhibit depicts the three institutional private equity providers relative to the investment stages and other criteria. There is some overlap between the providers and the stages (i.e., some venture firms invest in early- or later-stage deals, while some angels may get involved with start-ups).

EXHIBIT 24.6 Comparison of Private Equity Investors

Stage	Seed/Start-up	Early	Expansion	Later
Provider	Personal family/friends	Angels	Venture	PEGs, hedge, MFO
Deal acceptance %	10%–20%	20%–30%	<1%	1–2%
Typical investment	$50k–$100K	$100K–$2MM	$1MM–$10MM	>$3MM
Favored security		Common/convertible preferred Common	Convertible preferred	Common
Due diligence period	<4 weeks	<4 weeks	1–3 months	1–3 months
Expected returns	50%–60%	35%–40%	30%–35%	25%–30%
Control of company	Owner-manager	Minority	Minority	Control

Angels accept a larger percentage of the deals they are presented than do VCs and PEGs. This can be explained in two ways.

1. Angels do not get to see as many deals as the institutional investors, so the universe of deals they look at is smaller.
2. Angels often have nonmonetary reasons for making an investment, such as personal connection to the founder.

Typical investment sizes vary dramatically from one investor type to another. There is an overlap among the institutional providers. Unless there is an organized angel group involved, it is unlikely that more than $1 million to $2 million will be invested. Due to large amounts to invest, it is difficult for a VC, PEG, or hedge fund to invest less than $2 million to $3 million in a business for the deal to be worthwhile.

NEGOTIATING POINTS

Investees, the companies possibly receiving the funds, should not begin to negotiate a term sheet with private equity investors until they understand the offered terms. This is also a good time to get legal and other professional advice. The entire deal should be fully considered before specific clauses or provisions are discussed. Once the deal is understood, investees can expect to negotiate the next points.

Process of Developing the Valuation

Different investors value an interest quite differently, depending on their understanding of the risk of the investment. Investees should not negotiate a value or price offered for their shares until they understand the process used by the prospective investor. Even after the process is well understood, the valuation *process* should be negotiated rather than the final value.

Managing Multiple Offers

It is difficult to run auctions or other methods of generating multiple offers from equity investors. Part of the problem is that institutional investors talk to each other and often syndicate their deals. Another constraint is the time required by the investee to initiate and manage multiple offers. Managing multiple offers is more likely to be successful if the investee has engaged a representative. Even with professional assistance, it is probably wise to deal with investors who are widely separate geographically.

Board and Governance Issues

When investors have legal control, the board is mainly ceremonial. Minority equity investors often want the right to appoint a designated number of directors to a company's board. Doing so enables investors to better monitor their investment and have a say in running the business. Companies often resist giving equity investors control of, or a blocking position on, a company's board. A frequent compromise is to allow outside directors, acceptable to the company and investors, to hold the balance of power. Occasionally, board visitation rights, in lieu of a board seat, are granted.

A variety of governance issues should be described in the term sheet. These were discussed in Chapter 23.

Vesting of the Founders' Stock

Equity investors often insist that all or a portion of the stock owned or to be owned by the founders and key employees vest only in stages after continued employment with the company. This condition is often called an *earn-in* of stock. This can be an important issue even for later-stage companies when the value of the company is high. If forced to earn-in over time, managers should negotiate benchmarks that are within their control to achieve without further actions by the equity investor.

Employment Agreements with Key Founders

Management should negotiate employment agreements as part of the funding. Key issues often are compensation and benefits, duties of the employee and under what circumstances those duties can be changed, the circumstances under which the employee can be fired, severance payments on termination, the rights of the company to repurchase stock of the terminated employee and at what price, term of employment, and restrictions on postemployment activities and competition.

Special care should be taken to tie the employment agreement to the buy/sell agreement. For instance, if a manager is terminated without cause, that manager's stock should be repurchased at full value. However, if the manager is terminated with cause, the shares probably will be repurchased at a discount to full value. Managers should also negotiate to have the company pay for life and disability insurance that will fund the employment agreement and buy/sell.

Investor Transfer Rights

A number of investor transfer rights are negotiated. Some of these are:

- *Preemptive rights.* The right of the investor to acquire new securities issued by the company to the extent necessary to maintain its percentage interest on an as-converted basis.
- *Registration rights.* Investors typically receive certain registration rights for public offerings. Negotiations center around whether the investor receives piggyback and/or demand registration rights, and who pays the expenses of each such registration. Piggyback rights allow the investors to have their securities included in a company-initiated registration. Demand rights mean that the holder can require the company to prepare, file, and maintain a registration

statement. Normally, investors require the company to pay all of the holder's expenses regarding registrations.

- *Right of first refusal.* Right of the investor to be first offered securities to be sold by other shareholders and/or the company.
- *Right of cosale.* Right of the investor to sell its securities along with any securities sold by the company or the other shareholders.
- *Tag-along or drag-along right.* Right to obligate other shareholders to sell their securities along with securities sold by the investor.

These rights should be set forth in the term sheet and generally terminate upon an initial public offering of common stock by the company.

No Shop

Equity investors often insist on a *no-shop* period at the term sheet stage when the investors have a period of time (usually 30 to 60 days) where they have the exclusive right, but not the obligation, to make the investment. Viewed from the investee's perspective, it is the period within which the company or its agents cannot solicit other investor interest. The prospective investee does not want to grant such an exclusivity period, as it may prevent it from obtaining financing if the parties cannot reach agreement on a definitive deal. Ultimately the investee probably will agree to some no-shop period, which should not surpass 60 days. An investee might negotiate a benchmark for this no-shop period. For instance, at the end of 30 days, equity investors must sign off or release some part of their due diligence (e.g., the operating agreement or employment agreements must be agreed to in principle). If these agreements are not resolved at that point, the company can shop the deal again.

Private equity sources in the United States are sophisticated providers of various kinds of capital. Angels, venture capitalists, and PEGs tailor investments to achieve certain purposes, all leading to an expected return. The difficulty of generating these high returns cannot be overstated. Very few private companies can produce 30% compounded returns over a long period of time. This chapter shows that owners who wish to raise private equity should do so with great care.

TRIANGULATION

Private equity investors provide various types of capital to growing companies. The various equity providers align with the four stages of capital needs. Angels, venture capitalists, and PEGs typically invest in early-, expansion-, and later-stage companies, respectively. Many companies evolve from one capital provider to the next, as their capital needs change.

Companies in need of private equity are viewed in the world of market value. Value world collisions are the norm when private equity is sought. Founders and other shareholders tend to view value from the owner value world perspective, which often results in an overvaluation, at least from the perspective of the particular private equity provider. Many deals fail because this collision cannot be reconciled.

Family offices are an emerging player in private equity. They may be the perfect example of an investor that can maximize triangulation. They have access to substantial amounts of investible funds; their clientele typically has made or currently is making money from business ownership —so they have value creation and transfer know-how as well as vital global connections; and they can afford to take a longer-term view than the other private equity players. No other group can integrate capital, valuation, and transfer as effectively as family offices.

The goal of private equity is to produce significant value from investments. PEGs, hedge funds, and family offices share this mission. Each group uses different tactics to achieve this goal, however. A particularly interesting tactic involves PEGs and recapitalizations. In a recapitalization, an owner transfers most of the business to a company controlled by a PEG, which then funds an aggressive growth plan. This strategy allows an owner to sell the business twice: once to the PEG and once to the open market.

One manufacturer of highly engineered narrow woven fabrics chose a recapitalization structure to have enough capital to consolidate a segment of the textile industry and to partner with an investor who had a successful track record of growing companies and creating maximizing exit plans. Together, the original owner, with the backing of the PEG, acquired a number of smaller industry players and doubled the business in two years. Soon after this the partners were able to exit the business via a sale to a much larger player at a much higher-selling multiple than was possible as a small company.

From the moment a company receives private equity, it is in play to be transferred. Private equity providers are driven to invest by the probability of successful exits. They negotiate deals that increase the odds of a profitable transfer. As a last resort, the provider will transfer its shares back to the company at some future date. The more profitable exit for the investor, however, usually involves a public offering or sale to a synergistic acquirer. This can be another source of friction between shareholders and investors: Shareholders may wish to grow and hold, while investors want to grow and harvest. Both parties need to understand the other's motivations and plan accordingly.

NOTES

1. John K. Paglia, Pepperdine Private Capital Markets Project Survey Report, April 2010, bschool.pepperdine.edu/privatecapital.
2. Ibid.
3. Ibid.
4. Ibid.
5. Mark Long, *Raising Capital* (San Diego:Promotions Publishing, 1998), pp. 129–130.
6. Mark K. Thomas and Peter J. Young, "What Commercial Borrowers and Lenders Should Know about Private Equity vs. Hedge Funds," *CapitalEyes* (April 2006).
7. Taken from: www.magnum.com.
8. Ibid.

CHAPTER 25

Capital Structure: Conclusion

Since the ability to access capital directly affects the value of a business, owner-managers need to understand the ramifications of this value-capitalization relationship in the private capital markets. The previous chapters described the fundamental concepts underlying the capitalization of private businesses. This chapter builds on these fundamentals with a discussion of these issues:

- Capital providers use credit boxes and other devices to manage risk and return in their portfolios.
- Expected returns to institutional capital providers comprise the Pepperdine Private Capital Market Line.
- Private cost of capital emanates from the private capital markets.
- High cost of capital limits private company value creation.
- Intermediation is relatively ineffective in the middle market.
- Capitalization is triangulated to valuation and business transfer.

CAPITAL PROVIDERS MANAGE RISK AND RETURN IN THEIR PORTFOLIOS

Capital providers use credit boxes and other devices to manage risk and return in their portfolios. Institutional capital providers use portfolio theory to obtain this goal. Diversifying risk while optimizing return is the promise of portfolio theory. It is built on the premise that the risk inherent in any single asset, when held in a group of assets, is different from the inherent risk of that asset in isolation.

Capital providers employ credit boxes to filter asset quality and set return expectations. In other words, loans or investments that meet the terms of a provider's credit box should promise a risk-adjusted return that meets the needs of the provider. The provider then uses a number of devices to manage the risk and return of its portfolio. Exhibit 25.1 shows the relationship between the credit box and portfolio management.

Capital providers use a number of tools to manage their portfolios. Simple techniques, such as advance rates and loan terms, enable the provider to hedge risk. Providers use other measures to manage risk, such as interest rate matching and hedges, and diversify investments across geography and industries. Loan covenants are the major risk/return management tool for providers. By setting boundaries

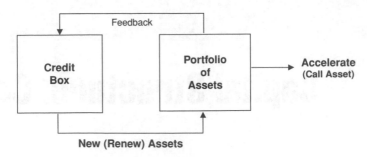

EXHIBIT 25.1   Credit Portfolio Management

around the behavior of a borrower or investee, a capital provider is better able to manage its portfolio. Borrowers who do not comply with covenants may have their loans accelerated. In other words, these borrowers are asked to find another source of capital. Providers monitor their portfolios and feedback information to their credit boxes to adjust the characteristics of new assets that enter the portfolio.

Lenders' and investors' portfolios constitute the limit of their expected returns, and managing this limit creates market fluctuations. Similarly, owners manage a balance sheet with a blend of equity and debt. In other words, owners manage a portfolio of equity and debt to maximize use of capital and manage exposure to risk. It is the day-to-day operation of these portfolios of investments through various market mechanisms that defines the market at any moment in time.

THE PEPPERDINE PRIVATE CAPITAL MARKET LINE COMPRISES EXPECTED RETURNS

The first edition of *Private Capital Markets* relied on anecdotal evidence to support the private capital access line, which graphed various expected returns of institutional capital providers. Describing the market via anecdotal evidence was insufficient, so the author partnered with Pepperdine University to conduct a series of surveys. These Pepperdine Private Capital Markets Surveys began in April 2009 and have continued every six months to the time of this writing. These surveys help overcome a major shortfall in the first edition of this book, which was based mainly on anecdotal evidence.

The Pepperdine survey project is the first comprehensive and simultaneous investigation of the behavior of the major private *capital types*. The surveys specifically examine the behavior of senior lenders, asset-based lenders, mezzanine funds, private equity groups, venture capital, angel investing, and factoring firms. The Pepperdine survey investigates, for each private capital type, the important benchmarks that must be met in order to qualify for capital, how much capital typically is accessible, and what the required returns are for extending capital in the current economic environment. This book incorporates empirical data from the surveys into the discussion wherever possible.

Capital types are segmented into various capital access points (CAPs). The CAPs represent specific alternatives that correspond to *institutional* capital

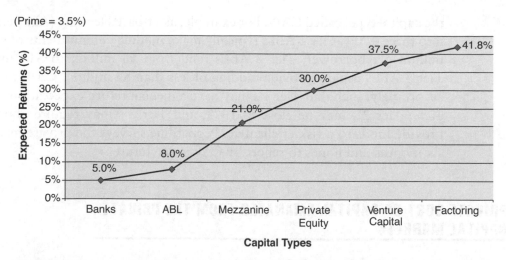

EXHIBIT 25.2 Private Return Expectations Viewed through the PPCML

offerings in the marketplace. For example, asset-based lending is a capital type, and Tier 1 or Tier 3 is an example of CAPs within that type. Exhibit 25.2 shows the capital types with corresponding CAPs that were surveyed, along with one capital type—equipment leasing—and a number of CAPs mentioned in this book that have not been surveyed. Examples of non-surveyed CAPs are government lending programs, such as Small Business Administration 7(a) or 504 loan programs. The author believes these nonsurveyed CAPs are derived mainly from programs that are readily observed in the marketplace.

Accessing private capital entails several steps. First, the *credit box* of the particular CAP is described. Credit boxes depict the criteria necessary to access the specific capital. Next, each CAP defines *sample terms*. These are example terms, such as loan/investment amount, loan maturity, interest rate, and other expenses required to close the loan or investment. Finally, by using the sample terms, an expected rate of return can be calculated. This rate is the expected, or "all-in," rate of return required by an investor. It is not adequate to consider the stated interest rate on a loan. Other factors, such as origination costs, compensating balances, and monitoring fees, add to the cost of the loan. Once all of the capital types are described and their expected returns determined, it is possible to graph the Pepperdine Private Capital Market Line (PPCML), shown in Exhibit 25.2.

The PPCML is stated on a pretax basis, both from a provider and from a user perspective. In other words, capital providers offer deals to the marketplace on a pretax basis. For example, if a private equity investor requires a 25% return, this is stated as a pretax return. Also, the PPCML does not assume a tax rate to the investee, even though many of the capital types use interest rates that generate deductible interest expense for the borrower. Capital types are not tax-effected because many owners of private companies *manage* their company's tax bill through various aggressive techniques. It is virtually impossible to estimate a generalized appropriate tax rate for this market.

The returns shown on the PPCML are median returns of the capital types. There can be substantial variances from the median based on segmentation within the capital type, called CAPs. For example, asset-based lending (ABL) is segmented into three CAPs. Tier 1 ABLs typically make funding commitments of at least $10 million per borrower; Tier 2 ABLs fund from $3 million to $10 million; and Tier 3 ABLs usually provide funding of less than $3 million. CAPs price for risk accordingly, such that Tier 1's may have a median return expectation of less than 10%; Tier 2's may be close to 13%; and Tier 3's may require above 15% to provide funds to a riskier clientele. Pepperdine surveys the private markets every six months and hopes to report by CAP in the future.

PRIVATE COST OF CAPITAL EMANATES FROM THE PRIVATE CAPITAL MARKETS

The temptation to use readily available public information to value private companies is strong. Note that within private capital markets, only academics and business appraisers use the guideline public company method. Other parties in private capital markets—business owners, lenders, investors, estate planners, and so on—rely on valuation methods that are specifically useful to making decisions in their markets.

Why do not parties in private capital markets employ public information in their decision-making process? Because these parties have real money in the markets; valuation is not notional to them. Making proper financing and investment decisions requires using theories and methods that are appropriate to the subject's market.

To help managers and others make better investment and financing decisions, the author created the Private Cost of Capital (PCOC) model, shown next.

$$PCOC = \sum_{i=1}^{N} \left[(CAP_i + SCAP_i) \times \frac{MV_i}{\sum_{j=1}^{N} MV_j} \right]$$

where: N = number of sources of capital
             CAP_i = median expected return for capital type i
         $SCAP_i$ = specific CAP risk adjustment for capital type i
            MV_i = market value of all outstanding securities i

This discount rate is empirically derived and threatens to alter professional, legalistic, compliance business appraisal in five ways. First, adjustments such as lack of marketability discounts and control premiums are not needed. These adjustments were created originally based on the faulty premise that public return expectations could be manipulated to derive private values. Once risk is defined using private return expectations, these public-to-private adjustments are unnecessary.

Second, PCOC provides a risk definition that can be applied across value worlds (standards of value). Each world also has an authority, which is the agent or agents that govern the world. The authority decides whether the intentions of the involved party are acceptable for use in that world and prescribes the methods used in that world. More specifically, "authority" refers to agents or agencies with primary responsibility to develop, adopt, promulgate, and administer standards of practice within that world. Authority decides which purposes are acceptable in its world, sanctions its decisions, develops methodology, and provides a coherent set of rules for participants to follow. Authority derives its influence or legitimacy mainly from government action, compelling logic, and/or the utility of its standards. Authorities from the various value worlds will have an empirically derived method of defining risk. It is hoped that these authorities will prescribe use of PCOC in their respective worlds.

Third, business owners will have the ability to determine their company's cost of capital. This knowledge will help them learn whether they are creating incremental business value (i.e., generating returns on invested capital greater than this cost). This should promote incremental business value creation as a practical and useful tool. Plus it opens an avenue for business valuators to consult with business owners to help them make better investment and financing decisions.

Fourth, the PCOC model will make business appraisal more relevant. Currently, an industry of business appraisers inhabits mainly the notional value worlds. Business owners need more help in competing in a global economy. Tools like the PCOC model will help the appraisal industry become more value-added.

Finally, by employing empirical data from the private capital markets to derive a private discount rate, we can better understand whether management actions are creating company value. The PCOC model enables users to view value in the incremental business value world, which, for the first time, will enable them to make decisions that generate returns on investment greater than their company's cost of capital.

HIGH COST OF CAPITAL LIMITS PRIVATE COMPANY VALUE CREATION

The author believes that most private business owners are not increasing the value of their firms.[1] This is an incredibly strong statement, since it means that the largest part of the American economy is slowly but surely underperforming to the point of going out of business.

Specifically, most business owners are not generating returns on investment greater than their company's cost of capital. Of course, substantial study needs to be done in this important area. But it should not come as a complete surprise that so little value is being created in the private capital markets. Until the recent Pepperdine surveys, no one knew how expensive private cost of capital really is. Also, most business owners do not know why it is important to know their company's cost of capital. These owners use payback or gut feel to make investment decisions, which are the equivalents of Stone Age tools used to build a skyscraper. Certainly we can do better in the twenty-first century.

For this discussion, it is important to distinguish between public and private cost of capital. As Exhibit 25.3 depicts, private cost of capital is more than twice

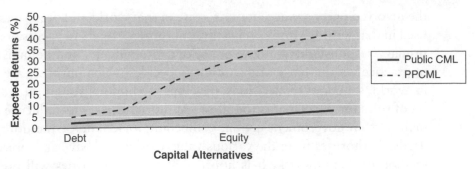

EXHIBIT 25.3 Public Capital Line versus Pepperdine Private Capital Market Line

as costly, on average, as large public companies' capital. In other words, to create incremental business value, private companies must generate returns on investment of more than twice as high as their public counterparts. With no investment decision-making framework to guide them, most business owners are not making maximizing value creation decisions.

Private company managers need to be educated and trained on cost of capital in a way that positively influences their decision making. This is especially important with global competition. Until this training occurs, it is likely that the private capital markets will continue to underperform financially.

INTERMEDIATION IS RELATIVELY INEFFECTIVE IN THE MIDDLE MARKET

Most capital that flows into the middle market is intermediated. This means that professionals, mainly private equity groups, venture capitalists, and mezzanine providers, raise monies from institutions and then invest in middle-market companies, with the hopes of earning a return that is commensurate with the risk of the investment. This investment model has not been effective, as Exhibit 25.4 depicts.

Intermediaries structure their investments in hopes of making an expected return. The expected returns from the most recent Pepperdine survey for several private investor types are listed in the exhibit.[2] It is important to note that these intermediaries issue term sheets and then fund opportunities with the goal of earning, on average, these expected returns (before costs). Venture capitalists earning a 38% return on their investments, for instance, would be considered successful.

EXHIBIT 25.4 Middle-Market Expected versus Realized Returns

Investments	Expected Returns	Realized Returns*		
		5 Year	10 Year	20 Year
Venture capital	38%	4.6%	−1.5%	17.8%
Mezzanine capital	21%	2.7%	2.3%	6.7%
Private equity	30%	5.8%	2.8%	11.3%

*Realized returns are net to investors after management fees and carried interest.

The realized returns from Exhibit 25.4 are taken from a Thomson Reuters study. For decades Thomson Reuters has collected data on actual public and private investment returns. Notice that none of the capital providers is meeting its investment goals over a 5- to 20-year investment horizon.[3] In fact, even if we add back the 5% to 7% for management fees, the realized return is dramatically lower than the expected returns for each provider. What are we to make of this shortfall?

Little research has been done in this area, but the author suggests several possible explanations. First, intermediaries themselves have typically not been educated or trained in private company value creation. More often than not, they have been educated at America's top MBA schools, which have historically not focused their curricula on growing private companies. Most MBA schools spend most of their time preparing students for life in a large public multinational corporation and not for the grind of growing a middle-market company.

Second, the intermediaries that cannot create value must rely on the skills of the owner-manager to do the work. But the vast majority of owner-managers have also not received any education or training on private company value creation and probably do not have a value creation framework on which to rely.

Finally, private cost of capital is so high that only handfuls of companies routinely generate returns on investment sufficient to create value. Therefore, intermediaries use a portfolio approach to value creation, where just a few winners are meant to overcome all of the losing investments. Over the past 20 years, this investment model has not worked, meaning that it has not created value for investors.

The foregoing suggests that the intermediaries that have realized substandard returns will not be able to raise new funds going forward and that a new investment model ultimately will replace the current intermediation construct.

TRIANGULATION

Triadic logic is a compelling logic holding the three conceptual sides of the private capital markets triangle together. It provides a powerful cohesion between the moving parts. An idea that originates on the capitalization leg of the triangle finds its opposite or counterpart in the valuation leg and transfer leg. Another way of looking at triangulation is that each side of the triangle creates a feedback effect, or loop, to the other sides. It is impossible to view capitalization without considering the influence of valuation and transfer. In a practical sense, this balancing act links private capitalization, valuation, and transfer.

The choice of capital structure matters to a private company. It directly influences a company's ability to create shareholder value because the balance sheet sets the minimum threshold for a company's cost of capital. Investments in the business must meet this threshold, or value is destroyed.

Ultimately, owner-managers can increase value by minimizing unsystematic risks. These are the risks that are company specific and cannot be diversified away. Building a functional organization is a good start, but maintaining a "balanced" balance sheet also limits unsystematic risks. In either event, these activities are within the owner-manager's control. Activities as simple as obtaining audited financial statements, paying attention to industry-generated ratios on key balance sheet items, and implementing an economic valuation method all work to reduce unsystematic risks.

Expected investor returns are derived from the capital side of the private capital markets. Owner-managers who ignore their balance sheets for the siren song of the income statement are likely to run underperforming businesses. Many companies run out of cash and go bankrupt because of failure to recognize the importance of the balance sheet. Most companies do not encounter these problems because they exhibit a lack of concern for the income statement. Owners who would not consider overpaying a supplier or overpaying for any other resource in the company frequently do not concern themselves with the effective use of their capital. This oversight makes just about all other business mistakes look inexpensive.

NOTES

1. Rob Slee, "Using the Incremental Business Value Model," *Valuation Strategies* (September 2010), pp. 20–25.
2. John K. Paglia, Pepperdine Private Capital Markets Project Survey Report, April 2010, John K. Paglia, bschool.pepperdine.edu/privatecapital.
3. Thomson Reuters Corporation, www.thomsoneuters.com, August 10, 2010.

Business Transfer

CHAPTER 26

Business Transfer: Introduction

Business transfer includes a spectrum of possibilities, from transferring the assets of a company to transferring partial or enterprise stock interests. Private business transfers take place in private capital markets. Because private markets are less visible than public markets, many observers do not recognize a structure in private markets. Yet a structure exists.

This chapter delineates the unique motives of public managers and private owners as well as the means to convert motives into action. The chapter also introduces the private business ownership transfer spectrum, which demonstrates the range of transfer alternatives available to private owners.

PUBLIC MANAGER AND OWNER MOTIVES

Motives that drive a public manager and private owner to transfer a business interest are unique to each party. Exhibit 26.1 compares public and private transfer motives. Understanding individual motives helps explain the behavior of the players.

The perspective of the players is the biggest difference between transfer motives of public manages and private owners. Public managers have an entity or corporate perspective, whereas private owners have personal transfer motives. Most private owners *sell out* because they are *burned out*. Public companies do not get tired. Private owners cannot easily replace themselves because they are so control-oriented. They also tend to wear so many hats that no one person can replace them. Public companies are organized functionally, so any one executive can be replaced without forcing the need to sell the business. Public companies are designed to last forever. Private companies usually do not outlast the founding owner.

Public entity motives are different from personal owner motives relative to diversification, legacy building, and likely retirement vehicles. Most public managers seek to diversify their businesses because diversification lessens ownership risk, thus increasing job security. As a result, public managers are more likely to diversify their businesses into unfamiliar territory. In contrast, private owners

EXHIBIT 26.1   Comparison of Transfer Motives

Public Managers Want to	Private Owners Want to
Meet entity transfer motives	Meet personal transfer motives
Diversify the business	Diversify their estate
Create a business legacy	Create a family legacy
Use 401(k) as main retirement vehicle	Use transfer of business as main vehicle
Have many shareholders	Have no partners

usually wish to diversify their estates, the majority of which is vested in the value of the businesses. Therefore, private owners are more likely to employ sophisticated estate planning techniques. For example, many private owners want to transfer the business to their children as a family legacy. There is no corresponding motive on the public side. Further, private owners typically forgo some compensation, especially in the early years, in order to reinvest earnings in the business; they are anticipating a major capital event. Public managers, however, look to maximize ordinary income and use 401(k)-type plans to build their retirement nest egg.

Finally, public managers operate in a market that trades small minority interests on a daily basis. A stated goal of most public managers is to increase the number of shareholders in their company. This creates a more fluid market for the stock while giving managers more control over the company since the ownership is spread out. Private owners, in contrast, are not motivated to sell small parts of their business. Private markets provide little support for this activity, and private owners typically do not want partners.

Motives alone do not create a successful transfer. The ability to convert motives into action is required. In other words, a participant needs the means to realize a motive in a market.

Means of Transfer

Having the *means of transfer* implies having the available tools to implement a transfer strategy. Certainly public managers have the means to transfer their businesses. Market makers ensure a liquid trading market. Every public company is only one vote by the board of directors away from selling out. There are scores of public investment bankers ready, willing, and able to assist in the transfer. The transparency of a public company's financial information enables the market to react quickly to a sale. Investment bankers are able to run highly public transfer processes, which add to the likelihood for a successful transfer.

Although the means of transfer is less fluid for private companies, the tools are available to the private owner to achieve the desired transfer result. Without a ready market, a private owner is much more involved in transfer planning and transfer implementation than a public manager. Several groups of transfer players assist the private owner. At the low end of the transaction curve, say, below $2 million, business brokers provide valuation and enterprise transaction support.

For medium-size transactions, mergers and acquisitions (M&A) intermediaries represent sellers and buyers and assist in limited capital-raising activities. For larger transactions, such as those above $10 million, private investment bankers arrange capital structures and provide the spectrum of valuation and transfer services.

A combination of factors has enabled financial engineering to impact the private capital markets. Financial engineering is the use of sophisticated financial methods to provide solutions to complex problems. Many transfer players employ financial engineering to provide a means of transfer to private owners. Estate planners engineer multivariable solutions to help owners minimize estate and other taxes. Many of the internal methods described herein are used for this purpose. Private investment bankers use financial engineering to service clients with diverse needs. For example, engineering a successful recapitalization requires an understanding of transfer processes as well as a command of market valuation and negotiation with private equity groups. Since most middle-market businesses are entangled with their owners' lives, their transfer techniques reflect that. The triangulation of valuation, capitalization, and business transfer proposed in this book enables owners to enjoy more sophisticated means of transfer services.

Business owners have a host of transfer alternatives from which to choose. The alternatives are organized as transfer channels and methods.

PRIVATE BUSINESS OWNERSHIP TRANSFER SPECTRUM

Most owners of private businesses think they have only a few transfer choices. Some intermediaries, and other industry professionals, enforce this limitation because they work in a narrow, specialized area and do not know the full range of options available. Owners and their teams may be advised that selling the entire business is the best solution when, in fact, this might be the least desirable alternative.

Exhibit 26.2 depicts the business ownership transfer spectrum. The macro private transfer options, called *transfer channels*, attract a cluster of specific alternatives, called *transfer methods*. Transfer methods—the actual techniques used to transfer a business interest—are grouped under transfer channels. Transfer channels and transfer methods provide a construct by which the range of business transfer options can be explained. Owners select transfer channels with the optimum potential, based on their motives for selling.

Transfer methods follow a specific set of steps, in a particular order, to achieve a goal. These methods are instruments, or sets of instruments, for accomplishing the objective of transferring a business. The criteria for developing a sound methodology are similar to those found in the world's argument. They include:

- What authority or logical structure holds the method together?
- What standards are prescribed or proscribed?

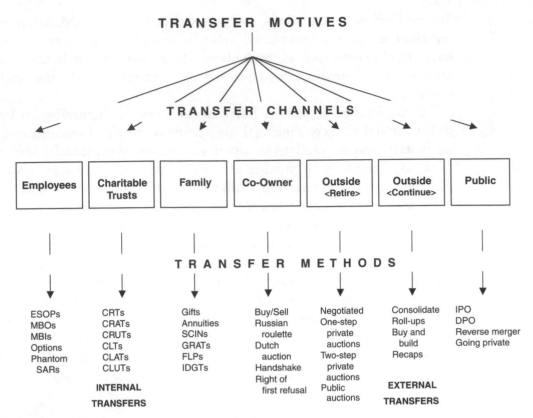

EXHIBIT 26.2   Business Ownership Transfer Spectrum

- What language is used in the method?
- How does choosing a method also determine the results?
- To what extent can the method be combined with other methods?

There is an authority that governs transfer methods and a language and logic that provides structure. The methods may be tax-driven, market-driven, or finance-driven, or a combination of all three. It is frequently possible to combine methods without violating the internal integrity of each, because transfer methods are not necessarily mutually exclusive.

Private business transfer exists within a discrete, niche market that often plays out in an ad hoc fashion. In other words, a menu of transfer alternatives is available for use by an owner. Motives of owners drive this market. Motives range from creating a family legacy to changing the landscape of an industry. A host of transfer players assist owners to meet their goals. The private markets largely provide owners with all of the means of transfer they need to convert motives into action. This rich range of alternatives, and the means to achieve those alternatives, has developed significantly in the past 10 to 15 years.

An owner has seven transfer channels from which to choose. They are:

1. Employees
2. Charitable trusts
3. Family

4. Co-owner
5. Outside, retire
6. Outside, continue
7. Public

The choice of channel is manifested by the owner's motives and goals. For instance, owners wishing ultimately to transfer the business to their children choose the family transfer channel. Owners who desire to go public choose the public transfer channel, and so on.

Each transfer channel contains numerous transfer methods. A transfer method is the actual technique used to transfer a business interest. For example, grantor-retained annuity trusts, family limited partnerships, and recapitalizations are methods by which an interest is transferred. Some methods are aligned exclusively with certain channels, such as an employee stock ownership plan (ESOP) within the employee channel. Other methods can be applied across channels, such as the use of a private annuity with either the family or outside channels.

When a business interest transfers within the company, it is called an *internal transfer*. These are custom-tailored solutions designed to transfer all or part of the business internally, without the uncertainty of finding an outside buyer for the business. Examples of internal transfer methods include management buyouts, charitable remainder trusts, family limited partnerships, and a variety of other estate planning techniques.

External transfers involve transferring business interests to a party outside the company. External transfers employ a process to achieve a successful conclusion. Examples of external transfers include negotiated sales, roll-ups, and reverse mergers. As an illustration, if an owner of a medium-size company wants to sell her business for the highest possible market price, she might employ a private auction process, which should produce the highest possible offers available in the market at that time.

The next chapters describe the business ownership transfer spectrum. Each transfer channel and method is described in detail, and the use of each method is illustrated. There is a discussion of negotiation points for each transfer method.

EMPLOYEE TRANSFER CHANNEL

Many owners of private companies wish to transfer their companies to their employees using the employee transfer channel. Transferring business interests to employees can be accomplished in a number of ways. For example, employees can buy stock directly, be given stock as a bonus, receive stock options, or obtain stock through a profit-sharing plan.

A few key transfer methods in the employee transfer channel are summarized next.

- *Employee stock ownership plan* is a qualified plan under the Employees Retirement Income Security Act of 1974. An ESOP is a defined-contribution, tax-qualified plan that has two distinguishing features: An ESOP is allowed to invest exclusively in the stock of its sponsoring company, and an ESOP can borrow money. A sponsoring corporation can contribute cash or stock to an ESOP on a tax-deductible basis, increasing cash flow. Owners of private companies can sell all or part of their stock to an ESOP at fair market value, often completely avoiding capital gains tax on the transaction.

- *Management buyouts* are acquisitions in which a company's incumbent management participates in the buying group. Because management has intimate knowledge of the company's markets and operations, transition issues generally revolve around pricing and financing of the acquisition. Since most management teams do not have the personal wealth to fund the transfer, they typically depend on an outside equity source, such as a private equity group, to raise the money.

- *Management buy-ins* (MBIs) occur when management teams from outside the target company buy a stake in the company. Normally a private equity group or other financing source backs a key manager or management team who is well known in the particular industry. These incoming managers receive significant ownership and daily operating control. MBIs typically occur when an owner wants to sell but feels that no incumbent manager is suited to own and manage the company. The seller benefits from an MBI because the deal usually is transacted confidentially, quickly, and with a high likelihood of continued success.

CHARITABLE TRUSTS TRANSFER CHANNEL

Charitable trusts enable business owners to transfer their businesses while benefiting from charitable giving. Since the business is the primary asset for most private owners, the disposition of this asset must be maximized. The use of a properly structured charitable trust enables owners to win an estate planning trifecta.

1. The owner transfers all or part of the business while possibly eliminating capital gains on the sale.
2. The owner earns ordinary income for life based on receiving some percentage of the sales proceeds and removes the asset from her estate.
3. The owner's heirs and charity of choice benefit from this technique.

There are two major types of charitable trusts:

1. A *charitable remainder trust* (CRT) is an irrevocable trust designed to convert an investor's appreciated assets into a lifetime income stream without generating estate and capital gains taxes. Basically, an owner of a C corporation gifts some or all of his stock to a CRT. After the gifting, the CRT can

sell the assets or stock of the company to a third party. Since the CRT is a non-taxpaying entity, no capital gains taxes are due from the sale.

When a CRT is established, the beneficiary, who is normally the business owner, receives income from the trust for life or for a term up to 20 years. When the trust ends, the remaining assets pass to the qualified charity or charities of the owner's choice.

2. A *charitable lead trust* (CLT) is the reverse of a charitable remainder trust. A CLT is an irrevocable trust that provides income to a charity for a specified period of time. The income interest to the charity must either be in the form of an annuity interest (CLAT) or a unitrust interest (CLUT). A CLAT is a trust that distributes a certain amount to a charitable beneficiary at least annually for a term of years or during the lives of one or more individuals living when the trust is created. The remainder of the trust is distributed to or held for the benefit of noncharitable beneficiaries. A CLUT is a trust that distributes a fixed percentage of the net fair market value of its assets valued annually. At the conclusion of the payment term, the CLUT trust property is distributed to the remainder, noncharitable beneficiaries, who can be anyone, including the donor. A number of other charitable trust variations are discussed in Chapter 29.

FAMILY TRANSFER CHANNEL

Transferring a business to the succeeding generation is a realization of an American dream. Although perhaps only 10% to 20% of private businesses actually transfer within the family from one generation to the next, this channel comprises thousands of transfers per year. Numerous methods are used to facilitate transfers to family. Probably more than any other transfer channel, family transfers require a long-term perspective on the part of the transferor, usually the parents, and the transferee, normally the children. There are several explanations for this lengthy transfer time span; most notably, the mechanics of several methods require several years to implement. Further, parents may not wish to relinquish control immediately or may choose to transfer control incrementally. Some of the transfer methods in this world are:

- *Gifting* stock interests is the most frequently used method of transferring stock in private companies. As of this writing, every person is entitled to give gifts of $13,000 each year to an unlimited number of donees, without incurring any gift tax. This $13,000 amount is adjusted for inflation in thousand-dollar increments. There is no limit on the number of permissible donees. Thus, if the donee has a large family, a significant amount of wealth can be transferred.
- According to Internal Revenue Service regulations, each person has a "unified credit" that allows up to $5 million worth of assets to be transferred during their lifetime and/or death without incurring gift or estate taxes. The portion

of the unified credit not used during a lifetime could be used at death. Gifts using the unified credit can be made in addition to gifts using the $13,000 annual exclusions.

- A *grantor retained annuity trust* is an irrevocable trust that pays an annuity to the term holder for a fixed time period. The annuity typically is paid to the grantor of the trust until the earlier of the expiration of a term of years or the grantor's death. After the expiration of the grantor's retained annuity interest, the trust assets are held in trust for the beneficiaries or paid outright to the remainder beneficiaries.

- *Family limited partnerships* (FLPs) have become an increasingly popular method for owners of private firms to transfer ownership indirectly to children without losing control of the company. FLPs are a dynamic estate planning tool for four key reasons.

  a. Parents control the distribution of cash flow generated by the partnership.
  b. Nearly all FLPs make it difficult for the children to sell the partnership interest.
  c. Using a partnership entity provides a high degree of protection from creditors. Creditors cannot get to the assets of the FLP or cause distributions to be made to the children.
  d. A gift of an ownership interest in an FLP may be made at a lower value than the interest's pro rata share of net asset value because the FLP interest is likely to be noncontrolling and nonmarketable. Thus, discounts for minority ownership and lack of marketability may be applied.

Other transfer methods described in the family channel include self-canceling installment notes, private annuities, and intentionally defective grantor trusts.

CO-OWNER TRANSFER CHANNEL

It is often necessary to buy out a partner. The co-owner transfers channel describes transfer methods available to purchase other shareholders' equal or unequal interests. Without a written ownership agreement signed by both parties prior to the point of need, a minority interest holder is at the mercy of the controlling shareholder. Further, 50/50 partners without a buy/sell agreement do not have the tools to settle serious disputes. The co-owner transfer channel includes buy/sell agreements, the right of first refusal provision, and other techniques available to transfer shareholder interests to partners. Chapter 31 focuses on several buy/sell provisions, such as Russian roulette and Dutch auction.

OUTSIDE, RETIRE, TRANSFER CHANNEL

Many owner-managers of private companies desire a lifestyle change and want to transfer their business to an outsider and retire. Although the ultimate transfer occurs to an outside investor, some of the transfer methods described in earlier sections can be incorporated into the sale. For example, it is possible to use charitable trusts, private annuities, or grantor-retained annuity trusts as vehicles for the transfer to an outside buyer.

The circumstances and needs of the owner lead to the selection of an appropriate marketing process for the business. The three broad marketing processes are negotiated sale, private auction, and public auction. A *negotiated* selling process is warranted when only one prospect is identified and the entire process is focused on that prospect. A *private auction* process is used when a handful of prospects are identified. A *public auction* process is appropriate when it makes sense to announce the opportunity to the market. The three marketing processes, as well as the players who assist in the transfer industry, are described at length in Chapter 32.

OUTSIDE, CONTINUE, TRANSFER CHANNEL

Some owner-managers of private companies wish to transfer all or part of their business to an outsider but continue operating the business with a financial interest in the business going forward. This condition exists for owners who need growth capital but do not want to bet their personal net worth in the process. To meet these goals, owners have two main choices.

1. They can transfer their business to an outside entity that is consolidating similar companies in their industry. When the consolidation occurs simultaneously with an initial public offering (IPO), the transfer is called a *roll-up*.
2. When owners transfer a business interest to a company controlled by a private equity group to fund aggressive growth, these transfers are called *recapitalizations*.

An equity sponsor that builds the company through acquisitions drives a *buy and build* consolidation. The consolidated company may remain private or go public later. A private seller may or may not have a continuing ownership position in a buy and build consolidation. Chapter 33 illustrates many points for an owner to consider before they take this important step.

GOING PUBLIC, GOING PRIVATE TRANSFER CHANNEL

Going public is the process of offering securities, generally common or preferred stock, of a private company for sale to the general public. The first time these securities are offered is referred to as an *initial public offering*. Some companies become public by merging with an existing public company. These deals, called *reverse mergers*, enable a private company to go public more quickly and less expensively than a traditional IPO. Less than 1% of the companies in the United States are publicly held. Yet going public remains the holy grail for a large percentage of private business owners. Chapter 34 describes the processes for going public and going private as well as points to consider before taking the first step.

The goal of this part of this book is to alert private business owners and their professionals to the large number of transfer options that actually exist. Motives of the owner usually lead to the choice of a transfer channel, and each channel comprises numerous transfer methods. The methods enable an owner to convert motives into actions. Because of the technical nature of business transfer, this part is written to give interested players an overview of the structure of various alternatives. Once a road map is conceived, an owner should engage experts in the particular area to tailor a solution to the need.

EXIT PLANNING

The first edition of this book helped launch a new industry called *exit planning*. Exit planning uses the linkage established in this book:

- Transfer motives or intentions of a business owner lead to a value world.
- Business owners have multiple transfer alternatives from which to choose.
- Specific transfer methods are connected to specific value worlds.
- Therefore, owner motives choose a range of values.

Thus, depending on their transfer motives, business owners actually choose the range of values within which their businesses will transfer. For example, owners motivated to transfer the business to employees via an ESOP receive a fair market valuation, or value determined through application of the hypothetical "willing buyer and seller rule"; those motivated to transfer via a management buyout are more likely to receive an investment valuation, or value that is specific to a particular investor. As is described in Chapter 2, an owner's motive for transferring part or all of the business determines the process by which the business interest is valued. Accordingly, a wide variety of transfer motives leads to a correspondingly large range of possible values for a business.

This discussion assumes that the business is large enough to access a number of transfer alternatives. Many personal service companies, such as a one-person marketing or medical practice, may not have many transfer options. However, a midsize advertising or medical firm may possess numerous transfer alternatives. Thus, financial planners should first assess if the client business has the characteristics necessary to qualify for a variety of transfers. This decision requires substantial experience and may necessitate conversations with other planners, business brokers, or investment bankers.

For exit planning to be effective, planners must be able to help clients identify their financial goals, develop strategies that will promote the realization of those goals, and ultimately execute tactics to achieve the goals. Understanding the linkage between transfer motives and business values empowers planners to help clients develop and execute their financial plans. This knowledge also enables planners to leverage existing skills, which creates value for the client and the planner.

TRIANGULATION

The ability to transfer a business interest is conditioned by the business's access to capital and the value world in which the transfer occurs. The transfer method determines the available choices of capital and often the corresponding value world. Exhibit 26.3 graphically depicts transfer triangulation.

The choice of transfer method may dictate or limit available capital types. For example, ESOPs typically employ bank debt whereas IPOs are linked to equity. Even if the transfer method does not correlate to a capital type directly, the transfer decision often determines the available choices of capital. A management buyout, for instance, qualifies for secured lending as well as mezzanine and private equity group capital. Many family transfers, meanwhile, are implemented without using any outside capital sources. The size of the transaction dictates if it qualifies for many of the government lending programs.

The choice of transfer method affects business value. Regulated transfer methods lead to regulated value worlds; unregulated transfer methods lead to unregulated value worlds. For instance, choosing an ESOP or estate planning technique, such as a charitable remainder trust, puts the seller in the world of fair market value. In contrast, choosing an auction or going public corresponds to market value.

Planning enhances the options available to owners to choose various transfer methods. In fact, the longer an owner plans, the more transfer options become

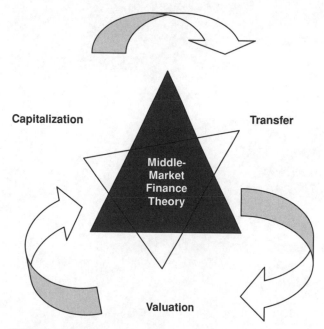

EXHIBIT 26.3 Triangulation

available. Some methods take years to implement. For example, preparing a qualified company to go public may take five years or more. Simpler methods, such as ESOPs, charitable trusts, or private auctions, may take more than a year to execute. However, owners who fail to plan usually have very few transfer options. One elderly owner of a chemical company had for many years intended to form his exit plan. Ultimately his health failed, causing him to spend months in the hospital. The only transfer option available was a low-ball bid to buy the company from a not-so-friendly competitor.

CHAPTER 27

Employee Stock Ownership Plans

Many owners of private companies desire partial shareholder liquidity without having to lose control of the business. These owners may also want to transfer beneficial ownership of their companies to their employees. This can be accomplished in numerous ways. Employees can buy stock directly, be given stock as a bonus, receive stock options, or obtain stock through a profit-sharing plan. A common form of employee ownership in the United States is the employee stock ownership plan (ESOP). The ESOP is popular because it can accomplish the transfer objective in a much more tax-efficient manner than the other methods. More than 11,000 companies now have these plans, covering more than 13 million employees. This chapter describes ESOPs in general, illustrates the issues surrounding ESOP implementation, and concludes with a discussion of points to consider regarding an ESOP creation.

The ESOP is at once a corporate finance tool and a qualified retirement benefit for employees; it is also a means of redistributing industrial wealth to workers in an effort to stimulate economic growth. Because of this, ESOPs have enjoyed continued support from both aisles of Congress since their creation several decades ago.

The modern-day ESOP parallels the theory first put forth by a prominent German economist, Johann Von Thunen, during the early days of the Industrial Revolution. Von Thunen put an ESOP of sorts into being when he set aside a share of his farm's profits for his employees. He invested the profits in machinery that would enhance earnings. A portion of the profits was then put in each worker's name. Earnings that were invested in other than capital equipment spun off interest, which was allocated and distributed to the employees as a second income. The principal itself expanded and was distributed to the employee at retirement.

Given the significant tax breaks afforded capital owners, the amplified retirement benefit afforded employees, and the resultant enhanced governance requirements, ESOPs are highly regulated by various government agencies. The Internal Revenue Service (IRS) enforces the tax issues surrounding ESOPs. The U.S. Department of Labor enforces many provisions of the Employee Retirement Income Security Act of 1974 (ERISA). ERISA established the ESOP as a type of tax-qualified retirement plan and continues to be the primary law overseeing its usage. Other governmental agencies, such as the Securities and Exchange

Commission (SEC) and Financial Industry Regulatory Authority (FINRA), may be involved, especially with regard to ESOPs in regulated industries.

Companies and their owners can use ESOPs for a variety of purposes. Structured properly, with an ESOP, the owner of a privately held company can:

- Sell stock of the company, pay no tax on the proceeds, and still keep control.
- Increase the company's working capital and cash flow with no cash expenditure and no productive effort.
- Buy out minority and majority stockholders with pretax dollars.
- Make acquisitions with pretax dollars that are tax free to the seller.
- Cut the cost of borrowing loan principal nearly in half by deducting principal payments as well as interest.
- Provide employees equity upside with no cash outlay on their part or the owner's part.
- Create the ESOP and achieve these objectives without the approval of employees.

Although ESOPs are used by public companies, this use accounts for less than 15% of all ESOPs. ESOPs are used most commonly to provide a market for the shares of departing owners of successful private companies, motivate employees, and take advantage of incentives to borrow money for acquiring new assets with pretax dollars. In almost every case, ESOPs provide beneficial stock ownership through *contributions* to the employee, *not* an employee purchase. Exhibit 27.1 shows the transfer matrix for ESOPs.

OVERVIEW

Technically, ESOPs are tax-qualified, defined contribution plans that are stock bonus plans or a combination of a stock bonus plan and a money purchase plan designed to invest primarily in the employer securities. Unlike other plans, they may borrow money to do so.

In an ESOP transaction, a corporation sets up a trust fund, called an employee stock ownership trust (ESOT), into which it contributes new shares of its own stock or cash to buy existing shares. Alternatively, the ESOP can borrow money to buy new or existing shares, with the company making cash contributions to the plan to enable it to repay the loan. Regardless of how the plan acquires stock, company contributions to the trust are tax-deductible and cannot exceed 25% of annual qualified payroll expenses.

ESOPs are tax-exempt entities for federal and state corporate income tax purposes. This enables the company to make cash and/or company stock contributions to the ESOT, which are then used to acquire stock of the company or other business assets on behalf of its employees. Through an ESOP, employees can be given beneficial ownership of employer stock without paying current income tax on the stock or typically ever actually owning the stock in the classic sense. This results because the contribution is made entirely by the company and is not

EXHIBIT 27.1   Transfer Matrix: Employee Stock Ownership Plans

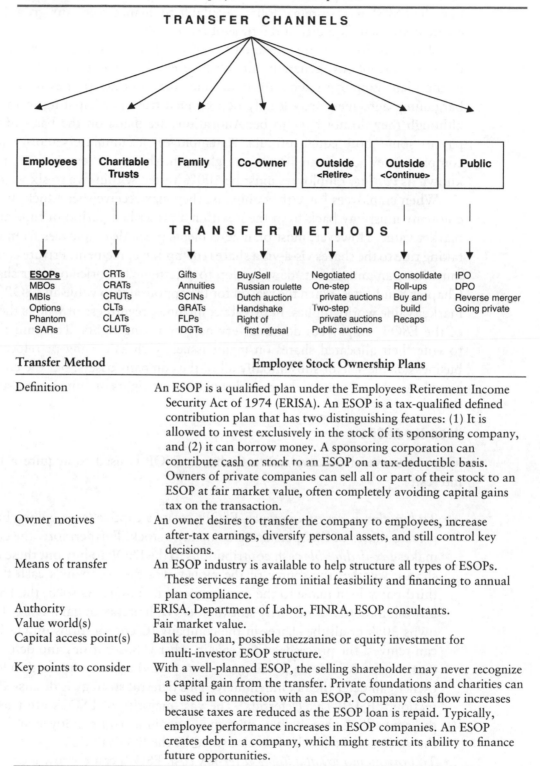

Transfer Method	Employee Stock Ownership Plans
Definition	An ESOP is a qualified plan under the Employees Retirement Income Security Act of 1974 (ERISA). An ESOP is a tax-qualified defined contribution plan that has two distinguishing features: (1) It is allowed to invest exclusively in the stock of its sponsoring company, and (2) it can borrow money. A sponsoring corporation can contribute cash or stock to an ESOP on a tax-deductible basis. Owners of private companies can sell all or part of their stock to an ESOP at fair market value, often completely avoiding capital gains tax on the transaction.
Owner motives	An owner desires to transfer the company to employees, increase after-tax earnings, diversify personal assets, and still control key decisions.
Means of transfer	An ESOP industry is available to help structure all types of ESOPs. These services range from initial feasibility and financing to annual plan compliance.
Authority	ERISA, Department of Labor, FINRA, ESOP consultants.
Value world(s)	Fair market value.
Capital access point(s)	Bank term loan, possible mezzanine or equity investment for multi-investor ESOP structure.
Key points to consider	With a well-planned ESOP, the selling shareholder may never recognize a capital gain from the transfer. Private foundations and charities can be used in connection with an ESOP. Company cash flow increases because taxes are reduced as the ESOP loan is repaid. Typically, employee performance increases in ESOP companies. An ESOP creates debt in a company, which might restrict its ability to finance future opportunities.

taxed to employees personally as it is allocated. The advantage to the company is that the ESOP makes pretax dollars available to finance company growth and/or create ownership liquidity at the time of retirement.

Shares in the trust are allocated to individual employee accounts. Although there are exceptions, generally all full-time employees over age 21 participate in the plan. Employees who are union members and are parties to a collective bargaining agreement may legally be excluded from participating in the ESOP, although they do not have to be. Allocations are made on the basis of relative pay or some more equal formula. As employees accumulate seniority with the company, they acquire an increasing right to the shares in their account, a process known as *vesting*. Employees must be 100% vested within five to six years.

When employees leave the company, they may receive their stock, which the company must buy back from them within a prescribed period of time at its fair market value. However, most plan agreements preclude employees from actually taking title to the shares vis-à-vis a share redemption agreement. Private companies must have an annual outside valuation to determine the price of their shares. As Chapter 8 indicates, when the reason for the appraisal is to value an ESOP, the fair market value world applies. In private companies, regardless of who is the trustee of the ESOT, employees do have very narrow voting rights. They must be able to vote their allocated shares on major issues, such as closing or relocating the business or the sale of substantially all of the company assets, but the company's board can choose whether to pass through voting rights on any other issues.

Uses for ESOPs

There are several primary reasons why an ESOP is used to acquire a business interest:

- *To buy the shares of an owner.* ESOPs create a captive, ever-willing buyer for private shares of the sponsoring company's stock. Furthermore, the company makes *tax-deductible* cash contributions to the ESOP to buy out these owner's shares, whether the source of the money was the company's cash flow or a third-party loan made to the company and its ESOP. As such, the ESOP can buy out minority or majority stockholders with pretax dollars. Once the ESOP owns 30% of all the shares in the company (C corporations only), the seller can reinvest the proceeds of the sale in other U.S. securities and defer any tax on the gain. By using a floating rate note (FRN) and a monetization loan, the owner can defer the tax indefinitely. This deferral strategy is discussed in next section, "ESOP Tax Deferral." The vast majority of ESOTs are trusteed by the controlling shareholder, who may remain a paid employee and controls the voting of the block of stock owned by the ESOP/ESOT.
- *To borrow money at a lower after-tax cost.* ESOPs can borrow money, which makes them unique among benefit plans. After the ESOP borrows money to purchase company shares, the company then makes tax-deductible contributions to the ESOP to repay the loan, meaning both principal and interest are deductible, within certain limits. For example, for each $1 million of

qualifying credit, the company can save approximately $700,000 (assuming a 30% tax rate). Deducting principal enables a company to effectively borrow much less expensively than conventional borrowing.

- *Acquire other companies with pretax dollars that are tax-free to sellers.* If the acquisition target (seller) sells her company's stock to the ESOP of the buyer, rather than directly to the buyer, and the target company would otherwise qualify for the ESOP tax deferral, then the target may legally elect the ESOP tax deferral. As the money used to acquire the target's shares was the ESOP money, the acquisition was done with substantially less (pretax) dollars, as well.

- *To create an additional employee benefit.* The stock in the ESOP provides employees equity upside (and downside) with no cash outlay on their part or on the part of the seller or provider of those shares. The shares in the ESOP do not have to have come from an owner selling the shares. The company can also issue new or treasury shares to an ESOP, deducting their value up to 25% of covered payroll expense from the company's taxable income. Or a company can contribute cash, buying shares from existing owners.

- *Increase working capital and cash flow.* For many companies, 25% of their annual payroll expense is equivalent to all or most of the company's taxable income. Thus, these tax-deductible contributions create a tax shield on the company's earnings, which increase the cash flow and therefore the working capital of the business by the amount that would of otherwise be paid in taxes. If the tax-deductible ESOP contributions were made in newly issued employer stock rather than cash, then these increases in assets and cash flow were made without a cash or productive expenditure. However, this would create dilution to existing shareholders.

ESOP Tax Deferral

Most owners are drawn to an ESOP initially because of the promise of deferring taxes on the sale. This deferral often represents a substantial tax savings. For example, a shareholder who owns stock worth $10, million, with a basis of $1 million, will pay almost $2 million in federal and state income taxes on a typical sale, assuming a combined federal and state tax rate of approximately 20% ($10 million – $1 million × 20%). In contrast, by selling stock to an ESOP, the shareholder will pay no federal income taxes and possibly no state income taxes on the sale. The selling shareholder will net $10 million on the sale, a tax deferral of $2 million. However, this ESOP tax deferral is available *only* if the next requirements are satisfied pursuant to Section 1042 of the Internal Revenue Code:[1]

- The selling shareholder must be an individual, a trust, an estate, a partnership, or a subchapter S corporation and must have owned the stock sold to the ESOP for at least three years.

- The selling shareholder must not have received the stock from a qualified retirement plan (e.g., an ESOP or stock bonus plan), by exercising a stock option, or through an employee stock purchase program.

- The company establishing the ESOP is a C corporation (not an S corporation).

- The sale must otherwise qualify for capital gains treatment but for the sale to the ESOP.
- The stock sold to the ESOP must (in general) be voting common stock or preferred stock that is convertible into voting common stock.
- For the 12 months preceding the sale to the ESOP, the company that establishes the ESOP must have had no class of stock that was readily tradable on an established securities market.
- After the sale, the ESOP must own at least 30% of the company that establishes the ESOP (on a fully diluted basis). The company also must consent to the election of 1042 tax-deferred treatment, and a 10% excise tax is imposed on the company for certain dispositions of stock by the ESOP within three years after the sale. There is also a 50% excise tax imposed on the company should there be a prohibited allocation of the stock purchased by the ESOP where the seller deferred the gain.
- Within a 15-month period beginning 3 months before the sale to the ESOP and ending 12 months after the sale, the selling shareholder must reinvest the sale proceeds in qualified replacement property (QRP), which are replacement securities (common or preferred stock, bonds, and/or debt instruments) issued by publicly traded or closely held domestic corporations that use more than 50% of their assets in an active trade or business and whose passive investment income for the preceding year did not exceed 25% of their gross receipts. Municipal bonds are ineligible reinvestment vehicles, as are certificates of deposit issued by banks or savings and loans, mutual funds, and securities issued by the U.S. Treasury. As of this writing, a bill is pending before Congress that would allow many of these ineligible securities to qualify under 1042.

Stock purchased by the ESOP may not be allocated to the seller, certain members of his or her family, or any shareholder in the company that establishes the ESOP who owns more than 25% of any class of company stock.

Careful reinvestment planning for the ESOP sale proceeds is extremely important. As the next section discusses, proper planning enables an owner to defer capital gains permanently. In the event of the selling owner's death after the ESOP sale, the heirs will receive a stepped-up basis on the replacement securities. In other words, taxation on the sale of the business is avoided forever.

Qualifying Replacement Property

To qualify for the capital gains tax deferral described previously, sellers must reinvest the proceeds into QRP within 12 months after the sale. The seller pays capital gains when the QRP ultimately is sold. This effectively creates a static buy-and-hold portfolio limitation on a seller. However, the QRP can be in the form of an FRN, which is a long-term note issued by certain AA and AAA companies. By using this technique, the seller can actively trade a portfolio of securities and defer capital gains permanently. Trading is possible because these notes can be margined up to 90%, which provides collateral for a loan to generate liquidity.

This method allows for some interesting strategies. For example, suppose Joe Mainstreet sells 30% of PrivateCo's stock to an ESOP for $2 million, the fair market value of the shares. The ESOP borrows $500,000 from a bank, and Joe takes back a note for $1.5 million. Joe then arranges a bridge loan for $1.5 million, buys a $2 million FRN, and simultaneously margins the note at 90%, or $1.8 million, which is used to repay the bridge lender.

As the company earns profits, it makes tax-deductible contributions to the ESOP for the repayment of principal and interest, which the ESOP then pays to the seller. The principal repayment is tax-free. The interest part is taxable to the seller, but receiving interest is generally not as bad as paying it.

The FRN pays a London Interbank Offering Rate (LIBOR) plus rate of interest to the owner, who pays a slightly higher rate on the borrowed funds. Since Joe borrows 90% and receives interest on 100%, this may result in nearly a "wash" cost. Joe can have an actively traded portfolio for the 90% value of the stocks sold without being taxed down to the original basis every time he sells a security.

LEVERAGED ESOPs

The most sophisticated use of an ESOP involves borrowed money and is called a *leveraged* ESOP. Exhibit 27.2 shows the leveraged ESOP transaction flow. In this approach, the company sets up an ESOT, which then borrows money from a lender. The company repays the loan by making tax-deductible contributions to the trust, which the trust pays to the lender. The loan must be used by the trust to acquire stock in the company. The stock is put into a *suspense* account, where it is released to employee accounts as the loan is repaid. After vested employees leave the company or retire, the company distributes to them the stock purchased on their behalf or its cash value. In practice, banks often require a second step in the loan transaction where the bank makes the loan to the company instead of the trust, with the company reloaning the proceeds to the ESOP.

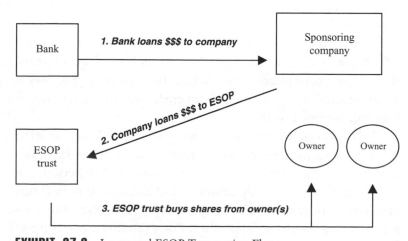

EXHIBIT 27.2　Leveraged ESOP Transaction Flow

In return for borrowing through the ESOP, the company gets two tax benefits, provided it follows the rules to ensure that employees are treated fairly.

1. The company can deduct the entire loan contribution it makes to the ESOP, within certain payroll-based limits described later. The company, in effect, can deduct interest *and* principal on the loan.
2. The company can deduct dividends paid on the shares acquired with the proceeds of the loan that are used to repay the loan itself. In other words, the earnings of the stock being acquired help pay for the stock itself.

The ESOP can also be funded directly by corporate contributions or cash to buy existing shares, or it simply may be funded by the contribution of shares. These contributions are tax deductible, generally up to 25% of the total eligible payroll of plan participants. For example, if a company has total eligible payroll of $5 million per year, the maximum annual amount that it can deduct is $1.25 million.

It is not a requirement to use an outside lender. If, for example, the company has accumulated funds under a profit-sharing plan, these funds may be rolled over into an ESOP and used to purchase company stock. Of course, this must be done carefully to ensure fiduciary compliance. In addition, the company or the seller may itself be the lender. By using one or more of these sources of internal cash, the company may be able to reduce or eliminate the necessity of borrowing from an outside lender.

How ESOP Shares Vest with Employees

Vesting rules can be fairly complicated, so readers are encouraged to review these rules before implementing an ESOP. In general, all employees over age 21 who work for more than 1,000 hours in a plan year must be included in the plan. If there is a union, the company must bargain in good faith with it over inclusion in the plan.[2]

Shares are allocated to individual employee accounts based on relative compensation. Generally, all W-2 compensation is counted. The allocated shares are subject to vesting. Employees must be 100% vested after five years of service, or the company can use a graduated vesting schedule not slower than 20% after two years and 20% per year more until 100% is reached after six years.

When participants who have participated in the plan for 10 years reach age 55, they may elect to diversify 25% of their stock account balance among at least three investment alternatives. When they reach age 60, they may elect to diversify an additional 25% of their plan benefit. As an alternative, the plan may pay the requisite amount to the employees.

Private companies must repurchase shares from departing employees at fair market value, as determined annually by an independent appraiser. The employee can exercise this put option in one of two 60-day periods, one starting when the employee receives the distribution, and the second period one year after that. The employee can choose which one to use. Quite often the company's bylaws carry a restriction on share ownership. For example, ownership may be limited to the ESOP and current employees, which may require the company to purchase the shares distributed immediately.

Repurchase Considerations

The legal obligation to repurchase shares of departing employees rests with the company, although the ESOP itself ultimately may purchase shares if required.

The repurchase obligation creates a continual need to plan for the repurchase of shares. Repurchase can be a major problem if companies do not anticipate and plan for it. A detailed repurchase study should be done periodically to help manage this process. The plan's third-party administrator may be able to provide these services as it has virtually all of the information necessary to conduct this study.

ESOPs IN S CORPORATIONS

Originally, ESOPs could own stock only in C corporations. Beginning in 1998, ESOPs could own stock in subchapter S corporations. While these ESOPs operate under many of the same rules as in a C corporation, there are two important differences.

1. Interest payments on ESOP loans count toward the contribution limits. They normally do not in C companies. Further, dividends paid on ESOP shares are also not deductible. Obviously, these two limitations dramatically affect the company's cash flow.
2. Most important, sellers to an ESOP in an S corporation do not qualify for the tax-deferred rollover treatment. To overcome this issue, many companies implement the ESOP as a C corporation and then convert the company to S corporation status once the statutory waiting period has been satisfied. The conversion generally is made in a subsequent fiscal year to avoid any challenge under the step transaction doctrine.

There are benefits, however, with S corporation ESOPs. The S corporation ESOP does not have to pay federal income tax on any profits attributable to it and may not have to pay state taxes. Thus, in the case of an S corporation that is 100% owned by its ESOP, the company's earnings are entirely tax exempt.

SETTING UP AN ESOP

There are several steps in implementing an ESOP. At each point, the decision maker can decide whether to stop or continue.[3]

Step 1. *Determine whether other owners are agreeable.* Many owners do not plan for the eventual sale of the business and, in co-ownership situations, do not wish to discuss a sale. There may be other owners of a private firm who will never agree to an ESOP, even if it seems appealing to the principal owners. ESOPs offer owner control and confidentiality, which should entice investors to at least consider it. Obtaining a consensus of the ownership upfront will make the process more meaningful.

Step 2. *Conduct a feasibility study.* This can range from a full-blown analysis by an outside consultant with detailed financial projections and management interviews to a business plan performed in-house. Historically, complete feasibility studies were needed only where there was some doubt about the ESOP's ability to repay the loan. Today, however, because of the baby boomer retirement wave that began in 2010, complete feasibility studies are recommended in nearly all cases as this demographical phenomenon creates a more material repurchase obligation to be modeled and understood. Any analysis, however, must look at three items.

    a. It must assess whether the ESOP will have adequate cash flow to repay the loan.

    b. It must determine if the company has adequate payroll for ESOP participants to make the ESOP contributions deductible.

    c. Estimates must be made regarding the repurchase liability and the position the company should be in to manage it, as noted.

Step 3. *Get a valuation.* The feasibility study will rely on a rough, informal valuation estimate to determine the adequacy of cash and payroll. The next step requires a formal valuation. A company may want to have a preliminary valuation done first to see if the range of values produced is acceptable, followed by a full valuation if it is acceptable. Getting a valuation is critical, since if the value is too low, sellers may not be willing to sell. If the price of the shares is too high, the company may not be able to afford it.

Step 4. *Engage an ESOP attorney.* If these first three steps are positive, the plan can be drafted and submitted to the IRS. Only experienced ESOP attorneys should be engaged. The IRS may take many months to issue a letter of determination on the plan, but the company can go ahead and start making contributions before then. If the IRS rules unfavorably, which rarely happens, normally the company can amend the plan.

Step 5. *Fund the plan.* There are several potential sources of funding, with the most likely source being a bank. ESOP lending is a specialty, so finding the right banker is important. Existing benefit plans are a second source of funding. Pension plans are not a practical source of funding, but profit-sharing plans sometimes are used. Profit-sharing assets are simply transferred in part or in whole to an ESOP. This must be done carefully because some employees may feel as if they lost a benefit. Finally, companies can make contributions outside of loan payments. A handful of licensed investment bankers in the United States focus on ESOP transactions and can be very helpful throughout all steps of this process, especially in arranging the debt to finance the transaction. As the ESOP transaction is considered a sale of stock by the SEC, it is imperative that the ESOP consultant be licensed and regulated by the SEC and FINRA to avoid governance liabilities.

It is relatively easy to determine if a company qualifies for an ESOP, as shown by the following:

DETERMINING ESOP FEASIBILITY

Several factors are involved in determining if a company is a good ESOP candidate.

- *Is the cost reasonable?* Setup costs for ESOPs typically run a minimum of $20,000 and up, depending on complexity and the size of the transaction. ESOPs tend to be more expensive to establish and maintain than other benefit plans. However, these costs generally are more than offset by the tax savings afforded both the company and its owners by establishing and maintaining the ESOP.

- *Is the payroll large enough?* Limitations on how much can be contributed to a plan may make it impractical to use to buy out a major owner or finance a large transaction. For instance, a $10 million purchase would not be feasible if the company has $800,000 of eligible payroll because annual contributions could be no larger than $200,000 (25%) per year, not enough to repay a loan for that amount.

- *Can the company afford the contributions?* Many ESOPs are used to buy existing shares, a practice that uses the company's capital in a nonproductive way. To afford the contributions, some owners may be required to forgo certain discretionary expenses, which may negatively affect their lifestyles.

- *Is management comfortable with the idea of employees as owners?* Private owners are typically partner-averse. The thought of employees as partners is a deal-killer issue for many owners.

Source: The National Center for Employee Ownership Web site, www.nceo.org.

Step 6. *Establish a process to operate the plan.* A trustee is chosen to oversee the plan. The trustee is often the president of the company. An ESOP committee directs the trustee. The critical step is getting employees involved in the process. Successful ESOPs involve the employees as owners from the beginning.

The following example describes an ESOP implementation.

EXAMPLE

Joe Mainstreet has decided to implement a 30% leveraged ESOP. A feasibility study indicates an ESOP can be successful. The fair market value of PrivateCo's equity is $9.2 million, as determined in Chapter 7. This figure is then adjusted to reflect a lack of control and possible lack of marketability.

Since the ESOP will own 30% of the outstanding stock of PrivateCo, a minority interest discount is warranted. ESOP company shares have better marketability than non-ESOP firms, however, because the ESOP provides a market, albeit not as active as a stock exchange. For this example, a combined 20% minority interest discount and lack of marketability discount is employed. Although simplified here, this valuation problem is not easy to solve in real life. Readers are encouraged to seek a fuller treatment of this issue if faced with this problem. Thus, for this illustration, the ESOP is valued at $2.2 million, rounded ($9.2 million × 30% interest × 20% discount).

Impact on the Owner

If Joe Mainstreet follows the ESOP rules, he will defer federal and state capital gains taxes on the 30% sale to the ESOP. Assuming his basis in the PrivateCo stock is $100,000 and the federal and state combined capital gains rate is 20%, this deferral is determined as shown.

Mainstreet 30% ESOP sale	$2,200,000
Basis in stock	100,000
Gain on sale	$2,100,000
Federal and state capital gains rate	20%
Deferred capital gain	$420,000

With proper planning, Joe Mainstreet can defer this $420,000 gain forever.

Impact on PrivateCo's Earnings

Joe learns that leveraged ESOPs borrow funds to purchase stock using a guarantee or other extension of credit from the company or the selling shareholder. The ESOP indebtedness is repaid via annual company contributions to the ESOP. A leveraged ESOP creates a tax shield that ultimately enhances the value of the equity of the company. The next table shows this economic benefit of a leveraged ESOP.

Benefits of a Leveraged ESOP

Assume:
1. PrivateCo is in a tax-paying position posttransaction.
2. PrivateCo borrows $2.2 million to fund the ESOP.
3. The loan is for seven years and bears an interest rate of 8%.
4. Annual ESOP contributions are $423,000.
5. The corporate tax rate is 30%.
6. The discount rate for present value calculations is 25%.

Tax Savings on ESOP Year	Contribution*	Present Value at 25%
2	126,900	81,216
3	126,900	64,973
4	126,900	51,978
5	126,900	41,583
6	126,900	33,266
7	126,900	26,613
Total	$928,200	$401,149

*$423,000 contribution times 30% tax rate.

Value of PrivateCo Equity

Pretransaction equity value	$9,200,000
Plus present value of ESOP benefit	401,000 (rounded)
Post-transaction equity value	$9,601,000

The tax savings associated with the ESOP contribution create a tax shield worth $401,000 on a present value basis. This tax savings increases the value of PrivateCo's equity.

Impact on PrivateCo's Balance Sheet

The ESOP loan is a liability of the company with an offsetting entry reflected as a contra-equity account. The accounting treatment for a leveraged ESOP may result in a company reporting a negative book value. The next table shows PrivateCo's summarized balance sheet before and after the ESOP.

PrivateCo Balance Sheet before and after ESOP		
	Before ESOP	**After ESOP**
Total assets	$2,568,350	$2,568,350
Current liabilities	$1,042,876	$1,042,876
Long-term debt		
Term loan	501,250	501,250
ESOP loan	0	2,200,000
Total liabilities	1,544,126	3,744,126
Equity	1,024,224	(1,175,776)
Total liabilities and equity	$2,568,350	$2,568,350

If PrivateCo adds $2.2 million in ESOP-related debt, it reports a negative book value of about $(1.2) million. A negative book value may have repercussions to the company relative to various financing relationships. PrivateCo should have its financial advisors involved with this situation to ascertain the impact of the ESOP debt on the balance sheet. Commercial banks that have been educated on the positive credit implications of an ESOP or are already experienced ESOP lenders are comfortable with the temporary negative book value issue.

POINTS TO CONSIDER

There are a number of points to consider for companies contemplating an ESOP. These points are broken into good points and not-so-good points.

Good Points to Consider

The next attributes make ESOPs highly desirable structures.[4]

- *Beneficial to typical sale.* Purchase of an owner's stock by an ESOP usually will be more financially beneficial to the owner than a sale or merger. This is especially true when banks are lending at low multiples of earnings before interest, taxes, depreciation, and amortization (EBITDA) or merger and acquisition transactions and the taxable alternative transactions to an ESOP do not compare well in after-tax dollars. Aside from the capital gains deferral associated with an ESOP, the owner can elect to maintain control of the company after the ESOP transaction. Assuming the company is highly profitable, the owner may not have to reduce discretionary expenses because of the ESOP.
- *Investment diversification.* ESOPs enable owners to take some chips off the table yet still keep an upside investment potential in the company. By using the FRN strategy described previously, owners can create and trade a public portfolio of securities, instead of having all of their wealth tied to a single illiquid asset.
- *The ESOP rollover provision* also solves the problem of the *locked-in* shareholder. Minority shareholders in a private company often would like to sell their shares, but the combination of no ready market plus capital gains taxes on the sale prohibit a transfer. ESOPs are perfect vehicles to purchase the shares plus provide tax relief.
- *Charitable contributions.* The ESOP can facilitate charitable giving. Every $1 of gift generates $2 of tax deduction. A stockholder can gift shares to a qualified charity and receive a charitable deduction personally in the amount of the gift. The ESOP makes a market for these shares and can purchase them from the charity at a later date, providing the charity with the cash it needs. Because the cash the ESOP uses to purchase this gifted stock was contributed to the ESOP on a tax-deductible basis, the corporation is able to deduct, dollar for dollar, the amount of the gift.

- *Private foundations.* The ESOP can also help a company owner transfer shares to a private foundation. Private foundation regulations prohibit the owner of a private business from contributing private securities directly to a private foundation. However, using an ESOP can overcome this problem. Owners may sell their securities to the ESOP and reinvest the proceeds tax-free into publicly traded securities. They then can transfer the public securities to a charity or to a private foundation without violating the rules regarding the acquisition and holding of employer securities.
- *Cash flow increase.* A company can reduce its corporate income taxes and increase its cash flow by issuing treasury stock or newly issued stock to an ESOP in any amount up to 25% of eligible payroll. As the example earlier in this chapter shows, a company increases its equity by the present value of these tax savings. If the contribution to the ESOP is made in lieu of cash contributions to a profit-sharing plan, the cash flow savings are even more dramatic.
- *Maximize employee performance.* At least one large study on the effects of ESOPs on private companies found that ESOPs appear to increase sales, employment, and sales per employee by about 2.3% to 2.4% per year over what would have been expected absent an ESOP.[5]

Not-So-Good Points to Consider

The principal disadvantages and possible problem areas that should be evaluated in considering an ESOP are listed next.[6]

- *Dilution.* If, by the company contributing newly issued stock to the ESOP rather than cash, the ESOP is used to finance the company's growth, the cash flow benefits must be weighed against the rate of dilution. For instance, if the owner sells 30% of the company's stock to the ESOP, will value be created due to the added growth?
- *Disclosure.* Once stock distributions are made, employees who hold stock are entitled to receive annual reports and attend shareholders' meetings. This level of participation makes many owners uncomfortable.
- *Valuation.* The stock must be valued annually to establish its value for purposes of purchasing, allocating, and distributing it. A qualified third party must prepare the valuation; normally this is someone certified by a national appraisal society. This valuation may cost $10,000 to $20,000 or more initially, with annual updates in the $5,000 to $15,000 range.

  An incorrect valuation affects the company's position. Overvaluation of the stock causes a reduction of the deduction that the company had taken for the contribution. If the ESOP purchased the stock, the deduction would not be affected, but the seller would be required to pay back the excess purchase price. Further, under ERISA, the seller is subjected to a penalty tax for each year that the stock was overvalued.
- *Liquidity.* Repurchasing stock in the future may be difficult for companies that experience substantial stock appreciation or earnings impairment. This is particularly important beyond the fifth year of the plan, since employees may

fully vest at this time. After the first five years, the ESOP normally will need to keep approximately one-third of the fund in liquid investments, to provide liquidity for retiring or terminating employees.

- *Stock performance.* If the value of the company does not increase, the employees may feel that the ESOP is less attractive than a profit-sharing plan. This may cause some employees to quit and seek more conventional employment. Of course, if the company fails, employees will lose their benefits to the extent that the ESOP is not diversified in other investments.
- *Leverage.* The ESOP normally borrows money from a financial institution to pay for the stock purchase from the shareholder. This is almost always a large transaction involving millions of dollars. The company will feel this pinch for at least one or two economic cycles. The debt will slow the company's ability to finance its operations in the future and, in some cases, prohibit it from growing.
- *Government as a partner.* Several government agencies oversee ESOPs, including the IRS, the Department of Labor, and possibly the SEC. In other words, by implementing an ESOP, owners must be prepared to deal with big government more than they currently do with their qualified plans in a non-ESOP status. At the very least, government is more of a partner in the ESOP scenario, positively and negatively.

BOTTOM LINE ON ESOPs

ESOPs are extremely powerful vehicles to assist owners in transferring part or all of their businesses. Unfortunately, they are also complex to implement and administer. An entire industry of ESOP professionals has emerged to help private owners deal with this complexity.

While there is no doubt that an ESOP is a powerful tool, the question becomes: Is implementing an ESOP worth the hassle? Perhaps. A business owner may spend years building a business only to give millions to the government in taxes. An ESOP can eliminate that tax burden. Owners should compare the after-tax liquidity they can receive from all transfer methods, including the ESOP, to help make this determination.

However, private business owners are not known for their tolerance and patience when dealing with the government. Many owners also bristle at the thought of having employees as partners. A certain amount of power is transferred with the beneficial ownership of the stock. All of a sudden, the owner owes a level of diligence not previously experienced to the employee-partners. When it comes to ESOPs, size does matter. Businesses with annual EBITDA of less than $1 million may find ESOPs too constricting from a financial perspective.

TRIANGULATION

The ability to transfer a business interest is conditioned by its access to capital and the value world in which the transfer takes place. ESOPs are especially affected by the value world in which they are viewed. The primary authority for ESOPs, the ERISA laws, decrees that they must be appraised in the world of fair market value. This means that ESOPs are valued in a notional regulated world, which has two ramifications.

1. The fair market value is a world without synergies, so the value an owner receives in an appraisal is likely to be less than the highest market value. Since most ESOPs own a minority interest of the sponsoring company's stock, value is further discounted to reflect lack of control and marketability.
2. ESOPs are the most highly regulated transfer method. Aside from ERISA, many governmental agencies are somehow involved with ESOPs.

Companies that implement ESOPs successfully tend to have many of the attributes of could-be-public companies. There is usually a good, functional management organization in place. The company generally outperforms competitors in its industry segment. Finally, the company has a place in the market, which means the owner is not crucial to the future success of the business.

Banks supply capital for most ESOP implementations. Most banks want their loans personally guaranteed. Owners selling into an ESOP are particularly vulnerable to these pressures since they are liquid borrowers. Many owners will extend credit or guarantee loans in the world of owner value, but they will not backstop a deal in the lesser world of fair market value.

The strength of the linkage between a regulated value world, such as fair market value, and regulated transfer method, as in ESOPs, is quite strong. Prospective sellers to an ESOP should consider long and hard whether they wish to trade being surrounded by the enhanced authority for liquidity when they want it without giving up control. Sellers who wish to share ownership with employees, and are willing to play by the rules, may find ESOPs a powerful tool.

NOTES

1. The National Center for Employee Ownership Web site, www.nceo.org.
2. Ibid.
3. Ibid.
4. R.K. Schaaf Associates Web site, www.rkschaaf.com.
5. Kruse/Blasi study, www.nceo.org/library/overview.html.
6. R.K. Schaaf Associates.

CHAPTER 28

Management Transfers

The term "management transfer" refers to two different situations. A management buyout (MBO) occurs when an existing management team purchases all or part of the company in which they are employed. A management buy-in (MBI) occurs when a management team buys all or part of a business in which it is not currently involved.

Successful management transfers rely on the valuation and capital structure formation areas of the triangular body of knowledge. All parties must first value the company. These valuations may take place in several different value worlds and involve various capital access points, depending on who is valuing what. For instance, the seller may value the company in the world of owner value while the managers value the company in the world of investment value or the financial subworld of market value.

Secured lenders value the company in the world of collateral value. Ultimately a deal is structured with the seller, possibly using other transfer methods, such as employee stock ownership plan (ESOPs). Finally, the deal must be financed, which may require assembling several capital types, such as bank, mezzanine, or equity capital.

Management transfers generally occur under three different circumstances:

1. *Corporate divestitures.* A corporate parent decides a division is no longer core to its strategic direction.
2. *Private owner.* The controlling shareholders of a private company decide to sell the business.
3. *Failed business.* A bankruptcy court or liquidator sells a business.

This chapter focuses on management transfers in corporate divestitures and buyouts from private owners. However, the motives of all players are similar, in that each wishes to maximize returns and minimize risk. In other words, each desires to play and win in the value world where it has maximum control, to finance at the optimal capital access point, and to utilize the most advantageous transfer methods.

Exhibit 28.1 provides a snapshot of management buyouts and depicts their position relative to other transfer methods.

EXHIBIT 28.1   Transfer Matrix: Management Buyouts

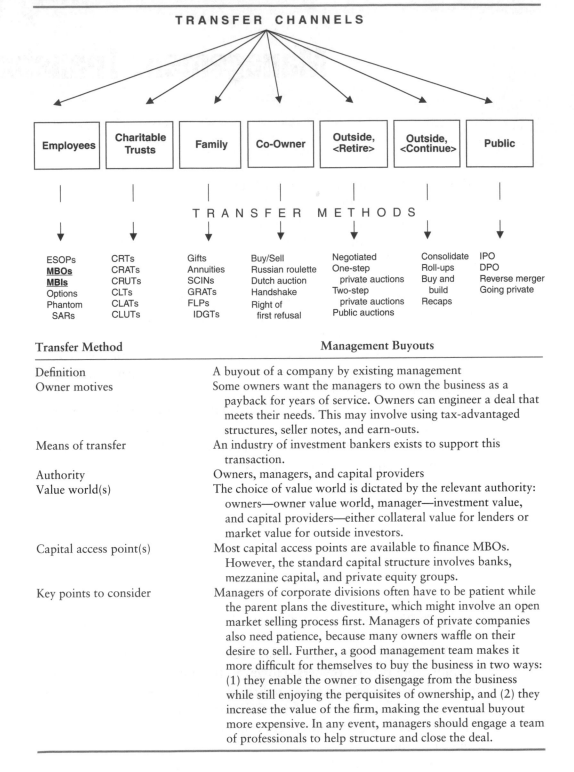

Transfer Method	Management Buyouts
Definition	A buyout of a company by existing management
Owner motives	Some owners want the managers to own the business as a payback for years of service. Owners can engineer a deal that meets their needs. This may involve using tax-advantaged structures, seller notes, and earn-outs.
Means of transfer	An industry of investment bankers exists to support this transaction.
Authority	Owners, managers, and capital providers
Value world(s)	The choice of value world is dictated by the relevant authority: owners—owner value world, manager—investment value, and capital providers—either collateral value for lenders or market value for outside investors.
Capital access point(s)	Most capital access points are available to finance MBOs. However, the standard capital structure involves banks, mezzanine capital, and private equity groups.
Key points to consider	Managers of corporate divisions often have to be patient while the parent plans the divestiture, which might involve an open market selling process first. Managers of private companies also need patience, because many owners waffle on their desire to sell. Further, a good management team makes it more difficult for themselves to buy the business in two ways: (1) they enable the owner to disengage from the business while still enjoying the perquisites of ownership, and (2) they increase the value of the firm, making the eventual buyout more expensive. In any event, managers should engage a team of professionals to help structure and close the deal.

DIFFERENCES BETWEEN MANAGEMENT BUYOUTS AND MANAGEMENT BUY-INS

The mechanics of acquiring a company are similar for an MBO and MBI. Differences between the two involve finding a deal, the perceived riskiness of the subject company, and the number of involved managers. Existing management teams have an advantage over outsiders for these reasons. Since they already manage the company, they can better assess its risk profile than outsiders. Outside management teams must search the marketplace for a company to buy. This search is usually more fruitful in the industry where they have experience. Most MBIs revolve around a single manager, who, if successful, may bring other managers into the deal. Many private equity groups will back an outside manager in the search and financing of a transaction. A number of industry roll-ups have occurred within this framework.

OTHER BUYOUT/BUY-IN TYPES

Two other buyout types are

1. *BIMBO: buy-in/management buyout.* This unfortunately named transfer type involves a transaction where a business is bought by a management team consisting of both existing management and incoming management.
2. *BIO: institutional buyout.* These transactions involve an equity sponsor who then introduces a management team. The team may be the existing team, a buy-in team, or a combination of the two.

Unless otherwise stated, this chapter refers to management transfers without differentiating between buyouts and buy-ins.

Industry Characteristics

A number of industry characteristics influence the likelihood of success in a management transfer. Characteristics such as predictable cash flows and stable operating environments are particularly important.

- *Established, mature industries are more suitable.* Emerging industries often require large investments in capital expenditures and working capital, and are less likely to receive transaction financing.
- *Less cyclical, nonseasonal industries are appealing.* The more stable the industry's sales cycle, the better. Industries that depend on seasonal selling periods, such as a Christmas retailer or ornament manufacturer, are difficult transactions to finance and close in a management transfer.
- *Both a stable technology and customer base are important.* High-technology companies are less suitable for management transfers because of the possibility of technological obsolescence. Industries with shifting customer bases, such as certain kinds of retail, are also not good candidates.

Of course, it is possible to effect management transfers in just about any industry. The issue raised here is the likelihood of closing the transfer and the ultimate long-term success of the acquisition. However, the individual company's characteristics are more important than industry characteristics.

Company Characteristics

The next company-specific attributes increase the likelihood of a successful transfer.

- Experienced management with a proven track record
- Management teams who invest substantial amounts of their own money
- Subjects with reliable cash flow streams
- Debts that can be serviced even during slow economic periods
- Predictable levels of capital expenditures and working capital investments
- Products or services that have some advantage in the marketplace

The best transfer candidates tend to have gross- and operating-profit margins above industry averages.

LIKELY DEAL STRUCTURES

There are two prevalent management transfer deal structures. The first is a leveraged buyout (LBO). The second is an equity-sponsored buyout. Both of these structures may involve tax-advantaged structures to the seller, such as the use of an ESOP or charitable remainder trust, the subject of Chapter 29. Both structures may also involve seller participation, either through seller notes or earn-outs.

EARN-OUTS

Earn-outs are a method for triggering changes in the purchase price based on future performance of the company. They are bridge tools to help buyers and sellers to reach a consensus on the purchase price.

Leveraged Buyouts

Leveraged buyouts use a relatively small amount of equity in the capital structure. For these purposes, LBOs rely on management's equity and nondilutive debt to pay for the acquisition. Exhibit 28.2 depicts capital contributions of the parties in a typical LBO capital structure.

The LBO capital structure is engineered to maximize the leverage of management's equity contribution. Management may contribute only 10% of the total capital needed. The team negotiates simultaneously with secured and unsecured

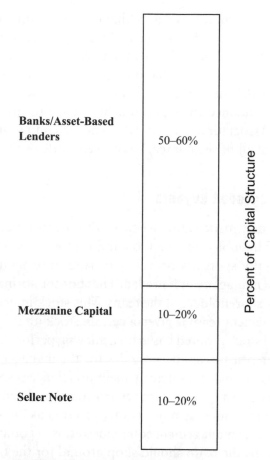

Banks/Asset-Based Lenders   50–60%

Mezzanine Capital   10–20%

Seller Note   10–20%

Percent of Capital Structure

EXHIBIT 28.2   Leveraged Buyout
Contributions to Capital Structure

lenders. The seller note is typically the last variable to be determined. Most sellers will not volunteer to finance a meaningful part of the structure because they are in a second or third lien position and basically incur equity-level risk while typically receiving only debt returns.

Sellers who finance a deal can protect themselves in a number of ways, such as:

- Finance less than 50% of the transaction.
- Require the buyer to obtain a life insurance policy naming the seller as beneficiary for the amount of the loan.
- Check the buyer's credit rating.
- Make sure the buyer has sufficient funds in the bank for operating costs.
- Receive a personal guarantee from the buyer.
- Limit the note to 60 months or less.
- Make sure the inter-creditor agreements with the other lenders allow for continued payments of the seller note, unless a major covenant break occurs.

An LBO structure is so highly leveraged that a company may fail with unforeseen losses or costs. Management team performance after the transaction is crucial. Successful teams realize that cash generation is the key. These teams structure deal terms to defer payments by using devices such as interest-only loans for a period of time. They also negotiate preferred payment terms with vendors and probably also attempt to speed up payments from customers.

In an LBO, managers trade added deal risk for an increased equity interest. They may enhance their position by using various programs, such as the Small Business Association 7(a) or 504 loan programs. In many cases, the managers obtain control of the company with very little of their own money.

Equity-Sponsored Buyouts

Many management teams partner with a private equity provider to complete a transfer. These buyouts tend to employ more conservative capital structures than LBOs. Equity sponsors provide expertise in financing the transaction as well as additional management if needed. The sponsor normally provides a carried interest to the key shareholders of the team. This stock interest comes in two forms. First, the management team is given a certain stock interest at the close, say, 10%, with additional stock granted based on achieving performance benchmarks. The second carried-interest possibility provides for the management team to purchase equity at attractive terms. This management preference is sometimes called an *envy ratio*. For instance, in a typical management transfer, the management team's investment may buy three times as much equity pro rata as the sponsor's money, for an envy ratio of 3. The management equity interest is negotiated up front with the sponsor, which means the team should shop around for the best sponsor.

The likely contributions in an equity-sponsored capital structure are shown in Exhibit 28.3. In this structure, the equity sponsor contributes 20% to 40% of the

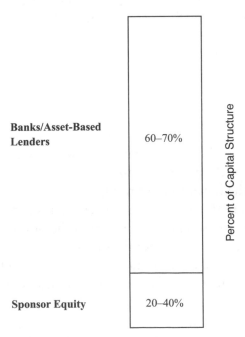

EXHIBIT 28.3   Equity-Sponsored Buyout Contributions to Capital Structure

capital while the managers contribute little or nothing. A strong equity sponsor may attract a senior lender to a deal and may entice the lender to loan a greater percentage of the capital needed at more attractive rates than an LBO structure might garner. Lenders may participate in this way because a greater percentage of equity in the deal reduces risk, and it may come as a surprise to learn that deeper pockets tend to get better deals.

DEALS

The need to arrange a number of deals simultaneously is a key difficulty in completing management transfers. Negotiating a deal with the seller is only the starting point. Agreements with the financing sources must occur to support the acquisition price. A variety of ownership agreements, such as shareholder agreements, buy/sells, and employment agreements, are necessary between the management team and equity sponsor or between the management participants themselves. Exhibit 28.4 shows these deal possibilities.

Dealing with the Seller

The primary preclosing document between the management team and seller is called a letter of intent (LOI). An LOI is generally a legally nonbinding agreement that describes all of the important terms of the deal. Most LOIs contain these key provisions:

- Description of what is being purchased (assets, stock, details)
- Description of what is excluded (specific assets)
- Proposed purchase price with possible adjustments
- Delivery terms of purchase price (cash at close, payment over time, seller note)
- Earn-out provisions (stated with as much precision as possible)
- Due diligence period (scope of the diligence plus time required)
- Conditions to proposed transaction (financing contingencies, other)
- Consulting and noncompete agreements (precise terms)

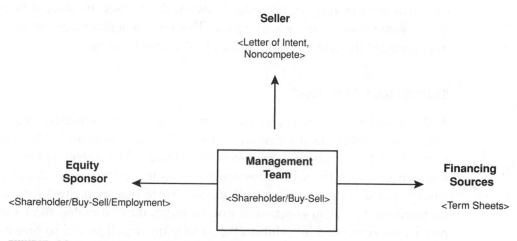

EXHIBIT 28.4 Simultaneous Deals Required

- Various representations
- Conduct of business until the closing (no material changes)
- Disclosure statements (no public announcements)
- No-shop agreement (exclusive dealing clause)
- Governing law (which state or country governs)
- Closing date

A properly constructed LOI contains all deal-killer issues. Appendix G contains an example LOI. The deal closing lawyers use the LOI to draft the final purchase and sale documents.

Dealing with Financing Sources

Management negotiates a term sheet with each financing source. This may involve players in several capital types, such as banks, asset-based lenders, factors, lessors, mezzanine capital, and private equity providers. Like letters of intent, term sheets describe the financing in some detail. Part Two of this book, "Capital Structure," discusses each of the capital types and negotiating tips for each of the capital access points. The information in Part Two also helps interested parties structure and negotiate financing term sheets.

Dealing with Equity Sponsors

Negotiating with equity providers is a major issue facing management teams. Many equity sponsors want to work out partnership agreements with the management after the seller signs the LOI. Management is better served by controlling the LOI process if possible. To accomplish this, management negotiates the deal with the seller and then cuts a deal with an equity sponsor. This enables management to obtain the best deal.

The deal with an investor is far from done once equity splits are negotiated. Equity splits represent how much of the equity each party owns in the acquired entity. But ownership agreements, such as shareholder, buy/sell agreements, and employment agreements are as important as the equity split. These agreements establish the working relationships between the parties and should be negotiated at the same time as the equity splits. The key ownership agreements used in a management transfer are summarized in the next sections.

Shareholder Agreement

A shareholder agreement sets the terms by which shareholders deal with each other (or members in the case of a limited liability company). The management team should draft the general terms of a shareholder agreement soon after the negotiations with the seller commences. Even if the transfer does not require an equity sponsor, the managers still should create this term sheet for use between themselves. The term sheet need not be much more detailed than the example provisions contained in Exhibit 28.5. The team is well served to hire a corporate

EXHIBIT 28.5 Example Tenets of a Shareholder (Member) Agreement Term Sheet

1. **Percentage Ownership Interest.** It is anticipated the equity will be split as follows:

   John Ambitious—10%

   Rick Underling—5%

   Dick Manager—5%

   PEGCo—80%

2. **Restrictions on Interest Transfer.** Interests cannot be freely transferred. The company has a right of first refusal to purchase the interest under terms no worse than those offered by a third party. If the company does not purchase the interests, the remaining shareholders may also purchase the interests under the same terms. If neither the company nor the shareholders purchase the interests, the interests may then be sold to a third party that is bound by this agreement.

3. **Tag Along.** The controlling shareholder cannot sell his interests unless the buyer agrees to purchase the minority interests at the same price and terms.

4. **Mandatory Buyout in Event of Death.** The company has an obligation to purchase the interests at death. The company will provide, if available, company-paid life insurance to cover this cost for the shareholders who are employees of the company. All valuation issues will be contained in the buy/sell agreement. In the event of a company purchase, the remaining shareholders will maintain their proportionate interest without dilution.

5. **Short-Term Disability.** Shareholders who are employed by the company will receive full salary for up to 12 months even if unable to work. If the disability extends beyond 6 months, then the disability will be classified as long term.

6. **Mandatory Buyout in the Event of Long-Term Disability.** The company has an obligation to purchase the interests in the event of a long-term disability by one of the employee-shareholders. For these purposes, disability will be determined by the definition in the disability insurance in force at that time. The parties will agree to a definition of disability in case no disability insurance is in force at the time of the disabling event.

7. **Optional Buyout in Certain Events.** A number of circumstances that *may* trigger the purchase of the interests include:

   a. Bankruptcy of a shareholder.

   b. Failure of a shareholder to perform duties as designated in an employment agreement or within the shareholder agreement.

   c. Voluntary withdrawal from the business, either through retirement or quitting.

   d. Divorce of the shareholder.

   In the event of a company purchase, the remaining shareholders will maintain their proportionate interest without dilution. Optional buyouts will require a supermajority of the shareholders voting interests to exercise the option.

8. **Dispute Resolution.** Disputes between the shareholders will be resolved by arbitration, with both sides paying equally for the services of the American Arbitration Association.

9. **Financing.** The primary source of borrowed funds for the company will be institutional lenders. A super majority of the board must agree to seek funds other than nondilutive debt.

10. **Distribution of profits and losses.** These will be divided per the original ownership percentages. Distributions for tax reasons will occur at the highest tax bracket.

11. **Managing the Business.** Issues that the management can decide without board inclusion:

    a. Hire/terminate nonshareholders.

    b. Spending less than $75,000 for capital projects.

    c. Changing benefit plans as long as the net effect is less than $75,000.

    d. Choosing and negotiating vendor and customer contracts.

    e. Arranging consignment agreements with customers and suppliers.

    f. Negotiating customer credits.

    g. All other issues not specifically contrary to paragraph 10 of the shareholders agreement.

(continued)

EXHIBIT 28.5   *(Continued)*

12. **Voting Rights.** Each shareholder will have voting rights based on ownership percentage of the entire entity on a pro rata basis.
13. **Duties.** The manager and other shareholders owe loyalty to the company. Specific job duties are described in the employment agreement term sheet.
14. **Corporate Governance.** The following decisions will require a supermajority (more than 66% of the outstanding shares) approval of the shareholders' voting interests:
    a. Elections of directors
    b. Issuance of new interests
    c. Sale of entire business
    d. Changes to share rights
    e. Distributions or dividends, except for normal tax distributions
    f. Incurring debts of more than $1 million
    g. Acquisition of another business
    h. Dissolution of the company
    i. Major changes in employee benefit plans
    j. Changes to the manager's compensation plan
    k. Optional buyouts
    l. Changes to the employment contracts, noncompete agreements, shareholder agreement, and buy/sell agreement

attorney to help construct terms appropriate to the circumstances. This lawyer also may represent the team in the negotiations with the equity sponsor.

Buy/Sell Agreement

This agreement controls the events that trigger a buyout, determines who can buy a shareholder's interest, and prices the interests that are purchased. Exhibit 28.6 presents some ideas management teams may wish to incorporate into their buy/sell term sheets.

As with the shareholder agreement example in Exhibit 28.5, the buy/sell example provisions are meant to provide ideas for managers to construct a suitable term sheet. Developing these term sheets is a test to determine if the managers can work together effectively. Once again, this term sheet is required for either LBOs or equity-sponsored buyouts. Working through these issues with prospective equity sponsors also sheds light on the viability of this future relationship.

Employment Agreements

As ownership term sheets are created, managers should construct terms for their continued employment after the closing. Exhibit 28.7 contains example tenets of an employment agreement term sheet. Although this step is vital with equity-sponsored transfers, it is also important in leveraged buyouts. The purpose of this term sheet is to define the duties and rights of the managers.

As with other agreements, managers should seek help from an employment contract lawyer when setting the employment terms.

The following example illustrates a management buyout.

EXHIBIT 28.6   Example Tenets of a Buy/Sell Agreement Term Sheet

1. **Triggering Event.** The following events involving a shareholder trigger the buy/sell agreement:
   a. Death
   b. Voluntary termination
   c. Personal bankruptcy
   d. Divorce
2. **Valuation of Interest.** The following process is used upon a triggering event. The value of 100% of the company is defined as the *greater* of the following values:
   a. An agreed-upon price set by March 31 of each year by a consensus of the board. This annual agreement must be in writing, and the agreed-upon price will remain in effect until the following March 31, unless changed in writing by a consensus of the board. It can be amended within the one-year time frame by written unanimous consent of the board.
   b. The insurance in force at the time of the triggering event.
   c. The net book value is determined by using generally accepted accounting principles, on an accrual basis, as of the most recent quarter's end to the date in question.
   d. The following formula will be used to value the company:
   i. 100% value = (earnings before interest and taxes for the most recent year-end × 4) − Long-term liabilities for the most recent year-end. "Long-term liabilities" are defined as those corporate liabilities that come due in more than one year from the statement date.
   I. Death
   The value of a shareholder's interest involving death shall be determined by using the value determined in paragraph 2 above times the shareholder's percentage of interest. The net proceeds of any life insurance payable to the shareholders for the purpose of redeeming the deceased shareholder's interests shall be the cash payment to the deceased shareholder's estate, up to value determined in paragraph 2 above times the shareholder's percentage of interest. If the value determined in paragraph 2 above times the shareholder's percentage of interest is more than the net proceeds of the life insurance payable to the shareholders, then the difference will be paid to the estate of the deceased shareholder.
   II. Voluntary Withdrawal or Retirement of the Manager
   The value of a manager's interest involving voluntary withdrawal or retirement shall be determined by using the value determined in paragraph 2 above times the manager's percentage of interest less 20%.
   III. Right to Call Interests
   The company maintains the right or option to purchase any or all shareholder interests that are subject to a third-party action, such as a personal bankruptcy or divorce of a shareholder. A consensus of the uninvolved shareholders will need to vote in writing to exercise this option to purchase. If an interest is called, the value and terms of purchase will be the same as an voluntary withdrawal, as described in paragraph II immediately above.
3. **Payment Terms.** In cases of a shareholder's death, the deceased shareholder's estate shall be paid 100% of the life insurance proceeds, if such insurance was in force at the time of death. If the insurance in force is insufficient to cover the valuation, the underinsured portion shall be paid under the same terms as the other triggering events as follows: the ownership interest valuation amount as determined by paragraph II above, payable monthly for five years from the triggering event at an annual interest rate of 7%.

EXHIBIT 28.7   Example Tenets of an Employment Agreement Term Sheet

1. **Term of Employment.** The following employees will be granted three-year employment agreements at the terms stated below.
2. **Salary.** The salary requirements for each manager is stated as follows:

   John Ambitious—$175,000 per year

   Rick Underling—$125,000 per year

   Dick Manager—$125,000 per year

   These salaries will increase each year by 3%.
3. **Bonus Plan.** In addition to the base salary, the key managers will participate in an "Annual Incentive Plan," which is described on a separate sheet.
4. **Employee Responsibilities.** A separate sheet is included on "Employee Responsibilities."
5. **Devotion of Full Attention and Energy.** Yes.
6. **Confidentiality.** Yes, executive will sign a C/A.
7. **Reimbursement of Business Expenses.** Yes.
8. **Reimbursement of Expenses.** Normal reasonable expenses furthering the company business will be reimbursed via itemized expense reports.
9. **Benefits.** The executives shall enjoy standard benefits in the following areas:
   a. Vacation days. Vested in same way as before the transaction.
   b. Health insurance.
   c. Disability coverage; short term versus long term.
   d. Life insurance.
   e. 401(k) plan.
10. **Termination of Agreement.**
    a. Without cause:
       Company may terminate with 18 months' notice.
       Employee may terminate with reasonable written notice for transition, but no less than 30 days.
    b. Termination as a result of business condition changes:
       Sales of assets or share of the company or material change in duties, remuneration, or benefits would be considered termination by company under clause (a) above.
    c. Disability: If unable to perform duties for more than 26 weeks, company may terminate agreement and company obligations cease without prejudice to employee rights under company disability programs or shareholder rights.
    d. Death: Agreement terminates and obligations cease.
    e. With cause: Company may terminate without notice for causes to be defined.
    f. In the event of termination without cause, employee shall be considered to have been given notice specified in (a) above and shall not be required to perform any duties during the notice period but shall receive all salary, prorated incentives, and fringe benefits as if the employee were a continuing employee.
11. **Settle Disputes.** By arbitration.
12. **Right to Work Product.** No.
13. **Noncompete Agreement.** For a period of 24 months after termination.
14. **Governing Law.** New York.

EXAMPLE

PrivateCo's president, John Ambitious, approaches Joe Mainstreet, PrivateCo's sole shareholder, about buying the business. Ambitious has managed PrivateCo for five years and believes he is now experienced enough to take this important step. Joe has no real desire to sell the company but cannot ignore the solicitation. Given the miserly approach to salaries at PrivateCo, Joe suspects Ambitious does not have money to buy the company. Ambitious says he will raise the money through a combination of debt and outside equity. Joe says he will not finance any part of the purchase price but will entertain a 100% buyout if the price is right.

The first step is to agree on this price. Joe is slow to talk about what he thinks PrivateCo is worth but eventually compiles the next valuation. (This is taken from the owner value world found in Chapter 14.)

PrivateCo Owner Value as Prepared by Joe Mainstreet	
	$000
Total compensation to owner, including bonuses	450
+ Pretax earnings of the business	1,800
+ Personal expenses passed through to the business[a]	75
+ Effect of close business contracts[b]	9
+ Covered expenses such as insurances, business vacations, etc.	25
+ Any other items that personally benefit the owner[c]	90
Benefit stream to owner	2,449

[a]Personal expenses equal vacations and conferences charged to company.
[b]Excess rent charged to PrivateCo by a company controlled by Joe Mainstreet.
[c]These equal donations ($74), legal ($9.9), and accounting ($6.5).

The benefit stream to Joe Mainstreet is $2,449,000. This is the amount that he expects to receive or control each year for the foreseeable future. Joe capitalizes this benefit stream at a low rate because he believes the risk of achieving this stream is low. In this case, Joe uses a 15% capitalization rate. This creates an owner value on a total capital basis of $16.3 million ($2.449 million by 15%). By deducting PrivateCo's long-term debt of $500,000 from the enterprise value, the value of Joe's equity in the owner value world is $15.8 million. This equates to about 6.5 times the benefit stream.

Joe tells Ambitious he will sell 100% of PrivateCo for $16 million *cash*. (Rounding up makes sense to Joe.) Ambitious is delighted that Joe has agreed to sell. He is uncertain, however, if $16 million is a fair price. When in doubt, hire an expert, thinks Ambitious. After hearing from an acquaintance that Dan Dealmaker is a fine fellow, Ambitious hires Dan to raise the money and close the deal. Ambitious tells Dan that he and two other managers can invest about $500,000 combined.

Dan believes this may be a record high amount for managers to invest in an MBO.

As a starting point, Dan reviews PrivateCo's balance sheet. After some study and calculations, Dan calculates PrivateCo's collateral value (also taken from Chapter 14). Dan's presentation is presented next.

		PrivateCo Collateral Value ($000)		
Asset Class	Stated Value	Loanable Value/Fair Market Value	Advance Rate	Collateral Value
Accounts receivable	$722	$686	80%	$549
Inventory	450	250	50%	125
Land/Building	442	2,200	70%	1,540
Machinery and equipment	866	450	65%	293
Total				$2,500

The "stated value" for each of the asset classes has been taken from PrivateCo's balance sheet (as shown in Chapter 5). The loanable value/fair market value column shows the amounts eligible for secured lending. Accounts receivable have been reduced from the stated value to reflect ineligible receivables, such as past due invoices or those generated from related companies. Inventory has been reduced to account for work-in-progress inventory, which is not eligible for lending. Land and building and machinery and equipment have been adjusted to fair market values.

Advance rates reflect the percentage of each asset class that a lender will actually loan against. For example, a lender may advance 80% against eligible receivables, 50% against eligible inventory, and so on. Eligibility can vary from lender to lender, and is explained in detail in Chapter 20. Finally, collateral value is the sum of the various asset class margined collateral. For PrivateCo, collateral value equals about $2.5 million (as rounded). With a $16 million need and only $2.5 million in traditional borrowing power, Dan Dealmaker quietly thanks his lucky stars that he took this assignment on an hourly plus success fee basis.

Considering management's investment of $500,000 and a $2.5 million borrowing capacity, Dan still needs $13 million to close the deal. The next step is to tap the mezzanine capital market. Dan contacts his golfing buddy, Tim, at MezzanineCo. Dan gives Tim these numbers on PrivateCo:

PrivateCo Summary Financials	
Book value (Chapter 5)	$1.0 million
Net asset value (Chapter 5)	2.4 million
Benefit stream	
Pretax earnings	$1.8 million
Prior owner compensation	.45 million
Prior owner discretionary expenses	.10 million
Depreciation	.4 million
Normalized capital expenditures	(.3) million
Adjusted EBITDA	$2.45 million
Expected stream growth in next 5 years: 15%	$5.0 million in year 5
Projected cash at end of year 5	$10.0 million

Tim reviews this information, along with the reams of backup information on PrivateCo that Ambitious created but Dan now claims as his own.

Somewhere deep in the bowels of MezzanineCo prowls an algorithm that determines how much mezzanine capital can be applied to the PrivateCo buyout. This simplified illustration assumes that MezzanineCo will not lend more than three times PrivateCo's adjusted earnings before interest, taxes, depreciation, and amortization (EBITDA), or about $7 million. The detailed pro formas show that the company can afford the $1 million per year in interest, and cash builds to $10 million by the end of the fifth year, more than enough to pay off the mezzanine loan.

MezzanineCo provides a term sheet to Dan that would choke a whale. Beyond the 14% current coupon payable quarterly, the warrant play amounts to 5% of PrivateCo's stock exercisable beginning in year 4. The warrants are valued using a formula that increases over time, thereby enticing Ambitious to buy them back as soon as possible. Dan expects PrivateCo will be worth at least $25 million in year 5 ($5 million EBITDA times a selling multiple of 5), so the warrants should be worth at least $1.25 million at that time. If the pro formas are correct, PrivateCo will be debt and cash free at the end of year 5 and will enjoy a strong earnings base.

Dan acts the part of an insulted broker for receiving such harsh terms. In reality, he is just one stop, and $6 million, away from raising the money needed to close the deal ($16 million purchase price less $500,000 management investment less $2.5 million asset-based loan less $7 million mezzanine loan). The last stop is private equity.

Ambitious watches Dan's progress and suddenly realizes he and the other two managers have a math problem. With a management investment of $500,000 and an equity need of $6 million, Ambitious and his team are staring at a 7.7% equity split ($500,000 divided by $6.5 million). It occurs to Ambitious, for the first time, that he might be better off working for Joe Mainstreet going forward and owning no stock than investing all of his money and owning about 4% of the company. (Ambitious has two management partners.) But wait! Dan Dealmaker is finally about to earn his money.

Dan knows a private equity group that specializes in backing management teams. PEGCo gives extra credit to the management team's investment. In other words, the management team's money is worth more than a pro rata share. After several meetings and two rounds of golf, PEGCo offers to cut the management team in for 20% of the equity. If management hits its financial targets, PEGCo will allow the management to *earn-in* another 2% per year over five years. Of course, PEGCo's senior partner says paying 6.5 times PrivateCo's adjusted EBITDA is too rich. This will necessitate a lengthy due diligence about PrivateCo and its industry.

There is a fairly disciplined approach relative to PEGCo's investment position. Assuming PEGCo is a typical private equity provider, it desires a 30% compounded rate of return on its investments. PEGCo believes PrivateCo will be debt free in year 5 and will earn about $5 million per year at that time. PEGCo is betting that it can sell PrivateCo for 6.5 times EBITDA in year 5, or $32.5 million. But PEGCo may only own 70% of the stock at that time, assuming management fully hits its bogeys. This 70% position is worth $22.8 million in year 5 ($32.5 million times 70%). Is this enough money to warrant a $6 million investment today? A financial calculator determines this compounded return is 31%. PEGCo is good to go.

In real life, PEGCo may have six to eight different deals under a letter of intent at the same time. The one deal that actually gets done is the one that shows the best potential during due diligence. This is disconcerting to members of a management team because they cannot hedge their bet. If the equity player decides not to close the transaction, management has to start over. It may take six months to arrange a complicated financing. Many owners are not patient enough to go through the capital-raising process again.

During due diligence, a PEGCo partner finds a problem. It looks like PrivateCo's industry is cyclical. Every 15 years or so the participants apparently lose their minds and begin a price war. PEGCo believes this might happen again in the next five to seven years. In an attempt to get Joe Mainstreet to accept less money because of this unforeseen risk, PEGCo decides it cannot move forward with the deal. Of course, Ambitious and the other managers are crushed. But they still have their old jobs.

What lessons can be learned from this hypothetical buyout?

1. Managers need to manage and leave the heavy deal making to a professional. A major backdrop issue with management transfers is that the managers *work for* the owner. It is imprudent for them to go nose to nose with their employer in negotiations. By hiring an investment banker, even if the deal fails, both sides can blame the dealmaker, and the relationship between employer and employee may continue as before.

2. The dealmaker should engineer a funding solution that simultaneously attacks the capital structure. All capital access points have credit boxes. This knowledge enables dealmakers to plan capital access. Next, each capital provider issues a term sheet for their proposed financing. The battle is won or lost at this point. A good dealmaker conducts this symphony of conflicted interests with a careful wand. Also, dealmakers need to incorporate the layered capital structure into the detailed projections. Doing this requires a thorough understanding of the effective returns for each capital access point.

3. The management team should sign the letter of intent with the owner, then shop the deal with a number of equity sources. Once again, the equity split and ownership term sheets are negotiated together.

POINTS TO CONSIDER

Management transfers are multivariable problems and require a structured approach to achieve success. There are many points to consider when approaching this task.

Number of Managers

The fewer managers involved in the transfer, the better. Many managers cannot make the transition from corporate minion to owner-manager. All managers think they work hard while in the big company. Owning a business, however, means a doubling of the workload and a tripling of the pressure. The key manager should bring on board only those players who have core competency skills. Another way to look at this is to invite only the managers whose skills cannot be readily purchased in the marketplace. In most cases, this limits the invitation list to less than five participants.

Fiduciary Responsibility

A primary difference between an MBO and MBI is the level of fiduciary responsibility required of the managers. For management buyouts, the key managers have a fiduciary duty to their employers. They must act honestly and respect the interests of the employer. The MBI team does not have this level of responsibility because its members cannot be fired for acting unprofessionally. Many sellers set ground rules for the managers at the beginning to head off these potential conflicts. For instance, they may set up front the terms of the deal, when the deal must close, and who may know about the situation. Sellers also may not allow the managers to bid on the business if the selling process is open because sellers do not want to scare away potential bidders. In some cases, managers have to be patient and let the auction process break down before putting their own deal together.

Earn-Outs

An earn-out is a method for triggering changes in the purchase price based on future performance of the subject company. It is useful in helping buyers and sellers reach a consensus regarding the purchase price. It is especially useful for management transfers, since a full down payment may not always be achievable. Earn-outs are fertile ground for downstream lawsuits, so great care must be used in their construction. A few of the more important points to consider when structuring an earn-out are listed next.

- Base the earn-out on services/products that exist at the closing, for some determined period of time, using terminology that exists in a third-party context, such as according to generally accepted accounting principles. A dealmaker or lawyer experienced with crafting earn-outs is needed at this point.
- Sellers typically want an earn-out to be based on net revenue rather than profits because the owner cannot control expenses post-closing. Buyers prefer a profit-based method earn-out because it better reflects whether the company can afford to pay the contingency. Because there are more variables in determining earnings than revenues, there is a greater likelihood that disputes may develop with the latter approach.

■ When disputes inevitably appear, private arbitration is preferable, using an arbitrator mutually agreeable to the parties. Using arbitration is usually faster and cheaper than settling a dispute in court, and the parties can choose an arbitrator with specific knowledge and expertise.

Much like seller financing, earn-outs should be used only by sellers in situations where they can live with the purchase price paid at closing, and any monies received postclosing are considered gravy.

Bridging the Purchase Price

Assuming the seller reads the prior paragraphs and refuses to provide seller financing or an earn-out, management still may be able to bridge a difference in purchase price. Managers are in a unique position to work with the seller to implement a tax-advantaged deal to the seller. Two choices exist. Managers can implement an ESOP–MBO structure, which may save the seller millions in taxes. Or managers can purchase the sellers shares from a charitable trust (the subject of Chapter 29), which may also save the seller a bundle. Chapters 27 and 29, on trusts, will give managers plenty to think about along these lines.

Who Has the Power

Managers who partner with an equity source should not cede operating control of the company, even if they are minority holders. Managers can negotiate certain rights with the equity sponsor so they do not get run over. Assume that PrivateCo will have a five-person board of directors post-buyout. PEGCo appoints three of the directors, and the management team appoints two. The next clause can be negotiated into the shareholder's agreement to block the majority from taking actions that might be detrimental to the managers.

Corporate Governance
The Board will have five members: PEGCo will appoint three; the Management team, two. PEGCo will appoint the chairman and CFO of the company. The following decisions will require a supermajority (at least four board votes) approval of the board:

Elections of directors

Issuance of new interests

Dilution of current interests

Sale of entire business

Changes to share rights

Distributions or dividends, except for normal tax distributions

Incurring debts of more than $1 million

Acquisition of another business

Dissolution of the company

> *Key employee hires*
>
> *Major changes in employee benefits*
>
> *Optional buyouts*
>
> *Changes to the employment contracts, noncompete agreements, operating agreement, shareholder agreement, and buy/sell agreement*
>
> *Job termination of a shareholder*

With this structure, managers cannot be forced to dilute their ownership interest or be terminated *unless* one of the management board members votes with the equity sponsor.

Legal Counsel

It takes a million lawyers to close a management transfer—at least it seems so. The management team has its own lawyer, who helps negotiate the deal with the seller and equity source. This lawyer also helps work out the deal between the managers, such as equity splits and employment agreements. Another lawyer represents the seller. Yet another lawyer represents the company being acquired. Scores of lawyers represent the various other parties: equity sources, financing sources, and so on. A smart management team incurs only out-of-pocket legal expenses for its particular lawyer. Other deal-related expenses are paid by the acquisition entity out of the closing proceeds.

Perhaps more than any other transfer method, management transfers contain a multitude of deal variables. The only thing standing between managers and complete chaos are term sheets. Well-constructed term sheets provide all interested parties with necessary information. Term sheets perhaps can be likened to a set of blueprints. Of course, the deal can be constructed without them, but chances are good that the foundation will sag and the structure ultimately will fail. The best advice is for managers and sellers to be represented by knowledgeable professionals. This is yet another time when good advice pays off handsomely.

TRIANGULATION

The ability to transfer a business interest is conditioned by its access to capital and the value world in which the transfer takes place. No other transfer method has as many capital options and possible value world combinations as management transfers. This variety of alternatives causes these transfers to be volatile and uncertain—and potentially rewarding.

Management transfers take place in several different value worlds simultaneously, depending on the perspective of the participants. Owners view the transaction through the world of owner value. They are the supreme authority in this world, so owners choose to transact in this world whenever possible. Although managers may view the deal in the world of investment value, they can get it financed only in the world of collateral value or, in the case of outside investors, the world of market value.

Too many perspectives in a deal can be dangerous. Value world collisions invariably result. One recent management buyout of a metal-stamping company exemplifies this dilemma. Although the owner believed the business was worth $20 million, the managers valued the company at $15 million. Secured lenders would lend only $10 million. This situation had the makings of a time-and-energy black hole. Yet the owner is the ultimate authority in management transfers. The owner decided to lend the managers, through a subordinated note, $10 million to complete the deal. Although the managers paid $5 million more than they thought the company was worth, the terms of the seller note were quite favorable, effectively causing the deal to consummate in the world of owner value.

Casual observers might blame the owner for taking such a large risk in the preceding example. To stay in the world of owner value, this particular owner decided to exert deal-making authority. The same observer might think less of the managers for overpaying and overleveraging the company. Are the players at risk here? Yes, but risk is better understood in management transfer than any other transfer method. Both owner and managers should understand and be able to measure and manage risk better than anyone else. Who better to judge the merits of the deal than the people who have shaped the company?

CHAPTER 29

Charitable Trusts

Charitable trusts enable business owners to transfer their businesses while enjoying the benefits of charitable giving. Since the business is the primary asset for most private owners, the disposition of this asset must be maximized. The use of a properly structured charitable trust enables owners to win an estate planning trifecta. First, the owner transfers all or part of the business while possibly eliminating capital gains on the sale. Second, the owner either earns ordinary income for life based on receiving some percentage of the sales proceeds or removes the asset from his or her estate. Finally, the owner's heirs and charity of choice benefit from implementing this technique. This chapter describes the two major charitable trust types, charitable remainder trusts (CRTs) and charitable lead trusts (CLTs), and discusses variations of these types.

Charitable trusts offer owners tremendous flexibility in planning the eventual transfer of a business interest. Incorporating charitable giving into an estate plan can be accomplished by a charitable trust. The transfer methods in this chapter rely on laws and supervision by the Internal Revenue Service (IRS). Since the U.S. government subsidizes business owners to use these trusts by reducing the donor's taxes, these rules must be followed to the letter. As with all areas that require detailed knowledge of the law and IRS codes, readers are encouraged to confer with experts before using any of the methods described here.

STRUCTURE OF CHARITABLE TRUSTS

Exhibit 29.1 describes the overall structure of the charitable trusts covered in this chapter. CRTs and CLTs each can be broken into variants that may differ slightly, but importantly, from each other. Each transfer method in Exhibit 29.1 is described in this chapter.

CHARITABLE REMAINDER TRUSTS

Transferring a business interest using a CRT is a way to both save taxes and reward a charity. A CRT is a transfer method that enables a donor to gift shares of private stock to a trust, generating a charitable gift deduction for the fair market value of the gift. When the shares are later sold by the trust, no capital gains are owed, since the trust is a non-taxpaying entity. Donors can receive distributions from the trust, within limits, during their lifetime.

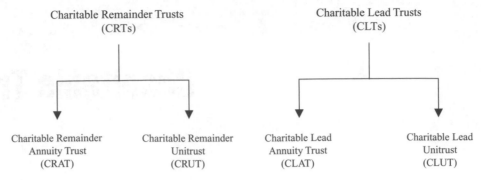

Charitable Remainder Trusts (CRTs)
— Charitable Remainder Annuity Trust (CRAT)
— Charitable Remainder Unitrust (CRUT)

Charitable Lead Trusts (CLTs)
— Charitable Lead Annuity Trust (CLAT)
— Charitable Lead Unitrust (CLUT)

EXHIBIT 29.1   Charitable Trusts

EXHIBIT 29.2   Transfer Matrix: Charitable Remainder Trusts

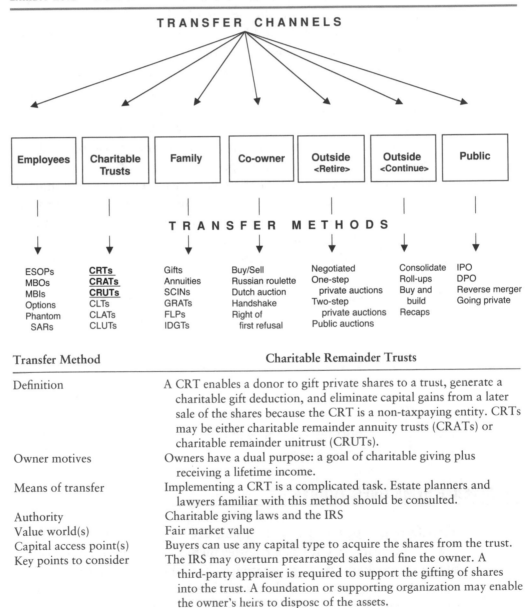

Transfer Method	Charitable Remainder Trusts
Definition	A CRT enables a donor to gift private shares to a trust, generate a charitable gift deduction, and eliminate capital gains from a later sale of the shares because the CRT is a non-taxpaying entity. CRTs may be either charitable remainder annuity trusts (CRATs) or charitable remainder unitrust (CRUTs).
Owner motives	Owners have a dual purpose: a goal of charitable giving plus receiving a lifetime income.
Means of transfer	Implementing a CRT is a complicated task. Estate planners and lawyers familiar with this method should be consulted.
Authority	Charitable giving laws and the IRS
Value world(s)	Fair market value
Capital access point(s)	Buyers can use any capital type to acquire the shares from the trust.
Key points to consider	The IRS may overturn prearranged sales and fine the owner. A third-party appraiser is required to support the gifting of shares into the trust. A foundation or supporting organization may enable the owner's heirs to dispose of the assets.

There are three rules regarding the use of a CRT.

1. All CRTs must be irrevocable.
2. The trust must function exclusively as a CRT from the date of its creation.
3. CRTs must distribute income at least once per year. Only the amount detailed in the trust agreement may be paid out during the term of the trust.

A trust must be either a charitable remainder annuity trust (CRAT) or a charitable remainder unitrust (CRUT) in every respect. Exhibit 29.2 provides the transfer matrix for CRTs.

STEPS TO IMPLEMENT A CRT

Step 1. A donor transfers stock or other property to an irrevocable trust. The trustee may be the donor. The trustee will pay income for life or the period of years specified in the trust document to the noncharitable beneficiaries the donor specified, typically husband and wife.

Step 2. The CRT can sell the property received and reinvest the proceeds without paying any capital gains tax. Thus, transfers of highly appreciated, low-income property are ideal. An example would include the stock of the donor's private company. The noncharitable beneficiary must receive an income interest of at least 5%. With a CRUT, the assets are revalued each year. Thus, if the value of the CRUT increases, the income increases.

Step 3. The gift to the CRT can qualify the donor for an income tax deduction in the year of the gift. The value of the deduction is measured by the present value of the charitable beneficiaries' right to receive the remaining assets at the end of the trust.

Step 4. Since the assets in the CRT can be reinvested or diversified, increased income often results over that being produced by the assets transferred by the donor. An obvious example would involve a gift of non–income-producing real estate that was subsequently sold by the CRT, without the payment of any capital gains tax, and then reinvested in high-income-producing stocks or other securities.

Step 5. At the end of the trust term, the charity will receive everything remaining in the CRT. These assets will be estate-tax-free.

Step 6. An irrevocable life insurance trust, sometimes called a wealth replacement trust, often is combined with a CRT to pay to the donor's children or grandchildren an amount equal to the assets in the CRT passing to charity. The insurance is intentionally excluded from the taxable estate of the donor. The increased income flow and income tax savings resulting from the CRT can be used to pay the insurance premiums involved.

A CRAT is a CRT that pays a fixed amount, either a dollar amount or a fixed percentage, of the initial fair market value of the CRT assets. A CRUT pays a fixed percentage of the CRT assets valued annually.

At the end of the trust term, the remainder interest must pass exclusively to or for the benefit of qualified charities. In either case, the payout amount of any CRT cannot be less than 5% or more than 50% of the initial fair market value of the trust assets.

The trust assets may either pass directly to the qualifying charity or continue in trust for charitable purposes. More than one charity may share in the remainder interest, and the donor may retain lifetime power to change the charitable beneficiaries of a CRT. The CRT can be established for one or more lives of individuals living at the time the trust is created or, alternatively, for a term not to exceed 20 years.

The company must be a C corporation to contribute stock to a CRT.

The following example illustrates the implementation of a charitable trust.

EXAMPLE

The always-busy Joe Mainstreet has decided to implement part of his estate plan. As such, Joe will give 20% of his shares in PrivateCo to a CRUT. To support this gifting, a certified business appraiser values the 20% interest in the world of fair market value. Since this gift is a minority interest, the appraiser can take a minority interest and lack of marketability discounts from the enterprise value. Even with these discounts, the fair market value of the 20% interest is $2 million.

After the transfer, a buyer is found for the company, and the stock is sold by the trust to the purchaser for $2 million. Joe avoids paying tax on the sale of the stock because the tax-exempt trust is the owner of the stock. Since the trust is the legal owner of the stock, it is also the legal owner of the $2 million in cash.

As the table in this example shows, by using the CRUT, Joe saves over $400,000 in federal and state capital gains taxes on the sale of the stock. In addition, he gets an immediate charitable deduction equal to the actuarial value of the remainder interest that would eventually pass to charity. Based on the life expectancy of the owner and his wife, this deduction was worth $350,000, or a tax savings of about $140,000 (based on a 40% tax rate).

Joe was at first hesitant to use a charitable trust because he thought he would be cutting his daughter out of his will. To solve this problem, Joe created another trust known as an irrevocable life insurance trust (sometimes known as a wealth replacement trust) that owns a second-to-die life insurance policy on the lives of Joe and his wife. At the death of the survivor of Joe or his wife, the life insurance policy is paid to the irrevocable life insurance trust for the benefit of the daughter. A properly structured irrevocable life insurance trust can receive life insurance proceeds without triggering any income or estate taxes.

Although the irrevocable life insurance trust owns the life insurance policy and pays the premium on the policy, Joe is indirectly responsible for the payment of premiums. Joe must transfer enough into the trust each year to pay the premiums. But since no income tax was paid on the sale of the stock, Joe's income interest on the $2 million in the CRUT is $20,000 larger than it would have been had Joe sold the stock himself and invested the after-tax proceeds. With this additional income, Joe has enough to pay the premiums on the life insurance policy and still meet his daily needs.

Comparison of Sales versus Charitable Gift		
	Outright Sale	Gift to CRUT
Value of business interest	$2,000,000	$2,000,000
Basis	0	0
Capital gain	2,000,000	2,000,000
Taxes (federal and state: 20%)	400,000	0
Net to reinvest	1,600,000	2,000,000
Annual income generated (5%)	80,000	100,000
Life insurance premiums	0	20,000
Additional annual income	0	80,000
Tax savings on charitable deduction	0	140,000
Gift to charity[a]	0	2,000,000
Inheritance to children net of estate taxes[a]	$1,000,000	$2,000,000

[a]Actual numbers depend on longevity of grantor, reinvestment of tax savings, appreciation rate on assets, and size of taxable estate.

With a CRUT, the retained interest withdrawal rate (i.e., the percentage of the CRT that the owner withdraws each year) is fixed at the time the CRT is created. This withdrawal rate must pass a reasonable person test and still allow for a substantial portion of the CRT to be available for eventual distribution to the charity. In this example, Joe has a life expectancy of about 15 years. Joe chooses a withdrawal rate of 10%, mainly because at the time the financial markets are returning in excess of this amount.

Joe and his wife will receive $80,000 per year for life ($100,000 income per year generated by the trust less $20,000 life insurance premium). In the year of the gift, Joe saves $140,000 in taxes. After they both die, their charity will receive the remainder interest, which in this case is at least $2 million. Joe's daughter will receive $2 million from the life insurance policy.

The ultimate transaction from the CRT must be a stock sale. Since most buyers prefer to buy the assets of a company, this may pose a problem. Yet the CRT holds another benefit. No federal estate tax is payable on the value of the charitable remainder interest in a CRT created during lifetime or at death. To maintain flexibility, it is best not to put all proceeds into the CRT, even if 100% of the company is sold. For example, a noncompete agreement or employment contract can be kept outside the CRT as well as some percentage of the total stock.

Using a CRUT to Transfer the Family Business to the Kids

Transferring a business to children raises the prospect of parents' paying gift taxes. By contributing their stock to a CRUT followed by a stock redemption, gift taxes can be avoided. For this technique to work, the children must own shares in the company prior to the corporation redeeming stock from the CRUT.

Assume that PrivateCo has 100 shares outstanding with a fair market value of $10 million. Joe Mainstreet has already gifted and sold 80 shares to his daughter and owns the remaining 20 shares. Joe wants to transfer his 20 shares to his daughter with little or no gift taxes and retain an income interest for the rest of his life. Joe can accomplish this goal if:

- He contributes 20 shares worth $2 million to a CRUT and names himself a joint income beneficiary.
- PrivateCo redeems the stock from the CRUT for $2 million cash.
- A trustee reinvests the $2 million, which pays Joe an income stream for life.

After the stock redemption, Joe's daughter owns 100% of the stock of PrivateCo. With this technique Joe Mainstreet wins the trifecta. In addition to transferring the company to his daughter, he creates a large income stream for life, reduces his taxable estate by $2 million, receives an immediate income tax charitable deduction, and ultimately helps the charity of his choice.

This is an aggressive estate planning technique. Readers should engage a tax expert before implementing this method.

POINTS TO CONSIDER FOR CRTs

Employing a CRT to transfer a business interest is a complex task. There are numerous points to consider. The next sections describe a few of the major issues.

No Prearranged Sales

A sale of stock from the trust must not be prearranged prior to the gift, or the IRS may undo the tax benefits of using the CRT. Normally the threshold is signing an agreement, such as a letter of intent, prior to gifting the stock into the trust. This prearranged sale doctrine does not prevent the donor from investigating potential buyers, however.

Use of a Private Foundation

Donors can use a private foundation as the charitable beneficiary in conjunction with a CRT gifting. This gives the donor, and probably the family, a method to control the proceeds for years after the gifting. The private foundation has a number of notable characteristics:[1]

1. A private foundation is a nonprofit, charitable organization.
2. A private foundation is not subject to regular income tax, but it does pay a 1% to 2% tax on net investment income.
3. No public support is necessary. However, cash contributions are deductible up to 30% of the donor's adjusted contribution base with a 20% limitation on capital gains property. Higher limitations generally apply to gifts to public charities.
4. Private foundations are subject to a number of potential excise taxes for self-dealing between the entity and certain individuals, including substantial contributors.
5. A minimum of 5% of the net investment assets must be distributed for charitable purposes annually.

Supporting Organizations

Some individuals find the administrative and reporting burdens as well as excise taxes and payout requirements of a private foundation are too onerous for their needs. A supporting organization may be a good alternative. A supporting organization is a charity that is classified as a public charity rather than a private foundation. This is because it "supports" a public charity such as a community foundation. A supporting organization can be classified as a public charity, even if there is only one donor or one family of donors.

A supporting organization is not treated as a private foundation because it does not, on its own, qualify as a public charity or charities. The primary advantages to establishing a supporting organization rather than a private foundation are listed next.

- The supporting organization is exempt from all private foundation excise tax and administrative requirements. This opens up many benefits to the donor who might want to use closely held stock or other assets prohibited in a private foundation.
- A donor can claim the more generous tax benefits of contributing to a public charity.
- There are great economies of scale through operating a supporting organization, especially in conjunction with a community foundation.

Supporting organizations have a separate name and identity within the nonprofit community and allow the donor an active role in managing the organization. Each supporting organization has its own board of directors on which the donor and relatives may serve.

Liquidation of Business

Some companies have a higher value in liquidation than in an outright sale. This can cause a tax problem for C corporations, because two levels of taxation occur upon a sale or liquidation: capital gains on any gain from the sale of capital assets and capital gains on liquidating distributions of cash and property in kind from the corporation. If the shareholders gift the stock of the company to a CRT and the trust liquidates the assets, the shareholders defer the second level of capital gains tax.

Unrelated Business Taxable Income

A CRT that holds private stock may be subject to unrelated business taxable income. This is especially important when the trust holds more than 50% of the stock of the private company. The unrelated business income tax was enacted to prevent unfair competition by tax-exempt organizations with for-profit businesses. To avoid this tax, readers should consult with an attorney.

Donor Age Matters

Younger donors may not be able to use CRTs. This is because the present value of the remainder interest must equal *at least* 10% of the net fair market value of the property on the date it is contributed to the trust. The math surrounding this rule may prohibit donors under 40 years of age from using a CRT. This is a situation based on facts and circumstances, and each donor should have the prospective CRT reviewed before implementation.

CHARITABLE LEAD TRUSTS

A CLT is the reverse of a CRT. A CLT is an irrevocable trust that provides income to a charity for a specified period of time. The income interest to the charity must either be in the form of an annuity interest (CLAT) or a unitrust interest (CLUT). A CLAT is a trust that distributes a certain amount to a charitable beneficiary at least annually for a term of years or during the lives of one or more individuals living when the trust is created. The remainder of the trust is distributed to or held for the benefit of noncharitable beneficiaries. A CLUT is a trust that distributes a fixed percentage of the net fair market value of its assets valued annually. At the conclusion of the term of the income payments, the CLT trust property is distributed to the remainder, noncharitable beneficiary. The remainder beneficiary can be anyone, including the donor.

Properly structured, a CLT allows donors to transfer assets to their favorite charity, and to their family or friends, without any gift or estate tax consequences. In most circumstances a CLT will not provide donors with any current charitable deduction for income tax purposes. Because of this, a CLT should be considered primarily an estate planning tool.

A CLT operates in this way:

- A donor funds the trust with cash or other assets, such as private company stock.

- One or more charities, which might include a private foundation, receive a specified amount from the trust each year.
- At the expiration of the charitable term, the remaining assets of the trust are distributed to the remainder beneficiaries.

Because the CLT is irrevocable and the donor retains no interest in or control over the assets transferred to the trust, no portion of the trust is subject to estate tax at the donor's death. Rather, gift tax is paid upon the funding of the trust, based on the value of the gift made to the remainder beneficiaries. With proper planning, a CLT can be structured in a manner that results in the gift to the remainder beneficiaries having little or no value for gift tax purposes. Thus, little or no gift tax is paid upon funding the trust and no estate tax is paid upon the donor's death.

There are 5 steps to implement a CLT as shown below.

STEPS TO IMPLEMENT A CLT

Step 1. A donor irrevocably transfers stock to an irrevocable trust. This is typically done at death, so that the donor can retain the use of the assets during life.

Step 2. The trustee will pay a set income of at least 5% of the fair market value of the trust assets for a period of years to a qualified charity.

Step 3. At the end of the trust term, the donor's heirs will receive everything remaining in the CLT.

Step 4. Because the value of the charitable interest is deductible for estate tax purposes, only the present value of the remainder interest is taxable in the donor's estate. The amount taxable depends on the percentage payable to charity, the length of the charitable payout term, and the monthly IRS interest rate at the time the CLT is established.

Step 5. A CLT can result in a zero estate tax for any size estate, depending on the terms of the charitable gift. For example, if a donor put $5 million into a CLT, with 6% payable to charity for 20 years, an estate tax deduction of $3.8 million would be available, assuming an applicable federal interest rate of 2%.* If the CLT earned 6% per year, over $6 million would remain at the end of the 20-year term for distribution estate-tax-free to the donor's children.

*To find the applicable federal rates, see www.brentmark.com/AFRs.htm.

To accomplish the most beneficial tax treatment, the annual charitable payout from the trust must be such that the actuarial value of the remainder interest is zero. The actuarial value of the remainder interest is the estimated value of the trust assets that will pass to the remainder beneficiaries, taking into account the charitable distributions made during that term. The actuarial value of the remainder interest is calculated using the assumed rate of return on the trust assets required under the Internal Revenue Code (the "applicable federal rate"). For a CLT to function properly, the assets in the trust must *outearn* the applicable federal rate. If the trust is structured so that there are no gift tax consequences, the remainder beneficiaries will receive trust assets to the extent that the trust outperforms the applicable federal rate. Exhibit 29.3 provides the transfer matrix for CLTs.

EXHIBIT 29.3   Transfer Matrix: Charitable Lead Trusts

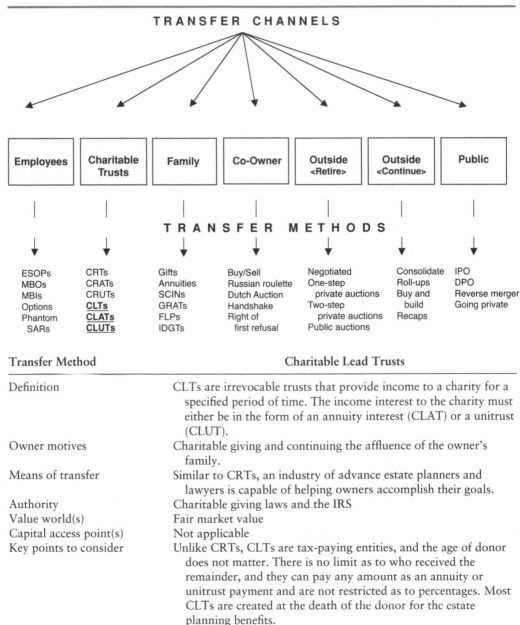

Transfer Method	Charitable Lead Trusts
Definition	CLTs are irrevocable trusts that provide income to a charity for a specified period of time. The income interest to the charity must either be in the form of an annuity interest (CLAT) or a unitrust (CLUT).
Owner motives	Charitable giving and continuing the affluence of the owner's family.
Means of transfer	Similar to CRTs, an industry of advance estate planners and lawyers is capable of helping owners accomplish their goals.
Authority	Charitable giving laws and the IRS
Value world(s)	Fair market value
Capital access point(s)	Not applicable
Key points to consider	Unlike CRTs, CLTs are tax-paying entities, and the age of donor does not matter. There is no limit as to who received the remainder, and they can pay any amount as an annuity or unitrust payment and are not restricted as to percentages. Most CLTs are created at the death of the donor for the estate planning benefits.

The following example describes a CLT implementation.

EXAMPLE
_____

Joe Mainstreet wishes to establish a CLT that pays his alma mater $60,000 a year for 15 years. At the end of the 15-year period, any assets remaining in the trust are to be distributed to Joe's daughter. Joe does not wish to pay any gift tax when funding the trust. If the applicable federal rate is 2%, Joe must transfer $1 million to the trust. Joe can gift this amount of PrivateCo stock to the trust. Later, when the stock is sold, possibly to Joe's daughter, and turned into cash, the contributions to the charity can begin. Assuming an actual annual rate of return on the trust assets of 6%, the charitable organization will receive $60,000 for 15 years, and Joe's daughter will receive approximately $1.2 million at the end of the charitable term.

By establishing a CLT during his lifetime, Joe effectively transfers over $1.2 million to his daughter free from any gift or estate tax. In addition, the charitable organization receives $900,000 over the 15-year term of the trust. It should be noted that Joe does not receive any income from the trust during the 15-year term, but he does receive nearly $1 million in tax benefits from the gift tax deduction and transfer tax savings.

POINTS TO CONSIDER FOR CLTs

Much like employing a CRT, using a CLT to transfer a business interest is a complex issue. There are numerous points to consider, which are discussed in the next sections.

CHARITABLE GIFT ANNUITIES
_____

A charitable gift annuity (CGA) is a contract between the donor and the charity that reserves for the donor or the donor's designee a life income interest. In exchange for cash, securities, or other property, the charity agrees to pay a specified sum each year for one or two lives, the present value of which is less than the value of the property transferred. The annuity amount promised by the charity generally depends on the donor's age, the size of the gift, whether the payments begin immediately or are deferred, and whether a second person receives annuity income.

Private Foundation Rule

The private foundation rule relating to excess business holdings applies to CLTs.[2] Therefore, the value of the trust cannot exceed 60% of the value of the private stock held in the trust. An exception to this rule occurs if the CLT disposes of the stock within five years of the gift. Another way to avoid this rule is to recapitalize the private company in order to shift voting control away from the CLT by limiting the CLT interest to 60% or less.

Select Appropriate Charitable Term

Along with the payout rate and applicable federal rates, the CLT's charitable term is one of the most significant factors in determining the actuarial present value of the charitable interest (APVCI). The shorter the charitable term, the smaller the APVCI. Conversely, the longer the charitable term, the greater the APVCI. The amount of the APVCI is a primary CLT design consideration. Because the term is one of the controllable inputs in the APVCI computation (along with the payout rate), the great majority of CLTs are designed to make the charitable payout for a term of years instead of for the lives of the donors.

Note that a longer charitable term increases the likelihood the CLT trustee will need to invade principal to make the payments. Also, the APVCI can never exceed 100% of the assets transferred to a CLT. Many CLTs do not list an integer as the charitable payout rate; rather, the payout rate in a typical CLT document will include precision to three or four decimal places based on an extensive financial analysis of the financial aspects of the CLT plan.

Redemptions

A donor can give private stock to fund a CLT and then redeem the stock. The charity must not be legally obligated to surrender its shares for this technique to stand the IRS scrutiny.

Gift Tax Strategy

A major advantage of a CLT is the very low gift tax cost of transferring wealth to younger generations. A properly constructed gift tax strategy attempts to maximize the use of the donor's unified credit or discounts the donor's gift and/or estate tax. The strategy involves transferring to a CLT assets that have the greatest potential for future appreciation and/or that may be valued at a substantial discount. Examples of the first category include start-up businesses and investments that have not quite turned the positive corner. The latter category includes assets such as minority interests in closely held businesses.

Generation Skipping

Another important consideration is the application of the generation-skipping tax (GST) to transfers made to CLTs. Any attempt to *skip* a generation and leave money or property to grandchildren will meet a 55% tax on that transfer above and beyond the 55% estate tax rate. However, each individual has an exemption indexed for inflation from this tax. If the assets of a CLT pass to grandchildren at the end of the trust term, and the donors allocate a portion of their GST exemption at the time the trust is established, the entire appreciated amount passes to the grandchildren without estate or GST tax at either the donors' or children's level.

As of this writing, each taxpayer possesses a $5 million exemption from the generation-skipping tax. That means that only aggregate gifts and bequests to grandchildren or younger beneficiaries in excess of $5 million (potentially $10 million for a married couple acting in concert) would be subject to the generation-skipping transfer tax. Readers are encouraged to seek current information on recent tax law changes.

COMPARISON OF CRTs AND CLTs

Both CRTs and CLTs can be used to transfer private stock with terms advantageous to the donor. These trusts are mirror images of each other; great care must be used in selecting the right vehicle. Exhibit 29.4 compares tenets of these trusts.

Perhaps the overriding difference between CRTs and CLTs is the intent of the donor. CLTs are for people who wish to give to charity and also want to ensure the continued affluence of family members. CRTs are most often used by people who wish to make charitable contributions but are more concerned with current income from the trust and may be less concerned with succeeding generations.

TRIANGULATION

Charitable trusts are regulated transfer methods designed by the government to encourage charitable giving. These methods are viewed solely in the world of

EXHIBIT 29.4   Comparison of CRTs and CLTs

	Charitable Remainder Trust	Charitable Lead Trust
Trust as taxable entity	CRTs are tax-exempt entities.	CLTs are tax-paying entities.
Donor needs income from trust	Donors typically need the income from the trust for retirement.	Donors are willing to forgo current income to realize long-term capital appreciation.
Structure of payments to charity	Limit of 20 years or can be on the basis of a life or lives.	No limit to term of years or can be on the basis of a life or lives
Limits of payments from trust	CRTs payouts are restricted to a minimum 5% payout or a maximum 50% payout.	CLTs can pay any amount out as an annuity or unitrust payment and are not restricted as to percentages.
Who receives remainder	Only qualified charities can receive remainder interest.	No limit as to who may receive the remainder interest.
Age of donor	Age of donor matters with CRTs. Young donors may not qualify.	Age of donor does not matter with CLTs.
Primary benefit to donor	Most CRTs are created during the life of the donor for the income tax benefits.	Most CLTs are created at the death of the donor for the estate planning benefits.

fair market value, which is also created by the government and highly regulated. Government as the authority in both circumstances means that users of these trusts need to follow specific rules or face sanctions. It also means that an industry of helpers has formed to assist owners comply with the regulations.

The intersection of a regulated transfer method and regulated value world causes the capital side of the triangle to float with the deal. In other words, no particular capital type is drawn to the transaction; rather, the most effective, and available, capital structure is employed. Buyers of stock from the charitable trust use whatever capital they can arrange.

An industrial distributor recently combined a CRT with a transfer of the business to key employees. First, the owner made sure the management team was interested in acquiring the business. Rather than dictate a selling price to the managers, this owner agreed to ask the trustee to transfer the shares at their fair market value. Next, he gifted all of the shares of his C corporation into a charitable trust, with a family foundation as the remainder beneficiary. His children directed the foundation. Finally, the managers created an acquisition company to buy shares out of the trust. The owner received an income for life from the interest on the proceeds.

NOTES

1. Jack Couzens et al., "All Estate Taxes Can Be Eliminated through Transfers Involving Charitable Gifts," found at: www.couzens.com, p. 2.
2. J. Lewis Perlson, Michael May, and Elizabeth B. Taylor, "Charitable Split Interest Giving Techniques," study prepared for the Northwestern Mutual Financial Network, 2001, p. 55.

CHAPTER 30

Family Transfers

Transferring a business to the succeeding generation is the realization of an American dream. Although it is likely that only 10% to 20% of private businesses actually transfer from one generation to the next, thousands of transfers are accomplished in the United States each year. There are numerous methods used to facilitate transfers to family. Family transfers, more than any other type, require a long-term perspective on the part of the transferors, usually the parents, and the transferees, typically the children. This lengthy time span has several explanations. The mechanics of several methods require several years to implement. Further, parents may not wish to relinquish control of the company immediately, so they may wait until some point in the future or may transfer control incrementally.

In late 2010, Congress passed the Tax Relief, Unemployment Insurance Reauthorization and Job Creation Act of 2010 (H.R. 4853), which created new rates and exemption amounts for estate, gift, and generation-skipping taxes. This new multibillion-dollar tax cut will greatly impact the transfer of private business interests. Some of the highlights of the new law, which applies only to years 2011 and 2012, are:

- $5 million exemption per person ($10 million for married couple) for estate, gift, and generation-skipping taxes (indexed for inflation in 2012).
- 35% top tax rate on transfers over the exemption limits.
- Federal capital gains and dividend rates remain at 15%.

For 2011 and 2012, a husband and wife can transfer $10 million of private company stock (or any asset) completely free of taxes during lifetime or death. Furthermore, the actual amount transferred can be increased exponentially over time once valuation discounts and advanced planning techniques are used, resulting in massive tax savings.

Before implementing any of the methods described in this chapter, readers are encouraged to seek professional help from a qualified estate planner familiar with these advanced planning techniques. Many of these transfer methods are highly regulated, technically complex, and subject to frequent changes by taxing authorities and the courts.

There are a variety of ways to transfer a business interest to family members. The main limitations are the transferor's ability to plan and execute the transfer. The most direct way is to sell the business to family members at its fair market value. While this is straightforward, it may be very costly. Suppose Joe Mainstreet sells 100% of PrivateCo's stock to his daughter for $4 million. Joe may owe up to $600,000 in federal capital gains tax on the sale plus state taxes. He still has over $3 million left in his estate, which may be subject to the newly enacted 35% estate tax on total estates in excess of $5 million when he dies. With proper planning, he can do better.

This chapter focuses on a handful of advanced estate planning techniques that enable private business owners to transfer their business to family members yet minimize taxes due on the sale. The transfer methods are categorized as *estate-freezing* techniques, which remove an asset from an estate and allow the beneficiary to realize the appreciation in the asset. The methods covered here are:

- Stock gifts
- Private annuities
- Self-canceling installment notes
- Grantor-retained annuity trusts
- Family limited partnerships
- Intentionally defective grantor trusts

STOCK GIFTS

Perhaps the most commonly used family transfer method involves gifting stock in the corporation (or membership interests). Gifting stock to family members is simplest and most direct transfer method. Gifting takes three forms: annual exclusion gifts, lifetime exemption gifts, and lifetime taxable gifts. Exhibit 30.1 provides the transfer matrix for stock gifts.

Annual Exclusion Gifts

As of this writing, every person is entitled each year to give gifts of $13,000 to an unlimited number of donees without incurring any gift tax. This $13,000 amount is adjusted for inflation, in thousand-dollar increments, for gifts made after 2011. There is no limit on the number of permissible donees. Donors with large families can transfer significant amounts of wealth. For example, if Joe Mainstreet of PrivateCo has two children and six grandchildren, he can transfer $104,000 of PrivateCo stock each year to these immediate family members.

When a gift is made by a married person to a third party, the spouse of the donor may allow the gift to be treated as if it was made one-half by each spouse. In the previous example, Joe's wife can agree to "gift-split," which effectively doubles the amount of these gifts to $208,000 each year without a gift-tax liability. The total amount of gifts reduces Joe's estate, and any appreciation of the gifted stock is credited to the donees.

Annual gifts require no paperwork and are income-tax-free to the recipient. But to qualify, the gift to each recipient must be a *present* interest gift with the

EXHIBIT 30.1   Transfer Matrix: Stock Gifts

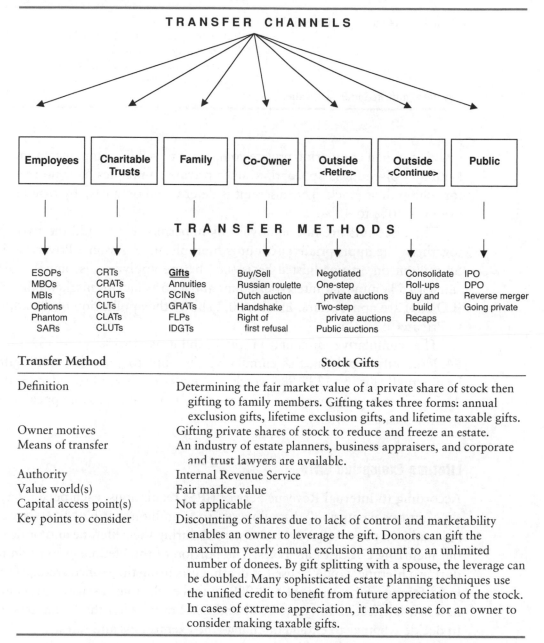

Transfer Method	Stock Gifts
Definition	Determining the fair market value of a private share of stock then gifting to family members. Gifting takes three forms: annual exclusion gifts, lifetime exclusion gifts, and lifetime taxable gifts.
Owner motives	Gifting private shares of stock to reduce and freeze an estate.
Means of transfer	An industry of estate planners, business appraisers, and corporate and trust lawyers are available.
Authority	Internal Revenue Service
Value world(s)	Fair market value
Capital access point(s)	Not applicable
Key points to consider	Discounting of shares due to lack of control and marketability enables an owner to leverage the gift. Donors can gift the maximum yearly annual exclusion amount to an unlimited number of donees. By gift splitting with a spouse, the leverage can be doubled. Many sophisticated estate planning techniques use the unified credit to benefit from future appreciation of the stock. In cases of extreme appreciation, it makes sense for an owner to consider making taxable gifts.

right to spend or use the property currently. It cannot be a promise of a future benefit.

An advantage of gifting minority interests, defined as stock positions of less than 50% of total outstanding voting shares in private companies, is the ability to discount the value of the stock prior to gifting.

The valuation for gifts occurs in the world of fair market value. Minority interests can be discounted substantially largely due to the inability to control the strategic decisions and finances of the company. In some cases, small interests have been discounted by more than 50% in comparison to the control position. In

EXHIBIT 30.2 Application of Adjustments

PrivateCo unadjusted indicated value:

Value on a control, marketable basis:	$4,000,000
Less minority discount (25%)	**(1,000,000)**
Value on a minority, marketable basis	$3,000,000
Less LOMD (25%)	(750,000)
PrivateCo adjusted indicated value	$2,250,000

addition, when comparing private companies to public companies, a lack of marketability discount is appropriate since private companies have no ready market for selling their stock. This discount is determined on a case-by-case basis, but it averages 20% to 40%.

The discounts are not additive; it is impermissible to add the two discounts together. The appropriate discount is multiplicative. Assume PrivateCo is worth $4 million on an unadjusted basis (i.e., before applying discounts). Further assume a 25% minority interest discount and a 25% lack of marketability discount (LOMD) are appropriate. Exhibit 30.2 shows the application of the adjustments to PrivateCo's value.

The cumulative discount in this exhibit is 43.7% (1 − ($2,250,000 ÷ $4,000,000)). Applying this cumulative discount to Joe's $104,000 gift means he is actually gifting $237,986 worth of PrivateCo stock, as rounded ($104,000 ÷ 43.7%). Discounting makes gifting minority stock interests an appealing alternative for business owners.

Lifetime Exemption Gifts

According to Internal Revenue Service (IRS) regulations, each person has a "lifetime gift tax exemption" that allows up to $5 million worth of assets per taxpayer ($10 million per couple) to be transferred during their lifetime and/or death without incurring gift or estate taxes. The portion of the lifetime exemption not used during a lifetime would be used at death. Gifts using the unified credit can be made in addition to gifts using the $13,000 annual exclusions discussed previously. The new law is effective for years 2011 and 2012 only. After that, Congress will need to decide whether to extend or change the exemptions and rates.

Lifetime gifts should be chosen carefully because they normally comprise appreciated property. They are subject to the same discounts as annual gifts.

Taxable Gifts

In some cases, it is prudent for an owner to make taxable gifts, even if the gift triggers an immediate tax. This might be the case for owners of rapidly appreciating businesses that have already used their lifetime exemptions. If a donor survives the gift date by three years, the gift tax paid will not be included in the donor's estate. As an example, assume Joe Mainstreet is in the 35% effective rate bracket for both gift and estate tax purposes. He makes a $1 million taxable gift to his daughter. This triggers a $350,000 gift tax to Joe, meaning that he had to part with $1.35 million to gift $1 million net of tax to his daughter.

Now assume Joe lives for another three years. Because a lifetime taxable gift imposes the tax on the donor, the tax on the gift is excluded from the tax base for the gift. This saves Joe $188,462 on the gift of $1 million net of tax to his daughter as compared to a gift from Joe's estate (which, because estate gifts are tax inclusive, would require $1,538,462 passing at 35% to net $1 million to Joe's daughter). Taxable lifetime gifts are tax exclusive while estate transfers are tax inclusive.

Often, a stock-gifting program is part of a larger estate plan. There are four points to consider when gifting.

1. An outside appraisal is required to support the value of the gift. Preferably a certified appraiser performs this appraisal annually.
2. The IRS prohibits undervaluing a stock for gifting purposes, assessing a penalty if a taxpayer's valuation is 50% or less than the IRS's valuation. The penalty is 20% of the taxpayer versus IRS difference and is in addition to the legal expenses that the taxpayer incurs.
3. Book value should not be used as the default value for stock gifting. This may cause an undervaluation of the subject's stock and lead to an IRS penalty.
4. A gift tax return should be filed to start the statute of limitations running on the valuation; otherwise, the IRS has no time limit for a challenge.

The following example illustrates a stock gifting.

EXAMPLE

Joe Mainstreet of PrivateCo wishes to gift stock to his daughter so she can eventually own the business. Joe wants to maintain control of the company until the final transfer point. He would like to create two classes of stock; he would own the A shares having voting rights while he would gift to his daughter the B shares containing no voting rights. The problem is that PrivateCo is an S corporation and therefore can have only one class of stock. However, an S corporation with a single class of stock can have some shares with voting rights and others with no voting rights.

Joe decides to recapitalize the company by, for example, exchanging the voting common stock for 2% voting common shares and 98% nonvoting common shares. He will then gift all of the nonvoting common shares to his daughter. Joe hires Ann Appraiser of AppraiseCo to determine the fair market value of the nonvoting common shares. These shares suffer from lack of voting rights because they cannot dictate corporate policy. And they lack marketability, since they are not readily transferable. Ann appraises the shares in this way:

PrivateCo Appraisal of Nonvoting Shares

Value on a control, marketable basis:	$4,000,000
Less minority discount (25%):	(1,000,000)
Value on a minority, marketable basis:	$3,000,000
Less LOMD (25%):	(750,000)
PrivateCo indicated value with voting rights:	$2,250,000
Less lack of voting rights (10%):	(225,000)
PrivateCo nonvoting shares indicated value:	$2,025,000

Joe can make a tax-free gift (below the $5 million exemption) of PrivateCo to his daughter while still maintaining control of the business. At some point in the future, probably when Joe retires, his daughter will acquire PrivateCo's voting shares.

PRIVATE ANNUITIES

Private annuities are another method used to transfer a business interest to a family member. Private annuities involve a transfer of stock by the seller in exchange for an unsecured promise by the buyer to make a stream of fixed payments for the life of the seller. Private annuities must be structured as an unsecured promise to pay, or an immediate tax obligation may be triggered. This transaction differs from the normal acquisition in that not only is no purchase price set, but also the number of annuity payments is uncertain, because the seller's life expectancy is uncertain.

There are two types of private annuities. The first is a single life annuity, with payments ceasing at the seller's death. The second is a joint or last survivor annuity, where payments continue until the death of the last survivor of a married couple. For example, suppose Joe Mainstreet opts to sell PrivateCo to his daughter for $4 million. Although she wants to buy the business, she has no money. Joe decides to use a single life annuity to accomplish the transfer. Joe will receive a fixed income stream for life. The stream will stop at his death, and the value of his estate will be reduced by the value of the business.

In 2006, a new rule was adopted by the IRS that greatly impacted private annuities. Rather than deferring any gain as payments are received over time, the seller's gain is to be recognized in the year the transaction is effected. For this reason there have been relatively few private annuity transactions since 2006. A private annuity may be a good strategy for a seller with a potentially short life expectancy. However, the planner needs to be careful of using the mortality component of the valuation tables to determine the present value of the private annuity. An individual who is known to have an incurable illness is considered terminally ill if there is at least a 50% probability of death within one year.

Exhibit 30.3 displays the transfer matrix for private annuities and self-canceling installment notes.

EXHIBIT 30.3   Transfer Matrix: Private Annuities and Self-Canceling Installment Notes

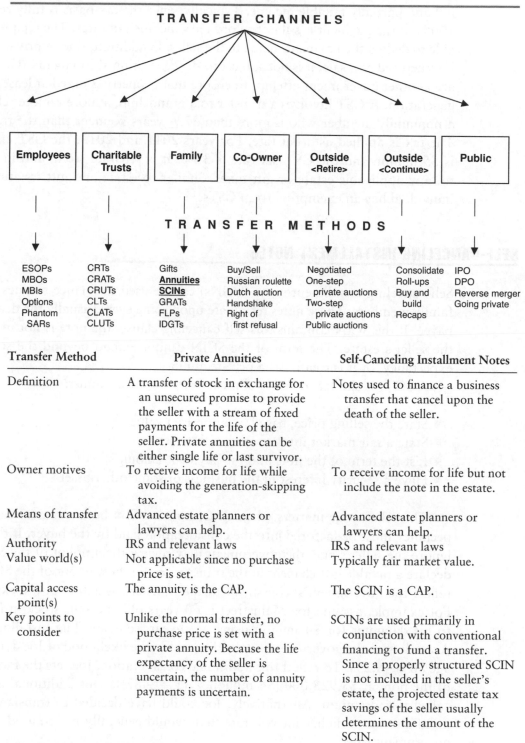

Transfer Method	Private Annuities	Self-Canceling Installment Notes
Definition	A transfer of stock in exchange for an unsecured promise to provide the seller with a stream of fixed payments for the life of the seller. Private annuities can be either single life or last survivor.	Notes used to finance a business transfer that cancel upon the death of the seller.
Owner motives	To receive income for life while avoiding the generation-skipping tax.	To receive income for life but not include the note in the estate.
Means of transfer	Advanced estate planners or lawyers can help.	Advanced estate planners or lawyers can help.
Authority	IRS and relevant laws	IRS and relevant laws
Value world(s)	Not applicable since no purchase price is set.	Typically fair market value.
Capital access point(s)	The annuity is the CAP.	The SCIN is a CAP.
Key points to consider	Unlike the normal transfer, no purchase price is set with a private annuity. Because the life expectancy of the seller is uncertain, the number of annuity payments is uncertain.	SCINs are used primarily in conjunction with conventional financing to fund a transfer. Since a properly structured SCIN is not included in the seller's estate, the projected estate tax savings of the seller usually determines the amount of the SCIN.

The IRS considers each payment received by the seller partially a return of capital and partially taxable income. Typically, once the tax basis is fully recovered, 100% of the payment is subject to ordinary income tax rates. The recipient is not able to deduct the payments made to the seller. In addition, since a private annuity is structured as a sale, it is not subject to the generation-skipping tax (GST). GSTs are another government attempt to ensure that property is taxed at least once per generation. A GST involves a transfer to a grandchild, a more remote relative, or a nonfamily member who is more than $37\frac{1}{2}$ years younger than the transferor. The tax is applied as a flat rate. For years 2011 and 2012, the GST exemption is $5 million and the GST tax rate is 35%. It is separate from, and in addition to, any applicable estate or gift taxes. Similar to estate and gift taxation, every individual has an exemption from GSTs.

SELF-CANCELING INSTALLMENT NOTES

Self-canceling installment notes (SCINs) can be used to finance business sales to family members. These notes terminate upon some event, usually the death of the payee. If the SCIN contains this self-canceling clause, the note is not included in the seller's estate. The term of the SCIN cannot extend beyond the seller's life expectancy, or it is treated as a private annuity.

A SCIN is similar to an installment note. As such, it must:

- State the selling price, based on appraised value
- State a fair market interest rate on the note
- List the term of the note and the payment amounts
- Have a security interest in the business or some other asset

The seller's age matters when structuring a SCIN because his or her life expectancy must be factored into the consideration paid by the buyer. If the parties ignore the seller's age, the government may review the amount of the SCIN and declare a taxable gift element in the transaction. So the amount of the SCIN must reflect the government's assessment of the transferor's actuarial life expectancy. For example, assume Joe Mainstreet is 60 years old and sells stock in PrivateCo to his daughter for $4 million using a 20-year, self-canceling installment note. According to the government's mortality tables, the likelihood of Joe dying before age 80 is 48.2%. To reflect this additional consideration, Joe sets the face amount of the note at $5,928,000 ($4 million × (1 + .482)). This additional amount is called risk premium. Alternatively, Joe could have decided to translate the risk premium into a higher interest rate than would generally be required under the government rules.

The capital gain consequences of a SCIN are the same as those of an ordinary installment sale. Yet the premium increases the amount of income the seller recognizes over the term of the note. Taxable income is reported as realized by the transferor as installments are received. The payment is apportioned between principal and interest in the same ratio as the transaction as a whole.

If the transferor dies before the entire gain is realized, the transferor's estate recognizes the unreported gain. Similar to a private annuity, the note is not included in the transferor's estate, because the note terminates at the transferor's death.

GRANTOR-RETAINED ANNUITY TRUSTS

A grantor-retained annuity trust (GRAT) is an irrevocable trust that pays an annuity to the term holder for a fixed time period. The annuity typically is paid to the grantor of the trust until the earlier of the expiration of a term of years or the grantor's death. After the expiration of the grantor's retained annuity interest, the trust assets are held in trust for the beneficiaries or paid outright to the remainder beneficiaries.

The transfer of assets to a GRAT is a taxable gift for the value of the remainder interest. In other words, the amount of the gift is the value of the property contributed to the GRAT less the value of the grantor's retained right to receive a stream of payments during the GRAT's term. The value of the grantor's retained income right is calculated based on several factors including the term of the trust, the amount of income the grantor will receive, and an assumed interest yield published monthly by the IRS, known as the Internal Revenue Code §7520 rate, which is 120% of the midterm applicable federal rate.

A good goal is to structure the annuity interest retained by the grantor so that the value of the remainder interest transferred is reduced for gift tax purposes, whereas the actual value of the trust property passing tax-free to the next generation is significant at the end of the term. This is why the private stock of a family business is suitable property for inclusion in a GRAT. The stock may be discounted for lack of marketability and minority interest, whereas the appreciated stock passes to the next generation without remaining in the grantor's estate. If the grantor dies within the term of the trust, the property is returned to the estate. If the grantor lives beyond the GRAT's term, the property passes on to the remainder beneficiaries at the GRAT's termination free of tax, including tax on the appreciation of the property held in the GRAT.

GRANTOR RETAINED UNITRUST

A grantor-retained unitrust is similar to a GRAT, except that the grantor's retained interest is a specified *percentage* of the trust's fair market value each year instead of a *fixed* dollar amount.

Since the annuity rate in the GRAT often exceeds the IRS published interest rate, the IRS assumes a portion of the trust corpus will be used each year to make up the difference. This reduces the present value of the remainder interest for valuation purposes and thus reduces the gift made by the grantor to a fraction of the fair market value of the trust property. In other words, a GRAT builds on the concept of a direct gift by taking advantage of valuation assumptions mandated in the IRS actuarial tables to "leverage" the gift.

BASIC MECHANICS OF A GRAT

1. The donor transfers an asset to a trust. In this case, the asset is the stock of a private company.
2. The donor retains a payment stream for a period of years (the "retained interest").
3. An annual income payment is made to the donor.
4. After the donor's income interest expires, the remainder interest in the trust passes to the named beneficiary, usually a family member.

Since the donor retains an interest, the gift tax value of the remainder interest will not be the entire fair market value of the property. For example, if the value of the asset upon transfer is $1 million, and the donor retains the right to receive 7% (or $70,000) per year for ten years, the value of the retained interest (at a 2% §7520 rate) is $589,288, and the taxable gift of the remainder interest is then $410,712 ($1,000,000 − $589,288). This gift of the remainder interest does not qualify under the annual gift tax exclusion because it is a future interest gift.

Using a lack of marketability discount, and a discount for minority interest, can reduce the value of property transferred to the GRAT. By gifting private stock interests, it is not uncommon to take combined discounts in the range of 25% to 50% of the value of private business interests transferred to the GRAT. Minority discounts should be permitted for transfers of private business interests even when, after the transfer, members of the same family control the business entity.

A grantor's retained annuity interest in a GRAT must consist of the right to receive one of a fixed amount, a fixed percentage, or a fraction of the initial fair market value of the trust assets payable no less frequently than annually. It is not required that the fixed dollar amount or percentage remain the same for each year of the GRAT's term. The only limitation is that the amount payable in one year cannot exceed 120% of the amount payable in the prior year.

In the following example Joe Mainstreet uses a GRAT as part of his estate plan.

EXAMPLE

Joe Mainstreet wants to transfer part of PrivateCo to his daughter. Assume the value of PrivateCo is appraised at $4 million. Joe transfers 45% of his interest to a GRAT and retains 55%. At the end of the preestablished ten-year period, the GRAT distributes the business interest to another trust established with his daughter as beneficiary.

Joe hires Ann Appraiser of AppraiseCo to value the interest in the GRAT. Ann appraises the 45% interest as shown.

Summary Value of GRAT

Fair market value of PrivateCo:	$4,000,000
Times 45% gifting:	1,800,000
Less minority discount (25%):	(450,000)
Value on a minority, marketable basis:	$1,350,000
Less LOMD (25%):	(337,500)
Value of GRAT interest after discounts:	$1,012,500
Value of remainder interest:	$160,137

Joe transfers a 45% interest in PrivateCo to the GRAT and retains an annuity income interest, which, at a 10% annuity payment, equals $101,250 per year for ten years, and which is valued at $852,363 (assuming a 2% §7520 rate). Only the present value of the remainder interest in the trust is subject to a gift tax. The gift of $160,137 is less than Joe's lifetime exclusion gift limit, so no gift tax is due.

Through the GRAT Joe transfers a large part of PrivateCo to his daughter, receives a fixed annuity stream for ten years, and removes a large asset from his taxable estate.

Advantages of a Grantor-Retained Annuity Trust

There are several good reasons to set up a GRAT:

- *High appreciation potential.* A GRAT is an especially useful transfer method in situations where the underlying assets are expected to appreciate significantly. If the earnings growth exceeds the IRS published interest rate, the valuation used to calculate the gift will lead to an undervaluation, which should cause significant value to pass to heirs free of gift or estate taxes.
- *Planning for a sale.* If an owner is contemplating the sale of a private company, she should consider transferring a minority interest in the company to a GRAT prior to the sale. This transfer should be based on a third-party valuation performed on the minority interest, incorporating the typical discounts. Once the company is sold, the minority interest appreciates substantially and the beneficiary gains from the circumstance. This is a case of enjoying a low valuation in the world of fair market value but realizing a high price in the world of market value.
- *Conservative technique.* A GRAT is largely specified by statute and regulation rendering it a fairly predictable and conservative transfer method.

Disadvantages of a GRAT

For the GRAT to work as intended, its assets must outperform the §7520 rate. If the grantor does not outlive the trust term, the assets will be included in the taxable estate. Therefore, a GRAT is not a good transfer technique for clients in poor health or who have a short life expectancy. Exhibit 30.4 provides the transfer matrix for GRATs and family limited partnerships.

EXHIBIT 30.4   Transfer Matrix: Grantor-Retained Annuity Trusts and Family Limited
Partnerships

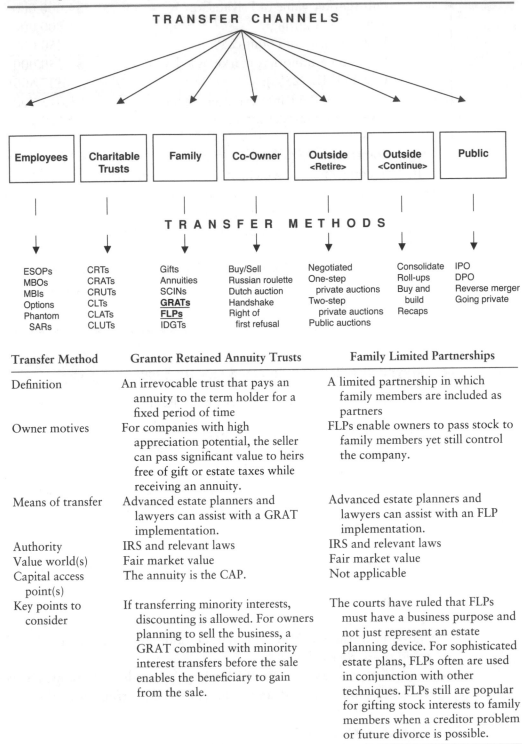

Transfer Method	Grantor Retained Annuity Trusts	Family Limited Partnerships
Definition	An irrevocable trust that pays an annuity to the term holder for a fixed period of time	A limited partnership in which family members are included as partners
Owner motives	For companies with high appreciation potential, the seller can pass significant value to heirs free of gift or estate taxes while receiving an annuity.	FLPs enable owners to pass stock to family members yet still control the company.
Means of transfer	Advanced estate planners and lawyers can assist with a GRAT implementation.	Advanced estate planners and lawyers can assist with an FLP implementation.
Authority	IRS and relevant laws	IRS and relevant laws
Value world(s)	Fair market value	Fair market value
Capital access point(s)	The annuity is the CAP.	Not applicable
Key points to consider	If transferring minority interests, discounting is allowed. For owners planning to sell the business, a GRAT combined with minority interest transfers before the sale enables the beneficiary to gain from the sale.	The courts have ruled that FLPs must have a business purpose and not just represent an estate planning device. For sophisticated estate plans, FLPs often are used in conjunction with other techniques. FLPs still are popular for gifting stock interests to family members when a creditor problem or future divorce is possible.

FAMILY LIMITED PARTNERSHIPS

A family limited partnership (FLP) is one in which only family members are included as partners. The FLP holds assets, in this case, of private stock transferred to it by the parents. The general partner or partners are usually the parents or the parent-owned corporation. The general partner typically holds a nominal general partnership interest, say, 1%. The limited partners, usually the children or trusts for children, hold the bulk of the equity in the form of limited partnership interests. The general partner controls the FLP and makes essentially all decisions. During the life of the FLP, the general partner can be paid to administer the partnership. Typically the rights of the limited partners are highly restricted.

The limited partners have limited liability. The most each limited partner has at risk is the amount he or she has invested in the partnership. This contrasts with an individual general partner, who may face personal liability in excess of his or her investment in the partnership.

There should be more than one individual general partner, or alternatively, the general partner should be an entity such as a corporation. A corporate general partner has the added advantage of minimizing the potential liability for the debts and obligations of the FLP. The partnership remains in place until the expiration of a fixed term designated in the partnership agreement, unless the partners vote to terminate it at an earlier date.

Unlike corporations and irrevocable trusts, a partnership is not a taxpaying entity. A partnership files an annual tax return setting forth its income, but it does not pay tax on its net income. Instead, each partner's proportionate share of income or loss is passed through from the partnership to the individual. Each partner claims his share of deductions or reports his share of income on his personal tax return.

The following example describes an FLP implementation.

EXAMPLE

Joe Mainstreet wants to gift $1.5 million of PrivateCo stock to his daughter through a family limited partnership. Joe creates Mainstreet Family Partnership, funding it with $1.5 million in PrivateCo stock. Joe then makes a gift of a 90% limited partnership interest to his daughter. Mainstreet hires Ann Appraiser, of AppraiseCo, who believes a 25% minority interest discount and 25% lack of marketability discount are warranted. Mainstreet ultimately files a gift tax return showing a $759,000 gift ($1.5 million × 90% = $1.35 million – 25% discounts, consecutively applied). The gift tax calculation is:

Family Limited Partnership Valuation

Original funding:	$1,500,000
Times 90% gifting:	1,350,000
Value on a control, marketable basis:	$1,350,000
Less minority discount (25%):	(337,500)
Value on a minority, marketable basis:	$1,012,500
Less LOMD (25%):	(253,125)
Value of limited partnership gift:	$759,375

> This $1.5 million funding is discounted to a rounded $760,000 gift, thus removing $760,000 from his estate in the first year. Joe Mainstreet must use his lifetime gift exemption to make this gift without triggering a gift tax.

Advantages of the FLP

There are a variety of advantages and disadvantages in using the FLP as a transfer method. Some of the more important advantages are discussed in the next sections.

Facilitates Annual Gifts   In some cases, gifting an asset to a donee fails to achieve the effects of more sophisticated gifting techniques. This occurs if the donor wishes to maintain control over the asset or if the asset is not easily divisible among multiple donees. Rather than gifting the asset itself, a donor may gift limited partnership interests in an FLP to which the asset has been transferred. Typically, the donor is the general partner of the FLP and retains control over the asset and the income. Limited partners have few, if any, rights to participate in the operations of the FLP.

Valuation Discounts   For gift and estate tax purposes, the value of a limited partnership interest is the price at which the interest can be sold to a hypothetical willing buyer. Because the limited partnership interests typically suffer from lack of marketability, lack of control, and few partnership rights, the interests can be discounted from the fair market value of the underlying FLP assets. These discounts are similar in nature and size to the discounts mentioned above with the gifting of private stock interests. Because of possible IRS scrutiny, the valuator must match the level of discounts with the restrictions specifically named in the partnership agreement.

Creditor Protection   Many families utilize an FLP to protect their assets from creditors. The FLP offers a general partner's ability to reinvest the FLP's income rather than distribute it. This is a major disincentive for creditors, whose main right is to receive the income distributed to the limited partner. It should be noted, however, that a transfer with the intent to defraud a creditor will not provide creditor protection. In addition, the liability of a limited partner for the debts and obligations of the partnership will not exceed his or her investment in the FLP.

Under the provisions of the Uniform Limited Partnership Act, the creditor of a partner cannot reach into the partnership and seize property or take specific partnership assets. The creditor has no rights to any property held by the partnership, since title to the assets is held in the name of the partnership and not the individual partner who is liable for the debt.

Disadvantages of the FLP

Although there are only a few disadvantages to an FLP, they are important considerations.

Internal Revenue Service View   The IRS requires a business purpose for establishing an FLP. The IRS is leery of estate planning techniques that enable taxpayers to dramatically reduce their estate tax while maintaining control of the assets in the estate. FLPs have the added distinction of using heavily discounted values as a basis for the giftings, which causes further IRS concern. Taxpayers should engage an experienced professional and use FLPs with care because the IRS continues to view them unfavorably.

Expense   FLPs are expensive to create. It is not unusual for the combined legal and valuation expenses to cost $25,000 or more. For FLPs to be cost effective, these techniques should be a major element of the estate plan.

No Step-up in Basis   Perhaps the biggest disadvantage with using an FLP, like other gifts, is that there is no step-up in tax basis allowed for heirs upon the death of the general partner. Often the private stock basis is low, and losing the potential step-up is quite costly. This is a major issue that should be taken into consideration together with the life expectancy of the general partner.

INTENTIONALLY DEFECTIVE GRANTOR TRUSTS

The final transfer method discussed here involves a private business sale to an intentionally defective grantor trust (IDGT) in exchange for a promissory note. Since the grantor recognizes no gain or loss, the sale is disregarded for income tax purposes, yet it is recognized for transfer tax purposes. If properly structured, the property, in this case the private stock of the company and all subsequent appreciation, is excluded from the grantor's estate. Only the note and any accumulated interest is included in the grantor's estate. Exhibit 30.5 contains the transfer matrix for IDGTs.

Life insurance owned by IDGT may be utilized in this technique. The insurance death benefit may be used to repay the obligation under the note to the seller's estate upon the seller's death, to fund an estate tax liability, provide assets for other estate liquidity needs, or to provide for future generations through the trust.

Mechanics of the IDGT

With an IDGT, the grantor first gifts a substantial sum of cash or other assets to the trust. While there is no official IRS guidance, commentators often recommend that this initial gift be at least 10% of the discounted value of the property to be sold to the trust. If necessary, the grantor pays gift tax on this gift.

EXHIBIT 30.5 Transfer Matrix: Intentionally Defective Grantor Trusts

TRANSFER CHANNELS

Employees	Charitable Trusts	Family	Co-Owner	Outside \<Retire\>	Outside \<Continue\>	Public

TRANSFER METHODS

ESOPs	CRTs	Gifts	Buy/Sell	Negotiated	Consolidate	IPO
MBOs	CRATs	Annuities	Russian roulette	One-step	Roll ups	DPO
MBIs	CRUTs	SCINs	Dutch auction	private auctions	Buy and	Reverse merger
Options	CLTs	GRATs	Handshake	Two-step	build	Going private
Phantom	CLATs	FLPs	Right of	private auctions	Recaps	
SARs	CLUTs	**IDGTs**	first refusal	Public auctions		

Transfer Method	Intentionally Defective Grantor Trust
Definition	An interest in a private business is sold to an IDGT for a promissory note.
Owner motives	The sale is not recognized for income tax purposes yet is recognized for transfer tax purposes. The stock and all subsequent appreciation are excluded from the seller's estate.
Means of transfer	Advanced estate planners and attorneys
Authority	IRS and applicable laws
Value world(s)	Fair market value
Capital access point(s)	Not applicable
Key points to consider	IDGTs are useful for generation-skipping transfers, as the GST exemption may be allocated to the trust for the "seed" gift, while the GST does not apply to a bona fide sale for full consideration. An installment sale to the IDGT allows the trust beneficiaries to receive tax-free the difference between the asset returns and the applicable federal interest rate. IDGTs are aggressive planning techniques and are susceptible to IRS scrutiny. Therefore, owners should seek professional advice before implementation.

The grantor then sells property, discounted when appropriate, to the grantor trust in return for a bona fide promissory note. Because the trust is a grantor trust for income tax purposes, no capital gain is recognized on the sale. The trust assumes the seller's tax basis in the assets.

The note pays the seller interest only, at the applicable federal rate, with a balloon payment of principal due at the end of the term. Once again, because the trust is a grantor trust, interest on the note is neither taxable to the seller nor deductible by the grantor trust. When properly structured, neither gift tax nor generation-skipping transfer tax is due on the transaction because it is truly a sale for full consideration and not a gift.

At the seller's death, the note and any accumulated interest are included in the seller's estate. Neither the trust property nor the property's postsale appreciation is included.

In the interim, the trust purchases insurance on the life of the seller. Ideally, the business interest that is the subject of the sale, plus the "seed" gift, generate enough cash flow to cover the insurance premium as well as principal and interest on the note. At the grantor's death, the death benefit is used to pay the corporation back its premium contributions and pay off the note owed to the seller's estate.

An IDGT is a sophisticated and powerful transfer method, as the following example illustrates.

EXAMPLE

Joe Mainstreet and his wife wish to transfer $4 million of PrivateCo stock to their daughter without paying any gift tax or capital gains tax. Joe creates a limited partnership and contributes $3.2 million of the stock to it. In exchange, he receives a 1% general partnership interest and a 99% limited partnership interest. Joe then creates an IDGT for the benefit of his daughter. Joe gives the trust $800,000 of PrivateCo stock. There is no gift tax because the gift is within the lifetime gift exemption amount.

Next, Joe gives his 1% general partnership interest to his wife. Joe hires Ann Appraiser to value his 99% limited partnership interest. Ann decides that the limited partnership interests should be discounted by 44% due to lack of marketability and minority interest restrictions. Ann appraises the limited partnership interest at $1.8 million ($3.2 million × 99%) = $3.17 million × (1 − 44%). Joe sells his 99% limited partnership interest to the trust for $1.8 million.

In lieu of cash, the trust pays Joe with a ten-year promissory note, paying interest only at the applicable federal rate (assume it is 3.53%), with a balloon payment of $1.8 million due at the end of the term. Since the trust is a grantor trust, the sale does not trigger capital gains tax.

The trust pays interest to Joe in the amount of $63,540 annually and at the end of the tenth year pays the balloon of $1.8 million. Now assume all assets within the trust (i.e., the gifted and sold assets) earn 9% (before interest payments on the note for the sold interests). On a nondiscounted basis, the trust owns $3,968,000 of PrivateCo stock (between gifts and sold FLP interests). Net of interest payments, this results in $4,460,340 of appreciation inside the trust before the IDGT note balloon payment. Net of the $1.8 million IDGT note balloon payment, this results in $6,628,340 inside the trust (at the end of the IDGT term) with no current gift tax, capital gains tax, or estate tax passing to his daughter.

Advantages of an Intentionally Defective Grantor Trust

The advantages of an IDGT are:

- *Generation-skipping tax planning.* Those wishing to use generation-skipping transfer tax planning will find an IDGT useful. Unlike a GRAT, the GST exemption may be allocated to the trust, because the grantor does not retain an interest in the trust.
- *Tax benefit of the sale.* The primary tax benefit of making the installment sale to the IDGT is that if the assets generate more than the applicable interest rate, the difference passes to the trust beneficiaries tax-free.

Disadvantages of the IDGT

Because the IDGT does not rely on statutory and regulatory authority, it is potentially more susceptible to IRS scrutiny. The fair market value of the promissory note at the grantor's death and any prior payments made to the grantor under the note are taxable in the grantor's estate. Further, if the grantor dies before the note has been paid, the IRS might assert that the property sold is included in the grantor's estate or that the capital gain on the sale is taxable to the grantor's estate when the balloon payment on the note is paid. Finally, the legal, valuation, and administrative costs of implementing this technique are significant.

COMPARISON OF FAMILY TRANSFER METHODS

Exhibit 30.6 compares the family transfer methods presented in this chapter on a number of criteria. All of the methods discussed in this chapter involve freezing or reducing the estate for estate tax purposes. In other words, the seller holds the value of the business at the date of transfer, and the grantee benefits from all appreciation of the stock after the transfer. Some of the transfer methods have "maybe" answers, indicating that the method may be subject to the characteristic if the seller has overused his or her exclusions or exemptions. Most owners' goals can be met with a properly engineered solution drawn from this variety of transfer methods.

EXHIBIT 30.6   Comparison of Family Transfer Methods

Characteristic	Gift	SCIN	GRAT	FLP	IDGT
Transfer method is an estate freeze.	Yes	Yes	Yes	Yes	Yes
Seller makes gift.	Yes	No	Yes	Yes	Yes
Seller keeps retained interest.	No	No	Yes	No	No
Transfer method involves promissory note.	No	Yes	No	No	Yes
Transfer method subject to estate tax.	Maybe	No	Maybe	No	No
Transfer method subject to gift tax.	Maybe	No	No	No	No
Transfer method subject to GST.	Maybe	No	Maybe	No	No
Value of business is removed from seller's estate.	Yes	Yes	Yes	Yes	Yes

ROLE OF INSURANCE IN FAMILY TRANSFERS

Managing risk is a critical factor in business success and transfer. Risk management protects the business, its owners, employees, customers, and suppliers and ensures continuity. Certain risks cannot be avoided entirely, while others can be transferred to a third party, such as an insurance company, at a relatively small incremental cost.

Owners are concerned about certain business risks:

- What if a family member, or other key personnel, dies or becomes disabled prior to a transfer?
- When I die, how will estate taxes be paid without forcing the liquidation of my business?
- I have a child actively involved in my business and a child who is not, how do I treat them fairly (not necessarily dollar for dollar) and equalize my estate? In some instances the active child inherits the business while the inactive child inherits the estate tax bill.
- If my business partner dies or becomes disabled, where will the cash come from to buy out his or her interest? Will cash drain the business? Will the bank call-in our outstanding loans/lines of credit?

These threats often can be addressed through proper insurance funding. There are many creative strategies to consider, often using the business itself to pay for the insurance. Even with business insurance already in place, coverage should be reviewed every few years to make sure it is cost effective and structured properly. The insurance marketplace has undergone many changes in recent years resulting in better coverage and more competitive pricing.

Properly structured business life and disability insurance can address the most significant threats to a business transfer plan. In conjunction with the sophisticated methods and techniques described in this chapter, it will help owners achieve their transfer goals.

TRIANGULATION

Family transfers are valued in the world of fair market value. This world and its trusts are highly regulated. The combination of a regulated transfer method and regulated value world makes for a strong bond. It also enables some unusual financial engineering to take place. Trusts are engineered techniques that create a buyer, usually the trust, to facilitate a transfer. In several cases, such as SCINs and GRATs, the transfer method becomes the capital for the transfer. This enables equity to transfer without any cash changing hands. When using intratransfers, the transfer method is a surrogate for the market. No outside market is necessary.

In estate planning, owners intentionally drive the value of the business down. An industry of estate planners is devoted to assist owners in their quest to balance the value of their estates. Gifting large blocks of private stock yet maintaining control of the purse strings motivates owners to employ sophisticated planning techniques. A number of trusts presented in this chapter enable owners to meet this goal.

There is a tension between authorities regarding many of the techniques discussed in this chapter. The IRS insists that estate planning be viewed within the strict confines of a business purpose. In other words, the IRS does not want owners to use these structures, especially FLPs, purely for tax avoidance. Lawyers and estate planners are constantly pushing the envelope on these issues, sometimes causing a tax court intervention. Since these transfer methods and corresponding value world do not emanate from the market, the courts must be the mechanism that both regulates and forces a balance between the parties.

CHAPTER 31

Co-Owner Transfers

At times, it becomes necessary to buy out a partner's interest. The methods available for purchasing other shareholder's interests are known as co-owner transfers. This discussion covers acquiring both equal and unequal partner interests. In the absence of a written ownership agreement, a minority interest holder is at the mercy of the controlling shareholder. Further, 50/50 partners without a buy/sell agreement will not have the tools to settle serious disputes. This chapter discusses buy/sell agreements, first refusal rights, and other techniques available to transfer shareholder interests to partners.

BUY/SELL AGREEMENTS

A buy/sell agreement among the owners of a business fixes the owners' rights with respect to each other and the business. A buy/sell agreement is important to the owners of a private business because it can serve the dual purposes of restricting the transfer of stock to undesirable parties and providing a ready market for the stock sale. If the agreement provides a practical framework for owners, it can resolve a number of issues that might otherwise lead to later conflict. The primary purposes of buy/sell agreements are to:

- Transition business ownership while continuing the operation of the business.
- Create liquidity and a market to sell a business interest.
- Determine the triggering events that will activate the buy/sell.
- Set a price, or formula for determining price, for the business interest.
- Protect against unwanted new partners.
- Provide for dispute resolution procedures prior to disputes occurring.
- Determine the payment terms once the buy/sell is triggered.

A well-constructed buy/sell agreement is similar to a premarital agreement because it is uncertain when one of the partners will want to part company. Dispute resolution procedures are relatively easy to agree on prior to the appearance of a dispute, but they become much more difficult once a dispute arises. Every business with multiple owners should have a buy/sell agreement.

A buy/sell agreement can establish the estate tax value of a private stock only if it satisfies specific conditions as set forth in Internal Revenue Service regulations. The regulations provide that agreements entered into before October 9, 1990, and not substantially modified thereafter will be considered in valuing the decedent's stock for estate tax purposes if both of these conditions are met:

- The agreement is a bona fide business arrangement.
- The agreement is not a device to pass the decedent's shares to the natural heirs for less-than-adequate consideration.

Insubstantial modifications include: those required by the agreement; discretionary changes, such as a company name change; modification of capitalization rates due to specified market interest rate changes; and adjustments to produce a closer approximation to fair market value. The decision whether to modify a grandfathered buy/sell agreement is important. It should be undertaken only with professional estate planning advice.

A decision hierarchy can be used to construct a buy/sell agreement properly. Exhibit 31.1 shows this process. The flow of decision making in the hierarchy indicates that the type of buy/sell agreement must be chosen before decisions are made regarding any corresponding provisions.

Provisions are then negotiated between the parties, reflecting the participants' intentions. Valuation mechanics are then constructed and applied in support of the provisions. These valuation mechanics are described in Chapter 11 and are not repeated here. Finally, buy/sell triggering events are defined, and appropriate funding techniques are chosen. This hierarchy forms the basis for the remaining discussion of buy/sell agreements in this chapter. Exhibit 31.2 provides the transfer matrix for buy/sell agreements.

EXHIBIT 31.1   Buy/Sell Decision Hierarchy

Determine type of buy/sell

↓

Decide major provisions

↓

Apply valuation mechanics
(See Chapter 11 for this discussion)

↓

Consider triggering events

↓

Choose funding technique

EXHIBIT 31.2 Transfer Matrix: Buy/Sell Agreements

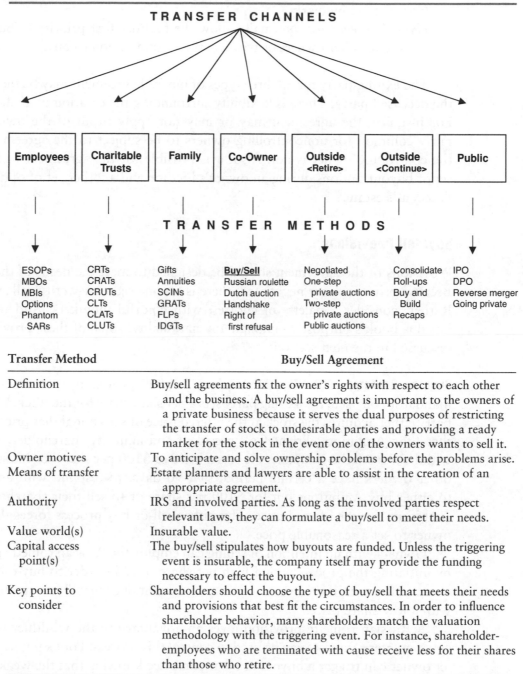

Transfer Method	Buy/Sell Agreement
Definition	Buy/sell agreements fix the owner's rights with respect to each other and the business. A buy/sell agreement is important to the owners of a private business because it serves the dual purposes of restricting the transfer of stock to undesirable parties and providing a ready market for the stock in the event one of the owners wants to sell it.
Owner motives	To anticipate and solve ownership problems before the problems arise.
Means of transfer	Estate planners and lawyers are able to assist in the creation of an appropriate agreement.
Authority	IRS and involved parties. As long as the involved parties respect relevant laws, they can formulate a buy/sell to meet their needs.
Value world(s)	Insurable value.
Capital access point(s)	The buy/sell stipulates how buyouts are funded. Unless the triggering event is insurable, the company itself may provide the funding necessary to effect the buyout.
Key points to consider	Shareholders should choose the type of buy/sell that meets their needs and provisions that best fit the circumstances. In order to influence shareholder behavior, many shareholders match the valuation methodology with the triggering event. For instance, shareholder-employees who are terminated with cause receive less for their shares than those who retire.

BUY/SELL TYPES

There are several types of buy/sell agreements.[1]

- *Repurchase agreements.* The entity (corporation, partnership, limited liability company, etc.) buys the interest from the exiting party.

- *Cross-purchase agreements.* One or more other individuals buy the interest from the exiting party.
- *Hybrid agreements.* Normally allow the founder first priority to buy the interest and other owners or partners the second option to buy.

The exiting party for all three types of buy/sell agreement may be the estate of the deceased party. There is flexibility surrounding the creation of an agreement. For instance, the agreement may or may not apply to all of the owners. It is fairly common for noncontrolling owners to be subject to the agreement while the controlling owner is not. Also, it is possible for the agreement to have one set of buyout options during an owner's lifetime and another set of options for a decedent's estate.[2]

Buy/Sell Provisions

Provisions of the agreement should be designed to meet the needs of the parties. Because provisions are negotiated, there is no one right answer for all situations. Rather, consider a palette of choices, with colorful monikers. And while it is not this book's purpose to impugn any nationality, some of these provisions are discussed in the next sections.

Russian Roulette   In a Russian roulette buy/sell provision, sometimes called a mandatory buy/sell, the exiting party sets a per share price for the stock.[3] The other party either acquires the stock at the offered price or sells out at that price. Assume that John Ambitious, PrivateCo's president and minority shareholder, wishes to withdraw from the company. He sets a price of $100 per share for his stock. The other owners have a certain period, say, 90 days, to respond with an election to either buy Ambitious out for $100 per share or to sell their shareholdings to Ambitious for the offered price. This either-sell-or-buy process forces the exiting owner to set a reasonable price.

Owners with no intention of selling can employ the Russian roulette provision by initiating the process with a high per share price in order to buy out another owner. However, if the owner wants to be bought out she will initiate the buy/sell with a low-share price.

A Russian roulette provision gives an advantage to the wealthier owner because greater resources can be used to control this process. For example, a wealthier owner can trigger a buyout at a bargain price knowing that the weaker owner will be unable to buy out the more affluent owner. To even the playing field, the use of a promissory note to purchase the shares is sometimes allowed.

Dutch Auction   In a Dutch auction provision, any owner can offer to buy the others' shareholdings. The responding owner must either accept the offer or make a counteroffer to buy at an even higher price. Assume once again that John Ambitious offers to buy out the other owners of PrivateCo for $100 per share. The auction provision indicates the minimum increase in price of the counteroffer.

EXHIBIT 31.3   Right of First Refusal Example Process

1. If a shareholder reaches agreement with any third party to sell shares of the company, that shareholder shall notify the company and all other shareholders in writing (the sales notice) with the following information:
   a. The terms of the proposed sale
   b. The date of the proposed sale
   c. The name and interest of the proposed buyer
2. The company shall have 10 days after delivery of the sales notice to notify the selling shareholder in writing that it elects to purchase the offered securities. If the company does not elect to purchase all of the offered securities, each of the remaining shareholders shall have 10 days after delivery of the company notice to notify the selling shareholder in writing that one or more of the shareholders elect to purchase all of the offered securities.
3. If electing to purchase, either the company or remaining shareholders must purchase the shares on the same terms and conditions set forth in the sales notice. If electing not to purchase, the selling shareholder shall have 90 days after the expiration of the notification period in which to complete the sale to the outside party.

The minimum addition can be a fixed amount, a percentage of the initial offer, or some other valuation formula. In this case, assume the other PrivateCo owners must respond within 90 days of the original offer and either accept Ambitious's offer, or counteroffer with a minimum increase of 120% of the original offer, or $120 per share. Normally, the counteroffer must satisfy the payment terms of the original offer.

One variation of this provision requires the initiating owner to accept the counteroffer without change. Following the example, this encourages Ambitious to offer a fair price on his first bid.

Right of First Refusal   The right of first refusal is another buy/sell provision. Under this practice, an owner *must* offer to sell his shares to other owners before selling shares to an outsider. The terms at which the current owners are entitled to buy the shares are predetermined. Generally a formal right of first refusal process is defined in one of the ownership agreements. Exhibit 31.3 is an example of the process.

A right of first refusal severely interferes with an owner's ability to sell the affected stock. Few outsiders will knowingly spend the time and effort to negotiate a stock purchase agreement if they have to wait and see if the existing owners are going to exercise their right of first refusal.

TRIGGERING EVENTS

A buy/sell agreement might sit idle for years until a triggering event occurs. A variety of triggering events activate the buy/sell agreement, including:

- Death
- Long-term disability

- Retirement with notice
- Voluntary termination
- Involuntary termination
- Third-party actions, such as personal bankruptcy or divorce

Other than death, these events need some further explanation. Typically someone is deemed to have a long-term disability according to the definition used in the disability insurance contract in force at the time of the disabling event. A typical disability insurance policy pays as long as the insured cannot perform the material duties of any occupation for which he or she is suited by training, education, or experience for some continuous period of time, say, six months. For example, if a night stockperson for a grocery store suffers injuries that prevent her from performing that function, she may collect disability payments only if she takes a position at less than 60% of her predisability income within 12 months of returning to work. This is called the *any occupation* definition, and many policies have a provision that limits payments in a variety of ways. In many cases, legal advice is necessary to create a disability definition that is appropriate to the user's circumstances.

Employee-owners who give at least one year's notice are said to retire with notice. As Chapter 11 describes, typically the retiring owner does not suffer a discount if he or she gives proper notice.

When the employee-owner freely chooses to quit or retire, this is known as voluntary termination. The board of the company may vote to purchase the shares of the exiting employee. The shareholder's ownership agreement will control the board's decision-making latitude regarding this purchase option.

Involuntary termination occurs when an owner, who is also an employee, is terminated against his or her will. This termination can be for "cause," meaning the owner violated the employment agreement, or "at will," meaning the employee was terminated without a specific reason. In either event, the ex-employee also becomes an ex-owner. This buyout frequently makes business sense because the employee may have become an owner originally because of employee contributions. Once these contributions cease, all attachments to the company also stop.

Third-party actions, such as a personal bankruptcy or divorce, also may trigger a buy/sell action. Most private company owners do not wish to have outsiders as owners, and this trigger protects the company against that kind of incursion. Again, it is typical for the board to vote on whether to call the shares, but the tenets of the ownership agreement should help decide this issue.

The triggering actions are also important because they may help determine value for the shares. For instance, if an employee-owner decides to quit without notice, thereby triggering the buy/sell agreement, the question arises of whether he or she should receive full value for owned shares. Many companies link the triggering event with both the value received and payment terms. This is illustrated in the next example.

EXAMPLE

Joe Mainstreet is selling a 10% stock interest to his president, John Ambitious. Joe realizes he needs to create a buy/sell agreement as part of the sale. Joe wants to link valuation discounts to either a voluntary or an involuntary termination triggering action. He wants to set up a system that would penalize Ambitious for actions not in the company's best interest. Joe believes there should be no discounts associated with Ambitious's death or disability. Joe decides a voluntary termination triggers a 35% discount from the full value of Ambitious's shares (as shown in Chapter 11), mainly because someone should not be able to walk off the job and receive full value. Involuntary termination receives the biggest discount, some 50%. According to Ambitious's employment agreement, only a major violation can cause him to be fired. Finally, Joe decides that third-party actions, such as divorce or personal bankruptcy, are treated as voluntary terminations for valuation purposes.

The PrivateCo ownership agreement might contain a great deal of flexibility regarding the discounting issue. For instance, the agreement might let the non-involved owners decide the level of discount in the triggering events, rather than enforce a hard and fast rule. An example of applying discretion is a third-party action that immediately gets resolved without the threat of an outsider wresting control of the involved owner's stock interest. In this case, the noninvolved owners might not even purchase the shares. Because of this, the buy/sell tenets cannot be viewed in isolation.

FUNDING TECHNIQUES

A company may choose to fund various triggering events differently. In the preceding example, death and disability of an owner may be funded in cash at the time of the event. All other triggering events may be paid over time. It is typical that payments are made monthly over three to five years at a market rate of interest. Generally a process is selected to vary this interest rate over time, such as using the rate set each January 1 as the *Wall Street Journal* prime rate plus some premium. For example, an involuntary termination payout of $200,000 would lead to monthly payments of $3,960 assuming a fixed 7% interest rate with 60 equal monthly payments.

Life insurance may be a source of funding for buy/sell agreements. Insurance provides liquidity, so the estate may be paid in cash without causing financial harm to the company. Also, if permanent life insurance is used, the cash value of the insurance becomes a valuable business asset.

To stay current with insurance needs to fund a buy/sell agreement, owners set an annual equity enterprise value. Without proper precautions, a death might trigger a buy/sell valuation that far exceeds the insurance in force, causing the company to borrow or sell assets to satisfy the claim.

The type of buy/sell agreement may determine how the insurance is paid. The company is the beneficiary of a repurchase agreement. Meanwhile, various stockholders are the beneficiaries in a cross-purchase agreement. Disability cases can be funded through the use of permanent disability insurance coverage or through the annuity or cash value of the life insurance policy.

WAYS TO HANDLE DEADLOCKS

A problem occurs when equal partners in a company need to settle disputes. This may involve two shareholders, each owning a 50% interest, or multiple shareholders polarized into two equal voting blocks. There are five possible ways to handle deadlocks regarding joint control of a company. In order of severity of the solution, they are:

1. *Tie-break director.* An independent "tie-break" director may be added to the board. Typically this director is appointed by mutual agreement of the partners, and she gets involved with a decision only if the partners have deadlocked. Often this director is appointed for a short time, such as one- to two-year term. This situation works best if the independent director is experienced with business and legal matters and does not know either partner.
2. *Mediation.* If a deadlock occurs, the parties hire a mediator who attempts to create a mutually acceptable solution in a short period of time. Typically the mediator's decision is not binding unless both partners agree.
3. *Binding arbitration.* The partners engage an arbitration association to settle the dispute. Each side presents its case, and the arbitrator's decision is binding. This option usually is chosen only after mediation has proven ineffective.
4. *Exercise a buy/sell transfer provision.* This option exists when the partners incorporate a transfer provision into their buy/sell agreement. A Russian roulette or Dutch auction provision serves to settle an intractable argument.
5. *Court-ordered dissolution.* This option is for truly frozen boards where every effort to break the deadlock has failed.

The process for settling disputes works best when it is stipulated and described in the buy/sell agreement. For instance, some agreements spell out the mediation and arbitration procedures, including the firms that will be hired. Other agreements stipulate formulas for dispute resolution.

WHEN NO BUY/SELL AGREEMENT EXISTS

Many companies do not have buy/sell agreements. Surprisingly, this situation is prevalent even in companies with 50/50 ownership. Fortunately, buy/sell agreements can be created at any point in a corporation's life. Readers in a no-buy/sell situation should drop what they are doing and start working on this serious oversight immediately. Once a dispute arises, it is extremely difficult for the parties to agree on a resolution process. Minority holders are especially vulnerable to a bad outcome because they have little or no leverage on the controlling shareholder. If the majority is oppressing the minority, or if the minority dissents from a majority decision, a fair value lawsuit may develop. This is discussed in Chapter 9.

TRIANGULATION

Ownership agreements such as buy/sell agreements provide a unique method of controlling the process of triangulation. When properly drawn, they stipulate the value world and methods to be used in arriving at a value. They also should incorporate the method of financing the transfer. Finally, they dictate the transfer method. In short, they can be used to integrate effectively all three legs of the triangle in a controlled process. Professional buyers, such as private equity groups, always use such agreements for their simplicity and power. Individual business owners seldom use these agreements.

The involved parties are primary authorities in co-owner transfers. The parties pick the value world. Sometimes this is chosen for them by the insurance company's involvement; however, for uninsured triggering events, the parties choose how to value a transfer. Since the deal is created while the parties are still civil and communicating with one another, valuation tends toward the friendly end of the spectrum.

The parties also choose the capital structure to support a transfer. Depending on the motives of the parties, they may require all-cash deals or engineer a financing solution. Defining capital structure for a buyout is especially important when 50/50 ownership is concerned. The 50/50 partners of a screen printer recently experienced the hazards of an ill-designed buy/sell agreement. The partners decided to divorce and agreed to let the tenets of the buy/sell settle the issue. While the agreement helped the partners determine a buyout price, it was silent as to the payment terms. Neither partner had the financial capability to use cash to buy out the other, yet neither would finance the purchase. Ultimately, the company was liquidated due to this impasse.

NOTES

1. Shannon P. Pratt, Robert F. Reilly, and Robert R. Schweihs, *Valuing a Business, The Analysis and Appraisal of Closely Held Companies*, 4th ed. (New York: McGraw-Hill, 2000), p. 624.
2. Ibid., p. 625.
3. A good source of information regarding buy/sell provisions is the Corporate Partnering Institute, "Shareholder Buy/Sell Agreements," www.corporate-partnering.com/info/shareholder-buy-sell-agreements.htm.

Outside Transfers: Retire

Many private company owner-managers transfer their business to an outsider prior to retirement. Often the owners want a lifestyle change. Even though the ultimate transfer occurs to an outsider, some of the transfer methods described in earlier chapters can be incorporated into the sale. For example, it is possible to use charitable trusts, private annuities, or grantor-retained annuity trusts as vehicles for the transfer to an outside buyer. This chapter discusses the proper timing for an outside transfer, the players that might assist with the transfer, the main approaches and marketing processes used to access the market, and the steps required to get to a satisfactory closing of the transaction.

Private business owners have a tendency to control most aspects of their companies. Controlling the transfer process is the last big challenge for an owner who probably has only one chance at the brass ring. Although there is an entire transfer industry at an owner's disposal, this process is too important to be blindly outsourced. The information presented in this chapter enables an owner to play an active part in the transfer.

In business, timing is often everything. This is especially true when a private business owner attempts to create an exit. Often it is difficult to transfer a private business. Most owners are surprised to find that it is easier to get into business than it is to get out. A multitude of variables must be aligned to enable a successful transfer. Even *timing* has multiple variables. Proper timing of any business transfer is paramount to achieving a maximizing solution. Transfer timing is comprised of personal, business, and market timing. Transfer timing can be likened to winning on a slot machine. Unless all three timing slots are aligned, there is no possibility of a big payout. Exhibit 32.1 depicts this gaming/timing metaphor.

The first slot represents the owner's personal timing. The owner must be physically, mentally, financially, and socially prepared to execute a transfer. The second slot is business timing. Good business timing exists when the company is well positioned to attract positive attention by virtue of its internal operations, management techniques, and financial performance. Market timing refers to the activity level for transferring a business interest in the marketplace. A "good" market is characterized by aggressive buyer activity both in terms of interest levels and acquisition multiples. The most successful transfer, from an owner's perspective, occurs when these three slots are in alignment.

Generally a less-than-satisfactory result occurs if any of the timing slots are out of calibration. For instance, owners who are not in a strong personal position to transfer the business may find it necessary to sell at less-than-optimum price or

EXHIBIT 32.1   Transfer Timing

terms. Of course, if the business is not ready to transfer, it is unlikely that outside offers will be attractive to the owner. If the market does not support the sales process, either the transfer will not occur or it will occur at less-than-optimal price and terms.

PREPARATION FOR A TRANSFER

There are a host of activities an owner can undertake to prepare for a transfer. Exhibit 32.2 shows the planning steps that correlate to the timing slots just described.

EXHIBIT 32.2   Preparation Steps for a Business Transfer

Personal	Business	Market
Reduce dependence of owner The owner should not be central to the operations of the business. The sales team should handle key customer accounts. The management team should be running the business. The owner spends the most time on strategic issues.	*Improve the financial records* Audited financial statements may be expensive, but they more than pay for themselves in the transfer process. Audited statements reduce risk from a buyer's perspective. Companies should also clean up all legal issues, such as lawsuits and environmental issues, prior to marketing a business.	*Ride the wave* Peak selling cycles in the overall private capital markets tend to happen every 5 to 7 years. Normally the crest of this merger wave occurs in the last 18 to 24 months of the cycle. Various investment banking organizations track these cycles.
Continue to take out money The owner can continue to take money out of the company, as these items will be recast. The key here is good record keeping so a buyer can trace all owner compensation.	*More and better systems* Financial and management systems should be upgraded. Companies should be able to track product line profitability, capacity requirements, sales forecasts by stock-keeping unit, etc. The more control a company has over its business, the more a buyer will respect the selling process.	*Consolidators may be watching* Many industries continue to consolidate, in some cases, on a global basis. Typically there are a handful of consolidating companies that intend to grow through acquisition. Often private equity groups control these acquirers. Owners should monitor the activities of consolidators, usually through trade associations and the media.
Get estate in order Estate planning can require years to effect. The best plans are proactive, not reactive. Owners wishing to implement sophisticated techniques should seek professional help.	*Clean up the place* Clean and organized facilities make a positive difference. In some cases, it makes sense for the owner to have phase I or II environmental audits performed before the selling process begins.	*Keep an eye open* The market may present itself at a moment's notice. Special one-time opportunities may knock on the owner's door.

Successful owners incorporate these action steps, in preparation for a business transfer, into their business plans. If retirement follows the closing of the deal, a capable management team must be in place. Obviously, building a quality management team takes years to accomplish. Owners who cannot remove themselves from daily operations tend to receive less for their company and face the privilege of signing a multiyear employment agreement with the new owner.

TRANSFER PLAYERS

There are thousands of business brokers, mergers and acquisitions (M&A) intermediaries, and investment bankers in the United States ready to assist owners in transferring their business. These players inhabit the private capital markets.

- *Business broker.* The International Business Brokers Association defines a business broker as one "who works with either buyers or sellers of businesses to help them realize their goals."[1] Business brokers provide a range of services including seller and buyer representation, arranging financing for a deal, and generating market valuations.
- *M&A intermediary.* M&A intermediaries focus on providing merger, acquisition, and divestiture services to middle-market companies. Hundreds of firms specialize in this area. For discussion purposes, all other practitioners are grouped in this category. For instance, some lawyers, CPAs, and financial consultants also act as M&A intermediaries.
- *Investment banker.* Investment bankers specialize in raising the capital that businesses require for long-term growth, and they advise firms on strategic matters involving mergers, acquisitions, and other transactions. Public investment bankers assist public companies in accessing the public capital markets. Private investment bankers help private companies access the private capital markets. This chapter describes only the latter.

Exhibit 32.3 shows a comparison between the various transfer players. Transaction size is the most obvious difference between the players. Business brokers typically complete transactions of less than $2 million. Both M&A intermediaries and private investment bankers work on deals up to $100 million or more. Public investment bankers normally work on larger transactions but may be involved in divestitures or other smaller deals.

The ability to raise capital also distinguishes the players. Business brokers and intermediaries may help arrange loans to close a deal, but typically they are not active with private placements or syndications or in raising equity. Private investment bankers normally can raise the entire capital structure offered in the private capital markets. Public investment bankers access the entirety of the private and public capital markets.

The size and sophistication of the goals influences whom to hire. Several questions help filter the players.

EXHIBIT 32.3 Comparison of Transfer Players

Characteristic	Business Broker	M&A Intermediary	Private Investment Banker	Public Investment Banker
1. Typical transaction size	<$2 million	$2 to $100 million	$2 to $100 million	>$50 million
2. Seller and buyer representation	Yes	Yes	Yes	Yes
3. Company valuations	Yes	Yes	Yes	Yes
4. Post an asking price	Yes	Maybe	No	No
5. Capital structure raising	No	No	Yes	Yes
6. Management buyouts	Maybe	Maybe	Yes	Yes
7. Recapitalizations	No	Maybe	Yes	Yes
8. Board advisory services	No	No	Yes	Yes
9. Reverse mergers	No	No	Maybe	Yes
10. Tenders offers	No	No	Maybe	Yes
11. Access public markets	No	No	No	Yes
12. Likely selling process	Negotiated	Negotiated/Private	Private auction	Public auction

- Is the firm familiar with all appropriate value worlds?
- Is the firm able to draw from all capital access points in assembling financing?
- Is the firm familiar with the rich variety of alternatives in the private transfer spectrum?

Answers to these questions and many others will help an owner determine the appropriate player to engage.

MARKETING PROCESSES

The circumstances and needs of the owner lead to the selection of an appropriate marketing process for the business. The three broad marketing processes are negotiated, private auction, and public auction. A negotiated selling process is warranted when only one prospect is identified and the entire process is focused on that prospect. A private auction process is used when a handful of prospects are identified. A public auction process announces the opportunity to the market. Further description of these processes is shown in Exhibit 32.4.

A seller should match her needs with one of these marketing processes. Hybrid forms can be used. For instance, a negotiated transfer process may involve several buyers simultaneously, each at different points in the process. Business brokers typically use this process. There may be a handful of buyers interested in purchasing the company, some of whom are making offers while a few may be meeting the owner for the first time. A private auction, however, may be used for as few as one or two prospective buyers but ideally involves more. In this case, the process is orchestrated to convince the buyers that an auction is under way.

Private and public auctions each have one- and two-step variations. A one-step auction is like herding cattle with prospective buyers playing the part of stampeding bovines. The intermediary attempts to maintain control and keep the procession as orderly as possible. With a fair amount of skill and some luck, a

EXHIBIT 32.4 Marketing Processes

Characteristic	Negotiated	Private Auction	Public Auction
Best to use when	There is one "perfect-fit" prospect. Confidentiality is at a premium.	A select group of buyers is identified. This may be consolidators or other synergistic players in the market.	Confidentiality is not important. This may involve troubled or public companies.
Summarized process	The parties work out a highly customized deal. Investment value and owner value must be aligned for a deal to work. There may be simultaneous due diligence and contract negotiations.	The buyer group is managed in an auction setting. Buyers receive information at the same time and are herded toward an offer at the same point. This works best if synergy value is quantifiable. Can be one or two steps.	Public announcements are made regarding the sale. The market is completely explored. General offering materials are provided. Buyers are quickly sorted. Can be one or two steps.
Seller perspective	Sellers control the process. Information is tailored to buyers' needs, while maintaining strict confidentiality.	Sellers still maintain control of the process, but there is some risk of a confidentiality break. The final result of the process may or may not yield the highest market price available in the broader market.	An intermediary directs traffic. Sellers oversee the process and should believe that the highest market price has been achieved.
Buyer perspective	Offer may preempt discussions with other prospects. Normally buyers can learn enough about the subject to measure cash flow and risk.	Buyers believe they have one shot to perform or the competition may prevail in the acquisition.	Buyers believe the business will be sold, usually in a short period of time. Sellers may dictate terms and conditions of the sale.

buyer might be corralled into paying a fair price. A two-step auction is more formal than the one-step auction. The two steps are staged with specified deadlines.

The negotiated and private auction marketing processes are described at length in the next section. The public auction process is quite similar to the private auction, except the former employs a mass marketing approach. Since this book is targeted at private companies, the public auction is not detailed here.

NEGOTIATED TRANSFERS

A negotiated transfer is a fairly flexible process since it is dependent on the wishes of the seller. However, Exhibit 32.5 depicts the steps that need to occur for a successful outcome.

Sellers should obtain a confidentiality agreement from the buyer. A confidentiality agreement, also called a nondisclosure agreement, restricts a buyer's use of any information supplied by the seller. Generally the seller or the seller's attorney supplies this document. Once the agreement is executed, the seller supplies information to the buyer, including financial statements, recast items, and whatever else helps the buyer get to the point of making an offer. It is the seller's choice as to whether to state an asking price for the business. The size of the transaction

Execute a confidentiality agreement

Information exchange

Execute a letter of intent

Buyer due diligence/drafting definitive agreements

Closing

EXHIBIT 32.5 Negotiated Transfer: Steps to Completion

and the orientation of the seller help make this decision. Typically smaller deals employ asking prices; therefore, most business-brokered transactions start with a price. Midsize and larger deals normally do not state a price because synergies may be incorporated into the price, and it is difficult to estimate these accurately in advance.

At some point the buyer may make an offer for the business, usually in the form of a letter of intent (LOI). A letter of intent is generally a legally nonbinding agreement that describes all of the important terms of the deal. Most LOIs contain these key provisions:

- Description of what is being purchased (assets, stock, details)
- Description of what is excluded (specific assets)
- Proposed purchase price with possible adjustments
- Delivery terms of purchase price (cash at close, payment over time, seller note)
- Earn-out provisions (stated with as much precision as possible)
- Due diligence period (scope of the diligence plus time required)
- Conditions to proposed transaction (financing contingencies, other)
- Consulting and noncompete agreements (precise terms)
- Various representations
- Conduct of business until the closing (no material changes)
- Disclosure statements (no public announcements)
- No-shop agreement (exclusive dealing clause)
- Governing law (which state or country governs)
- Closing date

A properly constructed LOI may be 5 to 20 pages long. It is recommended that all deal-killer issues be drafted into the letter. The deal-closing lawyers use the LOI to draft the final purchase and sale documents.

When an LOI is executed the buyer begins the due diligence stage. The buyer generates a due diligence list of required information. This list might be lengthy and will contain financial, operating, and legal questions. The due diligence period may last 60 to 90 days, and this timing should be spelled out in the letter of intent. About halfway through the due diligence period, the closing lawyers begin drafting the closing documents. As these are the final definitive legal agreements, care is taken to ensure that the will of the parties is correctly articulated. Typical closing documents include a purchase and sale agreement, possibly a short-term employment agreement with the seller, a noncompete agreement from the seller, and other agreements such as a real estate lease. Exhibit 32.6 provides the transfer matrix for negotiated transfers.

EXHIBIT 32.6   Transfer Matrix: Negotiated Transfers

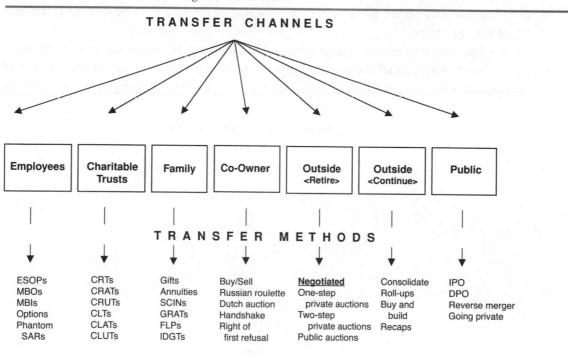

Transfer Methods	Negotiated Transfers
Definition	One or more buyer prospects are identified and negotiated with independently.
Owner motives	To maintain maximum confidentiality and transfer the business only if the deal is right.
Means of transfer authority	An industry of brokers and intermediaries are available to assist the owner, including business brokers, M&A intermediaries, and private investment bankers.
Value world(s)	Market value.
Capital access point(s)	Most CAPs are available to support a negotiated transfer.
Key points to consider	Negotiated transfers often are used for smaller deals, where an owner is a seller only if the deal is right. Either a buyer initiates the discussion with an owner or a broker contacts numerous buyers who have previously registered with the broker. The deal is highly customized and must align owner value and investor value for a successful conclusion.

PRIVATE AUCTIONS

The dictionary defines an auction as "the public sale at which goods or property are sold to the highest bidder." Intermediaries have modified the auction concept to sell private companies confidentially. In a private auction, the intermediary attempts to entice a limited number of buyers into a quiet auction setting. Unlike a public sale auction, where the bidders see each other and strategize based on this awareness, the private auction creates a bidding environment. A savvy intermediary orchestrates this process to the benefit of the seller, both in terms of confidentiality and a maximized selling price.

Private auctions may have one or two steps. A one-step auction concurrently encourages interest within a limited group of buyers. One-step auctions are most appropriate where the likely buyers are known prior to the auction. In all likelihood, they are synergistic buyers. Finally, the intermediary does not want to advertise an auction process is being employed for fear that buyers with the best fit will not play.

The one-step private auction typically uses the process shown in Exhibit 32.7.

Several aspects of the one-step private auction are different from the negotiated transfer process described earlier. The auction process generally relies on a selling

Execute a confidentiality agreement

Distribute a selling memorandum

Buyer visits

Call for offers

Negotiate synergy sharing

Execute a letter of intent

Buyer due diligence/definitive agreements

Closing

EXHIBIT 32.7 One-Step Private Auction: Steps to Completion

memorandum to disseminate information to the buyers. This document is created by the intermediary and basically tells the story of the subject company and the deal. The subject's financial statements are usually recast for discretionary and one-time expenses. The intermediary includes whatever information is necessary to enable a buyer to make an informed offer, without giving too much sensitive data away. For example, customer and employee names should not be included in the memorandum. Product-line profitability of the subject might be included as long as no cost-of-sales detail is provided. The intermediary and seller decide what information should be presented in the selling memorandum.

All interested buyers visit the seller within a fairly short period. This ensures buyers receive the same information at approximately the same time. For confidentiality reasons, visits are normally held outside of the seller's facility. If an intermediary is engaged, it is typical for buyers to interact directly with the seller only once prior to offer and agreement.

At some point after the last buyer visit, the intermediary calls for offers. The call may be a phone call, an email, or a letter. The intermediary states the desired format for the response. Depending on the circumstances, a phone conversation between the intermediary and decision maker for the prospective buyer may suffice. In other cases, a term sheet outlining the buyer's offer is warranted. Finally, a more formal letter of intent may be required. The intermediary's goal in the process is to foster competition, receiving multiple offers within the same week accomplishes this mission.

A deal really starts once the first offer is received. Unless one of the buyers makes a preemptive offer, the first-round offers are typically disappointing. A preemptive offer is an attempt to lock out the other bidders with a high purchase offer. While preemptive offers occur too often to be considered urban myths, most of the time the intermediary needs to improve one of several less-than-acceptable offers. Every deal maker has developed methods for dealing with this issue. Some will try to force or coerce a buyer into improving the offer. Intimidating buyers into paying more works well in the movies but not so well in the real world. A better approach is to discover how much more a buyer can afford to pay and still meet return expectations. This can be accomplished if the seller and buyer share synergies created by the deal. In other words, it can be accomplished when the deal is valued in the synergy subworld of market value.

The synergy subworld represents the market value of the subject when synergies from a possible acquisition are considered. Synergy is the increase in performance of the combined firm over what the two firms are already expected or required to accomplish as independent companies. From a valuation viewpoint, synergies are captured mainly from increases in the benefit stream of the combined firm.

A benefit stream may comprise earnings, cash flow, and distributions. This benefit stream is economic in that it is either derived by recasting financial statements or determined on a pro forma basis. Since the synergy subworld signifies the highest value available in the marketplace, the stream reflects the varied possibilities that exist in the market. The benefit stream for this subworld is:

$$\text{Recast EBITDA} + \text{Amount of enjoyed synergies}$$

Recast earnings before interest, taxes, depreciation, and amortization (EBITDA) is adjusted for one-time expenses and various discretionary expenses of the seller. These earnings are measured before interest since the valuation assumes a debt-free basis, and on a pretax basis since the market value world typically does not consider the tax status of either party. This lack of tax consideration is driven by the fact that many private companies are non-taxpaying flow-through entities, such as S corporations and limited liability companies. There are significant differences within the individual tax rates, such that tax rates for other parties cannot be determined with certainty. A pretax basis enables the parties to view the business on a similar basis. The amount of enjoyed synergies represents the synergies that a party can reasonably expect to realize, or receive credit for, in the acquisition. Chapter 7 shows how to analyze synergies in a market valuation setting.

Intermediaries attempt to use the private auction process to maximize synergy sharing on behalf of their clients. This is vital since only the numerator of the value equation can be influenced by the intermediary.

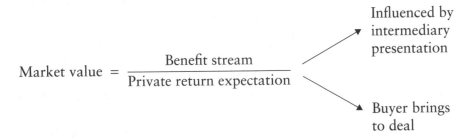

$$\text{Market value} = \frac{\text{Benefit stream}}{\text{Private return expectation}}$$

Influenced by intermediary presentation

Buyer brings to deal

The denominator of the valuation equation is the required rate of return needed by the buyer to compensate for the risk of making a particular investment. Once buyers understand the risk of an investment, they bring this expectation to the deal.

Another way of considering expected investor returns is to take the reciprocal of the buyer's expected rate of return, or capitalization rate, which then becomes a selling multiple. For example, an 18.0% weighted average cost of capital corresponds to an acquisition multiple of 5.6 (1/.18). This is a shorthand way of considering this issue, as the conversion does not incorporate long-term growth. In general terms, this prospective buyer could pay 5.6 times the benefit stream for an acquisition candidate and still meets its expectation. In this case, the buyer is betting that the benefit stream will continue for a minimum of 5.6 years. Increases in the benefit stream over the six years would increase the buyer's overall return.

The capitalization rate is somewhat fixed by a particular buyer, whereas the benefit stream varies with different buyers. Perhaps the following PrivateCo example can demonstrate this point.

EXAMPLE

Joe Mainstreet has decided to sell PrivateCo. On the suggestion of his lawyer, Joe hires Dan Dealmaker, a private investment banker, to assist in the sale. Dan believes PrivateCo is salable and a one-step private auction is the most suitable marketing process for the company. Dan researches the market and finds 12 prospective buyers for the business. Joe adds three to four companies that have periodically inquired about buying the business.

Dan sends a fact sheet and confidentiality agreement to the 16 companies that comprise the final prospect list. Of course, the fact sheet does not name PrivateCo.

Everything is coded to ensure confidentiality. Ten of the 16 prospects respond with an executed confidentiality agreement. Dan phones the ten to further discuss their acquisition programs and decides to cut three from this list for various reasons. The list is pared to seven.

Dan sends the seven interested parties a selling memorandum. Aside from the normal narrative, Dan recasts PrivateCo's income statement as shown (taken from Chapter 6).

Item	Y/E 20X3	Y/E 20X2	Y/E 20X1
Pretax profits	$1,800	$1,368	$1,950
Adjustments			
Depreciation	356	360	358
Normalized capital expenditures[a]	(300)	(300)	(300)
Excess owner compensation[b]	250	250	250
Management fees[c]	200	189	304
Interest[d]	95	99	97
Officer insurances[e]	5.0	4.5	4.6
Excess accounting[f]	6.5	10.5	8.5
Excess legal[g]	8.7	0	0
Excess rent[h]	9.9	9.6	12
Excess health insurance	8.2	14	14
Casualty loss—fire[i]	35	0	0
One-time consulting[j]	0	55	0
Donations[k]	74	69	72
Employee incentives[l]	125	115	117
Total adjustments	873	876	937
Recast EBITDA	$2,673	$2,244	$2,887

[a]Normalized capital expenditures have been deducted from depreciation to offset noncash charges.

[b]Since the majority owner is passive, all his compensation will be added back.

[c]Management fees are charged each year by another company that the majority owner also controls.

[d]Interest expense is added back to accurately depict cash flow.

[e]Officer insurances are added back since the majority shareholder will not be on the payroll after the sale.

[f]Some accounting services are performed by another company the majority owner controls and are billed to PrivateCo.

[g]One-time expense. Former employee illegally took blueprints, and PrivateCo successfully sued this person.

[h]Assumes current rent will not continue under new ownership.

[i]The uninsured part of a fire (one-time expense).

[j]A consultant was hired to perform design studies for a new product, which was not produced.

[k]The company gives donations each year to a charity the majority owner supports.

[l]Employee incentives includes bonuses that only a passive shareholder would institute.

Dan believes the prospects will buy into a recast EBITDA number of around $2.5 million. Some buyers give credit for certain adjustments while others do not. Dan also believes that, on the average, this group of buyers will view the risk of achieving the earnings at about 20%. PrivateCo's industry players pay about five times recast earnings, which further confirms his hypothesis. Multiplying the likely selling multiple (5) by the likely recast EBITDA yields a likely enterprise value of $12.5 million (5 × $2.5 million). Joe will pay off PrivateCo's long-term debt of $500,000 at the close, so Dan Dealmaker is expecting offers of *at least* $12 million.

Five companies decide to visit. Dan schedules all of the visits within a two-week period, to be held at his own office. Three of the buyers visit PrivateCo's facility at night. Two industry buyers choose not to visit the facility. There are few secrets in PrivateCo's industry. Several weeks after the final visit, Dan calls for offers. Three companies make offers by submitting term sheets. One offer is for $11 million, and the other two offers are for less than $10 million.

Fortunately, Dan is a veteran and knows it is show time. The highest bid comes from a company in PrivateCo's industry that can horizontally integrate Joe Mainstreet's operation into their own. Dan smells synergies. With Joe's help, Dan compiles the next list of probable synergies (taken from Chapter 7).

Anticipated Cost Savings Synergies Generated by PrivateCo/Horizontal Integrator			
Synergy	Total $ Amount	% Enjoyed by PrivateCo	$ Synergy for PrivateCo
1. Eliminate payables clerk	$35,000	30%	$10,500
2. Eliminate receivables clerk	35,000	30%	10,500
3. Payroll savings	30,000	30%	9,000
4. Eliminate controller	75,000	30%	22,500
5. Reduced health insurance costs	290,000	30%	87,000
6. Other insurance savings	235,000	30%	70,500
7. Facility consolidations	900,000	30%	270,000
8. Selling expense savings	150,000	30%	45,000
9. Interest savings	30,000	30%	9,000
Total synergies	$1,780,000	Total shared synergies	$534,000

Dan Dealmaker believes he can get credit from the buyer for about 30% of the total synergies, or $534,000. This increases PrivateCo's benefit stream to about $3 million. Dan employs a proprietary process that he has used successfully through the years to entice the buyer to share these synergies. After another month of hard work, Dan is able to negotiate a deal for about $13.5 million. Here are the numbers.

Original offer	$11 million
Original multiple offered	at 4.5 × recast EBITDA
Original recast EBITDA	$2.5 million
Ultimate offer	$13.5 million
Ultimate multiple offered	at 4.5 × recast EBITDA + shared synergies
Ultimate benefit stream	$3 million ($2.5 MM EBITDA + $.5 MM synergy)

> Of course, the deal craters during due diligence over some nitpicking drivel. But none of this should detract from the fine work performed by the hero of this story, the tireless but underappreciated private investment banker.

In this example, the buyer's return expectation does not change during the deal. Only the benefit stream changes to enable a higher purchase price. A real-world consideration: No buyer offers to pay a higher price without being pressured, even if it can afford to. It is the seller's responsibility to employ a transfer process that leverages its strengths so that a buyer will pay the maximum price.

TWO-STEP PRIVATE AUCTIONS

A two-step private auction is a more formal selling process than the one-step auction. A two-step auction process is most useful when the subject is so desirable that a formal auction process will not scare buyers away. Each step of the selling process is staged using deadlines. For instance, once a confidentiality agreement is executed and limited information is shared, the first stage calls for a written expression of interest. Only the top prospects are allowed to continue to the next step. In the second step, the prospects are allowed additional access to more detailed information about the target. Finally, the intermediary calls for a final offer, usually in the form of a formal letter of intent. The intermediary posts all rules for the two-step auction at the beginning of the process, complete with dates of completion for key events.

Exhibit 32.8 contains the transfer matrix for one- and two-step auctions.

Exhibit 32.9 depicts the two-step process. There are five important differences from the one-step process.

1. The two-step private auction uses dates and deadlines to move from one-step to the next. Unlike the one-step process, the buyers know they are in a rules-driven auction.
2. The universe of potential buyers is probably larger in a two-step auction. Instead of 5 to 15 prospects as in a one-step auction, there may be dozens of buyers introduced to the deal.
3. Once the buyers sign a confidentiality agreement and receive a selling memorandum, they have a relatively short period of time to submit an expression of interest including the price range they would be willing to pay. Exhibit 32.10 shows an example expression of interest letter. Of course, there are hedges on this value since the buyers have not talked with management on the subject nor reviewed any additional information other than what is presented in the memorandum. Based on the expression, the intermediary picks the top 6 to 10 prospects, who then enter the second step of the auction.

EXHIBIT 32.8   Transfer Matrix: One- and Two-Step Private Auctions

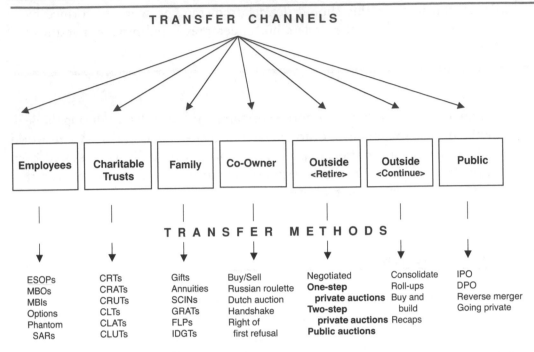

Transfer Methods	One-Step Private Auction	Two-Step Private Auction
Definition	This type of auction concurrently encourages interest within a limited group of buyers.	This type of auction uses stages and deadlines to manage a large group of interested buyers.
Owner motives	The owner believes only a handful of buyers are synergistic with the company. By approaching only a few buyers, confidentiality should be maintained.	The owner believes the company is highly desirable and is willing to subject the company to market-wide scrutiny.
Means of transfer	An industry of brokers and intermediaries are available.	An industry of brokers and intermediaries are available.
Authority	M&A intermediaries and private investment bankers	M&A intermediaries and private investment bankers
Value world(s)	Market value	Market value
Capital access point(s)	Nearly all CAPs are available.	Nearly all CAPs are available.
Key points to consider	One-step auctions are appropriate for industry buyers because the buyers are identifiable, synergistic, and paranoid about entering full-blown auctions.	Two-step auctions force an owner to forgo confidentiality in the hope of better offers. This process is suitable for divestitures and absentee owners.

4. The use of data rooms to support buyer visits is an additional difference. Some intermediaries use data rooms with a one-step auction, but they tend to be more prevalent with the more formal two-step process. A data room is just an area, often a digital warehouse, that contains mountains of data that a buyer can review to better understand the subject.

5. After the visits, the intermediary calls for offers. In some cases, the intermediary supplies the offer format for the buyer to use at this stage. The buyer is requested to fill in the price and other terms that are peculiar to their offer.

Execute a confidentiality agreement

Distribute a selling memorandum

Step 1: Formal expression of interest

Buyer visits—data room

Step 2: Call for offers—seller-supplied format

Negotiate synergy sharing

Execute a letter of intent

Buyer due diligence/definitive agreement

Closing

EXHIBIT 32.9 Two-Step Private Auction:
Steps to Completion

CLOSING THE DEAL

Closing a deal is usually an extremely difficult undertaking. Seemingly there are dozens of obstacles yet only two variables that promote a closing: the will of the parties. If both buyer and seller are not committed to fighting through the issues, especially those that arise on the day of closing, no deal will happen.

Once a letter of intent is executed and due diligence is mainly completed, the parties negotiate the definitive agreement. This is the legal agreement that contains the legal understanding between the parties. These negotiations are best performed in a team approach, with a lawyer taking the lead but with support from the intermediary, CPA, owner, and other professionals as needed. Issues that typically arise are:

- Representations and warranties by the parties
- Material adverse changes to closing (buyer can terminate the deal if major)

EXHIBIT 32.10   Example Expression of Interest Letter

To Dan Dealmaker:

ABC Industries, Inc. ("ABC") is pleased to confirm its interest in acquiring the business and assets of PrivateCo. Some of the assets that we would be acquiring include customer lists, trademarks, technology, formulations, process know-how, intellectual property, good work in process (if any), active raw materials, good finished goods, the manufacturing site, etc.

Based on the limited information provided to us, our indicative, nonbinding offering price for PrivateCo is $10 million, payable in cash. This value assumes that no cash would be included in the assets to be transferred and that the assets would be transferred on a debt-free basis. The cash to be paid by ABC would be obtained from internal and other sources in the usual course of business. No special financing would be necessary.

We also would structure the nonbinding offer to include a maximum earn-out of $5 million payable over a two-year period. The details of the earn-out would need to be discussed, but would be based on the business meeting its sales and EBITDA projections for FY 20X4 and FY 20X5.

In making this nonbinding offer, ABC has assumed that fiscal year 20X3 sales for PrivateCo would be approximately $25 million with a recast EBITDA of $2.5 million. Our nonbinding offer has further assumed that ABC, as the purchaser, would acquire the working capital. Our valuation assumed that PrivateCo would meet its sales forecast for the 20X4–20X6 time frame. Without any balance sheet information, ABC had to make estimates for PrivateCo's working capital.

ABC feels that we could bring sales and marketing synergies to PrivateCo, and we could obtain cost savings in administration, manufacturing, or raw materials. These synergies were included in our valuation.

In general, the ABC associates feel that the acquisition of PrivateCo could bring significant value to ABC.

This expression of interest is not to be considered, and is not, a binding offer, and is subject to ABC conducting due diligence as it deems appropriate. ABC is prepared to commence due diligence as soon as practicable for PrivateCo. Attached is a list of ABC's typical due diligence requirements. In any event, ABC shall have no legal obligations to PrivateCo, nor PrivateCo to ABC, unless and until definitive agreements have been executed and delivered.

ABC's nonbinding offer is further subject to: (i) the approval of ABC's Executive Committee and its Board of Directors, (ii) the approval by any required regulatory bodies or governmental agencies, and (iii) the negotiation of a definitive purchase agreement between the parties.

The submission of this indication of interest is made on a confidential basis. It is understood that neither the fact of this proposal or its terms, nor the identity of ABC as having submitted an indication of interest, will be disclosed other than in connection with the analysis of this proposal by PrivateCo and its advisors or as may be required to be disclosed, in the opinion of PrivateCo's counsel, by law.

ABC has made a number of acquisitions with a view to strengthening and expanding its Industrial Widget businesses. PrivateCo could represent an important extension of this strategy. ABC has the managerial experience and the resources to conclude this transaction expeditiously.

Very truly yours,

Tom Smith, President of ABC

- Indemnity provisions including caps and baskets (amount by which there will be no offset against the escrow)
- Escrow to secure indemnity; possible remedy beyond escrow
- Amount/period
- Survival of representations at least through escrow period, possibly longer
- Conditions to closing for both parties
- Minimum target net worth closing condition, with possible purchase price
- Adjustments based on changes to net worth at the closing

- One-way breakup fee (2%–4% of the purchase price is typical)
- Noncompetes from shareholders
- Employment agreements from key employees

It is not unusual for these negotiations to take several months. A successful tactic is to have weekly conference calls or meetings between the teams so that each issue is dealt with as part of the entire negotiation. Once the definitive agreement and other agreements, such as employment, noncompetes, and lease agreements, are executed, money changes hands and the deal is legally closed.

AFTER THE TRANSFER

This chapter assumes the goal of the owner-manager is to retire as soon as possible after the transfer. If the owner has a strong management team in place, departure may occur soon after the closing. This is another incentive for an owner to build a team. Without a strong team, the owner may need to stay with the company for two to three years after the closing to ensure a smooth transition. Some sellers view this period as equivalent to jail time. The new owner always seems to employ procedures that rub the old owner the wrong way. Owners in a long-term employment agreement position should negotiate a walk-away-without-pay-or-penalty employment agreement just in case they cannot take it anymore.

TRIANGULATION

It is an American dream to sell a business for a bundle and ride off into the sunset. This chapter discusses several strategies to enable owners to realize this dream.

In business, timing is everything. This is certainly true when it comes to business transfer. The timing trifecta occurs when personal, business, and market timing converge. Less-than-perfect solutions usually result if only one or two of the transfer timings are aligned. Since owners cannot control market timing, they must watch market movements.

Outside transfers occur in the open market and are valued in the world of market value. It is the unspoken goal of every owner to achieve a value in the synergy subworld of market value. In order to meet this goal, a company needs to be of sufficient size and complexity. Most companies fall short of this goal but still can be sold in the financial subworld.

Many investment bankers employ a one-step auction selling process and invite handfuls of strategic and nonstrategic buyers. The latter group serves as an insurance policy. Recently a medium-size industrial distributor was sold using this strategy. None of the industry players would share synergies with the seller, so the deal was valued in the financial subworld. The seller instead chose to sell 80% of his company to a private equity group. Rather than leaving the company at the closing, he decided to stay on the job and grow the business to another level. His hope is that the 20% remainder interest eventually will be worth as much as the 80% he received in the original sale. This recapitalization strategy is the subject of Chapter 33.

NOTE

1. www.ibba.org.

Outside Transfers: Continue

Many owner-managers of private companies wish to transfer all or part of their business to an outsider, but they plan to continue operating the business for the foreseeable future. Some owners want to continue to have a financial interest in the business going forward. Frequently they need growth capital but do not want to risk their personal net worth in the process. Owners can choose between two primary transfer methods to meet these goals.

1. They can transfer their business to an outside entity that is consolidating similar companies across the industry. When the consolidation occurs simultaneously with an initial public offering, the transfer is called a roll-up.
2. Owners can choose to transfer most of their business to a company controlled by a private equity group, which then funds an aggressive growth plan. These transfers are called recapitalizations.

This chapter describes these two transfer methods.

Even though the ultimate transfer occurs to an outside investor, some of the transfer methods described in earlier chapters can be incorporated into the sale. For example, it is possible to use charitable trusts, private annuities, or grantor-retained annuity trusts as vehicles for the transfer to an outside buyer. Many owners hire a business broker, mergers and acquisitions intermediary, or investment banker to assist in arranging the outside transfer. Further, the transfer processes described in Chapter 32 can be used to market the company to roll-up and recapitalization investors.

Discussing the nature of consolidations is a useful starting point for understanding outside transfers.

CONSOLIDATIONS

Consolidations involve the initial acquisition of one or more platform companies, followed by the purchase of add-on acquisitions. If the consolidation occurs simultaneously with an initial public offering (IPO), it is called a roll-up or a poof IPO. More common is the buy-and-build strategy, which uses private equity and debt for the initial acquisitions. "Buy and build" is the term used in the private equity industry for this method of consolidation. The participating owner, normally the owner of a platform company, might refer to this method as a recapitalization. Consolidations occurred in the first decade of this century in a wide variety of industries, such as metal distributors, staffing services, auto dealerships, and heating, ventilating, and air conditioning services.

Common characteristics of consolidations are

- High industry fragmentation.
- Substantial industry revenue base.
- Mature industry with decent profit margins.
- No dominant market leader and few, if any, national players.
- Critical mass is achievable with a manageable number of acquisitions.
- Achievable economies of scale.
- Ability to increase revenues with national coverage or brand.
- Large universe of willing sellers with profitable operations.

The ideal industry for a consolidation has one added characteristic—no existing consolidation players. The first consolidator should be able to scoop up the best companies and managers.

A consolidation creates numerous opportunities for earnings improvement of the consolidator.

- *Cost cutting*. Consolidations create redundancies. Eliminating these redundancies is a primary source of earnings improvement for these deals. There are surpluses in staff, administrative, and back-office functions, such as computer systems. Consolidators can obtain volume discounts and other vendor cost concessions in a wide range of areas.
- *Revenue growth*. The combination of acquisitions and organic growth enable consolidators to grow quickly. This growth is aided if the consolidator reaches critical mass by becoming large enough to service its industry on a national basis. In many industries, national companies have an advantage over smaller competitors.
- *Key management*. A successful consolidator often attracts the top managers in its industry. The combination of a high compensation package and opportunity to change the industry is often irresistible. These professional executives usually have experience managing hypergrowth situations.
- *Benefits of size*. Benefits accrue to the largest player in an industry. Aside from the ability to develop national accounts and attract the best employees, the consolidator may benefit from added rebates from vendors and the ability to create integrated systems and to establish national brands.

> ### CONSOLIDATIONS
>
> - *Roll-up.* Consolidation occurs simultaneously with an initial public offering. Sometimes called a proof roll-up. The original sellers trade control-level private equity for cash and a minority position in a public entity.
> - *Buy and build.* An equity sponsor builds the platform company through acquisitions. The consolidated company may remain private or go public later. The equity group calls these "buy-and-build consolidations." A private seller may or may not have a continuing ownership position in a buy-and-build consolidation.
> - *Recapitalization.* Shareholders transfer most of their business to a company controlled by a private equity group, which then funds an aggressive growth plan. A private company in a recapitalization may be the platform firm. The seller will have an equity stake going forward in a recapitalized company.

A consolidation can create a company that dominates smaller competitors. Exhibit 33.1 provides the transfer matrix for consolidations.

Pricing Arbitrage

The old investment axiom of "buy low, sell high" drives the public exit for many consolidations. A "private/public" pricing arbitrage opportunity is available to consolidators. Consolidators, from various industries, typically pay an average of about five to six times trailing recast earnings before interest, taxes, depreciation, and amortization (EBITDA) for acquired companies. By going public, those same consolidators may be able to resell those adjusted earnings at a multiple of 10 to 15, or more, depending on the industry. This private/public arbitrage allows consolidators to pay top prices for acquired companies. It also enables equity investors and lenders to achieve risk-adjusted returns on consolidation plays.

Players

A variety of participants are involved with creating and managing consolidations. These players are described in Exhibit 33.2. All of these players' movements must be orchestrated for the consolidation to succeed. The financial engineer arranges the activities, from valuing the various companies to determining the equity splits. Sometimes this engineer is an investment banker. The engineer attracts the equity sponsor to the consolidation and arranges the necessary debt. Most important, the engineer negotiates the first platform deal, which usually sets the tone for the consolidation. The key managers are hired early in the process. Part of the duties of these managers may include attracting other sellers to the consolidation. Various professionals, including lawyers and accountants, are required to assist with the deals. If the consolidation is taken public, an underwriter has a large voice in its structure.

EXHIBIT 33.1 Transfer Matrix: Consolidations

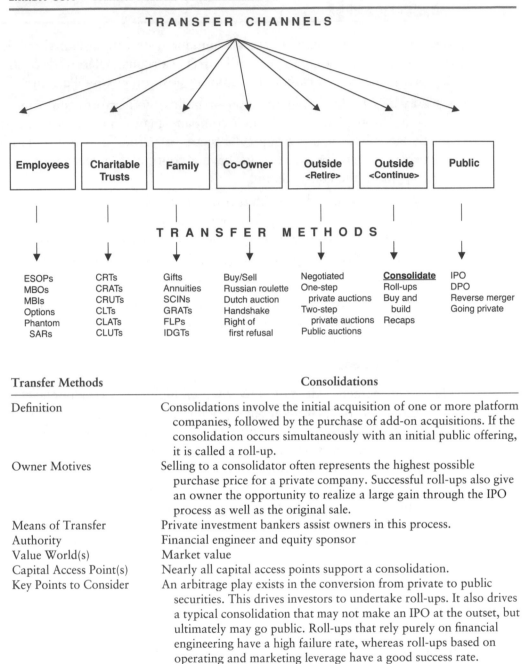

Transfer Methods	Consolidations
Definition	Consolidations involve the initial acquisition of one or more platform companies, followed by the purchase of add-on acquisitions. If the consolidation occurs simultaneously with an initial public offering, it is called a roll-up.
Owner Motives	Selling to a consolidator often represents the highest possible purchase price for a private company. Successful roll-ups also give an owner the opportunity to realize a large gain through the IPO process as well as the original sale.
Means of Transfer	Private investment bankers assist owners in this process.
Authority	Financial engineer and equity sponsor
Value World(s)	Market value
Capital Access Point(s)	Nearly all capital access points support a consolidation.
Key Points to Consider	An arbitrage play exists in the conversion from private to public securities. This drives investors to undertake roll-ups. It also drives a typical consolidation that may not make an IPO at the outset, but ultimately may go public. Roll-ups that rely purely on financial engineering have a high failure rate, whereas roll-ups based on operating and marketing leverage have a good success rate.

ROLL-UPS

A roll-up is the consolidation of several smaller businesses into one large operation, which is simultaneously taken public. A roll-up starts with an investment banker identifying several private companies operating in the same industry that wish to sell their businesses for some combination of cash and stock. A deal is created by which the owners of the founding companies agree to sell and be paid from the proceeds of the initial public offering of the newly created entity. A roll-up

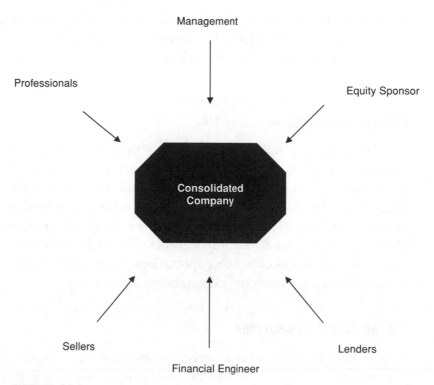

EXHIBIT 33.2 Consolidation Players

company is formed to acquire each founding company and initiate the IPO. Under typical buyout agreements, owners receive a combination of cash and stock in the newly formed company. Frequently, a portion of the debt also is paid off at this time. IPO proceeds also may be used to pay the firm that helped form the company. Founders who own platform companies often get the best price for their businesses.

Initial Public Offering

Going public is critical to consolidators for a number of reasons. The IPO provides the currency for add-on acquisitions because consolidators prefer to pay in stock instead of cash. There is a tax incentive for owners to do at least a 55% stock-for-stock exchange, since no capital gains taxes are triggered on that portion of the transaction. Of course, the downside to sellers is that they lose control over the stock price and probably will have restrictions on their ability to sell their position in a timely fashion. In addition, the IPO enables the realization of the earnings arbitrage mentioned earlier. Moreover, the IPO provides the promise of a large return for the equity sponsors and investors.

After the IPO

The primary challenge after the IPO is for the management team to integrate the acquisitions and impose the earnings discipline of a public company. The integration process is especially problematic, since the add-on acquisitions are not easily meshed into platform entities. The easier part of the integration is cost cutting of duplicate expenses. Unfortunately, many employees of the consolidating company may lose their jobs. The extent to which the former owners invest their energies and ambition in the consolidated company determines the ultimate success of the roll-up.

Roll-Up Performance

The 1990s were a roll-up heyday. More than two dozen industries were consolidated using this method. The financial performance of these roll-ups has been poor. One study examined the motivations and economic impact of 47 roll-ups initiated from 1994 and 1998.[1] It found that the long-term stock price performance substantially lags that of several benchmarks. While the operational performance of these roll-ups is no different from other firms in their respective industries, their initial valuations indicate that expectations were much higher. The firms in the sample fail to meet analysts' expectations, on average.

Roll-Up Points to Consider

Participating in a roll-up is a fairly high-risk endeavor, especially for the sellers. Potential sellers should consider the next points before signing up.

- *Many consolidations do not succeed.* For private owners to relinquish control over their company and plug into a public entity requires a leap of faith. Many owners are better off plotting their own independent course.
- *If an owner is determined to sell into a roll-up, it is best to sell early in the process.* The owner with a platform company usually gets the best deal.
- *Owners should not settle for a pure stock-for-stock transaction with the consolidated company.* They should receive enough cash to meet their minimum estate-planning requirements.
- *Owners should pick their partners carefully.* There is no substitute for experience. Some financial engineers and equity sponsors have better track records than others.

The best advice: Be wary of roll-ups because their risks may be too great to measure adequately.

BUY AND BUILD OR RECAPITALIZATIONS

The buy-and-build or recapitalization strategy is a more prevalent method of consolidating companies in an industry. Exhibit 33.3 shows the transfer matrix for buy and build and recapitalizations. The difference between buy and build and recapitalization is the perspective of the player; owners view it as a recapitalization while private equity groups (PEGs) view it as a buy and build. The buy-and-build strategy is a central business model for many PEGs. Most PEGs employ this strategy and may or may not eventually take the consolidated company public, depending on which alternative avenue maximizes their exit. A PEG usually acquires one or two platform companies in an industry and then makes a number of add-on "synergistic" acquisitions to build the company. The original platform sellers may or may not have a continuing ownership position in the consolidated company. The add-on company sellers probably will not have a continuing ownership position. With a recapitalization, some or all of the selling shareholders will have an ownership position in the consolidating company. Quite often the platform company in a buy-and-build strategy is recapitalized.

In a recapitalization, an owner sells part of the equity of the business in order to take some chips off the table while still operating the business. Recaps can involve the sale of any amount of company stock, but most involve a change of control. Most recap investors prefer to purchase at least 80% of the subject's stock at the outset. Doing so enables the investor to consolidate the subject's financial results to a holding company, which may have tax advantages to the investor.

Recaps can have numerous benefits. By employing a recap strategy, an owner hopes to achieve some or all of these goals:

- Increase personal liquidity.
- Continue operating the business while maintaining a significant equity position.
- Reduce personal risk by eliminating borrowing guarantees.
- Gain access to financial professionals who have experience in growing and exiting from businesses.
- Possibly receive nondiluting capital for growth. This last point is particularly important. In some cases owners are able to negotiate a provision whereby their equity is not diluted as more growth money is invested.

Mechanics

A typical change-of-control recap involves several steps. First, the subject is valued on an equity enterprise basis (100%). Recap valuations typically are conservative. Many recap investors value a company by applying no more than a five to six multiple against recast adjusted EBITDA, less long-term liabilities. Adjustments to EBITDA include seller discretionary items and one-time expenses. Potential deal synergies are not incorporated into the valuation.

Second, as part of the recap strategy, the original owner and the recap investor agree on a business plan for the recapped company (RecapCo) with fairly aggressive growth targets. This expansion usually is realized through a combination of one part organic growth and two parts add-on acquisitions. Recap investors normally expect to receive at least a 25% to 35% compounded rate of return on their investments, so the earnings growth of the RecapCo must be strong enough to support this return. The recap investor commits to fund the business plan, which may have a five- to seven-year horizon. Finally, the investor and original owner plan a liquidity event, usually near the end of the business planning period. This event could include a sale of the business or executing an initial public offering. Next we show the recap mechanics in more detail.

EXHIBIT 33.3   Transfer Matrix: Buy and Build and Recapitalizations

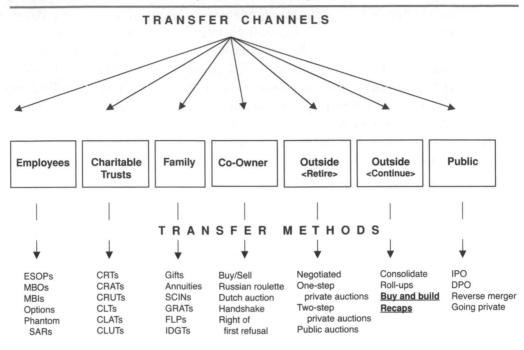

Transfer Methods	Buy and Build	Recapitalizations
Definition	A private equity group acquires one or more platform companies in an industry and then makes a number of add-on synergistic acquisitions to build the company.	An owner sells part of the equity of the business to a PEG but continues to operate the business.
Owner Motives	This strategy enables owners to get a high price and continue to operate the business without equity risk.	This strategy enables owners to get a fair price at the recap stage with the hope of making more money at the eventual exit.
Means of Transfer	An industry of PEGs and investment bankers exists to guide owners.	An industry of PEGs and investment bankers exists to guide owners.
Authority	PEGs, owners	PEGs, owners
Value World(s)	Market value for owner; investment value for PEG	Market value for owner, investment value for PEG
Capital Access Point(s)	Nearly all CAPs support a buy-and-build strategy.	Nearly all CAPs support a recap.
Key Points to Consider	Original owners probably do not have an ownership position going forward. Management is compensated with phantom stock and other deferred compensation plans. PEGs have a holding period of 5 to 7 years with these investments.	PEGs normally own 80% of the recap, so they can consolidate with other companies they control. Recaps are a good way for owners to take chips off the table yet still participate in the upside potential of the business.

EXAMPLE

Joe Mainstreet has been itching to do a deal for several chapters now. He sees tremendous growth opportunities for PrivateCo but does not want to give the company away for someone else to harvest the crop. Joe thinks a recapitalization may meet his needs.

Joe hires Dan Dealmaker to help market his company. Dan chooses a one-step private auction transfer process. Only PEGs are invited into the auction. Dan finds eight such groups, all of which are experienced players in the recap segment.

There are several key items that Dan negotiates with investors.

1. PrivateCo is valued on an all-cash basis.
2. The amount and type of funding that the recap investor will commit to the deal going forward.
3. The length of time and terms of Joe Mainstreet's employment agreement are considered.
4. What shareholder rights are available to Joe after the transfer as a minority shareholder? What decisions can he influence?

Dan Dealmaker supplies the equity groups with the next summarized information.

PrivateCo Summary Financials

Book value (taken from Chapter 5)		$1.0 million
Long-term debt		.5 million
Net asset value (Chapter 5)		2.4 million
Benefit stream		
Pretax earnings	$1.8 million	
Prior owner compensation	.45 million	
Prior owner discretionary expenses	.1 million	
Depreciation	.4 million	
Normalized capital expenditures	(.3) million	
	Adjusted EBITDA	$2.45 million

Dan asks each equity group to incorporate into their offer all of the key transfer points just mentioned. His private auction process nets several offers. After six weeks of further negotiation, Dan negotiates the next term sheet with PEGCo.

PEGCo Offer

PrivateCo value for 100% of the stock			$11 million
Mainstreet ownership position going forward			20%

Sources of Funds		**Uses of Funds**	
Debt	$5.0 million	Cash to Mainstreet	$9.8 million
PEGCo equity	4.8 million	Mainstreet retained	1.2 million
Mainstreet retained	1.2 million		
Total	$11 million	Total	$11 million

Ownership

PEGCo	$4.8 million (80%)
Mainstreet	1.2 million (20%)

Employment Agreement
Five-year agreement with a $200,000 base per year plus profit plan and full benefits.

Future Funding
PEGCo agrees to fund up to $10 million in additional capital within three years of the closing. No more than 50% of this will be comprised of debt. Joe will not be diluted from his 20% position within this funding limit.

Shareholder Rights
Joe will have a seat on the board. He will have veto rights regarding major corporate governance decisions, including acquisitions. He also has a put option to PEGCo that is exercisable beyond five years of the closing at a specified price and terms.

With this deal, Joe receives $9.8 million at the close and does not guarantee any of the company's debts going forward. He receives a salary of $200,000 per year, with a bonus potential of another $75,000. Joe is not diluted unless he agrees to spend more than $10 million in growth capital. Finally, he has veto powers over all key board decisions. All in all, it is a pretty sweet deal. Joe wonders how PEGCo can afford such a deal and still meet its return expectations.

Once again, Dan Dealmaker has an explanation. Dan believes that PEGCo desires at least a 30% compounded return on its investments. During the negotiations, it comes to Dan's attention that PEGCo believes the following about RecapCo:

PEGCo Return Calculation

RecapCo earnings in year 5	$ 5 million
Likely selling multiple	5
Likely selling price in year 5	$25 million (debt-free)
Times PEGCo ownership %	80%
Cash to PEGCo in year 5	$20 million
PEGCo investment in deal	$4.8 million
Compounded return to PEGCo	33%

If RecapCo achieves its goal of earning $5 million in the fifth year and the company is sold for five times its earnings, PEGCo will earn a 33% compounded return on its investment.

This deal also works for Joe Mainstreet. He receives $9.8 million at the close, then $5 million more in year 5 ($25 million selling price times 20%). Along the way, he collects more than $1 million in compensation for doing what he loves.

There are now thousands of institutional recap investors in the U.S. marketplace. The majority of PEGs participate as recap investors. These investors break down by size. Most investors focus on recap investments of $2 million to $10 million, which represents the minimum size range for institutional support. Another group invests primarily in deals with transactions between $10 million to $50 million. Finally, a few hundred investment firms participate in transactions greater than $50 million.

RECAPITALIZATION POINTS TO CONSIDER

A recapitalization is a complicated financial technique that should be used only if fully understood. The next points may help.

- *The subject's shareholders can choose individually whether to cash out or retain an equity position in the recapitalized company.* A shareholder can receive a mix of cash and continuing ownership.
- *Few managers have the vision and management ability to navigate a recapitalization successfully.* Owners need professional help in this area.
- *PEGs are constantly on the lookout for owners who have the right combination of industry knowledge and hypergrowth management ability.* Many successful recap managers have executive experience with a large company prior to transiting to an ownership role.
- *Too much leverage used in a recap is a dangerous thing.* Most recap investors use substantially more debt than equity in the recapitalization. Owners should require a conservative capital structure in the recap. This means employing a debt-to-equity ratio of no more than 2.5:1.
- *Owners should team only with experienced recap investors.* A recap investor needs experience and savvy in guiding aggressive growth plans and creating maximizing exits. It behooves an owner to interview at least six to eight investors before selecting one.
- *The valuation of the subject and cash received up front by the owner are the two items that draw the most attention.* As with management transfers, the terms of the deal are as important as valuation and price. If an owner is to be successful in the recap, shareholder rights issues, employment agreements, and future funding commitments must be considered.

Recaps are not for everyone. If selling a business once is not enough for an owner, however, a recap just might be the answer.

TRIANGULATION

To be successful, consolidators must understand how to value and capitalize acquisition opportunities. Buying in one value world and selling in another often creates value. For instance, most consolidators attempt to acquire in the financial subworld of market value and exit either in the synergy subworld of market value or through the public markets.

Some of the most successful consolidations involve buying groups of companies in the asset subworld, merging them into an operating company, and selling out to one of the higher-value worlds. Once critical mass is achieved, the exit can occur in the synergy subworld. Exiting at this level gives the consolidator a slightly higher selling multiple plus a higher synergized benefit stream. This is the logic behind recapitalizations.

Of course, consolidators need constant access to capital. Roll-ups access capital directly from the public capital markets. This is an insider's game with few acquirers having the Wall Street contacts to execute this strategy. The more likely consolidation is the buy and build version; hundreds of PEGs are ready to play this game. PEGs are capable of employing sophisticated capital structures to support their deals. For example, it is not unusual for PEGs to support their equity investment with senior lending and mezzanine capital. Manipulating capital structure is a critical success factor for consolidating companies.

NOTE

1. Keith Brown, Amy Dittmar, and Henri Servaes, "Roll-ups: Performance and Incentives for Industry-Consolidating IPOs," abstract, March 2001.

CHAPTER 34

Going Public, Going Private

Less than .1% of all companies in the United States are publicly held. Yet "going public" is the dream of many private business owners. It is like the dream of the sandlot player convinced he will be in the major leagues against all odds. The process of taking a private company public involves offering securities, generally common or preferred stock, for sale to the general public. The first time such securities are offered is generally referred to as an initial public offering (IPO). Some private companies offer public securities to the market, called direct public offerings (DPOs), but they remain private firms after the offering. Other companies become public by merging with an existing public company. Called a reverse merger, this transaction enables a private company to go public more quickly and less expensively than through a traditional IPO.

There are several good reasons to go public. The most likely reason is to raise capital for operational expansion at a lower cost of capital than otherwise possible. Other factors include the ability to use stock as currency for acquisitions, to diversify and liquefy personal holdings, and to burnish a company's reputation. Yet there are equally good reasons why a company should remain private. These include the intrusion of public shareholders into the company's affairs, the demand for short-term financial results, the high costs involved, and the probability that the benefits of going public are overrated. This last point is especially important and often misunderstood.

Most public companies do not enjoy all the benefits of public ownership. For instance, until a public company has a market value of outstanding shares of more than $300 million or so, its shares are thinly traded, and its access to public capital is limited. Since most companies sell only 20% of their shares to the public at the outset, the market value of the company must be more than $1 billion before the full advantages of public ownership are realized. Because the costs of being public often outweigh the benefits, thousands of public companies fall into the should-be-private category, which is the corollary to the could-be-public concept in Chapter 3. A number of should-be-private companies actually go private each year.

There are four primary ways for a private company to go public:

1. A DPO, which is a do-it-yourself IPO of sorts, in which securities are exempted from many of the registration and reporting requirements of the Securities and Exchange Commission (SEC). DPOs take a variety of forms, allow differing amounts of money to be raised within a 12-month period, and place varying restrictions on the investors.

2. An IPO on an American stock exchange.
3. Going public on a foreign exchange, such as the London Stock Exchange's AIM trading market for small business, or the Toronto Stock Exchange's TSX Venture Exchange.
4. A merger with an existing public company, commonly referred to as a reverse merger.

The first part of this chapter discusses DPOs. Next is a review the traditional IPO process, including the players, costs involved, and key points to consider. Then there is a description of reverse mergers. The chapter ends with a discussion of taking public companies private.

DIRECT PUBLIC OFFERINGS

The term *direct public offering* is almost a misnomer and is couched in confusion. DPOs are all based on amendments and exemptions to federal securities law known as Regulation D, Rules 504–506 and include Rule 147, which also encompass a significant portion of the private placement regulations.

DPOs, as with IPOs, allow the sale of stock or debt instruments to the general public and with some restrictions and disclosure requirements. DPOs allow a company to reach outside its immediate circle of friends, family, and acquaintances to sell stock. There is overlap in the definition and regulation of DPOs with Regulation D private placements. The major distinguishing difference is that Regulation D private placements require a "prior existing relationship" among other restrictions, to sell to investors.

The most common DPO is the Small Corporate Securities Offering Registration, or SCOR, which is a simplified DPO. The SCOR permits the sale of securities to an unlimited number of investors. For this reason, SCOR is known as a *registration by exemption*, because it is basically a hybrid between a public offering and a private placement, as are all DPOs. Stock sold under a SCOR offering can be freely traded in the secondary market, but it often has a limited float, has no market makers, and is quite difficult to find buyers, which yields limited liquidity and a lower valuation.

SCOR registrations use Form U-7, which is the general registration form for corporations registering under state securities laws. SCOR is designed for use by companies and their attorneys and accountants, who are not necessarily specialists in securities regulation.

Companies filing a SCOR are subject to certain requirements and an application process.

- The U-7 registration form has 50 questions. In some cases, the answers to these questions provide potential investors with adequate information about the company ownership, business practices, intentions, risks, competition, stock allocations, and proposed distributions if the company is already known to the potential investor. Often the lack of detail in the U-7 form about the business deters outside investors and leads to lower valuations.

- Before any stock can be sold, the completed U-7, together with supplemental exhibits including financial statements, needs to be approved by the state securities administrator in each state in which the stock is to be offered. On approval, the U-7 becomes the prospectus or offering circular and may then be photocopied and given to potential investors. An expensive printed prospectus is not required.
- A U-7 can be drafted by company officers, assisted by their attorney and CPA, and submitted for approval.

The offering price must be at least \$5 per share in most states, although some states allow \$1.[1] Moreover, the company may not split its stock or declare stock dividends for two years following the effective date of the registration, except with the permission of the securities administrator in connection with a subsequent registered public offering.

The securities registered and sold are freely transferable and tradable, but the company is limited to raising no more than \$1 million in any 12-month period. Due to the offering size and \$1 to \$5 per share minimum price, a public trading market is unlikely to arise. The Pacific Stock Exchange (PSE) received approval in May of 1995 from the SEC to list SCOR securities, which could have created a market for listed SCOR and other DPO securities. But in 2006, the PSE was merged with the New York Stock Exchange (NYSE) and the market for SCOR securities remains limited.

The SCOR offering is an early-stage venture financing, using public investors solicited by means of advertising and other general solicitation. If appropriate, the SCOR may be followed at some later stage by other DPOs or a conventional public offering that could result in the development of a publicly traded market. Depending on the state, SCOR may be used to register common or preferred stock, including convertible preferred and options, warrants or rights. After demonstrating that the company will be able to meet debt service, SCOR may be used to register debt securities, including convertible debt.

Under a SCOR offering, a company can advertise for investors and sell securities to anyone who expresses an interest. Obviously, this provides businesses a much-needed tool for raising capital. Small companies have successfully used SCOR to sell stock without using a securities underwriting firm. This method works particularly well for companies with an established customer base or other supportive source of investors.

Other DPOs or related offerings exist that allow companies to raise various amounts of capital on an annual basis include:

- SEC Regulation D, Rule 505, which enables a business to sell up to \$5 million in stock in a 12-month period to an unlimited number of accredited investors and up to 35 nonaccredited investors.
- SEC Regulation A offerings, which are "mini public offerings," and allow up to \$5 million raised and bypassing SEC registration.

- SB-1 allows up to $10 million raised.
- SB-2 allows an unlimited amount of securities to be sold in a 12-month period.

Finally, there is an intrastate filing exemption, Rule 147, which allows an unlimited amount of capital to be raised, as long as the stock is sold only in the primary state in which the company does business. Both the investors and the company must reside in the same state under Rule 147.[2]

Private companies use DPO offerings to access money from investors in a public venue. The issuing company does not become a public company because it uses a DPO. Public companies, a different breed, are covered next.

WHICH COMPANIES ARE PUBLIC?

A company is technically public if it must file public disclosures with the SEC. The federal securities laws require tens of thousands of companies to file reports with the SEC each year. These reports include quarterly reports on Form 10-Q, annual reports (with audited financial statements) on Form 10-K, and periodic reports of significant events on Form 8-K. A company *must* file reports with the SEC if *one* of the listed items is true:

- It has 500 or more investors and $10 million or more in assets.
- It lists its securities on these stock exchanges:
  - Boston Stock Exchange
  - Chicago Stock Exchange
  - Cincinnati Stock Exchange
  - Nasdaq
  - NYSE
  - NYSE Amex Equities
  - Pacific Exchange
  - Philadelphia Stock Exchange

Nasdaq and the NYSE are the largest and best known. Fewer than 8,000 companies are listed on these two national exchanges.[3] Due to a consolidation of ownership of the stock exchanges and increased competition for the listings of companies, many changes and lowering of listing standards have occurred recently. New markets have been created to allow the listing of smaller companies in search of public capital, with both NYSE and Nasdaq having alternative markets available for smaller companies.

Summarized listing requirements for the Nasdaq Capital Market are shown in Exhibit 34.1. Companies must meet all criteria under at least one of the standards shown in the exhibit.[4]

Nasdaq is comprised of several markets, including the Nasdaq Global Select Market, Nasdaq Global Market, and the Nasdaq Capital Market, all with differing listing requirements. As shown in Exhibit 34.1, a company with $5 million stockholders' equity, a $15 million value of 1 million publicly held shares, and

EXHIBIT 34.1 Nasdaq Capital Market Initial Listing Requirements

Requirements	Equity Standard	Market Value of Listed Securities Standard	Net Income Standard
Stockholders' equity	$5 million	$4 million	$4 million
Market value of publicly held shares	$15 million	$15 million	$5 million
Operating history	2 years	N/A	N/A
Market value of listed securities	N/A	$50 million	N/A
Net income from continuing operations (in latest fiscal year or in two of last three fiscal years)	N/A	N/A	$750,000
Bid price	$4	$4	$4
Publicly held shares	1 million	1 million	1 million
Shareholders (round lot holders)	300	300	300
Market makers	3	3	3
Corporate governance	Yes	Yes	Yes

two years of operating history without earnings can be listed on the Nasdaq Capital Market.

The NYSE is more restrictive than Nasdaq in a few key areas, including a minimum trailing earnings requirement of the NYSE and a greater number of initial shareholders. The NYSE also requires both a much larger market value of public float than Nasdaq and wider ownership of the listed firm's shares. Exhibit 34.2 shows NYSE listing requirements.[5]

INITIAL PUBLIC OFFERING TEAM

An IPO's success depends on selecting and assembling the right team. Exhibit 34.3 depicts the major players. Managers of the issuing company are normally fully engaged in the process. Just feeding the other professionals information is a full-time job for a number of the issuing company's managers. One of the primary differences between a successful and failed IPO is the management team's commitment to the process.

Hiring the investment banker or underwriter is the key initial decision. Aside from selecting an underwriter with access to the marketplace, it is important that this firm also has analysts who follow the industry of the issuing company. It is preferable for the issuing company to develop a relationship with several investment banking firms a number of years prior to the actual underwriting event. Doing this enables enough time to build relationships that are necessary once the IPO process begins. Ultimately, the company selects one investment banking firm to lead the offering.

The next criteria are useful in selecting the appropriate investment banker:

- The underwriter's track record
- Further services offered, such as debt placement and merger and acquisitions advice
- An analyst who understands the industry and is committed to following the company going forward

EXHIBIT 34.2   NYSE Listing Requirements

DISTRIBUTION AND SIZE CRITERIA (*Must meet all 3 of the following*)

Round-lot holders	400 U.S.
Public shares	1.1 million outstanding
Market value of public shares	
IPOs, spin-offs, carve outs, affiliates	$40 million
All other listings	$100 million
Stock price criteria	$4

FINANCIAL CRITERIA (Must meet 1 of these alternative standards: earnings test, valuation, affiliated company, or assets and equity)

Earnings Test

Aggregate pretax income for the last 3 years	$10 million
Minimum in each of 2 most recent years; third year must be positive	$2 million

OR

Aggregate pretax income for last 3 years	$12 million
Minimum in most recent year	$5 million
Minimum in next most recent year	$2 million

Valuation (Cash Flow or Revenues)
Cash Flow

Global market capitalization	$500 million
Revenue (most recent 12-month period)	$100 million
Aggregate adjusted cash flow for last 3 years (all 3 years must be positive)	$25 million

OR

Pure Valuation with Revenues

Global Market Capitalization	$750 million
Revenues (most recent fiscal year)	$75 million

Affiliated Company (for new entities with parent or affiliated company listed on NYSE)

Global market capitalization	$500 million
Operating history	12 months

Assets and Equity

Global market capitalization	$150 million
Total assets	$75 million
Stockholders' equity	$50 million

- The ability to distribute the stock to large institutions or individual investors through its retail arm
- A fair deal regarding the underwriter's compensation

OTC BULLETIN BOARD

The over-the-counter bulletin board (OTCBB) is an electronic quotation system that displays real-time quotes, last-sale prices, and volume information for many over the counter (OTC) securities that are not listed on Nasdaq Stock Market or a national securities exchange. Brokers who subscribe to the system can use the OTCBB to look up prices or enter quotes for OTC securities. Although the National Association of Security Dealers oversees the OTCBB, the OTCBB is not part of the Nasdaq Stock Market.

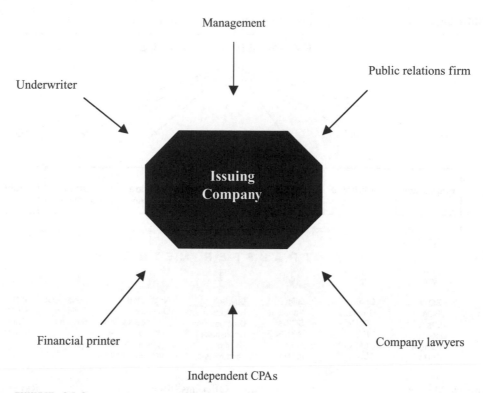

EXHIBIT 34.3 Initial Public Offering Team

The issuing company's board of directors normally makes the final choice of a lead investment banking firm. Once an investment banker is chosen, attention can be turned to the particulars of the offering. Particulars include the estimated offering price range for the securities being issued and whether the assignment will be on a firm-commitment or best-efforts basis.

With a *firm commitment*, the underwriter agrees to buy all of the issue and thereby assumes the risk for any unsold securities. The offering company prefers a firm commitment type of offering; this is used most frequently for larger offerings. The commitment is not made until the exact offering price is negotiated, which happens just prior to the effective date of the registration statement. This timing enables the price to be aligned with current market conditions. In a *best-efforts* offering, the underwriter agrees to use its best efforts to sell the issue but is not obligated to purchase any unsold securities. Best-efforts offerings put the offering company in the untenable situation of not knowing whether the offering will occur. If a company can achieve a best-efforts commitment only, it might be a good indicator that it should remain a private company.

IPO PROCESS

Exhibit 34.4 provides the transfer matrix for IPOs and reverse mergers. Here is a summary of the IPO process. Each of the seven steps involves a tremendous amount of detail. Companies interested in going public should consult with the appropriate lawyers and public investment bankers.

EXHIBIT 34.4   Transfer Matrix: Initial Public Offerings and Reverse Mergers

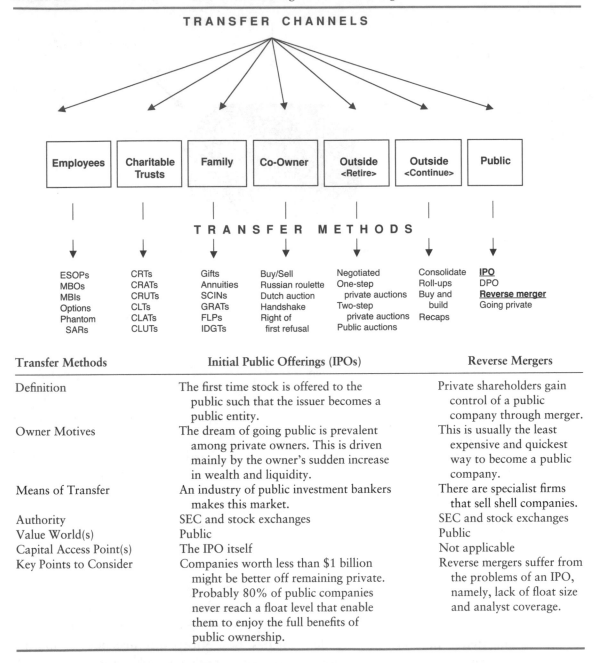

Transfer Methods	Initial Public Offerings (IPOs)	Reverse Mergers
Definition	The first time stock is offered to the public such that the issuer becomes a public entity.	Private shareholders gain control of a public company through merger.
Owner Motives	The dream of going public is prevalent among private owners. This is driven mainly by the owner's sudden increase in wealth and liquidity.	This is usually the least expensive and quickest way to become a public company.
Means of Transfer	An industry of public investment bankers makes this market.	There are specialist firms that sell shell companies.
Authority	SEC and stock exchanges	SEC and stock exchanges
Value World(s)	Public	Public
Capital Access Point(s)	The IPO itself	Not applicable
Key Points to Consider	Companies worth less than $1 billion might be better off remaining private. Probably 80% of public companies never reach a float level that enable them to enjoy the full benefits of public ownership.	Reverse mergers suffer from the problems of an IPO, namely, lack of float size and analyst coverage.

1. *Organizational meeting.* The company's IPO begins with an organizational meeting of the various parties involved in the transaction. The agenda of the organizational meeting generally consists of a discussion of the timetable for the offering, the general terms of the offering, and the responsibilities of the various participants.

2. *Registration statement.* Following the organizational meeting, the company's lawyers begin to draft the registration statement for ultimate submittal to the SEC. The front and back cover pages and the summary and risk factor sections of the prospectus must be written in plain English.

3. *Due diligence matters.* The due diligence process includes a review of existing agreements to determine whether any security holders have preemptive or registration rights that may be triggered by the offering. If so, the underwriters probably will require that such rights be waived. Similarly, company counsel reviews all other agreements that may affect the offering.

4. *Initial filing.* The SEC registration statement is filed via EDGAR, the SEC Web site. The company may issue a press release with respect to the filing. If the company elects not to issue a press release, the filing is referred to as a quiet filing. The initial SEC review typically takes 30 to 40 days but may last longer. At the end of the review period, the SEC staff will issue a comment letter containing both legal and accounting comments on the registration statement.

5. *Quiet period.* The filing of the registration statement commences the "quiet period" that continues until the registration statement is declared effective by the SEC. During this time, company representatives should refrain from providing any information about the company that is not included in the registration statement.

6. *Road show.* Once the preliminary prospectus is printed and distributed, several representatives of the company, usually the chief executive officer and chief financial officer, and the underwriters embark on a "road show" to major U.S. cities to meet with large institutional investors and market the offering. The road show for an IPO typically lasts two to three weeks. The offering is priced after the completion of the road show.

7. *Closing.* The date of the closing is determined according to when the offering is priced. If the offering is priced at any time during the day while the market is open, closing will take place three business days later; if pricing occurs after the market closes, closing will be four business days later (T + 3 rule).

MARKET MAKER

A *market maker* is a firm that stands ready to buy and sell a particular stock on a regular and continuous basis at a publicly quoted price. Market makers are known in the context of the Nasdaq or other OTC markets. Market makers that stand ready to buy and sell stocks listed on an exchange, such as the NYSE, are called *third market makers*. Many OTC stocks have more than one market maker.

The IPO process requires 6 to 24 months to complete. Bad planning or incorrect advice may cause delays of several months and additional costs. If the deal is not registered properly and executed smoothly, the stock can be underpriced, thereby potentially limiting the amount of equity raised and the market capitalization of the company.

Costs of a Traditional IPO

Performing an IPO is an expensive proposition. As a rule of thumb, it costs about 8% to 10% of the offering proceeds on larger-size transactions and considerably

EXHIBIT 34.5   Estimated Cost of a Traditional IPO

Item	$25 Million Offering	$50 Million Offering
Underwriting commissions	$1,750,000	$3,500,000
SEC fees	9,914	19,828
NASD fees	3,375	6,250
Printing and engraving	100,000	100,000
Accounting fees	160,000	160,000
Legal fees	200,000	200,000
Blue-sky fees	25,000	25,000
Miscellaneous	34,200	34,200
Nasdaq entry fees	63,725	63,725
Nasdaq annual fees	11,960	11,960
Transfer agent fees	5,000	5,000
Total	$2,400,000	$4,100,000

more on smaller transactions, ranging from 15% to 20%, on an all-in basis.[6] According to Nasdaq, the expenses shown in Exhibit 34.5 are typical for offerings of $25 million and $50 million.[7] But keep in mind that there are considerable pre-IPO expenses involved for accounting, outside consultants, preparation, and positioning of the company. Also, underwriting costs, as a percentage of money raised, can be as high as 18%, in addition to all other costs, with 10% for discounts, 5% accountable expenses, and 3% nonaccountable expenses.[8]

ADVANTAGES OF GOING PUBLIC

There are numerous advantages to going public. Some of the more important are:

- *Access to long-term capital.* One of the biggest advantages to going public is the ability to access the favorable financing terms in public capital markets. Public markets are larger, more liquid, and less costly than private capital markets.
- *Established value.* A public company is valued on a daily basis. This is helpful for a number of reasons, including the ability to use public stock as currency in acquisitions, diversification of owner's estate, liquidity, and the ability to use stock as loan collateral.
- *Ability to attract key personnel.* Employee incentive and benefit plans are more flexible and sophisticated for public companies. Stock options and stock appreciation rights are useful tools for attracting, motivating, and rewarding employees.
- *Public awareness.* Every shareholder is a potential customer. Many customers prefer to deal with public companies because of the perception of financial strength that often accompanies these firms.

DISADVANTAGES OF GOING PUBLIC

The disadvantages of going public are important to understand. Some of these are:

- *Lack of operating confidentiality.* All of the public disclosures give the competition access to information that a private company keeps secret. Some examples are compensation and holdings of officers, detailed financial information, borrowings, and major customers are all available to the public.
- *Loss of management control.* At some point the management may lose legal control of the public company. Since many private owners tend to be control-oriented, this loss of control may be hard to handle.
- *Pressure for short-term performance.* Meeting quarterly expectations is a far cry from living in the luxury of the long-term perspective a private owner can take toward the business. Because the report card is so frequent, the manager of a public company spends a large amount of time selling the investment potential of the company rather than managing the company.
- *Different accounting and tax issues.* Private owner-managers are driven to minimize reported earnings and thus taxes whereas public managers desire to maximize earnings. A public company's financial statements are always audited and must conform to generally accepted accounting principles. Additionally, the public company must follow all SEC rules for accounting and disclosure.
- *Costs of being public.* The initial costs of going public are enormous. The ongoing costs are substantial.
- *Potential liability.* Officers of public entities must follow securities laws, including the Sarbanes-Oxley requirements. Officers are also subject to possible insider trading charges.
- *Lock-up period for insiders.* Owners and pre-IPO stockholders of the company after going public will more than likely not be able to sell their stock for a period of time. A typical lock-up period is four to six months.
- *Potential undervaluation.* Despite the best of intentions and execution, in going public, a private company faces obstacles to getting its story and information disseminated. Unless it has been a highly visible and well-promoted company prior to going public, its acceptance by the investment community may not reflect the company's true value. Timing and uncontrollable events also can diminish value to a significant degree.
- *Sarbanes-Oxley compliance cost.* According to one survey that included 168 "accelerated filers"—companies with market capitalizations above $75 million—total average cost for Section 404 compliance was $1.7 million. The survey also revealed that total audit fees for U.S. filers averaged $3.6 million. These costs represent a major loss of value when a price/earnings ratio is applied.[9]

GOING PUBLIC KEY POINTS TO CONSIDER

Going public is a monumental decision with many related issues to consider, not the least of which is the motivation of the particular private owner. Why go public? Unless there are several specific goals that cannot be achieved as a private entity, the company should not go public. A few more points to consider are:

- *Size matters.* The size of the float matters. If a public company does not have hundreds of millions of dollars in float, it probably does not gain full access to the benefits of being public. Other companies are less likely to accept its stock as currency in acquisitions. The bond market may not be available. The stock may be too thinly traded to use effectively for employee benefit purposes. Further, stock analysts may not follow the stock.
- *The exchange matters.* Most public companies are not listed on a national exchange; rather, they are exchanged OTC or listed on a minor exchange. Many small-cap stocks are caught in financial purgatory. They cannot achieve sufficient orbital velocity to get to heaven, but they perform too well to sink to the depths. Unless a company qualifies for listing on a national exchange, owners may regret going public.
- *Shared vision.* In order to go public, the entire management team must share a corporate vision. This cannot be only one person's vision and be successful. Public companies require management depth because the team faces new responsibilities and new challenges. Transitioning from an executive in a private company to an executive in a public company is one of the more difficult metamorphoses in the business world.
- *Earnings growth.* To be a successful public company, it is necessary to have both a track record and forecast for high earnings growth. The stock market punishes companies that fail to meet their forecast or that experience average or no growth.
- *Market timing.* The market for IPOs runs in cycles. It is difficult to achieve a good price for an IPO stock in a down cycle. It is probably better to delay going public until the market is more receptive.
- *Benefits versus costs.* Owners must ask: Do the benefits of being a public entity outweigh the costs of achieving this status? Unless the answer is clear-cut, the owner probably is better off staying private.

The decision to go public should not be made in isolation. Fortunately, thousands of lawyers and investment bankers can assist in this discovery process.

GOING PUBLIC ON FOREIGN EXCHANGES

Foreign exchanges such as AIM or the TSX Venture Exchange have differing advantages, disadvantages, and costs from those of American exchanges. They should be thoroughly researched and evaluated as alternatives for even American companies considering going public. Since inception in 1995, more than 2,200 companies have had an average of over $20 million raised on AIM.[10] TSX Venture Exchange is a public venture capital marketplace for emerging companies. As of this writing, the exchange had listed 2,364 companies with an average market capitalization of $25.7 million.[11] It is of paramount importance to retain experienced legal, accounting, and investment banking expertise in connection with foreign exchange IPOs.

REVERSE MERGERS

The second method of going public is through a reverse merger. A reverse merger is a transaction whereby private company shareholders gain control of a public company by merging it with their private company. The private company shareholders receive a substantial majority of the shares in the public company (normally 80% to 90% or more) and control of the board of directors. The public corporation is called a shell. All that exists of the original company is the corporate shell structure and shareholders. The transaction in which a private company is taken public in a reverse merger can be accomplished quickly because it does not go through a review process with state and federal regulators. The predecessor public company has already completed the process.

"PINK SHEETS"

The pink sheets—named for the color of paper on which they have historically been printed—available by subscription from the National Quotation Bureau are daily listings of bid and ask prices for OTC stocks not included in the daily Nasdaq OTC listings. "Pink sheet" companies typically do not meet listing requirements.

Upon completion of the reverse merger, the name of the shell company usually is changed to the name of the private company. If the shell company has a trading symbol, it is changed to reflect the name change. If the shell company has no symbol, an application for a symbol usually is made to the Nasdaq bulletin board. The bulletin board has no financial requirements. A listing will be granted if the affairs of the company are in order and the company answers the questions posed by Nasdaq.

If the shell company is listed on the bulletin board, the registered shares can continue to trade. The company can do a private placement immediately. In order to offer new shares to the public, the newly combined public company must first register the shares with the SEC. This process takes three to four months and normally requires filing a registration statement with the SEC.

Mechanics of a Reverse Merger

There are many details involved in successfully concluding a reverse merger. A summary of the main steps is presented next.

First, a public vehicle normally acquires 100% of the outstanding stock of the private company in consideration for issuing to the private shareholders a negotiated number of restricted shares in the public company. The private company generally continues to operate as a wholly owned subsidiary of the public holding company.

Second, following the previous transaction, the total shares held by the private company's shareholders usually will equal a majority of the total outstanding stock in the public holding company. The officers and directors of the public company resign at the closing, and the officers and directors of the private company now manage the public company and continue to operate the wholly owned subsidiary.

The total time required for a private company with audited statements to become public via this process is approximately three to eight weeks. The fees involved in a reverse merger vary on a project-by-project basis and are dependent on many variables, including the type of vehicle used. The cost of acquiring a public shell ranges from $100,000 to $1 million, in addition to 5% to 40% of the stock in the company after merger.[12] Legal and accounting fees are additional expenses.

The primary advantages to going public via a reverse merger are speed to market and limited expense. A reverse merger may save 12 months and millions of dollars of costs that would be incurred in a traditional IPO. All of the disadvantages of being a public company mentioned earlier apply to an entity formed through reverse merger with one major addition: It is highly unlikely that security analysts will follow a company that enters the market through a reverse merger. If the market movers do not get behind a public company, it loses many of the benefits of being public.

GOING PRIVATE

A company goes private when it reduces the number of its shareholders to fewer than 300 and is no longer required to file reports with the SEC. About 500 companies each year deregister from a major exchange, or "go dark," as it is called, when their shareholders of record fall below 300 (or 500, if assets total less than $10 million). For many of these companies, total shareholders may number in the thousands. However, since recorded shareholders fall below the threshold, the company deregisters and is no longer a public entity.

A number of transactions can result in a company going private, including:

- Another company or individual makes a tender offer to buy all or most of the company's publicly held shares.
- The company merges with or sells the company's assets to another private company.
- The company can declare a reverse stock split that not only reduces the number of shares but also reduces the number of shareholders. In this type of reverse stock split, the company typically gives shareholders a single new share in exchange for a block of 10, 100, or even 1,000 of the old shares. If a shareholder does not have a sufficient number of old shares to exchange for new shares, the company usually pays the shareholder cash based on the current market price of the company's stock.

Athough SEC rules do not prevent companies from going private, the SEC does require companies to provide information to shareholders about the transaction that caused the company to go private. The company may be required to file a merger proxy statement or a tender offer document with the SEC.

SEC rules require public disclosure of the reasons for going private, alternatives the company may have considered, and whether the transaction is fair to all shareholders. The rules require disclosure of any directors who disagreed with the transaction and why they disagreed or abstained from voting. The company also must disclose whether a majority of directors who are not company employees approved the transaction.

Going-private transactions require shareholders to make difficult decisions. Some states have adopted corporate takeover statutes to protect shareholders and provide shareholders with dissenter's rights. These statutes provide shareholders the opportunity to sell their shares on the terms offered, to challenge the transaction in court, or to hold on to the shares. Once the transaction is concluded, shareholders may have a difficult time selling their retained shares because of a limited trading market.

HOW TO GET DELISTED FROM NASDAQ

There are several ways to get delisted from Nasdaq. Some of the key ways are listed next.

- The subject is taken over.
- A company can be delisted if its stock falls below a minimum trading price for a specific period of time and the company does not meet one of the other minimum standards.
- Once a company's stock price falls below $1 per share, it can be delisted solely based on its stock price. If a company's stock trades below $1 for 30 consecutive trading days or six weeks, Nasdaq will issue a deficiency notice. If during that 30-day period the stock climbs above a buck and then slips below it again, the clock is reset. In any case, the deficiency notice warns the company that it has 90 calendar days to bring its price up to $1 for 10 consecutive days. The company may accomplish this through various actions, such as a merger, acquisition, or a significant transaction or order with another company. If the company is unsuccessful, it could end with a delisting.[13]

Exhibit 34.6 displays the transfer matrix for going-private transactions.

GOING PRIVATE KEY POINTS TO CONSIDER

Going private may be an even more legalistic transaction than going public. This is because going private transactions exclude some shareholders from continuing to hold equity. The major risk is that shareholders may claim unfair treatment by

EXHIBIT 34.6   Transfer Matrix: Going Private

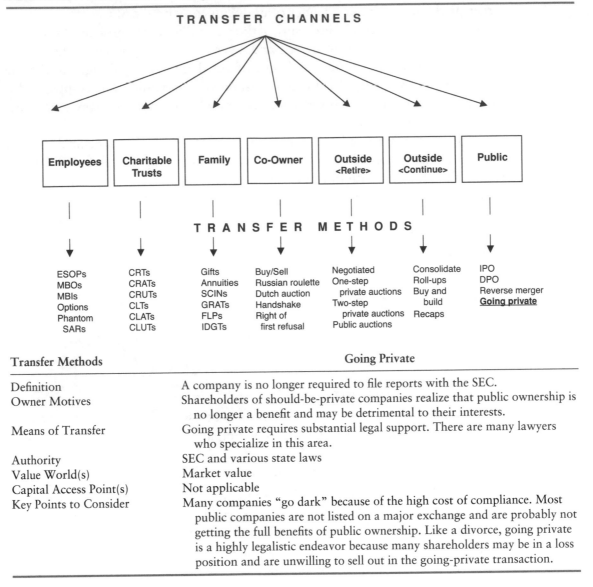

Transfer Methods	Going Private
Definition	A company is no longer required to file reports with the SEC.
Owner Motives	Shareholders of should-be-private companies realize that public ownership is no longer a benefit and may be detrimental to their interests.
Means of Transfer	Going private requires substantial legal support. There are many lawyers who specialize in this area.
Authority	SEC and various state laws
Value World(s)	Market value
Capital Access Point(s)	Not applicable
Key Points to Consider	Many companies "go dark" because of the high cost of compliance. Most public companies are not listed on a major exchange and are probably not getting the full benefits of public ownership. Like a divorce, going private is a highly legalistic endeavor because many shareholders may be in a loss position and are unwilling to sell out in the going-private transaction.

the acquiring party. As a result, going-private transactions must be structured to prevent the inherent danger that the control group will, whether intentionally or not, treat itself more favorably than the outsider group. The next points should be considered prior to taking the first step.

■ The transaction must be entirely fair. The price paid and the procedures used must be considered fair to an impartial observer.

■ The higher the premium paid for the outsiders' stock, the less likely a shareholder lawsuit will result.

■ SEC disclosure rules must be followed. The SEC requires the filing of a number of public disclosures. For instance, one report requires the proponents of a going-private transaction to explain publicly why they believe the transaction is fair.

- An external fairness opinion is needed. Those seeking to take the company private should engage a nationally known investment banking firm to perform a third-party fairness opinion. This is something of an insurance policy that may further discourage lawsuits.
- A law firm that specializes in going-private transactions is needed.
- Even if all rules are followed, there is a good chance that litigation will result. Some outside shareholders may have lost substantial money and wish to recoup their losses in court. Those taking companies private will not be disappointed if they anticipate litigation. The key is to prepare for it.

Thousands of public firms should be private companies. Only a small percentage of companies that go public achieve the critical mass necessary to make the decision worthwhile. Much like divorcing a business partner, the going-private process is certain to involve lawyers with all of the nastiness and cost associated with a divorce.

TRIANGULATION

An IPO signals the close of the private business spectrum but launches the public value world, as described in Chapter 14. Public markets have authorities and defined processes by which to value interests. Buyouts show that stock prices change based on perceptions of synergies and control. In fact, many of the same variables that drive private value also dictate public pricing.

As they take a company public, private owners trade the anonymity and private ownership control for the magnifying glass of the public markets. Many private owners go public because they believe private markets will not yield enough growth capital, at a reasonable dilution, to support their company's growth needs. Others go public because they would prefer to sell their business for double-digit multiples rather than the single digits the private markets will bear. Whatever the motivating cause, a relatively small percentage of public companies realize the ultimate goal of high liquidity and sustained wealth generation.

By going private, a company moves from the public value world to a private value world, probably the financial subworld of market value. Many of these should-be-private companies actually go private because they have been valued as a private company despite their public stature. Without an increased valuation, high level of liquidity, or active access to low-cost capital, there really is little reason to be a public entity. For these reasons, plus the higher costs of being public caused by adherence to the Sarbanes-Oxley law, thousands of smaller public companies will continue to go private in the coming years.

NOTES

1. Office of Securities, State of Maine, www.maine.gov/pfr/securities/small_business/scor.htm
2. www.sec.gov.

3. NASDAQ.com; NYSE.com.
4. Nasdaq: http://listingcenter.nasdaqomx.com/assets/nasdaq_listing_req _fees.pdf.
5. New York Stock Exchange Web site: www.nyse.com/regulation/nyse/1147474807344 .html.
6. www.referenceforbusiness.com.
7. www.nasdaq.com.
8. www.streetdirectory.com.
9. www.fei.mediaroom.com.
10. en.wikipedia.org/wiki/Alternative_Investment_Market.
11. en.wikipedia.org/wiki/TSX_Venture_Exchange.
12. www.accountingtools.com.
13. NASDAQ: http://listingcenter.nasdaqomx.com/assets/nasdaq_listing_ req_fees.pdf.

CHAPTER 35

Business Transfer: Conclusion

This chapter concludes the transfer section of this book with a number of observations that build on information provided throughout the preceding chapters. Because the ability to transfer a business interest directly affects the value of a business, owner-managers must understand the ramifications of this value-transfer relationship in the private capital markets. Further, the choice of transfer method often connects with specific types of capital available to support a transfer. The foregoing chapters described the fundamental concepts underlying the transfer of private businesses. This chapter builds on those fundamentals with a discussion of these issues:

- Transfer activity is segmented in private capital markets allowing for an arbitrage opportunity.
- Owner motives choose the range of values available for a transfer.
- Creating value in a private business requires planning.
- Transfer is triangulated to valuation and capitalization.

SEGMENTED TRANSFER ACTIVITY AND ARBITRAGE

There is no unified transfer market in private capital markets. Rather, the market for transferring business interests is segmented into several levels where the transfer is likely to occur. Each level has more or less access to each of the disparate capital access points, value worlds, transfer mechanisms, and market mechanisms. Each separate shop in the bazaar called the private capital markets can be accessed through various segments or levels. There is an overlap between these transfer segments. For example, different intermediaries assist owners within each segment but may provide services that overlap into other segments. Plus, although certain market mechanisms may be available to all segments, they may be more or less developed within a given segment. Exhibit 35.1 depicts the transfer segments in the lower-middle market.

The three transfer levels roughly correspond to annual sales ranges of less than $5 million, between $5 million and $50 million, and between $50 million and

EXHIBIT 35.1   Segmented Transfer Markets

	Sales		
	$0–$5 MM	**$5 MM–$50 MM**	**$50 MM–$150 MM**
Market needs	Local market access; owner dominated; buyer is buying a job; no synergies available.	Regional and national access; owner is less central to business; buyer is buying a business; possible synergies available.	National and international access; business practices are institutionalized; buyer is buying a market position; synergies available.
Likely intermediary	Business broker	M&A intermediary	Private investment banker
Strongest mechanism	Exchange	Intermediation	Information
Transfer methods	Negotiated	Negotiated and one-step auctions	Auctions
Likely value worlds	Owner value, asset and financial subworlds of market value	Financial and synergy subworlds	Financial and synergy subworlds
Likely capital access points	Banks, government programs	Banks, ABLs, some mezzanine and private equity at the higher sales end	All CAPs but IPO
Likely EBITDA multiple	2–3.5 times	4–6 times	5–7 times

$150 million. Although these market segments can be observed, they are not cast in stone. There are daily variations on the format presented in the table. However, a number of useful perceptions can be drawn from grouping the presentation in this manner.

First, each segment represents salient market needs. Companies with less than $5 million in sales usually transfer locally. However, companies doing more than $100 million may be sold to an international acquirer. Most small companies are sold using a negotiated selling process while larger companies typically transfer using an auction approach.

Second, different groups of intermediaries provide for shareholders' and investors' needs at various market levels. Business brokers are likely to arrange transfers at the low end; private investment bankers handle larger deals. There is a fair amount of overlap between the segments. For instance, some business brokers and merger and acquisitions (M&A) intermediaries handle larger deals.

Third, each segment is affected differently by the strength of the underlying market mechanisms. The lowest segment relies on exchange, since these deals are horse-traded events. Further, business brokers have done the best job of creating exchanges in their segment. Some states have multiple-listing-style services for small business sales. Midsize businesses rely heavily on intermediation. Information is opaque in these businesses, and M&A intermediaries must create the information environment for client companies by recasting the financial

EXHIBIT 35.2 Consolidation Math

Value World	Selling Multiples	Sales Segment
Asset subworld	Net asset value	
Investment value world	2.5–4 times EBITDA	$0–$5 million
Financial subworld	4–6 times EBITDA	$5–$50 million
Synergy subworld	5–7 times EBITDA	$50–$150 million
Public world	Greater than 10 times EBITDA	Above $150 million

statement and other means. When combined with the need for confidentiality, with respect to both to the market and employees, these middle deals require a tremendous amount of intermediation. Larger deals leverage existing information. The selling company probably has audited financial statements and accounts for product line profitability using systems that generate numerous management reports. Information regarding potential buyers is also better understood with larger deals.

Perhaps the most interesting aspect of the transfer segments involves the arbitrage play that exists for those who can transact in the proper value world. Buying in one value world and selling in another often creates value. For instance, most consolidators attempt to acquire in the financial subworld of market value and exit either in the synergy subworld of market value or through the public markets. A consolidation math, shown in Exhibit 35.2, can help conceptualize the arbitrage opportunity.

Some successful consolidations involve buying a group of companies in the asset subworld, merging them into a single operating company, and then selling out in one of the higher-value worlds. But the math still works for investors if the acquisitions are consummated in the financial subworld and the exit occurs in the synergy subworld. It should be noted that selling multiples is often the same in the financial and synergy market value subworlds, but it can be different as well. Exiting at the synergy market level may give the consolidator a slightly higher selling multiple plus a higher synergized benefit stream. This logic behind recapitalizations is further demonstrated in the next example.

One industrial distributor used consolidation math to its advantage in building a fair-size company in a short period of time. The owner noticed that gross profit percentages were falling for his company and his competitors. He reasoned that growth into a medium-size firm would shield his margins and grow his profitability. By using simple math, he was able to determine that companies in the $3 million to $4 million annual sales level would be unable to stay in business in the near term. Consolidating a number of these companies would solve his need for growth and help the owners get out of their investment. He hired an investment banking firm that contacted several dozen of these smaller firms. The investment bankers visited a number of companies and showed them the value-destroying math. Eventually they offered the same deal structure to eight companies: net asset value plus a three-year employment contract. Seventy percent of the purchase price would be paid in cash, with the remainder paid over three years earning 7%. Six of the eight companies agreed to sell representing about $22 million in additional sales.

	Industrial Distributor	
	Preconsolidation	Postconsolidation
Sales	$40,000,000	$62,000,000
EBITDA	4,000,000	8,000,000
Long-term debt (LTD)	0	8,000,000
Minimum market value (5 × EBITDA – LTD)	$20,000,000	$32,000,000

The consolidator gained four things by employing this strategy.

1. It had almost no cash out of pocket to fund these acquisitions. A tier 2 asset-based lender funded most of the required down payment.
2. The consolidator locked up the former owners as managers for several years, which greatly reduced operating risk going forward.
3. With another $22 million in sales, the consolidator was able to renegotiate rebates with vendors adding to profitability.
4. Most important, the distributor centralized accounting, computer operations, and other systems, saving millions of dollars per year.

After the dust settled, the distributor's owner figured he expanded his company dramatically and would recoup his investment in less than two years. Within five years, the owner plans to sell out in the synergy subworld, which is available because his company is now a threat in the marketplace to larger competitors.

OWNER MOTIVES CHOOSE THE RANGE OF VALUES

Private business owners actually choose the range of values within which their business will transfer. This choice of value is manifested by their underlying motives for the transfer, which leads to one or more value worlds. The appraisal process within a value world yields a likely value within a sea of possible values. Once again, private business valuation is a range concept; owner motives just narrow the range a bit. Some of the transfer motives of private owners are listed next.

- Meet personal transfer motives within a business setting
- Diversify their estate
- Create a family legacy
- Use transfer of business as main wealth-creating vehicle
- Grow the business without using personal cash
- Have no partners

Transferring a private business often is complicated because personal and business motives are intertwined. Many owners want to transfer their businesses to their children, yet perhaps only 10% to 20% of all businesses stay within the family. This is an obvious example of the conflict between personal and business motives. These contrasting motives drive the choice of transfer method. This tension causes owners to find a balance between their hearts and their wallets. It also explains the multitude of choices available in the transfer spectrum. A case can be made that because of the impact of owner motives, the private transfer spectrum is vastly more sophisticated than what is available in public markets.

Most private owners sell out because they are burned out. Private owners cannot easily replace themselves, partly because they are control-oriented but also because they tend to wear so many hats that no one person can replace them. This is a key reason why private companies frequently do not outlast the current owner. The private owner usually wishes to diversify her estate, the majority of which is vested in the value of the business. In fact, frequently the business and the personal life of the owner are intimately intertwined. Therefore, a private owner is likely to employ sophisticated estate planning techniques, particularly if her motive is to transfer the business to children as a family legacy. Further, private owners typically forgo some compensation in order to reinvest earnings in the business in the hope that a major capital event will occur someday. Finally, private owners usually are not motivated to sell small parts of their business. The private markets provide little support for this activity, and private owners typically do not want partners anyway.

Ultimately, a motive leads an owner to action. This action, in turn, causes the owner to choose a transfer channel. That choice of a transfer channel directly leads to the choice of a transfer method, which selects a value world. Exhibit 35.3 shows this chain of events.

Three interesting observations can be made regarding this causal chain.

1. Channels may house numerous methods, some of which select different value worlds. For instance, the employee channel houses employee stock ownership plans (ESOPs), viewed in fair market value, and management buyouts (MBOs), which may be viewed in market value, investment value, or owner value.
2. The left side of the chart largely involves regulated transfer methods, which lead to the fair market value world. The right side of the chart largely involves unregulated methods, which are viewed primarily in market value. The co-owner channel is the dividing line and can be viewed as part regulated, part unregulated.
3. Channels with multiple worldviews by definition have multiple world values. Thus, an owner wishing to transfer to an outsider and then retire might transact in market value, owner value, or investment value. Each world probably has a dramatically different value proposition.

The value range concept is extended when one considers that some transfer methods may apply to multiple channels, something that is not shown in Exhibit 35.3. For instance, the negotiated transfer method may be employed in the

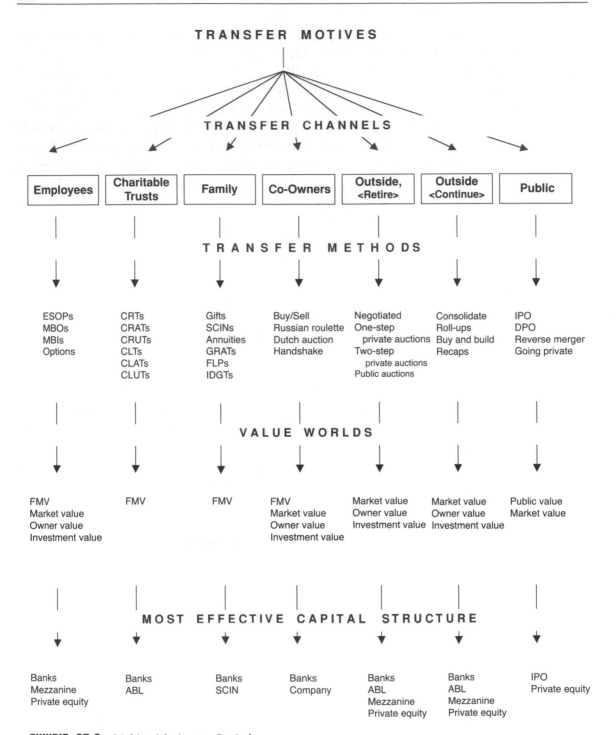

EXHIBIT 35.3 Linking Motives to Capital

employee, family, co-owner, and outside channels. Or management transfers may occur within the charitable trusts, family, or co-owner channels. Showing all possible linkages would quickly turn the chart into something only Jackson Pollock would recognize. Perhaps a PrivateCo example of this crossover linkage will help.

Assume Joe Mainstreet wishes to transfer PrivateCo to his son and daughter. Because all is well with the Mainstreet, clan the transfer occurs in the family

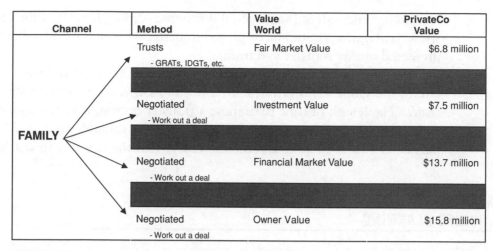

Channel	Method	Value World	PrivateCo Value
	Trusts - GRATs, IDGTs, etc.	Fair Market Value	$6.8 million
FAMILY	Negotiated - Work out a deal	Investment Value	$7.5 million
	Negotiated - Work out a deal	Financial Market Value	$13.7 million
	Negotiated - Work out a deal	Owner Value	$15.8 million

EXHIBIT 35.4 Mainstreet's Family Transfer Options

transfer channel. There are other transfer methods that Joe may employ beyond the family methods shown in the previous exhibit. Exhibit 35.4 shows Joe's transfer options, along with PrivateCo's value in the corresponding value worlds as calculated throughout Part One of this book.

If Joe is motivated to sell PrivateCo to family members, he chooses the family transfer channel. This may employ multiple transfer methods, such as a negotiated deal or the use of various trusts. In other words, Joe always can choose to work out a deal with his children or stay within the confines of a more structured method, such as a grantor-retained annuity trust. The main question is: In which value world will the transaction occur? These methods select four different value worlds, each with a different corresponding value. For this example, PrivateCo's values have been derived in Part One of the book. Joe can choose to transfer PrivateCo to his son and daughter for between $6.8 million to $15.8 million, depending on which value world he selects.

The ability to choose a particular value world in which to transact is similar to possessing a *put option*. In options lingo, a put is a right to sell something for a particular price at a particular time. The more options an owner has to transfer the business, the more puts she holds. As the range of values in Exhibit 35.4 shows, these puts are valuable. In general, the longer the exercise period and more certain the optioned event, the more valuable the option becomes. The lead time required to execute most transfer methods is not long, at least relative to the life of the business. For instance, implementing an ESOP in a company, arguably one of the most sophisticated methods, usually can be accomplished within one year. Further, most transfer methods are within an owner's control to launch. Other than going public, an owner can plan and execute all other methods.

Options theory may help explain the spectrum of business transfer and its multiplicity of choices. Business owners face a plethora of transfer alternatives. Each alternative has different risks, different values, and different outcomes. Weighting and valuing competing investment opportunities is the task for which options theory was developed. The financial community utilizes options theory on a daily basis. In fact, many companies use *real options* analysis, which is a technique for identifying and valuing managerial decisions. Although beyond the scope of this work, real options could be employed to better understand and value the options presented on the transfer spectrum.

Well-run businesses can choose from the spectrum of transfer options until late in the game. This is fortunate since most owners procrastinate on transfer issues. The length of time to exercise a transfer option, plus the high certainty of a successful execution, makes these options quite valuable to owners. Planning a particular course of action, based on a motive, is the key to a successful transfer.

CREATING VALUE IN A PRIVATE BUSINESS REQUIRES PLANNING

Company owners should be concerned with creating business value. Often value is not realized from a private business investment until a transfer of the enterprise occurs. Growing businesses are like hungry children: They must be fed. In this case, capital is the sustenance. Many owners choose to suffer personally along the way so their business can remain healthy. If only a transfer unleashes value, what can owners do to increase the value of their firms?

Readers who have read this far will recognize that no single activity is likely to create value in all value worlds. However, if it is possible to plan the value world in which to transact, as the previous section asserts, it is possible to determine how to grow the value of a business. As with most things that really matter, planning is the key.

Chapter 32 introduces the notion of transfer timing. This simply means that timing a transfer is critical to insuring a successful outcome. A multitude of variables must be aligned to enable a successful transfer. Even *timing* has multiple variables. Transfer timing is comprised of personal, business, and market timing. Transfer timing is like winning on a slot machine. Unless all three timing slots are aligned, the possibility of a big payout is limited. Exhibit 35.5 depicts these three slots.

The first slot represents the owner's personal timing. The owner must be physically, mentally, financially, and socially prepared to execute a transfer. The second slot is business timing. Good business timing exists when the company is well positioned to attract positive attention by virtue of its internal operations, management techniques, systems, and financial performance. Market timing refers to the activity level for transferring a business interest in the marketplace. A good market is characterized by aggressive buyer activity in terms of interest levels, acquisition multiples, and available financing. From an owner's perspective, the most successful transfer occurs when all three slots are in alignment.

EXHIBIT 35.5 Transfer Timing

Generally a less-than-satisfactory result occurs if any timing slots are out of calibration. For instance, owners who are not in a strong personal position to transfer the business may find it necessary to sell at less-than-optimum price or terms. Of course, if the business is not ready to transfer, it is unlikely that outside offers will be attractive to the owner. Finally, the owner and business may be ready for transfer, but if the market does not support the selling process, either the transfer will not occur or it will occur at less-than-optimal price and terms.

Personal Timing

Personal timing is largely within an owner's control. Obviously unexpected problems arise; there is no control over serious illness, accident, or other life-changing circumstances. Yet a good deal of control is possible with adequate planning. The business can be prepared for sale before the time comes when owners want to sell for estate purposes, liquidity, or retirement. Control can be achieved by setting the process in place and planning the event. Personal timing is partially within the control of the individual.

Although some events are beyond control, if the business is prepared for sale, the odds of an attractive sale price are improved. For example, in business cycles, it is possible to anticipate that downturns often follow peaks. If an economic downturn is on the horizon, the business is ready for sale, and personal timing is OK, an owner may control two and a half factors.

Personal timing is difficult to describe because it is different for each owner. The need for clarity in an owner's motive, however, is a commonality for a successful transfer. A number of items constrain an owner's ability to personally plan. Exhibit 35.6 shows some of these constraints.

Several constraints affect an owner's personal motives for transferring the business. For example, age is a constraint. The average age for sellers in the United States is approximately 52 years old. This age is down significantly from the prior generation, perhaps as much as 10 years. Either the new economy wears people out faster or baby boomers want to see the world while they are still young. It often takes a year or more to prepare a business for the transfer. Many owners must remain with the business after a transfer for two to three years. Owners who are 70 or older and have no succession plan probably will die in the business. Greed is insatiable. This causes many owners never to leave the world of owner value because no one else on earth values the business as highly as they do. These owners also have a tendency to die in the business, regardless of age. Most smart owners begin planning the transfer at least five years in advance of the transaction.

EXHIBIT 35.6   Personal Transfer Timing Constraints

Average age of seller in United States	Early 50s
Time to prepare a transfer	1–3 years
Average length of employment agreement	2.5 years
Average length of noncompete agreement	2–3 years
Fate of owners over 70 years old	Probable death in business
Chances of selling a greedy owner's business	Near zero

EXHIBIT 35.7   Actions that Affect Market Value

Goals	Value Drivers	Strategies
Increase recast EBITDA	Increase sales	Enter niche markets; patent new products to create barriers to entry; launch innovative products; consolidate competitors.
	Lower cost of goods sold	Develop scale economies; acquire captive access to raw materials; increase efficiencies in processes (production, distribution, services, and labor utilization); implement cutting-edge cost control systems.
	Control operating expenses	Budget and monitor expenses; identify fixed versus variable expenses; manage expenses at lowest level possible; keep track of recast items.
Reduce risk	Increase incremental value	Invest only in positive NPV/IBV projects.
	Decrease capital base	Withdraw or liquidate underperforming businesses, implement product line profitability capabilities to determine winners and losers.
	Reduce business risk	Perform at a higher operating level compared to competitors, long-term contracts, etc.; institute financial transparency; including the retention of audited financial statements.
	Reduce cost of capital	Maximize use of debt to support equity; possibly use less costly equity substitutes, such as mezzanine debt; reduce surprises (volatility of earnings); consistently test the market cost of debt; walk down the Pepperdine Private Capital Market Line whenever possible.
	Reduce customer concentration	No single customer should account for more than 25% of sales.
	Form management structure	Create a functional, possibly virtual, organization so the owner is not central to the business; develop a strong backup manager.
Increase acquisition attractiveness	Develop a place in the market	Always be considered a tough competitor, or roadblock, by larger players; become a company of niches.
	Obtain critical mass	Achieve minimum sales of least $10–15 million.
	Maintain high margins	Focus on maintaining higher gross and operating margins than the competition.
	Management team and systems add value	Owner is redundant so management team is considered self-sufficient.
	Create effective planning	Build an effective business model that links owner motives to employee actions.

Business Timing

Preparing a business for eventual transfer is enhanced by knowledge of the value worlds. Simply put, owners can increase the value of their business by choosing the value world for the transfer, then focusing on and maximizing the variables that drive value in the world.

Most owners should be concerned with increasing their company's market value. Exhibit 35.7 shows a number of variables sensitive to market value. The exhibit shows things owners can do to affect their company's market value. There are three general goals listed, which correspond to the market valuation process. To create market value, companies need to increase recast earnings before interest, taxes, depreciation, and amortization (EBITDA), decrease the risk of achieving the benefit stream, and generally increase its attractiveness to acquirers. The middle column lists actions that drive value. Finally, strategies are offered that will help owners meet their goals. Several of the value driver items deserve further explanation.

Increase Recast EBITDA

Increasing recast EBITDA is of primary importance since this is the metric that most directly affects market value. Owners can increase sales through internal or external growth, or a combination of the two. In either case, capital is a constraint. Aggressive owners are constantly in search of acquisition opportunities that are accretive and self-financing. This means that consolidation math works in their favor, particularly with a deal structure requiring little or no out-of-pocket cash.

Owners who focus on maximizing their company's gross margins often unlock substantial value. By definition, this means minimizing cost of goods sold. The best investment most owners can make is upgrading the company's purchasing function. Professional materials management pays for itself many times over and helps create market value. Companies can benefit greatly from installing cutting-edge inventory management and other throughput management systems.

Finally, most medium-size companies can create market value by better controlling operating expenses. Unfortunately, many of these companies do not maintain a flexible budget or tie their budgets to longer-term planning. Professional managers, however, are obsessive-compulsive about budgeting at the lowest possible level in the organization and then creating accountability for everyone involved. Ultimately, in most large companies, employee compensation is tied to success against the budget. This contrasts with many smaller private companies, which do not budget sales and expenses. Of course, always reacting to change is a management method that ensures that small companies remain small.

Reduce Risk

Market value increases as a company reduces its operating and financial risk. The starting point here is to manage risk/return by implementing a disciplined capital allocation system. The payback method works well for projects that return the investment within a year or so; however, complicated projects require a net present value or incremental business value approach. Owning a company gets progressively easier and more profitable when assets are deployed correctly.

The single most glaring weakness for most medium-size companies is the lack of vision regarding product and service line profitability. Simply put, many companies do not know where they make money. Outsiders correctly view this lack of control as risky. Once again, companies that budget effectively typically do not have this problem.

Another risk-reducing attribute is the elimination of customer concentrations above 25% or so. Concentrations above 25% are viewed as all-or-nothing accounts by the market and are discounted appropriately. Buyers view management concentration similarly.

Some owners are so central to the success of the business that buyers must plan to hire several additional people to replace them. This situation not only has a negative recasting impact but also adds tremendous risk to an assessment. In either event, concentrations reduce market value.

Increase Attractiveness

There are a variety of actions an owner can take to increase the attractiveness of her firm to the market. It is desirable to be viewed as a market roadblock by larger companies. Larger companies fanatically plan their businesses, especially regarding market share changes. Smaller companies exploit niches that larger companies cannot service effectively. A good value-added strategy for a small company is to position itself in a number of these niches. Larger companies may conclude that it is cheaper to acquire a small competitor than start a market war.

The synergy subworld requires critical mass from its participants. Most sellers cannot access this high-level value world unless they have annual sales of more than $10 million and preferably more than $20 million. Perhaps a perfect situation is a niche company with five to six niches, each selling $5 million to $7 million per year.

Finally, companies with effective business models are always in demand. A business model represents the way an entity is organized to meet a goal. Effective business models are almost always simply stated and understood. The linkage between owner motives and employee actions is taut, which leads to good communications and ability to quickly effect business changes in the market. In many cases, the acquirer adopts many of the business model attributes of the target. For example, a chemical manufacturer was able to convert advanced chemists to technical salespeople, thereby eliminating the need for nontechnical salespeople. A larger chemical company ultimately acquired the company, citing its increased profitability and service capabilities due to a more effective sales force.

How are effective business models developed? Such models start with an intuitive management approach and a keen sense of the market. Beyond this, it is not surprising that many of the strategies that form these business models are the same as the actions that create market value.

Market Timing

Market timing is no less important than personal and business timing. There are opportunities to transfer a business in almost any type of economy. The unexpected knock on the door from an overpaying consolidator, however, happens only to the guy three lockers down. Everyone else must increase their market savvy to realize their goals. To maximize a transfer, a healthy transfer market is a good place to start. The U.S. transfer market seems to run in ten-year cycles, as shown in Exhibit 35.8.

Ten-year transfer cycles represent the macroeconomic market cycle for enterprise transfers. It is no coincidence that the cycle mirrors general economic activity. Transfer cycles begin each decade with two to three years of deal

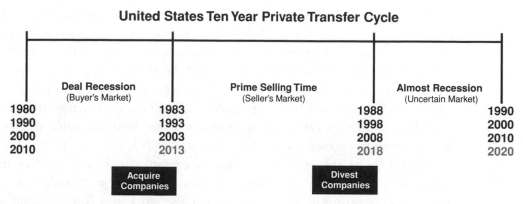

EXHIBIT 35.8 Ten-Year Transfer Cycle

recession. This period reflects an economy in recession that causes banks and other capital providers to lessen lending and investment activities. Large companies tend to focus on core businesses and curtail aggressive acquisition plans. For acquirers with cash, this is a buyer's market.

From a seller's perspective, the prime time to sell a business occurs during the middle years of the cycle. Capital is available for buyers to finance deals during these years. During this period, the MBA crowd has again convinced Wall Street to fund roll-ups and other consolidations. Big companies are back in the game, growing income statements and balance sheets through strategic acquisitions.

The smartest sellers typically wait until near the end of the seller's market before making a move. In this way they get the benefits of increasing profitability plus the highest transfer pricing. Economic storm clouds start forming after eight years or so of the cycle. Because of the economic uncertainty during this period, deals are harder to initiate and close; therefore, waiting too long is risky.

Deal periods in a transfer cycle are not binary switches. Rather, they are like leaky deal faucets. There are opportunities in every period for an owner to create and maximize an exit. However, sellers are most likely to get a good deal in a seller's market.

What is stopping more people from buying in the second and third year of each decade, then selling out in the seventh and eighth years? The answer depends on who they are. Most private business owners are emotionally tied to their businesses, and therefore buying and selling their firms is not something they do routinely. Most private equity groups do not synchronize their activities with the transfer cycle. (Typically this type of thing is not taught in MBA programs.) And large public companies are not concerned with the private transfer cycle.

Obviously, the overall economy in which business operates is not within individual control. However, each industry operates with its own macroeconomic characteristics. By attending industry meetings, reading industry literature, and studying general economic trends, it is possible to assess the health of an industry and where it is in its transfer cycle. With a serious look at the industry and the economy, it is possible to keep informed and exercise some control over when it is best to expose the business to the market.

Maximizing a transfer value usually requires balancing all three elements of timing. But it is somewhat unlikely that an owner is personally ready for a transfer at the same time that the business and market have peaked. It is more likely that a timing trade-off is required. For instance, if the business is growing 30% per year, will it be worth 30% more in a year? Where is the market for business sales and where it is likely to be? If, for example, the business is growing and the economy is declining, interest rates may be higher and the business value to a buyer may decline because financing costs have increased.

Therefore, if the current multiple of earnings is 5, and reduces to 4.5, an owner may have achieved a higher revenue base and profitability but receive a lower market multiple. It is possible to have worked a full year and added no incremental sale price to the business. However, if the economy is strong and growing, then perhaps it is wise to build if it is possible.

A what-if analysis is useful, for example, if the business is valued at $10 million and the owner's target is $12 million. It is possible to develop a plan to increase the business value to meet expectations. This is the art of controlling business timing while factoring in personal goals and personal timing. Business timing is almost entirely in the owner's control. The ancient wisdom here is that from the time an owner acquires or starts a business, he or she should be looking at its sale.

TRIANGULATION

Since most owners get only one shot at the brass ring, they must claim maximum benefits. Positioning for an effective transfer is the key. Yet this chapter shows that this level of planning is a daunting challenge, given the complexity and the multiplicity of transfer options. Continuing with circus analogies, transferring a business is like simultaneously balancing a number of plates spinning on sticks arrayed in a triangular fashion. The critical difference is that the transfer is doomed if just one plate falls. Each plate represents a valuation world, a capital access point, or a transfer method. Owners should understand that the most gifted juggler needs help preparing and implementing the task.

Owners must comprehend the material presented herein on valuation, capitalization, and transfer just to get the plates rotating. Owners should assemble a team with expertise in the respective areas. Keeping the plates spinning and balanced requires almost perfect timing and coordination. An owner needs to form a transfer team to share the load.

In the final analysis, transferring a business involves more art than science. The options include hundreds of possible combinations that could work to accomplish the ultimate objective. However, human folly abounds. Take, for example, a recent incident of an 85-year-old seller who "suddenly discovers" that his 62-year-old son does not want to own the business at exactly the point when the market for business is in its reversionary cycle. Or the rapidly growing cash-strapped $15 million company that chooses to do a reverse merger but still finds it necessary to factor its receivables. Consider the owner who has lived so long in the world of owner value that he has convinced himself it is the only value world that applies to his business. He will always be an owner instead of a seller because he passes up numerous opportunities to sell the business, missing market changes, and ultimately will die in the business or watch as the company goes under.

Selling a business is a process, not an event. The process begins long before any specific event occurs, and there is no second chance with a transfer. The best advice for owners: Clarify motives, choose the channel and methods, form a team, and grab the darn ring.

CHAPTER 36

Conclusion

Although it may be hard to believe, this book could easily be 500 to 1,000 pages longer. Nearly every chapter topic could be developed into a book. Since the first edition was released in 2004, many chapters have spawned numerous books. Perhaps the most important part of writing, however, is making hard choices.

Much of the thinking behind this book is based on several macro insights. First, corporate finance theory does not predict behavior in private capital markets. Appendix A contains a discussion of corporate finance principles and shows they are not particularly useful to private managers. Second, people who view valuation, capitalization, and transfer as discrete and unrelated areas do not grasp the larger picture and are likely to make incorrect financing and investment decisions.

Finally, the private capital body of knowledge is large and expanding. Its full practice is effectively limited to those who dedicate themselves to its study.

A number of important themes are presented in this book. Taken together, they form the basis for a fuller description of private capital markets and middle-market finance theory. Several themes are presented next. The chapter then concludes with a discussion of major issues that require further study.

THEME 1

Public and private capital markets are not substitutes for each other because they rely on different capital markets theories to explain market behavior.

Until now, private companies have been viewed in the literature as the unruly stepchildren of public markets. A select few of these children occasionally come of age and are allowed to eat at the public or grown-up table; however, most are not considered mature enough to converse with. This book demonstrates that private markets rely on a unique body of knowledge to explain its structure and activities. In other words, unique markets require unique market theories.

In the foreword, finance professor John Paglia describes his personal journey from believing corporate finance explained the behavior in all capital markets to his current understanding that middle-market finance better explains behavior in the middle market. Professor Paglia, like all finance PhDs, is a product of a system that officially recognizes only corporate finance as the theory that describes behavior in capital markets. Because the two market theories share a common lineage, there are bound to be similarities. However, as this book demonstrates, public and private capital markets are based on differing motives of the participants and maturity of market mechanisms and other factors.

Many underlying assumptions between corporate and middle-market finance are different and often severely at odds with each other. Several characteristics are particularly noteworthy:

- A market establishes value for public companies whereas private companies must rely on a point-in-time appraisal or a transaction to determine value.
- Public companies have ready access to capital, but private companies must create capital solutions one deal at a time, with little certainty of success.
- There are differences in ownership risk, return expectations, anticipated holding periods, and extent of owner participation between the two markets.

These and other mechanistic differences between corporate finance and middle-market finance point to the need for a separate financial theory for the private middle market. This is called middle-market finance theory.

THEME 2

Motives of private business owners initiate actions that function under rules imposed by various authorities.

Nothing happens in the private capital markets until an owner decides to act. Motives of private owners initiate action. Motives drive appraisal purpose, or choice of value world, because a private owner should not undertake a capitalization or transfer without knowing the value of her business. Motives also decide the best capital structure for a firm. Further, an owner's motive for a transfer leads to the choice of a transfer method, which yields a particular value. But motives alone do not dictate a final result. Authorities in the market must support the motive and provide it with additional momentum. No positive outcome is possible without this additional support. Authorities control both access and the rules of the game within their spheres of influence.

Who or what are these authorities? They are the traffic cops in the private markets. In valuation, for example, the Internal Revenue Service (IRS), courts, laws, investors, lenders, and other agents are in position to make the rules. Capital authorities provide money. Transfer authorities range from laws, such as the Employee Retirement Income Security Act or estate laws, to financial intermediaries. Owners who ignore authority do so at their own risk. Authority sanctions its decisions by veto power or denying access to the market. For example, the IRS is not always correct in its decisions, but the full power of the U.S. government still stands behind it.

Private owners need to understand the mutually exclusive features and functions of private capital markets. Once the motive initiates action, specific possibilities are opened and closed. By launching the initial motive without proper information, the owner unknowingly chooses a course of action that narrows future options. This restriction is further indication that knowing the rules of the game in advance is critical for success.

THEME 3

A private business value is relative to the value world in which it is viewed. These value worlds offer a range of possible values.

The value of a private businesses is extremely dynamic; it changes based on the financial fundamentals of the company but also on the reason for the appraisal. This is a startling observation. It suggests that every private business interest at a moment in time has a large range of correct values. The examples throughout the book show that PrivateCo is worth seven times more in the highest-value world as compared to the lowest-value world. Does this value relativity concept mirror reality?

Yes, every private business interest embodies an array of possible values. Proof of this statement is empirically evident. For instance, a private minority interest may have substantial fair value, a modicum of fair market value, and almost no market value. It seems strange to many observers that the same business interest at the same time can be correctly appraised at a host of different values. Yet due to a proliferation of appraisal purposes and functions, value, like beauty, is in the eye of the beholder.

Valuation is the language of private capital markets, but the players seem to speak different dialects. With all of these peculiar perspectives on value, how does business actually get transacted? In other words, how do parties ever agree on the value of a private business interest? The grimaced, chiseled faces of veteran intermediaries answers this question: Agreement occurs only when the parties transact in a neutral world, such as market value, or the party with the greater pull forces the other participant to play in its world. This is what happens every day in the world of owner value day. Typically, no deal is possible with owner-managers unless you play by their rules, or they get desperate and transact in a world other than their authoritarian stronghold.

THEME 4

The Pepperdine Private Capital Market Line (PPCML) describes risk and return in the middle market by showing how credit is rationed based on the provider's credit quality requirements.

Balancing risk and return is a key meta-financial concept in any market. Market players will not invest unless they have a method to measure and manage risk. This is a major problem in the private markets. Because information is opaque, no liquid or even semiliquid market is possible. But in the effort to get paid for taking risk, savvy investors have some useful tools at their disposal.

The primary tool is the credit box. Capital providers ration funds based on credit quality established in the credit box. Money is not lent or invested unless a prospect meets the requirements. The second tool is the portfolio or, more precisely, the ability to manage a portfolio effectively. All successful capital providers are adept at monitoring and managing their portfolios. Providers prune nonperforming investments from the portfolio and attempt to extend successful positions. Ultimately, the combination of a well-positioned credit box and sound portfolio management techniques enables capital providers to meet their return expectations.

The PPCML captures, on an empirical basis, the private return expectations of private institutional capital providers. This line provides a risk/return capital road map to private markets, specifically the middle market. This empirical description of risk/return is in contrast with much of the current literature that does not indicate a return difference in choosing venture capital over bank debt, for example. One book even promotes the use of private equity capital over bank debt because "it is better to have partners than put up with a bank's constant demands." While this may be true, it ignores the fact that private equity is probably three to five times more expensive than bank financing.

THEME 5

Business transfer comprises a spectrum of alternatives. Owners select a transfer channel and method based on their motives or goals.

Owners have dozens of alternatives to use in transferring their business. In most cases, a transfer can be engineered once an owner determines her goals. It turns out that choosing a goal is often the hardest part of the transfer process.

Many owners procrastinate before making the transfer decision. A somewhat exaggerated example involves an 85-year-old man who sought my firm's help to effect a transfer. The man was distraught because "Junior" had recently been offered the chance to buy the family business but had declined the opportunity. The elderly owner castigated the younger generation for its flimsy work ethic and lack of vision. I later discovered that Junior was 62 years old! Junior told me he had worked in the business for more than 30 years and had offered to buy the business more than 10 years before, but the "old man" would not even discuss it. The most revealing aspect to this story is that it occurs every day on Main Street. One can only wonder why.

The answer is based more in psychology than finance. Successful owner-managers are a different breed. They tend to want to control things. Their lives become so intertwined with the business that planning the transfer of their business is like planning the transfer of their existence. I refer to this phenomenon as "walking to the elephant graveyard." Many owners prefer to be carried out of their office in a box than face this walk. Even the elderly owner just mentioned did not really want to transfer his business to Junior or anyone else. It turns out he had a terminal disease and was motivated to control the transfer, just as he had controlled everything else in the business for more than 50 years.

PRIVATE CAPITAL MARKETS

These broad themes provide a framework that describes the private capital markets. Exhibit 36.1 is a graphical depiction of this market structure. Although private capital markets are unique, their boundary is more like a membrane than a brick wall. This permeable membrane enables participants to meet their primary goal: to get information and money into and out of private capital markets. Various market mechanisms provide the gears, or movement to the markets. In a sense, private markets are held together by exchange, allocation, intermediation, and regulation. Exchange provides the trading activity between the parties. Allocation provides the resources necessary to feed the market. Intermediation facilitates market transactions. Finally, regulation provides the market rules.

The motives of an involved party lead to action in the markets. This book is oriented toward owner-managers; therefore, most of the information presented herein looks at situations through their eyes. But millions of nonowners also inhabit private markets. Examples of involved nonowners are management teams, capital providers, lawyers, CPAs, and so on. For this schematic to be effective, it must work for all parties. For example, a banker's or investor's motives are subject to the same market forces as those of any other involved party.

The relevant authority tempers motives. This is fortunate, or capitalism would soon run amuck. The Wild West economic environment of modern-day Russia is an example of what happens when motives go unrestrained. However, there are things to consider within the concept of authority. There are competing authorities throughout the market. For example, the IRS and tax courts compete on a variety of valuation issues. In this case, the authority with the stronger logical argument *generally* carries the day.

Further, there are outside authorities that parachute edicts into the private markets. The Financial Accounting Standards Board mandated fair value onto private markets, even though this board was actually attempting to solve a public company issue. Finally, authorities control only their sphere of influence. Sometimes this is fairly limited, as in the case of investors whose only sanctioning power is to not invest. In other cases the authority's sphere is quite broad, such as that of the IRS. The influence of authority is felt in valuation, capitalization, and transfer issues.

Positive activity begins when authority is combined with motive; at this step an involved party's motive is empowered. This combination launches middle-market finance theory. This theory is the rotary engine of the private capital markets. Valuation, capital structure formation, and business transfer are interconnected to power the markets. Triangulation refers to the use of two sides of the middle-market finance theory triangle to help fully explain a point on the third side. The three-legged stool analogy seems to capture this image effectively.

Due to the lack of a trading market, private business appraisal is a difficult exercise. Much of the current literature suggests that fair market value is the default standard of value (value world). This has caused thousands of appraisers to rely on this *single standard* regardless of the reason for the appraisal. For instance, appraisers routinely determine open market values of business interests

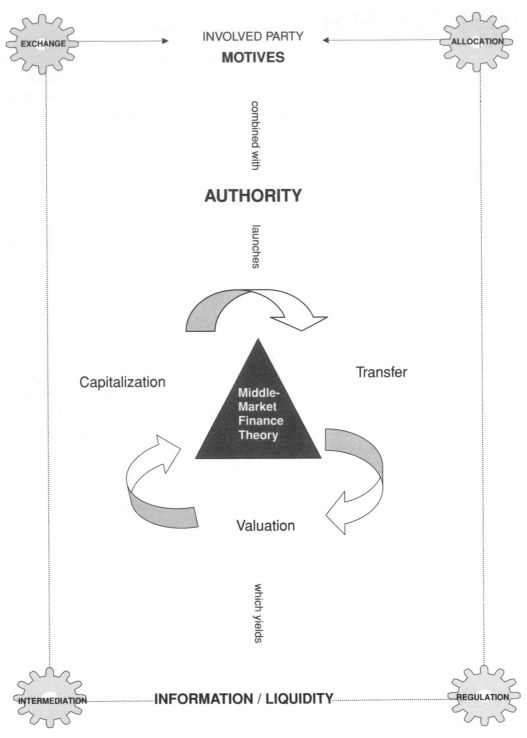

EXHIBIT 36.1   Structure of the Private Capital Markets

using fair market value. This leads to an overvaluation of minority interests and an undervaluation of control values. This book suggests a different approach.

Value world theory predicts that every private company embodies a wide range of values. Many observers are uncomfortable with this thought, presumably because it disrupts their every-business-has-one-true-value mentality. Many people also believe that public markets provide the necessary information to derive private value conclusions. This book shows, without hesitation, that private valuation is holistic and not driven by public capital markets.

Describing capital structure formation is less problematic than valuation since this source material is less theoretically driven. Several simple observations describe private capital: Private companies need capital; institutional capital providers have it; somehow parties occasionally negotiate a deal. Credit boxes, sample terms, and expected rates of returns explain this process. The analogy to a financial bazaar seems to best describe the actual workings of the private capital markets.

Business transfer is the most interconnected side of the private capital markets triangle. Transfer depends on the value world in which the transfer takes place and the availability of capital to make it happen. After more than 15 years providing private financial engineering services to the middle market, I am still amazed when a transfer deal actually closes. Everything seems to be against it. Only the will of the parties can overcome the obstacles. This is why both parties need to be somewhat equally motivated once the letter of intent is executed.

Although the gears and arrows on Exhibit 36.1 suggest market movement, the schematic cannot capture the velocity of the private capital markets. No diagram can. Ultimately private markets yield two precious commodities: information and liquidity. Information in private markets is like water in the desert. It is both necessary and scarce. Those who master it usually win the game. It is just that easy. Successful managers effectively gather, manage, and deploy information. Unsuccessful managers wonder why they are a step slow and never seem get a break.

To the victor goes liquidity. If information is the water, liquidity is the oasis. It is extremely difficult to get money into and out of private markets. Once again, well-conceived strategies enable this to happen. But strategies take time and require a certain single-mindedness. Nearly all owners possess these attributes; only some owners convert these qualities into liquidity.

WHAT WE DO NOT KNOW

A separate book is possible on what we do not know about private capital markets. So as not to outweigh the broad themes, only five particularly fertile research areas are discussed here.

1. *What factors motivate people to own and manage private businesses?* Perhaps only 1% of the population should own a business. Yet many more than this make the attempt. Why? What motivates people to seek the 24/7 lifestyle that comes with the owner-manager title? Certainly control of one's destiny is important to this group. For many, the risks associated with ownership outweigh likely returns. This might be another instance where the lack of good information causes people to understate risk and overstate return. A better understanding of the motivating factors of business ownership will lead to a better understanding of how owners make important decisions.

2. *What needs to occur to have efficient private capital markets?* Private capital markets are inefficient, at least when compared to public markets. Without an active trading market for private securities, it seems unlikely that private markets will ever be liquid, which is a precursor to efficiency. Each market mechanism would need to change for efficiency to occur. As a start the quality and quantity of information needs to dramatically improve. Regulation from the government might have to mandate this change. The mode of exchange needs to become more liquid. Intermediation needs to become more market maker oriented and less reliant on outside agents.

Market efficiency matters. Increased efficiency enables companies to maximize their resources. Perhaps the private markets will never be efficient, but further study of this issue might help make them more efficient than they are today.

3. *Why don't more business owners create value in their businesses?* The author believes that the majority of business owners are not increasing the value of their businesses. This lack of value creation has created a substantial "value gap" in the private markets. The value gap represents the difference between what an owner thinks or wants his or her business to be worth, versus what the market of investors thinks it is worth. The value gap is the result of long periods where companies have not generated returns on investment greater than their cost of capital. This alarming opinion was reached partly because most business owners do not even know what it means to increase the value of their firms. Owners and managers have not been educated on the framework described in this book. Why not? Private companies generate the majority of the U.S. gross domestic product. What are we waiting for?

$3^1/_2$. *Why are expected and realized returns so dramatically different?* Every institutional private capital provider expects to achieve an all-in rate that is much higher than the return actually realized. For instance, private equity groups (PEGs) expect to receive 25% to 30% but generally receive less than 10%. Venture capitalists structure their deals using a 35% to 40% return expectation yet receive about the same return as PEGs. This is an incredibly inefficient use of capital. What are we to make of this finding? Is this underperformance due to the difficulty of picking winners in private capital markets? Or are the institutional capital providers not adding enough value to their investments? Eventually this imbalance will cause sources of capital to find other intermediaries with new models that generate higher realized returns.

$3^3/_4$. *Does private cost of capital affect the lower-middle market's ability to compete against larger domestic companies and globally?* Private companies have a much higher cost of capital than large public firms. The comparison of the PPCML and public market line, discussed in Chapter 26, graphically displays the difference. The lack of liquidity in private markets only partially explains the difference. Information opacity is a further cause of private inefficiency that directly leads to higher return expectations for private capital providers. Does a higher cost of capital necessarily put private firms at a competitive disadvantage? There is some empirical evidence that it does. For example, factoring, which is the most expensive capital type, historically has been used extensively by textile and furniture manufacturers. This capital structure causes these manufacturers to have extremely high costs of capital. I believe this cost structure prevented the textile and furniture trades from reinvesting in their businesses, especially in production-enhancing technologies. Of course, these industries wilted under the onslaught of global competition.

It seems reasonable to believe that, all things being equal, a higher cost of capital limits the value-creating investment choices of a firm. Since the U.S. government is counting on small businesses as the job engine for the foreseeable future, this consideration is extremely important.

4. *How do owners use options to determine transfer alternatives?* Many owners avoid making the transfer decision to avoid walking to the elephant graveyard. Yet some owners do plan their exits. How do they make this decision? Do they internalize the business transfer spectrum and choose the option that best fits their motives? This seems somewhat unlikely to me. I have assisted in hundreds of private transfers and have found that it is difficult to get owners to concentrate on sophisticated planning options. It is just not where they live.

It has always been an American dream for parents to transfer the family business to their children. Something is amiss in America, however. Twenty years ago, perhaps 30% of private businesses transferred from one generation to the next. Now the number is likely closer to 10%. Why? Has something changed in the family unit to cause this low transfer percentage?

Will educating business owners regarding the dozens of transfer options available enhance their desire to plan the exit? There is no way to be certain, but planning must be preferable to selling out when it is no longer fun owning the company.

5. *Why don't our institutions support the private capital markets?* First, where are the academics? I speak on dozens of college campuses each year in America. Only rarely do I find a single traditional academic who knows anything about private capital markets, let alone the middle market. I constantly ask these academics: "Would you consider anyone who knows only half of their field of study to be an expert?" Of course they answer no. Then I point out that private markets generate more than 50% of the U.S. economy and that private markets are unique in behavior and almost totally separate from large public markets. What do I hear? Silence.

We cannot expect our students to become successful owners and operators of private companies when they are not introduced to even the most basic concepts in school. If academics will not engage the private capital markets body of knowledge, they need to admit that they are not experts in their fields and get out of the way of those of us who are.

Further, why does public policy largely ignore the private capital markets? To this end, why does government policy either ignore these markets or is just plain detrimental to them? It is strongly in the best interest of the United States to help grow private markets, as the vast majority of jobs are created there. Politicians constantly proclaim that small businesses are the engines of the economy, yet they then pass law after law that effectively stymies the growth of those businesses? Why?

A FINAL THOUGHT

I believe private capital markets are the last major uncharted capital frontier. This work is a conceptual Lewis and Clark–type survey. I hope others heed the call and expand our understanding of the terrain. This trailblazing adventure reminds me, in some ways, of the nineteenth-century rush to California. Upon seeing the Sierra Nevadas for the first time, the starry-eyed younger prospectors would whisper, "There's gold in them thar hills." The grizzled veteran miners would nod, then add a critical insight: "Eet's there all right . . . but only for them that know whar to look."

Corporate Finance Theory: Application to Private Capital Markets

Until the first edition of this book appeared in 2004, private market players had only corporate finance theories to explain the behavior of private capital markets. They were left to assume that corporate finance theories explain and *predict* actions in private markets. This book demonstrates otherwise. Left unsaid by academics is that corporate finance theories explain and organize public capital markets but were never intended to explain nonpublic capital markets. Private markets must be explained using theories tailored to experience in those markets.

Private Capital Markets is a Lewis and Clark–type survey of the theories and methods of middle-market finance. It is concerned with the manner in which these concepts relate to each other, to larger bodies of knowledge, and to what extent they may be mutually exclusive or internally limited. It connects the theoretical with the practical but never loses sight of its primary use in serving as a road map. For example, there is a valuation methodology developed in the world of market value. While we all know the world exists, standard valuation methods have not developed tools to chart or capture it.

A premise of this book is that middle-market finance theory holistically describes behavior in the private middle market. Further, much like corporate finance theory, middle-market finance theory emanates from meta-financial theory. Exhibit A.1 graphically represents the influence of meta-theories on corporate finance and middle-market finance theory.[1]

Thus, public and private capital market theories are theoretical siblings. Obviously, this assertion is not easily accepted by the academic community. Until the first edition of this book was released, private markets had not been viewed as stand-alone markets that required unique market theories to explain and predict behavior. Most academics still view private markets as the offspring of public markets and middle-market finance theory as the child of corporate finance theory. This book demonstrates otherwise.

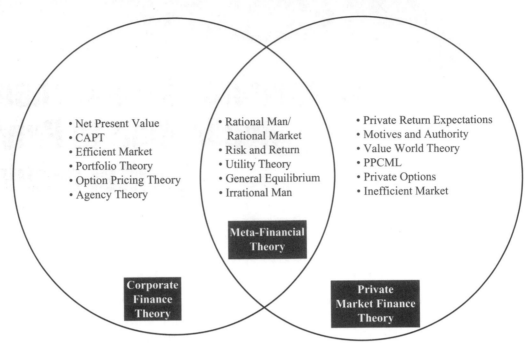

EXHIBIT A.1 Influence of Meta-Financial Theory

META-FINANCIAL THEORY

Meta theories are pervasive all-encompassing financial theories from which lower-level theories, methods, and tools are derived. Considered individually, they are powerful. Collectively, they reinforce one another and provide an open, systematic construct for the development of both corporate finance theory and private capital markets theory. Meta-theories are the theoretical parents of lower-level market theories. From a theoretical perspective, corporate finance theory and private capital markets theory are siblings. However, each capital markets theory is designed with particular needs and particular markets in mind.

Rational Man/Rational Market

Economists base a good deal of thought on the theory that rational men act in rational markets and make rational decisions. They posit that given timely and accurate information, individual economic actors, taken as a whole, will arrive at cogent, coherent decisions isomorphic with economic reality. This is the inherited tradition of economic thought derived from David Hume, Adam Smith, and John Stuart Mill.

Rational expectations take many forms. If one assumes that prices are not completely nonsensical, arbitrary, and unrelated to anticipated future value, then one is left to assume that investors base their decisions on anticipation or probability of those returns. Their assessment of the actions of others is relative to that judgment. If assets are systematically valued relative to future payouts, prices will be determined by individual assessment of the intrinsic value of those payouts.

The highest form of the rational expectation argument is that prices form on the basis of expected future payouts.

The rational actor assumption powerfully enables economic analysis; however, it prevents economists from explaining large parts of human behavior.

Risk and Return

The concept of risk and return permeates all finance theory. Firms operate in an uncertain environment, and any calculation of return on investment must take the level of risk into account. To justify risky investment, there must be a commensurate level of return. The basic concepts are intuitively available; however, the formal linkages between them are a bit more difficult.

Risk and return analysis can be used in relation to a single asset or in relation to a group of assets. More specifically, *return* is defined as the realizable cash flow earned during a specified period of time, normally stated as a percentage. *Risk* is a statistical concept derived through applying knowledge of probabilities. Return is an estimate of the probability distributions of certain outcomes. All finance theory concerns itself with quantifying and analyzing the elements of risk and return. Risk and return taken collectively form the boundary around finance theory.

Private return expectations and public return expectations each form a foundation and a boundary for their respective disciplines.

Utility Theory

Utility theory, originally developed by the utilitarian philosophers, is central to major theories of finance. It is integral to understanding the concepts of risk and return and expected rates of return in relation to the goals of investors. Utility theory provides a framework for describing decision making under uncertain conditions.

Marginal utility is the additional utility an investor receives from an incremental change in wealth. It is a measure of the increase or decrease in utility derived from a change in total wealth by one unit. Investors make decisions using the concept of diminishing marginal utility. That is, investors derive less and less incremental utility from each additional increment in total wealth. Perhaps this is why beer is sold in-six packs.

Most people invest to make the best use of their resources. They hope to maximize their utility by investing in risky investments that increase wealth and contribute to their happiness. In short, they seek the maximum utility for their investment. The capital asset pricing model (CAPM) and Private Cost of Capital Model developed in the first part of this book are derived from utility theory.

General Equilibrium Theory

General equilibrium theory can be traced back to the work of Leon Walras (1837–1910). He developed a mathematical theory of general equilibrium that is a major tenet of current economic thought. His model demonstrated the exact conditions under which equilibrium might be achieved, with everyone acting on individual self-interest, in a perfectly competitive market with complete flexibility in shifting resources from one use to another. In this theory, an economy is in equilibrium when production is matched with consumer preferences, and the highest level of benefit is achieved given existing resources and technology.

The Walras equilibrium theory led to a theory of supply and demand in a system of equilibrium similar to Adam Smith's but on stronger theoretical and empirical footing. For example, when funds are allocated between savers and investors, at a price commensurate with the risk involved, that is an efficient market because risk and return are in equilibrium. In equilibrium, the supply of funds equals the demand for funds, or the supply of business for sale equals the demand for these businesses.

An efficient market is a market in equilibrium. Levels of market efficiency are discussed throughout this work. Capital market efficiency is concerned with the behavior of prices in a free market system. This leads to the fundamental question of the efficient market theory, a pillar of corporate finance theory: Do prices of assets in a particular market accurately reflect all of the necessary information available? Better and more timely information renders the public capital markets more efficient than the private markets. It is less clear, however, what role asymmetric information plays in determining private market pricing efficiency.

Equilibrium theory pervades all financial theories. It is found in the principle of substitution necessary for market theories of value comparison. For the concept of substitution to work, substituted values must be equivalent. Failure to meet this equilibrium or substitution principal may subject an argument to the logical fallacy of irrelevance.

Irrational Man

Motives of individual owners ground private capital markets theory. Occasionally those motives are not easily accessible through rational explanation. Since the time of Aristotle, thinkers have focused on the dichotomy sometimes identified as the mind/body problem and other times cast as rational/irrational man. Irrational behavior also can be studied, but doing so requires different approaches and methods.

Some economists offer rational choice theory as an assumption. But it is a huge assumption adopted in order to make economics more like the physical sciences in terms of explanatory and predictive power. The assumption entails a normative assessment as to how people should act as opposed to how they actually act. Adam Smith chose a narrative approach to the subject rather than a strictly analytical approach and developed useful insights. Charles Kindelberger, in *Manias, Panics and Crashes*, presents a brilliant description of man as an economic actor when he is acting less than rational.[2]

An active school of economic theory now is reflected in recent Nobel Prizes in Economics. In 2002 Vernon Smith and Daniel Kahneman received the Nobel Prize for their work in experimental economics. Their major contribution was developing experimental methods for explaining why people do not behave as economic theory suggests they should. In his 2001 Nobel Prize acceptance speech, George Akerlof brought to economics insights from other disciplines, including fairness, reciprocity, loss aversion, and procrastination, to help explain why real economic actors do not always do what general equilibrium theory predicts they will do.

Motives set economic processes in motion. For the individual owner of a middle-market business, motives initiate the process of triangulation, whether those motives are rational and well considered or not. Motives can be studied even if they are in blatant disregard to economic theory.

A number of meta-theories other than those just named influence public and private capital markets theories. Several deserve mention. *Information theory* is central to all markets. Availability, accuracy, and access to information shape market mechanisms and directly affect market efficiency. *Decision theory* explains how people acquire and analyze information before making decisions. In its capitalist form, decision theory argues that preferences among risky alternatives can be described by maximizing expected monetary value. Obviously this is the basis for investor decision making. *Game theory* explains decision making in conflict situations, involving two or more decision makers. Game theory illustrates the behavior of decision makers with different objectives or those who share the same resources. In other words, it studies how players act in a market. Further, *mechanism design theory*, or *market design theory*, asks about the consequences of different sets of rules. The design of certain market mechanisms, such as auctions or credit allocation devices, affects players' ability to meet goals.

Corporate finance principles and theories are taught in all business schools. A great deal of work and research has been done in all areas of corporate finance theory and the applications of that theory. Much of the methodology at work within public capital markets is directly derived from, or conditioned by, these corporate finance theories.

Middle-market finance theory, and its related methods and practice, is currently taught in universities around the world, but to a much lesser degree than corporate finance. Although there are hundreds of thousands of individuals working in private capital markets as appraisers, financing sources, or various intermediaries, little academic attention is provided to the area. Therefore, only a scant body of organized theoretical knowledge is available. This book addresses that situation.

The remainder of this appendix describes various corporate finance theories and shows the implications and applications of these theories to the private capital markets.

CORPORATE FINANCE THEORY

Numerous theories comprise corporate finance theory. Summaries of some of these theories are discussed next.

Net Present Value

Net present value (NPV) is an elementary concept for treating the time value of money. A dollar received immediately is preferable to a dollar received at some future date. As a capital budgeting technique, it is necessary to determine the expected net cash flows of an investment, discounted at the marginal (or some risk-adjusted discount rate) cost of capital, then subtract from that the initial cost outlay of the project. A project would meet the selection criteria if its NPV were greater than or equal to zero. A project with a positive NPV earns more than the required rate of return. In this circumstance, equity holders earn all excess cash flows because debt holders have only a fixed claim. Equity holders' wealth increases by exactly the NPV of the project. It is this direct link that renders NPV important in financial decision making.

Capital Asset Pricing Theory

Capital asset pricing theory is a fundamental financial theory that defines the opportunity cost of a firm's capital budgeting decisions. It is designed to specify the expected relationship between rates of return and risk where the required return is the risk-free rate plus a risk premium. This theory, and the models derived from it, provides useful estimates of the rates of return required on risky public securities.

Developed in the 1960s, capital asset pricing theory, or the CAPM, is an extension of Harry Markowitz's portfolio theory. Measuring total risk is accomplished by determining the variance of portfolio returns. Measuring risk in an individual security in equilibrium is accomplished by determining its contribution to total risk. Two individuals, Sharpe and Linter, demonstrated that this relationship to total risk is measured by the covariance of the individual return on the portfolio of all assets. *Systematic risk* is the term given to describe this risk measure. Asset pricing theory analyzes the opportunity cost of capital for the firm's capital budgeting decisions. The CAPM concept can also be applied to an arbitrage pricing model. First developed by Ross in 1976, the arbitrage pricing model allows the use of multiple factors to explain security returns.

Efficient Market Theory

The efficient market theory is an analysis of the behavior of prices in a free market system. It is concerned with whether prices accurately reflect all of the necessary information to determine that scarce resources are efficiently allocated among a variety of competing uses. In a perfectly efficient market, it would be impossible to make an excessive profit by trading on information not available to all interested parties. In a perfectly efficient market, the net present value of a transaction is zero. The immediate availability of inexpensive relevant information is a linchpin of the efficient market theory. According to the theory, when markets reach this efficiency, they are said to be in equilibrium.

The efficient market theory is among the most extensively studied theories in all of corporate finance, particularly as it relates to equity prices in the public markets. Often it is separated into three levels of strength according to the strength and timeliness of the impact of information availability on prices: strong-form efficiency, semi-strong efficiency, and weak-form efficiency. The efficient market theory indicates that prices should fully reflect all relevant information, but it does not necessarily describe the process for arriving at efficiency.

Portfolio Theory

Portfolio theory is built on the premise that the risk inherent in any single asset, when held in a group of assets, is different from the inherent risk of that asset held in isolation. Rumor has it that portfolio theory is like the bookie at the racetrack who "lays off," or hedges, a bet in order to bring total risk to a level he is comfortable with. The basic concept of portfolio theory is intuitively available and has been used for centuries. The specific applications discussed here rely on the development of probability theory and modern statistics.

Harry Markowitz introduced the basic concepts of portfolio theory in the 1950s. He developed an analysis of how it is possible to select the optimum combination of assets to maximize return while minimizing risk. Assuming an efficient market, that is, that all relevant information is available, Markowitz's portfolio theory demonstrates that by using two parameters of distributions—the mean or expected value, and the variance or standard deviation—it is possible to assemble a portfolio that achieves maximum utility. The analysis provides a formal approach to the measurement of diversification. Mean variance analysis is used to measure the contribution of the covariance among returns and risks and establishes rules for building an efficient portfolio.

Portfolios are combinations of assets that offer the advantage of reducing risk through diversification. Portfolio theory analyzes the relationship between the diversified components, so that positive standard deviation levels are available at every level of expected return. Through this analysis, it is possible to develop accurate understandings that range beyond financial assets such as stocks and bonds. The analysis is applicable to physical assets and other capital budgeting questions and is also used in a variety of other applications.

Option Pricing Theory

Option pricing theory builds on the CAPM linking current asset prices with expected economic benefit streams. Many decisions faced by managers involve knowledge of the value of assets that are contingent on the value of other assets. Call options are options that give the holder the right to buy a stipulated number of securities at a given price for a fixed time. In 1973, Black and Scholes developed a model to value call options. Their theory indicates that a risk-free position is possible by maintaining a hedge between an option and its stock when the hedge can be adjusted continuously over time. Under the Black-Scholes model, the return to the hedge must equal the market risk-free rate yielding an expressed value for the equilibrium call price.

Extending the Black-Scholes analysis, assuming a firm's cash flow distribution is fixed, option-pricing analysis can be used to value other contingent assets, such as equity and debt of a leveraged firm. The equity of a leveraged firm could be treated like a call option on the total value of a firm's assets, with an exercise value equal to the value of the debt and an expiration date equal to that of the maturity of the debt. The Black-Scholes model could be used as a valuation model for a firm's equity and debt. This covariance indicates that an increase in a firm's asset value increases the economic benefit stream to the equity and also increases the debt coverage, thus increasing the current value of both. Conversely, an increase in the value of the debt increases the debt holder's claim in the firm's assets, thus increasing the value of the debt while reducing the value of the equity. Time is the third covariant; increasing the repayment schedule of the debt increases the riskiness of the debt and lowers its return.

Agency Theory

Agency theory is that area of corporate financial theory that is concerned with examining the relationship that occurs when principals engage other individuals to perform some service on their behalf, and it involves delegating some decision-making authority. It examines the costs to owners when others manage the firm. It includes questions such as monitoring expenditures to restrict inappropriate behavior by managers while providing sufficient incentives for them to perform. In the case of large public companies, agency theory analyzes the relationship between those who manage the firm on behalf of those who own the equity of the firm. The theory is concerned with aligning the incentives of owners and managers to overcome the inherent conflict in the situation.

Modern agency theory developed in the 1970s with the work of Jensen and Meckling, who defined agency costs as the sum of all costs involved in structuring contracts including bonding costs, expenditures by the agent, compensation including bonuses and warrants, and all residual costs. Jensen and Meckling indicate that the agency analysis can be used to resolve conflict of interest between owners or principals and managers or agents. Inherent in the agency theory is the modern theory of the firm where management and risk sharing are often separated.

APPLICATION OF CORPORATE FINANCE THEORY TO PRIVATE CAPITAL MARKETS

Exhibit A.2 compares the application of a number of corporate finance theories to the private capital markets. Since public and private theories have the same parent, they share many similarities. For instance, private capital providers use the tenets of portfolio theory to manage their portfolios and diversify risk. Conversely, portfolio theory does not uniformly explain behavior in the private capital

EXHIBIT A.2   Application of Corporate Finance Theory to the Private Capital Markets

Corporate Finance Theory	Application to the Private Capital Markets
Net present value	Theoretically correct for all firms. Used primarily by public companies. Less than 10% of private companies use NPV to make investment decisions. Research shows this is mainly because small companies are unaware of the tool.
Capital asset pricing theory	Measuring risk and return is a core concept for all markets. The use of beta and other assumptions lessen the utility of the capital asset pricing model for private companies.
Efficient market theory	Applies to both private and public markets. Private capital markets are much less efficient than public markets.
Portfolio theory	Value worlds view the firm as a portfolio of risky assets and liabilities, each with an expected return that can be calculated. Requires diversification of assets to minimize portfolio risk, which is impossible for a private owner-manager. Portfolio theory is widely used by private capital providers to manage risk and return.
Option pricing theory	Options theory is primarily used for corporate finance. Since private companies do not trade on an exchange, volatility, the degree to which stock price changes exceed their historical average, cannot be measured to support the theory. Used by private firms to assess business options, including stock options, lease options, and buy/sell provisions. A version of options theory helps explain the valuation of transfer alternatives faced by private owners.
Agency theory	Agency theory explains how to best organize relationships in which one party determines the work, which another party undertakes. Strong management adds to the value of a private firm. Issues exist even for owner-managed private firms. Authorities in the private capital markets can be viewed as agents that provide constraints and rules to the parties.

markets. For example, private owners cannot use portfolio theory to diversify their ownership risk because they have nearly all of their wealth tied to one asset.

Net Present Value

Net present value incorporates the time value of money into the investment decision process. There is no dispute about its theoretical utility. Do private companies use NPV to make investment decisions? The answer is usually no. Obviously, no matter how great the concept, its usefulness is limited if not applied.

Researchers Walker, Burns, and Denson studied 213 private manufacturing firms with fewer than 500 employees. They found only 9% used discounted cash-flow techniques, of which NPV is the major tool.[3] The other 91% use simpler methods for making investment decisions, including project payback, accounting rate of return and, of course, gut feel.

The Walker research found 66% of small firms studied are unaware of the NPV method. This figure is surprisingly high and probably will improve as more business school graduates flock to small, private companies. Interestingly, they found 26% of small firms familiar with NPV decide not to use it for several reasons.

The authors found perceived success rates in capital budgeting of non-NPV users were higher than the rates of NPV users. The authors think that this may be misleading, since the smallest firms in the survey may not collect data in a manner that would enable them to make such a claim accurately.

Regardless of the reasons, small private companies do not routinely use NPV analysis. It is possible successful business owners, who shun NPV, normally compensate with an excellent *gut feel* for return on investment. Even project payback is a reliable analysis of return on investment if the payback period is less than two years.

Capital Asset Pricing Theory

The capital asset pricing model measures the rate of return required on risky securities. There are several difficulties in using the CAPM to measure risk in the private capital markets. Notably, none of the assumptions listed next supporting the CAPM are usable in the private capital markets. Further, the only way to test the CAPM directly is to see whether the market portfolio is efficient. Unfortunately, because the market portfolio contains all assets (marketable and nonmarketable, human capital, coins, houses, bonds, stocks, options, etc.) it is impossible to observe directly.[4] Seven of the assumptions behind the CAPM are:

1. All investors have identical investment horizons, expected holding periods.
2. All investors have identical expectations about variables such as expected rates of return and the method of generating capitalization rates.
3. There are no transaction costs.
4. There are no investment-related taxes, although there may be corporate income taxes.
5. The rate received from lending money is the same as the cost of borrowing money.
6. Rational investors seek to hold efficient, fully diversified portfolios.
7. The market has perfect divisibility and liquidity. Investors can readily buy or sell any desired fractional interest.

Beyond the difficulties with the assumptions, there are a handful of problems with measuring beta (the measure of market risk):[5]

- There is no single accepted source of data or method for measuring beta. Various services report different estimates of beta for the same industry and even the same individual stock.
- Betas are typically measured infrequently; therefore, they can be out of date.
- Betas are not available for many stocks, particularly for thinly traded securities. Stocks of thousands of public companies are not followed by a financial reporting service.

The most troubling assumption about investors in private companies is that they behave in the same manner as investors in public companies with well-diversified portfolios. Owners of private firms usually have most of their personal wealth invested in the business and therefore are not well diversified. CAPM is not strictly applicable for cost of equity or required return estimates for private companies. Therefore, it is incorrect to assume that investors have diversified all other sources of risk, both systematic and nonsystematic, and face only systematic risk that cannot be diversified. This fact alone destroys the CAPM's direct applicability to the private capital markets. Clearly, owners of private companies face both systematic and unsystematic risk, and risk/return models appropriate for private equity required returns should reflect this fact. The private markets apparently do not respond to CAPM.

Finally, the assumption that the market has perfect liquidity (assumption 7 listed earlier) is particularly troubling, given the lack of marketability for private stocks discussed in the next section.

Efficient Market Theory

The efficient market theory is an analysis of the behavior of prices in a free market system. An efficient capital market means security prices accurately reflect available information and respond rapidly to new information as soon as it becomes available. The private capital markets are far less efficient than their public counterparts. The primary difference is that pricing for private company securities occurs in a static market. Efficient market pricing depends on a dynamic market where information immediately impacts pricing. With no public exchange to ascertain current pricing, the private capital markets offer no such dynamism.

In fact, not only is there a substantial pricing efficiency difference between public and private stocks, there are built-in differences in their pricing. These differences make any direct pricing comparison between private companies and their public cousins problematic.

Price Difference: Stock Marketability

Investors are most interested in the marketability of an investment. It is difficult to sell an existing investment without an established trading market. The more difficult it is to liquidate an investment, the longer the implied investment holding period. In a long-term investment, the risk is greater. That greater risk requires a lower price to attract investors. According to many studies, the lack of marketability for private stocks, when compared with public stocks, should be a discount of at least 35% and probably considerably more.

Ready marketability adds value to a security. Conversely, lack of marketability diminishes its value. Private businesses do not enjoy the ready market of publicly traded stock. This difference must be considered when evaluating an interest in a private business with reference to prices of publicly traded stocks. Risks associated with illiquidity include the inability to dispose of an interest in the face of deteriorating company or industry conditions as well as the inability to sell the interest if the investor's personal situation demands it. The lack of marketability for a private company's stock can be examined from either restricted stock studies or pre–initial public offering (IPO) studies. A number of studies quantify the marketability difference between public and private securities.

Restricted Stock Studies

Restricted stock studies examine the issuance of restricted common stock of companies with actively traded public shares. The restricted shares issued are identical to the freely traded common shares of the public companies in every way except marketability. These restricted shares have some legal limitations related to their marketability.[6]

In 1977, the Internal Revenue Service took a position on this matter in the form of a revenue ruling (Rev. Rul. 77-287, 1977-2, C.B.319). This ruling, based on a study conducted by the Securities and Exchange Commission, states: "This research project provides some guidance for measuring the discount in that it contains information, based on the actual experience of the marketplace." The ruling outlines four factors for guidance on the amount of discount that should be taken relative to the price of the registered counterparts of the stock in question.[7]

The factors outlined in the ruling include earnings, sales, trading market, and resale agreement provisions. In general, lower total sales or earnings of the issuer result in a higher discount to the registered stock. The more active the market in which the stock trades, the lower the discount. Nonreporting, over-the-counter issues demonstrated the highest discounts, while stocks with counterparts traded on the New York Stock Exchange had the lowest discounts.

In the Securities and Exchange Commission study, approximately 44% of over-the-counter companies experienced discounts over 30%, and almost 60% experienced discounts over 20%. Because of their smaller size, companies traded over the counter are more comparable to private businesses than the companies listed on the New York Stock Exchange.

A number of studies examine the magnitude of the discount for lack of marketability applicable to the appraisal of private stock:

- Milton Gelman studied 89 purchases of restricted shares by four closed-end investment funds over a two-year period; the discounts averaged 33%.[8]
- Robert E. Moroney studied 146 purchases of restricted securities sampled from 10 investment companies; the discounts ranged up to 90%. Most letter stock purchases were discounted between 15% and 35%.[9]
- J. Michael Maher studied the prices of restricted stocks compared with market prices of unrestricted stocks. The mean discount for lack of marketability was approximately 35%.[10]

There are a number of other restricted stock studies from the late 1960s and early 1970s. The studies provided average discounts from freely traded values of issuing companies ranging from 23% to 45%. The average of the nine major studies is 33%.

Pre-IPO Studies

A stock valuation's marketability discount can be determined by analyzing the relationship between share prices of companies whose shares initially were offered to the public in IPOs and the prices at which their shares traded immediately prior to their public offerings. John Emory conducted the first comprehensive study of this type.

Emory studied private transactions occurring within the five months prior to 593 IPOs completed from January 1, 1980, to December 30, 2000. The 593 companies used in the study were later-stage companies and were financially sound prior to the offering. Private sales and transactions took place at a 47% average discount from the price at which the stock subsequently came to market. Marketability discounts ranged from 3% to 94%, with a median of 48%.[11] As the Emory studies show, even private companies that could go public suffer from a serious lack of liquidity.

Willamette Management Associates, a major appraisal firm, also analyzed pre-IPO studies using data from 1975 to 1993. It concluded that average discounts varied from time to time but were higher in all cases than the average discounts shown for restricted stocks of companies with an established public trading market. That is exactly the result one would expect. Of the hundreds of transactions analyzed, the discounts ranged from 24% to 55%, with a median of 46%.[12]

The evidence from the Emory and Willamette studies taken together is compelling. The studies covered hundreds of transactions over 19 years. They discovered that average differentials between private transactions prices and public market prices varied under different market conditions with a range from about 40% to 63%, after eliminating the outliers. This finding strongly supports the hypothesis that fair market values of minority ownership interests in private entities are greatly discounted from their publicly traded counterparts.[13]

In conclusion, private companies suffer from a lack of marketability because there is no ready market for their shares. This is the single biggest built-in difference between public and private stock valuation.

Price Difference: Cost of Liquidity

The cost of obtaining access to an established trading market is substantial. Flotation costs, or cost of selling stock in a public offering, often are used as a benchmark for quantifying the discount for lack of marketability for controlling interests. Flotation costs can amount to more than 10% of the offering, when all of the underwriting expenses are considered. A public corporation, even with no assets, has a high value attributable to its ability to raise equity capital without significant additional flotation costs.

Public companies also get more attention when they are for sale, primarily due to auction pricing. Majority interests in public companies transfer at substantial premiums over their normal trading ranges. Studies by *Mergerstat Review*, a publication that measures control premiums, show the average control premium paid in the past ten years has been in the 35% to 45% range.[14]

Since there is no active market for shares of private companies, pricing is set by buyers aware of the situation. This lack of marketability depresses a private company's stock in two ways.

1. It prohibits private companies from participating in a public auction of their shares, resulting in a greatly reduced premium, if any premium is realized at all.
2. It forces buyers to create a market price for private shares called point-in-time pricing. Most buyers reduce their risk by setting a low price for the stock.

Efficient market theory does not apply to private companies in the same way it applies to public companies because the markets are structurally different. Chapter 1 contains a discussion of these structural differences.

Portfolio Theory

Applications of portfolio theory are apparent in other areas of the private capital markets. Generally, in the value worlds, it is possible to view the firm as a portfolio of risky assets and liabilities, each with an expected level of return that can be calculated. Treating the firm to be valued as a portfolio of assets, liabilities, risks, rewards, and related income streams is a far more sophisticated approach than treating it as a single isolated asset. For example, in the world of economic value, it is possible to measure the contribution to margin of a product line, where the strategic array of products is treated as a portfolio of investments.

Private capital is allocated based on segmentation of risk and the development of specialized instruments, methods, and personnel to achieve the optimum return at a given a level of risk. Segmenting risk and pricing it accordingly allows financial institutions to create a portfolio with optimum returns. Most banks and other lenders today utilize sophisticated portfolio management techniques to manage returns and insure that those returns exceed their hurdle rates. With these portfolio tools, lending institutions are able to ration credit more selectively. Banks, for example, may be driven by yield rather than a strict reliance on balance sheet decision making.

Option Theory

Option pricing theory as applied to the public markets cannot be ported to the private markets. Many of the variables associated with the Black-Scholes option model simply do not exist since private companies do not trade on an exchange. Once again, however, options are used every day in the private markets. Many equipment leases have options associated with end-of-lease decisions. Stock options are used throughout the private markets. Chapter 35 suggests private owners have transfer options that have value. Much more work needs to be done in this area. But it is clear that option theory is implied and applied in many ways to the private markets.

Obviously, most middle-market private firms have little use for options pricing theory because they do not issue stock to the public and do not utilize these sophisticated capitalization techniques in assembling their capital structure. However, if Black-Scholes is understood in its broadest sense as a method of covariant analysis, a number of applications are possible in the middle market.

In the value worlds, a central argument of the current work is that value is a range concept. Not only are there a number of mutually exclusive worlds with divergent value ranges, values can range within each world. Therefore, covariance is an integral concept beginning with the discussion of the application of Monte Carlo simulation as a method for calculating the probability distribution of possible values of a firm. As indicated earlier, the Black-Scholes model can be used as a valuation model for a firm's equity and debt.

In private capital, a manager has some ability to choose among capital access points, and that choice is amenable to a covariant analysis. Within a number of worlds, Black-Scholes analysis or something similar to it is used regularly. In equipment leasing, leasing companies have used Black-Scholes analysis for years. That lessees do not use it only indicates that they approach the question using less sophisticated analysis. Asset-based lenders have the prerogative of using a form of Black-Scholes analysis in assembling their portfolio of investments. Business owners seeking financing often have the prerogative of determining the level of equity versus asset-based loans and mezzanine financing. Clearly layered financing requires an analysis of multiple variables.

In business transfer, business owners have their widest latitude to choose the channel they wish to accomplish the transfer in. Understanding this choice involves analyzing multiple variables of risk and return within and between the value worlds. Initially the project is too complex for an analysis like Black-Scholes, but as the number of choices is narrowed, there is no reason why a sophisticated analysis in not appropriate. Some transfer techniques directly involve option pricing theory. Buy/sell agreements frequently involve puts and calls that are, of course, directly amenable to Black-Scholes analysis. Employee stock ownership plans use calls by employees on the stock of the firm also rendering such analysis appropriate.

There is no question that option pricing theory was developed for, and is applicable to, the corporate finance needs of large public companies and investors in those companies. It is also clear that there are areas in the private capital markets where it applies. Moreover, it is likely that as middle-market finance theory matures, there will be more opportunities to apply option analysis in this market.

Agency Theory

In the middle market, most firms are owner-managed; therefore, approaches through agency theory require some modification. Owners often are confronted with the question of how to appropriately reward or compensate key employees and consider granting stock as a possibility. Management teams clearly add value to a company; balancing the cost of that value increment against the cost is an appropriate question for agency theory.

Private firms incur agency costs. In 2001, Schulze, Lubatkin, Dino, and Buchholtz published a research article concluding that family-managed firms incur agency costs as they invest in internal controls.[15] The authors found midmarket firms are exposed to agency risks that are increased by the necessity for self-control rather than controls imposed by the market for corporate control.

In the value worlds, a fundamental rift is found between the world of owner value and other worlds involving investor value. Owners experience less agency cost and typically view less risk than investors. In a sense, the business actually may be worth more absent agency costs. However, management teams do add value, particularly in the world of market value where investors are more likely to pay a premium for a business whose management team helps ameliorate risk in the eyes of the investors.

Questions central to agency theory and common to owners of businesses of all sizes are: What form of equity should a firm issue? and Under what parameters and constraints should it be issued? As financing moves along the capital access pricing line, away from asset-based financing and toward financing involving intangible assets, the greater is the role of the management team. Mezzanine financing is based on two things that actually reduce to one thing: business plans and the management teams who conceive and implement them. Equity and mezzanine investors base their funding decisions on the efficacy of the agents they are funding. In short, they bet on management teams.

Agency theory also plays a considerable role in transfer. A strong management team allows an owner a broader choice as to which transfer world is available. Not only is it possible for management teams to add value, as discussed, but they can render a buyer's transition and ongoing operations more stable and less risky; thus, a broader range of buyers, and a broader range of transaction types, may be available.

SUMMARY

Corporate finance theory was developed in the 1960s to explain the behavior of large companies in the public capital markets. Economists who originally developed these tools never intended for them to be used to predict the behavior of other markets. Certain corporate finance theories, such as net present value, the capital asset pricing theory, and efficient market theory, either are not used by owners of private companies or do not apply to private markets. Applying these theories in private markets is like utilizing the wrong tools in a tool box. Corporate finance tools were designed specifically to work on public market mechanisms.

Market theories are designed to organize and predict behavior in an underlying self-contained market. Each structure rests on a foundation of the purposes for which the activity is undertaken. Employing powerful theories in the wrong context leads to frustration and a loss of utility. For example, assessing risk using a theoretical structure applicable to one market while expecting a return in another market is serious disconnect. Middle-market finance theory is designed to reflect the reality of the private capital markets. It is also the beneficiary of a rich intellectual tradition conditioned by powerful meta-financial theories.

NOTES

1. Robert T. Slee, *Private Capital Markets: Valuation, Capitalization, and Transfer of Private Business Interests*, (Hoboken, NJ: John Wiley & Sons, 2004), foreword.
2. Charles P. Kindleberger, *Manias, Panics, and Crashes: A History of Financial Crises* (New York: John Wiley & Sons, 2000).
3. Joe Walker, Rick Burns, and Charles Denson, "Why Small Manufacturing Firms Shun DCF," *Journal of Small Business Finance* (1993), pp. 233–249.
4. Thomas Copeland and J. Fred Weston, *Financial Theory and Corporate Policy* (Boston: Addison-Wesley, 1998), p. 211.
5. Shannon P. Pratt, Robert F. Reilly, and Robert R. Schweihs, *Valuing a Business, The Analysis and Appraisal of Closely Held Companies*, 4th ed. (New York: McGraw-Hill, 2000), p. 180.
6. A good source of information on this topic is: Christopher Z. Mercer, *Quantifying Marketability Discounts* (Brockton: Peabody Publishing, 1997.)
7. "Discounts Involved in Purchases of Common Stock (1966–1969)," Institutional Investor Study Report of the Securities and Exchange Commission. H.R. No. 64, Part 5, 92d Cong., 1st Sess. 1971, pp. 2444–2456.
8. Milton Gelman, "An Economist-Financial Analyst's Approach to Valuing Stock of a Closely Held Company," *Journal of Taxation* (June 1972): 353.
9. Robert E. Moroney, "Most Courts Overvalue Closely Held Stock," *Taxes* (March 1973): 144–154.
10. J. Michael Maher, "Discounts for Lack of Marketability for Closely-Held Business Interests," Taxes (September 1976), pp. 562–571.
11. John D. Emory, "Expanded Study of the Value of Marketability as Illustrated in Initial Public Offerings of Common Stock," *Business Valuation News* (December 2001).
12. Pratt, Reily, and Schweihs, pp. 344–348.
13. *Ibid*, 348.
14. *Mergerstat Review 2000*, Los Angeles, p. 24.
15. William S. Schulze, Michael H. Lubatkin, Richard N. Dino, and Ann K Buchholtz, "Agency Relationships in Family Firms: Theory and Evidence," *Organizational Science*, 12 (2), (March-April 2001).

As the purchaser of this book, *Private Capital Markets: Valuation, Capitalization, and Transfer of Private Business Interests*, you have access to the supporting Web site: www.wiley.com/go/privatecapital

The Web site contains files for:

Appendix B, Principle of Substitution. The principle of substitution underlies nearly all appraisals. According to the principle of substitution, value is determined by the cost of acquiring an equally desirable substitute. This appendix explains that from an investment viewpoint, transaction prices are relevant to the value of private businesses when they are similar with respect to the degree of risk, the liquidity of the investment, and the involvement of management.

Appendix C, IBA Standards. The Institute of Business Appraisers (IBA) is the oldest professional society devoted solely to the appraisal of private businesses. To support business appraisers, IBA and other professional appraisal organizations have developed and published appraisal standards. These standards provide much of the structure for the practice of valuation. Every person in need of a private business appraisal should review this appendix before engaging an appraiser.

Appendix D, Private Equity Securities. There are many types of private equity securities. Each type of security may have numerous permutations and features. This appendix explains different securities, including common and preferred stock, phantom stock, and stock appreciation rights.

Appendix E, Sample Preferred Stock Offering Term Sheet. Term sheets outline the key tenets of a deal. These documents can be very complex, and generally employ unfamiliar language. This appendix provides an example preferred stock offering term sheet, which indoctrinates the uninitiated to the confines of private equity.

Appendix F, Private Placements. A private placement is a nonpublic offering of securities exempt from full Securities and Exchange Commission registration requirements. Prior to formally offering private securities to the market, managers should understand and follow the appropriate securities laws. This appendix gives an overview of the laws and various types of private placements and discusses marketing strategies for a successful offering.

Appendix G, Sample Management Buyout Letter of Intent. A letter of intent is the primary preclosing document between the management team and the seller. This letter is generally a legally nonbinding agreement that describes all of the important terms of the deal. Similar to the term sheet contained in Appendix E, the sample letter in this appendix will help those unfamiliar with the management buyout process.

Glossary. The glossary contains hundreds of definitions of important terms used in the book. Words introduced in *Private Capital Markets* are marked with an asterisk.

The password to enter this site is: private